TASK SWITCHING AND COGNITIVE CONTROL

TASK SWITCHING AND COGNITIVE CONTROL

EDITED BY JAMES A. GRANGE

AND

GEORGE HOUGHTON

OXFORD
UNIVERSITY PRESS

OXFORD
UNIVERSITY PRESS

Oxford University Press is a department of the University of Oxford.
It furthers the University's objective of excellence in research, scholarship,
and education by publishing worldwide.

Oxford New York
Auckland Cape Town Dar es Salaam Hong Kong Karachi
Kuala Lumpur Madrid Melbourne Mexico City Nairobi
New Delhi Shanghai Taipei Toronto

With offices in
Argentina Austria Brazil Chile Czech Republic France Greece
Guatemala Hungary Italy Japan Poland Portugal Singapore
South Korea Switzerland Thailand Turkey Ukraine Vietnam

Published in the United States of America by
Oxford University Press
198 Madison Avenue, New York, NY 10016

A copy of this book's Catalog-in-Publication Data is on file with the Library of Congress
ISBN 978-0-19-992195-9

9 8 7 6 5 4 3 2 1
Printed in the United States of America
on acid-free paper

CONTENTS

CONTRIBUTING AUTHORS

Erik M. Altmann
Michigan State University, USA

Catherine M. Arrington
Lehigh University, USA

Eveline A. Crone
Leiden University, the Netherlands; Leiden Institute for Brain and Cognition, the Netherlands; and University of Amsterdam, the Netherlands

Abhijit Das
Kessler Research Foundation, USA; Rutgers University, USA

Michel D. Druey
University of Zurich, Switzerland

Miriam Gade
University of Zurich, Switzerland

Nicola K. Ferdinand
Saarland University, Germany

James A. Grange
Keele University, UK

George Houghton
Bangor University, UK

Sharna D. Jamadar
Monash University, Australia

Frini Karayanidis
University of Newcastle, Australia

Alexander Kirkham
University of York, UK

Iring Koch
RWTH Aachen University, Germany

Jutta Kray
Saarland University, Germany

Gordon D. Logan
Vanderbilt University, USA

Paloma Marí-Beffa
Bangor University, UK

Nachshon Meiran
Ben-Gurion University of the Negev, Beer-Sheva, Israel

Sabine Peters
Leiden University, the Netherlands; Leiden Institute for Brain and Cognition, the Netherlands

Susan M. Ravizza
Michigan State University, USA

Kaitlin M. Reiman
Lehigh University, USA

Franziska R. Richter
University of Oxford, UK

Ruth E. Salo
University of California Davis, USA

Darryl W. Schneider
Purdue University, USA

Stefanie Schuch
RWTH Aachen University, Germany

Starla M. Weaver
Kessler Foundation Research Center, USA

Glenn R. Wylie
Kessler Research Foundation, USA; University of Medicine and Dentistry of New Jersey, USA

Nick Yeung
University of Oxford, UK

1

Task Switching and Cognitive Control

An Introduction

JAMES A. GRANGE AND GEORGE HOUGHTON ■

INTRODUCTION

Humans live in an increasingly busy, multitask environment, requiring frequent switching between different cognitive operations and tasks. Driving, for example, presents us with an incredibly complex environment in which many subtasks—e.g., speed monitoring, interpretation of abstract road signs, planning the best route, etc.—must be organized and deployed appropriately to arrive at our destination safely. Even simple acts require effective scheduling and deployment of cognitive operations: For example, making a cup of coffee requires memory retrieval (Where did I store the coffee?), planning (fill the kettle with water *before* turning it on), mental rotation (read the coffee labels to avoid selecting the "de-caf"), coordination of both hands to open the coffee jar, and so on. Yet, despite the hustle and bustle, humans are able to act in a goal-directed manner. The question thus arises as to how humans are able to organize and control the selection and deployment of ongoing cognitive processes to ensure successful performance in multitask environments.

This problem is confounded because stimuli in our environment typically afford more than one action, making stimulus-dependent responding impossible; many of these competing actions are often totally irrelevant for the current task. For example, sat at a computer with the intention to write a book manuscript—how do we select this task in the face of competing tasks such as checking our email, browsing an online bookstore, or playing *just one more* game of online chess before we begin our work?

The cognitive system must be able to select the appropriate task based on current goals and intentions, rather than relying on stimulus-evoked actions. Such selection sometimes fails, as we have all likely experienced in the form of "action slips" (Reason, 1984)—putting a tea bag in your mug instead of coffee is one common example. Pathologically, damage to the prefrontal cortex has been shown to be sometimes associated with "utilization behaviour" (Lhermitte, 1983), where patients are not able to resist goal-irrelevant actions afforded by stimuli presented to them; walking past a light switch, a patient with utilization behavior might not be able to resist the urge to switch it on, even if lights are not required.

Thus, some form of top-down control is required to *select* the goal-relevant task in the face of competing alternatives. This *cognitive control* is imperative to ensure behavior is not stimulus driven. However, selection of relevant tasks is only one problem that the cognitive system must solve. Once a relevant task *has* been selected, how is this task able to dominate behavior so that competing tasks are not able to intrude? There would be little use for a system that can select relevant tasks with ease but is unable to maintain this task once competitors are present (otherwise, book manuscripts would never be finished). Therefore, the system needs to ensure the *stability* of task-relevant representations once a task has been selected. Somewhat paradoxically, although task representations must be stable, they must also be *flexible*, so that the representation can be removed and replaced when goals change. Failure to remove and update relevant task representations would lead to perseveration of action. The tension between these opposing demands has been called the *stability–flexibility dilemma* (Goschke, 2000), and it is a challenge for researchers of cognitive control to understand the mechanisms that allow the balance to occur. A system that solves the stability–flexibility dilemma would be well placed to adapt to changing situations and to act in a goal-directed manner.

THE TASK SWITCHING PARADIGM

The present volume is dedicated to a discussion of one set of tools that researchers of cognitive control have used to try to understand the mechanisms that allow a resolution to the plethora of demands placed on the cognitive system in multitask environments. The *task switching paradigm* has garnered much research interest over the past 20 years, driven by the potential that it allows measurement of cognitive control processes in operation (Kiesel et al., 2010; Meiran, 2010; Monsell, 2003; Vandierendonck, Liefooghe, & Verbruggen, 2010). In task switching paradigms, participants are typically presented with stimuli that afford more than one action (e.g., numbers) and are required to perform one of two tasks on the stimuli (e.g., odd/even judgments and lower-than-5/higher-than-5 judgments). Successful performance in such situations requires careful selection and maintenance of the currently relevant task and the flexibility to update tasks when goals change. It is a well-replicated finding in such task switching experiments that switching tasks induces a performance cost—typically manifesting in slower response times (RTs) and increased errors—compared with repeating tasks. Many researchers (though far from all) have taken this so-called *switch cost* as reflecting the time-course of a—or a set of—cognitive control processes dedicated to task switching (Meiran, 1996; Meiran, Chorez, & Sapir, 2000; Rogers & Monsell, 1995;

cf. Altmann & Gray, 2008, Allport, Styles, & Hsieh, 1994, Logan, 2003), and—by inference—that this cost is an important phenomenon with which to explore cognitive control. Thus, the growth in task switching research reflects interest in the possibility that understanding the nature of the switch cost will allow us to understand the cognitive processes that solve the stability–flexibility dilemma and to understand how efficient goal-directed behavior is produced.

The boom of interest in task switching research is highlighted by examining citation records of key task switching articles. For example, a key publication that reinvigorated research into task switching (Rogers & Monsell, 1995) has been cited 1,213 times[1]; a review in 2003 from the same group (Monsell, 2003) has been cited 774 times. Lest readers think interest in task switching is fading, two updated reviews of task switching—both published as recently as 2010—(Kiesel et al., 2010; Vandierendonck et al., 2010) have already accrued impressive citation counts in such a short time (124 and 77 citations, respectively). It is thus timely that a volume be dedicated to the research conducted on task switching.

CHAPTER OVERVIEW

The purpose of the present chapter is to provide the reader with a broad overview of task switching in general and to provide an overview of some of the different task switching paradigms available to the researcher, together with brief discussion of key empirical phenomena that are measured in these paradigms and how each is thought to be related to key cognitive control processes. Although some of these paradigms and empirical phenomena are the subject of dedicated chapters in this book—specifically, Chapters 3 (Meiran), 4 (Marí-Beffa & Kirkham), 5 (Altmann), and 6 (Arrington, Reiman, & Weaver)—we provide brief overviews here to give the reader sufficient background knowledge to tackle this book in any order. The overview is designed to be rather superficial, mainly highlighting the main trends in task switching research, making it as accessible as possible to new researchers to task switching. As we have noted, two excellent and comprehensive systematic reviews of task switching were recently published (Kiesel et al., 2010; Vandierendonck et al., 2010) that provide in-depth coverage of everything discussed in this chapter; however, we still aim to give a reasonably broad overview of the field here to ensure the book can stand alone.

After reviewing the paradigms and main empirical phenomena of task switching research, we provide an overview of the chapters in the present volume. We have been fortunate that each chapter is written by groups of leading authorities in their respective specialties; thus, this volume provides the reader with state-of-the-art knowledge of task switching research. Not only does each chapter provide comprehensive reviews, but they also are full with ideas for future directions in task switching research. Thus, these chapters will also provide the reader with many avenues with which to explore in their own research program.

Broadly, the book can be considered to be presented in three sections. The first "section" (Chapters 2 to 8) addresses key task switching paradigms and phenomena/concepts in more detail than the current chapter; these paradigms and effects reflect important areas of task switching research, and as such warrant their own chapters. This section also provides an overview of computational/mathematical models of task switching, which reviews the efforts of researchers to model and integrate key task switching effects. The second section (Chapters 9 and 10) deals with the neuroscience of task switching, focusing on the temporal (Chapter 9) and spatial (Chapter 10) localization of cognitive control processes during task switching. These chapters provide comprehensive reviews of the neural correlate of task switching performance in healthy populations. Section 3 addresses research on task switching and cognitive control in atypical research populations, including those with executive dysfunction (Chapter 11) and psychiatric disorders (Chapter 12). This section also includes comprehensive reviews of the developmental trajectory of task switching and cognitive control throughout the life span, covering research of task switching in childhood/adolescent populations (Chapter 13) and older adults (Chapter 14). It is hoped that the broad scope of topics covered in this book will appeal to readers from a wide range of research disciplines, including cognitive psychology, cognitive neuroscience, cognitive neuropsychology, clinical psychology, developmental psychology, human factors, and cognitive science.

TASK SWITCHING AND COGNITIVE CONTROL: PARADIGMS AND EMPIRICAL PHENOMENA

This section provides a chronological overview of trends in task switching research to date. Along the way, we highlight key experimental paradigms that have been used to measure cognitive control during task switching. Empirical phenomena in such paradigms have led researchers to hypothesize as to the nature of the control processes operating, although some of these processes are still hotly debated today.

Early Work and the Concept of Task Sets

The work of Jersild (1927) is typically cited as among the first empirical investigations into task switching (although Meiran, 2010, mentions earlier work by Ach, 1910). He presented participants with lists of stimuli (e.g., numbers) and required participants either to work through the list using just one task for all stimuli (repetition list, hereafter referred to as "pure" blocks or "pure" lists; e.g., add 3 to each number) or to alternate between two tasks (alternation list; e.g., add 3 to the first number, subtract 6 from the second, and repeat this pattern until the list is complete). Jersild's results showed that list-completion time was slower when participants were required to switch between two tasks than when just one task was required (see also Spector & Biederman, 1976), an effect the reader can replicate in Figure 1.1.

8—11—6—16—15—19—12—17—9

Figure 1.1 An example of the list paradigm (Jersild, 1927). Time yourself in two conditions. In the first condition, work through the list of numbers, adding 3 to each number (task repetition or "pure" list). In the second condition, work through the list of numbers, adding 3 to the first number, subtracting 6 from the second number, and repeating this pattern until you reach the end of the list (alternation list). Your list-completion times should be slower for the alternating list than for the repetition list.

Jersild (1927) suggested that to perform successfully on this paradigm, participants must establish in their mind a set of task rules and representations that allow correct performance. For example, when performing the addition task, the participant must activate in working memory some form of representation of "addition" that allowed successful execution of this task. Establishing new mental sets takes time, as reflected in the slower list-completion times for alternation lists compared with pure lists: Alternation lists require updating of mental set on every stimulus, whereas pure lists require maintaining the same mental set throughout. To Jersild, then, the list-alternation cost reflected the time taken to update one's mental set.

The concept of mental set has been expanded in recent years and is now typically referred to as a *task set*. Although the operational definition of task set varies with researcher (or goes undefined/underspecified; see Logan & Gordon, 2001; Schneider & Logan, 2007a; Schneider & Logan, Chapter 2, this volume), there are some definitions to be found in the task switching literature. Rogers and Monsell (1995), for example, define a *task set* as "form[ing] an effective intention to perform a particular task" (p. 207). Logan and Gordon (2001)—in their model of executive control of visual attention in dual task situations (ECTVA)—suggest that a task set consists of a set of programmable parameters critical for successful task performance that affect task processes, such as response selection, attentional bias, etc.; when the task changes, these parameters must be updated. Mayr and Keele (2000) offer a similar definition, stating a task set is "the configuration of perceptual, attentional, mnemonic, and motor processes critical for a particular task goal" (p. 5). Meiran (2010) has more recently suggested that a task set consists of five main elements[2]: (a) a goal state, (b) selection of task-relevant information through attention, (c) activation of task-relevant semantic information (e.g., in the case of the example in Figure 1.1, performance of an addition task requires activation of relevant numerical information [addition rules, etc.]), (d) activation of response information affording readiness to respond (e.g., in modern studies, participants might have to learn to associate a left key press with either an odd or a lower-than-5 response; depending on the currently relevant task; so-called *stimulus–response rules*), and (c) activation of correct response rules for presented stimulus (e.g., stimulus is odd, so press left).

Despite these somewhat inhomogeneous definitions, they all share the implicit assumption that task sets must be updated when the relevant task changes.

Establishment of a robust task set has been shown to shield the cognitive system effectively from distracting elements in multitask situations (Dreisbach, 2012; Dreisbach & Haider, 2008, 2009). For example, if a participant has firmly established the task set of "color naming," then they should be less prone to interference during a Stroop task (Stroop, 1953) when presented with the word "GREEN" written in red ink (and, with relevance to the example provided earlier, establishing the task set of "writing book chapter" should reduce interference from email distractions). Thus, establishing a suitable task set seems one way to ensure stability of task performance.

Alternating Runs Paradigm and Task Set Reconfiguration

At first, it seems the list paradigm is a suitable tool to measure the cognitive control processes required to update task sets when a change in task occurs: It produces a robust cost to performance, which is thought to index the time required to update task sets in working memory. However, despite it still being used sporadically (e.g., Baddeley, Chincotta, & Adlam, 2001; Bryck & Mayr, 2005; Emerson & Miyake, 2003), fundamental shortcomings with its construct validity render the list paradigm largely absent from modern task switching research. There exist other demands on the cognitive system than the requirement to switch task sets in the alternating lists compared to pure lists. One important factor is the differential load on working memory in the two list conditions: Pure lists require the maintenance of just one task set in memory, whereas alternating lists require participants to keep two task sets in a state of preparedness (Los, 1996; Philipp, Kalinich, Koch, & Schobotz, 2008; Poljac, Koch, & Bekkering, 2009; Rubin & Merian, 2005).

Indeed, later research demonstrated that task repetition RTs in pure lists (e.g., *AAAA*. . .) are faster than task repetitions in mixed lists (e.g., *AABB*. . . ; see later for more elaboration on mixed lists), even though both are strictly task repetitions. This *mixing cost* has been rather neglected in task switching research (but see seminal studies by Los, 1996; Rubin & Meiran, 2005; and more recent investigations: Marí-Beffa, Cooper, & Houghton, 2012) but could reflect important cognitive control processes. For example, Mari-Beffa and Kirkham (Chapter 4, this volume) argue that the mixing cost is an important measure of sustained mental control processes in multitask situations. Regardless of the true cause of the mixing cost, its presence complicates the issue when comparing pure and alternating lists in the Jersild (1927) paradigm as the costs to performance might not reflect the time-course of task set updating—and are thus potentially not an important signature of cognitive control, because the cost might reflect the extra demands on working memory during alternating lists.

To overcome this problem, Rogers and Monsell (1995)—in a seminal report that reinvigorated interest in task switching—introduced the *alternating runs paradigm*; this allowed investigation of responses to task repetition and task switching trials while equating working memory load (cf. Jersild, 1927). The alternating runs paradigm required participants to switch between two simple tasks every

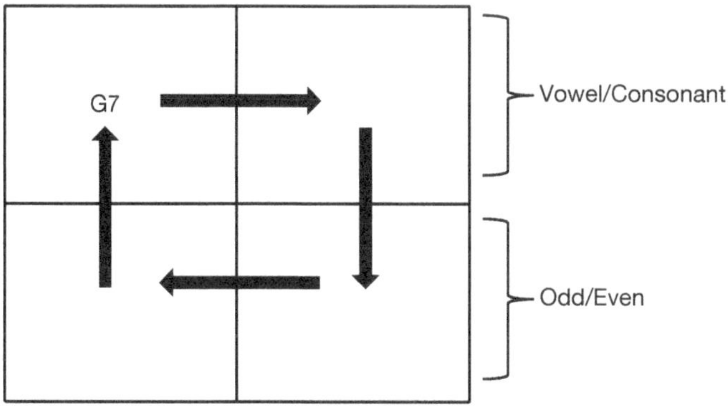

Figure 1.2 Example of the alternating runs paradigm (Rogers & Monsell, 1995). The stimulus location rotated in a predictable clockwise fashion on every trial, with the task switching when the stimulus crossed the horizontal mid-section. Performance in the upper-left and the lower-right squares thus reflects task switch trials, whereas performance on the upper-right and the lower-left squares reflects task repetition trials.

second trial in a predictable manner (e.g., AABBAABB. . ., etc.). Memory load was reduced in this experiment by presenting participants with a 2 × 2 grid with the location of the imperative stimulus rotating clockwise every trial (see Figure 1.2). If the stimulus appeared in either of the two upper squares, participants had to perform one task (e.g., vowel/consonant judgment on the letter), and when the stimulus appeared in the lower squares, participants had to perform the other task (e.g., odd/even judgment on the number stimulus; see Figure 1.2): Task switches occurred when the imperative stimulus moved across the horizontal mid-section, and other trials are task repetitions (e.g., moving from top-left to top-right requires repeating the vowel/consonant task). Thus, task switches and task repetitions occur in the same block of trials and memory load is equated (cf. Jersild, 1927).

As stimuli were mostly bivalent (in that the stimulus equally afforded both tasks), task performance required establishing a relevant task set. Thus, the finding of increased RTs and error rates to task switches compared to task repetitions led Rogers and Monsell (1995) to posit that this switch cost reflected the time taken for the cognitive system to reconfigure the relevant task set in memory; that is, the task set parameters relevant to the previous trial need to be removed and replaced with parameters relevant for the current trial. This time-consuming *task set reconfiguration* is required only on switch trials, as the previously applied task set is no longer relevant; repetition trials do not require any reconfiguration as the previous task set is applicable to the current trial. Using subtraction logic of RT analysis (e.g., Sternberg, 1969)—that responses to switch trials required only the addition of a task set reconfiguration stage, in comparison to task repetition trials, which do not—Rogers and Monsell hypothesized that the switch cost reflects the temporal signature of cognitive control in operation (although, as we will see, this has not met with consensus in the literature).

In apparent confirmation of the reconfiguration hypothesis, Rogers and Monesll (1995) found that the switch cost was significantly reduced if participants were given sufficient preparation time prior to target onset; this is consistent with a reconfiguration account as preparation time allows the time-consuming reconfiguration process to occur prior to target presentation (for an excellent overview of task preparation and its associated empirical evidence, see Kiesel et al., 2010).

Preparation time in the alternating runs paradigm is manipulated by varying the *response–stimulus interval (RSI)*: the time between the response to one task and the onset of the stimulus for the next task. The authors varied the RSI between 150 milliseconds (ms) and 1,200 ms and found that switch cost was indeed reduced at longer RSIs. This *reduction in switch cost (RISC)* has been taken as strong evidence for a reconfiguration process (Monsell, 2003; but see Logan & Bundesen, 2003, and the rejoinder Monsell & Mizon, 2006). However, even at prolonged RSIs, a small but consistent switch cost remained; this *residual switch cost* was subject to a flurry of investigation in subsequent years, with two main hypotheses for its presence: that it reflected a fundamental limit of reconfiguration based on sufficient task preparation (e.g., De Jong, 2000) and that there was an influence of the task stimulus on performance (Mayr & Kliegl, 2003; Rogers & Monsell, 1995; Rubinstein et al., 2001).

Rogers and Monsell (1995) supported the latter, suggesting that task set reconfiguration consisted of an endogenously driven reconfiguration process and a second, exogenous, component that must wait for stimulus presentation to commence. This two-stage account is in line with Mayr and Kliegl (2000, 2003), who suggested that task switching requires retrieval of task rules—a "relatively abstract description of what has to be done with the next stimulus" (Jost, Mayr, & Rösler, 2008, p. 75)—from long-term memory (together with their installation into working memory) and the application of these rules to the stimulus (e.g., if the stimulus is odd, press the left response key, and if the stimulus is even, press the right response key). The former process can be achieved ahead of target presentation (accounting for the large RISC with increased preparation time), but the latter process must wait for target presentation to be completed (thus accounting for the residual switch cost, but see Jost et al., 2008, and Monsell & Mizon, 2006, for evidence that this process can begin earlier than target onset).

Other authors suggested the residual switch cost reflected a fundamental limit of task preparation. Rather than reflecting a two-stage process that must wait for target onset to be completed, these theories suggest that full reconfiguration is possible before target onset but that it does not occur for a variety of reasons. The most influential theory in this respect is De Jong's (2000) *failure to engage* (FTE), which posits that full advanced reconfiguration is possible but participants do not engage this preparation on all trials. FTE suggests that preparation is an all-or-none process (cf. Lien et al., 2005) and that performance during task switching therefore consists of a mixture of fully prepared and unprepared trials. This transient nature of preparation was suggested to be driven by one of three (or any combination thereof) factors: (a) absence of goal-driven intention (i.e., motivation is lacking), (b) low environmental support (e.g., in the alternating runs paradigm, requiring to hold a task sequence in memory rather than being cued by stimulus position on screen), and (c) fatigue.

Task-Set Inertia

The hypotheses of the switch cost discussed so far assume it reflects an endogenously driven cognitive control process, namely task set reconfiguration. However, around the same time as Rogers and Monsell's (1995) investigation, Allport and colleagues (Allport, Styles, & Hsieh, 1994; Allport & Wylie, 2000) were also beginning to investigate task switching, developing their *task set inertia* (TSI) hypothesis. TSI explains switch cost not as a time-consuming reconfiguration process but rather as arising from familiar memory processes such as priming and interference (see also Altmann, 2002, 2003a, 2003b, Altmann & Gray, 2002, 2008). From this perspective, the switch cost can—on a task switch trial—be explained by persisting activation of the previous, but now irrelevant, task from the previous trial; this persisting activation—together with negative priming of the relevant task (see later)—hinders implementation of the currently relevant task, creating interference. The switch cost from the TSI perspective thus reflects the time taken to resolve this interference and establish the desired task set. Note also that this account provides an elegant explanation of the residual switch cost: that it is caused by proactive interference from elements of the previous task, independent of any preparation time (see Vandierendonck et al., 2010, for elaboration). Although the TSI account does not deny the requirement of cognitive control during task switching (Logan, 2003), it *does* deny that the switch cost directly measures the time-course of cognitive control operations. The cognitive system faces the same challenge on task switch trials that it also faces on task repetition trials: that of ensuring the relevant task is the most active among all competitors (see also Altmann & Gray, 2008).

Support for this hypothesis comes from the so called *asymmetric switch cost*: The observation that—when switching between tasks of unequal difficulty—the switch cost is greater when switching from the difficult to the easy task compared with switching from the easy task to the difficult task. Allport and colleagues suggested this cost arises as performance of the difficult task when switching from the easy task is hindered by the dominant activation of the easy task, causing interference; this interference needs to be resolved, by activating the difficult task (which takes time due to its difficulty) and negatively priming (i.e., inhibiting) the easy task. When switching back from the difficult task to the easy task, the activation of the difficult task persists, as does the inhibition of the easy task. Together, the inhibition of the relevant task (negative priming) and the increased interference from the irrelevant task (positive priming) cause uncertainty in the system, which takes time to resolve; the net effect is a large switch cost. Conversely, when switching from a difficult to an easy task, because the easy task is so dominant, there will be less necessity to strongly activate it (leading to reduced positive priming on the next trial) and the difficult task would require less/no inhibition (leading to reduced negative priming on the next trial). This effect replicates well (Arbuthnott, 2008a; Meuter & Allport, 1999; Monsell, Yeung, & Azuma, 2000; Yeung & Monsell, 2003; but see Schneider & Anderson, 2010, for an alternative interpretation of this cost). These data present a strong challenge to the reconfiguration hypothesis (see Gilbert & Shallice, 2000), which would predict a greater switch cost in switching from the easy task to the difficult task (as more needs to be "reconfigured"); the reconfiguration account also predicts no "carry-over" of previous (i.e., irrelevant) task activation once reconfiguration has occurred, contrary to what is observed.

The TSI account explains reduction of switch cost at extended preparation intervals (the RISC) by the dissipation of activation of irrelevant tasks (plus the dissipation of inhibition of the relevant task). During switch trials at short RSIs, the previous task's representation will still be very active, generating proactive interference. At extended RSIs, the previous task's activation will have decayed, eliciting less proactive interference. Thus, according to this view, observation of reduced switch cost with extended preparation time does not suggest a reconfiguration mechanism is in operation.

Both the TSI and reconfiguration hypotheses mimic each other in predicting a reduction of switch cost at extended RSIs. The reconfiguration account states this reduction is due to preparation-based reconfiguration of task sets (and thus the switch cost reflects cognitive control), whereas the TSI account predicts the reduction due to reduced proactive interference (and thus the switch cost does not reflect cognitive control). As extending the RSI in the alternating runs paradigm increases time for preparation *and* time for the previous tasks' activation to decay, it was clear that this paradigm was not suited to differentiate the competing hypotheses; as such, the alternating runs paradigm is seldom used in modern task switching research (see Altmann, 2007, for further important shortcomings of the alternating runs paradigm).

Explicit Cuing Paradigm

Meiran (1996; see also Chapter 3, this volume) and Meiran, Chorev, and Sapir (2000) used the *explicit cuing paradigm* (see also Sudevan & Taylor, 1987) to differentiate between the reconfiguration and TSI account of the switch cost. In this paradigm, participants must switch between two (or more) tasks on multivalent stimuli. Task presentation is random (cf. the fixed structure of the alternating runs), and participants know which task is currently relevant by a valid task cue that instructs them as to which task to perform. Trials are categorized into switch or repeat trials by comparing the cue on the previous trial with that of the current trial. Meiran's task presented participants with a 2 × 2 grid, with a target appearing in one of the four quadrants of the screen. The tasks were to either judge whether the stimulus appeared in the upper or lower two quadrants (up/down judgment) or in the left or right two quadrants (right/left judgment). The cues presented were two arrows, either pointing up and down (to cue the up/down task) or pointing left and right (to cue the left/right task).

This elegant paradigm allows researchers to separate the contributions of preparation-based processes (e.g., advanced reconfiguration) and TSI on the switch cost. Instead of manipulating the RSI, researchers now have control over two experimental parameters: The *cue–stimulus interval (CSI)* and the *response–cue interval (RCI)*. The CSI is the time between the onset of the task cue and the appearance of the trial target; extension of this period affords more time for task-specific preparation. The RCI is the time between the response to the previous task and the onset of the cue for the next task; extension of this period affords more time for the previous task's activation levels to decay (but see Horoufchin, Philipp, & Koch, 2011). Importantly, extension of the RCI does not affect task-specific preparation, as task presentation is randomized so participants are unaware of the upcoming task during this period. In this paradigm, the RSI—still defined as the time between the response on the previous trial and the stimulus for the next trial—is not manipulated directly but rather is a byproduct of CSI and/or RCI manipulations. This empirical isolation of RCI and CSI highlights that the alternating runs' main manipulation of the RSI is an inseparable synthesis of RCI and CSI. Thus, the cuing paradigm provides the researcher with greater control over preparation time.

Meiran (1996) manipulated the CSI while keeping the RSI constant (which controls the degree of proactive interference from the preceding trial; see Chapter 3, this volume, for more detail on this manipulation) and found significant reductions in switch cost at extended preparation intervals, consistent with a reconfiguration account. Note this finding is inconsistent with a TSI account, which predicts equivalent performance in conditions with constant RSI. However, despite examining preparation intervals of up to 1,908 ms (see Experiment 5), a significant residual switch cost remained. Meiran et al. (2000) suggested this residual cost reflected a contribution of interference from the preceding trial exerting itself (i.e., TSI), suggesting that both reconfiguration *and* TSI contribute to the switch cost.

Meiran et al. (2000) examined this hypothesis by varying the RCI while holding the CSI constant; holding the CSI constant between conditions equates the opportunity for preparation. Variation of the RCI is thought to manipulate the degree of interference from the previous trial: Short RCIs present a cue for the next trial while the previous task is assumed to still be very active, thus leading to greater interference than a condition with a long RCI, which allows the previous task's activation to decay, leading to reduced interference. Meiran et al. found reduced switch cost at longer RCIs, suggesting TSI can account for a portion of the switch cost. Based on these results, Meiran et al. suggested the switch cost consists of three components: (a) an active preparatory process (i.e., task set reconfiguration) that sets the system for a change of task, (b) passive decay of the activation levels of previous (irrelevant) tasks, and (c) a residual component.

Although it might seem that only the preparatory component should be of interest to researchers of cognitive control, all three components are tightly linked to task set preparation (and, hence, cognitive control). For example, it has already been mentioned that the residual component has been hypothesized to arise from failure to deploy preparatory processes (and, hence, cognitive control; De Jong, 2000; Nieuwenhuis & Monsell, 2002; but see Verbruggen, Liefooghe, Vandierendonck, & Demanet, 2007). In addition, interference from the preceding task's activation may be overcome by cognitive control processes (e.g., Logan, 2003) such as inhibition, which serves to reduce the interfering activation (Grange & Houghton, 2010b; Houghton et al., 2009; Koch, Gade, Schuch, & Philipp, 2010; see also Chapter 7, this volume).

Inhibition in Task Switching

Despite the concept of behavioral inhibition in cognitive psychology being rather controversial (see, for example, Gorfein & Brown, 2007; MacLeod, Dodd, Seard, Wilson, & Bibi, 2003; Nigg, 2000; Tipper, 2001), the evidence for inhibitory control being required during task switching is compelling. Recall that the TSI hypothesis of Allport and colleagues (Allport et al., 1994; Allport & Wylie, 2000; Wylie & Allport, 2000) suggested that the switch cost was caused not only by the persistent activation of the irrelevant task but also by the persisting inhibition of the relevant task. However, Mayr and Keele (2000) were the first to provide definitive evidence for inhibition in task switching. They contrasted two types of task switching sequence: an AB*A* sequence required performing a task recently performed after one intervening trial; this was compared with a CBA sequence, where task A has not been performed so recently. The idea is that—in an ABA sequence—switching from task A to task B requires activation of B, together with inhibition of task A; if task A is inhibited, it should take longer to reactivate when it is required soon after. In contrast, in a CBA sequence, task A has not been inhibited recently and should therefore be relatively easy to activate. Across several experiments (and many replications since; see Koch et al., 2010, and Gade et al., Chapter 7, this volume), it was shown that ABA sequences do elicit a slower RT than CBA sequences. This effect was called *backward inhibition* by Mayr and Keele (2000), but the more theoretically neutral term *n–2 repetition cost* is preferred today (Koch et al., 2010).

Note that this n–2 repetition cost is not congruent with the notion that task switching merely requires activating the relevant task (e.g., Altmann & Gray, 2008), as this would produce an ABA *benefit* as task A's activation will persist and prime performance (Grange, Juvina, & Houghton, 2013). Thus, this cost is the best evidence for a role for inhibitory processes in aiding task switching. Inhibition and activation together provide an elegant solution to the stability–flexibility dilemma mentioned at the outset of this chapter: *Stability* of a task's representation is achieved by maintaining its activation; *flexibility* is achieved by inhibiting tasks once a switch is required.

Problems With the Cuing Paradigm

Although the cuing paradigm remains perhaps the most popular choice among researchers interested in cognitive control, there are a number of important limitations of the paradigm. The first is that it typically confounds task switching with *cue switching*, and the second is that RTs conflate cue-related processes and target-related processes (e.g., Altmann & Gray, 2008).

Confounding Task Switching and Cue Switching

A fundamental shortcoming of the cuing paradigm with one cue per task is that task switching and cue switching are confounded: A task switch is always coupled with a cue switch (e.g., odd/even—*low/high*) and a task repetition with a cue repetition (odd/even—*odd/even*). A solution to this issue is to use two cues per task, which creates three possible sequences: *Cue repetition* (both the cue and the task repeat), *cue switch* (the cue switches, but the task required repeats, e.g., low/high—*magnitude*), and *task switch* (both the cue and the task switches, e.g., low/high—odd/even). The contribution of cue switching to the switch cost can now be estimated by comparing cue repetition RTs with cue switch RTs; "true" task switching costs (i.e., independent of cue switch effects) can now be estimated by comparing cue switch RT with task switch RT (Logan & Bundesen, 2003; Mayr & Kliegl, 2003). Costs associated with switching cues have been reliably shown to be substantial, due to residual priming of cue encoding processes during cue repetitions (Grange & Houghton, 2010a; Logan & Bundesen, 2003; Mayr & Kliegl, 2003); cue switches do not benefit from direct priming and thus must be encoded fully. However, the task switch cost has been found to be less reliable than previously thought. Some studies find that task switches show a cost which cannot be explained by switching cues (Altmann, 2006; Arrington, Logan, & Schneider, 2007; Grange & Houghton, 2010a; Jost et al., 2008; Mayr & Kliegl, 2003; Monsell & Mizon, 2006), while others report that task switches are just as costly as cue switches (Arrington & Logan, 2004a; Logan & Bundesen, 2003, 2004; Logan & Schneider, 2006b; Schneider & Logan, 2005).

Indeed, Logan and colleagues have presented this latter finding as evidence that explicit cuing paradigms do not measure cognitive control processes. They suggest that the same processes are deployed on switch trials as on repetition trials (cf. reconfiguration theories, which state reconfiguration is deployed on switch trials, but not on repetition trials): All that is required for successful performance is to encode the cue in short-term memory (STM), encode the target, and use this cue–stimulus compound to probe long-term memory (LTM) for the correct response. For example, after practice, the cue "odd/even" and the stimulus "2" uniquely retrieve the response "even" from LTM. From this perspective, task switching is merely cue switching: Cue switches (and also task switches) require encoding of a new cue into STM, which takes time. Cue repetition trials benefit from priming of STM contents (as the relevant cue is already encoded), whereas cue switch and task switch trials require encoding a new cue into STM; this theory was formalized mathematically by Schneider and Logan (2005; see also Logan & Schneider, 2010, and Schneider & Logan, 2009; see Chapter 8, this volume, for more detail about these models). Note this theory predicts identical performance for cue switch and task switch trials (which was indeed what Logan & Budnesen, 2003, reported); however, more recent evidence has suggested cue switch and task switch performance can be dissociated behaviorally (Arrington et al., 2007; Grange & Houghton, 2010a; Mayr & Kliegl, 2003) and at the neural level (Jost et al., 2008).

Mayr and Kliegl (2003) suggested that the cue switch cost arises from priming of a cue-specific retrieval route that obtains task rules from LTM and installs them into working memory. By this theory, when a cue repeats, the retrieval route is primed, contra to when a cue switches, which requires the use of a new (and unprimed) retrieval route. Thus, cue switch costs arise from priming of control processes that establish a working memory representation of what to do. Grange and Houghton (2010a) also provided evidence that cue switch costs arise from cognitive control processes responsible for establishing a working memory representation of what to do.

Although the cue switch–versus–task switch area of research has become incredibly controversial over recent years, the cuing paradigm remains a powerful tool for researchers of cognitive control, if used with the above constraints in mind. Meiran (Chapter 3, this volume) provides an excellent "recipe" for researchers interested in using this paradigm.

Separating Cue-Related Processes From Target-Related Processes

Performance on the standard explicit cuing paradigm—i.e. responses to unitary stimuli following a valid task cue—is a combination of cue-related processing and target-related processing; thus performance differences could be due to changes in cue processing or target processing (or a mixture of both). Although cue-related and target-related processes can be separated theoretically (e.g., see the mathematical models of Logan & Bundesen, 2003, and Schneider & Logan, 2005), empirical separation would be beneficial.

The work of Altmann has championed one such empirical paradigm that allows such separation (Altmann, 2002, 2006, 2007; Altmann & Gray, 2002, 2008; see also Chapter 5, this volume). This *extended runs paradigm* presents a cue that signals which of two (or more) tasks is relevant for a given "run." On this run, the cue is only presented with the first target; after this, targets are presented in isolation, and the relevant task must be maintained in memory (e.g., C_AAAAA where C_x is the cue for task x). Cues can either indicate a repetition of the previously relevant task (e.g., C_AAAAA—C_AAAAA) or a switch from the previous task (e.g., C_AAAAA—C_BBBBB). Using this paradigm, only trial one conflates cue-processing with target-processing, whereas uncued trials only reflect target processing.

Typical findings from this paradigm largely mirror those found in the standard cuing paradigm on trial one of the run (i.e., the cued trial); for example, switch RTs are slower than repetition RTs. However, there are some findings that are unique to this paradigm. For example, if the cue signals a repetition of the previous task, trial one RT is much larger than the RT for cueless trials, indicating a substantial cost of processing the cue independent of any switch of task. This *restart cost* (Allport & Wylie, 2000; Altmann, 2002, 2006, 2007; Altmann & Gray, 2002, 2008; Gopher Armony, & Greenshpan, 2000; Poljac et al., 2009) is thought to reflect the time the cognitive system needs to reactivate task representations that may have decayed since the last cue presentation. The restart cost is important theoretically, as it suggests that encoding and activation processes are run on repetition trials as well as switch trials (a view formalized by Altmann & Gray, 2008; see also Chapter 5, this volume), a view not compatible with a reconfiguration view of a dedicated set of processes that run on switch trials only (Meiran, 1996; Rogers & Monsell, 1995). It suggests the cognitive system faces the same problem on switch trials *and* repetition trials of ensuring the relevant task is the most active among all competing representations (see Chapters 5 and 8, this volume, for more information about this).

A related finding is that RTs slow steadily over a run of cueless trials (Altmann, 2002, Altmann & Gray, 2002, 2008). This *within-run slowing* is theorized to reflect the system attempting to access a decaying task representation (which becomes more difficult over time due to passive decay, and hence slows responses); the restart cost is thought to reflect the time needed to reactivate the decayed representation on repetition runs.

Newer Paradigms

Due to the problems inherent with the explicit cuing paradigm—and due to the growing consensus that it is not sensitive enough to measure cognitive control processes (Logan, 2003)—researchers have begun to investigate alternative paradigms capable of capturing cognitive control processes in operation. Such alternatives are briefly discussed below.

The *transition-cuing paradigm*, in which cues are presented that merely inform participants whether to "switch" or "repeat" tasks; that is, the participant must retain in memory the currently relevant task so that the next transition cue can be interpreted and acted on appropriately. This paradigm—introduced by Forstmann, Brass, and Koch (2007; but see Rushworth, Hadland, Paus, & Sipila, 2002)—thus allows the examination of potentially more "high-level" control in operation (Jost, De Baene, Koch, & Brass, 2013). Among the paradigm's immediate appeal is that the cues used are themselves not tied to one particular task (cf. standard task cues) but are merely associated with transition requirements; thus, the cues are signaling the required behavior and cannot—*prima facie*—be used in conjunction with the stimulus to drive compound-cue retrieval of the response from LTM (although see Schneider & Logan, 2007b, for how this might be achieved in conjunction with mediator retrieval—the process of retrieving a meaningful task name in response to a nontransparent cue, Logan & Schneider, 2006a). In addition, transition cuing also allows the occurrence of a task switch being signaled by a cue repetition (e.g., "Switch" → "Switch"), which is not possible with the standard 2:1 cue–task mapping procedure. Although there remain methodological issues to overcome (see, e.g., Schneider & Logan, 2007b), it seems that transition cuing is an interesting—and, as yet, relatively unexplored—avenue with which to research cognitive control.

The *task-span procedure*—introduced by Logan (2004; see also Logan, 2006)—ensures that cognitive control is being used during task switching by having participants remember a short list of task names (e.g., parity—parity—magnitude—parity—magnitude—magnitude. . .) and then execute these tasks on stimuli that follow (e.g., 6—7—2—9—8—6. . .). As a consequence of such lists, some responses will be task repetitions (responses 2 and 6 in the example) and some will be task switches (responses 3, 4, and 5). This procedure is thought to require cognitive control as the participant must control access to memory elements so as to retrieve the correct task name on the current trial, as well as implementing task switches should the need arise (Logan, 2006). However, it is possible that the task names recalled could be used to drive compound-cue retrieval (Logan & Schneider, 2010), so, although certainly interesting—especially if one is interested in exploring the relationship between the processes dedicated to task switching and the processes dedicated to working memory maintenance/access—the task-span procedure might face the same problems as the explicit cuing paradigm (Mayr, 2010). As this paradigm is still relatively underresearched, further work is required to establish whether the task-span procedure shares the explicit-cuing paradigm's fate.

Leading the way in the endeavor of finding an alternative paradigm is the work of Arrington and colleagues, who developed the *voluntary task switching (VTS) paradigm* (Arrington & Logan, 2004b; see Chapter 6, this volume). In this paradigm, no cues are presented to participants (which immediately alleviates the problem of cue switching), but rather participants must choose which of two (or more; see Lien & Ruthruff, 2008) tasks to perform on a random basis. Presented with a stimulus on an experimental trial, participants are typically instructed to choose which task to perform as if flipping a coin decided the outcome; so, on some trials participants will be switching from the task they performed on the previous trial, and on some trials they will be repeating the task they performed on the previous trial. By separating the responses for the two tasks to separate hands (i.e., respond with the left hand using the "D" and "F" keys if performing task A, and respond with the right hand using the "J" and "K" keys if performing task B), the researcher is able to easily establish which task was attempted by the participant. As task choices require cognitive control (see Chapter 6, this volume), it is thought that the VTS paradigm might capture these active processes during performance (see Arrington & Logan, 2004, 2005). Together with standard dependent variables typical to task switching—RTs and error rates to task repetitions and to task switches—VTS paradigms introduce a unique dependent variable, that of the probability of choosing a task repetition [*p*(repetition)]. *P*(repetition) should be.5 if the task choice truly is random (as task repetitions should be just as frequent as task switches), yet research has consistently shown a *repetition bias* (Chapter 6, this volume), hinting at some fundamental limitation in choosing task switches compared with task repetitions. This *p*(repetition) can be used to investigate what factors influence task choice. Although choice in the VTS is under some degree of top-down control, several studies have shown that exogenous, bottom-up factors can influence task choice (e.g., Arrington, 2008; Arrington &

Rhodes, 2010; Arrington, Weaver, & Pauker, 2010; Butler, Arrington, & Weywadt, 2011; Demanet, Verbruggen, Liefooghe, & Vandierendonck, 2010; Mayr & Bell, 2006; Yeung, 2010), suggesting there might be some limitation to the belief that VTS paradigms completely capture top-down processing. However, the paradigm appears to be an increasingly popular tool with which to explore cognitive control during task switching.

CONCLUSION AND OVERVIEW OF CHAPTERS

Even though this chapter intends to provide merely a *broad* overview of the main trends in task switching research, the reader would be right to be already forming the impression that the task switching field is deep and expansive, with a plethora of clever empirical designs and comprehensive theoretical advances. The present volume brings together experts across the wide field of task switching research, with chapters dedicated to each author's subdomain of expertise. It is hoped that this volume will aid consolidation of knowledge gleaned from research efforts so far and highlight important areas for future research. Here, we provide an overview of the chapters that make up this volume. We had originally planned to end the book with a chapter on future directions for research on task switching and cognitive control. However, all of the authors have done a superb job of highlighting important areas in each of their respective topics that deserve more attention in future research; as such, the reader will find an abundance of important and unresolved questions that need attention.

In Chapter 2, **Schneider and Logan** discuss the important—but often neglected—topic of what actually constitutes a task; coupled with this, it has long been suggested that task switching requires implementing a task set (e.g., Jersild, 1927; Rogers & Monsell, 1995), but the nature of the task set itself often goes unspecified. How can we tell whether task set reconfiguration has occurred if we are not clear on what a task set really is? At first glance, what constitutes a task seems simple, but Schneider and Logan argue that task switching research—and its associated theorizing—has been hampered by poor definitions of what are tasks and task sets. Schneider and Logan provide an elegant distinction between the two: A task is the representation of a set of instructions required to perform an activity accurately; a task set is the set of representations and processes that enable execution of the task. Schneider and Logan argue that—contrary to the often-held assumption that switching between two tasks in a task switching paradigm requires switching between two task sets—tasks and task sets do not necessarily have a one-to-one mapping. The authors provide recommendations for how to explore the nature of the relationship between tasks and task sets.

In Chapter 3, **Meiran** provides a user's guide for using the explicit-cuing paradigm, arguably the most popular choice among researchers interested in cognitive control. As stated in this introductory chapter, there are many issues that a researcher new to the area needs to be aware of when using this paradigm; with this user guide, researchers are treated to excellent recommendations for designing a task switching study, answering important questions such as "How many tasks should I use?" "How should I estimate mixing cost?" "What cues should I use?" "How do I empirically separate the retrievability of the previous task and the preparation for the current task?" This chapter also has a section on what actually constitutes a task (cf. Schneider & Logan, this volume); thus, this topic is clearly gaining traction in the minds of researchers. Closely following the recommendations set out in this chapter will allow researchers to produce valid experimental procedures capable of tapping important cognitive control processes.

In Chapter 4, **Marí-Beffa and Kirkham** provide an overview of the mixing cost, the finding of increased RTs to task repetitions in mixed blocks than in pure blocks. The chapter reviews current work and major findings regarding this cost and discusses key methodological difficulties in measuring it (together with some practical recommendations for the reader). Marí-Beffa and Kirkham take this cost to be indicative of sustained mental control processes that are activated when participants expect to have to switch between task sets; as such, the mixing cost is an interesting effect with which to explore cognitive control processes.

Chapter 5 provides an overview of the empirical and theoretical advantages of using the extended-runs paradigm. As **Altmann** highlights, this paradigm allows separation of cue-related processes and stimulus-related processes on performance; this separation (and the associated effects) highlights important constraints on models of cognitive control during task switching. In this chapter, Altmann discusses these effects in relation to his recent model of task switching (Altmann & Gray, 2008; see also Chapter 8 this volume).

In Chapter 6, **Arrington, Reiman, and Weaver** provide an excellent overview of one of the newest variants of task switching paradigms, the VTS paradigm. Although in its relative infancy as a paradigm, the VTS procedure has garnered considerable interest among researchers, and a wealth of empirical investigation has already accumulated. The promise is that this paradigm captures nuances of cognitive control not measurable with other task switching paradigms, such as control over task choice. Arguably, this puts task switching research into more "ecologically valid" scenarios: In everyday life, humans often take control over which task to execute at a given moment rather than being instructed to do so; the VTS aims to uniquely capture the processes that give rise to volitional behavior. This chapter provides an overview of the empirical contributions, as well as detailed discussion of the theoretical accounts of VTS performance; open questions in this important area of research are also highlighted, providing fruitful avenues for the next wave of research.

In Chapter 7, **Gade, Schuch, Druey, and Koch** provide a comprehensive overview of inhibitory control during task switching. Inhibition has become an increasingly controversial concept in cognitive psychology (Gorfein & Brown, 2007; MacLeod, Dodd, Seard, Wilson, & Bibi, 2003; Nigg, 2000; Tipper, 2001), but there is convincing evidence for a robust role for inhibitory mechanisms during task switching; this makes the task switching paradigm an ideal vehicle to explore inhibitory control in typical and atypical populations. The authors discuss two lines of evidence for inhibition in task switching: Response repetition effects and the n–2 repetition cost, with the latter being the least ambiguous line of evidence. There is convincing evidence—reviewed in this chapter—that inhibition is a flexible process targeting whichever aspect of the trial structure (cue, target, response) that generates interference when the task switches (Houghton et al., 2009); however, the exact nature of the inhibitory input itself (is it lateral inhibition? is it self-inhibition?) remains largely unclear. This area remains a fertile ground for research, and Gade and colleagues highlight many unanswered questions requiring researchers' attention going forward.

In Chapter 8, **Grange and Houghton** provide an overview of the key models of cognitive control during task switching. Models of cognition allow researchers to peer inside the "black box" that is human cognition. Thus, models of task switching allow researchers to investigate and test formal theories of how cognitive control is deployed to allow efficient goal-directed behavior in multitask environments. This chapter reviews the most influential and successful models of task switching. We provide an overview of the architecture of each model, before discussing how each model explains key theoretical and empirical concepts that have accumulated in the field of task switching. In a final section, we discuss critical general shortcomings of extant models and propose some promising future directions for modeling efforts. In particular, we note that the formal modeling of inhibitory processes in task switching—a process with considerable empirical support—is a notable omission from many models and is an essential area for future research.

Chapter 9 marks the start of the second section, focusing on neuroscientific examination of cognitive control during task switching. In this chapter, **Karayanidis and Jamadar** review the electrophysiological evidence, focusing on event-related potentials (ERPs). ERPs provide the researcher with superb temporal resolution, tracking neural activity at the scalp with millisecond precision. As behavioral measures (e.g., RTs) usually only collect a response from the subject at the end of a sequence of events (e.g., an experimental trial in task switching, which consists of task cues and stimuli), inferences about the participant's responses to the various components of the trial are inevitably somewhat indirect. The use of ERP recording, on the other hand, allows the collection of electrophysiological measures through an experimental trial, whether or not a participant makes an overt response. The high temporal resolution of these methods mean that it is feasible to separate out the brain responses to events occurring within less than 100 ms of each other. Hence, for instance, brain responses to task cues can be separated from those to stimuli, and the effects of task switching manipulations on the various components of a trial structure can be separated. Thus, ERPs allow an unprecedented examination as to the time-course of cognitive control during task switching.

In this chapter, **Karayanidis and Jamadar** review the ERP evidence of proactive and reactive control during task switching. Proactive control refers to processes deployed during preparatory intervals in task switching, which ready the system for the upcoming task; reactive control refers to control processes that serve to reduce interference during stimulus onset. The evidence reviewed leads the authors to suggest that proactive control requires general task preparation (i.e., not specific to switching) and switch-specific preparation (i.e., dedicated processes that only run on switch trials). In terms of reactive control, the evidence suggests switch-specific modulation of response preparation and response implementation. The chapter also provides coverage of multi-modal studies which mix ERP measurements with other neuroscientific techniques.

In Chapter 10, **Richter and Yeung** provide an overview of functional magnetic resonance imaging (fMRI) studies of task switching. The advent of noninvasive neuroimaging techniques with high spatial resolution has had a tremendous and continuing impact on cognitive psychology, and task switching is being extensively studied using (usually) event-related fMRI designs. While not enjoying the temporal resolution of ERPs, fMRI provides a high degree of spatial resolution, allowing the brain areas involved in the maintenance and switching of task rules to be investigated. In this chapter, the authors provide a meta-analysis of 34 fMRI task switching studies to elucidate the neural regions responsible for task switching. In addition, the authors continually refer to how evidence from fMRI studies shapes and constrains our theorizing of cognitive control in task switching. One striking conclusion from this chapter is that there is very little evidence from the studies reviewed that switch-specific (i.e., reconfiguration) processes are recruited during task switching.

In Chapter 11, **Das and Wylie** review the effect of executive dysfunction on task switching performance. As task switching is generally thought to require recruitment of cognitive control processes, it is an excellent paradigm with which to explore the broader domain of executive functioning in atypical populations. Das and Wylie examine the current literature on task switching and executive dysfunction, focusing on stroke, Parkinson disease, Huntington disease, traumatic brain injury, and schizophrenia. Exploring a range of executive dysfunction populations allows the authors to elucidate to what extent the disorders differentially affect cognitive control in task switching (with some populations showing surprising "sparing" of task switching ability). The investigation of neurological pathology complements the work of neuroimaging, which can only be taken so far; for example, demonstrating activation of region X in an fMRI study cannot differentiate whether the activation in region X is a cause or a consequence of a particular cognitive process. Finding patients with damage to region X—and investigating their performance on task switching—can bridge the gap between research on healthy and atypical populations in elucidating the neural underpinnings of task switching.

In Chapter 12, **Ravizza and Salo** review the literature on task switching in psychiatric disorders. As many psychiatric disorders are associated with deficits in executive function, and task switching is thought to require executive control, these populations become an important area for investigation. In this chapter, the authors review evidence from task switching studies in four populations: schizophrenia, autism spectrum disorder, attention-deficit/hyperactivity disorder, and major depression. There exist dissociable processes during task switching that are selectively affected by some disorders and not others, constraining both theoretical models of task switching and models of the effects of clinical disorders on cognition.

Chapter 14 focuses on cognitive flexibility in childhood and adolescence. In this chapter, **Peters and Crone** review the behavioral and neural development of two types of cognitive flexibility: instructed flexibility (more typically measured by the standard task switching paradigm) and adaptive flexibility (measured with performance-monitoring paradigms). Both approaches provide insights into resolution of the stability–flexibility dilemma. Studying the development of cognitive control during childhood provides important insights, as the neural architecture thought to serve cognitive control (e.g., the frontal lobes) is not fully developed in adolescence. By reviewing the evidence, the authors conclude that both types of flexibility are dissociable when comparing adults with typically developing children, and provide ideas for future research.

Chapter 15 focuses on the effect of healthy aging on task switching performance. In a world where the average life expectancy is consistently rising, the implications of healthy aging on cognitive performance are becoming more germane. In this chapter, **Kray and Ferdinand** review the literature on task switching and aging, concentrating their discussion on three focused areas: To what extent are there process-specific limitations of older adults in task switching (e.g., impairments of task maintenance and selection)? Which factors module age-related impairments in these processes? Which cognitive interventions are useful for improving them.

NOTES

1. All searches conducted in PsycINFO on August 8, 2013.
2. There is a sixth, but it only applies to multistep procedures that are not discussed in this chapter (but see Luria & Meiran, 2003, 2006; Schneider & Logan, 2006a).

REFERENCES

Ach, N. On volition (T. Herz, Trans.). (Original work published 1910) Available at: University of Konstanz, Cognitive Psychology Web site: http://www.uni-konstanz.de/kogpsych/ach.htm. 2006.

Allport, A., Styles, E. A., & Hsieh, S. (1994). Shifting intentional set: Exploring the dynamic control of tasks. In C. Umilta & M. Moscovitch (Eds.), *Attention and performance XV. Conscious and nonconscious information processing* (pp. 421 452). Cambridge, MA: MIT Press.

Allport, A., & Wylie, G. R. (2000). Task switching, stimulus–response bindings, and negative priming. In S. Monsell & J. Driver (Eds.), *Control of cognitive processes: Attention and performance XVIII* (pp. 35–70). Cambridge, MA: MIT Press.

Altmann, E. M. (2002). Functional decay of memory for tasks. *Psychological Research*, 66, 287–297.

Altmann, E. M. (2003a). Task switching and the pied homunculus: Where are we being led? *Trends in Cognitive Sciences, 7*, 340–341.

Altmann, E. M. (2003b). Think globally, ask functionally. *Behavioral & Brain Sciences, 26*, 602–603.

Altmann, E. M. (2006). Task switching is not cue switching. *Psychonomic Bulletin & Review, 13*, 1016–1022.

Altmann, E. M. (2007). Comparing switch costs: Alternating runs and explicit cuing. *Journal of Experimental Psychology: Learning, Memory, and Cognition, 33*, 475–483.

Altmann, E. M., & Gray, W. D. (2002). Forgetting to remember: The functional relationship of decay and interference. *Psychological Science, 13*, 27–33.

Altmann, E. M., & Gray, W. D. (2008). An integrated model of cognitive control in task switching. *Psychological Review, 115*, 602–639.

Arbuthnott, K. D. (2008a). Asymmetric switch cost and backward inhibition: Carryover activation and inhibition in switching between tasks of unequal difficulty. *Canadian Journal of Experimental Psychology, 62*, 91–100.

Arrington, C. M. (2008). The effect of stimulus availability on task choice in voluntary task switching. *Memory & Cognition, 38*, 991–997.

Arrington, C. M., & Logan, G. D. (2004a). Episodic and semantic components of the compound stimulus strategy in the explicit task cuing procedure. *Memory & Cognition, 32*, 965–976.

Arrington, C. M., & Logan, G. D. (2004b). The cost of a voluntary task switch. *Psychological Science, 15*, 610–615.

Arrington, C. M., & Logan, G. D. (2005). Voluntary task switching: Chasing the elusive homunculus. *Journal of Experimental Psychology: Learning, Memory and Cognition, 31*, 683–702.

Arrington, C. M., Logan, G. D., & Schneider, D. W. (2007). Separating cue encoding from target processing in the explicit task-cuing procedure: Are there "true" task switch effects? *Journal of Experimental Psychology: Learning, Memory, and Cognition, 33*, 484–502.

Arrington, C. M., & Rhodes, K. M. (2010). Perceptual asymmetries influence task choice: The effect of lateralized presentation of hierarchical stimuli. *Laterality, 15*, 501–513.

Arrington, C. M., Weaver, S. M., & Pauker, R. L. (2010). Stimulus-based priming of task choice during voluntary task switching. *Journal of Experimental Psychology: Learning, Memory, and Cognition, 36*, 1060–1067.

Baddeley, A., Chincotta, D., & Adlam, A. (2001). Working memory and the control of action: Evidence from task switching. *Journal of Experimental Psychology: General, 130*, 641–657.

Bryck, R. L., & Mayr, U. (2005). On the role of verbalization during task set selection: switching or serial order control? *Memory & Cognition, 33*, 611–623.

Butler, K.M., Arrington, C.M., & Weywadt, C. (2011). Working memory capacity modulates task performance but has little influence on task choice. *Memory & Cognition, 39*, 708–724.

De Jong, R. (2000). An intention-activation account of residual switch costs. In S. Monsell & J. Driver (Eds.), *Attention and performance XVIII: Control of cognitive processes* (pp. 357–376). Cambridge, MA: MIT Press.

Demanet, J., Verbruggen, F., Liefooghe, B., Vandierendonck, A. (2010). Voluntary task switching under load: Contribution of top-down and bottom-up factors in goal-directed behavior. *Psychonomic Bulletin & Review, 3*, 387–393.

Dreisbach, G. (2012). Mechanisms of cognitive control: The functional role of task rules. *Current Directions in Psychological Science, 21*, 227–231.

Dreisbach, G., & Haider, H. (2008). That's what task sets are for: Shielding against irrelevant information. *Psychological Research, 72*, 355–361.

Dreisbach, G., & Haider, H. (2009). How task representations guide attention: Further evidence for the shielding function of task sets. *Journal of Experimental Psychology: Learning, Memory, and Cognition, 35*, 477–486.

Emerson, M. J., & Miyake, A. (2003). The role of inner speech in task switching: A dual-task investigation. *Journal of Memory and Language, 48*, 148–168.

Forstmann, B. U., Brass, M., & Koch, I. (2007). Methodological and empirical issues when dissociating cue-related from task-related processes in the explicit task-cuing procedure. *Psychological Research, 71*, 393–400.

Gilbert, S. J., & Shallice, T. (2002). Task switching: A PDP model. *Cognitive Psychology, 44*, 297–337.

Gopher, D., Armony, L., & Greenshpan, Y. (2000). Switching tasks and attention policies. *Journal of Experimental Psychology: General, 129*, 308–339.

Gorfein, D. S., & Brown, V. R. (2007). Saying no to inhibition. In D. S. Gorfein & C. M. MacLeod (Eds.), *Inhibition in cognition* (pp. 103–124).

Goschke, T. (2000). Intentional reconfiguration and involuntary persistence in task set switching. In S. Monsell & J. Driver (Eds.), *Control of cognitive processes: Attention and performance* (Vol. 18, pp. 331–355). Cambridge, MA: MIT Press.

Grange, J. A., & Houghton, G. (2010a). Cue-switch costs in task-switching: Cue priming or control processes? *Psychological Research, 74*, 481–490.

Grange, J. A., & Houghton, G. (2010b). Heightened conflict in cue–target translation increases backward inhibition in set switching. *Journal of Experimental Psychology: Learning, Memory, and Cognition, 36*, 1003–1009.

Grange, J. A., Juvina, I., & Houghton, G. (2013). On costs and benefits of n–2 repetitions in task switching: towards a behavioural marker of cognitive inhibition. *Psychological Research, 77*, 211–222.

Houghton, G., Pritchard, R., & Grange, J. A. (2009). The role of cue–target translation in backward inhibition of attentional set. *Journal of Experimental Psychology: Learning, Memory and Cognition, 35*, 466–476.

Horoufchin, H., Philipp, A. M., & Koch, I. (2011). The dissipating task-repetition benefit in cued task switching: Task-set decay or temporal distinctiveness? *Journal of Experimental Psychology: Human Perception and Performance, 37*, 455–472.

Jersild, A. T. (1927). *Mental set and shift. Archives of Psychology, 89*(entire issue).

Jost, K., De Baene, W., Koch, I., & Brass, M. (2013). A review of the role of cue processing in task switching. *Zeitschrift für Psychologie, 221*, 5–14.

Jost, K., Mayr, U., & Rosler, F. (2008). Is task switching nothing but cue priming? Evidence from ERPs. *Cognitive, Affective, and Behavioral Neuroscience, 8*, 74–84.

Kiesel, A., Steinhauser, M., Wendt, M., Falkstein, M., Jost, K., Philipp, A., & Koch, I. (2010). Control and interference in task switching—a review. *Psychological Bulletin, 136*, 849–874.

Koch, I., Gade, M., Schuch, S., & Philipp, A. M. (2010). The role of inhibition in task switching—A review. *Psychonomic Bulletin & Review, 17*, 1–14.

Lhermitte, F. (1983). Utilization behaviour and its relation to the frontal lobes. *Brain, 106*, 237–255.

Lien, M.-C., & Ruthruff, E. (2008). Inhibition of task set: Converging evidence from task choice in the voluntary task-switching paradigm. *Psychonomic Bulletin & Review, 15*, 1111–1116.

Lien, M.-C., Ruthruff, E., Remington, R. W., & Johnston, J. C. (2005). On the limits of advance preparation for a task switch: Do people prepare all the task some of the time or some of the task all the time? *Journal of Experimental Psychology: Human Perception and Performance, 31*, 299–315.

Logan, G. D. (2003). Executive control of thought and action: In search of the wild homunculus. *Current Directions in Psychological Science, 12*, 45–48.

Logan, G. D. (2004). Working memory, task switching, and executive control in the task span procedure. *Journal of Experimental Psychology: General, 133*, 218–236.

Logan, G. D. (2006). Out with the old, in with the new: More valid measures of switch cost and retrieval time in the task span procedure. *Psychonomic Bulletin & Review, 13*, 139–144.

Logan, G. D., & Bundesen, C. (2003). Clever homunculus: Is there an endogenous act of control in the explicit task-cuing procedure? *Journal of Experimental Psychology: Human Perception and Performance, 29*, 575–599.

Logan, G. D., & Bundesen, C. (2004). Very clever homunculus: Compound stimulus strategies for the explicit task-cuing procedure. *Psychonomic Bulletin & Review, 11*, 832–840.

Logan, G. D., & Gordon, R. D. (2001). Executive control of visual attention in dual-task situations. *Psychological Review, 108*, 393–434.

Logan, G. D., & Schneider, D. W. (2006a). Interpreting instructional cues in task switching procedures: The role of mediator retrieval. *Journal of Experimental Psychology: Learning, Memory, and Cognition, 32*, 347–363.

Logan, G. D., & Schneider, D. W. (2006b). Priming or executive control? Associative priming of cue encoding increases "switch costs" in the explicit task-cuing procedure. *Memory & Cognition, 34*, 1250–1259.

Logan, G. D., & Schneider, D. W. (2010). Distinguishing reconfiguration and compound-cue retrieval in task switching. *Psychologica Belgica, 50*, 413–433.

Los, S. A. (1996). On the origin of mixing costs: Exploring information processing in pure and mixed blocks of trials. *Acta Psychologica, 94*, 145–188.

Luria, R., & Meiran, N. (2003). Online order control in the psychological refractory period paradigm. *Journal of Experimental Psychology: Human Perception and Performance, 29*, 556–574.

Luria, R., & Meiran, N. (2006). Dual route for subtask order control: Evidence from the Psychological Refractory Period paradigm. *Quarterly Journal of Experimental Psychology: Section A, 59*, 720–744.

MacLeod, C. M., Dodd, M. D., Sheard, E. D., Wilson, D. E., & Bibi, U. (2003). In opposition to inhbition. *Psychology of Learning & Motivation, 43*, 163–214.

Marí-Beffa, P., Cooper, S., & Houghton, G. (2012). Unmixing the mixing cost: Contributions from dimensional relevance and stimulus-response suppression. *Journal of Experimental Psychology: Human Perception and Performance, 38*, 478–488.

Mayr, U. (2010). The surface structure and the deep structure of sequential control: What can we learn from task-span switch costs? *Psychonomic Bulletin & Review, 17*, 693–698.

Mayr, U., & Bell, T. (2006). On how to be unpredictable: Evidence from the voluntary task switching paradigm. *Psychological Science, 17*, 774–780.

Mayr, U., & Keele, S. W. (2000). Changing internal constraints on action: The role of backward inhibition. *Journal of Experimental Psychology: General, 129*, 4–26.

Mayr, U., & Kliegl, R. (2000). Task-set switching and long-term memory retrieval. *Journal of Experimental Psychology: Learning, Memory, and Cognition, 26*, 1124–1140.

Mayr, U., & Kliegl, R. (2003). Differential effects of cue changes and task changes on task-set selection costs. *Journal of Experimental Psychology: Learning, Memory, and Cognition, 29*, 362–372.

Meiran, N. (1996). Reconfiguration of processing mode prior to task performance. *Journal of Experimental Psychology. Learning, Memory, and Cognition, 22*, 1423–1442.

Meiran, N. (2010). Task switching: Mechanisms underlying rigid vs. flexible self control. In R. Hassin, K. Ochsner, & Y. Trope (Eds.). *Self control in society, mind and brain* (pp. 202–220). New York, NY: Oxford University Press.

Meiran, N., Chorev, Z., & Sapir, A. (2000). Component processes in task switching. *Cognitive Psychology, 41*, 211–253.

Meuter, R. F. I., & Allport, A. (1999). Bilingual language switching in naming: Asymmetrical costs of language selection. *Journal of Memory and Language, 40*, 25–40.

Monsell, S. (2003). Task switching. *Trends in Cognitive Sciences, 7*, 134–140.

Monsell, S., & Mizon, G. (2006). Can the task-cuing paradigm measure an endogenous task-set reconfiguration process? *Journal of Experimental Psychology: Human Perception and Performance, 32*, 493–516.

Monsell, S., Yeung, N., & Azuma, R. (2000). Reconfiguration of task-set: Is it easier to switch to the weaker task? *Psychological Research, 63*, 250–264.

Nieuwenhuis, S., & Monsell, S. (2002). Residual costs in task switching: Testing the failure-to-engage hypothesis. *Psychonomic Bulletin & Review, 9*, 86–92.

Nigg, J. T. (2000). On inhibition/disinhibition in developmental psychopathology: Views from cognitive and personality psychology and a working inhibition taxonomy. *Psychological Bulletin, 126*, 220–246.

Philipp, A. M., Kalinich, C., Koch, I., & Schubotz, R. I. (2008). Mixing costs and switch costs when switching stimulus dimensions in serial predictions. *Psychological Research, 72*, 405–414.

Poljac, E., Koch, I., & Bekkering, H. (2009). Dissociating restart cost and mixing cost in task switching. *Psychological Research, 73*, 407–416.

Reason, J. T. (1984). Lapses of attention. In R. Parasuraman, R. Davies, & J. Beatty (Eds.), *Varieties of attention* (pp. 515–549). Orlando, FL: Academic Press.

Rogers, R. D., & Monsell, S. (1995). Costs of a predictible switch between simple cognitive tasks. *Journal of Experimental Psychology: General, 124*, 207–231.

Rubin, O., & Meiran, N. (2005). On the origins of the task mixing cost in the cuing task-switching paradigm. *Journal of Experimental Psychology: Learning, Memory, and Cognition, 31*, 1477–1491.

Rubinstein, J. S., Meyer, D. E., & Evans, J. E. (2001). Executive control of cognitive processes in task switching. *Journal of Experimental Psychology: Human Perception and Performance, 27*, 763–797.

Rushworth, M. F. S., Hadland, K. A., Paus, T., & Sipila, P. K. (2002). Role of the human medial frontal cortex in task switching: A combined fMRI and TMS study. *Journal of Neurophysiology, 87*, 2577–2592

Schneider, D. W., & Anderson, J. R. (2010). Asymmetric switch costs as sequential difficulty effects. *Quarterly Journal of Experimental Psychology, 63,* 1873–1894.

Schneider, D. W., & Logan, G. D. (2005). Modeling task switching without switching tasks: A short-term priming account of explicitly cued performance. *Journal of Experimental Psychology: General, 134,* 343–367.

Schneider, D. W., & Logan, G. D. (2006a). Hierarchical control of cognitive processes: Switching tasks in sequences. *Journal of Experimental Psychology: General, 135,* 623–640.

Schneider, D. W., & Logan, G. D. (2007a). Defining task-set reconfiguration: The case of reference point switching. *Psychonomic Bulletin & Review, 14,* 118–125.

Schneider, D. W., & Logan, G. D. (2007b). Task switching versus cue switching: Using transition cuing to disentangle sequential effects in task-switching performance. *Journal of Experimental Psychology: Learning, Memory, and Cognition, 33,* 370–378.

Schneider, D. W., & Logan, G. D. (2009). Selecting a response in task switching: Testing a model of compound cue retrieval. *Journal of Experimental Psychology: Learning, Memory, and Cognition, 35,* 122–136.

Spector, A., & Biederman, Y. (1976). Mental set and mental shift revisited. *American Journal of Psychology, 89,* 669–679.

Sternberg, S. (1969). The discovery of processing stages: Extensions of Donders' method. *Acta Psychologica, 30,* 276–315.

Stroop, J. R. (1935). Studies of interference in serial verbal reactions. *Journal of Experimental Psychology, 18,* 643–662.

Sudevan, P., & Taylor, D. A. (1987). The cuing and priming of cognitive operations. *Journal of Exerimental Psychology: Human Perception and Performance, 13,* 89–103.

Tipper, S. P. (2001). Does negative priming reflect inhibitory mechanisms: A review and integration of conflicting views. *Quarterly Journal of Experimental Psychology, 54A,* 321–343.

Vandierendonck, A., Liefooghe, B., & Verbruggen, F. (2010). Task switching: Interplay of reconfiguration and interference control. *Psychological Bulletin, 136,* 601–626.

Verbruggen, F., Liefooghe, B., Vandierendonck, A., & Demanet, J. (2007). Short cue presentations encourage advance task preparation: A recipe to diminish the residual switch cost. *Journal of Experimental Psychology: Learning, Memory, and Cognition, 33,* 342–356.

Wylie, G., & Allport, A. (2000). Task switching and measurement of "switch costs." *Psychological Research, 63,* 212–233.

Yeung, N. (2010). Bottom-up influences on voluntary task switching: The elusive homunculus escapes. *Journal of Experimental Psychology: Learning Memory and Cognition, 36,* 348–362.

Yeung, N., & Monsell, S. (2003). The effects of recent practice on task switching. *Journal of Experimental Psychology: Human Perception and Performance, 29,* 919–936.

2

Tasks, Task Sets, and the Mapping Between Them

DARRYL W. SCHNEIDER AND GORDON D. LOGAN ■

INTRODUCTION

The copious research on task switching over the past several years has been fueled by the belief that understanding how people switch tasks will shed light on the broader question of how the mind exercises control over cognition. However, the hodgepodge of empirical phenomena (for reviews, see Kiesel et al., 2010; Vandierendonck, Liefooghe, & Verbruggen, 2010) and the lack of theoretical integration in the task switching domain lead one to wonder how much light has actually passed through the semiopaque window of task switching. We contend that the opacity is a consequence of fundamental inadequacies in how researchers think about and discuss task switching. *Tasks* and *task sets* (the means by which tasks are performed) are often poorly defined, and the mapping between them is usually given superficial analysis. As a result, it is difficult to link theory to data and to determine when and how the cognitive control purportedly reflected by task switching is being exercised. Our goal in this chapter is to draw attention to these issues in an effort to stimulate critical thinking about key concepts in task switching research and facilitate progress toward achieving a better understanding of cognitive control.

WHAT IS A TASK?

> "We acknowledge that it is difficult to define with precision, even in the restricted context of discrete reaction tasks, what constitutes a 'task.'"
>
> —Rogers and Monsell (*1995, p. 208*)

The difficulty of defining a task was recognized early by Rogers and Monsell (1995), but since then it has largely been ignored. We think part of the reason the issue has been neglected is that researchers are free to call anything a "task" and, by extension, refer to even the smallest of transitions as "task switching." For example, consider an experiment in which subjects learn a simple pair of stimulus–response mappings (e.g., press key *1* for stimulus *A* and key *2* for stimulus *B*) then perform trials on which they see either an *A* or a *B* displayed in either green or red font. When the stimulus is green, they have to respond according to the learned mapping, but when the stimulus is red, they have to respond according to the reversed mapping (e.g., press key *2* for stimulus *A* and key *1* for stimulus *B*). Does this experiment involve one task (with a set of four stimulus–response mappings) or two tasks (defined by color)? When the stimulus changes color across trials, does that constitute a task switch? If so, then is there any evidence of a *switch cost*—a longer response time or higher error rate for color switches compared with color repetitions?

Some insight regarding the answers to these questions has been provided in studies by Dreisbach and colleagues (Dreisbach, Goschke, & Haider, 2006, 2007; Dreisbach & Haider, 2008). They conducted experiments in which word stimuli appeared in different-colored fonts across trials, with each color cuing a specific task (e.g., green cued an animal–nonanimal judgment on the referent of the word and red cued a consonant–vowel judgment on the first letter of the word). The key manipulation was that one group of subjects (the "two-task" group) was informed of the two tasks represented by the color–task mappings, whereas another group of subjects (the "stimulus–response" group) was merely instructed to memorize all the stimulus–response mappings. The main result was a switch cost in performance (associated with color change) for the two-task group but not for the stimulus–response group. Interestingly, when the stimulus–response group was later informed of the color–task mappings, they began to show a switch cost (Dreisbach et al., 2007). Thus, despite subjects experiencing identical trial conditions, their behavior was influenced by whether they were instructed about the existence of different tasks.

Another example of how instructions can influence behavior in task switching situations was provided by Logan and Schneider (2006a). In a previous study of ours (Schneider & Logan, 2005), subjects switched between a parity task (judging whether a digit stimulus was odd or even) and a magnitude task (judging whether a digit stimulus was lower or higher than 5) that were cued by their stimulus categories (i.e., *odd* and *even* were separate cues for the parity task and *Low* and *High* were separate cues for the magnitude task). We observed a cue–target congruency effect such that performance was better when the cue and the target digit were associated with the same category (congruent; e.g., *odd* and *3*) than when they were associated with different categories (incongruent; e.g., *even* and *3*). To investigate the role of instructions in producing this effect, Experiment 2 of our 2006a study involved subjects performing parity and magnitude tasks that were cued by the second or the third letters of the stimulus categories (i.e., *D* for *odd*, *V* for *even*, *W* for *low*, and *G* for *high*). We reasoned that this nontransparent mapping between cues and stimulus categories would produce a negligible congruency effect, which is what we observed in the first half of the experiment. However, after subjects were informed of the relationship between the letter cues and the stimulus categories midway through the experiment, there was a substantial congruency effect in the second half. We argued that the new information about the cues altered how they were interpreted, leading subjects to use categorical mediators to guide their behavior.

The findings of Dreisbach and colleagues and of Logan and Schneider (2006a) draw attention to the importance of instructions in task switching situations. As we noted near the end of our 2006a article, the ability to give and to receive instructions is a powerful tool in the human cognitive repertoire, such that "five minutes of verbal instructions can put a human in a state of preparation to perform a task that would take 5 months of training to establish in a monkey" (p. 362). Whether something is considered a task depends on the nature of those verbal instructions, consistent with Logan and Gordon's (2001) definition of a *task* as a propositional representation of instructions for performance. Indeed, the instructions given to subjects in an experiment must define the task(s) at a level that permits comprehension of what has to be accomplished.

In Table 2.1, we offer a definition of a task as a representation of the instructions required to achieve accurate performance of an activity. We also provide a corresponding interpretation in the context of Marr's (1982) theoretical framework for understanding complex information-processing systems. Marr proposed that an information-processing activity can be understood at three levels. The *computational* level addresses the problem to be solved by an information-processing system. The *algorithmic* level addresses the representation of information and the algorithms used to transform that representation (e.g., by translating input into output) to solve the problem. The *implementational* level addresses the physical instantiation of representations and algorithms in information-processing systems such as the brain. We propose that tasks are associated with the computational level in that they are similar to problems that have to be solved. To foreshadow, we associate task sets with the algorithmic level and the neural substrates of task sets with the implementational level (see Table 2.1).

Table 2.1 DEFINITIONS OF *TASK* AND *TASK SET*

Concept	**Definition**	**Level(s) of Marr's (1982) framework**
Task	Representation of the instructions required to achieve accurate performance of an activity.	Computational: The problem to be solved by an information-processing system.
Task set	Set of representations and processes capable of performing a task, including the parameterization of those processes and the identification of their neural substrates.	Algorithmic and implementational: Representation of information and the algorithms used to transform that representation to solve the problem, including their physical instantiation.

Tasks can also be associated with different time scales of human action. Newell (1990; see also Anderson, 2002) considered a "task" to be an activity that is performed in a span ranging from a few minutes up to several hours, which corresponds to one of his bands of cognition—the Rational Band. The tasks that are typically studied in task switching experiments correspond more closely with his Cognitive Band, where he differentiated between "unit tasks" that take about 10 seconds, "simple operations" that last 1 second, and "deliberate acts" on the order of 100 ms. For example, the parity and magnitude judgments studied by Schneider and Logan (2005) each took about 1 second and would be considered simple operations under Newell's categorization.

Even at the time scale of 1 second, there is some latitude regarding how one defines a task. The flexibility and richness of language allow one to express instructions at many different levels of abstraction, similar to how one can categorize objects (Brown, 1958; Rosch, 1978; Rosch, Mervis, Gray, Johnson, & Boyes-Braem, 1976), classify events (Morris & Murphy, 1990; Rifkin, 1985; Zacks & Tversky, 2001), and identify actions (Vallacher & Wegner, 1985, 1987) at a variety of levels. Figure 2.1 shows different levels at which one can define the tasks used in the studies by Schneider and Logan (2005, 2007a). As mentioned earlier, the 2005 study involved judging whether a digit stimulus was odd or even on some trials or lower or higher than 5 on other trials. These judgments can be considered different tasks—parity and magnitude judgments, respectively—if tasks are defined at the level of stimulus categories (odd and even versus low and high). However, both judgments can also be regarded as versions of the same higher-level task (semantic classification of numbers), although instructions framed at that level would likely be inadequate for accurate task performance. The 2007a study involved judging whether a digit stimulus was lower or higher than 2 on some trials or lower or higher than 7 on other trials. Both judgments can be considered the same magnitude task at the level of stimulus categories (low and high). However, they can also be regarded as different lower-level tasks—relative judgments involving either 2 or 7 as reference points (see also Schneider & Verbruggen, 2008). From extreme perspectives, the tasks in both studies could also be given the high-level task label of doing a psychology experiment or the low-level task label of making keypress responses to stimuli (see Figure 2.1), with the latter corresponding to the level of task definition used for the stimulus–response group in the studies by Dreisbach and colleagues. Thus, tasks can be defined at multiple levels, with the level of abstraction varying with one's perspective. A similar point was made by Morris and Murphy (1990) in the context of event classification:

> Events often do not have ready-made names for them, as objects do. When someone asks you what you are doing, there is often no single name that is the conventional label for that activity. One might easily respond with a number of names that focus on different aspects of the activity, at different levels of abstraction and including more or fewer actions (p. 417).

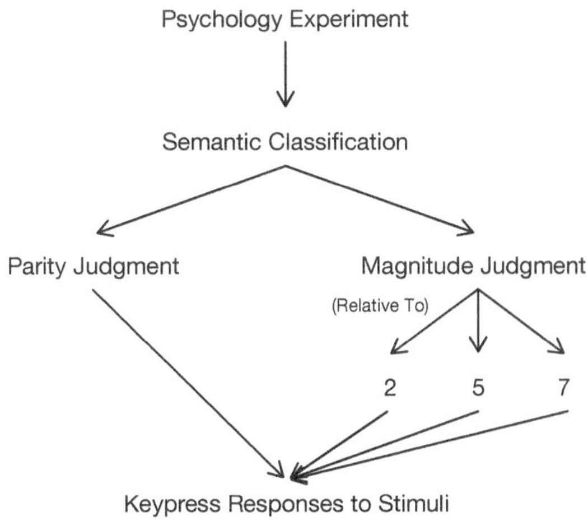

Figure 2.1 Examples of different levels at which tasks can be defined in a typical task switching experiment.

Although there is flexibility when it comes to labeling something as a task, such flexibility does not necessarily portend uncertainty in task definition. In principle, a task can be defined at different levels of abstraction (see Figure 2.1), but in practice, there may be a single level that is prepotent in the minds of most subjects (and researchers). The level at which a task is defined for practical purposes is likely constrained by a number of considerations, three of which we discuss here.

First, there may be a consensus as to what represents a task in an experimental situation. In many studies, relatively good agreement in level of classification has been found among subjects who were instructed to name event-based stories (Morris & Murphy, 1990), identify scenes comprising scripts (Bower, Black, & Turner, 1979), list daily events (Rosch, 1978), or identify breakpoints in filmed event sequences (Newtson & Engquist, 1976; see also Baird & Baldwin, 2001). Tasks may be defined the same way by most subjects in an experiment. Furthermore, there seems to be an implicit consensus among researchers regarding the identities of tasks in many task switching experiments. For example, to our knowledge, nobody has argued that magnitude and parity judgments are the same task. Later in this chapter we argue that both tasks can be performed with the same task set, but that is a different proposition that can be appreciated only if one makes a clear distinction between tasks and task sets.

Second, there may be a *basic level* at which tasks are defined across a range of experimental situations, mirroring the basic levels that have been found or suggested for objects (Rosch, 1978; Rosch et al., 1976), events (Morris & Murphy, 1990; Rifkin, 1985), and scripts (Abbott, Black, & Smith, 1985). The basic level is the level of abstraction at which different entities (e.g., objects, events, or tasks) tend to be categorized. For example, an object may be categorized as a chair at the basic level but as furniture at a superordinate level or as a kitchen chair at a subordinate level (Rosch et al., 1976). The basic level represents a compromise between distinctiveness and informativeness (Morris & Murphy, 1990), providing maximal cue validity while at the same time minimizing cognitive load (Rosch, 1978; Rosch et al., 1976). The net result is that the basic level may be "the most useful level of categorization" (Rosch et al., 1976, p. 435) and, as such, the level that is typically used to categorize items (Brown, 1958) or to make inferences (Abbott et al., 1985). A basic level for tasks has yet to be explicitly identified, but it would likely map onto the same level at which subjects and researchers mutually distinguish between different tasks, as discussed earlier. For example, magnitude and parity judgments may correspond to a basic level of task definition.

Third, there may be a constraint on the highest level at which a task can be defined. As mentioned earlier, what constitutes a task is often determined by instructions. For subjects to respond appropriately in an experiment, they must receive instructions that contain the minimum amount of information required to enable accurate task performance. If a task is defined too abstractly, then subjects may be unable to identify many of the task's attributes (Morris & Murphy, 1990; Rifkin, 1985; Rosch et al., 1976) and, as a result, they may be unable to achieve the desired balance between distinctiveness and informativeness (Morris & Murphy, 1990). For example, if subjects are instructed to perform "semantic classification" of numbers but they are not informed of the relevant semantic attributes (e.g., parity and magnitude), then they will likely be unable to perform the task accurately in the absence of feedback. A clear conception of the experiment can be achieved only if tasks are defined at a lower level that provides sufficient information (e.g., the relevant stimulus categories) for performance. Thus, one could argue that there is an upper-level informational constraint on the hierarchy used to define tasks.

Despite these constraints on task definition, it can be difficult to firmly establish what the tasks are in an experiment. Instructions may be expressed in different ways that convey all the relevant information but produce divergent effects on behavior, as seen in the work of Dreisbach and colleagues and of Logan and Schneider (2006a). In the context of writing or reading instructions, there may not be a consensus among researchers or subjects on whether a given experiment involves one or two or more tasks. Similarly, researchers or subjects may not agree on a basic level for defining tasks in a specific domain.

However, uncertainty about task definition need not be a crippling problem for task switching research. Indeed, the ever-growing body of literature on task switching—in the absence of clear *task* definitions—indicates that the field has not been hindered. Regardless of whether one considers an experiment to have one or two tasks, it is generally the case that one can establish what constitutes accurate task performance. That is, most experiments involve clearly defined mappings of stimuli to responses, enabling the researcher to determine whether subjects are following instructions and performing the task(s) as designed. From this perspective, the critical element is not how a task is defined but rather how it is performed. In the context of Marr's (1982) levels of analysis, the problem specified at the computational level may not be as important as how it is solved at the algorithmic level. In the domain of task switching, the algorithmic level—which indicates how a task is performed—is represented by the task set.

WHAT IS A TASK SET?

> "What constitutes a task set is seldom explained, the differences between task sets are rarely identified, and the distinction between tasks and task sets is hardly ever discussed."
>
> —Schneider and Logan *(2007a, p. 118)*

Despite its prevalence as a theoretical construct, precise definitions of task set are as rare today as they were in the past (see Dashiell, 1940; Gibson, 1941). In task switching research, a *task set* has been loosely defined as a set of internal control settings, a state of preparation, a collection of stimulus–response or category–response mapping rules, or a configuration of perceptual, cognitive, and motor processes that enables achievement of a task goal, especially in the context of competing goals and other sources of interference (e.g., Allport, Styles, & Hsieh, 1994; Mayr & Keele, 2000; Rogers & Monsell, 1995). We say "loosely defined" because there is no agreed-upon definition of task set and most of the definitions themselves are ill-defined. For example, what is a "set of internal control settings?" What is it about one set of internal control settings that makes it different from another? What changes are made to internal control settings to accomplish "task-set reconfiguration" (e.g., Monsell & Mizon, 2006)? These questions highlight some of the ambiguity that one finds with verbal theorizing in the domain of task switching.

We think this ambiguity can be avoided and task sets can be placed on firmer ground by defining them in the context of computational models. A computational model is a formal specification of the representations and the processes needed to perform a task. In other words, it instantiates a task set in precise terms that can be realized by computer simulation or expressed as mathematical equations (which might characterize processes that could also be simulated). Computational models help one avoid some of the pitfalls associated with verbal theorizing, such as ambiguities in the mapping of words to meanings and the treatment of labels as explanations (Hintzman, 1991). In so doing, they can improve reasoning about the aspects of cognition represented in the model and facilitate shared understanding of ideas between researchers (Farrell & Lewandowsky, 2010). Computational models also have the advantages of generating quantitative predictions that can be compared with behavioral data (e.g., response time and error rate) and potentially revealing nonintuitive, complex interactions among different processes.

Fortunately, several computational models of task switching have been developed in recent years (e.g., Altmann & Gray, 2008; Brown, Reynolds, & Braver, 2007; Meiran, Kessler, & Adi-Japha, 2008; Schneider & Logan, 2005; Sohn & Anderson, 2001). The models differ in many ways, ranging from their assumptions to their scope of application, and are even instantiated in different types of modeling frameworks (e.g., mathematical model—Schneider & Logan, 2005; neural network—Brown et al., 2007; production system—Sohn & Anderson,

2001). Despite these differences, all the models define task sets at a level of detail sufficient to perform the tasks of interest. Consistent with this view, Logan and Schneider (2010) defined a *task set* as a "set of parameters in a computational model that is sufficient to program the model to perform particular task-relevant computations" (p. 416). In Table 2.1, we offer a broader definition of a *task set* as a set of representations and processes capable of performing a task, including the parameterization of those processes and the identification of their neural substrates.

For example, consider the model of task switching developed by Schneider and Logan (2005), which is a member of a broader class of models subsumed under the Executive Control Theory of Visual Attention (ECTVA; Logan & Gordon, 2001) and the Instance Theory of Attention and Memory (ITAM; Logan, 2002; see also Logan, 2004). The model assumes that task switching performance reflects two key processes: cue encoding and compound cue retrieval. Cue encoding is the process by which a semantic, categorical representation of a task cue is formed (Arrington, Logan, & Schneider, 2007; Logan & Bundesen, 2003; Schneider & Logan, 2005). Priming of cue encoding by repetition or association has been shown to be at least partly responsible for observed switch costs in cued task switching performance (e.g., Logan & Bundesen, 2003; Logan & Schneider, 2006b; Schneider & Logan, 2006, 2007b, 2011). The representation of the cue is used in conjunction with a semantic, categorical representation of the target stimulus (Schneider & Logan, 2010) to select a response. Compound cue retrieval is the process by which information from the cue and the target is combined to probe memory for evidence in favor of one response or another (Logan & Schneider, 2010; Schneider & Logan, 2005, 2009a). The way in which conflicting information from the cue and the target affects compound cue retrieval has been shown to account for several congruency effects seen in task switching performance (e.g., Schneider & Logan, 2005, 2009a).

In the context of Schneider and Logan's (2005) model, a task set is a set of internal control settings but it is one that is clearly defined in terms of various model parameters. For example, two important parameters in compound cue retrieval are the bias and the criterion. The bias parameter controls the strength of the bias toward a specific response category, such that increasing the bias for a response category makes the model more likely to select that response. The criterion parameter controls how much evidence is needed for one response category over the other before termination of the decision process for response selection (modeled as a random walk; see Ratcliff, 2001). Increasing the criterion makes the model select a response more slowly but also more accurately, thereby allowing it to trade speed for accuracy. Changing either the bias or the criterion qualifies as task-set reconfiguration because those parameters partly define the task set (see Logan & Gordon, 2001). Thus, rather than speculating about task-set reconfiguration in a task switching situation, one can investigate whether and which parameters of the model need to change to accommodate different tasks.

An example of such an investigation was provided by Logan and Schneider (2010). In that study, we focused on modeling the target functions for the magnitude and parity tasks in the data from Schneider and Logan (2005). A target function is a pattern of performance across different target stimuli that presumably reflects differences in how targets are either represented or processed. The target function for the magnitude task revealed that performance improved as the distance of the target from 5 (the reference point for making the magnitude judgment) became longer. This finding corresponds to the well-known *distance effect* in numerical judgments (Moyer & Landauer, 1967; for reviews, see Banks, 1977; Moyer & Dumais, 1978). The target function for the parity task revealed that performance was better overall for even targets than for odd targets, consistent with previous research (Hines, 1990).

The different target functions might be used to infer that the tasks require different task sets (and, by extension, that switching between the tasks requires task-set reconfiguration), but Logan and Schneider (2010) presented modeling results showing that this need not be the case. More specifically, we demonstrated that two versions of our model of compound cue retrieval—of which one involved task-set reconfiguration and one did not—provided equivalent fits to the empirical target functions. The reconfiguration version of the model involved changing the bias parameter to favor the task-relevant categories (e.g., *odd* and *even* when the parity task was relevant), whereas the nonreconfiguration version of the model could accommodate the different target patterns with no change in bias by having the cue representation "gate" the evidence from the target to favor the task-relevant categories. The shapes of the target functions were determined by assumptions about how magnitude and parity are represented in memory (e.g., Dehaene, Bossini, & Giraux, 1993; Miller & Gelman, 1983; Shepard, Kilpatric, & Cunningham, 1975). The bias parameter and the cue representation each allowed the model to emphasize one representation over the other, resulting in the production of different target functions. Thus, we were able to use computational modeling to show that magnitude and parity tasks could be performed with either the same task set or different task sets.

Task sets and their reconfiguration can also be explored in the context of other computational models (e.g., Altmann & Gray, 2008; Brown et al., 2007; Gilbert & Shallice, 2002; Kieras, Meyer, Ballas, & Lauber, 2000; Meiran et al., 2008; Sohn & Anderson, 2001), so researchers do not need to endorse our model or subscribe to a specific modeling framework. Moreover, even though various models may differ at a superficial level, many of them share deeper similarities in their assumptions about how task sets are represented and how task information is processed. Such similarities at the algorithmic level of Marr's (1982) framework may prove useful in understanding how task sets are represented at the implementational level in the brain. That is, research on the neural basis of task sets (e.g., Dosenbach et al., 2006; Miller & Cohen, 2001; Yeung, Nystrom, Aronson, & Cohen, 2006; for an overview, see Schneider & Logan, 2009b) may benefit from a better understanding of the mechanistic basis of task sets, and vice versa.

MAPPINGS BETWEEN TASKS AND TASK SETS

Despite the fact that the terms "task" and "task set" are often used interchangeably, the preceding text indicates that they can and should be distinguished (e.g., see Table 2.1). A task is an instruction-based representation of what to do that can be conceptualized at a computational level of analysis. A task set is a delineation of the representations and processes involved in doing a task, often cast in the form of a computational model, which can be conceptualized at algorithmic and implementational levels of analysis. Once this distinction is recognized and appreciated, one can begin to think more critically about the mapping between tasks and task sets in different experimental situations. More specifically, one can abandon the commonplace assumption that there is a one-to-one mapping of tasks to task sets.

The one-to-one mapping assumption is that every task is associated with a unique task set, which implies that task switching always involves task-set reconfiguration. The assumption is prevalent among many formal and informal theories of task switching and is often implicit in how researchers interpret their task switching data. For example, in a task switching experiment involving two nominally different tasks, switch costs are frequently interpreted by default as either direct or indirect evidence that task-set reconfiguration has occurred. Although there are many situations in which the one-to-one mapping assumption is likely valid, we think it is prudent to consider situations in which it may be invalid; that is, situations in which there may be many-to-one or one-to-many mappings of tasks to task sets.

A many-to-one mapping is a case of different tasks being performed with the same task set. For example, consider the tasks of judging whether a famous name is that of a male or a female or that of a musician or an actor. The tasks are associated with distinct semantic attributes—gender and occupation—and they can be labeled as nominally different tasks. However, both tasks can be performed by memory retrieval, using the name to probe a vast store of semantic knowledge in memory about famous people. If the tasks were to be modeled with compound cue retrieval (Schneider & Logan, 2005, 2009a), then the target name would access several different semantic attributes in memory and the task cue would constrain retrieval of those attributes to the one that is most relevant. This retrieval mechanism would function in the same way regardless of the task, providing an example of how two tasks can be accomplished with a single task set.

We made a similar argument in previous work involving tasks such as magnitude and parity judgments (e.g., Schneider & Logan, 2005). We argued that magnitude and parity information could be retrieved from memory using a common task set, and we presented a "proof of concept" by showing that it could be done in the context of a computational model that provided satisfactory fits to empirical data. This led us to give our 2005 article the provocative title "Modeling Task Switching Without Switching Tasks," but a more appropriate title would have been "Modeling Task Switching Without Switching *Task Sets*." Thus, even we are guilty of conflating tasks and task sets in the past.

Many-to-one mappings of tasks to task sets are not restricted to task switching situations; they can also be found in other domains of cognitive psychology. For example, analogical problem solving is based on the idea that it may be possible to use the solution to one problem to solve another problem (i.e., there is a many-to-one mapping of problems to solutions), even if the problems differ in their surface features. In a classic study, Gick and Holyoak (1980) explored analogical transfer from a military story about attacking a fortress to a medical story about using radiation to destroy a tumor. A many-to-one mapping arose from the fact that the dispersion solution to the fortress problem (e.g., divide the army into small groups that converge simultaneously on the fortress from multiple roads) could be applied to the tumor problem (e.g., use low-intensity rays that are directed simultaneously toward the tumor from multiple angles), demonstrating that a relatively abstract task set was not restricted to a single situation. The instantiation of a many-to-one mapping in analogical problem solving may depend on being able to map the relational structure of one problem to that of another (Gentner, 1983) or being reminded of the applicability of a previous solution to a current problem (Ross, 1984), but the overarching point is that such mappings exist.

A one-to-many mapping is a case of the same task being performed with different task sets. For example, consider the task of judging whether a number is odd or even. At least two different task sets could be developed to perform this parity judgment. One task set could be based on an algorithm that involves dividing the number by 2 and checking to see whether there is a remainder. An alternative task set could involve engaging in direct memory retrieval, drawing on the knowledge that any number with a 0, 2, 4, 6, or 8 in the units position is an even number. These distinct mechanisms for determining parity provide an example of how a single task can be accomplished with different task sets.

However, the mechanisms underlying the task sets for performing the task do not necessarily have to be different. Two task sets could be based on the same mechanism but involve different parameterizations of it. Recall that *task sets* are defined as sets of parameters in the family of models of which our task switching model is a member (e.g., ECTVA; Logan & Gordon, 2001; ITAM, Logan, 2002). We mentioned two of the parameters in the task set (the bias and the criterion), but there are additional parameters such as a priority parameter that determines the attention weights given to stimuli and a feature-catch parameter that determines the proportion of features that are "caught" in the perceptual organization of the stimulus display (Logan, 1996; Logan & Gordon, 2001). It may be possible for the performance of a given task to be controlled in similar ways by different parameters. For example, Logan and Gordon noted that the bias and the priority parameters operate in the same manner, acting as gain controls on the evidence acquired from stimuli. Thus, there are likely circumstances under which equivalent task performance can be achieved by either modulating the bias parameter while holding the priority parameter constant or modulating the priority parameter while holding the bias parameter constant. Each parameter combination would be considered a different task set that accomplishes the same task.

An example of a proposed one-to-many mapping in the task switching literature was provided in a study by Schneider and Logan (2007a). As mentioned earlier, that study involved judging whether a digit stimulus was lower or higher than 2 on some trials or lower or higher than 7 on other trials, and both judgments can be considered the same magnitude task at the level of stimulus categories (low and high). However, we argued that the task required different task sets, with the key parameter being an internal control setting associated with the reference point (2 or 7). Indeed, in unpublished modeling work analogous to the work presented in Logan and Schneider (2010), we found that the target functions in Schneider and Logan's (2007a) data, which took the form of distance effects that changed with the reference point (see also Dehaene, 1989; Holyoak, 1978), could be modeled only by changing the bias parameter in compound cue retrieval. In other words, different task sets were needed to model a magnitude task that involved reference point switching.

One-to-many mappings of tasks to task sets can also be found in other domains of cognitive psychology. For example, some theories of automatization in skill acquisition are based on the idea that the same task can be performed in different ways (e.g., Logan, 1988; Rickard, 1997; see also Anderson, 2007). Consider the task of alphabet arithmetic (Logan & Klapp, 1991), which involves verifying equations of the form M + 3 = Q (determining whether Q is three letters down the alphabet from M). Novice subjects typically perform alphabet arithmetic using a counting algorithm: Starting at the initial letter (M), they count through the alphabet for a number of steps equal to the digit addend (3) and then compare the true sum (P) with the presented sum (Q) to determine whether the equation is true or false. Subjects could also use a letter–digit translation algorithm, translating letters into digits (M = 13) on which standard arithmetic can be performed (13 + 3 = 16) and then translating digits back into letters (16 = P) for comparison with the presented sum. However, similar to determining a number's parity, alphabet arithmetic can also be performed by memory retrieval. With practice, alphabet arithmetic facts become stored in memory, enabling direct retrieval of correct responses when presented with studied equations. Automatization of tasks such as alphabet arithmetic has been argued to reflect a transition from an algorithm to direct memory retrieval (Logan, 1988; Rickard, 1997), which is only possible in the context of a one-to-many mapping of tasks to task sets.

It is even possible to have both one-to-many and many-to-one mappings in the same situation. Returning to the domain of problem solving, Luchins (1942; Luchins & Luchins, 1950) conducted experiments in which subjects had to determine how to obtain a specific volume of fluid by pouring fluid into and out of containers of assorted sizes. The same solution method (sequence of operations) could be used for the first few problems (i.e., a many-to-one mapping of problems to solutions), but subsequent problems could each be solved in multiple ways (i.e., a one-to-many mapping of problems to solutions). The question of interest was whether the original solution method was used to solve the later problems that afforded multiple solution methods, with the result being that many subjects persisted in using the original method. Luchins and Luchins (1950) considered the persistent use of the original method to reflect "a special kind of mental set" (p. 279), which is consistent with how we have defined *task set*.

These examples of many-to-one and one-to-many mappings of tasks to task sets challenge the one-to-one mapping assumption implicit in much of the task switching literature. To be clear, the challenge is not that one-to-one mappings do not exist, but that they are not the only possible mappings; therefore, one cannot assume by default that a given situation involves a one-to-one mapping and, by extension, that task switching always involves task-set reconfiguration. However, if one cannot assume that the data from a task switching experiment directly or indirectly reflect task-set reconfiguration, then how can the task switching paradigm be used as a tool for understanding cognitive control?

THE WAY FORWARD

We believe that task switching can serve as a useful paradigm for studying cognitive control if researchers are cognizant of what a task is at the computational level of analysis (e.g., how tasks are defined by instructions), but they focus on how task sets are realized at both the algorithmic and the implementational levels (see Table 2.1). Instead of speculating about whether a given situation involves one or two or more tasks, it may be more fruitful to investigate how the performance of the task(s) can be accomplished by a computational model and how that model might be physically instantiated in the brain.

Despite recent progress, we contend that there is much to be gained from continued development and testing of computational models of task switching. A task set can be explicitly defined in such models (e.g., as a set of parameters) and task-set reconfiguration can be made concrete (e.g., as a change in parameters). If a model requires different task sets to accommodate the data from different tasks, then one is on firmer ground for arguing that the data reflect cognitive control due to task-set reconfiguration. Moreover, given that the nature of the reconfiguration can be specified (e.g., changing a bias or an attention weight in the model), one can make inferences about the nature of the cognitive control process (e.g., response biasing or attention shifting). A researcher would then be in a better position to proceed to the implementational level and investigate whether the hypothesized cognitive control processes involved in task-set reconfiguration depend on the same neural substrates that have been identified for those control processes using other paradigms (e.g., through meta-analyses of neuroimaging results; Buchsbaum, Greer, Chang, & Berman, 2005; Lenartowicz, Kalar, Congdon, & Poldrack, 2010; Wager, Jonides, & Reading, 2004).

An overarching consideration that may serve to guide future research is the recognition that cognitive control in task switching is the outcome or end-product of processing that may or may not involve task-set reconfiguration. That is, cognitive control may be achieved by means of task-set reconfiguration, but it need not be. We discussed this point earlier in relation to our model of task switching and its compound cue retrieval mechanism for response selection (e.g.,

Logan & Schneider, 2010; Schneider & Logan, 2005, 2009a). The model can accurately perform nominally different tasks without engaging in task-set reconfiguration because it uses the combination of cue and target information to control what is retrieved from memory, with the cue serving a gating function by favoring task-relevant target categories. The outcome of this "information gating" can be interpreted as cognitive control, even though it does not involve task-set reconfiguration. Thus, cognitive control and task-set reconfiguration are separable entities that can and should be distinguished, perhaps with the aid of computational models. There are many paths to cognitive control and task-set reconfiguration is just one of them. We think further progress in research on task switching and cognitive control may come from traveling "off the beaten path" and exploring alternative possibilities regarding how the human mind is able to control itself.

REFERENCES

Abbott, V., Black, J. B., & Smith, E. E. (1985). The representation of scripts in memory. *Journal of Memory and Language, 24*, 179–199.

Allport, A., Styles, E. A., & Hsieh, S. (1994). Shifting intentional set: Exploring the dynamic control of tasks. In C. Umiltà & M. Moscovitch (Eds.), *Attention and performance XV* (pp. 421–452). Cambridge, MA: MIT Press.

Altmann, E. M., & Gray, W. D. (2008). An integrated model of cognitive control in task switching. *Psychological Review, 115*, 602–639.

Anderson, J. R. (2002). Spanning seven orders of magnitude: A challenge for cognitive modeling. *Cognitive Science, 26*, 85–112.

Anderson, J. R. (2007). *How can the human mind occur in the physical universe?* New York, NY: Oxford University Press.

Arrington, C. M., Logan, G. D., & Schneider, D. W. (2007). Separating cue encoding from target processing in the explicit task-cuing procedure: Are there "true" task switch effects? *Journal of Experimental Psychology: Learning, Memory, and Cognition, 33*, 484–502.

Baird, J. A., & Baldwin, D. A. (2001). Making sense of human behavior: Action parsing and intentional inference. In B. F. Malle, L. J. Moses, & D. A. Baldwin (Eds.), *Intentions and intentionality: Foundations of social cognition* (pp. 193–206). Cambridge, MA: MIT Press.

Banks, W. P. (1977). Encoding and processing of symbolic information in comparative judgments. In G. H. Bower (Ed.), *The psychology of learning and motivation* (Vol. 11, pp. 101–159). New York, NY: Academic Press.

Bower, G. H., Black, J. B., & Turner, T. J. (1979). Scripts in memory for text. *Cognitive Psychology, 11*, 177–220.

Brown, J. W., Reynolds, J. R., & Braver, T. S. (2007). A computational model of fractionated conflict-control mechanisms in task-switching. *Cognitive Psychology, 55*, 37–85.

Brown, R. (1958). How shall a thing be called? *Psychological Review, 65*, 14–21.

Buchsbaum, B. R., Greer, S., Chang, W.-L., & Berman, K. F. (2005). Meta-analysis of neuroimaging studies of the Wisconsin card-sorting task and component processes. *Human Brain Mapping, 25*, 35–45.

Dashiell, J. F. (1940). A neglected fourth dimension to psychological research. *Psychological Review, 47*, 289–305.

Dehaene, S. (1989). The psychophysics of numerical comparison: A reexamination of apparently incompatible data. *Perception & Psychophysics, 45*, 557–566.

Dehaene, S., Bossini, S., & Giraux, P. (1993). The mental representation of parity and number magnitude. *Journal of Experimental Psychology: General, 122*, 371–396.

Dosenbach, N. U. F., Visscher, K. M., Palmer, E. D., Miezin, F. M., Wenger, K. K., Kang, H. C.,... Petersen, S. E. (2006). A core system for the implementation of task sets. *Neuron, 50*, 799–812.

Dreisbach, G., Goschke, T., & Haider, H. (2006). Implicit task sets in task switching? *Journal of Experimental Psychology: Learning, Memory, and Cognition, 32*, 1221–1233.

Dreisbach, G., Goschke, T., & Haider, H. (2007). The role of task rules and stimulus–response mappings in the task switching paradigm. *Psychological Research, 71*, 383–392.

Dreisbach, G., & Haider, H. (2008). That's what task sets are for: Shielding against irrelevant information. *Psychological Research, 72*, 355–361.

Farrell, S., & Lewandowsky, S. (2010). Computational models as aids to better reasoning in psychology. *Current Directions in Psychological Science, 19*, 329–335.

Gentner, D. (1983). Structure-mapping: A theoretical framework for analogy. *Cognitive Science, 7*, 155–170.

Gibson, J. J. (1941). A critical review of the concept of set in contemporary experimental psychology. *Psychological Bulletin, 38*, 781–817.

Gick, M. L., & Holyoak, K. J. (1980). Analogical problem solving. *Cognitive Psychology, 12*, 306–355.

Gilbert, S. J., & Shallice, T. (2002). Task switching: A PDP model. *Cognitive Psychology, 44*, 297–337.

Hines, T. M. (1990). An odd effect: Lengthened reaction times for judgments about odd digits. *Memory & Cognition, 18*, 40–46.

Hintzman, D. L. (1991). Why are formal models useful in psychology? In W. E. Hockley & S. Lewandowsky (Eds.), *Relating theory and data: Essays on human memory in honor of Bennet B. Murdock* (pp. 39–56). Hillsdale, NJ: Erlbaum.

Holyoak, K. J. (1978). Comparative judgments with numerical reference points. *Cognitive Psychology, 10*, 203–243.

Kieras, D. E., Meyer, D. E., Ballas, J. A., & Lauber, E. J. (2000). Modern computational perspectives on executive mental processes and cognitive control: Where to from here? In S. Monsell & J. Driver (Eds.), *Control of cognitive processes: Attention and performance XVIII* (pp. 681–712). Cambridge, MA: MIT Press.

Kiesel, A., Steinhauser, M., Wendt, M., Falkenstein, M., Jost, K., Philipp, A. M., & Koch, I. (2010). Control and interference in task switching—A review. *Psychological Bulletin, 136*, 849–874.

Lenartowicz, A., Kalar, D. J., Congdon, E., & Poldrack, R. A. (2010). Towards an ontology of cognitive control. *Topics in Cognitive Science, 2*, 678–692.

Logan, G. D. (1988). Toward an instance theory of automatization. *Psychological Review, 95*, 492–527.

Logan, G. D. (1996). The CODE theory of visual attention: An integration of space-based and object-based attention. *Psychological Review, 103*, 603–649.

Logan, G. D. (2002). An instance theory of attention and memory. *Psychological Review, 109*, 376–400.

Logan, G. D. (2004). Cumulative progress in formal theories of attention. *Annual Review of Psychology, 55*, 207–234.

Logan, G. D., & Bundesen, C. (2003). Clever homunculus: Is there an endogenous act of control in the explicit task-cuing procedure? *Journal of Experimental Psychology: Human Perception and Performance, 29*, 575–599.

Logan, G. D., & Gordon, R. D. (2001). Executive control of visual attention in dual-task situations. *Psychological Review, 108*, 393–434.

Logan, G. D., & Klapp, S. T. (1991). Automatizing alphabet arithmetic: I. Is extended practice necessary to produce automaticity? *Journal of Experimental Psychology: Learning, Memory, and Cognition, 17*, 179–195.

Logan, G. D., & Schneider, D. W. (2006a). Interpreting instructional cues in task switching procedures: The role of mediator retrieval. *Journal of Experimental Psychology: Learning, Memory, and Cognition, 32*, 347–363.

Logan, G. D., & Schneider, D. W. (2006b). Priming or executive control? Associative priming of cue encoding increases "switch costs" in the explicit task-cuing procedure. *Memory & Cognition, 34*, 1250–1259.

Logan, G. D., & Schneider, D. W. (2010). Distinguishing reconfiguration and compound-cue retrieval in task switching. *Psychologica Belgica, 50*, 413–433.

Luchins, A. S. (1942). Mechanization in problem solving. *Psychological Monographs, 54* (entire issue 248).

Luchins, A. S., & Luchins, E. H. (1950). New experimental attempts at preventing mechanization in problem solving. *Journal of General Psychology, 42*, 279–297.

Marr, D. (1982). *Vision*. New York, NY: W. H. Freeman.

Mayr, U., & Keele, S. W. (2000). Changing internal constraints on action: The role of backward inhibition. *Journal of Experimental Psychology: General, 129*, 4–26.

Meiran, N., Kessler, Y., & Adi-Japha, E. (2008). Control by Action Representation and Input Selection (CARIS): A theoretical framework for task switching. *Psychological Research, 72*, 473–500.

Miller, E. K., & Cohen, J. D. (2001). An integrative theory of prefrontal cortex function. *Annual Review of Neuroscience, 24*, 167–202.

Miller, K., & Gelman, R. (1983). The child's representation of number: A multidimensional scaling analysis. *Child Development, 54*, 1470–1479.

Monsell, S., & Mizon, G. A. (2006). Can the task-cuing paradigm measure an endogenous task-set reconfiguration process? *Journal of Experimental Psychology: Human Perception and Performance, 32*, 493–516.

Morris, M. W., & Murphy, G. L. (1990). Converging operations on a basic level in event taxonomies. *Memory & Cognition, 18*, 407–418.

Moyer, R. S., & Dumais, S. T. (1978). Mental comparison. In G. H. Bower (Ed.), *The psychology of learning and motivation* (Vol. 12, pp. 117–155). New York, NY: Academic Press.

Moyer, R. S., & Landauer, T. K. (1967). Time required for judgments of numerical inequality. *Nature, 215*, 1519–1520.

Newell, A. (1990). *Unified theories of cognition*. Cambridge, MA: Harvard University Press.

Newtson, D., & Engquist, G. (1976). The perceptual organization of ongoing behavior. *Journal of Experimental Social Psychology, 12*, 436–450.

Ratcliff, R. (2001). Diffusion and random walk processes. In *International encyclopedia of the social and behavioral sciences* (Vol. 6, pp. 3668–3673). Oxford, UK: Elsevier.

Rickard, T. C. (1997). Bending the power law: A CMPL theory of strategy shifts and the automatization of cognitive skills. *Journal of Experimental Psychology: General, 126*, 288–311.

Rifkin, A. (1985). Evidence for a basic level in event taxonomies. *Memory & Cognition, 13*, 538–556.

Rogers, R. D., & Monsell, S. (1995). Costs of a predictable switch between simple cognitive tasks. *Journal of Experimental Psychology: General, 124*, 207–231.

Rosch, E. (1978). Principles of categorization. In E. Rosch & B. B. Lloyd (Eds.), *Cognition and categorization* (pp. 27–48). Hillsdale, NJ: Erlbaum.

Rosch, E., Mervis, C. B., Gray, W. D., Johnson, D. M., & Boyes-Braem, P. (1976). Basic objects in natural categories. *Cognitive Psychology, 8*, 382–439.

Ross, B. H. (1984). Remindings and their effects in learning a cognitive skill. *Cognitive Psychology, 16*, 371–416.

Schneider, D. W., & Logan, G. D. (2005). Modeling task switching without switching tasks: A short-term priming account of explicitly cued performance. *Journal of Experimental Psychology: General, 134*, 343–367.

Schneider, D. W., & Logan, G. D. (2006). Priming cue encoding by manipulating transition frequency in explicitly cued task switching. *Psychonomic Bulletin & Review, 13*, 145–151.

Schneider, D. W., & Logan, G. D. (2007a). Defining task-set reconfiguration: The case of reference point switching. *Psychonomic Bulletin & Review, 14*, 118–125.

Schneider, D. W., & Logan, G. D. (2007b). Task switching versus cue switching: Using transition cuing to disentangle sequential effects in task-switching performance. *Journal of Experimental Psychology: Learning, Memory, and Cognition, 33*, 370–378.

Schneider, D. W., & Logan, G. D. (2009a). Selecting a response in task switching: Testing a model of compound cue retrieval. *Journal of Experimental Psychology: Learning, Memory, and Cognition, 35*, 122–136.

Schneider, D. W., & Logan, G. D. (2009b). Task switching. In L. R. Squire (Ed.), *Encyclopedia of neuroscience* (Vol. 9, pp. 869–874). Oxford, UK: Academic Press.

Schneider, D. W., & Logan, G. D. (2010). The target of task switching. *Canadian Journal of Experimental Psychology, 64*, 129–133.

Schneider, D. W., & Logan, G. D. (2011). Task-switching performance with 1:1 and 2:1 cue–task mappings: Not so different after all. *Journal of Experimental Psychology: Learning, Memory, and Cognition, 37*, 405–415.

Schneider, D. W., & Verbruggen, F. (2008). Inhibition of irrelevant category–response mappings. *Quarterly Journal of Experimental Psychology, 61*, 1629–1640.

Shepard, R. N., Kilpatric, D. W., & Cunningham, J. P. (1975). The internal representation of numbers. *Cognitive Psychology, 7*, 82–138.

Sohn, M.-H., & Anderson, J. R. (2001). Task preparation and task repetition: Two-component model of task switching. *Journal of Experimental Psychology: General, 130*, 764–778.

Vallacher, R. R., & Wegner, D. M. (1985). *A theory of action identification*. Hillsdale, NJ: Erlbaum.

Vallacher, R. R., & Wegner, D. M. (1987). What do people think they're doing? Action identification and human behavior. *Psychological Review, 94*, 3–15.

Vandierendonck, A., Liefooghe, B., & Verbruggen, F. (2010). Task switching: Interplay of reconfiguration and interference control. *Psychological Bulletin, 136*, 601–626.

Wager, T. D., Jonides, J., & Reading, S. (2004). Neuroimaging studies of shifting attention: A meta-analysis. *NeuroImage, 22*, 1679–1693.

Yeung, N., Nystrom, L. E., Aronson, J. A., & Cohen, J. D. (2006). Between-task competition and cognitive control in task switching. *Journal of Neuroscience, 26*, 1429–1438.

Zacks, J. M., & Tversky, B. (2001). Event structure in perception and conception. *Psychological Bulletin, 127*, 3–21.

3

The Task-Cuing Paradigm

A User's Guide

NACHSHON MEIRAN

INTRODUCTION

Task switching paradigms have become the method of choice in studying cognitive flexibility and task representations. There is a large variety of task switching paradigms that differ from one another in many respects. An important dimension along which the paradigms differ concerns the manner in which tasks are instructed. In some paradigms, the task sequence is known in advance. For example, in Jersild's (1927) experiments, the tasks alternate, namely the task order (with Tasks A and B) is A-B-A-B.... In Rogers and Monsell's (1995) alternating runs paradigm, there are runs of fixed length in which the task remains the same, and these runs alternate. For example, with run length of two, the sequence is A-A-B-B.... In Logan's (2004) task-span paradigm, a long sequence of tasks is instructed. There are other paradigms in which the participants choose the task to perform. For example, in Arrington and Logan's (2004) paradigm, the participants are asked to choose one of two tasks while trying to maintain an equal proportion of trials in each task. In Kessler et al.'s (2009) paradigm, participants chose the task without any constraint. In the third group of paradigms, the paradigms involve some degree of task uncertainty. In Altmann and Gray's (2002, 2008) randomized runs paradigm, the trials are arranged in runs of trials of variable length such that all the trials in the run involve the same task and the task is announced at the beginning of the run. In the cuing paradigm (Biederman, 1972; Meiran, 1996; Shaffer, 1965), the tasks are randomly ordered and each trial begins with task instructions. From the few studies that formally compared different task switching paradigms (e.g., Altmann, 2007a; Arrington & Logan, 2005; Mayr & Bell, 2006; Monsell et al., 2003; Tornay & Milan, 2001), we already know that analogous effects that are obtained in different paradigms may represent different underlying processes.

Here, I provide a *user-oriented* review of the cuing paradigm that appears to have become among the most widely used task switching paradigms. Unlike the three recent reviews that focused on the main findings and their interpretation (Kiesel et al., 2010; Meiran, 2010; Vandierendonck et al., 2010), the present review is more methodological. It focuses on issues one needs to consider when designing task switching experiments. I end each section with some tentative recommendations. Given the fact that this essay concerns the cuing paradigm, the first recommendation is to never take it for granted that analogous effects obtained in the cuing paradigm reflect the same underlying process as that in other paradigms.

The intent of the next few paragraphs is to equip readers with some necessary terms and notions. Briefly, the cuing paradigm involves asking participants to switch between randomly ordered tasks. Typically, the target stimuli on which the tasks are executed afford all the tasks and the responses are also shared between the tasks (see more on this issue later). Thus, unlike in other paradigms in which the serial position of the trial indicates which task is required, in the cuing paradigm, each trial begins with task instructions. Thus, the paradigm involves two stimuli: the stimulus used to instruct of the task and the stimulus on which the instructed task is performed, referred as "cue" and "target," respectively. For example, the cue could be the stimulus "WORD?" indicating that the required task is lexical decision and the target could be a letter string that is either a word or a nonword.

The most interesting blocks in the experiment are the blocks in which there is task switching. These blocks are sometimes called "mixed" (Fagot, 1994). In these blocks, it is possible to examine the role of *task* transition, which should be distinguished from other transitions such as those involving targets and responses. In describing the various transition conditions, I will refer to the current trial (the trial in which performance is recorded) as Trial n, and preceding trials as Trial n-1, Trial n-2, etc.

Two transition conditions have attracted most of the research: The "repeat" condition includes trials in which the task rule was the same in Trials n and n-1. The "switch" condition includes trials in which the tasks in Trials n and n-1 differ. Comparing switch and repeat trials provides the most widely studied transition effect, *switching cost*, which is the (usually) poorer performance in switch trials compared with repeat trials. Another relatively widely studied sequential effect is the lag-2 task repetition cost (Mayr & Keele, 2000; see Koch et al., 2010, for review), but additional, more complex forms of transitions are being studied as well (see Meiran et al., 2010, for a formal taxonomy of some of these effects), and I anticipate additional progress in this direction in the future.

Mixing tasks in a block presumably allows researchers to study the hypothetical process of "set switching." "Set" (see Gibson, 1941) is a key term in the task switching literature and it refers to a particular state of the mind that readies it to carry out particular operations. "Task sets" consist of a special kind of mental sets that are presumably adopted when participants need to execute a particular task. Sets can be described as parameter configurations. Consider, for example, the mindset involved in executing a lexical decision task. Its parameters would include "attend to a particular location"; "keep in mind that the right key indicates WORD and the left key indicates NONWORD"; "place your index fingers on the right/left keys and be prepared to press the keys"; "refer the string on the screen to your lexical knowledge"; "maintain a high level of accuracy"; etc. Although the term "task-set" has proved to be very useful, it is important to keep in mind that there is no consensual definition of the term. Moreover, it is debated whether task sets comprise unitary representations or are merely ad-hoc configurations of these parameters. Perhaps because of the lack of consensual definition of "task set," many essays adopt a somewhat loose and intuitive definition. Others incorporate rather precise definitions, but these definitions are tightly linked to a particular theory (e.g., Altmann & Gray, 2008; Logan & Gordon, 2001; Meiran, 2000a; Meiran et al., 2008).

ADVANTAGES AND DISADVANTAGES ASSOCIATED WITH USING THE CUING PARADIGM

Before continuing, I wish to first address what is probably the core question: What are the advantages and disadvantages of the cuing paradigm? Regarding advantages, at least three answers come to mind. The first advantage concerns the ability to independently control two critical intervals: (a) the interval between the previous (n-1st) response and the current (nth) cue, which is the *response-cue interval* (RCI) and the interval between the nth cue and the nth target, the *cue-target interval* (CTI) (Meiran, 1996; Meiran et al., 2000). The second advantage is associated with the random ordering of tasks. Nonrandom orders run the risk that participants would learn the task sequence (Gotler et al., 2003; Heuer et al., 2001; Koch, 2001) or parts of it, a fact that might change the unit of behavior that makes a "task." Specifically, consider the alternating runs paradigm of Rogers and Monsell (1995). In this paradigm, the tasks are arranged in alternating runs of fixed length (typically two) forming orders (with tasks A and B) such as AA-BB-AA.... It is reasonable to assume that the unit making a task becomes the entire run, for example. Using a random task order overcomes this issue (although it does not overcome the possibility that participants would treat the entire block or experiment as a "task," see more on this issue later). Finally, I am mentioning a third advantage despite the fact that it was not widely acknowledged: The cuing paradigm provides an interesting tool to study the processes underlying following simple instructions, a process deserving researchers' attention in its own right.

The task-cuing paradigm also has some disadvantages. At least in its current format, it does not allow the study of self selected actions. Moreover, in most studies, the cues indicate the identity of the task; hence, performance is, in a sense, exogenous (triggered by the environment) and not endogenous. The ability to self-initiate a task is sometimes most critical and may be overlooked when using explicit task cuing (e.g., see Logan, et al., 2007, for a related critique). For example, in a classic article, Brown and Marsden (1988) showed that Parkinson's disease patients were impaired in task switching only when they had to initiate the task from memory and not when the task was explicitly cued. It seems to me that this potential shortcoming of the cuing paradigm can be addressed with some relatively minor modifications.

One such modification is the use of transition cues indicating whether to remain on the same task or to shift to the other task (Forstmann et al., 2005, 2006; see more on this topic later). Another technique that has been used is instructing a series of tasks rather than just one task (Logan, 2004; Sohn & Carlson, 2000).

A BRIEF HISTORY

Allport et al.'s (1994) article demarks the transition from a period of relatively sporadic research on task switching into a period in which this topic became a major theme in psychology and neuroscience. In this section, I cover the early era. To the best of my knowledge, Shaffer (1965) has introduced the cueing paradigm. In his experiment, the target stimulus was a light that appeared either on the right or the left side of the fixation point, and the two task rules were to press (a) the compatibly located key (Rule 1) or (b) the key on the opposite side (Rule 2). His focus was on the difference in performance between the two rules, but his results indicate poorer performance in switch relative to repeat trials. In other words, there was switching cost. Moreover, this switching cost was numerically smaller when the task cue preceded the target stimulus compared with when it appeared simultaneously with it. Similar findings were later reported by Hartley et al. (1990) and de Jong (1995; see also Keele & Hawkins, 1982).

Aside from the aforementioned conditions, Shaffer has also included in his study two conditions that have only rarely been included in subsequent work. In one condition, the target stimulus came before the task cue (see Ruge et al., 2009, for a recent application), and in another condition, the cue came simultaneously with the target but there was a noninformative warning stimulus, making it possible to differentiate between general nonspecific preparation and task-specific preparation.

Another notable early study was conducted by Biederman (1972), in which the stimuli varied along three dimensions: size, color, and line-tilt. The values along one of these dimensions (such as "green" and "red") indicated which one of the other two dimensions was relevant. Thus, one dimension was the cue while the two other dimensions served as the target. Importantly, Biederman counterbalanced the dimensions' roles, meaning that, across the entire group of participants, each dimension was equally likely to be the cue and the target. This made it possible to compare between cues and targets while controlling for their physical characteristics. Biederman found that the repetition of the task cue (which indexes the "task switching cost") was associated with a larger reaction-time (RT) effect compared with target repetition, already suggesting that these two repetition effects may be mediated by different processes.

A SCHEMATIC REPRESENTATION OF THE CUING PARADIGM

At the block level, the cuing paradigm includes mixed blocks and (sometimes also) single-task (or "pure") blocks. At the trial level, each trial involves a cue and a target. The total duration of a trial is typically described as beginning with the response that was given in the preceding trial (Trial n-1) and ending with the response that is given in the current trial (Trial n). This duration is subdivided as follows: the first interval begins with the *n*-1st response and ends with the *n*th cue (RCI). The second interval begins with the *n*th cue and ends with the *n*th target (CTI). The final interval is the RT, beginning with the *n*th target and ending with the *n*th response.[1]

CONSIDERATIONS IN DESIGNING CUING PARADIGMS

In what follows, I list the various considerations involved in designing a cuing task switching paradigm. This overview is essentially limited given the enormous (and rapidly growing) literature on this topic. The considerations are subdivided into two sections. The first section covers considerations that apply to any task switching paradigm, not just a cuing paradigm. The second section covers considerations that pertain just to the cuing paradigm. In the following discussion, I distinguish between relatively abstract structural aspects of the experiment and relatively concrete elements. The abstract elements include trial and block structure as well as other non–task-specific elements such as the type of information provided by the cue and whether the target stimuli afford more than one task, for example. The more concrete elements are at the level of the tasks themselves.

Considerations That Apply to Any Task Switching Paradigm

This section will first deal with the relatively abstract aspects of the experiment including block and trial structure of the experiment. Then I will deal with more concrete considerations, including (a) How many tasks are involved? (b) Which tasks are involved? and (c) How are the tasks related to one another?

Estimating Mixing Cost

Task switching experiments often involve two types of experimental blocks: single-task blocks (or "pure" blocks) and mixed-tasks blocks. The mixed-tasks blocks involve switch trials and repeat trials. This basic design thus involves three conditions: switch, repeat, and single-task, which are used to define alternation-cost, switching cost, and mixing cost. *Switching cost* is the difference in performance between switch trials and repeat trials. *Mixing cost* (also called "global cost") is the (usual) processing impairment in repeat trials relative to the single-task conditions, despite the fact that in both cases the current task is the same as the preceding task. *Alternation cost* is the joint cost, defined as the decrement in performance in switch trials relative to single task trials (see Fagot, 1994). Note that from the statistical point of view, three conditions have only 2 degrees of freedom and can be defined by two orthogonal contrasts. Switching cost and mixing cost, as described earlier, are nonorthogonal. The vector of

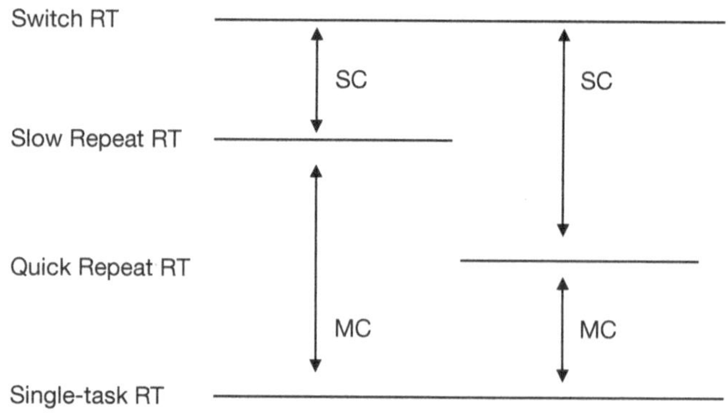

Figure 3.1 Why mixing cost and switching cost are dependent by definition (SC = switching cost; MC = mixing cost).

contrast weights describing switching cost is "1, −1, 0" (for switch, repeat, and single-task, respectively). The vector of contrast weights describing mixing cost is "0, 1, −1." When these vectors are multiplied, the dot-product is −1, meaning that they are negatively correlated. This becomes apparent when considering a case in which two conditions that are being compared have equal switch RT and single-task RT. Slowed repeat RT in one condition would be accompanied by smaller switching cost and equally larger mixing cost than in the other condition (see Figure 3.1). The fact that switching cost and mixing cost are nonorthogonal is especially important in correlational studies (although it is relevant in any study), because if a negative correlation is found between switching cost and mixing cost, this would reflect the manner in which the costs are defined more than revealing anything about nature. This problem is resolved when using a modified definition of mixing cost, "1, 1, −2," in which the mean single-task RT is subtracted from the mean RT in switch and repeat trials, combined (e.g., Kray & Lindenberger, 2000).

Demonstrating mixing cost is associated with some methodological challenges. Several different designs were used, each associated with its own advantages and disadvantages. One design is between subjects, in which one group of participants performs single-task blocks and the other group receives mixed-task blocks (e.g., Marí-Beffa et al., 2012). The drawback is obvious: poor statistical power due to the between-group design and inability to assess mixing cost at the level of individual participants. For these reasons, this design is likely to be impractical when studying special populations, in correlation studies and in imaging studies. The advantages of the between-subjects design are also obvious: In this design, there are no carryover effects. These carryover effects may be quite substantial, as discussed later.

The other designs mentioned next have potential carryover effects. There are two types of carryover effects: from the mixed-tasks blocks to the single-task blocks, and vice versa. Concerning the first category of carryover effects, we currently know that the stimuli become bound with the task (Waszak et al., 2003; see also Gade & Koch, 2007) or even with the experimental context (Woodward et al., 2003), and when the stimuli are encountered or the context is encountered, this leads to an automatic retrieval of that task. Moreover, having just experienced mixed-tasks conditions induces task uncertainty and may lead to a conflict regarding which task to execute. Such a conflict may even be present in conditions in which it was absent beforehand (Allport et al., 1994, Experiment 4; Braverman & Meiran, 2010). The carryover from the mixed-tasks conditions is also seen in the "fadeout effect" (Mayr & Liebscher, 2001). Mayr and Liebscher have shown that the transition from the mixed-tasks condition to the single-task condition is characterized by a marked initial slowing and a gradual acceleration until the original levels of single-task performance are attained. While this transition is rather quick among healthy young adults, it is slow among the elderly (Mayr & Liebscher) and among some psychiatric populations (Meiran et al., 2011a). One interpretation of this barely studied effect is that it reflects a process of disengagement from a mind-set associated with task switching (see Marí-Beffa et al., 2012).

The carryover effects may also work in the opposite direction, namely from the single-task condition to the mixed-tasks condition. For example, Philipp and Koch (2006) have shown that experiencing task repetitions may be sufficient to eliminate the backward inhibition effect (Koch et al., 2010), and we have similar unpublished results. Recent results from my lab suggest yet another type of carryover effect from single-task to mixed-tasks conditions. Specifically, Erel and Meiran (2011) showed that following instructions regarding a single two-choice task resulted in subsequent drastic impairments in executive functioning, including rule finding, task switching, feedback evaluation, and ideational fluency.

Three within-subjects designs have been used to study mixing cost. Braver et al. (2003) intermixed single-task blocks and mixed-tasks blocks (see also Koch et al., 2005). This design was probably adopted because of the constraints of functional magnetic resonance imaging, but it is likely to diminish the differences between the two types of blocks because of the various carryover effects (see Los, 1996). A compromise is the sandwich design (Rubin & Meiran, 2005) in which the single-task blocks start and end the experiment and the mixed-tasks blocks are in the middle. There are two notable advantages to this design. One is that, on average, the amount of task training is equal in the mixed-tasks and the single-task conditions. The other advantage is the ability to detect carryover effects that come from the mixed condition to the last single-task condition by comparing the early and late single-task blocks. Since the training effects are expected to result in better performance in the late blocks than in the early blocks, a reverse trend is indicative of carryover effects (e.g., Mayr & Liebscher, 2001). If such carryover effects are observed, the early portion of the late blocks can be discarded. Finally, in my lab, we often use a design in which the single-task block comes last in the experiment. We often observe that the first single-task trials are relatively slow, indicating fadeout effects, and we eliminate these trials (e.g., Yehene & Meiran, 2007). This design completely overcomes the problems associated with carryover effects from the single-task condition to the mixed condition. It additionally permits discarding the initial single-task trials to eliminate the influence of fadeout effects, but it does not enable the relatively precise assessment of the carryover effects in the single-task trials due to the lack of a baseline condition. This last design has the drawback of confounding mixing cost with practice. The direction is toward an underestimate of the mixing cost since the slower condition (mixing) enjoys more practice. This problem can be nearly completely resolved by comparing the last mixed-tasks trials with the single-task block, because at this point, task practice effects are negligible.

Recommendation: As seen from this review, none of the aforementioned designs is fault free. Thus, a clear recommendation cannot be given except perhaps noting that the choice depends on the constraints and the experimental questions. Just try to ensure that focal issues in your study are not the ones associated with the aforementioned shortcomings. Take, for example, a case in which one wishes to estimate the correlation between mixing cost and some brain pathology. In such a study, the focus is likely to be on differences between patients or between them and controls, and the absolute mixing cost is less important. Moreover, maximizing statistical power is critical given the typical rareness of patients. In such a case, a within-subjects design seems more appropriate.

Transition Probability

Several studies have shown that when task switches are rare, switching costs become larger than when task switches are common (e.g., Logan et al., 2007; Meiran et al., 2000; Monsell & Mizon, 2006). The exact reasons are debated but may include a variety of factors, including the known tendency for quicker responses to more likely events (e.g., Logan et al.); the fact that in the cuing paradigm, RT tends to decrease gradually in the course of the run (Meiran et al.; Monsell et al., 2003; Tornay & Milàn, 2001) combined with the fact that when switch probability is low, runs tend to become longer (resulting in facilitated average repeat RT), etc. This issue has an impact on a number of related issues such as run length (longer runs being associated with lower switch probability) and number of tasks (see later). Actually, the relative frequency of events is an issue spanning beyond just task switching probability (e.g., see Altmann, 2011).

Number of Tasks

Mixing cost (in which a single-task condition is compared with an n-task condition) may be conceived of as a special case of a more general issue concerning the number of tasks. Without conducting a formal review, my impression is that the majority of the studies used two-task designs. Yet, the use of two-task designs is limited because there are important effects that can be demonstrated only with three or more tasks. Aside from not being able to estimate these effects, the use of two-task designs may contaminate switching cost and other effects. In detail, three tasks are required to observe the lag-2 repetition effects ("backward inhibition"; Koch et al., 2010). Briefly, this effect is based on comparing two kinds of switch trials: those involving lag-2 repetition (e.g., A-B-A) and those that do not (e.g., C-B-A). This definition makes it obvious that one needs at least three tasks (A, B, and C) to observe lag-2 repetition costs. An additional inhibitory effect is the competitor rule suppression effect (CRS; Meiran et al., 2010, also called dimension-suppression, see Astle et al., 2012). To understand what CRS means,

I need to first define the term *competitor rule*. A task rule is an irrelevant rule that produces a wrong response. One means to prevent this wrong response from getting executed is to suppress the competitor rule. This suppression is then seen in poorer performance when the competitor rule becomes the relevant rule in the next trial. One cannot, however, simply compare trials in which the shape rule is a competitor rule with trials in which this rule is not a competitor rule. Such a comparison would be between trials following a response conflict and trials without a response conflict—hence, one confounding general nonspecific control adaptation (e.g., Botvinick et al., 2001) and the specific suppression of the competitor rule. To demonstrate CRS, one needs to include trials in which a third rule was a competitor rule, namely trials following a response conflict but without next applying the competitor rule. Thus, to demonstrate CRS, one needs at least three tasks.

Recommendation: My suggestion is to use at least three tasks, while keeping in mind that the number of tasks has been shown to influence performance (Biederman, 1973; Dixon, 1981; Meiran et al., 2002). One should, however, also keep in mind that when the tasks are randomly ordered, an increase in the number of tasks is associated with a corresponding decrease in the proportion of task repetitions (i.e., it influences transition probability).

Which Tasks?

The task switching literature often focuses on the relatively abstract structural characteristics of the experiment such as the type of switching paradigm and disregards the tasks themselves. This has been true since the beginning of the new era of task switching research. For example, we (Meiran et al., 2000) tried to reconcile Allport et al.'s (1994) notion regarding task-set dissipation and Rogers and Monsell's (1995) notion regarding advance task reconfiguration. Yet, these two groups used different tasks. Allport et al. studied Stroop (color versus word) task switching. Rogers and Monsell asked participants to switch between vowel–consonant judgments and odd–even judgments. We used spatial tasks (vertical and horizontal).

The practice of focusing on abstract structural issues of the paradigm may be somewhat justified given the similar pattern of results that is usually obtained with different tasks (e.g., Yehene & Meiran, 2007); the fact that the behavioral effects load on the same individual differences factor (Friedman & Miyake, 2004; Miyake et al., 2000); and the overlapping brain activation (e.g., Derrfuss et al., 2005; Dosenbach et al., 2006). Nonetheless, as knowledge accumulates, it appears that the tasks themselves play a quite substantial role in performance. An important early example is Mayr and Kliegl's (2000) finding concerning larger switching costs when the tasks involved episodic retrieval as compared with semantic retrieval, a result which led the authors to conclude that task preparation involves episodic retrieval of task rules. An additional example is the atypical elimination switching cost (given a long preparation, known as "residual switch cost") when the tasks involve eye movements (pro-saccade versus anti-saccade, Hunt & Klein, 2002; see especially Hunt et al., 2006). Similarly, switching the relevant dimension in same-different judgments showed no preparation-related reduction in switch cost (Meiran & Marciano, 2002) despite using the exact same stimuli that, in another study, showed marked reduction in switch costs when the tasks involved speeded classification (Meiran et al., 2002). Next, I discuss some of the more salient task dimensions in the extant literature.

Stimulus Valence

A major consideration involves the choice of target stimuli. The typical design involves targets that afford all the possible tasks, such as colored shapes when switching between a shape task and a color task. The literature often regards them as "bivalent" but I think that a more proper term should be "multivalent," thus covering any number of tasks. The alternative is to use *univalent* targets that afford only one task. Target valence has been shown to play a major role in switching costs (e.g., Mayr, 2001; Meiran, 2000b) and mixing costs (Rubin & Meiran, 2005), and the inclusion of bivalent targets in the block has shown to influence univalent performance as well (Woodward et al., 2003).

Although not often discussed in the task switching literature, one should take into consideration how to design multivalent targets. In some studies, a single perceptual object is used. Some early examples are the use of colored letters when switching between a letter task and a color task (Hartley et al., 1990). The alternative is to use targets that comprise of several objects such as Rogers and Monsell's (1995) letter-digit combinations (such as "G7"). An advantage of using integrated objects is the enhanced selection difficulty (Kahaneman & Henik, 1981). An advantage of using multielement displays is ease of applying a separate manipulation on each element. This advantage has been used by Rogers and Monsell, for example, in designing univalent stimuli by replacing one of the elements by an asterisk (e.g., "G*" instead of "G7").

It is important not to confuse "valence" with "dimension" and to appreciate the potential role of target repetition. Regarding valence versus dimension, it is possible to design univalent multidimensional targets. For example, it is possible to present univalent colored shapes in an experiment involving a shape task and a color task if the shape is not among the shapes in the shape task. Actually, the literature suggests that while bivalency is challenging, the presence of never-relevant target dimensions does not appear to substantially increase switching challenge among adults (Meiran et al., 2012b; Rubin & Meiran, 2005), although it may do so among preschoolers (e.g., Brooks et al., 2003). Additionally, when the targets are multivalent, there might be target repetitions even in switch trials. However, when the targets are univalent, target repetitions are possible only in repeat trials. This issue should be seriously considered given the strong influence of target repetition in switching costs (Waszak et al., 2003) as well as in other effects (e.g., Waszak et al., 2008).

Response Valence

A related task-element is response valence. Just as the stimuli can be shared among the various tasks, so can the responses. While many studies used an overlapping set of responses (multivalent response setups), some studies used a separate set of response keys. Like with stimulus multivalence, response multivalence has shown to increase switch costs (Meiran, 2000b) sometimes in combination with stimulus bivalence (Mayr, 2001). Nonetheless, even when the responses of the tasks are separated, their cognitive codes (such as "inner" and "outer") may overlap and this has also been shown to influence performance (Druey & Hübner, 2008; Hübner & Druey, 2008; Schuch & Koch, 2004).

Relative Task Dominance

Another relatively widely discussed issue concerns the relationship between the tasks—most specifically, their differential difficulty or dominance. Allport et al. (1994), who studied switching between a (dominant) word task and a (nondominant) color task that were performed on Stroop stimuli, were the first to report the phenomenon of *switch asymmetry*. This phenomenon is the fact that switching cost is larger in the easy/dominant task than in the difficult/nondominant task. Analogous findings were found regarding mixing costs in the literature on stimulus–response compatibility (e.g., Shaffer, 1965; van Duren & Sanders, 1988; see Los, 1996, for review). For example, in Shaffer's (1965) experiment described earlier, performance was better in the compatible task than in the incompatible task, reflecting a spatial compatibility effect. This spatial compatibility effect was eliminated in the mixed-tasks condition. However, when the target stimulus was preceded by a cue (the CTI was 333 ms), the compatibility effect was found even in the mixed condition. It should be noted that switch asymmetry is not always found (Monsell et al., 2000), and its presence seems to depend on high levels of intertask conflict (Yeung & Monsell, 2003). Finally, an analogous effect has been reported even when there was a difficulty level switch without task switching (Bryck & Mayr, 2008).

Several additional task-level variables have been shown to influence performance, sometimes quite markedly. These include stimulus repetition (especially Waszak et al., 2003), response repetition (e.g., Kleinsorge & Heuer, 1999; Rogers & Monsell, 1995), the combined effects of both (e.g., Mayr & Bryck, 2005), task expectancy (e.g., Dreisbach et al., 2002), and the proportion of in/congruent trials (e.g., Meiran, 1996).

Recommendation: The simple recommendation is to consider the tasks themselves and their interrelations, not just the abstract structure of the experiment. Additionally, if one wishes to focus on what I called "structural" aspects of the paradigm, I recommend studying several task combinations rather than base the conclusions on a single assembly of tasks to ensure the generality of the conclusions.

Single-Step Tasks Versus Multistep Tasks: What Makes a "Task"?

Researchers often use a rather intuitive definition of a *task*, but as the later review suggests, the unit of work that makes a "task" depends to a large extent on subtle environmental cues, which are mostly perceptual in nature. In this regard, the vast majority of the studies on task switching used single-step tasks typically involving one stimulus and one response. However, a few studies have focused on multistep tasks that could be motor sequences (Hayes et al., 1998), a pair of stimuli (a letter and a color patch) requiring two responses (Luria & Meiran, 2003), or a single multidimensional stimulus requiring a series of responses, each referring to a different dimension (Luria et al., 2006). An informal observation suggests that in many of these instances, the stimuli and responses were integrated into a multistep task by perception. This observation is supported by several studies (Ellenbogen & Meiran, 2011; Koch et al., 2006; Lien & Ruthruff, 2004). In Lien and Ruthruff's study, it was shown that when a pair of trials could be grouped on the basis of perceptual features and temporal proximity, switch costs turned into switch benefits. This is due to the fact that when the pair of trials was considered as one unit, the switch condition (between Task A and Task B) made a pair repetition (A→B then A→B). The critical role of task construal is dramatically demonstrated in Dreisbach et al.'s (2006, 2007) studies in which participants performed the exact same task switching paradigm in two conditions. In one condition (SR), the instructions were given in terms of stimulus–response pairs (e.g., this word corresponds with that response). In another condition (task switching, or TS), participants were told that the color of the words indicates which stimulus dimension is relevant: the beginning letter (vowel versus consonant) or whether the word represents an animate-versus-inanimate object. The results showed switching costs (as well as several additional indications such as goal shielding, Dreisbach & Haider, 2009) only in the TS condition, not in the SR condition.

A related issue has been discussed in the task switching literature under the term "task-space" (Kleinsorge & Heuer, 1999). The essence of the concept as I see it is that, when asked to perform several tasks, participants form an abstract representation of all the tasks that they encounter in the paradigm. In Kleinsorge and Heuer's study, the representation was arguably hierarchical, with the relevant stimulus dimension at the top of the hierarchy, the type of response rule underneath, and the response itself at the very bottom. Corroborating evidence comes from the developmental literature on the Dimensional Card Sorting task that is actually a task switching paradigm. In it, the ability to form a hierarchical task representation arguably determines preschoolers' ability to switch tasks (Frye et al., 1998; Zelazo & Frye, 1998). An intriguing possibility is that what is construed as a "task" may actually be the switching situation itself. In other words, the "task space" may actually represent a high-order task set. This notion accords with the fadeout effect, already mentioned. In this regard, I suggest that the unit of behavior making a task is akin to what we (Meiran et al., 2012b) termed "plan-to-execution event," which begins with the formation of a behavioral plan and ends when this plan has been completed. Although the term *event* is rather elusive, there is marked agreement between observers regarding event boundaries and considerable objective support for the psychological reality of these boundaries (e.g., Zacks et al., 2007). The link between the concept of a "task" and the concept "plan-to-execution event" is supported by findings showing that a goal change demarks event boundaries (Zacks & Swallow, 2007) and the evidence suggesting that the contents of working memory are (partly) refreshed at these boundaries (e.g., Swallow et al., 2009).

Recommendation: My recommendation is to consider the fact that what the experimenter is defining as a "task" may not be construed as a task by the participants and vice versa. For example, beware of how the tasks are grouped in time and space and whether sequences of tasks repeat many times in the course of the experiment, since grouping and sequence repetitions are likely to change the subjective construal of "task." I additionally repeat one of the aforementioned advantages of the cuing paradigm, namely the random ordering of the tasks that seems to prevent any systematic influence of task sequence representations that form a special case of high-order task sets.

Aspects That Are Uniquely Linked to the Cuing Paradigm

RCI AND CTI: SEPARATING THE RETRIEVABILITY OF THE *N*-1 TASK SET AND THE PREPARATION OF THE *N*TH TASK SET

Early theoretical conceptions made a distinction between two sets of processes that contribute to switching costs. The first set refers to the ease of retrieval of the previous ($n-1$) and no-longer relevant task set (Allport et al., 1994; Allport & Wylie, 2000). The other set of processes includes "reconfiguration"—the setting the cognitive system according to the demands of the current (nth) task (Rogers & Monsell, 1995). I think that given the theoretical and empirical progress in this field, it becomes clear that the aforementioned distinction may be inaccurate. This is so because aspects of the current task set (which is presumably what is prepared as a part of the reconfiguration) involve the suppression of the previous task set (Brown et al., 2007; Mayr & Keele, 2000; Meiran et al., 2010; cf. Koch & Allport, 2006; Meiran & Daichman, 2005).

The cuing paradigm made it possible to disentangle the aforementioned processes. The rationale was that the temporal distance between the n-1 response and nth target (Response-Target Interval) influences the ease of retrieval of the n-1st task set during Trial n. In contrast, the CTI influences reconfiguration. Two methods to study the time course of reconfiguration were accordingly developed. In one method, the CTI is manipulated within a fixed response-target interval (Meiran, 1996). The other method (Meiran et al., 2000) involves two steps. In the first step, CTI is fixed (and short) and RCI varies. This step yields a function relating switch-costs to RCI. This function often indicates that switching costs become smaller with increasing RCI but that the function appears to reach asymptote after a certain RCI (Meiran et al., 2000). In other studies it was a flat function, indicating insensitivity of switch costs to RCI increase (e.g., Luria & Meiran, 2003). Either way, it is possible to determine an RCI beyond which any further increase in RCI has only negligible influence on switch costs. For example, in Meiran et al.'s study, the RCI was barely influence switching costs when the RCI ranged between ~1 sec and ~3 sec. This justified using a fixed RCI of ~1 sec in subsequent experiments.

Although the first method has become more popular, I actually recommend the second (two-stage) method. The reason is that, when examining the articles using the first method, when the CTI was long, RCI was typically extremely short (i.e, ~100 ms) making it possible that cue processing efficiency was compromised because processing resources were temporarily depleted (Muraven & Baumeister, 2000)[2] or were yet unavailable because of post response processing (e.g., Kafry & Kahneman, 1977, as well as processes involved in the Error Related Negativity, Yeung et al., 2004, for a recent review). Another drawback of the first method is that (when CTI is manipulated within blocks, hence varies randomly) the cue comes at an unexpected point in time, again compromising its processing efficiency. As detailed below, this is especially true for the short-RCI-long-CTI condition.

RCI/CTI Blocking and Range of Values

Other considerations of the CTI and RCI manipulations concern the blocking of these variables, the range of values and their distribution. Two lines of reasoning pertain to blocking and range of values. One line concerns the temporal predictability of stimulus onset. The other line concerns temporal distinctiveness.

Temporal Predictability

Preparation is known to rely on several distinct processes (e.g., Jennings & van der Molen, 2005; Meiran et al., 2000). Moreover, subtle cues may indicate that one preparation mode may be relatively more efficient than another. This can be exemplified in the cuing paradigm in which the cue provides at least two pieces of information: task identity information and timing information regarding when the target stimulus is likely to appear (Meiran et al., 2000). Cue presentation can thus give rise to at least two distinct forms of preparation: a non-specific form ("arousal") associated in part with predicting target onset and a task-specific form in which task unique features are prepared. These include the retrieval of stimulus–response mapping information (Mayr & Kliegl, 2000) and the redirection of attention towards the relevant stimulus dimension (Meiran, 2000a, 2000b). Based on the extant literature it seems that certain conditions differentially emphasize one preparation mode relative to the other.

The influence of temporal predictability has been sztudied in relation to the CTI. Specifically, when the CTI is blocked, target temporal predictability is generally high (given the certainty concerning CTI duration). It is important to note that knowing the CTI is not enough since in order to make use of this information, participants need to estimate the CTI. Since, according to Weber's Law, prediction error is proportional to estimated interval, prediction accuracy decreases with increasing CTI. In other words, predicting target onset is likely to be relatively discouraged when the CTI is very long even when it is blocked.

When the CTI varies between trials, the ability to predict stimulus onset is further decreased due to uncertainty. Intuitively, many people to whom I explained the paradigm thought that when trials involving different CTIs are equally frequent, the CTIs become unpredictable, but actually this is not the case. In fact, target predictability increases with CTI in these conditions. This is so because target predictability is a function of the *conditional* probability that the target will appear in the next CTI given that the shorter CTIs have already passed, an effect termed "aging foreperiod" (see Meiran et al., 2000). Such "aging" effects can be overcome by using exponentially distributed CTIs such that the most frequent CTI is the shortest CTI, so called "non-aging" conditions. This issue has been discussed in the literature on the foreperiod effect (e.g., Los & van der Heuvel, 2001; Niemi & Naatanen, 1981).

Meiran et al. (2000) compared "aging" and "non-aging" CTIs and found that this manipulation did not influence switching costs. Rather it influenced switch and repeat RTs equally. With aging CTIs, RT continued to decrease throughout the entire CTI range. When the CTI was "non-aging," RT was influenced by CTI only in the shorter CTIs. One hypothesis that we considered in that paper was that task specific preparation and preparing towards target onset are processes that compete over common resources. The idea was rejected in that paper based on the null influence of "aging" on switching costs. Nonetheless, the "aging" manipulation is not the strongest possible manipulation of temporal predictability since when the CTI varies between trials, target onset remains somewhat uncertain regardless of "aging." A much more drastic manipulation of expectancy is CTI blocking. Actually, some studies show that when the CTI is blocked, CTI does not influence switching costs (Altmann, 2004; Koch, 2001, but see Meiran et al., 2012, for a case in which between-participants manipulation influenced switching costs).[3] This result is compatible with the idea that when the CTI is blocked, target onset is certain, a fact that may motivate participants to adopt a preparation strategy that relies on the prediction of target onset instead of on task-specific preparation.

An additional related issue is the difference between between-subject manipulations versus blocking of the CTI. Specifically, when the CTI (or the RCI) are manipulated between-subjects, each participant is exposed to a single CTI (or RCI). However, when the CTI (or RCI) is blocked, participants are exposed to CTI (or RCI) variation in the course of the experiment. Being exposed to the CTI/RCI variation might attract attention to these variables, a fact that might further encourage non-task-specific preparation (Gotler, 2004).

Although temporal predictability has not yet been considered in relation to RCI manipulations, there is no reason why it should not be considered. Specifically, participants may try to predict cue onset as well. If my speculation is correct, it impacts on experiments in which the CTI is manipulated within blocks and within a fixed Response-Target Interval (see above). This manipulation creates differential cue-onset uncertainty. Specifically, cue onset is less predictable when the RCI is short (and the CTI is long) than when the RCI is long (and the CTI is short).

Range of CTIs/RCIs

Several theories suggest that the range of CTI/RCI values may also influence performance. Los and van der Heuvel (2001) studied the influence of foreperiod which, when regarding target onset predictability, is analogous to CTI. These authors showed that performance depends on the combined effects of the *n*th and the *n*-1st foreperiod. Horufchin et al. (2011) studied the influence of RCI in task switching experiments. According to these authors, the n-1st task set does not decay passively as previously suggested by Allport et al. (1994) and Meiran et al. (2000). Rather, its availability in Trial n (and hence, the interference in switch trials) depends on the strength of the temporal retrieval cue, which depends on the $RCI_n/RCI_{n\text{-}1st}$ ratio. For obvious mathematical reasons, this ratio depends on RCI blocking (when blocked, the ratio always equals one) and on the range of RCIs when RCI is not blocked. While most of the published studies support Horufchin et al.'s theory (see their paper for review) our original results (Meiran et al., 2000) do not accord with this prediction since RCI blocking did not significantly change the function relating switching costs to RCI. Perhaps this is another example for a result that depends on the tasks themselves?

Finally, a related consideration is how many CTIs (or RCIs) one should use. Many experiments used only two extreme intervals (Meiran, 1996; Shaffer, 1965) since their focus was to merely show that preparation exists. In contrast, other experiments used many CTIs in an effort to trace the time course of the preparation process (e.g., Logan & Bundesen, 2003; Sudevan & Taylor, 1987). Just beware of the fact that the choice of number of intervals impacts on interval predictability when the CTI (or RCI) vary within a block, as explained.

Preparedness and Overcoming Interference

In this section I would like to discuss a commonly held assumption that preparation reduces switching/mixing costs because of mental work that is performed ahead of the target stimulus. According to this assumption, the kind of processing that takes place is similar in the prepared and less-prepared states, except that some of this work has already been done ahead of the RT measurement in the prepared state (e.g., Meiran, 1996, 2000a; Rogers & Monsell, 1995; Rubinstein et al., 2001). This idea has been challenged by several authors including Ruge et al. (2005) who used fMRI methodology and by Meiran et al. (2008) who used mathematical modeling. The alternative that has been suggested is that short and long CTIs elicit different control modes in line with Braver's (2012) distinction between proactive and reactive control.

Recommendation: It is obvious that manipulating RCI/CTI in different ways changes the context and that context *can* have an effect. Ideally, studies should manipulate these temporal variables in different ways to ensure that they reach a conclusion that is true regardless of a specific design. Since this recommendation cannot often be followed, researchers should at least mention the limitations when listing their conclusions.

What Cues to Use?

Obviously, the task cues are a critical component of the cuing paradigm. Broadly speaking, two types of cues are used: task cues and transition cues. Task cues indicate task identity whereas transition cues indicate whether the next trial involves a task repetition or a task switch (e.g., Dreisbach et al., 2002; Forstmann et al., 2005, 2006, 2007).

Several studies compared different types of task cues. An early example is a study by Mayr and Kliegl (2000, Experiment 3). In one condition, the cues indicated the identity of the task and nothing else. The authors reasoned that in this condition, participants must retrieve from memory the rules that mapped categorizations (e.g., "this is a word describing a living thing") to physical responses (e.g., "press the right key"). The other cues provided this mapping directly by placing the relevant categorization on the right/left side of fixation (e.g., "LIVING + NONLIVING"), rendering mapping retrieval unnecessary. The results of this experiment indicated much larger switching costs with task-identity cues than with mapping cues, and mostly so when the tasks themselves involved heavy memory retrieval demands. More generally, one may distinguish between cues that provide more (vs. less) information about the task. When less information is provided directly, more information needs to be retrieved from memory.

Along a similar line, Logan and Bundesen (2004) showed differential performance when comparing between cues that provided the task name versus letter cues that just reminded of the task name. They showed larger "true switch costs" (see below) when the cues did not specify the task identity directly than when task information was provided directly. This distinction between more or less transparent cues is reminiscent of the distinction between more and less compatible stimulus–response arrangements (see Kornblum et al., 1990, for a review and taxonomy). Compatible stimulus–response arrangements such as "respond to the right light by pressing the right key" are such that the target stimulus provides a strong retrieval cue for the response. Similarly, transparent cues are ones which provide a strong retrieval cue for the task set.

According to this line of reasoning, changing the arbitrary cue-to-task mapping in the middle of the experiment should lead to increased switch costs because of the associated difficulty in task identity retrieval (Gade & Koch, 2007). A similar manipulation has also been shown to increase backward inhibition effects (Grange & Houghton, 2010b) in line with the results suggesting that these effects are linked to the level of the abstract task identity rather than the concrete level of the cue percept (e.g., Altmann, 2007b). Finally, Arbuthnott (2005) found differential performance when the tasks were indicated by the position of the target stimulus as compared to when the task was indicated by means of a verbal cue indicating the response alternatives (e.g. "Odd/Even").

How Many Cues Per Task? How Many Tasks Per Cue??

A number of studies have employed two cues per task (also known as 2:1 cue-task mapping) and one study employed 1:2 mapping in which each cue indicated two different tasks (Hydock & Sohn, 2011). Logan and Bundesen (2003) and Mayr & Kliegl (2003) noted that in earlier studies employing the cuing paradigm, when the task repeats from the previous trial, so does the task cue. Thus a portion of the switch costs, as measured using these earlier paradigms might be attributable to the priming of cue processing in repeat trials. Logan & Bundesen as well as Mayr and Kliegl have thus introduced an alternative cuing procedure in which there are 2 cues per task, creating two types of task repetitions: with and without cue repetition. This design makes it possible to obtain separate estimates of cue repetition effects (cue and task repetition versus cue switch with task repetition) and "true" task switch effects (cue switch with task switch versus cue switch with task repetition).

Both studies indicated a cue switch effect (RTcue-switch>RTcue-repetition). However, in Logan and Bundesen's paper, the cue switch effect accounted for nearly all the task switching cost, and there was barely any "true" task switch effect (RTswitch—RTcue-switch). In contrast, Mayr & Kliegl found a reliable "true" task switch effect over and above the cue switch effect. Mayr and Kliegl conceived of the cue repetition effect as priming of task rule retrieval. The initial claims made by Logan, Bundesen and Schneider (especially Schneider & Logan, 2005) were quite radically different from those made by Mayr and Kliegl. They argued that there is no task switching in the cuing paradigm. Their idea (known as "the compound cue hypothesis") was that participants encode the cue and the target and use the cue-target compound to retrieve the response. Nonetheless, later publications from this group expressed much less radical views. For example, Arrington et al. (2007) concluded that the task cues access abstract task representations and Schneider and Logan (2005, 2009) assumed that the responses that are being retrieved represent abstract task-specific categorizations such as ODD, EVEN, HIGH, etc. Thus, the current view of this group is that task switching in the cuing paradigm entails a switch in at least two elements: the abstract task representation that guides response retrieval and the subgroup of categorizations. My impression is that such a switch would be regarded as a task-set switch by researchers coming from the other "camp."

Logan and Bundesen's (2003) hypothesis has led researchers to find ways to overcome the "problem" of cue repetition. For example, Forstmann et al. (2007) used transition cues in order to factorially manipulate task repetition and cue repetition. This approach may be somewhat limited because transition cues introduce a confounding variable that is related to the task sequence (Schneider & Logan, 2007b). Consider, for example a paradigm involving Tasks A, B. In such a paradigm, a condition with task switch and cue repetition is one in which Trial n and Trial n-1 both involved a task switch (e.g., an A-B-A sequence). In contrast, a task switch with a cue switch means that Trial n-1 was a repeat trial and Trial n was a switch trial (e.g., a B-B-A sequence). Because such transitions are known to strongly influence performance, this questions the validity of the transition-cues approach in overcoming cue-repetition effects.

Monsell and Mizon (2006) suggested to simply eliminate cue repetitions altogether. This is possible by employing the 2:1 design (such that two cue types are used for each task) but regularly alternating cue type (e.g., "parity"→ "odd/even"→ "size"→"high/low" etc.). One can think of additional solutions such as cuing pairs of trials so that the second trial in the pair does not have a task cue at all (see Sohn & Carlson, 2000, for a related paradigm). Additionally, in Altmann & Gray's

(2002, 2008) randomized runs paradigm, which can be conceived of an extension of the cuing paradigm, cue repetition is not confounded with task repetition (see also Gopher et al., 2000).

Perhaps one of the best solutions is using *tasks* in which the compound-cue strategy or analogous strategies are disabled. This approach has been used quite extensively, intentionally or unintentionally. Examples are studies using the odd-item out task (e.g., Mayr & Keele, 2000) target localization (Grange & Houghton, 2010b), and same-different judgments (Meiran & Marciano, 2002).

Should One Attempt to Get Rid of Cue Repetition Effects?

In a sense, what has happened in the literature with the cue repetition effects resembles the neglect of mixing costs in the early studies of the new era (especially Meiran, 1996; Rogers & Monsell, 1995). These early studies considered mixing cost a nuisance; something to avoid in an attempt to capture the "real" executive aspects of task switching. Yet, later studies suggested that mixing cost may be quite important to cognitive control (see Rubin & Meiran, 2005, for a partial review).

Along a similar line of reasoning, I suggest that "cue repetition effects" may reflect important aspects of cognitive control (Grange & Houghton, 2010a) possibly for the same reasons that the decision to execute a given task (or the retrieval of this task's identity) obviously represents cognitive control. Actually, Mayr & Kliegl (2003) suggested that the cue repetition effect represents the primed retrieval of the task set. These and similar ideas are supported by recent studies showing that the CTI involves what we call "control processing." This includes behavioral evidence that the CTI is related to the resolution of a conflict regarding which task to execute (Braverman & Meiran, 2010). Additionally, there are studies that focused on cue-locked event-related potentials. Astle et al. (2008) showed differential cue evoked brain activity pattern depending on cue type. Meiran et al. (2011b) showed that cue evoked brain activity depended on whether the *n*th task rule has generated a response conflict in the preceding trial.

Cues Versus Primes

Sudevan and Taylor (1987) distinguished between "cues" and "primes." "Cues" are instructions, indicating the task with certainty while "primes" indicate which task is *likely* to appear. There are only very few studies which employed primes in the task switching literature. One difficulty with using primes is of course that, when primes are used there must also be cues to indicate the task otherwise participants would not know which task to execute. Ruthruff et al. (2000) solved this problem by using univalent target stimuli that require no cues. The drawback of this approach is that it is unclear if participants switch tasks at all when all the target stimuli are univalent. Alternatively, they may consider it as a single task. Sudevan and Taylor (1987) presented a prime and then a cue. An inherent difficulty associated with primes is that the prime might only influence cue processing rather than lead to task preparation.

WHERE NEXT?

In this last section, I highlight two issues that are among the issues that need further consideration.

Switch Costs Versus Other Effects

One issue concerns the exaggerated focus on task switching costs. As has been argued by other authors, there are many other, potentially very important phenomena to study in this paradigm. For one, task switching poses a serious and very interesting inhibitory challenge. This seems to be especially true for randomly ordered tasks because participants are faced with a conflict. On the one hand, they need to be prepared to execute any one of several tasks. Yet, when the next trial arrives, only one of the tasks is required and all the other potential tasks become (temporarily) irrelevant. Being prepared to execute tasks potentially increases the competition that comes from these tasks.

Task Switching Versus Set Switching

Perhaps the most important issue concerns the distinction between "set switching" and "task switching." As I see it, task switching paradigms have been introduced as a means to operationalize set switching (Gibson, 1941). As in the case of other operational definitions, this made it possible to make considerable progress in the study of a rather illusive term. However, a major drawback in overcommitting ourselves to this operational definition is that we sometimes forgot the broader issue at stake. Consequently, theoretical developments that have attempted to integrate the empirical findings emphasized rather concrete aspects of the term "set"—tied to specific tasks and task-specific processes. This is certainly true for most of the formal theories (e.g., Altmann, 2008; Gilbert & Shallice, 2003; Logan & Gordon, 2001; Meiran, 2000; Meiran et al., 2008; Sohn & Anderson, 2000). Specifically, in all these theories, the various empirical phenomena are explained in terms of task-specific representations. This may be a development in the wrong direction since it appears that set switching may refer to much more abstract representations. In addition, several reports suggest that switching effects span well beyond task switching. There are switching effects even when the task remains the same, and there is a change at the global/local level in which the target appears (Ward, 1982), the sensory modality (Sutton & Zubin, 1965), the response modality (Philipp & Koch, 2005), the decision criterion (Schneider & Logan, 2007a), and so forth. Thus, we currently know that task switching may not lead to switch costs unless it is accompanied by a set switch (Dreisbach et al., 2006, 2007) and that there is a switch cost when there is a set switch even in the absence of a task switch.

AUTHOR'S NOTE

This research was supported by a research grant from the Israel Science Foundation.

NOTES

1. Some authors call the CTI in other terms such as *stimulus onset asynchrony* (SOA) or, more frequently, *cue-stimulus interval* (CSI). I think these terms are imprecise. The first term is imprecise because it overlooks the distinction between the cue and the target and its use may thus lead to confusion as when there are two cues (e.g., Sudevan & Taylor, 1987) or two sequentially presented targets (Meiran & Marcinao, 2002). The CSI term is also inaccurate because it refers to the target as a stimulus but the cue is also a stimulus.
2. Most of the literature on dual-task interference focuses on conditions in which the tasks overlap temporarily, suggesting that this temporal overlap is responsible for the slowing observed in the second response. Nonetheless, there are some old studies showing a similar slowing with a gradual speeding as SOA increases even without temporal overlap between the tasks (e.g., Kafri & Kahaneman, 1977), in line with the resource depletion idea.
3. I acknowledge the fact that the RCI in that study was fixed and there was no preliminary experiment to demonstrate that it was asymptotic. Nonetheless, the value of this RCI was rather high (500 ms) and the reduction in switching cost was quite substantial (e.g., from 275 ms to 142 ms), much more than would be expected from an RCI increase alone. I think that, like in many other cases, the pattern of results depends on other features of the paradigm such as the tasks.

REFERENCES

Allport, A., Styles, E. A., & Hsieh, S. (1994). Shifting intentional set: Exploring the dynamic control of tasks. In C. Umiltà & M. Moscovitch (Eds.), *Attention and performance. XV: Conscious and unconscious processing* (pp. 421–452). Cambridge, MA: MIT Press.

Allport, A., & Wylie, G. (2000). 'Task-switching', stimulus-response bindings and negative priming. In S. Monsell & J. Driver (Eds.), *Attention and performance. XVIII: Control of cognitive processes* (pp. 35–70). Cambridge, MA: MIT Press.

Altmann, E. M. (2004). Advance preparation in task switching: What work is being done? *Psychological Science, 15*, 616–622.

Altmann, E. M. (2007a). Comparing switch costs: Alternating runs and explicit cuing. *Journal of Experimental Psychology: Learning, Memory, & Cognition, 33*, 475–483.

Altmann, E. M. (2007b). Cue-independent task-specific representations in task switching: Evidence from backward inhibition. *Journal of Experimental Psychology: Learning, Memory, and Cognition, 33*, 892–899.

Altmann, E. M. (2011). Testing probability matching and episodic retrieval accounts of response repetition effects in task switching. *Journal of Experimental Psychology: Learning, Memory, and Cognition, 37*, 935–951.

Altmann, E. M., & Gray, W. D. (2002). Forgetting to remember: The functional relationship of decay and interference. *Psychological Science, 13*, 27–33.

Altmann, E. M., & Gray, W. D. (2008). An integrated model of cognitive control in task switching. *Psychological Review, 115*, 602–639.

Arbuthnott, K.D. (2005). The influence of cue type on backward inhibition. *Journal of Experimental Psychology: Learning, Memory, and Cognition, 31*, 1030–1042.

Arrington, C. M., & Logan, G. D. (2004). The cost of a voluntary task switch. *Psychological Science, 15*, 610–615.

Arrington, C. M., & Logan, G. D. (2005). Voluntary task switching: Chasing the elusive homunculus. *Journal of Experimental Psychology: Learning, Memory & Cognition, 31*, 683–702.

Arrington, C. M., Logan, G. D., & Schneider, D. W. (2007). Separating cue encoding from target processing in the explicit task cuing procedure. Are there "true" task switch effects? *Journal of Experimental Psychology: Learning, Memory, & Cognition, 33*, 484–502.

Astle, D. E., Jackson, G. M., & Swainson, R. (2008). The role of spatial information on advance task-set control: A dense-sensor ERP study. *European Journal of Neuroscience, 28*, 1404–1418.

Astle, D. E., Jackson, G. M., & Swainson, R. (2012). Two measures of task-specific inhibition. *Quarterly Journal of Experimental Psychology, 65*, 233–251.

Biederman, I. (1972). Human performance in contingent information processing tasks. *Journal of Experimental Psychology, 93*, 219–238.

Biederman, I. (1973). Mental set and mental arithmetic. *Memory and Cognition, 1*, 383–386.

Botvinick, M. M., Braver, T. S., Carter, C. S., Barch, D. M., & Cohen, J. D. (2001). Evaluating the demand for control: Anterior cingulate cortex and crosstalk monitoring. *Psychological Review, 108*, 624–652.

Braver, T. S. (2012). The variable nature of cognitive control: A dual-mechanisms framework. *Trends in Cognitive Sciences, 16*, 106–113.

Braver, T. S., Reynolds, J. R., & Donaldson, D. I. (2003). Neural mechanisms of transient and sustained cognitive control during task switching. *Neuron, 39*, 713–726.

Braverman, A., & Meiran, N. (2010). Task conflict effect in task switching. *Psychological Research, 74*, 568–578.

Brooks, P. J., Hanauer, J. B., Padowska, B., & Rosman, H. (2003). The role of selective attention in preschoolers' rule use in a novel dimensional card sort. *Cognitive Development, 18*, 195–215.

Brown, R. G., & Marsden, C. D. (1988). Internal versus external cues and the control of attention in Parkinson's disease. *Brain, 111*, 323–345.

Brown, J. W., Reynolds, J. R., & Braver, T. S. (2007). A computational model of fractionated conflict-control mechanisms in task switching. *Cognitive Psychology, 55*, 37–85.

Bryck, R. L., & Mayr, U. (2008). Task selection cost asymmetry without task switching. *Psychonomic Bulletin and Review, 15*, 128–134.

De Jong, R. (1995). Strategical determinants of compatibility effects with task uncertainty. *Acta Psychologica, 88*, 187–207.

Derrfuss, J., Brass, M., Neumann, J., & von Cramon, D. Y. (2005). Involvement of the inferior frontal junction in cognitive control: Meta-analyses of switching and Stroop studies. *Human Brain Mapping, 25*, 22–34.

Dixon, P. (1981). Algorithms and selective attention. *Memory and Cognition, 9*, 177–184.

Dosenbach, N. U. F., Visscher, K. M., Palmer, E. D., Miezin, F. M., Wenger, K. K., Kang, H. C.,... Petersen, S. E. (2006). A core system for the implementation of task sets. *Neuron, 50*, 799–812.

Dreisbach, G., & Haider, H. (2009). How task representations guide attention: Further evidence for the shielding function of task sets. *Journal of Experimental Psychology: Learning, Memory, and Cognition, 35*, 477–486.

Dreisbach, G., Haider, H., & Kluwe, R.H. (2002). Preparatory processes in the task-switching paradigm: Evidence from the use of probability cues. *Journal of Experimental Psychology: Learning, Memory and Cognition, 28*, 468–483.

Dreisbach, G., Goschke, T., & Haider, H. (2006). Implicit task sets in task switching? *Journal of Experimental Psychology: Learning, Memory, & Cognition, 32*, 1221–1233.

Dreisbach, G., Goschke, T., & Haider, H. (2007). The role of task rules and stimulus-response mappings in the task-switching paradigm. *Psychological Research, 71*, 383–392.

Dreisbach, G., & Haider, H. (2009). How task representations guide attention: Further evidence for the shielding function of task sets. *Journal of Experimental Psychology: Learning, Memory, and Cognition, 35*, 477–486.

Druey, M.D., & Hübner, R. (2008). Effects of stimulus features and instruction on response coding, selection, and inhibition: Evidence from repetition effects under task switching. *Quarterly Journal of Experimental Psychology, 61*, 1573–1600.

Ellenbogen, R., & Meiran, N. (2011). Objects and events as determinants of parallel processing in dual tasks: Evidence from the backward compatibility effect. *Journal of Experimental Psychology: Human Perception and Performance, 37*, 152–167.

ErEl, H., & Meiran, N. (2011). Mindset changes lead to drastic impairments in rule finding. *Cognition, 119*, 149–165.

Fagot, C. (1994). *Chronometric investigations of task switching.* Unpublished Ph.D. thesis, University of California, San Diego.

Forstmann, B. U., Brass, M., & Koch, I. (2007). Methodological and empirical issues when dissociating cue-related from task-related processes in the explicit task-cuing procedure. *Psychological Research, 72*, 393–400.

Forstmann, B. U., Brass, M., Koch, I., & von Cramon, D. Y. (2005). Internally generated and directly cued task sets: an investigation with fMRI. *Neuropsychologia, 43*, 943–952.

Forstmann, B., Brass, M., Koch, I., & von Cramon, D. Y. (2006). Voluntary selection of task-sets revealed by functional magnetic resonance imaging. *Journal of Cognitive Neuroscience, 18*, 388–398.

Friedman, N., & Miyake, A. (2004). The relations among inhibition and interference control functions. *Journal of Experimental Psychology: General, 133*, 101–135.

Frye, D., Zelazo, P. D., Burack, J. A. (1998). I. Cognitive complexity and control: Implications for theory of mind in typical and atypical development. *Current Directions in Psychological Science, 7*, 116–121.

Gade, M., & Koch, I. (2007). Cue-task associations in task switching. *Quarterly Journal of Experimental Psychology, 60*, 762–769.

Gibson, J. J. (1941). A critical review of the concept of set in contemporary experimental psychology. *Psychological Bulletin, 38*, 781–817.

Gilbert, S. J., & Shallice, T. (2002). Task switching: A PDP model. *Cognitive Psychology, 44*, 297–337.

Gopher, D., Armony, L., & Greenshpan, Y. (2000). Switching tasks and attention policies. *Journal of Experimental Psychology: General, 129*, 308–339.

Gotler, A. (2004). *On the control of executive processes: Evidence for non-intentional cognitive control.* Ph.D. Thesis, Ben-Gurion University of the Negev, Beer-Sheva, Israel.

Gotler, A., Meiran, N., & Tzelgov, J. (2003). Nonintentional task-set activation: Evidence from implicit task sequence learning. *Psychonomic Bulletin & Review, 10*, 890–896.

Grange, J. A., & Houghton, G. (2010a). Cue-switch costs in task-switching: Cue priming or control processes? *Psychological Research, 74*, 481–490.

Grange, J. A., & Houghton, G. (2010b). Heightened conflict in cue–target translation increases backward inhibition in set switching. *Journal of Experimental Psychology: Learning, Memory & Cognition, 36*, 1003–1009.

Hartley, A. A., Keiley, J. M., & Slabach, E. H. (1990). Age differences and similarities in the effects of cues and prompts. *Journal of Experimental Psychology: Human Perception & Performance, 16*, 523–538.

Hayes, A. E., Davidson, M. C., Keele, S. W., & Rafal, R. D. (1998). Toward a functional analysis of the basal ganglia. *Journal of Cognitive Neuroscience, 10*, 178–198.

Heuer, H., Schmidtke, V., & Kleinsorge, T. (2001). Implicit learning of sequences of tasks. *Journal of Experimental Psychology: Learning, Memory & Cognition, 27*, 967–983.

Horoufchin, H., Philipp, A. M., & Koch, I. (2011). The dissipating task-repetition benefit in task switching: Task-set decay or temporal distinctiveness? *Journal of Experimental Psychology: Human Perception and Performance, 37*, 455–472.

Hübner, R., & Druey, M. D. (2008). Multiple response codes play specific roles in response selection and inhibition under task switching. *Psychological Research, 72*, 415–424.

Hunt, A. R., & Klein, R. M. (2002). Eliminating the cost of task set reconfiguration. *Memory and Cognition, 30*, 529–539.

Hunt, A., Ishigami, Y., & Klein, R. (2006). Eye movements, not hypercompatible mappings, are critical for eliminating the cost of task set reconfiguration. *Psychonomic Bulletin and Review, 13*, 932–937.

Hydock, C., & Sohn, M.-H. (2011). Dissociating the components of switch cost using two-to-two cue–task mapping. *Journal of Experimental Psychology: Human Perception and Performance, 37*, 903–913.

Jennings, J. R., & Van der Molen, M. W. (2005). Preparation for speeded action as a psychophysiological concept. *Psychological Bulletin, 131*, 434–459.

Jersild, A. T. (1927). Mental set and shift. *Archives of Psychology, 14*, 81.

Kafry, D., & Kahneman, D. (1977). Capacity sharing and refractoriness in successive reactions. *Perceptualand Motor Skills, 44*, 327–335.

Kahneman, D., & Henik, A. (1981). Perceptual organization and attention. In M. Kubovy & J. R. Pomerantz (Eds.), *Perceptual organization* (pp. 181–211). Hillsdale, NJ: Erlbaum.

Keele, S. W., & Hawkins, H. L. (1982). Explorations of individual differences relevant to high level skill. *Journal of Motor Behavior, 14*, 3–23.

Kessler, Y., Shenkar, Y., & Meiran, N. (2009). Choosing to switch: Spontaneous task switching despite associated behavioral costs. *Acta Psychologica, 131*, 120–128.

Kiesel, A., Steinhauser, M., Wendt, M., Falkenstein, M., Jost, K., Philipp, A. M., et al. (2010). Control and interference in task switching—A review. *Psychological Bulletin, 136*, 849–874.

Kleinsorge, T., & Heuer, H. (1999). Hierarchical switching in a multi-dimensional task space. *Psychological Research, 62*, 300–312.

Koch, I. (2001). Automatic and intentional activation of task sets. *Journal of Experimental Psychology: Learning, Memory & Cognition, 27*, 1474–1486.

Koch, I. (2005). Sequential task predictability in task switching. *Psychonomic Bulletin & Review, 12*, 107–112.

Koch, I., & Allport, A. (2006). Cue-based preparation and stimulus-based priming of tasks in task switching. *Memory & Cognition, 34*, 433–444.

Koch, I., Gade, M., Schuch, S., & Philipp, A. M. (2010). The role of inhibition in task switching—A review. *Psychonomic Bulletin & Review, 17*, 1–14.

Koch, I., Philipp, A. M., Gade, M. (2006). Chunking in task sequences modulates task inhibition.*Psychological Science, 17*, 346–350.

Koch, I., Prinz, W., & Allport, A. (2005). Involuntary retrieval in alphabet-arithmetic tasks: Task-mixing and task-switching costs. *Psychological Research, 69*, 252–261.

Kornblum, S., Hasbroucq, T., & Osman, A. (1990). Dimensional overlap: Cognitive basis of stimulus-response compatibility—A model and taxonomy. *Psychological Review, 97*, 253–270.

Kray, J., & Lindenberger, U. (2000). Adult age differences in task-switching. *Psychology and Aging, 15*, 126–147.

Lien, M.-C., & Ruthruff, E. (2004). Task switching in a hierarchical task structure: Evidence for the fragility of the task repetition benefit. *Journal of Experimental Psychology: Learning, Memory, and Cognition, 30*, 697–713.

Logan, G. D. (2004). Working memory, task switching, and executive control in the task span procedure. *Journal of Experimental Psychology: General, 133*, 218–236.

Logan, G. D., & Bundesen, C. (2003). Clever homunculus: Is there an endogenous act of control in the explicit task-cuing procedure? *Journal of Experimental Psychology: Human Perception and Performance, 29*, 575–599.

Logan, G. D., & Bundesen, C. (2004). Very clever homunculus: Compound stimulus strategies for the explicit task-cuing procedure. *Psychonomic Bulletin & Review, 11*, 832–840.

Logan, G. D., & Gordon, R. D. (2001). Executive control of visual attention in dual-task situations. *Psychological Review, 108*, 393–434.

Logan, G. D., Schneider, D. W., & Bundesen, C. (2007). Still clever after all these years: Searching for the homunculus in explicitly cued task switching. *Journal of Experimental Psychology: Human Perception and Performance, 33*, 978–994.

Los, S. A. (1996). On the origin of mixing costs: Exploring information processing in pure and mixed blocks of trials. *Acta Psychologica, 94*, 145–188.

Los, S. A., & Van Den Heuvel, C. E. (2001). Intentional and unintentional contributions to nonspecific preparation during reaction time foreperiods. *Journal of Experimental Psychology: Human Perception & Performance, 27*, 370–386.

Luria, R., & Meiran, N. (2003). Online order control in the psychological refractory period paradigm. *Journal of Experimental Psychology: Human Perception and Performance, 29*, 556–574.

Luria, R., Meiran, N., & Dekel-Cohen, C. (2006). Stimulus cued completion of reconfiguration and retroactive adjustment as causes for the residual switching cost in multi-step tasks. *European Journal of Cognitive Psychology, 18*, 652–668.

Marí-Beffa, P., Cooper, S., & Houghton, G. (2012). Unmixing the mixing cost: Contributions from dimensional relevance and stimulus-response suppression. *Journal of Experimental Psychology: Human Perception and Performance, 38*, 478–488.

Mayr, U. (2001). Age differences in the selection of mental sets: The role of inhibition, stimulus ambiguity, and response-set overlap. *Psychology and Aging, 16*, 96–109.

Mayr, U., & Bell, T. (2006). On how to be unpredictable? Evidence from the voluntary task switching paradigm. *Psychological Science, 17*, 774–780.

Mayr, U., & Bryck, R.L. (2005). Sticky rules: Integration between abstract rules and specific actions. *Journal of Experimental Psychology: Learning, Memory, and Cognition, 31*, 337–350.

Mayr, U., & Keele, S. W. (2000). Changing internal constraints on action: The role of backward inhibition. *Journal of Experimental Psychology: General, 129*, 4–26.

Mayr, U., & Kliegl, R. (2000). Task-set switching and long-term memory retrieval. *Journal of Experimental Psychology: Learning, Memory and Cognition, 26*, 1124–1140.

Mayr, U., & Kliegl, R. (2003). Differential effects of cue changes and task changes on task-set selection costs. *Journal of Experimental Psychology: Learning, Memory, & Cognition, 29*, 362–372.

Mayr, U., & Liebscher, T. (2001). Is there an age deficit in the selection of mental sets? *European Journal of Cognitive Psychology, 13*, 47–69.

Meiran, N. (1996). Reconfiguration of processing mode prior to task performance. *Journal of Experimental Psychology: Learning, Memory and Cognition, 22*, 1423–1442.

Meiran, N. (2000a). Modeling cognitive control in task-switching. *Psychological Research, 63*, 234–249.

Meiran, N. (2000b). The reconfiguration of the stimulus task-set and the response task set during task switching. In S. Monsell & J. Driver (Eds.), *Attention and performance. XVIII: Control of cognitive processes* (pp. 377–400). Cambridge, MA: MIT Press.

Meiran, N. (2005). Task rule congruency and Simon-like effects in switching between spatial tasks. *Quarterly Journal of Experimental Psychology: Section A, 58A*, 1023–1041.

Meiran, N. (2010). Task switching: Mechanisms underlying rigid versus flexible self control. In R. Hassin, K. Ochsner, & Y. Trope (Eds.), *Self control in society, mind and brain* (pp. 202–220). New York, NY: Oxford University Press.

Meiran, N., & Chorev, Z. (2005). Phasic alertness and the residual task-switching cost. *Experimental Psychology, 52*, 109–124.

Meiran, N., Chorev, Z., & Sapir, A. (2000). Component processes in task switching. *Cognitive Psychology, 41*, 211–253.

Meiran, N., Cole, M. W., & Braver, T. S. (2012a). When planning results in loss of control: Intention-based reflexivity and working-memory. *Frontiers in Human Neuroscience, 6*, 104. doi:10.3389/fnhum.2012.00104

Meiran, N., & Daichman, A. (2005). Advance task preparation reduces task error rate in the cueing task-switching paradigm. *Memory and Cognition, 33*, 1272–1288.

Meiran, N., Diamond, G. M., Todder, D., & Nemets, B. (2011a). Cognitive rigidity in unipolar depression and obsessive compulsive disorder: Examination of task switching, Stroop, working-memory updating and post-conflict adaptation. *Psychiatry Research, 185*, 149–156.

Meiran, N., Dimov, E., & Ganel, T. (2012b). Selective attention to perceptual dimensions and switching between dimensions. *Journal of Experimental Psychology: Human Perception and Performance*. doi:10.1037/a0027638

Meiran, N., Hommel, B., Bibi, U., & Lev, I. (2002). Consciousness and control in task switching. *Consciousness and Cognition, 11*, 10–33.

Meiran, N., Hsieh, S., & Chang, C.-C. (2011b). Smart inhibition: Electrophysiological evidence for the suppression of conflict-generating task rules during task-switching. *Cognitive, Affective, & Behavioral Neuroscience, 11*, 292–308.

Meiran, N., Hsieh, S., & Dimov, E. (2010). Resolving task rule incongruence during task switching by competitor rule suppression. *Journal of Experimental Psychology: Learning, Memory, and Cognition, 36*, 992–1002.

Meiran, N., Kessler, Y., & Adi-Japha, E. (2008). Control by Action Representation and Input Selection (CARIS): A theoretical framework for task switching. *Psychological Research, 72*, 473–500.

Meiran, N., & Marciano, H. (2002). Limitations in advance task preparation: Switching the relevant stimulus dimension in speeded same-different comparisons. *Memory & Cognition, 30*, 540–550.

Miyake, A., Friedman, N. P., Emerson, M. J., Witzki, A. H., Howerter, A., & Wager, T. D. (2000). The unity and diversity of executive functions and their contributions to complex "frontal lobe" tasks: A latent variable analysis. *Cognitive Psychology, 41*, 49–100.

Monsell, S., & Mizon, G. A. (2006). Can the task cuing paradigm measure an "endogenous" task set reconfiguration process? *Journal of Experimental Psychology: Human Perception and Performance, 32*, 493–516.

Monsell, S., Sumner, P., & Waters, H. (2003). Task-set reconfiguration with predictable and unpredictable task switches. *Memory and Cognition, 31*, 327–342.

Monsell, S., Yeung, N., & Azuma, R. (2000). Reconfiguration of task-set: Is it easier to switch to the weaker task? *Psychological Research, 63*, 250–264.

Muraven, M. R., & Baumeister, R. F. (2000). Self-regulation and depletion of limited resources: Does self-control resemble a muscle? *Psychological Bulletin, 126*, 247–259.

Niemi, P., & Nataanen, R. (1981). Foreperiod and simple reaction time. *Psychological Bulletin, 89*, 133–162.

Philipp, A. M., & Koch, I. (2005). Switching of response modalities. *Quarterly Journal of Experimental Psychology A: Human Experimental Psychology, 58A*, 1325–1338.

Philipp, A. M., & Koch, I. (2006). Task inhibition and task repetition in task switching. *European Journal of Cognitive Psychology, 18*, 624–639.

Rogers, R. D., & Monsell, S. (1995). The cost of a predictable switch between simple cognitive tasks. *Journal of Experimental Psychology: General, 124*, 207–231.

Rubin, O., & Meiran, N. (2005). On the origins of the task mixing cost in the cuing task switching paradigm. *Journal of Experimental Psychology: Learning, Memory, & Cognition, 31*, 1477–1491.

Rubinstein, J. S., Meyer, D. E., & Evans, J. E. (2001). Executive control of cognitive processes in task switching. *Journal of Experimental Psychology: Human Perception and Performance, 27*, 763–797.

Ruge, H., Braver, T., & Meiran, N. (2009). Attention, intention and strategy in preparatory control. *Neuropsychologia, 47*, 1670–1685.

Ruge, H., Brass, M., Koch, I., Rubin, O., Meiran, N., & von Cramon, D. Y. (2005). Advance preparation and stimulus induced interference in cued task switching: Further insights from BOLD fMRI. *Neuropsychologia, 43*, 340–355.

Ruthruff, E., Remington, R. W., & Johnston, J. C. (2001). Switching between simple cognitive tasks: The interaction of top down and bottom-up factors. *Journal of Experimental Psychology: Learning, Memory, & Cognition, 27*, 1404–1419.

Schneider, D. W., & Logan, G. D. (2005). Modeling task switching without switching tasks: A short-term memory priming account of explicitly cued performance. *Journal of Experimental Psychology: General, 134*, 343–367.

Schneider, D. W., & Logan, G. D. (2007a). Defining task-tet teconfiguration: The case of reference point switching. *Psychonomic Bulletin and Review, 14*, 118–125.

Schneider, D. W., & Logan, G. D. (2007b). Task switching versus cue switching: Using transition cuing to disentangle sequential effects in task-switching performance. *Journal of Experimental Psychology: Learning, Memory, and Cognition, 33*, 370–378.

Schneider, D. W., & Logan, G. D. (2009). Selecting a response in task switching: Testing a model of compound cue retrieval. *Journal of Experimental Psychology: Learning, Memory, and Cognition, 35*, 122–136.

Schuch, S., & Koch, I. (2004). The cost of changing the representation of action. *Journal of Experimental Psychology: Human Perception and Performance, 30*, 566–582.

Shaffer, L. H. (1965). Choice reaction with variable S-R mapping. *Journal of Experimental Psychology, 70*, 284–288.

Sohn, M. H., & Anderson, J. R. (2001). Task preparation and task repetition: Two-component model of task switching. *Journal of Experimental Psychology: General, 130*, 764–778.

Sohn, M. H., & Carlson, R. A. (2000). Effects of repetition and foreknowledge in task-set reconfiguration. *Journal of Experimental Psychology: Learning, Memory and Cognition, 26*, 1445–1460.

Sudevan, P., & Taylor, D. A. (1987). The cueing and priming of cognitive operations. *Journal of Experimental Psychology: Human Perception and Performance, 13*, 89–103.

Sutton, S., & Zubin, J. (1965). EVect of sequence on reaction time in schizophrenia. In A. T. Welford & J. E. Birren (Eds.), *Behavior, aging, and the nervous system* (pp. 562–579). Springfield, IL: Charles C Thomas.

Swallow, K. M., Zacks, J. M., & Abrams, R. A. (2009). Event boundaries in perception affect memory encoding and updating. *Journal of Experimental Psychology: General, 138*, 236–257.

Tornay, F. J., & Milàn, E. G. (2001). A more complete task-set reconfiguration in random than in predictable task switch. *Quarterly Journal of Experimental Psychology, 54*, 785–803.

Vandierendonck, A., Liefooghe, B., & Verbruggen, F. (2010). Task switching: Interplay of reconfiguration and interference. *Psychological Bulletin, 136*, 601–626.

Van-Duren, L. L., & Sanders, A. F. (1988). On the robustness of the additive factors stage structure in blocked and mixed choice reaction designs. *Acta Psychologica, 69*, 83–94.

Ward, L. M. (1982). Determinants of attention to local and global features of visual forms. *Journal of Experimental Psychology: Human Perception and Performance, 8*, 562–581.

Waszak, F., Hommel, B., & Allport, A. (2003). Task-switching and long-term priming: Role of episodic stimulus-task bindings in task-shift costs. *Cognitive Psychology, 46*, 361–413.

Waszak, F., Wenke, D., & Brass, M. (2008). Cross-talk of instructed and applied arbitrary visuomotor mappings. *Acta Psychologica, 127*, 30–35.

Woodward, T. S., Meier, B., Tipper, C., & Graf, P. (2003). Bivalency is costly: Bivalent stimuli elicit cautious responding. *Experimental Psychology, 50*, 233–238.

Yehene, E., & Meiran, N. (2007). Is there a general task switching ability? *Acta Psychologica, 126*, 169–195.

Yehene, E., Meiran, N., & Soroker, N. (2005). Task alternation cost without task alternation: Measuring intentionality. *Neuropsychologia, 43*, 1858–1869.

Yeung, N., Botvinick, M. M., & Cohen, J. D. (2004). The neural basis of error detection: Conflict monitoring and the error-related negativity. *Psychological Review, 111*, 931–959.

Yeung, N., & Monsell, S. (2003). Switching between tasks of unequal familiarity: The role of stimulus-attribute and response-set selection. *Journal of Experimental Psychology: Human Perception and Performance, 29*, 455–469.

Zacks, J. M., Speer, N. K., Swallow, K. M., Braver, T. S., & Reynolds, J. R. (2007). Event perception: A mind/brain perspective. *Psychological Bulletin, 133*, 273–293.

Zacks, J. M., & Swallow, K. M. (2007). Event segmentation. *Current Directions in Psychological Science, 16*, 80–84.

Zelazo, P. D., & Frye, D. (1998). II. Cognitive complexity and control: the development of executive function.*Current Directions in Psychological Science, 7*, 121–126.

4

The Mixing Cost as a Measure of Cognitive Control

PALOMA MARÍ-BEFFA AND ALEXANDER KIRKHAM

INTRODUCTION

Many essays in this volume are concerned with processes that influence the *transient* mental adaptations needed to switch from one task to another. In everyday life, such processes are central to our continual adaptation to a complex and changing social environment; allowing us to switch from, for instance, updating our Facebook page to writing a report. Yet in everyday life, we frequently experience a contrasting problem, that of *sustaining* attention on a given task when faced with other, possibly more enjoyable or pressing, alternatives—for instance, continuing to write the report while ignoring Facebook! This essay focuses on the more *sustained* mental processes that affect multiple events and actions within some period of time. We are thus concerned with how people can maintain task set in a context of changeable demands, avoiding distraction and maintaining their concentration through time.

The last 50–60 years has seen a considerable increase in our understanding of the mechanisms involved in the control of mental processes. Indeed, issues concerning automaticity and control have repeatedly gone in and out of fashion in an almost cyclic mode, including terminology and operational definitions (Los, 1996; Marí-Beffa, Fuentes, Catena, & Houghton, 2000). One highly reliable finding is that continuously repeating the same task over some period of time requires less concentration than repeating the same task in a context in which task switches also occur. In the first scenario (pure repetition context), we can gradually drop vigilance and let already learned actions take precedence under a more or less automatic mode. In the second (or mixed) scenario, the presence of task switches encourages a state of heightened vigilance or surveillance. This state not only influences switch trials but also affects task repetitions, typically producing a slowing of reaction times compared with the pure repetition context. This effect has been termed the *mixing cost* (Los, 1996). Compared with the various kinds of switch cost, the mixing cost has attracted little attention. The aim of this essay is to show how it can be used to investigate the mechanisms that promote sustained concentration on task goals.

In what follows, we review the main empirical findings on the mixing cost and suggest ideas for further theoretical development. We concentrate on behavioral studies (where most work has been done), with only limited coverage of research in neuroimaging. The mechanisms that produce mixing costs are currently poorly understood, with a lack of formal modeling studies. Therefore, we emphasize those effects that we believe are in most urgent need of explanation by future models.

Historical Background

Behavioral manifestations of mixing costs have been reported repeatedly since the first task switching studies (Allport, Styles, & Hsieh, 1994; Bertelson, 1961; Biederman, 1972; Jersild, 1927; Shaffer, 1965; Spector & Biederman, 1976). From the very beginning, however, it was methodologically and conceptually confounded with the switch cost. Indeed, mixing costs are observed every time a list paradigm is used. In its original version (Jersild, 1927), performance in a pure-task list (AAAA or BBBB [A, B, etc. denote tasks]) was compared against a switch- (or mixed-) task list (ABABABA). Performance in the latter was consistently poorer because of the additional processing demands involved. During the mixed-task list, participants not only need to switch tasks (resulting in switching costs) but also must maintain two task sets in working memory and avoid interference between them. The latter processes we study now under the mixing cost paradigm.

It could be said that, in the context of the task switching paradigm, mixing costs were first acknowledged in 1995 when Rogers and Monsell tried to remove them from the Jersild paradigm, to get a purer measure of switch cost. Indeed, they noted that participants in the switching list may perceive the block as more difficult, leading to "greater arousal, effort, and so forth" (Rogers & Monsell, 1995). To prevent these additional factors from contaminating the switch cost, they created the alternating runs paradigm, where runs of two trials from each task appeared predictably within the same block of trials, that is, AABBAA... (the underlined trials are the switch trials and the nonunderlined are the repeat trials). Here, both switch and repeat trials are extracted from the same (mixed) block, with the switch cost defined as the difference in performance between them (switch minus repeat). The repeat trials are treated as the control or baseline with respect to which switch costs are measured. The idea was that both switch and repeat conditions would now be *equally* affected by any "extra demands" involved in maintaining more than one task set, with the switch cost reflecting only transient task set reconfiguration. However, in principle, a problem will arise if some experimental manipulation differentially affects performance on the *repeat* trials. This will be recorded as a change in the switch cost (rather than "repetition benefit") and so likely be interpreted in terms of task switch processes.

A concrete example of this is the way in which the repeat trials in the mixed-task block can benefit from becoming predictable. In earlier studies, when task repetitions were included in the mixed block, the design combined both switch *and repeat* trials in a random sequence (Shaffer, 1965). Although this method has continued to be used (Mayr, 2001; Mayr & Keele, 2000; Meiran, 1996; Meiran, Chorev, & Sapir, 2000; Miyake, Emerson, Padilla, & Ahn, 2004; Monsell, Sumner, & Waters, 2003; Rubin & Meiran, 2005; Rubinstein, Meyer, & Evans, 2001; Tornay & Milan, 2001), the importance of task sequence and predictability cannot be ignored. In the original Jersild list paradigm, the alternation between tasks was predictable (ABABAB). But when task switches are mixed with repetitions, task uncertainty increases (e.g., AABABBBA). Therefore, part of the overall difficulty in the mixed block comes from a lack of preparation that affects all trial types. Importantly, however, repeat trials could benefit more from predictable sequences than do switch trials (Koch, 2005). This would produce a variation in the "switch cost" that is actually due to *benefits* in the repeat trials, or baseline.

If we are to remove uncertainty and lack of preparation from the mixed block, then the alternating runs paradigm is the design of choice (de Jong, 2000; Mayr & Kliegl, 2000; Meiran, 2000; Rogers & Monsell, 1995, Waszak, Hommel, & Allport, 2003). However, when differences in switch costs are reported, it is still difficult to know simply from the mixed block itself whether this is due to changes in the switch or the repeat trials. Any potential variations in repeat trials are better assessed by comparing them against a pure block of single-task trials. Note now that comparison takes place between two types of task repeat: those within the pure and the mixed blocks. Regardless of the exact switching paradigm used, the inclusion of a pure condition permits any variation in the mixed-repeat baseline to be measured (Kirkham, Breeze, & Marí-Beffa, 2012).

Several authors have used a different methodology (and often terminology) in the study of these costs. Mixing costs have been referred to as "non–switch specific" or "general" (Altmann, 2004; Kiesel et al., 2010) to represent the fact that all trials in the mixed block (whether they repeat the same task or switch to a new one) deteriorate in performance. In contrast, switch costs are referred to as "switch-specific" or "local." This terminology was used after it was noted that several manipulations lead to differences not only in the switch trials but also in the repeat trials within the mixed-task block. Here, the mixing cost is measured by comparing mixed-repeat trials under different conditions. Altmann (2004), for example, found that increasing the interval between the instructional cue and the target reduced response times (RTs) in both switch and repeat trials, concluding that task preparation is not switch specific. However, the study does not demonstrate whether this preparation is specific to mixed blocks. Although unlikely in this case, there is a chance that similar benefits might also be found in pure blocks, where trial-by-trial task preparation is not considered necessary. If this were so, then the benefits of preparation time in mixed blocks could be interpreted as something other than better task preparation—for instance, more peripheral stimulus–response (SR) adaptations. For this reason, in this review, we mostly focus on mixing costs that are measured relative to a pure block, although we try to integrate such findings with results from studies testing mixed repeat trials only.

Finally, Braver, Reynolds, and Donaldson (2003) refer to "sustained" and "transient" switch costs. This distinction is more theoretically motivated, proposing that the underlying mechanism responsible for each cost is either active throughout an entire block of trials (sustained) or is short-lived and fast acting to enable adaptations from trial to trial (transient).

Why Study Mixing Costs?

The importance of measuring mixing costs while studying task switching can be illustrated with some recent research conducted in our lab. We were studying mechanisms of executive control in patients affected by Parkinson's disease, comparing them with an age-matched control group. At first we aimed to evaluate task switching capabilities using the alternating runs paradigm. For the tasks, participants had to respond to bivalent stimuli according to their colour or shape. To maximize task preparation (and minimize working memory load), not only was the sequence predictable but also a task cue specifying the response options ("Blue/Red" or "Square/Circle") was presented, with plenty of time to prepare (>1000 ms).

The results showed the rather paradoxical effect of larger switch costs for the control group, with minimal switch costs in the patient group (see Figure 4.1). The small (almost absent) switch cost in the patient group did not fit the existing body of research, which commonly reports executive control problems in patients with Parkinson's disease that should have made switching difficult for them (Cools, Barker, Sahakian, & Robbins, 2001; Hayes, Davidson, Keele, & Rafal, 1998). On closer inspection, we saw a disproportionate increase between the groups in the time taken to complete the repeat trials in the mixed block. To test for this, we included a pure block of trials in further experiments, finding that the Parkinson's group showed greater mixing cost, rather than displaying reduced switch costs. In this respect, the mixed-block repeat trials constitute an experimental condition in their own right and do not provide a stable baseline to measure the switch cost (cf. Wylie & Allport, 2000, pp. 221–222).

Hence, the patients with Parkinson's disease actually exhibited *minimal repetition benefit*, resulting in highly similar responses for the repeat and switch trials. The control group displayed substantially smaller mixing costs, indicating that they were capable of *maintaining* the correct task set across repeat trials, leading to repetition benefits. In this sense, the patients realigned themselves for every trial, unaware of whether the following trial would be a repeat or a switch. Informally, it appeared as "if they switch on every trial," as lack of preparation would render minimal benefits for repetitions (Koch, 2005).

A similar case can be found in a much-cited study on bilingualism and task switching by Metuer and Allport (1999, see also Campbell, 2005, Costa & Santesteban, 2004; Costa, Santesteban, & Ivanova, 2006; Finkbeiner, Almeida,

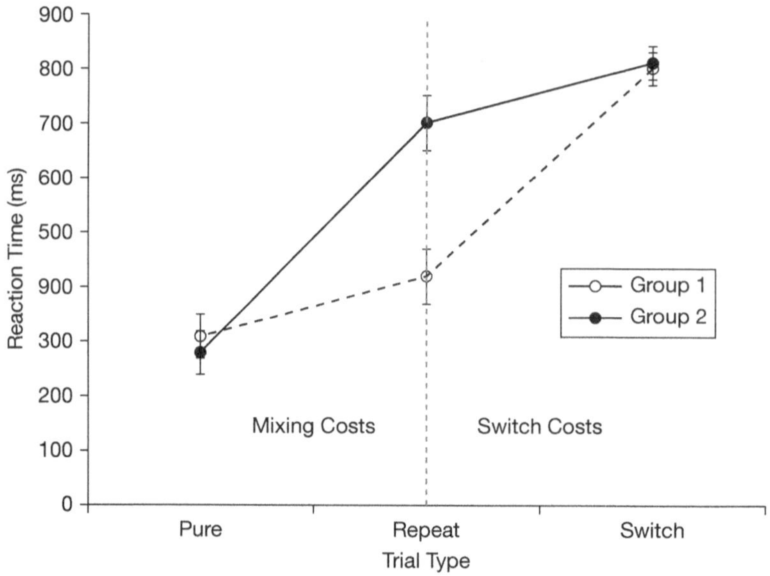

Figure 4.1 A representative example of the statement made in this section, presented in line graph format for clarity only. If relying solely on the alternating runs block of trials, we only pay attention to the results in the right area. Based solely on these figures, we would determine that Group 2 is superior at switching. However, by checking performance using pure block trials, we note that the two groups performed with great similarity in these trials but differ substantially during the mixed repeat trials.

Janssen, & Caramazza, 2006; Philipp, Gade, & Koch, 2007). This study has been widely cited as providing evidence of inhibitory mechanisms of selection when switching between languages in bilinguals. The authors reported greater switch costs when participants had to switch to their mother language (L1) than when they switched to their second language (L2). These results were interpreted as follows: because L1 is more dominant, it is automatically accessed and it needs to be suppressed to access L2. When, after responding to L2, participants are asked to use L1 again, this inhibition results in a greater reactivation cost. Interestingly, when looking at the results, there are differences in both repeat and switch trials but acting in different directions. When looking at the pattern of results from those participants with great language proficiency, for example, it is clear that switching to either of the two languages displays identical performance and that the greatest difference occurs with the repeat trials, where repeating L1 produces much *faster* RTs than repeating L2. Indeed, the increased switch cost with L1 may not be due to any special difficulty in switching to L1 but rather to greater benefits when repeating it (Yeung & Monsell, 2003). Without a pure block for all these conditions, it is difficult to obtain a stable baseline, so the results cannot be confidently interpreted.

Therefore, the switch cost can be seen as a subsidiary measure to the mixing cost and it cannot be unambiguously interpreted unless we verify that the

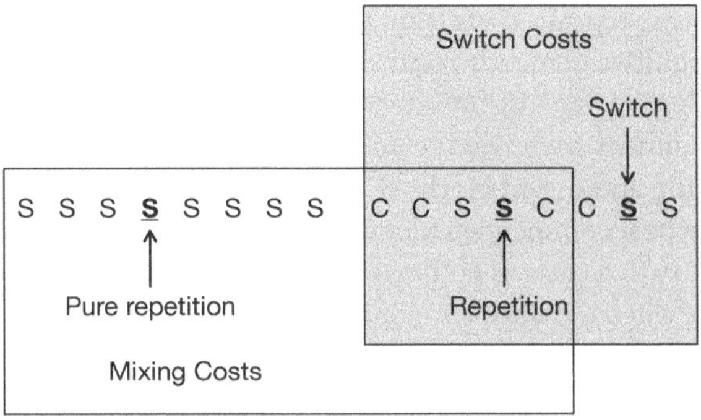

Figure 4.2 Illustration of the procedure to measure mixing costs and its relationship with the switch costs.

manipulation at hand does not have an impact on mixing costs (Rubin & Meiran, 2005; Ruthruff, Remington, & Johnston, 2001; Sohn & Anderson, 2001). That is not to say that the mixing cost can be used without issue. Measuring an adequate baseline in the pure block remains a challenge. Importantly, mixing costs are measures that are fairly free from confounds influencing trial-to-trial transitions, as both pure and mixed trials are based on task repetitions. But the greatest difficulty resides in trying to match the pure and mixed blocks on variables influencing the block as a whole (e.g., length). In the next section, we review some important methodological issues that should be taken into account in such designs. If measures of both the mixing and switch costs are considered separately, they provide two different indexes of cognitive control that complement each other.

FACTORS INFLUENCING MIXING COSTS

In this section, we review some key variables that influence the size of the mixing costs, while also referencing a body of research that functionally dissociates mixing from switch costs. Some of these variables are important for both theoretical and methodological reasons, so we will critically discuss them as they are introduced.

Traditional task switching studies compared performance between blocks of single task repetition trials (pure blocks) and a mixed block consisting of only switch trials, a list paradigm (Allport, Styles, & Hsieh, 1994; Bertelson, 1961; Biederman, 1972; Jersild, 1927; Shaffer, 1965; Spector & Biederman, 1976). To calculate mixing costs, the mixed block must include switch trials *and* repeat trials, as in the alternating runs paradigms (de Jong, 2000; Mayr & Kliegl, 2000; Meiran, 2000; Rogers & Monsell, 1995; Waszak et al., 2003) or random-cuing paradigms (Mayr, 2001; Mayr & Keele; Meiran, 1996; Meiran et al., 2000; Miyake et al., 2004; Monsell et al., 2003; Rubin & Meiran, 2005; Rubinstein et al., 2001; Shaffer, 1965; Tornay & Milan, 2001). The measurement of mixing costs relies on comparisons between the responses on the pure block trials and the mixed-block repeat trials.

Although both are repeats, costs from the mixed block are interpreted as an index of the extra cognitive demands required to maintain multiple tasks within working memory, despite presumably attending to only one on any given trial.

Still, some authors have tried to measure mixing costs as general differences between the pure and mixed blocks (Koch, Prinz, & Allport, 2005); however, this practice cannot be recommended for the strong contamination of the measure with more transient switch costs as outlined earlier. Therefore, the most important constraints we face when measuring mixing costs are that (a) there *must* be pure-block trial runs for each task and (b) the mixed block *must* contain repeat trials.

The Pure Block

Although the mixed block has been the center of most of the theoretical research (as it is meant to carry the experimental manipulation), the design of the pure block "baseline" poses challenges that are even greater than those in the mixed block. In this section, we will review the main variables to consider in the pure block.

Number of Trials

Take, for example, a standard alternating runs paradigm: If the mixed block contains 80 repetition trials, then 40 would normally be used for task A and 40 for task B. To keep constant the number of trials per condition, the pure repeat condition should be taken as the average of two pure blocks, one for each task, of 40 trials each. This method has been repeatedly used (Kirkham et al., 2012; Kray & Lindenberger, 2000; Rubin & Meiran, 2005).While it guarantees an equal number of trials per condition, it differs enormously in total block length across them. In the example under consideration, the pure blocks contain 40 trials and the mixed block contains 160 (80 repeat and 80 switches). Clearly, at the end of the mixed block, participants will be more tired than at the end of the pure block, and vigilance levels would fluctuate even more than expected by the mixing manipulation simply because of the unequal length. To avoid this, one might equalize the number of pure block trials for each task (Koch, Prinz, & Allport, 2005), to match the total number of trials within the mixed block (both repeats and switches). This would duplicate the number of pure trials to 80 for each task, resulting in twice as many pure trials as mixed repeats. This is likely to increase the amount of practice and priming in the pure block, speeding mean RTs and hence amplifying the estimation of the mixing cost (Marí-Beffa, Cooper, & Houghton, 2012). If several variables are manipulated and the experiment becomes quite long, such a large number of pure block repeat trials can result in fatigue or boredom, also affecting performance. For these reasons, this way of constructing the pure blocks would only be recommended when specific forms of analysis are required or as demanded by the specific purpose of the study. For purposes of a standard task switching study composed of analyses of mixing and switch costs, the initial design, equating the number of trials of each repeat condition, may be favored.

Furthermore, during the pure block trials, the participant is focusing solely upon the one task, and thus performance is likely to be rapidly optimized (especially if practice trials are included). Considering the majority of research analysis in this sector involves the calculation of mean RT measures, if optimum responding is reached quickly the measure is unlikely to change dramatically regardless of the number of trials, unless fatigue becomes a factor. Indeed, sometimes the number of trials in the pure block could be even less than that in the mixed block (Emerson & Miyake, 2003).

Response Mappings

Consider the example given in which bivalent objects were responded to with respect to their color (Blue/Red) or shape (Square/Circle). If we keep the tasks as such across the pure and mixed blocks, then within each of the pure blocks we only have two S–R mappings, but for the mixed block we have four. Differences in RT may result exclusively from the added number of mappings. This possibility was tested recently in our lab (Marí-Beffa et al., 2012), where mixing costs were compared against two different baselines; one with two S–R mappings for each pure block (Blue/Red, and Square/Circle) and another with four mappings (Blue/Red/Yellow/Green and Square/Circle/Triangle/Diamond). The pattern of performance was essentially the same for the two baselines, although, overall, RTs were slightly raised in the four mappings baseline, yielding slightly smaller mixing costs.

These parameters are relatively underexplored and it is likely that in certain paradigms their impact will be stronger than in others. Because it would be impossible to match pure and mixed blocks on every single variable, it is advisable to run a few pilots or controls specific for each study, as there might not be a standard approach that can be universally accepted.

Sequential Effects

Although this variable is not exclusive to the pure block, it is worth considering how intertrial facilitatory priming effects are greatly potentiated in the pure block. In essence, any stimulus or response property that repeats from trial to trial results in a speeding of RTs, and especially so if the identical object is repeated. In a pure-task block, this will mean that the response is also repeated (see Marí-Beffa et al., 2012, for a full analysis of repetition effects in the pure block). The mixed block does not benefit from this facilitation to the same extent. This raises a simple theoretical and practical question: Are these primed fast trials representative of the pure repeat condition used to measure mixing costs? If the answer is "Yes," then we need to consider the proportion of these repetitions, especially full object repetitions, in each individual design. If the answer is "No," then we need to exclude them and base our measure exclusively on trials that do not contain any repetition effect. This issue has largely been ignored in previous studies and there is no simple solution. We would recommend the use of multiple baselines to demonstrate the stability and robustness of the measure across different variations in the proportion of repetitions, mappings, or number of trials (Marí-Beffa et al., 2012).

The Mixed Block

RANDOM VERSUS ALTERNATING

The mixed block is the one that has received the most attention in the experimental literature. One of the earliest observations is that performance on the mixed block largely depends on the paradigm that we use. As discussed earlier, it should not come as a surprise that where an alternating runs paradigm is used, mixing costs are usually smaller than if a random-cuing paradigm is used—an example of how task expectancy influences mixing costs (Los, 1996). Although both paradigms contain repeat and switch trials, the alternating runs design benefits from the predictability of the task sequence. If the participant is capable of maintaining the task sequence within working memory, he or she can be expected to be aware of the upcoming task trial and hence prepare adequately to facilitate a swift response (Dreisbach, Haider, & Kluwe, 2002; Meiran et al., 2002; Ruthruff et al., 2001). This could affect both switch and repeat trials, but the influence could be even greater for the repeat trials themselves (Koch, 2005).

This benefit on repetitions from preparation and predictability could be described as analogous to playing tennis; after playing a shot, the player generally returns to the centre of the baseline, the direction of the return ball being unpredictable. By returning, they are in the best location if the ball is returned in the opposite direction—analogous to preparing for a switch trial. However, by doing so, they deny themselves the benefit of holding their position in case the ball is returned in the same direction—analogous to cost on (unpredictable) repetition trials. Consequently, the random cuing paradigm is expected to produce larger mixing costs and smaller switch costs than the alternating run design (Koch, 2005); in essence, every trial is treated as a potential switch trial, although some repetition benefits do remain, perhaps due to task-recency facilitation (Allport & Wylie, 1999).

TASK PREPARATION

Preparation for the upcoming task on a particular trial is a process that is largely believed to influence switch trials exclusively, as reflected by the vast literature on task preparation and switch costs. But, as acknowledged by Kiesel et al. (2010), failure to engage in task preparation can be seen not only on switch trials but also on repetition trials, to a lesser extent. For example, Altmann (2004, see also Koch, 2001, 2004; Koch & Allport, 2006) found that increasing the cue–stimulus interval (CSI) from 200 to 900 ms in a mixed block produced benefits for the repetition trials as much as for the switch trials, failing to produce the expected reduction in switch costs. Indeed, this effect is more commonly found than originally expected and reflects the fact that participants also prepare for the repetition trials in mixed contexts. Importantly, this benefit from repetition trial preparation was not observed if the CSI was manipulated between groups but was observed exclusively when both intervals were experienced by the same participants, whether it is from one block to the next or from trial to trial (Altmann & Gray, 2008). This result strongly suggests that the mechanisms that modulate preparation for repetition trials are context specific, adapting to individual block demands, rather than on a trial-by-trial basis, conclusions that are fully compatible with the role of serial order expectancy on the mixing costs suggested by Bryck and Mayr (2005). However, as we mentioned earlier, the lack of a pure block of trials against which to compare these results somewhat diminishes the strength of the explanation, although it is perfectly coherent with most of the research on mixing costs.

Object Bivalency/Task Ambiguity

A very important finding is that univalent stimuli do not normally produce mixing costs (Allport & Wylie, 2000; Jersild, 1927; Wylie & Allport, 2000). With bivalent stimuli, an additional rule needs to be mapped onto the same objects, so the stimulus itself cannot trigger the response rule (S–R rules), and additional memory needs to be recruited to process these conjunction rules (Woodward, Meier, Tipper, & Graf, 2003). This explanation is very much in line with the extra demands and memory resources proposed by Rogers and Monsell (1995, Monsell, Yeung, & Azuma, 2000), but it highlights the need to create rules that include the sequence or the cue as part of it in a format such as cue–stimulus–response (C-S-R). As discussed earlier, a further consequence of presenting bivalent stimuli is the presence of S–R conflict if the cue or the upcoming task is not fully integrated in the rule. This conflict is made evident in the incongruent trials, where the response associated to the target property is different than the one triggered by the alternative (now irrelevant) one. In the pure-task block, where only one S–R mapping rule is in place, the irrelevant property is never mapped to a particular response, so performance in the incongruent trials should not differ from the congruent ones. But when two incompatible S–R mappings are active in the mixed block, interference in the incongruent trials is now evident, obviously contributing to the overall increase in RTs in the mixed block. This source of mixing cost can be interpreted as a bottom-up influence that cannot be solely attributed to sustained vigilance on task or rule maintenance, as it emerges from S–R interference of previously learned mappings.

But critically, univalent stimuli that normally do not produce mixing costs do so when mixed with a small percentage of bivalent trials (De Jong, 2000, Experiment 2; Fagot, 1994, Experiments 3 and 4; Kray & Lindenberger, 2000; Mayr, 2001, Experiment 2, Woodward et al., 2003). Therefore, although part of the mixing costs could be triggered by S–R interference, its influence expands to other noninterfering trials, suggestive of a more strategic or sustained process that is applied to all trials in a block. Bottom-up and top-down processes, rather than being independent in their contribution toward mixing costs (Mayr & Kiegel, 2003; Ruthruff et al., 2001), seem to be linked and depend on each other (Rubin & Meiran, 2005). Indeed, when different properties from the same object automatically trigger responses associated to different tasks, there is a strong possibility that the participant adopts a qualitatively different mental set or strategy to cope with the new conflicting situation. The slower and more cautious way of responding in the mixed block, triggered by the bottom-up presence of conflict, may nevertheless correspond to the onset of a more controlled, top-down, way of processing information that would expand to all trials in the block, regardless of whether they generate conflict (Marí-Beffa et al., 2012). When using bivalent stimuli exclusively, a possible strategy is to check that the effects generalize to congruent trials, when S–R interference is greatly reduced (Kirkham et al., 2012).

Enhanced Inhibition in the Mixed Block

Negative Priming

If a previously ignored property becomes the target of an action on the next trial, then responses may be slowed due to negative priming (due to either suppression of the property, an incompatible response, or both; Houghton & Mari-Beffa, 2005). This should in principle affect only switch trials, because during task repetitions there is no change in the dimensions to attend. However, there is a chance that the irrelevant property in the previous trial is partially attended to in a mixed block. Some "spill of attention" may reach the to-be-ignored dimension with more probability in the mixed block than in the pure block (the intraselection account, Brown & Braver, 2005). If this property had been previously ignored, then even a task repetition trial might be subject to negative priming. This idea was tested by Marí-Beffa et al. (2012), who found evidence of neither positive nor negative priming from the repetition of the irrelevant property in the mixed block in a manner that matched the pure block. However, in this study the task sequence was completely predictable and it is quite possible that in more random contexts, when participants cannot anticipate whether the upcoming task is a repetition or a switch, this inhibition is continuously applied to all trials, influencing repetitions as well as switches. In fact, when manipulating the task probability ratios, mixing costs have been found to increase as the probability of the task reduces (Rubin & Meiran, 2005), a result that would be compatible with the intraselection, negative priming account. Still, no study has attempted to measure priming from the irrelevant property in the random mixed block, so the influence of this source of bottom-up inhibition is still under debate.

Antiperseveration Suppression Mechanism

A different source of inhibition has been tagged as responsible for the general deterioration of performance in the mixed block. To better understand its function, we need to clarify the role of practice in both pure and mixed blocks. In pure blocks, performance improves with consistent practice. As the context does not change, the optimal strategy would be to take advantage of any repetition. Automatisms will quickly set in, and temporary loss of attention is more likely to err to the participant's advantage (triggered by well-learned S–R mappings, reliable in 100% of the trials). In the mixed block, these automatisms cannot be trusted, as in 50% of the trials they will lead to an error. Therefore, an important mechanism in the mixed block is the suppression of automatisms. As we mentioned earlier, Marí-Beffa et al. (2012) measured repetition priming within the mixed and the pure block, demonstrating that a substantial positive priming in the pure block, arising from the repetition of both object and responses, was heavily reduced (or even inverted, Cooper & Marí-Beffa, 2008) in the mixed block. This suppression of the repetition priming effects was not observed when nonrelevant properties of the object repeated as it was specific to the repetition of target information and responses that were relevant for the task. The results supported the idea of an antiperseveration mechanism that is triggered by the detection of conflict in the mixed block (Cooper & Marí-Beffa, 2008; Grzyb & Hübner, 2013; Marí-Beffa et al., 2012).

STRATEGIC AND INDIVIDUAL FACTORS

The previously analyzed variables are very important methodologically when trying to use the mixing cost as an *absolute* index of the amount of concentration or task vigilance. However, in most cases, we would not be so concerned with the presence or absence of the underlying processes but rather with changes in its size, so it would be used more as a *relative* index of cognitive performance to compare across different groups of people or across different strategies.

Verbalizations

It is common to internally verbalize the goals of the task when performing multiple or complex tasks, but the reasons why we do so are still uncertain. We recently studied different ways in which participants processed verbal cues in a task switching paradigm and measured their impact on mixing costs (Kirkham et al., 2012): (a) silently read the cue, (b) articulatory suppression of it (repeating "blah, blah, blah" out loud during the task), and (c) reading the cue aloud. The three cues were physically identical, and the only difference was how they were processed. The results clearly demonstrated that the size of the mixing cost was greatest when participants performed the articulatory suppression task, being considerably reduced when silently reading the cue (see also Bryck & Mayr, 2005; Emerson & Miyake, 2003; Saeki & Saito, 2004, for related findings). More importantly, the mixing costs were reduced even further when participants read the cues aloud. This demonstrates that cue processing and/or interpretation does not happen the same way for every trial within a block. This is of special relevance in the case of the silent reading condition, where performance was less than optimum. If reading the cue is advantageous for the task (as demonstrated by the Reading Aloud Condition), why don't participants consistently use it? The best answer seems to be: because it is demanding and tiring. In an additional unpublished study, we administered a questionnaire exploring the subjective feeling of tiredness experienced before and after each cue processing condition to different groups of individuals. Participants reported being significantly more tired after performing the Reading Aloud condition than for either of the other two. This may seem paradoxical, as they were faster and more accurate when reading aloud, but this observation offers some insight into the nature of the processes measured by the mixing costs. This measure seems to be highly sensitive to top-down concentration on tasks. These processes are demanding and difficult to keep functioning at maximum performance for long periods of time. If participants are not forced to keep attending to the cue, performance would naturally drop. By asking them to read it aloud, we managed to keep them better focused for longer, and because of this, they felt tired. This link between concentration and cue processing will become more evident in the next section.

Vigilance

Vigilance can be described as the capability of maintaining attention and concentration towards a task over an extended period of time (Davies & Parasuraman, 1982). As we mentioned earlier, the decreasing ability to maintain this concentration over longer periods is limited and variable. This inconsistency in concentration (or impossibility to predict whether a given individual is going to concentrate on a particular trial) happens not only when comparing different participants but also within the same participant in two separate sessions. In an attempt to study the impact that this fluctuation of vigilance has on mixing costs, we recently conducted a study in which we used cumulative distribution frequency measures (CDF; Ratcliff, 1979) to analyze the RTs. The traditional methods of averaging the RTs across multiple trials make it impossible to isolate high and low vigilance trials, as they are all considered for the average as long as they are correct. Conversely, the CDF analysis creates bins of correct-trial RTs after sorting them according to their speed. If we consider that each bin is indicative of a different degree of preparedness (De Jong, 2000), then it could be argued that they will manifest in different sizes of mixing costs corresponding to more or less efficient strategies. For example, where the fastest RTs are obtained, these trials are considered as being fully prepared (De Jong, 2000; Grange & Houghton, 2011; Houghton & Grange, 2011); the participant is knowledgeable of the upcoming task, has activated the required task-set configuration, and can thus give a fast and accurate response. However, at the slower end of the spectrum, preparation and vigilance are gradually poorer.[1] We found that the switch costs did not change depending on the bin, whereas the mixing cost linearly increased (even after normalizing the RTs for each bin; Grange, Lody, & Bratt, 2012). When considering the different levels of verbal processing of the cue (as described in the previous section), results demonstrated an unequal number of bins (percentage of trials) for which there was no mixing costs at all; that is, responses in the mixed repeat trials were as fast as those in the pure blocks. Articulatory suppression of the cue resulted in only the fastest 10% of the trials (one bin) from the pure and mixed repeat conditions not being significantly different from each other. Silently reading the cue drastically increased the number of fast trials where no mixing costs were observable to 40% of the trials (fastest four bins), becoming even higher after reading aloud (50%, fastest five bins). Even more important, even in the 50% slow trials where mixing

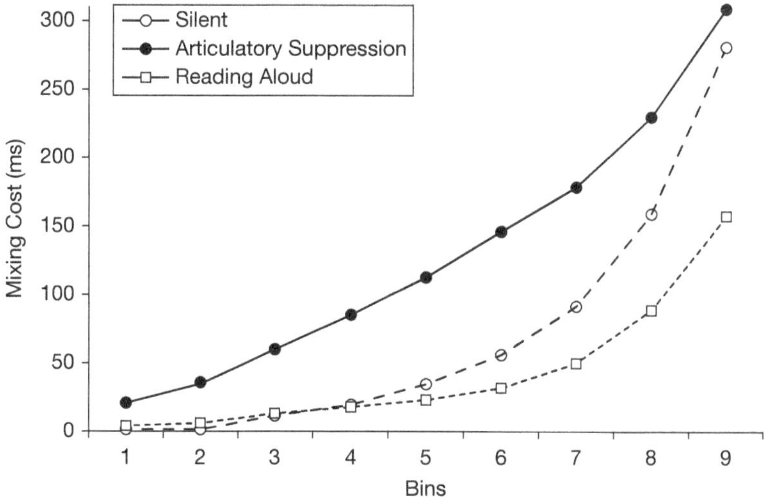

Figure 4.3 Results from the CDF study (see text for details) on mixing cost distributions across nine different bins of ranked RTs from fastest (Bin 1) to slowest (Bin 9). Mixing costs are shown in each of these bins for the three variations of task performance condition. The same pattern of results was obtained after normalizing the RTs for each bin average (e.g., Grange, Lody, & Bratt, 2012).

costs where noticeable after reading aloud the cue, the size of it was significantly smaller than when in silent reading or articulatory suppression (see Figure 4.3). This pattern of improved mixing costs associated with increased vigilance was completely absent when plotting the switch costs, which remained unchanged across the bins.

These results demonstrated a very strong link between the mixing costs and vigilance on task, a process heavily linked to strategic, top-down mechanisms of cognitive control. This interpretation is consistent with those studies that found no differences in mixing costs associated with type of stimuli or type of tasks (Lupker, Kinoshita, Coltheart, & Taylor, 2003) but on general processes influencing the entire block of trials (such as experimentally induced stress, Steinhauser, Maier, & Hübner, 2007).

Older Adults

Because individual strategies can lead to different distributions of mixing costs across trials, it is also reasonable to expect individual differences across different populations in the way these strategies are being applied. Across the life span, for example, we know that peak concentration is achieved at about 20 years old, shortly before it starts declining after 29 years of age. Later deterioration is variable but generally progressive, establishing it as the best predictor of cognitive dysfunction in the elderly (De Luca & Leventer, 2008). Therefore, we should observe a developmental pattern of mixing costs that reflects these changes. Kray and Lindenberg (2000) evaluated age-related performance of mixing and switching costs in a high-power study involving 120 participants (aged 20–80). In this large-scale study, each participant was also measured on 17 different measures of cognitive control, including reasoning, perceptual speed, knowledge, primary memory, and working memory. The results clearly indicated that aging was linked to an increase in mixing costs that was more profound than in switching costs. More specifically, mixing costs demonstrated a high correlation with reasoning and perceptual speed. This study demonstrated that one of the main signs of cognitive deterioration with age refers to the general ability to maintain two task sequences in memory, rather than on the more trial-to-trial specific preparation for a task. This ability to maintain two tasks in working memory fits very nicely with the mechanisms used to gain vigilance or concentration on task goals described earlier.

According to these results, we would easily expect that any population that displays problems with task control and concentration will display disproportionately large mixing costs effects. However, the study of mixing costs in special populations is still hardly explored.

Patients with Parkinson's Disease

As we mentioned earlier, patients with Parkinson's disease represent one of the populations that also presents greater mixing costs than age-matched controls, while showing no difference in switch costs (Werheid, Koch, Reichert, & Brass, 2007). In many ways, this is not surprising as the basal ganglia, the structure most affected in Parkinson's disease, has long been associated with processes such as planning and sequencing. Indeed, these patients have specific difficulties when having to use internal cues to initiate an action but not when the cue is external. As we mentioned earlier, one way in which mixing costs can be reduced is by knowing the task sequence, taking full advantage of task repetitions (Bryck & Mayr, 2005, Koch, 2005). This is a role commonly linked to the basal ganglia frontostriatal loops but also to the functioning of Broca's area (Ullman, 2006). We have already seen how verbalizations can reduce the mixing costs and promote task concentration, so here we have the possibility that this function is mediated by the basal ganglia (via a potential Broca-striatal connectivity (Ullman, 2006).

In a further attempt to gather some evidence in this direction, we recently compared articulatory suppression of the instructional cue with reading it aloud in 12 patients affected by hemi-Parkinson's (6 showing symptoms only on the left side of the body, and 6 showing symptoms exclusively on the right). Figure 4.4a shows the basic pattern of results for the control group. Reading the cue aloud (open circles) reduces the switch cost (Switch minus Mixed Repeat), but it completely abolishes the mixing cost (Mixed Repeat minus Pure), revealing again the beneficial effect that relevant articulations have on rule maintenance or task concentration. Participants with the damage in the right hemisphere (sparing any link between Broca's area and the basal ganglia) fully benefitted from reading aloud, with a performance remarkably close to that observed in the control group (see Figure 4.4b). Following articulatory suppression, however, participants demonstrated disproportionately high levels of mixing costs, as expected from the role that basal ganglia have on goal-directed behavior (Alexander & Crutcher, 1990; Middleton & Strick, 2000).

Left hemisphere patients (in whom the postulated left Broca–basal ganglia link would be disrupted) showed a similar pattern of deficits following articulatory suppression (Figure 4.5a, closed circles). This time, however, reading the cue aloud was not beneficial in any form and, instead, performance was impaired across all conditions. This dissociative pattern between reading aloud and the side of the lesion was very robust, being present in every patient. We interpreted these data as evidence for a link between cortical verbal structures from the left hemisphere and the frontostriatal system of control. But, more importantly, its influence seems to be more specific over performance influencing entire blocks of trials (mixing costs) rather than on a trial-by-trial basis (switch costs). These results strongly suggest that there is a neurocognitive system that uses verbalizations to hold task representations in working memory. This system is not involved in the retrieval or activation of task rules, as there is no modulation of switch costs. Instead they seem to be involved in expectancy, prediction, and maintenance of task goals, all processes that are involved in sustained concentration.

Taken together, results in this section are difficult to reconcile with a bottom-up locus of the mixing costs effects and instead speak to the involvement of top-down processes that can be modulated endogenously or by variables that influence an individual's ability to implement these processes (e.g., age, stress, or disease). If this link between mixing costs and top-down cognitive control is real, then by studying these variables, we are also studying how to improve planning, sequencing, and task concentration, providing potentially promising tools to be applied in more clinical settings.

NEUROIMAGING OF THE MIXING COSTS

Data from neuroimaging studies on the mixing cost are scarce, but they also point to a vigilance-based network of control that is very different from that being tested by studies of the switch cost.

Functional Magnetic Resonance Imaging

We will first review evidence from studies using functional magnetic resonance imaging (fMRI). Broadly speaking, insights on the neural basis of mixing costs arise mostly from studies that fail to show different loci for repeat and switch trials in the mixed block. It is normally reported that activation from task repetition trials is found in areas identical to those in the switch trials within the mixed block (for a review, see Ruge, Jamadar, Zimmermann, & Karayanidis, 2013). In fact, there is

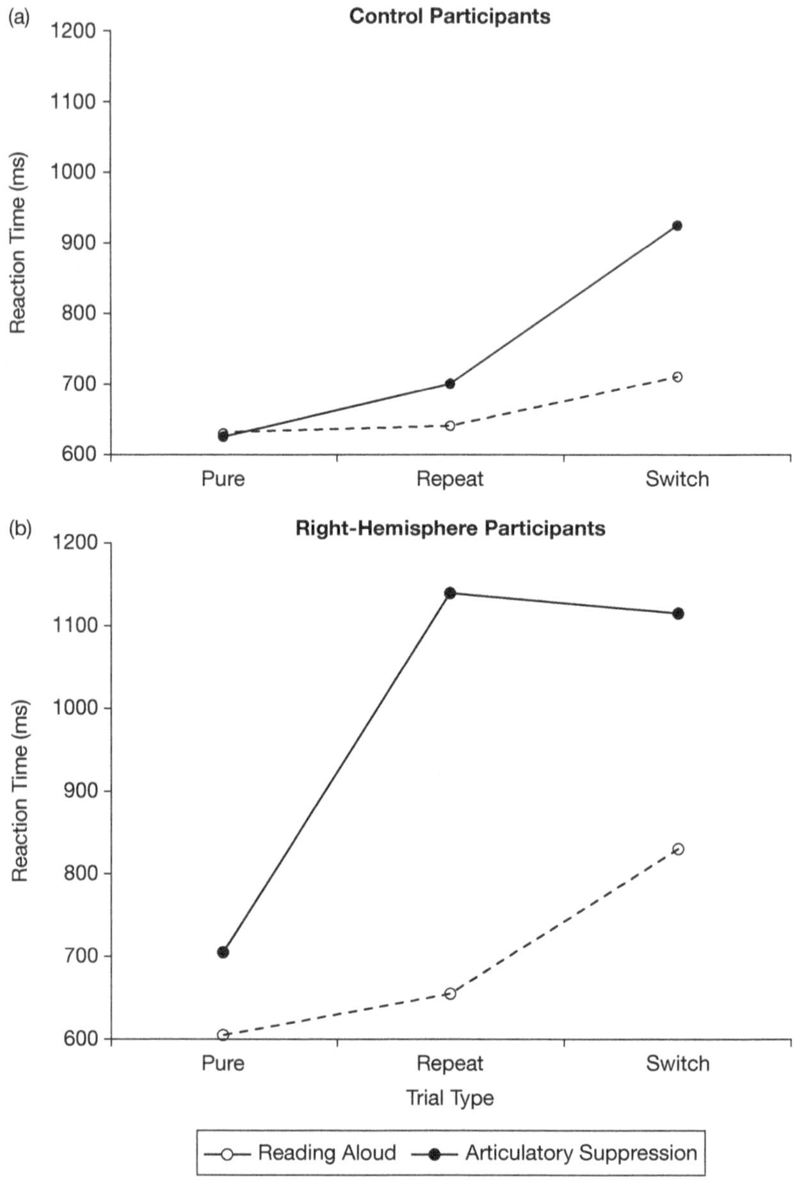

Figure 4.4 Overall RT performance for the right hemisphere Parkinson's disease patients and age-matched controls. The dashed line represents performance when participants had to read the cue aloud. The solid line represents the condition in which participants had to repeat a nonmeaningful syllable ("blah, blah, blah") while performing the task. Language contribution on cognitive control is expected when reading aloud only.

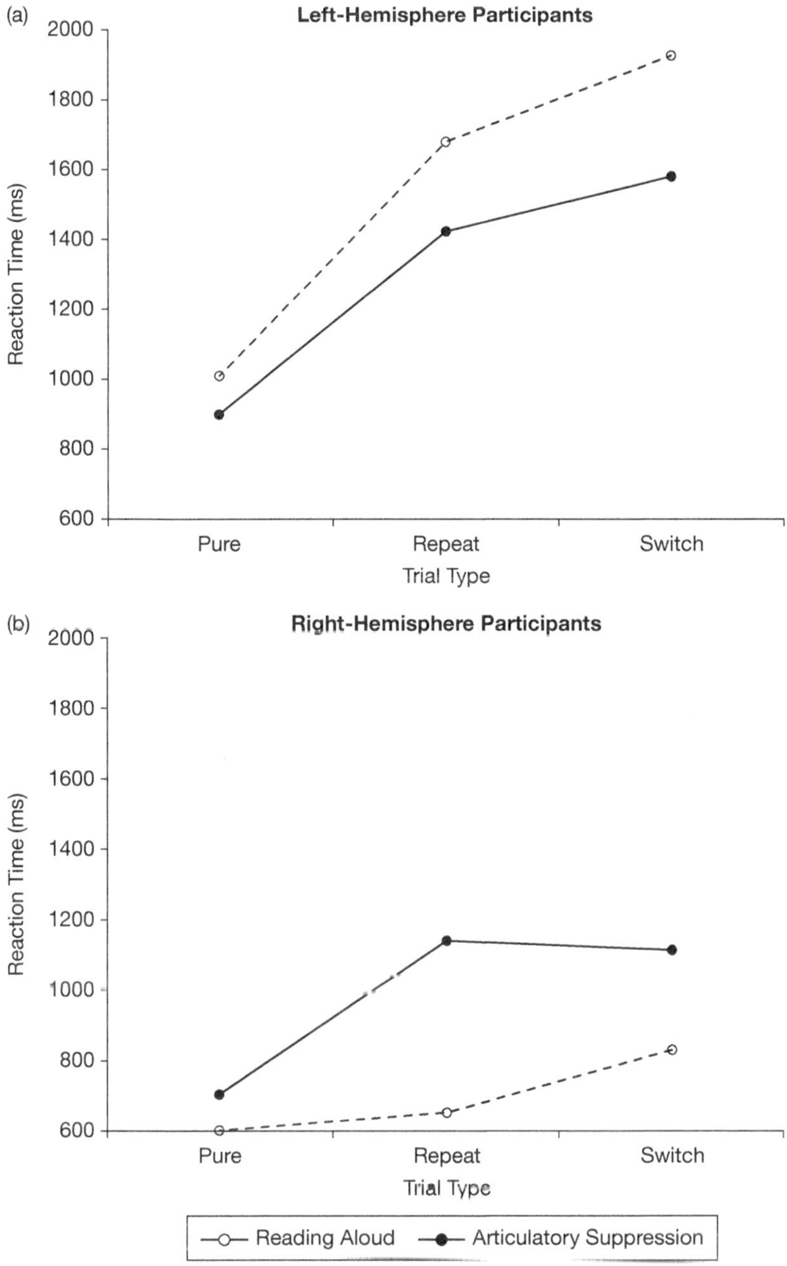

Figure 4.5 Overall RT performance for the left and right hemisphere Parkinson's disease patients. Note that data for right hemisphere patients are identical to those displayed in Figure 4.4, but the *y*-axes have been rescaled to allow cross-group comparison.

only one study that found brain areas that activate in switch trials exclusively but not in the repeat ones (the medial superior parietal lobe, Chiu & Yantis, 2009). The areas common to the two task types, which affect general performance in the mixed block but *presumably* would not be expected to do so in a pure-task block, have been repeatedly found at the inferior frontal junction (see, for example, Brass & von Cramon, 2002, 2004), with a stronger activation on the left (Broca's area) than on the right. This activation seemed to be linked to the processing of the cue, rather than the target, supporting the idea that one of the strategies used to maintain task sequencing during the mixed block could be the internal verbalization of the cues or instructions to complete the tasks. This line of research has produced a wealth of data supporting the recruitment of similar preparatory processes when switching as when repeating in the mixed block, an idea also defended in the more behavioral literature (Koch & Allport, 2006; see Kiesel et al., 2010, for a review).

From a theoretical perspective, it is difficult to base our interpretations on the activation of areas that produce null results between switch and repeat trials. We may be able to point to the brain areas that are not, apparently, involved in switch-specific processes, but this does not make them specific to mixed blocks. As far as we are aware, there is only one fMRI study, already 10 years old, differentiating brain structures recruited during the mixed block that do not appear in the pure block (Braver, Reynolds, & Donaldson, 2003). All the regions were found in the right hemisphere, including the ventral anterior cingulate cortex and the anterior prefrontal cortex. Interestingly, these regions appeared with the block analysis, showing little discrimination in the event related analysis, suggesting a more tonic activation, rather than a phasic, trial-specific one. More specifically, the anterior prefrontal cortex did not show any sign of heightened activity during the pure block, suggesting that its role is exclusively related to performance in the mixed block.

The right anterior prefrontal cortex is classically linked to sustained attention (Posner & Petersen, 1990), to planning in the Tower of London task (Baker et al., 1996), and to other tasks with high maintenance demands, such as remembering a sequence of positions or numbers in reverse order (Sakai & Passingham, 2002). These results support the idea of the mixing cost as an index of task sequencing and maintenance, processes that benefit from appropriate monitoring of instructional cue-related information when predictable (Brick & Mayr, 2005; Kirkham, et al., 2012).

Unfortunately, the low temporal resolution of fMRI cannot separate brain activity linked to cue and target processing at the temporal intervals typically used in behavioral studies. To further understand the role of instructional (cue) processing and its sustained monitoring during the mixed block, we need to review some recent findings with event-related potentials (ERPs).

ERP Studies

In contrast to fMRI research, the past decade has seen a few more studies evaluating the neurocognitive basis of mixing costs using ERPs (Eppinger, Kray, Mecklinger, & John, 2007; Goffaux, Phillips, Sinai, & Pushkar, 2006; Kray,

Eppinger, & Mecklinger, 2005; Ruge, Stoet, & Naumann, 2006; West, 2004; Wylie, Murray, Javitt, & Foxe, 2009). Most of them have found that the mixed repeat trials (compared with pure repeats trials) showed greater amplitude in a positive wave that peaks around 300 ms over centroparietal electrodes. Because its topographical and temporal distribution closely resembles the P3b attentional component (Sutton et al., 1967), this result has been simply interpreted as increased attention toward cues in the mixed-task block compared with the pure-task block (West, 2004). Interestingly, this mixing positivity is also present in switch trials, supporting the idea of similar processes involved in switch and repeat trials in the mixed block (Ruge et al., 2006) but different from the pure blocks. Wylie et al (2009) went a step further and performed source localization (LAURA) on this component and found that the difference between switch and repeat trials in the mixed block resided mainly in the strength of the response but not in the brain areas that generated them. There was a bilateral posterior activity present in all trials, pure and mixed, but the mixed ones also showed a wide frontoparietal network that was absent in the pure blocks.

Interestingly, Wylie et al. (2009) interpreted similar results not so much as evidence of increased attention toward the cue in the mixed block but rather as increased competition in the system. In their study, they manipulated the amount of interference from previously learned S–R associations and found increased amplitudes in this P3b component when participants had to overcome previously learned incompatible S–R associations.

However, we could also interpret this result as the increased attention to the cue that is required because the system detects higher levels of interference (Marí-Beffa et al., 2012). In support of this interpretation, we need to observe that this component is elicited by the instructional cue, before any target stimulus carrying the interfering information appears. The cue tells you to repeat the task, but it does not carry in itself the competition arising from incompatible S–R mappings or rules. Unfortunately, in this context, the authors never analyzed separately congruent and incongruent trials. If this P3 modulation arises from competition or interference, then we would expect the activation for congruent trials (where there is no competition) to be similar to that observed in the pure block, and emerging mostly in the target stimulus but not so much for the cue processing.

CONCLUDING REMARKS

The mixing cost is an important tool in the study of mechanisms of cognitive control and provides a useful counterpoint to the more frequently studied switch cost. Whereas the switch cost generally indexes transient adjustments required to link the appropriate stimulus with its corresponding response on a trial-by-trial basis, the mixing cost is usually interpreted as an index of a more sustained, general control mechanism. However, the idea of a "general" control process runs the risk of confounding too many variables or subprocesses that contribute to the size of the mixing cost. In this essay, we have highlighted a number of such subprocesses that have both theoretical and practical importance, with the focus on experimental designs where both a pure and a mixed block are presented. Obviously, the mixed condition contains the experimental manipulation, but it is important that the pure-task baseline be as stable and free from confounds as possible. Hence, we have emphasized that certain design parameters, such as block length, priming, or number of S–R mappings, can produce changes in the single-task baseline that should not be interpreted as changes in cognitive control, as indexed by the mixing cost.

The inclusion of a pure block baseline is also important to interpret switch costs. Indeed, there are circumstances where the repeat and the switch trials in the mixed block are differently affected by the manipulation (e.g., Meuter & Allport, 1999). When this happens, it is simply not possible to interpret changes in switch costs as changes in the ability to switch task. If we have a pure-task block that is stable and reliable to compare against, then we can study variables that influence exclusively the mixed block.

Generalized Interference from the Secondary Task Elements in the Mixed Block

One of the most important factors in mixed-task conditions is the bivalency of the stimulus, as it triggers a level of S–R competition that is largely absent in the single-task condition (Allport & Wylie, 2000; Jersild, 1927; Wylie & Allport, 2000). One precautionary measure is to test mixed-block effects only in the congruent trials, although this has rarely been reported. Observations from our lab show that mixing costs are substantial in congruent trials, in agreement with the finding that the mixing costs from bivalent stimuli generalize to univalent ones when they occur in the same block. This generalization of effects is a clear marker of a sustained process that exerts its influence on all trials, regardless of whether they generate conflict. It seems clear that once the participant perceives heightened conflict in a given experimental context, then the usual reaction is to increase "vigilance" to minimize mistakes. However, whether this reaction causes the generalization of effects from conflicting to nonconflicting items is still a matter of debate.

Increased Inhibition in the Mixed Block

One way in which the risk of making a mistake can be minimized is by increasing the suppression mechanisms that prevent the system from "relaxing" and taking full advantage of previously learned habits. This idea has been confirmed by recent studies demonstrating that the benefit of repetition trials found in single-task blocks is dramatically reduced or even converted to a cost in the mixed block (Cooper & Mari-Beffa, 2008; Mari-Beffa, Cooper, & Houghton, 2012; Grzyb & Hübner, 2013). The best explanation for this is to assume that one of the control mechanisms used during the mixed block is an anti-perseveration suppression mechanism acting on automatic associations. This inhibition produces an effect that mostly disappears when both stimuli and responses change in the mixed block.

Failure to Maintain the Sequence and Tasks in Working Memory

This inhibition mechanism could be a low-level mechanism that, to be applied, requires concentration and vigilance. Vigilance on task cannot be sustained homogeneously across all trials in a block but is aided by verbalization of the instructions (or the cue). When participants cannot use verbal self-cueing (e.g., with articulatory suppression), we have found mixing costs to be present in over 80% of the trials, but when they can (reading aloud), the costs are found on less than 50% of them. One possibility is that verbalizations aid the prediction of the upcoming task (Bryck & Mayr, 2005). Mixed repeat trials have been found to benefit from predictability (Koch, 2005) and time to prepare (Altmann, 2004). This fits well with the idea that when the sequence is stable and predictable, one strategy is to verbally rehearse the sequence, obtaining maximum benefit when the task repeats as there is no uncertainty (Kirkham, Breeze, & Marí-Beffa, 2012).

Of special interest is the highly specific deterioration of mixing costs (but not switch costs) in the Parkinson population (Werheid, Koch, Reichert, & Brass, 2007). Patients with Parkinson's disease are well known for displaying bradyphrenia, or very slow cognitive processing that leads to a specific difficulty to switch to new tasks or initiating movements when they are endogenously guided (Peavy, 2010). The fact that these patients exhibit specific deficits in mixing costs suggests that a basal ganglia frontostriatal network could be supporting the mechanisms linked to vigilance, sequencing, inhibition, and maintenance of task sets. There is very little evidence from neuroimaging on the neural basis of these processes, but the mechanisms involved in vigilance could be supported by the right anterior prefrontal cortex, which is selectively activated in mixed, but not in pure, blocks (Braver et al., 2003). Also, the verbal rehearsal of task instructions, rules, or sequences seems to be linked to the left inferior frontal junction, or Broca's area (Brass & Crammon, 2002, 2004). Data from ERPs indicate that the control mechanisms used during the mixed block are activated by the task-cue, prior to stimulus onset (the "mixing positivity," Wylie et al., 2009).

Despite this progress, the processes responsible for the mixing costs are far from being fully understood, with many gaps in the experimental literature. The research conducted so far indicates that this is one of the most promising and intriguing indexes of cognitive control. No theory of task switching is complete without considering the "global" changes that take place when the participant needs to deal with more than one task. Our view is that these changes are better studied via the mixing costs, rather than the switch cost, and, indeed, that the latter cannot be properly understood, or even measured, without taking into account the effects on repetition trials of having to maintain more than one task set in readiness. Thus, the study of the mixing cost should help elucidate not only how we change between tasks when required to do so but also how we stay on task when there are other tasks demanding our attention.

NOTE

1. As we are only considering correct trials, it could be argued that participants can be correct by chance and that more risky responses might have been rushed in the fastest bins, so the contamination or lucky hits might be unequally distributed across the blocks. In this case, a speed–accuracy tradeoff check can be used to detect this, as slowest bins should contain the highest levels of accuracy. With this system, we found no speed accuracy tradeoff.

REFERENCES

Alexander, G. E., & Crutcher, M. D. (1990). Neural representations of the target (goal) of visually guided arm movements in three motor areas of the monkey. *Journal of Neurophysiology, 64*(1), 164–178.

Allport, A., Styles, E. A., & Hsieh, S. (1994). Shifting attentional set: Exploring the dynamic control of tasks. In C. Umilta & M. Moscovitch (Eds.), *Conscious and nonconscious information processing: Attention and Performance. XV* (pp. 421–452). Cambridge, MA: MIT Press.

Altmann, E. M. (2004). The preparation effect in task switching: Carryover of SOA. *Memory & Cognition, 32*(1), 153–163.

Altmann, E., & Gray, W. (2008). An integrated model of cognitive control in task switching. *Psychological Review, 115*(3), 602–639.

Baker, S. C., Rogers, R. D., Owen, A. M., Frith, C. D., Dolan, R. J., Frackowiak, R. S. J., & Robbins, T. W. (1996). Neural systems engaged by planning: A PET study of the Tower of London task. *Neuropsychologia, 34*(6), 515–526.

Bertelson, P. (1961). Sequential redundancy and speed in a serial two-choice responding task. *Quarterly Journal of Experimental Psychology, 13*(2), 90–102.

Biederman, I. (1972). Human performance in contingent information-processing tasks. *Journal of Experimental Psychology, 93*(2), 219.

Brass, M., & von Cramon, D. Y. (2002). The role of the frontal cortex in task preparation. *Cerebral Cortex, 12*(9), 908–914.

Brass, M., & Von Cramon, D. Y. (2004). Decomposing components of task preparation with functional magnetic resonance imaging. *Journal of Cognitive Neuroscience, 16*(4), 609–620.

Braver, T. S., Reynolds, J. R., & Donaldson, D. I. (2003). Neural mechanisms of transient and sustained cognitive control during task switching. *Neuron, 39*, 713–726.

Brown, J. W., & Braver, T. S. (2005). Learned predictions of error likelihood in the anterior cingulate cortex. *Science, 307*(5712), 1118–1121.

Bryck, R. L., & Mayr, U. (2005). On the role of verbalization during task set selection: Switching or serial order control? *Memory & Cognition, 33*(4), 611–623.

Campbell, J. I. (2005). Asymmetrical language switching costs in Chinese–English bilinguals' number naming and simple arithmetic. *Bilingualism: Language and Cognition, 8*(01), 85–91.

Chiu, Y. C., & Yantis, S. (2009). A domain-independent source of cognitive control for task sets: Shifting spatial attention and switching categorization rules. *The Journal of Neuroscience, 29*(12), 3930–3938.

Cools, R., Barker, R. A., Sahakian, B. J., & Robbins, T. W. (2001). Mechanisms of cognitive set flexibility in Parkinson's disease. *Brain, 124*(12), 2503–2512.

Cooper, S., & Marí-Beffa, P. (2008). The role of response repetition in task switching. *Journal of Experimental Psychology – Human Perception and Performance, 34*(5), 1198–1211.

Costa, A., & Santesteban, M. (2004). Lexical access in bilingual speech production: Evidence from language switching in highly proficient bilinguals and L2 learners. *Journal of Memory and Language, 50*(4), 491–511.

Costa, A., Santesteban, M., & Ivanova, I. (2006). How do highly proficient bilinguals control their lexicalization process? Inhibitory and language-specific selection mechanisms are both functional. *Journal of Experimental Psychology: Learning, Memory, and Cognition, 32*(5), 1057.

Davies, D. R., & Parasuraman, R. (1982). *The psychology of vigilance* (pp. 107–117). London: Academic Press.

De Luca, C. R., & Leventer, R. J. (2008). Developmental trajectories of executive functions across the lifespan. In V. Anderson, R. Jacobs, and P.J. Anderson (Eds.), *Executive functions and the frontal lobes: A lifespan perspective*,(pp. 23–56). New York, NY: Psychology Press.

De Jong, R. (2000). An intention-activation account of residual switch costs. In S. Monsell & J. Driver (Eds.), *Control of cognitive processes: Attention and Performance. XVIII* (pp. 357–376). Cambridge, MA: MIT Press.

Dreisbach, G., Haider, H., & Kluwe, R. H. (2002). Preparatory processes in the task-switching paradigm: Evidence from the use of probability cues. *Journal of Experimental Psychology: Learning, Memory, and Cognition, 28*, 468–483.

Emerson, M. J., & Miyake, A. (2003). Memory and language: The role of inner speech in task switching: A dual-task investigation. *Journal of Memory and Language, 48*(1), 148–168.

Eppinger, B., Kray, J., Mecklinger, A., & John, O. (2007). Age differences in task switching and response monitoring: Evidence from ERPs. *Biological Psychology, 75*(1), 52–67.

Fagot, C. (1994). Chronometric investigations of task switching. PhD thesis, University of California, San Diego.

Finkbeiner, M., Almeida, J., Janssen, N., & Caramazza, A. (2006). Lexical selection in bilingual speech production does not involve language suppression. *Journal of Experimental Psychology: Learning, Memory, and Cognition, 32*(5), 1075.

Goffaux, P., Phillips, N. A., Sinai, M., & Pushkar, D. (2006). Behavioural and electrophysiological measures of task switching during single and mixed-task conditions. *Biological Psychology, 72*(3), 278–290.

Grange, J. A., & Houghton, G. (2011). Task preparation and task inhibition: A comment on Koch, Gade, Schuch, & Philipp (2010). *Psychonomic Bulletin and Review, 18* (1), 211–216.

Grange, J.A., Lody, A., & Bratt, S. (2012). Cost-benefit and distributional analyses of accessory stimuli. *Psychological Research, 76*(5), 626–633.

Grzyb, K. R., & Hübner, R. (2013). Excessive response-repetition costs under task switching: How response inhibition amplifies response conflict. *Journal of Experimental Psychology: Learning, Memory, and Cognition, 39*(1), 126.

Hayes, A. E., Davidson, M. C., Keele, S. W., & Rafal, R. D. (1998). Toward a functional analysis of the basal ganglia. *Journal of Cognitive Neuroscience, 10*(2), 178–198.

Houghton, G., & Grange, J. (2011). CDF-XL: Computing cumulative distribution functions of reaction time data in Excel. *Behavior Research Methods, 43*(4), 1023–1032.

Houghton, G. & Marí-Beffa, P. (2005). Dissociating object- and response-based components of negative priming through effects of practice. *Perception and Psychophysics, 67*(8), 1423–1436.

Jersild, A. T. (1927). Mental set and shift. *Archives of Psychology, 89*.

Kiesel, A., Steinhauser, M., Wendt, M., Falkenstein, M., Jost, K., Philipp, A. M., & Koch, I. (2010). Control and interference in task switching—A review. *Psychological Bulletin, 136*(5), 849.

Kirkham, A. J., Breeze, J. M., & Marí-Beffa, P. (2012). The impact of verbal instructions on goal-directed behaviour. *Acta Psychologica, 139* (1), 212–219.

Koch, I. (2005). Sequential task predictability in task switching. *Psychonomic Bulletin & Review, 12*(1), 107–112.

Koch, I., & Allport, A. (2006). Cue-based preparation and stimulus-based priming of tasks in task switching. *Memory & Cognition, 34*(2), 433–444.

Koch, I., Prinz, W., & Allport, A. (2005). Involuntary retrieval in alphabet-arithmetic tasks: Task-mixing and task-switching costs. *Psychological Research, 69*(4), 252–261.

Kray, J., Eppinger, B., & Mecklinger, A. (2005). Age differences in attentional control: An event—related potential approach. *Psychophysiology, 42*(4), 407–416.

Kray, J., & Lindenberger, U. (2000). Adult age differences in task switching. *Psychology and Aging, 15*(1), 126–147.

Linden, D. van der Frese, M., & Meijman, T. (2003). Mental fatigue and the control of cognitive processes: Effects on perseveration and planning. *Acta Psychologica, 113*(1), 45–65.

Los, S. (1996). On the origin of mixing costs: Exploring information processing in pure and mixed blocks of trials. *Acta Psychologica, 94*(2), 145–188.

Lupker, S. J., Kinoshita, S., Coltheart, M., & Taylor, T. E. (2003). Mixing costs and mixing benefits in naming words, pictures, and sums. *Journal of Memory and Language, 49*(4), 556–575.

Marí-Beffa, P., Cooper, S., & Houghton, G. (2012). Unmixing the mixing cost: Contributions from dimensional relevance and stimulus–response suppression. *Journal of Experimental Psychology: Human Perception and Performance, 38*(2), 478–488

Marí-Beffa, P., Fuentes, L. J., Catena, A., & Houghton, G. (2000). Semantic priming in the prime task effect: Evidence of automatic semantic processing of distractors. *Memory & Cognition, 28*(4), 635–647.

Mayr, U. (2001). Age differences in the selection of mental sets: The role of inhibition, stimulus ambiguity, and response-set overlap. *Psychology and Aging, 16*, 96–109.

Mayr, U., & Keele, S. W. (2000). Changing internal constraints on action: The role of backward inhibition. *Journal of Experimental Psychology: General, 129*, 4–26.

Mayr, U., & Kliegl, R. (2000). Task-set switching and long-term memory retrieval. *Journal of Experimental Psychology: Learning, Memory & Cognition, 26*, 1124–1140.

Meiran, N. (1996). Reconfiguration of processing mode prior to task performance. *Journal of Experimental Psychology: Learning, Memory & Cognition, 22*, 1423–1442.

Meiran, N. (2000). Reconfiguration of stimulus task sets and response task sets during task switching. In S. Monsell & J. Driver (Eds.), *Control of cognitive processes: Attention and performance. XVIII* (pp. 377–399). Cambridge, MA: MIT Press.

Meiran, N., Chorev, Z., & Sapir, A. (2000). Component processes in task switching. *Cognitive Psychology, 41*, 211–253.

Meuter, R. F., & Allport, A. (1999). Bilingual language switching in naming: Asymmetrical costs of language selection. *Journal of Memory and Language, 40*(1), 25–40.

Middleton, F. A., & Strick, P. L. (2000). Basal ganglia output and cognition: Evidence from anatomical, behavioral, and clinical studies. *Brain and Cognition, 42*(2), 183–200.

Miyake, A., Emerson, M. J., Padilla, F., & Ahn, J. C. (2004). Inner speech as a retrieval aid for task goals: The effects of cue type and articulatory suppression in the random task cuing paradigm. *Acta Psychologica, 115*, 123–142.

Monsell, S., Sumner, P., & Waters, H. (2003). Task-set reconfiguration with predictable and unpredictable task switches. *Memory & Cognition, 31*(3), 327–342.

Monsell, S., Yeung, N., & Azuma, R. (2000). Reconfiguration of task-set: Is it easier to switch to the weaker task? *Psychological Research*, 63(3–4), 250–264.

Parasuraman, R. (1986). Vigilance, monitoring, and search. In K. Bo, L. Kaufman, & J. Thomas (Eds.), *Handbook of human perception and performance: Vol. II. Cognitive processes and performance* (pp. 43.1–43.39). New York, NY: Wiley.

Peavy, G. M. (2010). Mild cognitive deficits in Parkinson disease: Where there is bradykinesia, there is bradyphrenia. *Neurology, 75*(12), 1038–1039.

Philipp, A. M., Gade, M., & Koch, I. (2007). Inhibitory processes in language switching: Evidence from switching language-defined response sets. *European Journal of Cognitive Psychology, 19*(3), 395–416.

Posner, M. I., & Petersen, S. E. (1990). The anterior system of the human brain. *Annual Review of Neuroscience, 13*, 25–42.

Ratcliff, R. (1979). Group reaction time distributions and an analysis of distribution statistics. *Psychological Bulletin, 86*(3), 446–461.

Rogers, R. D., & Monsell, S. (1995). Costs of a predictable switch between simple cognitive tasks. *Journal of Experimental Psychology: General, 124*(2), 207–231.

Rubin, O., & Meiran, N. (2005). On the origins of the task mixing cost in the cuing task-switching paradigm. *Journal of Experimental Psychology: Learning, Memory, and Cognition, 31*(6), 1477–1491.

Rubinstein, J. S., Meyer, D. E., & Evans, J. E. (2001). Executive control of cognitive processes in task switching. *Journal of Experimental Psychology: Human Perception and Performance, 27*(4), 763–797.

Ruge, H., Jamadar, S., Zimmermann, U., & Karayanidis, F. (2013). The many faces of preparatory control in task switching: Reviewing a decade of fMRI research. *Human Brain Mapping, 34*(1), 12–35.

Ruge, H., Stoet, G. T., & Naumann, E. (2006). Attentional set mixing: Effects on target selection and selective response activation. *Psychophysiology, 43*, 413–421.

Ruthruff, E., Remington, R. W., & Johnston, J. C. (2001). Switching between simple cognitive tasks: The interaction of top-down and bottom-up factors. *Journal of Experimental Psychology: Human Perception and Performance, 27*(6), 1404–1419.

Sakai, K., & Passingham, R. E. (2002). Prefrontal interactions reflect future task operations. *Nature Neuroscience, 6*(1), 75–81.

Saeki, E., & Saito, S. (2004). Effect of articulatory suppression on task switching performance: Implications for models of working memory. *Memory, 12*(3), 1–1.

Shaffer, L. (1965). Choice reaction with variable S–R mapping. *Journal of Experimental Psychology, 70*, 284–288.

Sohn, M. H., & Anderson, J. R. (2001). Task preparation and task repetition: Two-component model of task switching. *Journal of Experimental Psychology: General; Journal of Experimental Psychology: General, 130*(4), 764.

Spector, A., & Biederman, I. (1976). Mental set and mental shift revisited. *American Journal of Psychology, 89*(4), 669–679.

Steinhauser, M., Maier, M., & Hübner, R. (2007). Cognitive control under stress: How stress affects strategies of task-set reconfiguration. *Psychological Science, 18*(6), 540–545.

Sutton, S., Tueting, P., Zubin, J., & John, E.R. (1967). Information delivery and the sensory evoked potential. *Science, 155*, 1436–1439.

Tornay, F., & Milan, E. G. (2001). A more complete task-set reconfiguration in random than in predictable task switch. *Quarterly Journal of Experimental Psychology, 54*, 785–803.

Ullman, M. T. (2006). Is Broca's area part of a basal ganglia thalamocortical circuit? *Cortex*, 42(4), 461–658.

Waszak, F., Hommel, B., & Allport, A. (2003). Task-switching and long-term priming: Role of episodic stimulus-task bindings in task-shift costs. *Cognitive Psychology, 46*(4), 361–413.

Werheid, K., Koch, I., Reichert, K., & Brass, M. (2007). Impaired self-initiated task preparation during task switching in Parkinson's disease. *Neuropsychologia, 45*(2), 273–281.

West, R. (2004). The effects of aging on controlled attention and conflict processing in the Stroop task. *Journal of Cognitive Neuroscience, 16*(1), 103–113.

Woodward, T. S., Meier, B., Tipper, C., & Graf, P. (2003). Bivalency is costly: Bivalent stimuli elicit cautious responding. *Experimental Psychology, 50*(4), 233.

Wylie, G., & Allport, A. (2000). Task switching and the measurement of "switch costs". *Psychological Research, 63*(3–4), 212–233.

Wylie, G. R., Murray, M. M., Javitt, D. C., & Foxe, J. J. (2009). Distinct neurophysiological mechanisms mediate mixing costs and switch costs. *Journal of Cognitive Neuroscience, 21*(1), 105–118.

Yeung, N., & Monsell, S. (2003). The effects of recent practice on task switching. *Journal of Experimental Psychology: Human Perception and Performance, 29*(5), 919.

5

The Extended-Runs Procedure and Restart Cost

ERIK M. ALTMANN

INTRODUCTION

Task switching procedures provide a means to study the interplay between goal-directedness and cognitive flexibility at a fine temporal grain. On each trial, the participant performs a simple "task," often judging a digit stimulus as even or odd (one task) or as higher or lower than 5 (the other task). The task can switch between one trial and the next, requiring the cognitive system to configure itself so that it can apply the current task rules correctly (and thus show goal-directedness) but also accommodate changes to these task rules (and thus show flexibility).

The most commonly used task switching procedures are the explicit-cuing procedure (e.g., Chapter 3, this volume) and, to a lesser extent, the alternating-runs procedure (introduced by Rogers & Monsell, 1995). In the explicit-cuing procedure, a randomly selected task cue is presented perceptually on every trial, often shortly before the imperative stimulus to allow time for cue related task preparation. To perform the task correctly, the participant has no option but to process this task cue, so this procedure is useful for examining the time course and other characteristics of cue processing. It does not allow close scrutiny of processes triggered by the imperative stimulus, because any cue processing that continues past onset of the imperative stimulus will obscure them.

In the alternating runs procedure, there is typically a perceptual cue to the current task available on every trial (e.g., Rogers & Monsell, 1995; cf. Koch, 2003), effectively giving participants strategic options about where to acquire task information. That is, they could encode a memory representation of the current task at the start of a run, to last for the duration of the run until the task switches, or they could rely on the external cue available on every trial. This strategic option helps explain some of the variability in findings from this procedure, and in general makes the data from this procedure difficult to interpret (Altmann, 2007; Altmann & Gray, 2008).

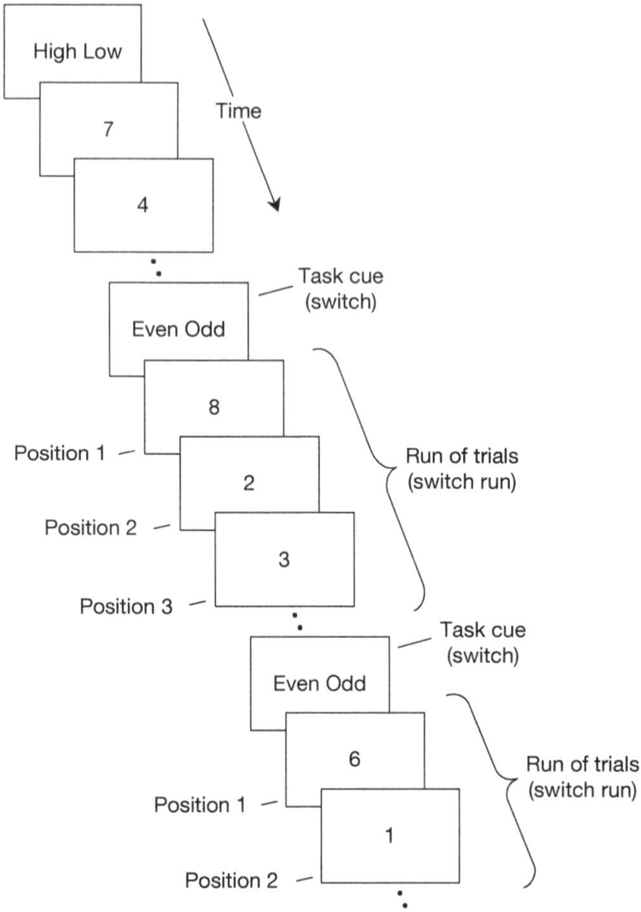

Figure 5.1 Illustrative timeline of trials in the extended-runs procedure.

The extended-runs procedure (also known as the randomized-runs, instructed-switch, and multiple-trials procedure) solves some of these problems, while possibly introducing its own. A perceptual cue, randomly selected from the different candidates as in explicit cuing, is presented at the start of a run of trials that are to be performed according to that task. The cue is then withdrawn for the duration of the run, such that retaining a memory of the cued task is a requirement for performance. Figure 5.1 illustrates, showing three consecutive runs of trials. The first run is governed by the "high/low" task (to judge a digit stimulus as higher or lower than 5), and the second two governed by the "even/odd" task (to judge a digit stimulus as even or odd). The second run represents a switch run, because the task switches relative the run that preceded it. The third run represents a repeat run, because the task continues from the run that preceded it.

In Figure 5.1, each trial is labeled with a serial position relative to the task cue that started the run. As depicted in the figure, the Position 1 trial begins only after the task cue offsets. This is the usual arrangement in extended-runs studies but also represents a difference relative to the explicit cuing procedure. In a purely procedural sense, explicit cuing can be viewed as a special case of extended runs in which the run length is always one. However, often in explicit cuing, the task cue offsets together with the imperative stimulus, which here would correspond to the cue offsetting with the Position 1 stimulus, instead of before it. Nonetheless, despite this difference, I will refer to the Position 1 trial as the cued trial and trials on later positions as uncued trials, because the Position 1 trial in the design schematized in Figure 5.1 shows basically the same behavioral effects as an explicit cuing trial.

One benefit of the extended-runs procedure is that processes linked to stimulus processing and processes linked to cue processing can be measured independently. There is also less strategic variability possible than there is in the alternating-runs procedure, because a perceptual strategy for acquiring task information is not an option. One potential cost of the extended-runs procedure is simply that episodic memory processes are required. This is a "cost" in the sense that memory processes are not required in procedures where a cue is always perceptually available, so models of processing in the extended-runs procedure may not generalize. However, theoretical arguments suggest they do, an issue I return to in Concluding Issues.

The extended-runs procedure has roots in two early lines of work. Gopher and colleagues (Gopher, Armony, & Greenshpan, 2000; Gopher, Greenshpan, & Armony, 1996) first demonstrated that most of the cost of switching was borne on the first trial following the task cue. They also found response latencies highly elevated on the first trial of a run regardless of whether the task switched or repeated from the previous run. In the repeat case, they termed this finding "reconsideration cost," but the term "restart cost" (Allport & Wylie, 2000) has since taken root. Gopher and colleagues treated trials other than the first of a run as baseline trials used strictly for comparison purposes and did not analyze performance on them in detail for its own sake.

Separately, Allport and colleagues (Allport & Wylie, 1999, Allport & Wylie, 2000; Waszak, Hommel, & Allport, 2003) explored the role of interference driven by stimulus priming, using what they referred to as the "before-after" task. One study in particular illustrates the contribution from including uncued trials in this procedure. Waszak et al. (2003) manipulated whether specific stimuli had, on earlier trials, been presented with the alternative task. When the stimulus presented on current trial had been presented with the alternative task on earlier trials, response latencies on the current trial were highly elevated. However, this effect differed depending on the task. The stimuli were Stroop-like picture–word compounds, and the two tasks were picture naming and word reading. If a stimulus had been presented with the picture-naming task on earlier trials, response latency was elevated when that stimulus was presented again with the word reading task—but only when the stimulus was presented on the first trial of a run of word reading trials. In the reverse case, if the stimulus was presented first with the word reading task, response latency was elevated when it was then presented with the picture naming task—but for all trials of the run, not just the first.

Waszak et al. (2003) interpreted their findings in terms of stimulus priming of the currently irrelevant task, modulated by differences in representational strength of the two tasks. The picture-naming task was hypothetically weaker and therefore more vulnerable to interference when a stimulus primed the alternative task. The word-reading task was hypothetically stronger, so it had to be inhibited to allow the picture-naming task to be performed at all, and this inhibition required a single trial of performance to overcome. On that trial only, performance of the task was hypothetically vulnerable to additional interference when the stimulus primed the alternative task. Regardless of the exact theoretical interpretation, this dissociation between the two tasks, which represents a potentially important constraint on how tasks are represented, could not have been discovered using the explicit-cuing procedure, in which there is effectively only one trial per run.

Subsequently, Poljac, Koch, and Bekkering (2009) returned to the constructs of restart cost and "mixing cost," showing that they could to some extent be dissociated. Mixing cost is the cost of performing a task in a mixed-task context, measured by comparing performance of a task on repeat trials interleaved with switch trials with performance of the same task when only that task is performed. In the critical condition, participants performed a predictable number of repeat runs in a row before switching to the other task (then back again, etc.). In this condition, there was no mixing cost, defined as a difference in performance on uncued trials between this condition and a pure-task condition in which there was only one task switch, midway through the experimental session. There was, however, still restart cost, defined as a difference between the first and second trials of a repeat run. Restart cost was absent in the pure-task condition. The authors took this pattern to mean that restart cost reflects the process of activating a representation of the current task in episodic memory, under conditions in which the task can change, if predictably. Mixing cost, in contrast, was linked to conditions in which there was some uncertainty about what the next task would be. A key insight here was that mixing cost under conditions of uncertainty about the next task was associated with trial processing as well as cue-related processing. Thus, these results identified control-related mechanisms that could not have been identified using the explicit cuing procedure, in which trial processing and cue processing cannot be separated.

In the balance of the essay, I focus on a particular theory that addresses performance on uncued trials in some details. This theory sets up some predictions for specific behavioral measures, which I then examine in context of new data. The aim is to have a close look at some subtle and not-so-subtle empirical patterns associated with the extended-runs procedure.

EXISTING THEORY

To date, the only detailed model of performance on uncued trials in the task switching context is the cognitive control model (CCM) of Altmann and Gray (2008). I review some of the basic elements of the theory here, to motivate an

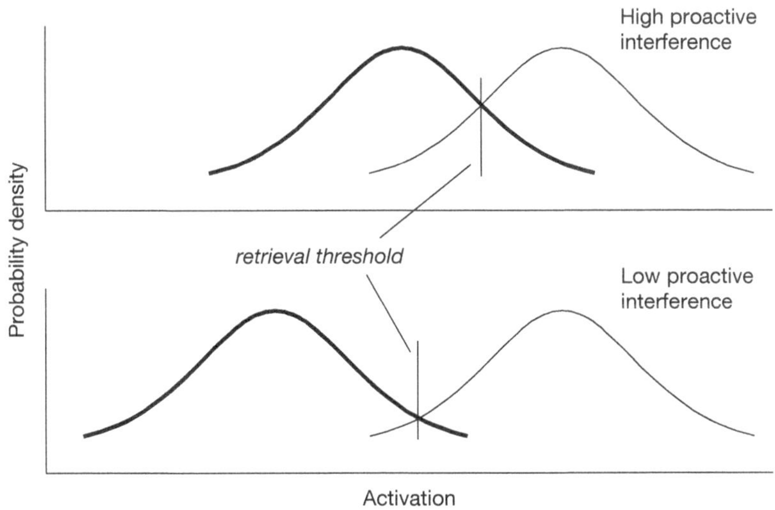

Figure 5.2 Abstract representation of activation dynamics in the cognitive control model (Altmann & Gray, 2008). In each panel, the right-hand probability density function represents the activation of the currently correct task in episodic memory, and the left-hand probability density function represents the activation of the most active old task code in episodic memory, which is a source of proactive interference. See text for details.

experiment that illustrates some of core extended-runs phenomena that have been reported since the beginning and that replicates some other effects demonstrated only more recently.

Figure 5.2 shows the basic logic of CCM. In the top panel, which is representative, there are two probability density functions, each representing the activation of a code in episodic memory. The abscissa of the figure represents activation level, and the ordinate represents probability density. Thus, each density function represents activation noise: The memory code corresponding to that density function is usually at its mean level of activation (located at the peak of the function) and less often more active or less active (the tails). The right-hand density function is the activation of the code for the most recently presented task cue. This is the code that should govern performance during the current run of trials. The left-hand density function is for the activation of the most active code for a previously presented task cue. That is, the left-hand function represents the competing control code that is most likely to intrude on the target control code during performance of a trial in the current run. In general there are many competing control codes, one for each old task cue. However, under conditions that apply here, a set of density functions can be represented by a single density function that is right shifted (Anderson & Lebiere, 1998).

The remaining construct in Figure 5.2 is the retrieval threshold, located at the intersection of the two density functions. The retrieval threshold is a high-pass filter that allows only those codes with activation above threshold to be visible to the system. The performance of the system, as measured in response latency and the error rate, depends on how much of each of the two density functions is above threshold (Altmann & Gray, 2008). In general, assuming that the retrieval threshold remains at the intersection point of the two densities, performance will be better (faster and more accurate) as the greater is the separation between the two density functions (just as in signal detection theory, on which the decay model is based). In more familiar terms, the greater the separation between the two density functions, the less the *proactive interference* from old task cues.

The two panels of Figure 5.2 represent performance conditions differing in terms of amount of proactive interference. In the bottom panel, relative to the top panel, more of the right-hand density function is above threshold, making the target code more accessible, and less of the left-hand density function is above threshold, making the competing code less accessible.

The dynamics represented in Figure 5.2 make clear that some process, or set of processes working together, must ensure that the two density functions are separate—that proactive interference does not increase to the point where the densities lie on top of one another, or, in signal detection terms, that d′ does not go to zero. The specific proposal incorporated in CCM is that decay is one of these processes: as soon as a code for the current task is encoded in episodic memory, in response to presentation of a task cue, that code begins to decay, such that its role in generating proactive interference in future is reduced. In terms of Figure 5.2, this decay is represented simply as the right-hand density function shifting left along the abscissa. Note that in principle, a process like inhibition could substitute for decay in maintaining a functional situation in which the target code is more active than the most active competitor.

The empirical test for a decay process is whether there are changes in behavioral measures as the activation of the target code decays gradually across trials within a run. The specific behavioral effects that reflect decay are *within-run slowing* (for response latencies) and *within-run error increase* (for error rates). In terms of Figure 5.2, the decay causing these effects involves the density function for target code gradually shifting left past the retrieval threshold, progressively reducing the area of the density function that is above threshold, and also the proportion of the total area across the two density functions that is represented by the right-hand function. (Because decay is curvilinear, older codes lose activation less quickly. In effect, the right-hand density can be viewed as stationary, such that its area above threshold does not change.)

The contrast between the two panels of Figure 5.2 makes a prediction concerning the rate at which response latency and error rates should increase across trials in a run—that is, concerning the slopes of within-run slowing and error increase. The decay rate—the rate at which the density function shifts leftward in the two panels—is assumed to be an architectural parameter and not influenced by conditions. However, what governs performance is the area of the right-hand density function that is above threshold, and this will change more slowly (with a fixed decay rate) in the bottom panel than in the top panel. This is because the retrieval threshold intersects the right-hand density function at a lower density level in the bottom panel than in the top panel. Thus, within-run slowing and error increase should have flatter slopes under conditions of lower proactive interference, as represented in the bottom relative to the top panel of Figure 5.2.

In Altmann and Gray (2008), we manipulated proactive interference by manipulating the average number of trials per run. The more trials per run, the lower is the rate of new task cues being presented and the greater is the time between task cues—both factors that should reduce proactive interference. Thus, longer compared with shorter runs hypothetically created the situation in the bottom panel of Figure 5.2 compared with the top panel. Within-run slowing and within-run error increase were indeed both flatter with longer runs (Altmann & Gray, 2002, 2008).

The experiment reported next takes a different approach to manipulating proactive interference. The approach of manipulating the number of trials per run does introduce a confounding factor, which is simply that the number of trials per run varies inversely with the frequency and recency of task cues. In principle, then, the larger number of trials per run could have been the causal factor, though a mechanism for this is not apparent. Nonetheless, a useful converging operation would involve controlling number of trials per run while manipulating proactive interference.

Here, I manipulated proactive interference by extending time per run directly, by adding a 500-ms lag between each response and onset of the next stimulus. The duration of this lag roughly the response latency of a single uncued trial, and thus the effect is roughly to double the time between task cues for a given number of trials per run. The result should be flatter slopes for within-run slowing and error increase in the lag condition compared with the no-lag condition.

EXPERIMENT

Method

Forty Michigan State University undergraduates participated in exchange for credit toward a course requirement.

The stimulus on each trial was a digit selected randomly from the set (1, 2, 3, 4, 6, 7, 8, 9), subject to the constraint that a stimulus could not repeat between trials.

As illustrated in Figure 5.1, the two candidate tasks were to judge whether the stimulus digit was even or odd or whether it was higher or lower than 5. A task cue was either “even/odd” or “high/low.”

Participants responded to each stimulus by pressing either the C or the M key on a QWERTY keyboard. For each task, the two candidate responses mapped to the two response keys, with the mapping randomized between participants. The left–right order of the words in the task cue was congruent with the response mapping for that participant.

Each participant performed 192 experimental blocks of 20 trials each. Each block was divided into two runs of trials. The block began with a task cue giving the task for the first run of the block. After the last trial of the first run, another task cue was presented giving the task for the second run. The location of the task cue for the second run was randomly selected to occur after the 7th trial of the run but before the 13th trial of a run, such that every run contained at least 7 trials.

A task cue was presented for 500 ms and then withdrawn. Following cue offset, the first trial of the run began immediately. After the last trial of a block, a feedback screen was presented, giving participants their accuracy for that block. If this was below 90% (18/20 trials correct), participants were asked to be more accurate. Participants pressed either trial response key to continue to the first task cue for the next block. Blocks on which accuracy was below 90% were excluded from analysis.

Each experimental session was divided in half. In one half (96 blocks), each response on a trial was immediately followed by the next event (another trial, a task cue, or a feedback screen). In the other half, each response was followed by a 500-ms lag before onset of the next event. Midway through the session, the computer informed the participant of the change. The order of lag and no-lag conditions was counterbalanced between participants.

Results and Discussion

Figure 5.3 shows median response latencies on correct trials (top panel) and error percentages (bottom panel), separated by position of the trial within the run (abscissa) and by level of the lag manipulation (lines). The figure shows some of the standard patterns found in extended-runs studies. One is that response latency is much higher on Position 1 of a run—what I have been referring to as the cued trial—than on later, uncued trials. A second finding is the dissociation between response latency and error rates on Position 1, with error rates being lower on Position 1 than on later trials. The CCM model (Altmann & Gray, 2008) accounts for this in terms of cue-encoding processes, which cost time but do not affect errors as they do not participate in the judgment about the imperative stimulus.

Figure 5.3 also shows a main effect of the lag manipulation on response latencies, which were faster with a lag than without, $F(1,38) = 74.5, p <.001, \eta_p^2 = .662$. For errors there is the opposite trend, though this was not significant, $F(1,38) = 1.7$, $p = .202, \eta_p^2 = .042$. The main effect of lag for latencies was not expected, in that the analogous manipulation in Altmann and Gray (2008), where we varied the number of trials per run to affect proactive interference, had only a small main effect, to the point that it was null on Position 2. Here, the opposite trend for errors hints at a speed–accuracy tradeoff. Participants may have grown a little impatient with the lag between trials and hurried their response, with a negligible effect on accuracy. Alternatively, response-related processes (e.g., Philipp, Jolicoeur, Falkenstein, & Koch, 2007; Schroder, Moran, Moser, & Altmann, in press; Steinhauser & Hubner, 2006) or other sequential effects (Brown, Reynolds, & Braver, 2007) may have contributed to response latency in the no-lag condition but been factored out in the lag condition.

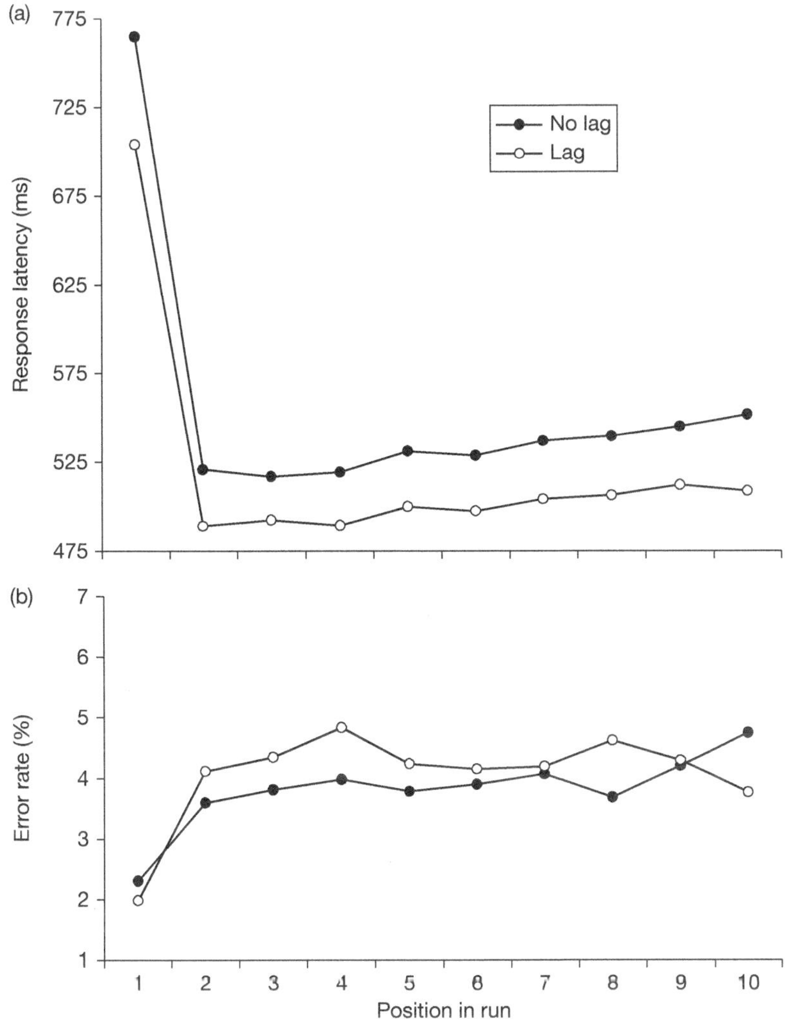

Figure 5.3 Response latency and error data from the experiment, separated by the position of a trial within a run (abscissa) and whether or not there was a 500-ms lag between trials (lines).

Within-run slowing is visible in the top panel of Figure 5.3, starting from Position 2. (On theoretical grounds, I leave Position 1 out of the analysis of within-run slowing, assuming that latency on this position reflects cue-encoding processes.) The size of the effect is small compared with the large difference between Position 1 and other trials, and this may have led to be it being overlooked in early work with this procedure. However, there was a main effect of Position across Positions 2–10, $F(8,304) = 35.8$, $p < .001$, $\eta_p^2 = .485$. Within-run slowing has proved to be robust and has replicated in other labs (Ikeda & Hasegawa, 2012; Poljac et al., 2009).

Within-run slowing is sometimes also found in procedures other than extended runs. Within the domain of task switching, there is one case in which it was significant in the alternating-runs context (Altmann, 2002). In Experiment 6 of Rogers and Monsell (1995)—in which runs were longer than two trials, and thus long enough to measure within-run slowing—there was a nonsignificant trend.

In domains that are less clearly task switching, within-run slowing has been found even when it is not so clear what the memory load is that is decaying over trials in a run (Experiment 3 of Pashler, 1994; Schroder et al., in press). These instances suggest either that a decay account, as incorporated in the CCM model, is incorrect—or, in the alternative, that control information encoded in episodic memory for control information is more pervasive than one might have thought. Under the latter view, essentially any behavior that involves some sort of constancy over time may be governed by episodic memory representations that decay over time. A high-level functional argument supporting this position is that the controller for a mobile organism in a dynamic environment might serve the organism best if it incorporates an architectural process that keeps the system from completely locking into behavioral ruts. Architectural decay is well-suited to this purpose, because it applies to any control information, and thus cannot be "left out" of the configuration for a particular task, yet is gradual and thus affords plenty of opportunity for the system to reevaluate any rut it is in and *decide* that continuing in that rut is appropriate.

Within-run error increase is visible in the bottom panel of Figure 5.3, though the effect is largely driven by Position 1. (I include Position 1 in the analysis of within-run error increase, because, unlike with response latencies, there is no reason not to.) Statistically, there is a main effect of Position across Positions 1–10, $F(9,342) = 10.4$, $p < .001$, $\eta_p^2 = .215$. In general, within-run error increase is much more variable than within-run slowing, sometimes showing trends in the opposite direction (e.g., Poljac et al., 2009).

The prediction of the theoretical analysis earlier was that slopes of within-run slowing and within-run error increase should be flatter with an intertrial lag than without. No such difference is readily apparently in Figure 5.3. However, the difference for latencies is clearer in Figure 5.4. There, latencies are plotted on a finer-grain scale, and best-fitting linear functions are shown for both latencies and errors (see legends for slopes and intercepts). Statistically, for latencies, across Positions 2–10, there was a significant Position × Lag interaction, $F(8,304) = 2.6$, $p = .010$, $\eta_p^2 = .063$. For errors, across Positions 1–10, the Position × Lag interaction was also significant, $F(9,342) = 1.9$, $p = .048$, $\eta_p^2 = .048$. Thus, the results converge with those of Altmann and Gray (2008) to support the specific activation and interference dynamics characterized in Figure 5.2.

One methodological criticism of the procedure used here is that the length of a run was "aging," meaning that each successive trial in the current run—specifically after the seventh trial, which was the last guaranteed trial in a run—was more likely than its predecessor to be the last. This dynamic, known as an increasing hazard function (Luce, 1986), arose because runlengths were uniformly distributed across the range of 7–13. An increasing hazard function offers an alternative

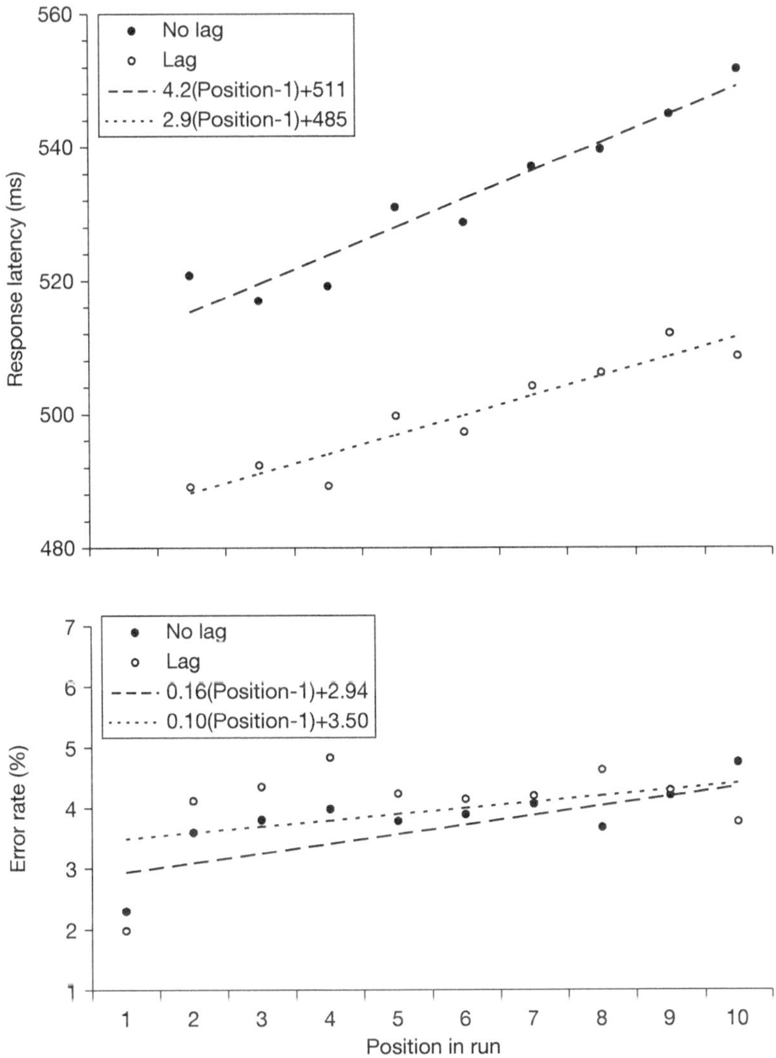

Figure 5.4 The data from Figure 5.3 re-plotted to show response latencies for Positions 2–10 on a finer-grain temporal scale and with best-fitting linear functions for each measure and lag condition (slopes and intercepts appear in figure legends).

account of at least within-run slowing in this study; the effect could have reflected increasing anticipation as the end of the run approached. However, why errors would also increase as the end of the run approached, under this account, is not clear. More to the point, within-run slowing also occurs with a flat hazard function (Altmann, 2002), though an empirical question that has not been explored is the extent to which within run slowing is modulated by the precise form of the hazard function.

Figure 5.5 shows some additional patterns in this data set, some of which have replicated many times and some of which were uncovered by Altmann and Gray

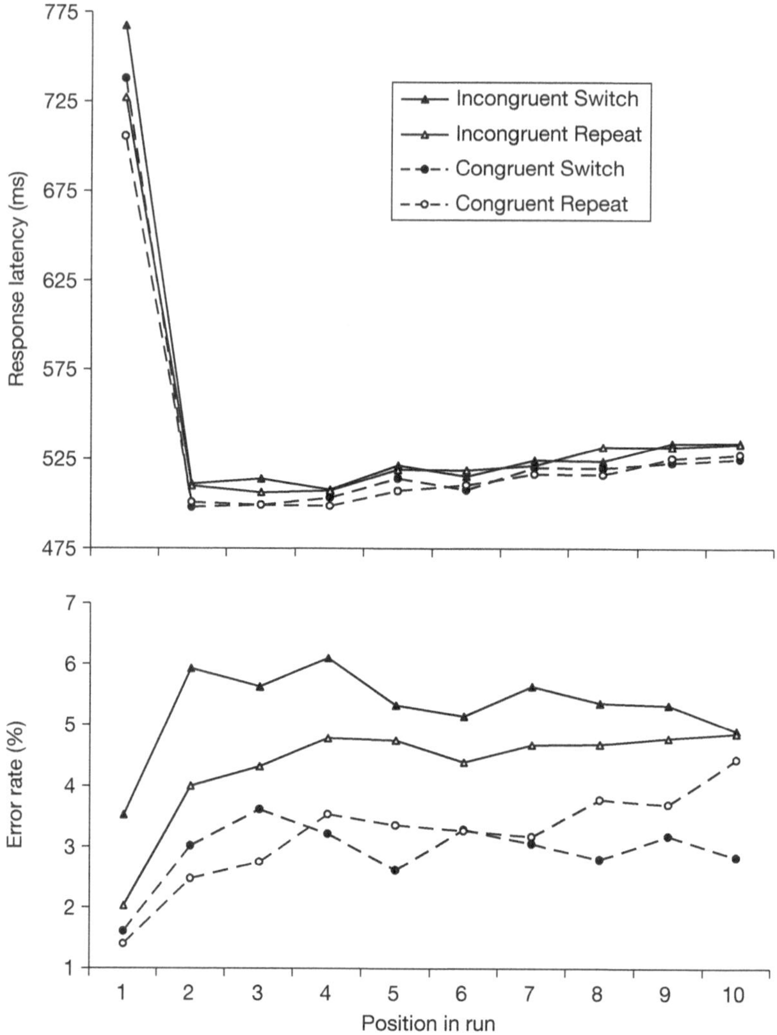

Figure 5.5 Response latency and error data from the experiment, separated by position (abscissa), and by switching (whether or not the task switched from the previous run) and congruency (whether or not the correct response is the same under both tasks).

(2008) and tested again here for only the second time. The data in Figure 5.5 are averaged over lag condition but separated by *switching* and by *congruency*. Switching is defined with respect to the preceding run: If the task on the current run is the same as the task on the preceding run, then the current run is a repeat run, otherwise it is a switch run. Congruency is defined with respect to the stimulus/task/response constellation for the current trial: If the response to the stimulus would be the same under either task, then the trial is congruent, but if the response to the stimulus would differ by task, then the trial is incongruent.

The switching and congruency factors are useful together are a means for identifying conditions under which the previous task is influencing performance. This influence should register specifically on incongruent switch trials, because the previous task implies the currently-incorrect response. In contrast, on congruent trials both tasks imply the same response, and on repeat trials the previous task is the same as the current. Thus, evidence for the previous task influencing performance takes the form of a switching x congruency interaction.

In Figure 5.5, latency switch cost was limited to Position 1. Statistically, Switching interacted with Position, $F(9,342) = 10.9$, $p < .001$, $\eta_p^2 = .223$, and had a significant effect on Position 1, $F(1,38) = 22.1$, $p < .001$, $\eta_p^2 = .368$, but no effect across Positions 2–10, $F < 1$. Gopher et al. (2000) found a similar pattern, and only occasionally does latency switch cost extend beyond Position 1 (Ikeda & Hasegawa, 2012). Latencies showed a main effect of Congruency for Positions 1–10, $F(1,38) = 20.9$, $p < .001$, $\eta_p^2 = .335$. Congruency interacted with Position, $F(9,342) = 2.5$, $p = .008$, $\eta_p^2 = .062$, but was significant for Position 1, $F(1,38) = 9.4$, $p = .004$, $\eta_p^2 = .198$, and (unlike Switching) for Positions 2–10, $F(1,38) = 17.9$, $p < .001$, $\eta_p^2 = .320$. Finally, latencies for Positions 1–10 showed no Switching × Congruency interaction, $F < 1$, suggesting that switch cost (present only on Position 1) and congruency effects reflect independent processes—at least for response latencies.

For errors, switch cost was not limited to Position 1. Statistically, for Positions 1–10, there was a main effect of Switching, $F(1,38) = 6.9$, $p = .012$, $\eta_p^2 = .154$, and a Switching × Position interaction, $F(9,342) = 2.8$, $p = .004$, $\eta_p^2 = .068$. However, Switching was still significant for Positions 2–10, $F(1,38) = 4.3$, $p = .046$, $\eta_p^2 = .101$. Errors showed a robust effect of Congruency for Positions 1–10, $F(1,38) = 35.7$, $p < .001$, $\eta_p^2 = .484$, but no Congruency × Position interaction, $F < 1$. Finally, errors for Positions 1–10 showed a large Switching × Congruency interaction, $F(1,38) = 17.7$, $p < .001$, $\eta_p^2 = .318$. This is evident in the bottom panel of Figure 5.5, where switch cost registers for Incongruent trials (across the first several Positions) but not for Congruent trials. Indeed, for Positions 1–10, Switching was significant for Incongruent trials, $F(1,38) = 18.1$, $p < .001$, $\eta_p^2 = .323$, but not for congruent trials, $F(1,38) = 1.6$, $p = .112$, $\eta_p^2 = .065$.

The results in Figure 5.5 have two important implications. First, influence of the previous task—measured by the switching × congruency interaction—registered for errors but not latencies. In the CCM model (Altmann & Gray, 2008), the influence is through memory for the previous task (the left-hand density in either panel of Figure 5.2) intruding on trial processing. Such an intrusion triggers the incorrect response only on incongruent switch trials, per the earlier analysis. Such an intrusion does not affect response latencies, because these depend only on the activation, at the moment, of whichever task representation guides performance.

A second, related implication of the results in Figure 5.5 is that error switch cost and latency switch cost stem from different processes. Error switch cost occurs on cued and uncued trials alike, so it is best interpreted as reflecting processes that begin with stimulus onset. Consistent with this interpretation, error switch cost is qualified by a switching x congruency interaction, which reflects the influence of the previous task on the processes that interpret the stimulus and select a response. In contrast, latency switch cost is limited to cued trials, and thus is best interpreted as reflecting the process of encoding the task cue. (In CCM, latency switch cost is represented simply as repetition priming that facilitates cue encoding.) Whatever the best theoretical explanation of this dissociation between switch costs turns out to be, the dissociation itself could only be discovered with the inclusion of uncued trials in the procedure.

CONCLUDING ISSUES: EPISODIC MEMORY IN COGNITIVE CONTROL

An open question is whether the same mechanisms support cognitive control in the extended-runs procedure as in other task switching procedures. The question is easiest to frame with respect to the explicit cuing procedure, which in procedural terms is a special case of the extended-runs procedure in which the runlength is one. On all the other dimensions, such as random selection of task cues, the procedures are largely the same. In terms of functional requirements, however, the explicit cuing procedure does not require memory for the current task, because a perceptual task cue is available on every trial. Thus, all that is functionally required for performance is to combine the task cue with the stimulus in a compound cue that retrieves the response (Logan & Bundesen, 2003).

Nonetheless, in the CCM model we assumed that, even when a task cue was always available perceptually, the current cue was encoded in memory and from there governed stimulus interpretation and response selection (Altmann & Gray, 2008). This mechanism turned out to provide adequate fits to explicit cuing performance, because this performance was quite similar to that on the cued trial of the extended-runs procedure. For response latencies in particular, the overall magnitudes are similar in the two procedural contexts, and the switching and cue–stimulus interval factors have basically the same effects, to the point that whether the two factors interact depends whether cue–stimulus interval is manipulated within or between subjects (Altmann, 2004). Recent empirical evidence suggests that the influence of the previous task, as measured by the switching x congruency interaction for errors, is greater under explicit-cuing conditions than under extended-runs conditions (Altmann, in press)—hypothetically because the previous task stored in memory is more recent and therefore less decayed.

The theoretical implication of this evidence is that episodic memory processes might play a more basic role in cognitive control than previously thought. In other words, in a broad range of situations, including those in which the environment always indicates what task is currently relevant, goal-directedness and cognitive flexibility might reduce to fine-grained memory processes delivering the right information at the right time. This is not a new idea; one of the earliest studies in this domain identified "task-set inertia"—a form of proactive interference—as a core constraint on performance (Allport, Styles, & Hsieh, 1994). Since then many effects have been discovered and many mechanisms postulated (Kiesel et al., 2010; Vandierendonck, Liefooghe, & Verbruggen, 2010), and future work with the extended-runs procedure should help determine which of these are ultimately linked to episodic memory processes and which are not.

REFERENCES

Allport, A., Styles, E. A., & Hsieh, S. (1994). Shifting intentional set: Exploring the dynamic control of tasks. In C. Umilta & M. Moscovitch (Eds.), *Attention and performance XV: Conscious and nonconscious information processing* (pp. 421–452). Cambridge, MA: MIT Press.

Allport, A., & Wylie, G. (1999). Task-switching: Positive and negative priming of task-set. In G. H. Humphreys, J. Duncan & A. Treisman (Eds.), *Attention, space, and action: Studies in cognitive neuroscience* (pp. 273–296). New York, NY: Oxford University Press.

Allport, A., & Wylie, G. (2000). Task-switching, stimulus–response bindings, and negative priming. In S. Monsell & J. Driver (Eds.), *Control of cognitive processes: Attention and performance XVIII* (pp. 35–70). Cambridge, MA: MIT Press.

Altmann, E. M. (2002). Functional decay of memory for tasks. *Psychological Research, 66*, 287–297.

Altmann, E. M. (2004). Advance preparation in task switching: What work is being done? *Psychological Science, 15*, 616–622.

Altmann, E. M. (2007). Comparing switch costs: Alternating runs and explicit cuing. *Journal of Experimental Psychology: Learning, Memory, and Cognition, 33*, 475–483.

Altmann, E. M. (2013). Fine-grain episodic memory processes in cognitive control. *Zeitschrift für Psychologie/Journal of Psychology, 221*, 23–32.

Altmann, E. M., & Gray, W. D. (2002). Forgetting to remember: The functional relationship of decay and interference. *Psychological Science, 13*, 27–33.

Altmann, E. M., & Gray, W. D. (2008). An integrated model of cognitive control in task switching. *Psychological Review, 115*, 602–639.

Anderson, J. R., & Lebiere, C. (1998). *The atomic components of thought*. Hillsdale, NJ: Erlbaum.

Brown, J. W., Reynolds, J. R., & Braver, T. S. (2007). A computational model of fractionated conflict-control mechanisms in task-switching. *Cognitive Psychology, 55*, 37–85.

Gopher, D., Armony, L., & Greenshpan, Y. (2000). Switching tasks and attention policies. *Journal of Experimental Psychology: General, 129*, 308–339.

Gopher, D., Greenshpan, Y., & Armony, L. (1996). Switching attention between tasks: Exploration of the components of executive control and their development with training *Proceedings of the HFES 40th annual meeting* (pp. 1060–1064). Philadelphia, PA: Human Factors and Ergonics Society.

Ikeda, K., & Hasegawa, T. (2012). Task confusion after switching revealed by reductions of error-related ERP components. *Psychophysiology, 49*, 427–440.

Kiesel, A., Steinhauser, M., Wendt, M., Falkenstein, M., Jost, K., Philipp, A. M., & Koch, I. (2010). Control and interference in task switching. A review. *Psychological Bulletin, 136*, 849–874.

Koch, I. (2003). The role of external cues for endogenous advance reconfiguration in task switching. *Psychonomic Bulletin & Review, 10*, 488–492.

Logan, G. D., & Bundesen, C. (2003). Clever homunculus: Is there an endogenous act of control in the explicit task-cuing procedure? *Journal of Experimental Psychology: Human Perception and Performance, 29,* 575–599.

Luce, R. D. (1986). *Response times: Their role in inferring elementary mental organization.* New York, NY: Oxford.

Pashler, H. (1994). Overlapping mental operations in serial performance with preview. *Quarterly Journal of Experimental Psychology, 47A,* 161–191.

Philipp, A. M., Jolicoeur, P., Falkenstein, M., & Koch, I. (2007). Response selection and response execution in task switching: Evidence from a go-signal paradigm. *Journal of Experimental Psychology: Learning, Memory, and Cognition, 33,* 1062–1075.

Poljac, E., Koch, I., & Bekkering, H. (2009). Dissociating restart cost and mixing cost in task switching. *Psychological Research, 73,* 407–416.

Rogers, R. D., & Monsell, S. (1995). Costs of a predictable switch between simple cognitive tasks. *Journal of Experimental Psychology: General, 124,* 207–231.

Schroder, H. S., Moran, T. P., Moser, J. S., & Altmann, E. M. (in press). When the rules are reversed: Action-monitoring consequences of reversing stimulus–response mappings. *Cognitive, Affective, & Behavioral Neuroscience.*

Steinhauser, M., & Hubner, R. (2006). Response-based strengthening in task shifting: Evidence from shift effects produced by errors. *Journal of Experimental Psychology: Human Perception and Performance, 32,* 517–534.

Vandierendonck, A., Liefooghe, B., & Verbruggen, F. (2010). Task switching: Interplay of reconfiguration and interference control. *Psychological Bulletin, 136,* 601–626.

Waszak, F., Hommel, B., & Allport, A. (2003). Task-switching and long-term priming: Role of episodic stimulus-task bindings in task-shift costs. *Cognitive Psychology, 46,* 361–413.

6

Voluntary Task Switching

CATHERINE M. ARRINGTON, KAITLIN M. REIMAN, AND STARLA M. WEAVER ■

INTRODUCTION

Humans show a remarkable flexibility in responding to environmental stimuli under varying conditions and goals. Changes in both the external environments and internal goals may alter how individuals respond to specific stimuli. Executive control processes regulate which particular behavior is carried out when multiple tasks, or pathways of responding, are available for action on a given stimulus (Norman & Shallice, 1986). One of the ways that this adaptive behavior is captured in the laboratory is through the use of task switching paradigms. It has become clear in the almost 20 years of accumulated use of these paradigms that shifting mental sets likely engages a variety of cognitive operations, both active and passive in nature (Kiesel et al., 2010; Vandierendonck, Liefooghe, & Verbruggen, 2010). However, a common perception of many researchers using the paradigm as well as other researchers in the field, is that task switching engages the executive control mechanisms that allow for adaptive behavior and thus, in some way, taps into a key aspect of human volitional behavior (Monsell, 2003; cf. Haggard, 2008).

VOLUNTARY TASK SWITCHING

We focus on the voluntary task switching paradigm (Arrington & Logan, 2004). This version of task switching involves selection by the participant of which task to perform on each trial in a multitask environment, which is in contrast to other task switching paradigms that use cues or memorized sequences to indicate the appropriate task. Standard task switching methods provide tight experimental control of factors such as preparation time and transition type, which allows for systematic investigation of parameters that influence set shifting processes. In contrast, voluntary task switching trades control over these parameters for a less constrained environment in which task selection becomes a component of behavior. This tradeoff expands the range of questions that can be addressed within a task switching paradigm beyond performance measures, such as response time (RT) and accuracy, to measures of task choice. This modification to the task switching paradigm has proved particularly successful in considering the mechanisms supporting task selection. A full understanding of the flexibility in cognitive control must necessarily address not only the ability to perform various actions on a particular stimulus but also the choice of which action to perform.

Experimental Paradigm

The voluntary task switching procedure bears many structural similarities to other task switching paradigms, in particular explicitly cued task switching. The procedure generally involves performance of two or more simple categorization tasks (e.g., parity and magnitude judgments of single digit numbers). A multivalent target stimulus appears on each trial and subjects must categorize the target based on one of the possible tasks. Responses are typically made using manual key presses—responses made with the left hand using the *d* and *f* keys, for example, would indicate "even" and "odd," while responses made with the right hand using the *j* and *k* keys would indicate "low" and "high." Hand to task mapping is usually counterbalanced across subjects. Timing intervals between the response on trial *n*-1 and the onset of the target stimulus on trial *n* are controlled by the experimenter and can be varied parametrically to evaluate the influence of preparation time on behavior. The key difference between voluntary task switching and explicit task-cuing paradigms is that the task to be performed on a trial-to-trial basis is chosen by the participant rather than dictated by the experimenter in the form of a cue. Participants typically receive global instructions to select tasks in a random or unpredictable manner. In our instructions to subjects in the first voluntary task switch study (Arrington & Logan, 2004), we suggested that subjects equate the choice to a coin toss.

A variant of the voluntary task switching procedure referred to as the double registration procedure requires the participant to make an explicit response indicating the task choice on each trial (Arrington & Logan, 2005). Generally, a prompt stimulus such as a question mark is presented at the beginning of a trial and remains on the screen until a response is made indicating which task the subject intends to perform on the upcoming target or whether they intend to repeat or switch tasks (Kessler, Shencar, & Meiran, 2009). Task choice and task performance are executed using separate hands (Arrington & Logan, 2005). For example, participants may be assigned to use their left hand and the keys *s* and *d* to indicate whether they will perform the magnitude or parity task on the upcoming trial and their right hand and the *j* and *k* keys to respond to the target using the chosen task. The double registration paradigm has the advantage of having a response associated with task choice that is separate from the subsequent response resulting from the performance of that task on the target stimulus. This procedure is thought to allow for better isolation of processes associated with task selection and task performance.

Dependent Measures

The novel contribution of the voluntary task switching procedure to the broader task switching literature is the ability to measure choice processes. Two measures of choice are common: task choice and task transition. Task choice refers to the identity of the task selected on trial *n*. Task choice in a standard single response voluntary task switching study is coded based on the response to the target. That is, if subjects make a response associated with the parity task, then the trial is coded as if parity was the selected task. For the double registration paradigm, the response to the prompt stimulus is used to code the task choice. Task choice can be used to examine the factors that influence the selection of one task over other competing tasks. Task transition refers to the relationship between the task selected on trial *n*-1 and the task selected on trial *n*. Task repetitions and task switches are the most common values for the task transition measure, and the probability of switching or *p*(switch) is commonly reported for voluntary task switching studies.

Additionally, more complex task transition designations have been considered. Arrington and Logan (2005) considered chosen repetitions versus instructed repetitions in a paradigm that required subjects to repeat a selected task for two or three target presentations. In this case, task performance was compared in order to rule out the possibility that subjects make a choice only on trials on which they decide to switch tasks. Also, in an examination of hierarchical task representations, Weaver and Arrington (in press) distinguished between task switches that were within an aggregate task or between two aggregate tasks. In this case, choice patterns were compared in order to determine if participants were representing tasks hierarchically in a voluntary task switching environment. Finally, Lien and Ruthruff (2008) examined the effect of backwards inhibition in task selection by examining task transitions based on trial *n*-2 task selection. In this case, the frequency of *n*-2 repetitions was compared with the frequency of *n*-2 switches to determine how inhibition impacts voluntary choice. In these examples the focus of the researchers is on how subjects choose to transition between tasks, although the transition patterns are not as straightforward as simply switching and repeating tasks.

Standard task performance measures of RT and accuracy can also be examined in voluntary task switching. However, in this context, there are some caveats to considering these measures. RT can be measured for the response both to the target stimulus and, when using the double registration paradigm, to the prompt. A strong assumption is that prompt RTs provide a measure of the time engaged in performing the task choice, while target RTs measure the time required to establish the appropriate task set and perform the discrimination task (Arrington & Logan, 2005). Accuracy may also be measured in voluntary task switching, although it should be done with care. As noted earlier, task choice is coded based on the response that is performed by subjects on a given trial. Error trials raise some concerns about how to code task choice. Did the error result from confusion about which button to press on the correct hand for the intended task, or which hand to use for the intended task? Arrington and Logan (2004) argue that within-hand errors (e.g., an error mistaking "even" for "odd") are more likely than between-hand errors (e.g., an error mistaking "even" for "larger than 5") and therefore accordingly coded task choice based on the hand used to make the response. However, a cautious researcher may wish to discard all error trials from choice and RT analyses due to the concern about how to code the task. Finally, when analyzing the task performance measures, researchers often compare trials based on the task choice measures, such as comparing task repetition and task switch trials. Thus, a variable that serves as a dependent measure when examining choice probabilities also serves as an independent variable when examining performance measures.

OVERVIEW OF BASIC VOLUNTARY TASK SWITCHING FINDINGS

In the following overview of findings from past voluntary task switching studies, we focus on the choice-dependent measures. A number of researchers have asked questions focused on performance measures, such as contrasting the switch costs found in voluntary task switching compared with cued task switching (Liefooghe, Demanet, & Vandierendonck, 2009), but a comprehensive review of these effects is outside the scope of this work.

Repetition Bias

A key and robust result from voluntary task switching studies is the repetition bias. The instructions to perform tasks randomly should result in an equal number of task repetitions and task switches. However, when free to choose which task to perform on a given trial, participants tend to repeat tasks more than switch tasks resulting in a p(switch) value of <.5. The deviation from chance does not just reflect an underlying difficulty in producing random sequences. When producing a random sequence of events, subjects tend to vary from chance in the direction of producing too many switches, whereas the repetition effect in voluntary task switching shows the opposite pattern. More specifically, Arrington and Logan (2004) asked subjects to produce a random sequence of Hs and Ts to represent a series of flips of a coin. The same subjects who had just shown a repetition bias in voluntary task switching showed the typical bias toward switches when the events did not require performing a series of tasks.

Manipulating the time between the response on the previous trial and the onset of the target stimulus on the current trial, response to stimulus interval

(RSI), influences the magnitude of the repetition bias. The repetition bias is larger when the time between trials is shorter. This finding occurs both when the RSI is manipulated between blocks (Arrington & Logan, 2004; Yeung, 2010) and when it is manipulated within blocks (Arrington & Logan, 2005; Liefooghe et al., 2009). Typically, in these studies, the RSIs range from 0 to approximately 1000 ms. Across this range, shorter RSIs (those less than 500 ms) tend to result in repetition biases that are statistically different from the expected value of .5, while longer RSIs (those greater than 500 ms) often fail to show significant or even mathematical repetition biases (Arrington & Logan, 2005).

Stimulus-Based Effects

A variety of stimulus-based effects have been uncovered in task choice and task transition, suggesting that bottom-up factors do affect choice during voluntary task switching. Mayr and Bell (2006) reported large stimulus repetition effects in a voluntary task switching paradigm involving left/right and up/down judgments of a stimulus appearing in a 2 × 2 grid. Subjects showed a marked increase in the repetition bias on trials when the stimulus repeated position. When the paradigm involves tasks with a larger number of targets (e.g., eight target stimuli in the commonly used number judgments of parity and magnitude), stimulus repetitions are diminished but still significant (Butler, Arrington, & Weywadt, 2011; Demanet, Verbruggen, Liefooghe, & Vandierendonck, 2010; Mayr & Bell, 2006). The stimulus repetition effect even extends to features of a stimulus that were not explicitly categorized on trials *n* and *n*-1. Yeung (2010) had subjects categorizing targets based on the location or shape of the target. A repetition of the target location increased the likelihood of repeating the task, even when the task that subjects performed was the shape task.

The accessibility of a stimulus or stimulus feature to the cognitive system also appears to influence task selection. Arrington (2008) examined the effect of stimulus availability by offsetting the timing between the presentations of two components of a target display. This manipulation is referred to as stimulus onset asynchrony (SOA). Subjects were biased to choose the task associated with the first stimulus to appear with a probability that increased as the SOA increased. As with the repetition bias described here, this bias to choose the task associated with the first stimulus decreased as the RSI increased, suggesting that preparation time could buffer against the bottom-up influence of stimulus availability. Arrington and Rhodes (2010) further examined the role of stimulus accessibility on task choice through a manipulation of how specific features of a compound target stimulus are processed. Stimuli with both global and local features (e.g., a large H made up of small 'T' elements) were presented to the left or right visual field. Such lateralized presentation influences how quickly the different levels of the compound stimulus are processed (Navon, 1977). Subjects were more likely to choose to perform the task (identification of the stimulus at the global or local level) associated with the feature more efficiently perceived on the given side of presentation.

The identity of a stimulus can influence the choices that subjects make about what task to perform on a stimulus. The influence of stimulus identity is seen particularly in the context of past experience with stimuli both within the context of the experiment (Arrington, Weaver, & Pauker, 2010; Demanet et al., 2010) and outside the experiment (Gollan & Ferreria, 2009). When performing judgments of animacy and size on a large number of concrete nouns, subjects bias task choice for a particular stimulus toward the task performed on that stimulus at its first experimental exposure. This effect occurs both when the task performed on first exposure was selected by the subject and when instructed by the experimenter in the context of practice with individual tasks (Arrington et al., 2010), as well as when the first exposure required a response in a different modality from later voluntary task switching performance (i.e., vocal versus manual responding; Demanet et al., 2010). These results suggest that episodic binding between stimuli and tasks can bias task choice in voluntary task switching. Additionally, extraexperimental stimulus characteristics influence choice. In the Arrington et al. study, particular words elicited biased choice patterns across subjects when initial exposures involved task choice (e.g., "aspirin" was far more likely to be categorized as *small* than as *nonliving*.) The pattern of choice across items was suggestive of an influence of semantic associations on choice. Gollan and Ferreria similarly suggested that lexical accessibility of words influenced task choice in a language switching version of voluntary task switching performed with bilingual subjects.

Task-Based Effects

The specific tasks being performed and the relationships among tasks also influence subjects' task choices and task transitions. Several studies have shown that task difficulty influences task selection in surprising ways. Using Stroop stimuli with word reading and color naming tasks, Liefooghe, Demanet, and Vandierendonck (2010) demonstrated that subjects choose to perform the more difficult color naming task on a larger proportion of trials. They attribute this bias toward a mechanism that inhibits the more dominant word reading task when switching from that task. Yeung (2010) replicated this finding with a pair of tasks in which task strength was manipulated based on response compatibility, highlighting the importance of interference between tasks in driving this choice effect. This work has recently been extended to a double registration paradigm showing that task selection was influenced by interference between tasks even when the choice was made prior to the onset of the target stimulus (Millington, Poljac, & Yeung, in press). Both sets of researchers note that the strength of the task set for the more difficult or weaker task must be enhanced in the face of competition from the less difficult or stronger task and that it is this increased strength of the task set that influences the choice to repeat that task. This same mechanism appears to account for trial-by-trial changes in the task repetition bias in a paradigm addressing conflict adaptation effects on task choice (Orr, Carp, & Weismann, 2011). Subjects were more likely to repeat tasks following high conflict trials when the task set would need to be more strongly instantiated to guide correct task performance.

The task effects extend beyond the strength or difficulty of specific tasks to the larger structure of the task space in which they are represented. The relationships among tasks within a task hierarchy also influence task selection (Weaver & Arrington, in press). In a four-task environment, subjects learned that two tasks were mapped arbitrarily to one aggregate-level task goal while the other two tasks were mapped to a second aggregate-level task goal. Simple discriminations tasks performed on single visual objects (i.e., size, shape, fill, and orientation) were arbitrarily grouped into aggregate-level tasks based on temporal, spatial, and explicit instructions cues during practice with the tasks. During voluntary task switching when instructed to perform all tasks equally often in a random order, subjects were more likely to make switches between tasks that were within-aggregate switches than between-aggregate switches even when cues to the hierarchical mapping of the tasks were absent.

Memory-Based Effects

Task choice and task transition in voluntary task switching have both shown variation as a function of concurrent working memory loads. Across three experiments, Demanet et al. (2010) embedded short runs of voluntary task switching trials between the study and recall phases of a six letter working memory load. The repetition bias increased under working memory load conditions, particularly on those trials where the stimulus repeated, thus providing a strong external cue to task repetition. Weywadt and Butler (2013) more closely examined the nature of the working memory effect by varying the type of concurrent load. An articulatory suppression condition, assumed to load verbal working memory, resulted in a larger decrement in switching than a nonverbal foot tapping condition; again, the effect was particularly exaggerated when the stimulus switched. We recently examined the impact of a concurrent working memory load in a related voluntary task span procedure. In this paradigm, modeled from the Logan (2004) task span procedure, subjects generate a six-task sequence (three shape and three height judgments) and then carry out the tasks on a subsequent series of stimuli. Subjects are instructed to try to generate all of the possible sequences (20 total) in a random fashion. Concurrent working memory loads result in the generation of less complex tasks sequences, generally associated with fewer switches between tasks (Reiman & Arrington, in preparation).

While the previous studies show general effects of load on the probability of switching tasks, other research has shown more specific effects of the type of information held in working memory on the selection of particular tasks. Weaver and Arrington (2010) had subjects hold either identity or spatial information in working memory while performing a series of voluntary task switching trials that involved either identity or spatial judgments on a series of letter and number stimuli appearing in different locations. Task selection was biased such that subjects were more likely to select the task that matched the type of information being maintained in working memory. This result demonstrates that the contents of working memory can have a direct effect on the task selection process.

Individual Differences

Researchers are showing growing interest in using the voluntary task switching paradigm to investigate individual differences in task selection in volitional behavior. Two different general approaches will be reviewed here. First, the correlation of task choice behavior in voluntary task switching with individual differences measures of various cognitive processes has been used to examine what processes are critical for volitional task choice. Second, voluntary task switching has been used to consider how volitional behavior may vary for individuals in different groups (e.g., individuals with autism).

Researchers have examined individual differences in task choice and performance in voluntary task switching with three cognitive processes: inhibition, working memory, and executive control. In considering individual differences in task choice and task performance measures, Mayr and Bell (2006) found a moderate correlation between local switch costs and switch rate, and a large correlation between global switch costs and switch rates. They interpret this later correlation as evidence of differential involvement of inhibition in task choice and task performance with subjects who better inhibit the previous trial showing both slowed performance on repetition trials relative to a single task condition (global switch costs) and a greater probability of switching tasks. Butler et al. (2011) examined the relationship between individual differences in working memory capacity and task choice and performance in voluntary task switching. Individual differences in working memory capacity showed only very weak and inconsistent correlations with task choice, which is surprising given the effect of experimental manipulations of working memory load on task choice. However, in the voluntary task span procedure described earlier, a correlation between working memory capacity and sequence complexity (measured in terms of number of switches) did appear (Reiman & Arrington, in preparation). In sum, these results suggest a relationship between working memory capacity and choice in voluntary task selection that is small and may not be robust across choice environments. Executive control, as measured in the attention network test (Fan, McCandliss, Sommer, Raz, & Posner, 2002) as the ability to resolve response conflict from incompatible distractors, correlates with task choice in both voluntary task switching (Arrington & Yates, 2009) and voluntary task span (Reiman & Arrington, in preparation) procedures, with more efficient executive control being associated with choices involving greater switching.

In addition to individual-differences studies focused on the relationship between task choice and specific measures of various cognitive functions, researchers have examined voluntary task switching behavior in populations where deficits in executive functioning are suspected. During voluntary task switching, the switch rate is lower for older adults than for young adults (Terry & Sliwinski, 2012) and for individuals with higher scores on an Autism-Spectrum Quotient questionnaire than for those with lower scores (Poljac, Poljac, & Yeung, 2012). Interestingly, in both studies, the differences between groups were limited to task choice measures and did not appear in the RT switch costs.

Neuroanatomical and Neurophysiological Studies

Researchers interested in the neural underpinnings of volitional behavior have begun using the voluntary task switching paradigm in a small number of neuroimaging and electrophysiological recording studies.[1] An early functional magnetic resonance imaging (fMRI) study by Forstmann, Brass, Koch, and von Cramon (2006) contrasted no choice versus two- or three-alternative task choice conditions. During voluntary task selection, regions of the frontal and parietal cortices were active. In particular, these researchers focused on the role of a portion of the midcingulate cortex referred to as the rostral cingulate zone (RCZ). Noting that this region has previously been associated with error detection and conflict monitoring, Forstmann et al. suggest that in the context of voluntary task switching, the activity in this region may be associated with task-level response conflict. A recent fMRI investigation expanded on this work to show that the involvement of RCZ in task choice varied as a function of the nature of that choice for particular stimuli (Demanet, De Baene, Arrington, & Brass, 2013). When subjects chose to perform a task that was highly practiced for a particular stimulus, RCZ activity was lower than when subjects chose the unpracticed task. Interestingly, this pattern of modulation when choice was biased by past experience only occurred in RCZ and not in other frontal and parietal regions active during voluntary task selection. Neither of these fMRI studies considered differences in activation as a function of task repetition versus task switch conditions, however, leaving open an important avenue of investigation for future research.

The temporal dynamics of selection processes in voluntary task switching have been studied using event-related potentials (ERPs). Building on their fMRI work highlighting the key role of RCZ in voluntary selection, Forstmann and colleagues (Forstmann, Ridderinkhof, Kaiser, & Bledowski, 2007) recorded ERPs time-locked both to a cue indicating whether a choice would be needed and the target stimulus. In support of the previous fMRI results, the authors found a preparatory medial frontal modulation that appears to be associated with the process of voluntary task selection. More recently, two important insights into the selection process in voluntary task switching have come from an ERP study conducted by Vandamme, Szmalec, Liefooghe, and Vandierendonck (2010). First, they found a larger contingent negative variation on switch trials compared with repetition trials. Importantly, this difference occurred in a 600-ms interval prior to stimulus onset, indicating that task preparation precedes stimulus onset. Second, examination of the lateralized readiness potential (LRP), when the two tasks were mapped to different hands, indicated that activity on task switches was suggestive of an initial tendency to repeat tasks that must be overcome. Again, this foreperiod LRP peaked prior to stimulus onset suggestive of a tendency to repeat tasks that was overcome on switch trials with advance preparation.

THEORETICAL ACCOUNTS OF TASK CHOICE

In light of the empirical work described here, it appears clear that task selection processes are influenced by both top-down (controlled) and bottom-up (automatic) factors. In line with these observations, recent theorizing about the processes of task selection in voluntary task switching focus on two components: (a) a controlled process of task selection that involves selecting or retrieving tasks from long-term memory to match some general idea of a random sequence and (b) an automatic process that occasionally overrides the controlled task selection.

Competing Heuristics

Arrington and Logan (2005) conceived of the selection process as a race between two competing heuristics. The first is a representativeness heuristic built from a model of randomness developed by Rapoport and Budescu (1997). This heuristic operates as a controlled process involving the maintenance of a series of recently performed tasks in working memory and the selection of the task on the current trial to make that sequence match most closely the idea of a random sequence. This mechanism should ultimately lead to more switches than expected based on chance performance given the generally skewed representation of randomness for most subjects. There is some evidence that at long RSIs when there is time to carry out this controlled search process, the repetition bias can actually reverse (Arrington & Logan, 2005). The second is an availability heuristic (Baddeley, 1996), which operates automatically to select the task that is most available in working memory at the point when a choice is required. Generally, the task with the highest level of activation and therefore most available in working memory is the task that was just performed on the previous trial, thus allowing for the operation of the availability heuristic to account for the repetition bias. Further evidence suggests that a variety of other factors that increase task availability also make it more likely that selection of that task will occur (e.g., Arrington, 2008; Arrington et al., 2010; Yeung, 2010). Finally, the balance between the two heuristics can be shifted depending on the characteristics of the decision environments. Factors that decrease the ability to carry out the controlled representativeness heuristic should result in choices biased toward availability. The effects of limited preparation time (Arrington &

Logan, 2005) and concurrent working memory load (Demanet et al., 2010) on the repetition bias support this view.

Chain-Retrieval Model

More recently, Vandierendonck, Demanet, Liefooghe, and Verbruggen (2012) proposed a more formal chain-retrieval model of task selection that also implements both controlled and automatic processes. The primary mechanism for task selection is the retrieval of a chunk or chain of tasks from long-term memory. As with the competing heuristics view, the development of this component of the chain-retrieval model was heavily influenced by the work of Rapoport and Budescu (1997). Foundation models of random generation focus on retrospective monitoring and correction of sequences, whereas the chain-retrieval model focuses on prospective choice, which is able to account for the difficulty of actually switching tasks and include this information in the predicted choice patterns. The frequency with which particular chains are retrieved conforms to a representation of random sequences. However, the ease of performance of the sequence of tasks also determines selection of a chain, such that chains with more repetitions are favored. The retrieval of task chains is a controlled process and is limited by working memory capacity. Additionally, tasks can be triggered in an automatic fashion by the appearance of a stimulus that strongly affords a particular task. In such cases, the triggered task can serve to override the next task in the chain. The authors captured these assumptions in a model with three free parameters representing working memory, chain bias, and bottom-up priming. While the initial evidence supports the basic assumptions of this model, more work is needed to test the specific parameters of the model. For example, future research should test the assumptions made during the development of the model parameters. For one, the parameter related to chain bias assumes that participants' past experience leads them to believe that repetitions are easier than switches, thereby leading to their selection of chains of tasks with more repetitions. Such a bias should be demonstrated in other contexts. Similarly, straightforward relationships between working memory capacity and typical chain length would provide evidence for the working memory parameter.

OUTSTANDING QUESTIONS

While the voluntary task switching technique has been widely used for almost ten years, there are still a number of outstanding methodological and theoretical questions that need consideration as the field moves forward. In this section we address two of these questions. The first is a more methodological question: How do the global task instructions influence choice behavior? The second is a more theoretical question: What is the relationship between task selection and task preparation in voluntary behavior?

TASK INSTRUCTIONS AND TASK CHOICE

The term *voluntary* in the voluntary task switching procedure refers to the fact that on a trial-by-trial basis there is no externally determined "correct" task. Unlike the alternating runs or explicit task-cuing procedures, the experimenter provides no guidance as to the task to perform on each trial. However, it is worth considering that the subjects are always operating under some instructions about how to perform in the task environment more generally. In the initial Arrington and Logan (2004) study, we considered a variety of global instructions designed to ensure that both task repetition and task switch trials would occur, thus allowing sufficient data for analysis. We settled on instructing subjects to perform the tasks randomly and published the verbatim instructions including, "You should try to perform each task on about half of the trials and should perform the tasks in a random order" and an example of a coin toss with the task names on the sides of the coin. Across the majority of subsequent research, researchers have largely duplicated these original instructions or similar instructions such as to be "unpredictable." While these instructions do not specify a particular task on a given trial, they do constrain the appropriate proportion of task choices and task transitions across the run of the experiment.

Little attention has been placed on considering the role that these global instructions have on task selection in voluntary task switching. There are two exceptions. In a study of the persisting activation of task sets, Liefooghe et al. (2010) contrasted performance under the standard task switching instructions with a modified condition in which subjects were instructed to perform tasks equally often but were given no instruction to perform tasks randomly. Switching was slightly less frequent in the modified instruction condition, $p(\text{switch}) = .312$, than in the standard condition, $p(\text{switch}) = .410$. Kessler et al. (2009) demonstrated that switching among tasks would occur in an environment where no global instructions were provided to constrain the choice. Subjects received training on three categorization tasks and were then instructed to perform just one task on each trial. Switching tasks was allowed and was indicated either by a button press that selected the upcoming task (Task Group) or a button press that indicated that a switch to a new task instruction was requested (Switch Group). Switching across conditions ranged between .004 and .132.

Based on the results of these studies, our laboratory has conducted a series of experiments addressing the need for a systematic consideration of the influence of global task instructions on task choice. The first two experiments contrasted global instructions while holding the task environment the same. Experiment 1 used a partially modified instruction requiring that the tasks be performed equally often but not specifying a random order. Experiment 2 used a fully modified instruction placing no constraints on task choice. The second two experiments varied the task environment while using the same fully modified version of the global instructions. Experiment 3 included single-task trials to force both tasks to be maintained actively in memory throughout the experiment. Experiment 4 used tasks in which stimuli might be preferentially associated with one task or another.

In all respects except for the global task instructions, Experiments 1 and 2 used methods similar to those of Arrington (2008) Experiment 1. Subjects performed simple categorization tasks on bivalent stimulus displays that included a number and a letter. As the original focus of the Arrington paper was on the influence of stimulus availability, the onset of the two stimuli was staggered with a varying SOA, though we do not consider those effects at present. The RSI was either 200 or 1000 ms. Following single-task practice, subjects were introduced to the voluntary task switching environment with the following instructions:

> Now that you have practiced each one of the tasks individually, you will do a block of trials where you will be mixing together these two tasks within a single block of trials. You will see both a letter and a number on each trial. You only need to do one task on each trial, either the letter or the number task. You have to choose which task to perform on each trial. We do want you to try to perform the two tasks about equally often, but on any given trial, you get to decide which task to do.

Experiment 1 included the full instructions. Experiment 2 excluded the final sentence. Following the presentation of the instructions, subjects completed 640 trials in ten blocks. For the purposes of the current discussion, we focus only on two dependent measures: task bias and *p*(switch). Task bias refers to the proportion of time that the most frequent task was selected.

Task choice under the standard voluntary task switching instructions used in Arrington (2008) serves as a comparison of task choice behavior for the current series of experiments. Table 6.1 provides the summary data (mean and standard deviation) for task bias and *p*(switch) for Arrington (2008) as well as for the current experiments. Under standard voluntary task switching instructions, subjects' choices appeared to fairly closely follow the global instructions. The task bias was small indicating that subjects performed tasks nearly equally often. The *p*(switch) showed a slight repetition bias. In Experiment 1, subjects again showed compliance with the instruction to perform the tasks equally often. However, under these partially modified instructions that placed no external constraints on task transitions, subjects were almost half as likely to generate task switches. In Experiment 2 with the fully modified instructions, subjects began to display a substantial bias toward performing one of the tasks more frequently than the other. Interestingly, individual differences now appeared in the task bias measure as can be seen in the large standard deviation. Finally, when no global instructions regarding task selection were provided for subjects, there was a marked decrease in the probability of switching between tasks.

In Experiment 3, we addressed the question of whether the reduction in task switching under the fully modified instructions might arise because subjects

Table 6.1. Mean and Standard Deviation (SD) Values for Task Bias and p(Switch) Measures Across Five Studies

	Previous*	Experiment 1	Experiment 2	Experiment 3	Experiment 4
Task bias					
Mean	.514	.517	.692	.743	.720
SD	.012	.015	.265	.195	.156
p(switch)					
Mean	.466	.258	.086	.161	.257
SD	.105	.193	.115	.093	.202

*Data from Arrington (2008).

in that condition allow one of the tasks to be discarded from memory (or even discarded at a more mechanical level by removing one hand from the response keys). We tested this idea by requiring subjects to maintain readiness for both tasks throughout the blocks of trails by interspersing single-task trials with choice trials. On one-ninth of trials, only a letter or number appeared along with a $ symbol at the other target location. On these trials, subjects were forced to perform the task appropriate for the univalent stimulus. Otherwise, the procedures were identical to Experiment 2 including the fully modified instructions. If the large task bias and small *p*(switch) in Experiment 2 were a result of subjects failing to actively maintain task readiness for both tasks, then we would expect to see these effects diminished under the current conditions. This did not occur. Subjects again showed a large bias toward performing the preferred task. Furthermore, while the *p*(switch) value appeared to show an increased choice of task switching, this increase was largely driven by the switching that occurred on or following single task trials. When these tasks were removed the *p*(switch) value dropped to .089, virtually the same as for Experiment 2. These data suggest that subjects switched tasks away from the preferred task when forced to by a single-task trial but returned immediately to the preferred task. Thus, the lack of task switching occurring under fully modified instructions cannot be attributed to simply failing to maintain both tasks.

In a final experiment, we considered whether choice behavior in the absence of specific global instructions would be influenced by a change in the nature of the tasks. The letter and number tasks used in the first three experiments are simple categorization tasks in which the stimulus displays contain separate elements affording each task, thus allowing subjects to ignore one aspect of the stimulus display and perform only one categorization task. Experiment 4 used a different set of tasks: animacy and size judgments of concrete nouns. In this environment, a single stimulus affords both tasks, perhaps making it more difficult for subjects to focus on the performance of just one task while excluding the other dimension of the stimulus. The stimuli in this experiment were 36 concrete nouns divided evenly into categories created by crossing living/nonliving and small/

large categories. Following single task practice (using a different set of practice words), subjects received the fully modified instructions and performed eight blocks of 72 trials each. The results of this study showed that while still maintaining a strong task bias toward one of the tasks, subjects also performed far more task transitions than were seen in either of the other experiments using the fully modified instructions. Further investigation of the pattern of task choice suggested that subjects may have been switching tasks to accommodate particular words that tended to more consistently result in the performance of one task over another (Arrington et al., 2010). Thus, in richer task environments that may draw on past semantic associations between stimuli and tasks, subjects demonstrated a three-fold increase in the degree of spontaneous switching.

In sum, the global instructions provided during voluntary task switching studies do indeed have a large impact on the choice behavior of subjects in terms both of a bias toward performing a particular task and a marked decrease in task switching behavior. Interestingly there was also evidence of some increase in variability across subjects as the constraints of global instructions relaxed (though this effect was not seen in increased standard deviations across all situations), suggesting that in less constrained environments more individual differences may influence task choice. This finding suggests that researchers interested in examining individual differences in voluntary behavior may wish to use modified instructions. Finally, the nature of the task also influenced the choice behavior, indicating the need for researchers to consider the generality of their conclusions about volitional behavior for studies using a single type of task.

Task Selection versus Task Preparation in Voluntary Behavior

The processes that control behavior in multitask environments are bound to be multifaceted. Allport and Wylie (2000) describe one distinction between "endogenous control of task set, in the sense of controlling *which task* is performed" and " 'task readiness'. . . measured by speed of performance" (p. 36). The selection of which task to perform may be governed by processes that are separate from those that configure the attention, decision making, and motor systems to optimally perform that task. In a model where task selection and task preparation are considered as separate processes, it makes sense to consider the relationship between these processes. Logically, task selection should precede and guide task preparation processes. The distinction would be similar to that made in the model of Logan and Gordon (2001) between task-level representation and parameter-level representation of task sets. The task-level representation is a proposition maintained in working memory and linked to the task goal. This task-level representation may be construed as the intention to perform a given task. Thus at one level, task selection can be thought of as the formation or activation of a task-level representation for a given task. The parameter-level representation, which is both present in working memory and transmitted to the subordinate systems, represents preparation of a given task and ultimately determines task performance in the presence of the stimulus. Within this framework, task selection occurs at the task-level representation that will then influence the parameter-level task set that is transmitted to the subordinate systems, thus preparing the system to perform the selected task. The formation of a propositional task-level goal may instantiate the act of voluntary selection, while establishing the parameter-level representation and transmitting the parameters to the subordinate systems implements the current task goal in a manner consistent with the idea of task preparation or readiness.

In standard task switching studies, a sequence retrieved from memory or an external cue provides the endogenous control over which task is selected for performance. Examination of various types of task cues suggests that such cues must be interpreted prior to the establishment of the intended task set (Arrington, Logan, & Schneider, 2007). The processes of task selection are likely to be even more complex in voluntary task switching when the control over which task to perform on a trial-by-trial basis is not imposed by the experimenter but rather is freely selected by the subject on any given trial with only global task instructions. While task selection is under the control of the subject in the sense that no explicit cue is provided on a trial to trial basis indicating the task to be performed, it does not rule out the possibility that stimuli in the environment will be incorporated into and even guide task selection processes. When no task cue is provided, task selection is further removed from and less directly influenced by the environment (Brass & Haggard, 2008). As described here, numerous external factors can influence task selection, and while these effects have all been replicated and are robust, they generally result in relatively small changes in task selection (e.g., 2% to 10%) and thus account for a small portion of the total variability in selection, unlike explicit task cues that determine which task is performed on an almost one-to-one basis. Thus, the presence of these bottom-up effects does not remove the possibility of volitional action being present in the task selection measures; rather, it provides interesting insight into how the external environment is used by the individual in guiding volitional behavior.

Task performance measures in voluntary task switching show robust switch costs, just as in other task switching procedures, though some differences in the time course and occurrence of these switch costs do differ from other paradigms (Arrington & Logan, 2005; Liefooghe et al., 2009). Differences in the preparation to perform a particular task result in differences in RT on task repetition and task switch trials. More weakly prepared task sets, such as occur on task switch trials, lead to slower responding that is more likely to be influenced by stimulus–response incompatibility. Switch costs during voluntary task switching appear to be primarily the result of task preparation processes rather than reflecting the time that it tasks to select a new task (Arrington & Logan, 2005).

The dissociation between task selection and task preparation in voluntary task switching environments can be seen in the relatively small correlations between choice and performance measures. In studies that correlate the switch costs and *p*(switch) values, the correlations range between −.12 and −.45 and are not consistently significant (Arrington & Yates, 2009; Mayr & Bell, 2006). Furthermore, examination of the relationships between these measures and individual differences measures of executive control and working memory show different patterns of correlation. Executive control measures correlated with task choice but not task performance (Arrington & Yates, 2009), while working memory measures correlated with task performance but not task choice (Butler et al., 2011). These findings suggest that these different types of behavioral measures available from voluntary task switching studies may tap into different underlying aspects of volitional control of behavior. Further work directly addressing the distinction between task selection and task preparation should provide interesting insights into volitional behavior.

CONCLUSION

The current volume attests to the wide use of task switching paradigms to study executive control functions. Here, we focus on the growing body of work using the voluntary task switching variant of these paradigms. In a way that other task switching paradigms do not, voluntary task switching goes beyond just addressing how control mechanisms allow for set shifting to examine the conditions under which those shifts will be performed in settings allowing for volitional behavior. Researchers studying questions of executive control should consider the following question, "Do voluntary choice measures tell us something about this process that forced-choice performance measures do not?" If the answer is "Yes," then voluntary task switching may be the appropriate technique.

NOTE

1. In this section, we focus exclusively on studies that have specifically used a voluntary task switching paradigm. However, there are a number of closely related studies that have examined the neural underpinnings of voluntary selection in closely related paradigms such as response selection in a voluntary go/nogo task (e.g., Karch et al., 2010) or in a finger-tapping task (Zhang, Hughes, & Rowe, 2012). Many of these studies complement the basic findings of the research using voluntary task switching.

REFERENCES

Allport, A. & Wylie, G. (2000). Task switching, stimulus–response bindings, and negative priming. In S. Monsell & J. Driver (Eds.), *Control of cognitive processes: Attention and performance. XVIII.* (pp. 35–70). Cambridge, MA: MIT Press.

Arrington, C. M. (2008). The effect of stimulus availability on task choice in voluntary task switching. *Memory & Cognition*, *38*, 991–997.

Arrington, C. M., & Logan, G. D. (2004). The cost of a voluntary task switch. *Psychological Science, 15*, 610–615.

Arrington, C. M., & Logan, G. D. (2005).Voluntary task switching: Chasing the elusive homunculus. *Journal of Experimental Psychology: Learning, Memory, and Cognition, 31*, 683–702.

Arrington, C. M., Logan, G. D., & Schneider, D. W. (2007). Separating cue encoding from target processing in the explicit task-cuing procedure: Are there "true" task switch effects? *Journal of Experimental Psychology: Learning, Memory, and Cognition, 33*, 484–502.

Arrington, C. M., & Rhodes, K. M. (2010). Perceptual asymmetries influence task choice: The effect of lateralized presentation of hierarchical stimuli. *Laterality, 15*, 501–513.

Arrington, C. M., Weaver, S. M., & Pauker, R. L. (2010). Stimulus-based priming of task choice during voluntary task switching. *Journal of Experimental Psychology: Learning, Memory, and Cognition, 36*, 1060–1067.

Arrington, C. M., & Yates, M. M. (2009). The role of attentional networks in voluntary task switching. *Psychonomic Bulletin & Review, 16*, 660–665.

Baddeley, A. (1996). Exploring the central executive. *The Quarterly Journal of Experimental Psychology: Human Experimental Psychology, 49*(A), 5–28.

Brass, M., & Haggard, P. (2008). The what, when, whether model of intentional action. *The Neuroscientist, 14*, 319–325.

Butler, K. M., Arrington, C. M., & Weywadt, C. (2011). Working memory capacity modulates task performance but has little influence on task choice. *Memory & Cognition, 39*, 708–724.

Demanet, J., DeBaene, W., Arrington, C. M., & Brass, M. (2013). Biasing free choices: The role of the rostral cingulate zone in intentional control. *Neuroimage, 72*, 207–213.

Demanet, J., Verbruggen, F., Liefooghe, B., Vandierendonck, A. (2010). Voluntary task switching under load: Contribution of top-down and bottom-up factors in goal-directed behavior. *Psychonomic Bulletin & Review, 3*, 387–393.

Fan, J., McCandliss, B. D., Sommer, T., Raz, A., & Posner, M. I. (2002). Testing the efficiency and independence of attentional networks. *Journal of Cognitive Neuroscience, 14*, 340–347.

Forstmann, B. U., Brass, M., Koch, I., & von Cramon, D. Y. (2006). Voluntary selection of task sets revealed by functional magnetic resonance imaging. *Journal of Cognitive Neuroscience, 18*, 388–398.

Forstmann, B. U., Ridderinkhof, K. R, Kaiser, J., & Bledowski, C. (2007). At your own peril: An ERP study of voluntary task set selection processes in the medial frontal cortex. *Cognitive, Affective, & Behavioral Neuroscience, 7*, 286–296.

Haggard, P. (2008). Human volition: Towards a neuroscience of will. *Nature Reviews Neuroscience, 9*, 934–946.

Gollan, T. H., & Ferreira, V.S. (2009) Should I stay or should I switch? A cost–benefit analysis of voluntary language switching in young and aging bilinguals. *Journal of Experimental Psychology: Learning, Memory, and Cognition, 35*, 640–665.

Karch, S., Feuerecker, R., Leicht, G., Meindl, T., Hantschk, I., et al. (2010). Separating distinct aspects of the voluntary selection between response alternatives: N2- and P3-related BOLD responses. *Neuroimage, 51*, 356–364.

Kessler, Y., Shencar, Y., & Meiran, N. (2009). Choosing to switch: Spontaneous task switching despite associated behavioral costs. *Acta Psychologica, 131*, 120–128.

Kiesel, A., Steinhauser, M., Wendt, M., Falkenstein, M., Jost, K., Philipp, A. M., & Koch, I. (2010). Control and interference in task switching—A review. *Psychological Bulletin, 136*, 849–874.

Liefooghe, B., Demanet, J., & Vandierendonck, A. (2009). Is advance reconfiguration in voluntary task switching affected by the design employed? *The Quarterly Journal of Experimental Psychology, 65*, 850–857.

Liefooghe, B., Demanet, J., & Vandierendonck, A. (2010). Persisting activation in voluntary task switching: It all depends on the instructions. *Psychonomic Bulletin & Review, 17*, 381–386.

Lien, M.-C., & Ruthruff, E. (2008). Inhibition of task set: Converging evidence from task choice in the voluntary task switching paradigm. *Psychonomic Bulletin & Review, 15*, 1111–1116.

Logan, G. D., & Gordon, R. D. (2001). Executive control of visual attention in dual-task situations. *Psychonomic Bulletin & Review, 15*, 1111–1116.

Mayr, U., & Bell, T. (2006). On how to be unpredictable: Evidence from the voluntary task switching paradigm. *Psychological Science, 17*, 774–780.

Millington, R., Poljac, E., & Yeung, N. (2013). Between-task competition for intentions and actions. *The Quarterly Journal of Experimental Psychology, 68*, 1504–1516.

Monsell, S. (2003). Task switching. *TRENDS in Cognitive Sciences, 7*, 134–140.

Navon, D. (1977). Forest before the trees: The precedence of global features in visual perception. *Cognition, 9*, 353–399.

Norman, D. A., & Shallice, T. (1986). Attention to action: Willed and automatic control of behavior. In R. J. Davidson, G. E. Schwartz & D. Shapiro (Eds.), *Consciousness and self-regulation: Advances in research and theory* (Vol. 4, pp. 1–18). New York: Plenum Press.

Orr, J. M., Carp, J., & Weismann, D. H. (2011). The influence of response conflict on voluntary task switching: A novel test of the conflict monitoring model. *Psychological Research, 76*, 60–73.

Poljac, E., Poljac, E., & Yeung, N. (2012). Cognitive control of intentions for voluntary actions in individuals with high level of autistic traits. *Journal of Autism and Developmental Disorders, 42*, 2523–2533.

Rapoport, A., & Budescu, D. V. (1997). Randomization in individual choice behavior. *Psychological Review, 104*, 603–617.

Reiman, K. M., & Arrington, C.M. (n.d.). Executive control, working memory and action planning: An individual differences approach. Manuscript in preparation.

Terry, C. P., & Sliwinski, M. J. (2012). Aging and random task switching: The role of endogenous task selection. *Experimental Aging Research, 38*, 87–109.

Vandamme, K., Szmalec, A., Liefooghe, B., & Vanderindonck, A. (2010). Are voluntary switches corrected repetitions? *Psychophysiology, 47*, 1176–1181.

Vandierendonck, A., Demanet, J., Liefooghe, B., & Verbruggen, F. (2012). A chain-retrieval model for voluntary task switching. *Cognitive Psychology, 65*, 241–283.

Weaver, S. M., & Arrington, C. M. (In press). The effect of hierarchical task representations on action selection in voluntary task switching. *Journal of Experimental Psychology: Learning, Memory, and Cognition.*

Weaver, S. M., & Arrington, C. M. (2010). What's on your mind: The influence of the contents of working memory on choice. *The Quarterly Journal of Experimental Psychology, 63*, 726–737.

Weywadt, C., & Butler, K. M. (2013). The role of verbal short term memory in task selections: How articulatory suppression influences task choice in voluntary task switching. *Psychonomic Bulletin & Review, 20*, 334–340.

Yeung, N. (2010). Bottom-up influences on voluntary task switching: The elusive homunculus escapes. *Journal of Experimental Psychology: Learning Memory and Cognition, 36*, 348–362.

Zhang, J., Hughes, L. E., & Rowe, J. B. (2012). Selection and inhibition mechanisms for human voluntary action decisions. *Neuroimage, 63*, 392–402.

7

Inhibitory Control in Task Switching

MIRIAM GADE, STEFANIE SCHUCH, MICHEL D. DRUEY, AND IRING KOCH

INTRODUCTION: WHY ASSUME INHIBITION IN COGNITIVE CONTROL?

In cognitive control, we are interested in selection problems: how do participants chose their next action? And how do they prevent other actions to be performed instead? To gain some understanding of how people solve those problems, the task switch paradigm has become a valuable methodological tool (see, e.g., Kiesel et al., 2010; Monsell, 2003; Vandierendonck, Liefooghe, & Verbruggen, 2010, for recent reviews). In this paradigm, participants are required to perform at least two different tasks (i.e., judging whether a digit is odd or even or whether it is larger or smaller than 5) in random order. Which task is currently relevant is indicated either by a valid task cue (see Meiran, this volume for a description of the procedure) or by position in a memorized sequence. Participants then implement the task set (i.e., the cognitive representation of the currently relevant task; see, e.g., Logan & Bundesen, 2003; Rogers & Monsell, 1995) and produce a response in accordance with the given stimulus–response mapping (see, e.g., Kiesel et al., 2010, for a description of different task switch procedures). The basic finding is an increase in reaction time in task switch trials compared with task-repetition trials. Most theoretical accounts deal with the processes that give rise to these switch costs and the possibility to reduce or counteract them (see Kiesel et al., 2010).

Answers to questions of how the cognitive system achieves a successful selection of task sets come from theories like the one of Norman and Shallice (1986). According to this theory, the cognitive system selects the most activated task set (or schema, in the terminology of Norman and Shallice). In their model, selection thus follows a winner-takes-it-all logic. The most activated schema wins the selection and takes over control. However, to keep the system flexible and allow switching of tasks, which people can perform quite successfully, it is not sufficient to assume activation of task sets as the only mechanism. Imagine two task sets of roughly equal current activation, which one will be selected in the end is probably a matter of chance. One task set might get just a bit more activation, perhaps because other, irrelevant features in the environment further boost its activation. To make sure that it is not chance that decides which task set is most activated, but that we implement the task set indicated by our current goals or by the instructions, inhibition of competing task sets is beneficial in addition to activation of the relevant task set (yet not mandatory, as suggested by Altmann & Gray, 2008, who assume only activation processes but no inhibition). In the model of Norman and Shallice, this inhibition dampens the activation of concurrently active schemata and therefore ensure that the intended or cued schema is selected (see also Houghton & Tipper, 1996, for a comparable model). In sum, with rare exceptions (e.g., Altmann & Gray, 2008), the notion of inhibition in the context of selection is at the bottom of many theories (e.g., Houghton & Tipper, 1996; Klein, 2000; McKay, 1987), and it is therefore not surprising that it has been proposed to also play a role in task switching. The aim of this essay is to provide an overview of inhibitory phenomena that are found when switching among tasks.

The inhibitory mechanism assumed in most models of action selection is *lateral inhibition*, meaning that the strongest competitor(s) of the currently relevant task set is suppressed so that it can no longer compete for selection (Houghton & Tipper, 1996; Norman & Shallice, 1986). Apart from lateral inhibition, *self-inhibition* is also widely assumed to contribute to the success of sequential behavior. The idea behind the principle of self-inhibition is that after selection of a task set, it is inhibited by a negative feedback-loop that is tied to it (e.g., Houghton & Tipper, 1994) to avoid erroneous reexecution or perseveration (Arbuthnott, 1996; Li, Lindenberger, Rünger, & Frensch, 2000; McKay, 1987). Furthermore, proactive and retroactive inhibition can be distinguished (see, e.g., Nigg, 2000). Proactive inhibition acts top-down and is linked to cues or task preparation (e.g., Mayr & Keele, 2000). Retroactive inhibition acts bottom-up and serves to resolve conflict during task performance (e.g., Koch, Gade, Schuch, & Philipp, 2010; Schuch & Koch, 2003).

In the next section, we discuss the role of inhibition in task switching. We will then provide a model case by which we aim to enlighten the problems and solutions arising when invoking inhibitory explanations. The final section is devoted to *n*-2 repetition cost, the most commonly used and widely accepted marker for inhibitory processes in task switching. In the concluding remarks, we briefly discuss the role of inhibitory processes in formal models proposed to account for task switch performance.

METHODOLOGICAL PROBLEMS IN ASSUMING INHIBITION

In this section, we discuss several phenomena in the field of task switching that have been attributed to inhibitory processes. However, as will be shown, for most of these phenomena, activation-only based explanations cannot be ruled out successfully. Therefore, caution seems warranted when attributing performance decrements, such as increases in reaction time (RT) or error rate (ER) to the influence of inhibition.

Performance Decrements as Markers of Inhibition in Task Switching

The empirical marker of inhibition, on a behavioral level, is commonly thought to be the increase in RT and ER when switching to a recently inhibited task set (or task set component), relative to switching to a less recently inhibited task set (component) (Mayr & Keele, 2000). The increase in RT and ER is assumed to be due to persisting inhibition of the task set, such that its activation takes longer to rise above threshold again, which then ensures selection and implementation. If one takes this increase in RT and ER as a marker of inhibition, then there are several phenomena that can be explained as inhibitory aftereffects.

Task Switching Phenomena Attributed to Inhibition

The primary empirical phenomenon in task switching is the task switch cost, denoting a prolonged RT (and increased ER) after a task switch compared with a task repetition. Inhibitory explanations of switch costs have been around from the very beginning, for instance in the initial paper by Allport and Wylie (1999). They assume that negative priming (a classical inhibitory effect from the attention literature, cf. Tipper, 2001) on the level of task sets causes these switch costs, apart from persisting activation of recently performed tasks.

Later on, the measure of task set inhibition became more specific. Only increases in switch costs after incongruent trials, not those after congruent trials, were taken as a measure of task inhibition (Goschke, 2000). The reasoning is that in incongruent trials, the irrelevant task set needs to be inhibited to avoid interference. If the task switches in the following trial, this formerly irrelevant task set becomes relevant, and therefore persisting inhibition needs to be overcome (Meiran, Hsieh, & Chang, 2011; see also Astle, Jackson, & Swainson, 2012; Meiran, Hsieh, & Dimov, 2010, for further refinements of this inhibitory explanation to account for RT (and ER) increases after incongruent trials).

A similar logic serves to explain asymmetric switch costs: When switching between an easier (dominant) and a harder (nondominant) task, switch costs are higher for the dominant than for the nondominant task (Meuter & Allport, 1999). The reasoning is that, when performing the nondominant task, the dominant task needs to be inhibited more strongly than vice versa. Therefore, more inhibition needs to be overcome when switching to the dominant task than when switching to the nondominant task, leading to larger switch costs (but see Schneider & Anderson, 2010, for an alternative explanation).

A common idea behind all these phenomena is that the competing task set is inhibited to ensure a successful switch to the "weaker" (i.e., less dominant, primed to a lesser degree, less well practiced, less S–R compatible, or simply more flexible; cf. Allport & Wylie, 1999; Goschke, 2000; Schuch, Werheid, & Koch, 2012; Yeung & Monsell, 2003a) task set.

Problems for the Assumption of Inhibition as Cause for RT Differences

Although plausible, the assumption of inhibition based on slower RT in a task switch compared with a task-repetition trial bears several problems. The first and most important one constitutes the definition of a proper baseline. The second one refers to the target of inhibition.

With regard to the first problem, the definition of a baseline, it has been pointed out (Philipp, Gade, & Koch, 2007a) that using just two tasks does not warrant to infer inhibitory mechanisms, as differences in RT can be also explained by different levels of initial activation of task sets and the need to achieve a certain activation level that ensures selection and implementation of the task set (cf. Yeung & Monsell, 2003b, for a similar argument). If, for example, participants are asked to switch to a "weaker," less well-trained task, the levels of activation that render the "weaker" and the "stronger" task set to be executable may differ because of long-term practice (Monsell, Yeung, & Azuma, 2000). This means that switching to the weaker task set requires the cognitive system to activate this task set more than the stronger task set. If one further takes into account the winner-takes-it-all logic that most selection models inherit (e.g., Norman & Shallice, 1986), this means that even the usually faster, more-trained (i.e., stronger) task set might need to be activated to ensure its proper implementation when switching from the weaker task set. This reactivation takes some time (or to be more precise, the resolution of conflict between a highly activated, albeit "weaker" task set and a less activated "stronger" task set by means of overall activation in the cognitive system) and might be reflected in asymmetric switch costs. Please note that this explanation in terms of activation differences holds true for any difference in RTs when assessing just two tasks. Therefore, although inhibitory mechanisms might provide a straightforward explanation, a valid alternative explanation relies on activation differences only (Philipp, et al., 2007a).

Alternative Explanation of Increased RT Based on Memory

MacLeod et al. (2003) point to another important source of activation differences that might erroneously be taken as indication of inhibitory processes—the role of episodic memory and the impact of the most recent use of stimuli and responses that might prime (and therefore activate) currently encountered tasks (Koch & Allport, 2006; Waszak, Hommel, & Allport, 2003). According to this account, recently encountered stimuli and responses have an activation advantage compared with those less recently encountered. If now participants are asked to switch among tasks on bivalent stimuli (stimuli that can be used in both tasks), stimulus processing automatically primes the last encountered task set associated with these stimuli, which, in case of a task switch, happens to be the wrong task. Therefore, participants first have to counteract this wrong task activation and raise the activation of the currently relevant task to a sufficient degree for successful performance. This is reflected in prolonged RT (and increased ER). However, this prolongation in RT arises solely because of memory-based activation differences that needed to be counteracted to ensure successful and correct task set implementation and execution.

One field of research in which the debate over which account—associative learning, inhibition, or episodic retrieval—represents the best explanation of the observed pattern of results is the study of response–repetition effects. In the following, we will outline the theoretical lines discussed in this field and the data supporting either one of these accounts. The field of response–repetition effects is a model case about how the same basic data can be explained with or without reference to inhibitory mechanisms.

RESPONSE REPETITION EFFECTS IN TASK SWITCHING

In addition to task switch costs, another standard effect in task switching refers to the pattern of response–repetition effects: Repeating the same response from one trial to the next usually leads to facilitated performance (i.e., decreased RT and lower ER) than switching the response, as long as the task stays the same. When the task switches, however, repeating the same response leads to performance costs (i.e., increased RT and higher ER) relative to switching the response (see, e.g., Hübner & Druey, 2006; Meiran, 2000; Rogers & Monsell, 1995; Schuch & Koch, 2004).

As an example, consider switching between two tasks: categorizing a digit as odd or even and categorizing a digit as larger as or smaller as 5 (see Figure 7.1). Assume that the same left and right response keys are used for responding in both tasks (see also Meiran, this volume). The parity task may require a left key press for "odd" and a right key press for "even"; the magnitude task may require a left key press for "larger" and a right key press for "smaller." When participants press left for "odd" in one trial, they take longer and are more likely to make an error when they have just pressed the same left key for "larger" in the trial before than when having just pressed the right key for "smaller" (see, e.g., Schuch & Koch, 2004).

What is the cause of these response–repetition costs? Do they constitute another empirical marker of inhibitory processes involved in task switching? Over the last two decades, several theoretical accounts of response–repetition costs have been offered, some including inhibitory processes, others not. In the following, we give a short overview of the main theoretical accounts of response-repetition costs.

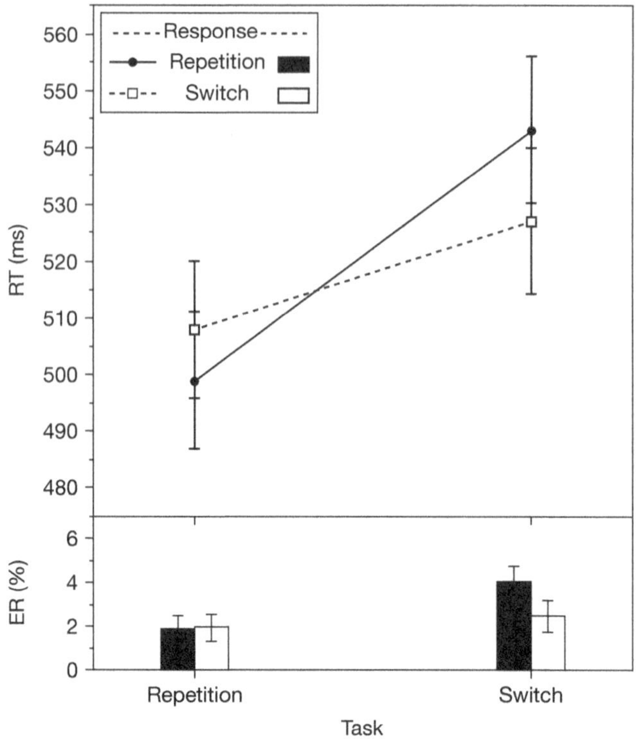

Figure 7.1 The interaction of task sequence and response sequence. Error bars represent 95% within-subject confidence intervals.
Example data are replotted from Table 2 of Hübner and Druey (2008).

Associative Learning Account

Rogers and Monsell (1995) offered several explanations for the observed pattern of response-repetition benefits versus costs in task repetitions versus task switches, respectively. One idea was that the strengths of associations between stimulus categories and responses are continuously modified over time. Every time a response is selected, the association between this response and the current task-relevant stimulus category is strengthened. If, on the next trial, the same response needs to be selected, but in the context of a different task, there is interference between the different category–response associations that refer to the same response; this interference is reflected in response–repetition costs. Schuch and Koch (2004, 2010) further elaborated this idea and suggested that response–repetition costs reflect interference of task-specific response codes. That is, the left response is associated with the category "odd" in one task but with the category "larger" in the other task, and there is interference when the same response needs to be reinterpreted during a task switch. Meiran (2000) developed a computational model of such "response recoding" processes in task switching. In his connectionist model, the weights of the respective category–response associations are readjusted during every response process, with the currently relevant category–response association being strengthened.

The associative-learning account can be interpreted as an inhibitory account in the sense that it involves lateral inhibition on the level of category–response associations in the course of response selection. In particular, Schuch and Koch (2004) suggested that the category–response associations that refer to the same response are competing and therefore mutually inhibit each other during response selection.

That is, according to this suggestion, inhibition of the competing response code persists over time, leading to performance costs when this response code becomes relevant on the next trial. Note, however, that response–repetition costs do not provide unambiguous evidence for lateral inhibition, due to a lack of baseline. As was outlined here, a difference in RT between two conditions might be due to inhibition of one representation or activation of another.

Response Inhibition Account

Another idea put forward by Rogers and Monsell (1995) is that responses are inhibited after they have been executed to prevent perseveration tendencies. A similar explanation in the context of response repetition effects in simple choice RT tasks has already been suggested by Smith (1968) and can be found in several models on language production (MacKay, 1987), negative priming (Houghton & Tipper, 1996), mental arithmetic (Arbuthnott, 1996), sequential Stroop task (Juvina & Taatgen, 2009), or random number generation (Baddeley, Emslie, Kolodny, & Duncan, 1998). However, how can response inhibition explain the whole pattern of task and response sequence effects? If there was only response inhibition, one would always expect costs for response repetitions relative to response switches, irrespective of the relation between the currently relevant task and the previous task. So, what then is the reason for the response repetition benefit in the task repetition trials? A careful analysis of this situation reveals that response repetitions in task repetition trials necessarily bring along a simultaneous repetition of the relevant stimulus category. Thus, taking up the example given here, if the task in two subsequent trials is to judge digits according to their parity and if both digits require a left response, this means that both digits were odd. Under the assumption that this stimulus category remains active from one trial to the next, the negative effects of response inhibition are counteracted by residual stimulus category activation. Depending on the relative strengths of residual activation and inhibition, the negative effects of response inhibition might not only be compensated but even reversed by priming, thus resulting in a net benefit for response repetitions in task-repetition trials. Hence, in this framework, two opposing mechanisms account for the response repetition costs in task switch trials and the response–repetition benefits in task-repetition trials: response inhibition and stimulus category priming (Druey & Hübner, 2008; Hübner & Druey, 2006; Steinhauser, Hübner, & Druey, 2009; see also Koch, Schuch, Vu, & Proctor, 2011).

In a recent study, Oberauer, Souza, Druey, and Gade (2013) extended this framework and partly integrated it with the association learning accounts. In their study, they showed that stimulus category priming is usually not sufficient to reverse the response inhibition effects. But there is a second mechanism adding to the positive priming effects in task repetition trials and thus counteracting response inhibition: the strengthened association between stimulus category and response. Together, these two mechanisms are usually sufficiently strong to produce response repetition benefits in task repetition trials. Moreover, this extension of the original model provides an interesting integration of the associative learning and the inhibition accounts (cf. Schuch & Koch, 2004).

The inhibitory process proposed in this framework is not simply lateral response inhibition, because lateral inhibition in this context would result in an increased activation difference in favor of the just executed response and not to its disadvantage. Rather, the just executed response is specifically inhibited. Two possibilities can be considered in producing such an effect: first, automatic self-inhibition and, second, strategic preparation-linked inhibition. By now, the question of which of these options is actually valid cannot be answered conclusively. Whereas Steinhauser et al. (2009) in a lateralized readiness potential study provided evidence in favor of a strategic-like explanation, where response inhibition is directly linked to the preparation of the new upcoming task, computational models dealing with mechanisms preventing perseveration usually implement the respective inhibitory processes according to the concept of automatic self-inhibition (e.g., Houghton & Tipper, 1996; Logan & Gordon, 2001).

Episodic Retrieval Account

A third account for the response–repetition effects in task switching has recently been proposed by Altmann (2011). He argues that the pattern of response–repetition costs and benefits can be explained by an episodic retrieval account. An episode is one trial in a task switch experiment, which involves a set of features, such as task cue, task, stimulus, and response. Altmann assumes that all features of an episode become associated and bound together. If, in the future, a feature of a previous episode is repeated, this feature activates the whole previous episode (cf. Hommel et al., 2001; Waszak et al., 2003). This leads to facilitation if the whole previous episode is repeated but to interference if the present episode differs in some features from the previous episode. The more similar the number of repeating and nonrepeating features, the larger is the interference. In particular, the actual amount of interference is determined by a matching process, with the number of mismatches relative to the number of matches reflecting the degree of interference.

As a concrete example, consider the scenario described here, where switching between a parity and a magnitude task is required. Assume further that the same digit cannot be repeated from one trial to the next (as is often the case in task switching studies; cf. Altmann, 2011). Let us first consider task repetitions: in response repetitions, the task cue, the task, and the response repeat; in response switches, only the task cue and the task repeat. Hence, three of four features repeat in response repetitions, but only two of four repeat in response switches. The number of repeating and nonrepeating features is less similar in the former (three and one) than in the latter (two and two) case, which explains why performance is better in response repetition than in response switch trials. Second, consider task switches: In response repetitions, only the response repeats (i.e., one of four features). In response switches, no features repeat (i.e., none of four features). The number of repeating and nonrepeating stimuli is more similar in response repetitions (one versus three) than in response switches (none versus four), which explains why performance is more impaired in the former than in the latter condition.

A possible weakness of the episodic retrieval account is that it is not clear how many features compose an episode. For instance, in the given scenario, one could ask why the stimulus category is not considered as an additional feature. Furthermore, some of the results in the literature (e.g., the previous-trial congruency effect; Altmann, 2011; Druey & Hübner, 2008) can only be explained with the help of several additional assumptions regarding the weighting of the mismatching features.

Does the episodic retrieval account of response repetition effects in task switching involve inhibitory processes? At first sight, it does not seem to. At second sight, however, inhibitory processes might play a role in this model, too. In particular, when episodic binding takes place, a feature that is currently bound within one episode is less accessible for binding within another episode (see Hommel et al., 2001; Stoet & Hommel, 1999). Being "less accessible," however, might as well be conceived of as "being inhibited" (cf. Schuch & Koch, 2004).

A crucial aspect of the episodic retrieval account is that the response is also a feature of the present episode (cf. Altmann, 2011). As a consequence, the response, once it is selected, also serves as a retrieval cue, activating features that previously have been associated with it. Thus, the correct response can be selected (presumably by rule-driven processes?) and only after the response has been selected the episodic matching process comes into play. That is, according to this model, response–repetition effects in task switching reflect processes that take place *after* a response has been correctly selected. This is in fact in accord with the assumptions of the associative learning models (cf. Meiran, 2000, Philipp, Jolicoeur, Falkenstein, & Koch, 2007b; Schuch & Koch, 2004) as well as with the inhibition account, according to which a response is inhibited after it has been selected and executed (cf. Hübner & Druey, 2006).

Integrative Perspective

Although the three theoretical accounts of response repetition effects in task switching outlined here differ in a number of ways, they have two important aspects in common. First, they all involve some kind of "inhibition," at least if inhibition is defined on a functional level as some mental representations being less accessible than others. The inhibition account explicitly proposes that previously executed responses are inhibited. The associative learning and episodic retrieval accounts do not explicitly refer to the concept of inhibition. Nevertheless, some mechanisms within these models are functionally equivalent to inhibition (i.e., lateral inhibition of competing stimulus–response associations in the course of response selection; responses bound into one episode being less accessible for binding into a new episode).

Second, all three theoretical accounts agree that response–repetition costs in task switches reflect processes that take place *after* a response has been (correctly) selected. This is true for the episodic retrieval model (Altmann, 2011), the associative learning models (cf. Meiran, 2000; Philipp et al., 2007b; Schuch & Koch, 2004), as well as for the inhibition account, according to which a response is inhibited after it has been selected and executed (Hübner & Druey, 2006; Druey, 2014).

Hence, although the exact mechanisms underlying response–repetition effects in task switching are still under debate, a common picture is emerging (see Oberauer et al., 2013, for a suggestion). More research is needed to further enable integration of the different accounts (cf. Tipper, 2001).

INHIBITION IN TASK SWITCHING AS MEASURED BY *N*-2 REPETITION COSTS

To disentangle accounts relying on episodic memory and associative learning from those assuming inhibitory mechanisms, clever experimental designs are required. One such clever design includes the introduction of a third task, which allows establishing a proper comparison between task sequences and leads to a less ambiguous proof of inhibitory mechanisms in task switching. The remainder of this essay is dedicated to this inhibitory effect, the research it has generated, and the questions it answers.

In a task switching study using three different tasks, Mayr and Keele (2000) introduced an odd-item out paradigm. In this paradigm, participants were asked to indicate the location of the item differing from the other items in the cued dimension (e.g., size, tilt, or colour). Mayr and Keele used three-dimensional stimuli, so that they could compare performance in trial *n* (in the following examples indicated as underlined dimension) after an *n*-2 change (i.e., sequences of the type CB*A*, whereby C, B, and A denote different dimensions) to performance after an *n*-2 repetition (i.e., sequences of the type AB*A*). In a series of experiments, they observed *n-2 task repetition costs*, showing that it was harder to return to a recently performed task (*n*-2 task repetitions) than to switch to a less recently performed task (*n*-2 task nonrepetition). Mayr and Keele (2000) termed these observed costs "backward inhibition," but we prefer to use the theoretically more neutral term "*n*-2 repetition costs" (Koch et al., 2010). Using three tasks instead of two allowed establishing a valid marker of inhibitory processes, because it provided conditions in which an activation-based account and an inhibition-based account make different predictions.

For an activation-based account, switching back to a recently performed task (i.e., AB*A*) should be beneficial compared with switching to a less recently performed task (i.e., CB*A*); thus, an *n*-2 repetition benefit should emerge. On the other hand, an inhibition account, which states that the last performed task (or last attended-to stimulus dimension) should be suppressed to prevent interference while establishing a new task/attending to a new dimension, predicts *n*-2 repetition costs because the recently inhibited task still suffers from residual inhibition and therefore RT (and ER) will be increased.

The introduction of a third dimension (or task) thus allows for the comparison of *n*-2 repetition and *n*-2 switches, which in turn allows testing inhibition-specific predictions. In their study, Mayr and Keele (2000) could also show that other well-known inhibitory phenomena like negative priming (Tipper, 2001) and inhibition of return (Klein, 2000) could not account for *n*-2 task repetition costs. Using this new paradigm, researchers set out to further clarify the role of inhibition in task switching. In the following section, we briefly review the most important findings (see Koch et al., 2010, for a comprehensive review). There is little discussion that inhibition leading to *n*-2 repetition costs reduces the conflict among tasks and ensures successful implementation of the now relevant task set. The main interest of the studies reported here refers to the question as to the processing stage at which conflict among tasks arises. Related to this question of the functional locus of conflict is the question as to the target of inhibition: Is inhibition applied to task sets as a whole, or only to specific parts of the task set such as cue-, stimulus-, or response-related elements of the task set?

Cue-Related Processing

If we break down the elements of a trial in cued task switching, the first elements participants encounter is a cue that indicates which task to perform next. Based on work of Logan and colleagues (e.g., Schneider & Logan, 2005), we not only know that cues might actually influence performance by indicating the task but also that its processing has been shown to affect the size of the switch costs (Logan & Bundesen, 2003; see Jost, de Baene, Koch, & Brass, 2013, for a review). Therefore, studies investigating the role of the cue for the occurrence of *n* 2 repetition costs, and whether it is a target of the inhibitory process, seemed warranted. In the original study by Mayr and Keele (2000), there was a 1:1 mapping between dimension and cue. Mayr and Kliegl (2003) used a 2:1 cue-to-task mapping and found no significant influence of cue repetition or cue change on *n*-2 task repetition costs, although *n*-2 repetition costs were numerically absent with cue repetitions. They accounted for this modulation of *n*-2 repetition costs by cue sequence (repetition vs. switch) as positive priming from the repeated cue. However, Altmann (2007) and Gade and Koch (2008) also used two cues per tasks, and both studies revealed no evidence for cue-related task set inhibition (see Philipp & Koch,

2009, for supporting evidence in language switching). That is, *n*-2 repetition costs were observed, regardless of whether the specific cue repeated or changed. Furthermore, the lack of cue-related inhibition also suggest that task inhibition is not applied proactively (i.e., top-down, Mayr & Keele, 2000) but rather reactively, bound to the emergence of conflict due to persisting activation of stimulus or response categories (see Koch et al., 2010, for a discussion).

Another cue-related variable that might influence the observation of *n*-2 repetition costs was investigated by Druey and Hübner (2007). They found that in all studies reporting *n*-2 repetition costs, the cue remained on the screen and thus temporally overlapped with the target, and concluded that this feature of experimental design might have influenced *n*-2 repetition costs. Therefore, Druey and Hübner (2007) contrasted conditions in which the cue occurred only briefly and participants had to memorize it for performing the correct task with those in which the cue remained on the screen until the response was given. Brief cue presentation requires participants to encode and memorize the cue immediately. Druey and Hübner (2007) found that indeed the continued presence of the cue seems to foster the observation of *n*-2 repetition costs. However, in a replication, Grange and Houghton (2009) showed that temporal overlap between cue and target is not necessary to observe *n*-2 repetition costs.

The previous studies referred to cue identity in *n*-2 task repetitions or the cue-target overlap, but there is also evidence regarding the influence of the type of cue. That the type of cue can influence *n*-2 repetition costs was repeatedly shown by Arbuthnott and colleagues (Arbuthnott, 2005, 2008; Arbuthnott & Frank, 2000; Arbuthnott & Woodward, 2002). In their studies, the actual task was cued by symbols, words, shapes, or, using a column for stimulus presentation, by spatial cues. For spatial cues, no *n*-2 repetition costs were observed. This was taken as evidence that spatial cuing renders the tasks more distinct from each other and reduces between-task conflicts, which then lead to less need for inhibitory mechanisms.

The influence of cue type on the amount of conflict was further investigated by Houghton, Pritchard, and Grange (2009). Using an odd-item out paradigm like Mayr and Keele (2000), they found that cue-transparency, referring to the format of the cue (e.g., a depiction of the dimension of interest) modulated the size of *n*-2 repetition costs. For highly transparent cues, where no "translation" of cue to stimulus was required (e.g., both contained the odd shape), *n*-2 repetition costs were absent, whereas the costs increased with increasing translation demands (e.g., a word cue and a visual stimulus, see also Grange & Houghton, 2011).

To sum up, although studies using a 2:1 cue-to-task mapping showed that the cues themselves seem to be an unlikely target of inhibition, the type of cue nonetheless alters the amount of conflict among tasks and therefore determines the occurrence of *n*-2 repetition costs or alters their size. Yet, the presentation of cues is not necessary to observe *n*-2 repetition costs. Lien and Ruthruff (2008) found evidence for *n*-2 repetition costs in a voluntary task switching paradigm (see Arrington, Reiman, & Weaver, this volume) in which no cues appear because participants can freely select which task to perform.

Stimulus-Related Processing

After the cue the actual target stimulus is presented. In most studies investigating *n*-2 repetition costs, stimuli were multivalent (e.g., Gade & Koch, 2005; Schuch & Koch, 2003), so that participants could not decide based on the stimulus alone which tasks they have to perform. However, there is just one other study examining the effects of stimulus valence on the occurrence of *n*-2 repetition costs. In their study, Sdoia and Ferlazzo (2008) found no evidence for *n*-2 repetition costs with univalent stimuli (i.e., color patches), but *n*-2 repetition costs were observed again when the univalent stimuli were combined with other stimuli yielding trivalent stimuli again, suggesting that multivalent stimuli increase conflict among tasks (Hübner, Dreisbach, Haider, & Kluwe, 2003; Lien, Ruthruff, & Kuhns, 2006; Woodward, Meier, Tipper, & Graf, 2003). Consequently, inhibition is required to resolve this conflict. In a recent study, Gade and Koch (2012) used a paradigm with 25% univalent trials which were randomly interspersed among trivalent trials, if univalent trials lead to less conflict univalent stimuli in trial *n*-1 should lead to less interference. However, that was not was Gade and Koch (2012) found; *n*-2 repetition costs were observed regardless whether participants encountered a univalent trial in *n*-1 or a trivalent trial, with a tendency to observe numerically larger costs after univalent stimulus in trial *n*-1. Thus, conflict during stimulus processing yielded inconsistent pattern so far and seems to require further investigation.

Response-Related Processing

After having processed cue and stimulus, the participant in the experiment is required to select a response (i.e., which key to press to indicate to which category the stimulus belongs to or which of the four targets differs in the indicated dimension). First evidence of the role of response selection for *n*-2 repetition costs came from a study by Schuch and Koch (2003). They asked participants to perform digit classification tasks (i.e., odd/even, smaller/larger than 5, or inner/outer on the number line from 1 to 9) and unpredictably interspersed no-go trials in 25% of all trials. In some experiments, the authors replaced the no-go requirement with the requirement to perform a task-unspecific response ("double press"; i.e., pressing both response keys simultaneously) instead of a task-specific response. In both conditions, they found no *n*-2 repetition cost after a no-go (or double-press) trial (see Figure 7.2), despite clear evidence for cue-based task preparation (i.e., effect of cuing interval) in those trials that turned out to be go trials. This decrease of *n*-2 task repetition costs following no-go trials suggest that *task-specific* response selection in trial *n*-1 is critical for *n*-2 repetition costs to be observed (see also Philipp, Jolicoeur, Falkenstein, & Koch, 2007b).

In another study, Gade and Koch (2007) observed no *n*-2 repetition costs when the response categories were different for the task in trial *n*-1. They instructed participants on four tasks, three of which relied on trivalent stimuli that called for responding to size, color, or type of stimuli by saying "left" or "right," while

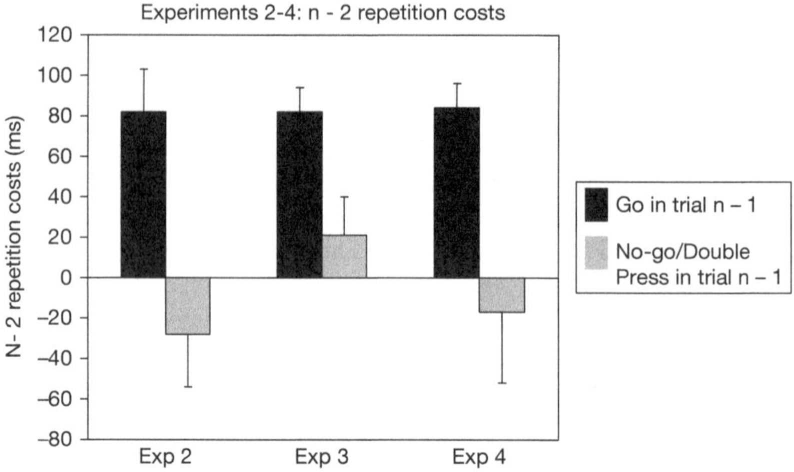

Figure 7.2 The *n*-2 repetition costs in the go and no-go/double-press (DP) conditions, respectively, averaged across cue–stimulus interval conditions. Error bars refer to the standard error of the mean.
Data from Schuch and Koch (2003) for experiments 2 to 4.

the fourth task relied on univalent stimuli requesting participants to judge the fill of a rectangle (i.e., saying "filled" or "empty" or "up" and "down" in different experiments, respectively). In these conditions, there were no significant *n*-2 task repetition costs, but when the response sets for all four tasks overlapped (i.e., participants said "left" or "right" in response to any stimulus as indicated by the S–R mapping), *n*-2 repetition costs were observed even if the fill task with univalent stimuli (i.e., nonoverlapping stimulus sets) was performed in trial *n*-1.

Further evidence for response-related conflict as trigger of inhibitory processes leading to *n*-2 repetition costs was provided by studies from Philipp and colleagues (2007b), who highlighted the role of response execution using a *go-signal procedure*. In this procedure, a go/no-go tone was presented a variable time after stimulus presentation to inform participants to either execute or withhold the response. The authors found clear *n*-2 repetition costs following go-trials, but no or clearly reduced *n*-2 repetition costs were observed after no-go trials even when the signal delay was very long (1500 ms; i.e., with fully prepared responses). This result suggests that processes even later than response selection, such as response initiation or response evaluation, are crucial trigger conditions for inhibition of the preceding task.

Further evidence for response-related conflict as triggering conditions for *n*-2 repetition costs comes from studies assessing switching among response modalities (i.e., manual, pedal, and vocal; Philipp & Koch, 2005) or experiments that differed in response requirements, i.e., asking participants to perform a double key press response for one task (Koch, Philipp, & Gade, 2004).

In sum, there are several studies that suggest that processes of response selection and response execution invoke conflict among tasks that require inhibition of the most recently performed task to solve this conflict. These studies explored the role of manipulations of the type of representation and their overlap across tasks in task inhibition. In the next section, we discuss studies focusing on the influence of temporal variations of the cuing interval or the overall trial duration.

The Influence of Preparation Time and Response Cue Interval on *n*-2 Repetition Costs

Mayr and Keele (2000) speculated that *n*-2 repetition costs contribute to residual task switch costs (i.e., the switch costs that remain even after ample preparation time). One reason for this claim was the observation that *n*-2 repetition costs did not decrease significantly with longer preparation time (e.g., cue–target interval [CTI]). This finding has been replicated several times (e.g., Gade & Koch, 2008; Philipp & Koch, 2006; Schuch & Koch, 2003), suggesting that prolonging preparation time did not affect *n*-2 repetition costs reliably (Koch et al., 2010).

However, Grange and Houghton (2011) suggested a different way of analysis using cumulative distribution functions that provides some evidence that preparation has an effect on the distribution of prepared and unprepared trials. In their analysis, fast responses (which, in their argument, arise from optimally prepared tasks) showed no *n*-2 repetition costs, whereas *n*-2 repetition costs became larger with longer RTs (but see Prior, 2012, for conflicting findings). That is, for the fastest responses, *n*-2 repetition costs were absent, even though the actual preparatory state of these responses must remain undetermined in this purely correlational analysis.

There are three further studies in which *n*-2 repetition costs were reduced to a nonsignificant level with longer CTI. In one study (Koch, Philipp, & Gade, 2004), participants were required to respond with a double key-press for one of the tasks. In the second study, which examined language switching (Philipp et al., 2007a), participants were asked to name digits in German, English, or French. In the third study (Gade & Koch, 2012), participants were required to perform classification tasks (letter, digit, and symbol classification), but univalent stimuli were presented in 25% of trials. That is, all three studies differed in some respect from the standard paradigm used to assess *n*-2 repetition costs. These differences might account for the finding of significantly reduced *n*-2 repetition costs, but the exact role of these differences in the influence of prolonged preparation time on *n*-2 repetition costs is not yet fully conclusive and warrants further investigation.

Another timing interval that can be manipulated in task switching is the response–cue interval (RCI; Meiran, Chorev, & Sapir, 2000). The duration of this interval has been found to affect *n*-2 repetition costs (Gade & Koch, 2005; Mayr, 2002; Mayr & Keele, 2000). The *n*-2 repetition costs are reliably smaller after a long RCI compared with a short RCI. More specifically, though, Gade and Koch showed, using a trial-by-trial manipulation of RCI, that the duration of the RCI in trial *n*-2 instead of that in trial *n*-1 is crucial for the amount of inhibition observed. They proposed that the decrease in task activation during a long RCI leads to less

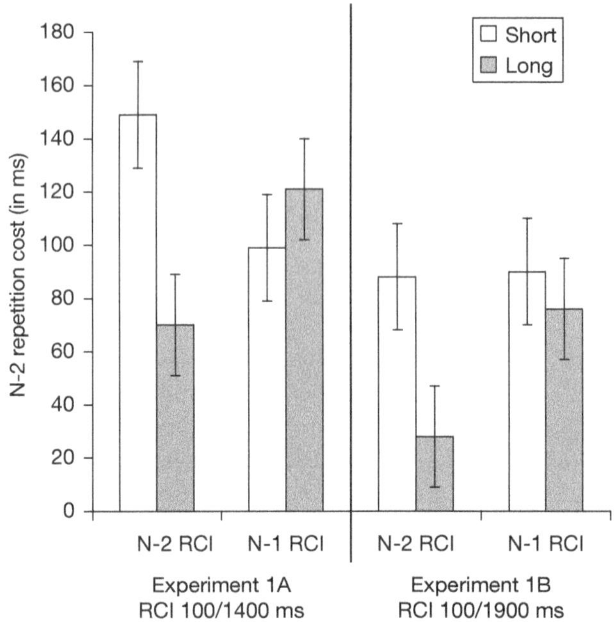

Figure 7.3 Experiment 1A used short RCI of 100 ms, compared with a long RCI of 1400 ms. In Experiment 1B, short RCI was again 100 ms and long RCI was 1900 ms. Error bars refer to standard error of the mean.
Data from Gade and Koch (2005).

conflict when establishing the task in trial *n*-1, so that less inhibition of the previous task is required. This provides further evidence for the above mentioned linkage between the amount of conflict experienced and the size of *n*-2 repetition costs (see also Arbuthnott, 2008; Philipp et al., 2007a, for a similar argument).

In sum, with respect to timing manipulation, *n*-2 repetition costs have been found to be largely unaffected by prolonged preparation time in some studies but not in other studies, so that the pattern of results is not fully conclusive. In contrast, *n*-2 task repetition costs seem to decrease with long RCI, suggesting that inhibition dissipates over time, even though, again, the underlying mechanism is not yet fully understood.

Clinical Populations and Elderly Participants

The prefrontal cortex is commonly assumed to be the neural substrate of executive functions (Dreher & Berman, 2002; Miller, 2000). Therefore, studies in patients with lesions in the prefrontal cortex (PFC) or psychiatric or neurologic disorders affecting prefrontal functions seem to be informative with respect to the role of PFC in task inhibition. Mayr et al. (2006), for instance, examined task set selection and inhibition in patients with right and left prefrontal lesions. Patients with lesions in the left PFC exhibited deficits in task set selection (i.e., increased switch costs), whereas patients with lesions in the right PFC were found to have weaker task set inhibition (i.e., lack of *n*-2 repetition costs), which points to a critical role of the right PFC in inhibition (cf. Aron, Robbins, & Poldrack, 2004). The notion of right PFC involvement in task inhibition has also found empirical support in a neuroimaging study (Dreher & Berman, 2002) in a paradigm requiring participants to switch among three tasks.

Another neuroanatomical structure that is of interest when searching for the neural correlates of task inhibition are the basal ganglia which are known to have strong connections to the frontal lobes (Alexander, De Long, & Strick, 1986). Moritz et al. (2004) found no evidence for diminished inhibitory abilities in patients with obsessive-compulsive disorder, and Fales et al. (2006) investigated patients with Parkinson's disease and found increased ER for *n*-2 repetitions but no difference in RT. That is, with respect to patients' studies, there are some hints that task inhibition as measured by *n*-2 repetition costs can be altered by pathological conditions affecting either frontal lobes or strongly connected regions, but further investigation seems needed.

Another population of participants known to suffer from decline of PFC function are elderly participants (West, 1996). If one assumes that intact PFC functioning is crucial for *n*-2 repetition costs to be observed, it is surprising that no decline in *n*-2 repetition costs in elderly participants (over 60 years of age) was found, although the study of Mayr (2001) as well as a recent study by Lawo, Philipp, Schuch, and Koch (2012) found impairments in dealing with task interference in task switching (Mayr, 2001) or decreased preparation benefits (Lawo et al., 2012).

Taken together, the data of patients thought to suffer from impaired PFC function or from decrement of basal ganglia functions show no consistent evidence for an impairment of task inhibition. Likewise, studies examining *n*-2 repetition costs in elderly participants did not find evidence for a decrease in the ability to inhibit a competing task set.

Summary and Final Remarks

From the very beginning, theorizing on task switching invoked explanations based on the inhibition of competing task sets (e.g., Allport & Wylie, 1999). However, for many seemingly inhibitory phenomena, there are viable noninhibitory accounts, and lively debates regarding this issue are still going on. Furthermore, as pointed out by our review and discussion of response–repetition effects in task switching, integrative accounts combining memory-based and inhibitory mechanisms are clearly desirable but yet not fully developed.

To our knowledge, *n*-2 repetition costs are the only nondisputed inhibitory phenomenon in task switching. They have been observed in many studies and across different paradigms (see Koch et al., 2010, for a review). Given the robustness of this inhibition effect across various paradigms, we propose that *n*-2 repetition costs represent a marker of inhibition in sequential task performance. However, this does not imply that the absence of (significant) *n*-2 repetition costs indicates a lack of inhibition (see Grange, Juvina & Houghton, 2012, for a profound discussion and a formal model on this issue). Rather, the finding of small or even slightly reversed *n*-2 repetition costs might be due to inhibition and activation counteracting each other (as in all two process models, see Druey & Hübner, 2008).

One important step in research on inhibition of task sets is the incorporation of *n*-2 repetition costs in models of task switching (cf. Altmann & Gray, 2008; Gilbert & Shallice, 2002). So far, the published models only comprise two-task situations, and most of them incorporate lateral inhibition mechanisms to deal with competition among tasks. A first attempt to model *n*-2 repetition costs has been made by Grange and colleagues (2012) and will for sure further nourish the discussion about the exact underlying mechanisms and the type of inhibitory processes involved.

Existing research on *n*-2 repetition costs has been fruitful in identifying triggering conditions for task-related inhibition. However, because of the flexibility of task inhibition (it is observed after cue-, stimulus-, or response-triggered conflict), its exact target within the cognitive representation of a task remains to be specified. Possible targets of the inhibition could be the task cues, responses, stimuli, or the complete task set, and the exact target might vary with the source of conflict in the particular experimental situation.

REFERENCES

Alexander, G. E., DeLong, M. R., & Strick, P. L. (1986). Parallel organization of functionally segregated circuits linking basal ganglia and cortex. *Annual Review of Neuroscience*, *9*, 357–381. doi:10.1146/annurev.ne.09.030186.002041

Allport, A., & Wylie, G. (1999). Task-switching: Positive and negative priming of task-set. In G. W. Humphreys, J. Duncan & A. M. Treisman (Eds.), *Attention, space and action: Studies in cognitive neuroscience* (pp. 273–296). Oxford, UK: Oxford University Press.

Altmann, E. M., & Gray, W. D. (2008). An integrated model of cognitive control in task switching. *Psychological Review*, *115*, 602–639. doi:10.1037/0033-295X.115.3.602

Altmann, E. M. (2007). Cue-independent task-specific representations in task switching: Evidence from backward inhibition. *Journal of Experimental Psychology: Learning, Memory, & Cognition*, *33*, 892–899. doi:10.1037/0278-7393.33.5.892

Altmann, E. M. (2011). Testing probability matching and episodic retrieval accounts of response-repetition effects in task switching. *Journal of Experimental Psychology: Learning, Memory, and Cognition*, *37*, 935–951. doi:10.1037/a0022931

Arbuthnott, K. D. (1996). To repeat or not to repeat: Repetition facilitation and inhibition in sequential retrieval. *Journal of Experimental Psychology: General*, *125*(3), 261–283. doi:10.1037/0096-3445.125.3.261

Arbuthnott, K., & Frank, J. (2000). Executive control in set switching: Residual switch costs and task-set inhibition. *Canadian Journal of Experimental Psychology*, *54*, 33–41. doi:10.1037/h0087328

Arbuthnott, K., & Woodward, T. S. (2002). The influence of cue-task association and location on switch cost and alternating-switch cost. *Canadian Journal of Experimental Psychology*, *56*, 18–29. doi:10.1037/h0087382

Arbuthnott, K. (2005). The influence of cue type on backward inhibition. *Journal of Experimental Psychology: Learning, Memory, & Cognition*, *31*, 1030–1042. doi:10.1037/0278-7393.31.5.1030

Arbuthnott, K. (2008). Asymmetric switch costs and backward inhibition: Carryover activation and inhibition in switching between tasks of unequal difficulty. *Canadian Journal of Experimental Psychology*, *62*, 91–100. doi:10.1037/1196-1961.62.2.91

Aron, A. R., Robbins, T. W., & Poldrack, R. A. (2004). Inhibition and the right inferior frontal cortex. *Trends in Cognitive Sciences*, *8*, 171–177. doi:10.1016/j.tics.2004.02.010

Astle, D. E., Jackson, G. M., & Swainson, R. (2012). Two measures of task-specific inhibition. *The Quarterly Journal of Experimental Psychology*, *65*(2), 233–251. doi:10.1080/17470210903431732

Baddeley, A., Emslie, H., Kolodny, J., & Duncan, J. (1998). Random generation and the executive control of working memory. *The Quarterly Journal of Experimental Psychology*, *51A*, 819–852. doi:10.1080/027249898391413

Dreher, J.-C., & Berman, K. F. (2002). Fractionating the neural substrate of cognitive control processes. *Proceedings of the National Academy of Sciences of the United States of America*, *99*, 14595–14600. doi:10.1073/pnas.222193299

Druey, M., & Hübner, R. (2007). The role of temporal cue-target overlap in backward inhibition under task switching. *Psychonomic Bulletin & Review*, *14*, 749–754. doi:10.3758/BF03196832

Druey, M. D., & Hübner, R. (2008). Response inhibition under task switching: its strength depends on the amount of task-irrelevant response activation. *Psychological Research*, *72*, 515–527. doi:10.1007/s00426-007-0127-1

Druey, M. D. (2014). Stimulus-category and response-repetition effects in task switching: An evaluation of four explanations. *Journal of Experimental Psychology: Learning, Memory, and Cognition*, *40*(1), 125–146. doi:10.1037/a0033868

Fales, C. L., Vanek, Z. F., & Knowlton, B. J. (2006). Backward inhibition in Parkinson's disease. *Neuropsychologia*, *44*, 1041–1049. doi:10.1016/j.neuropsychologia.2005.11.002

Gade, M., & Koch, I. (2005). Linking inhibition to activation in the control of task sequences. *Psychonomic Bulletin & Review*, *12*, 530–534. doi:10.3758/BF03193800

Gade, M., & Koch, I. (2007). The influence of overlapping response sets on task inhibition. *Memory & Cognition*, *35*, 603–609. doi:10.3758/BF03193298

Gade, M., & Koch, I. (2008). Dissociating cue-related and task-related processes in task inhibition: Evidence from using a 2:1 cue to task mapping. *Canadian Journal of Experimental Psychology*, *62*, 51–55. doi:10.1037/1196-1961.62.1.51

Gade, M., & Koch, I. (2012). Inhibitory processes for critical situations—The role of n-2 task repetition costs in human multitasking situations. *Frontiers in Physiology*, *3*, 159. doi:10.3389/fphys.2012.00159

Gilbert, S. J., & Shallice, T. (2002). Task Switching: A PDP model. *Cognitive Psychology*, *44*, 297–337. doi:10.1006/cogp.2001.0770

Goschke, T. (2000). Intentional reconfiguration and involuntary persistence in task-set switching. In S. Monsell & J. Driver (Eds.), *Attention and performance. XVIII. Control of cognitive processes* (pp. 333–355). Cambridge, MA: MIT Press.

Grange, J. A., & Houghton, G. (2009). Temporal cue-target overlap is not essential for backward inhibition in task switching. *Quarterly Journal of Experimental Psychology, 62*, 1068–2079. doi:10.1080/17470210802696096

Grange, J. A., & Houghton, G. (2010). Heightened conflict in cue-target translation increases backward inhibition in set-switching. *Journal of Experimental Psychology: Learning, Memory, & Cognition, 36*, 1003–1009. doi:10.1037/a0019129

Grange, J. A., & Houghton, G. (2011). Task preparation and task inhibition: A comment on Koch, Gade, Schuch & Philipp (2010). *Psychonomic Bulletin & Review, 18*, 211–216. doi:10.3758/s13423-010-0023-3

Grange, J. A., Juvina, I., & Houghton, G. (2012). On costs and benefits of n-2 repetitions in task switching: Towards a behavioural marker of cognitive inhibition. *Psychological Research*, 1–12. doi:10.1007/s00426-012-0421-4

Hommel, B., Müsseler, J., Aschersleben, G., & Prinz, W. (2001). The theory of event coding (TEC): A framework for perception and action. *Behavioral and Brain Sciences, 24*, 849–937. doi:10.1017/S0140525X01000103

Houghton, G., & Tipper, S. (1994). A model of inhibitory mechanisms in selective attention. In D. Dagenbach & T. Carr (Eds.), *Inhibitory processes in attention, memory and language* (pp. 53–112). San Diego, CA: Academic Press.

Houghton, G., & Tipper, S. P. (1996). Inhibitory mechanisms of neural and cognitive control: Applications to selective attention and sequential action. *Brain and Cognition, 30*, 20–43. doi:10.1006/brcg.1996.0003

Houghton, G., Pritchard, R., & Grange, J. A. (2009). The role of cue-target translation in backward inhibition of attentional set. *Journal of Experimental Psychology: Learning, Memory, & Cognition, 35*, 466–476. doi:10.1037/a0014648

Hübner, M., Dreisbach, G., Haider, H., & Kluwe, R. H. (2003). Backward inhibition as a means of sequential task-set control: Evidence for reduction of task competition. *Journal of Experimental Psychology: Learning, Memory, & Cognition, 29*, 289–297. doi:10.1037/0278-7393.29.2.289

Hübner, R., & Druey, M. D. (2006). Response execution, selection, or activation: What is sufficient for response-related repetition effects under task shifting? *Psychological Research, 70*, 245–261. doi:10.1007/s00426-005-0219-8

Jost, K., De Baene, W., Koch, I., & Brass, M. (2013). A review of the role of cue processing in task switching. *Zeitschrift Für Psychologie, 221*(1), 5–14. doi:10.1027/2151-2604/a000125

Juvina, I., & Taatgen, N. A. (2009). A repetition-suppression account of between-trial effects in a modified Stroop paradigm. *Acta Psychologica, 131*(1), 72–84. doi:10.1016/j.actpsy.2009.03.002

Klein, R. M. (2000). Inhibition of return. *Trends in Cognitive Sciences, 4*, 138–147. doi:10.1016/S1364-6613(00)01452-2

Koch, I., Gade, M., & Philipp, A. M. (2004). Inhibition of response mode in task switching. *Experimental Psychology, 51*, 52–58. doi:10.1027/1617-3169.51.1.52

Koch, I., Gade, M., Schuch, S. & Philipp, A. M. (2010). The role of inhibition in task switching. A review. *Psychonomic Bulletin & Review, 17*, 1–14. doi:10.3758/PBR.17.1.1

Koch, I., Schuch, S., Vu, K.-P., & Proctor, R. W. (2011). Response-repetition effects in task switching—Dissociating effects of anatomical and spatial response discriminability. *Acta Psychologica, 136*, 399–404. doi:10.1016/j.actpsy.2011.01.006

Lawo, V., Philipp, A. M., Schuch, S., & Koch, I. (2012). The role of task preparation and task inhibition in age-related task-switching deficits. *Psychology & Aging*, in press. doi:10.1037/a0027455

Li, Z. H., Lindenberger, U., Rünger, D., & Frensch, P. A. (2000). The role of inhibition in the regulation of sequential action. *Psychological Science, 11*, 343–347. doi:10.1111/1467-9280.00268

Lien, M. C., Schweickert, R., & Proctor, R. W. (2003). Task switching and response correspondence in the psychological refractory period paradigm. *Journal of Experimental Psychology: Human Perception and Performance, 29*, 692–712. doi:10.1037/0096-1523.29.3.692

Lien, M. C., Ruthruff, E., & Kuhns, D. (2006). On the difficulty of task switching: Assessing the role of task-set inhibition. *Psychonomic Bulletin & Review, 13*, 530–535. doi:10.3758/BF03193881

Lien, M. C., & Ruthruff, E. (2008). Inhibition of task set: Converging evidence from task choice in the voluntary task-switching paradigm. *Psychonomic Bulletin & Review, 15*, 1111–1116. doi:10.3758/PBR.15.6.1111

Logan, G. D., & Gordon, R. D. (2001). Executive control of visual attention in dual-task situations. *Psychological Review, 108*(2), 393–434. doi:10.1037//0033-295X.108.2.393

Logan, G. D., & Bundesen, C. (2003). Clever homunculus: Is there an endogenous act of control in the explicit task cuing procedure? *Journal of Experimental Psychology: Human Perception & Performance, 29*, 575–599. doi:10.1037/0096-1523.29.3.575

MacLeod, C. M., Dodd, M. D., Sheard, E. D., Wilson, D. E., & Bibi, U. (2003). In opposition to inhibition. *The Psychology of Learning and Motivation, 43*, 163–214. doi:10.1016/S0079-7421(03)01014-4

MacKay, D. G. (1987). *The organization of perception and action: A theory for language and other cognitive skills*. New York, NY: Springer.

Mayr, U. (2001). Age differences in the selection of mental sets: The role of inhibition, stimulus ambiguity, and response-set overlap. *Psychology and Aging, 16*, 96–109. doi:10.1037/0882-7974.16.1.96

Mayr, U. (2002). Inhibition of action rules. *Psychonomic Bulletin & Review, 9*, 93–99. doi:10.3758/BF03196261

Mayr, U., & Keele, S. W. (2000). Changing internal constraints on action: The role of backward inhibition. *Journal of Experimental Psychology: General, 129*, 4–26. doi:10.1037//0096-3445.129.1.4

Mayr, U., & Kliegl, R. (2003). Differential effects of cue changes and task changes on task-set selection costs. *Journal of Experimental Psychology: Learning, Memory, & Cognition, 29*, 362–372. doi:10.1037/0278-7393.29.3.362

Mayr, U., Diedrichsen, J., Ivry, R., & Keele, S. W. (2006). Dissociating task-set selection from task-set inhibitionin the prefrontal cortex. *Journal of Cognitive Neuroscience, 18*, 14-21. doi:10.1162/089892906775250085

Meiran, N. (2000). Modeling cognitive control in task-switching. *Psychological Research, 63*, 234–249. doi:10.1007/s004269900004

Meiran, N., Chorev, Z., & Sapir, A. (2000). Component processes in task switching. *Cognitive Psychology, 41*, 211–253. doi:10.1006/cogp.2000.0736

Meiran, N., Hsieh, S., & Dimov, E. (2010). Resolving task rule incongruence during task switching by competitor rule suppression. *Journal of Experimental Psychology: Learning, Memory, and Cognition, 36*(4), 992–1002. doi:10.1037/a0019761

Meiran, N., Hsieh, S., & Chang, C. C. (2011). "Smart inhibition": electrophysiological evidence for the suppression of conflict-generating task rules during task switching. *Cognitive, Affective, & Behavioral Neuroscience, 11*(3), 292–308. doi:10.3758/s13415-011-0037-y

Meuter, R. F. I., & Allport, A. (1999). Bilingual language switching in naming: Asymmetrical costs of language selection. *Journal of Memory and Language, 40*, 25-40. doi:10.1006/jmla.1998.2602

Miller, E. K. (2000). The prefrontal cortex and cognitive control. *Nature Reviews. Neuroscience, 1*(1), 59–65. doi:10.1038/35036228

Monsell, S., Yeung, N., & Azuma, R. (2000). Reconfiguration of task-set: Is it easier to switch to the weaker task? *Psychological Research, 63*, 250–264. doi:10.1007/s004269900005

Moritz, S., Hübner, M., & Kluwe, R. (2004). Task switching and backward inhibition in obsessive-compulsive disorder. *Journal of Clinical and Experimental Neuropsychology, 26*, 67-683. doi:10.1080/13803390490504317

Nigg, J. T. (2000). On inhibition/disinhibition in developmental psychopathology: Views from cognitive and personality psychology and a working inhibition taxonomy. *Psychological Bulletin, 126*, 220–246. doi:10.1037//0033-2909.126.2.220

Norman, D. A., & Shallice, T. (1986). Attention to action: Willed and automatic control of behavior. In Davidson, R. J., Schwartz, G. E., & Shapiro, D. (Eds.), *Consciousness and self-regulation: Advances in research and theory* (Vol 4, pp. 1–18). New York, NY/London, UK: Plenum Press.

Philipp, A. M., Gade, M., & Koch, I. (2007a). Inhibitory processes in language switching? Evidence from switching language-defined response sets. *European Journal of Cognitive Psychology, 19*, 395–416. doi:10.1080/09541440600758812

Philipp, A. M., Jolicoeur, P., Falkenstein, M., & Koch, I. (2007b). Response selection and response execution in task switching: Evidence from a go-signal paradigm. *Journal of Experimental Psychology: Learning, Memory, and Cognition, 33*, 1062–1075. doi:10.1037/0278-7393.33.6.1062

Philipp, A. M., & Koch, I. (2006). Task inhibition and task repetition in task switching. *European Journal of Cognitive Psychology, 18*, 624–639. doi:10.1080/09541440500423269

Philipp, A. M., & Koch, I. (2005). Switching of response modalities. *Quarterly Journal of Experimental Psychology, 58A*, 1325–1338. doi:10.1080/02724980443000656

Philipp, A. M., & Koch, I. (2009). Inhibition in language switching: What is inhibited when switching among languages in naming tasks? *Journal of Experimental Psychology: Learning, Memory, & Cognition, 35*, 1187–1195. doi:10.1037/a0016376

Prior, A. (2012). Too much of a good thing: Stronger bilingual inhibition leads to larger lag-2 task repetition costs. *Cognition, 125*(1), 1–12. doi:10.1016/j.cognition.2012.06.019

Oberauer, K., Souza, A., Druey, M. D., & Gade, M. (2013). Analogous mechanisms of selection and updating in declarative and procedural working memory: Experiments and a computational model. *Cognitive Psychology, 66*(2), 157–211. doi:10.1016/j.cogpsych.2012.11.001

Rogers, R. D., & Monsell, S. (1995). Costs of a predictable switch between simple cognitive tasks. *Journal of Experimental Psychology: General, 124*, 207–231. doi:10.1037//0096-3445.124.2.207

Schneider, D. W., & Anderson, J. R. (2010). Asymmetric switch costs as sequential difficulty effects. *The Quarterly Journal of Experimental Psychology, 63*(10), 1873–1894. doi:10.1080/17470211003624010

Schneider, D. W., & Logan, G. D. (2005). Modeling task switching without switching tasks: A short-term priming account of explicitly cued performance. *Journal of Experimental Psychology: General, 134*, 343–367. doi:10.1037/0096-3445.134.3.343

Schuch, S., & Koch, I. (2003). The role of response selection for inhibition of task sets in task shifting. *Journal of Experimental Psychology: Human Perception & Performance, 29*, 92–105. doi:10.1037//0096-1523.29.1.92

Schuch, S., & Koch, I. (2004). The costs of changing the representation of action: response repetition and response-response compatibility in dual tasks. *Journal of Experimental Psychology: Human Perception & Performance, 30*, 566–582. doi:10.1037/0096-1523.30.3.566

Schuch, S., & Koch, I. (2010). Response-repetition effects in task switching with and without response execution. *Acta Psychologica, 135*, 302–309. doi:10.1016/j.actpsy.2010.07.016

Schuch, S., Werheid, K., & Koch, I. (2012). Flexible and inflexible task-set-sets: Asymmetric interference when switching between emotional expression, sex, and age classification of perceived faces. *The Quarterly Journal of Experimental Psychology, 65*, 994–1005. doi:10.1080/17470218.2011.638721.

Sdoia, S., & Ferlazzo, F. (2008). Stimulus-related inhibition of task set during task switching. *Experimental Psychology, 55*, 322–327. doi:10.1027/1618-3169.55.5.322

Smith, M. C. (1968). Repetition effect and short-term memory. *Journal of Experimental Psychology, 77*(3), 435–439. doi:10.1037/h0021293

Steinhauser, M., Hübner, R., & Druey, M. D. (2009). Adaptive control of response preparedness in task switching. *Neuropsychologia, 47*(8–9), 1826–1835. doi:10.1016/j.neuropsychologia.2009.02.022

Stoet, G., & Hommel, B. (1999). Action planning and the temporal binding of response codes. *Journal of Experimental Psychology: Human Perception and Performance, 25*, 1625–1640. doi:10.1037/0096-1523.25.6.1625

Tipper, S. P. (2001). Does negative priming reflect inhibitory mechanisms? A review and integration of conflicting views. *The Quarterly Journal of Experimental Psychology, 54A*, 321–343. doi:10.1080/02724980042000183

Waszak, F., Hommel, B., & Allport, A. (2003). Task-switching and long-term priming: Role of episodic stimulus-task bindings in task-shift costs. *Cognitive Psychology, 46*, 361–413. doi:10.1016/S0010-0285(02)00520-0

West, R. L. (1996). An application of prefrontal cortex function theory to cognitive aging. *Psychological Bulletin, 120*, 272–292. doi:10.1037//0033-2909.120.2.272

Woodward, T., Meier, B., Tipper, C., & Graf, S. (2003), Bivalency is costly: Bivalent stimuli elicit cautious responding. *Experimental Psychology, 50*, 233–238. doi:10.1026//1618-3169.50.4.233

Yeung, N., & Monsell, S. (2003a). The effects of recent practice on task switching. *Journal of Experimental Psychology: Human Perception and Performance, 29*(5), 919. doi:10.1037/0096-1523.29.5.919

Yeung, N., & Monsell, S. (2003b). Switching between tasks of unequal familiarity: The role of stimulus attribute and response-set selection. *Journal of Experimental Psychology: Human Perception and Performance, 29*, 455–469. doi:10.1037/0096-1523.29.2.455

8

Models of Cognitive Control in Task Switching

JAMES A. GRANGE AND GEORGE HOUGHTON ■

INTRODUCTION

The ultimate goal in the field of cognitive science/psychology is to understand the workings of the human/animal mind. How do we selectively attend to goal-relevant stimuli? How do we remember such vast amounts of information? How do we plan and coordinate complex plans of action? Researchers address these problems by describing behavior, through observation and experimentation. At a higher level, researchers aim to predict behavior: only a solid understanding of a phenomenon allows successful prediction of future behavior in differing contexts. Prediction is a key tool for assessing whether our understanding of a phenomenon is sufficient.

Understanding cognitive phenomena is challenging as the human mind is impossibly complex; thus, researchers develop models of cognition, that abstract away from unnecessary details while emphasizing the factors thought to underlie the phenomena under investigation (Fum, Missier, & Stocco, 2007). For example, a model of memory might not describe how the memoranda are perceptually encoded or how the motor system produces a response at the end of an experimental trial (although, of course, they might, as is the case in cognitive architectures such as ACT-R; see Anderson, 2007) but would emphasize in detail how memories are formed, maintained, and accessed (e.g., Oberauer, Lewandowsky, Farrell, Jarrold, & Greaves, 2012). Examination of the model's behavior provides a window onto the more complex system that it is representing, increasing our understanding of that system (Dawson, 2004). As there is little utility in replacing one system we do not understand (i.e., human cognition) with another system equally as complex, models of cognition must be simpler than the system they are representing. But, with simplicity comes greater opportunity for understanding the system being modeled.[1]

Development of cognitive models to aid understanding of cognitive control during task switching is important because the control processes are not themselves directly observable (Logan & Schneider, 2010). Take, for example, the hypothesis of Rogers and Monsell (1995; see also Meiran, 1996) that task switching requires a discrete task set reconfiguration phase that alters the cognitive system allowing it to adapt to the new task demands (see Grange and Houghton, this volume). As reconfiguration is an unobservable process that likely occurs at some point between cue onset (which signals a change in task is required) and response output, its presence can only be inferred, via switch costs and other phenomena. As the reconfiguration mechanism is a latent variable, it makes understanding the nature of reconfiguration—or, indeed determining whether reconfiguration even occurs (Logan & Bundesen, 2003; Schneider & Logan, 2005)—difficult. By specifying the nature of reconfiguration in a cognitive model (e.g., Logan & Gordon, 2001; Logan & Schneider, 2010; Sohn & Anderson, 2001)—that is, explicitly stating its function and what job it is doing (and when)—one can explore the verisimilitude of such a process in more detail, increasing our understanding of that process.

Relatedly, expressing theories in explicit computational/mathematical models forces the researcher to be exact in describing the process under investigation; this increases both the clarity of exposition of the theory, and the opportunity for falsification. Clarity of exposition naturally follows as other researchers can investigate the specifics of a theory by examining the computer code and/or the model equations. As noted by Farrell and Lewandowsky (2010), verbal theories can be problematic due to their vague nature, leading to little more than a game of "telephone" when communicating theories among researchers (leading to the "I didn't mean that" problem when theories are misinterpreted). The vague nature of verbal theories also increases their flexibility in explaining empirical observation, leading to problems with falsification as flexible theories can fit any arbitrary data set (Roberts & Pashler, 2000). This flexibility is a by-product of the underspecification of verbal theories; explicit computational models are less flexible as decisions *must* be made for all aspects of the model. For example, as elegantly demonstrated by Lewandowsky and Farrell (2011), although the phonological loop component of Baddeley's (1986) Working Memory Model is thought to be a unitary component of a larger system, formal implementation of this component leads to at least 144 possible models. The large number arises from the number of possible decisions about aspects of the model that are not detailed in the verbal theory (When does rehearsal begin? Do memories decay linearly or as a power function? How is the threshold for successful recall set?); different choices produce different models. The sheer variety of possible models that can stem from an underspecified verbal theory demonstrates how hard they can be to falsify (if model number 96 is falsified, the "that's not what I meant" problem means another variant can be offered: number 112; Farrell & Lewandowsky, 2011).

The precision required of the modeler in instantiating a theory into a computational/mathematical model allows development of quantitative predictions of human behavior, meaning that competing models can be directly compared as to how they fit empirical observation. Thus, models with differing assumptions as to the nature/presence of latent variables can be directly compared, allowing a degree of model selection. Logan and Schneider (2010) used this advantage to show that a model that assumed a discrete task set reconfiguration stage did not fit the observed data any better than a model that assumed no reconfiguration stage; as such, Logan and Schneider argued that task switching does not require reconfiguration. Such a direct comparison and evaluation of theories is largely impossible with verbal theories.

GENERAL OVERVIEW

The purpose of this chapter is to review the efforts of theorists in developing and testing formal (i.e., not purely verbal) models of cognitive control during task switching. As has been highlighted in the previous chapters, there are a plethora of well-established empirical effects in the task switching literature that serve to constrain the space of plausible models of cognitive control. The chapter proceeds as follows. First, we provide an overview of the architecture of extant models of task switching, describing the nuts and bolts of each. To ease exposition, we group discussion of the different models into three classes: mathematical models, computational models, and neural network models. The second section then covers key empirical/theoretical concepts in the task switching literature, discussing how the models explain them. In particular, we focus on each model's explanation of task sets and the switch cost. All models discussed have something to say on these issues. We also discuss "run" effects (see Altmann, this volume), which are only explicitly covered by the Altmann and Gray (2008) model; we believe these run effects provide important constraints for theories of task switching. By organizing the discussion in this way—architecture first, then discussion of how findings are explained by the different models—the reader will be able to compare and contrast models more closely than if each model (and their explanation of concepts/effects) were discussed separately. By providing an overview of how effects/concepts are explained by the models, we are able to highlight areas that they do not cover or that require more elaboration in future modeling work. This is the focus of the third and final section.

We conclude that, despite the impressive progress made on the development of theories of task switching, there are important and rather neglected aspects that need to be addressed in future models. One important direction is the formalization of inhibitory processes during task switching; although there are many empirical effects that provide convincing evidence for the role of inhibitory mechanisms during task switching (which serve to reduce interference from competing, but irrelevant, tasks; see Gade, Schuch, Druey, and Koch, this volume), most models do not address these effects.

OVERVIEW OF MODEL ARCHITECTURES

In this section, we provide overviews of each model's architecture; the coverage is grouped by the model's class: mathematical, computational, and artificial neural (connectionist) networks.

Mathematical Models

In contrast to computational models (which we discuss next), mathematical models do not *reproduce* behavior; rather, mathematical models of task switching aim to *describe* how cognitive control might be exerted in the system by estimating parameters in the model that represent key control processes. In this section, we describe—without recourse to the mathematical details—key mathematical models of task switching.

Meiran's Models

Meiran and colleagues (Meiran, 2000; Meiran, Kessler, & Adi-Japha, 2008) have developed a number of mathematical models of cognitive control during task switching. The experimental paradigm they model has a very small stimulus set (four possible stimuli), so different actions are required to identical stimulus input. Thus, the cognitive system must somehow be able to be biased toward the task-relevant action and not be controlled by environmental stimuli alone. The paradigm (see Meiran, 1996) presents participants with a 2 × 2 grid, with a stimulus appearing in any one of the four quadrants with equal probability. The possible tasks are a vertical judgment (does the stimulus appear in the top or bottom two squares?) and a horizontal judgment (does the stimulus appear in the left or right two squares?). Arrows serve as cues, which could be pointing up and down (vertical task) or left and right (horizontal task). The response mappings are bivalent—that is, the response keys change their meaning with the task. For example, using the numerical part of a standard keyboard, the "7" key might represent an "up" and a "left" response (depending on the cued task), and the "5" key might represent "down" and "right". The stimuli are also bivalent, and can be *congruent* or *incongruent*. Stimuli are congruent when the response for the relevant task and the irrelevant task both map on to the same key (e.g., a stimulus appearing in the top-left quadrant requires a "7" response, regardless of the task); stimuli are incongruent when the response for the relevant and irrelevant task are different (e.g., a stimulus appearing in the top-right requires a "7" response if the task is vertical, and a "5" response if the task is horizontal). Several studies have shown that response times (RTs) are faster and more accurate to congruent stimuli than to incongruent stimuli (e.g., Rogers & Monsell, 1995). Importantly, the stimulus display alone on incongruent trials does not uniquely signal a particular response, and so some internal representation/process must be used to disambiguate the stimulus in order to make an accurate response. Although the models of Meiran (2000) and Meiran et al. (2008) share some similarities, there are critical differences and so they shall be discussed separately.

Meiran's (2000) Model

The core assumption of Meiran's (2000) model is that task switching requires a switch in how stimuli and/or responses are interpreted. The model assumes that these two changes in interpretation are independent and have different temporal loci. At the center of the model are mental representations of the physical stimuli being presented and of the two possible responses (i.e., representing up/left and bottom/right). These representations are formed by filtering the physical presentation of stimuli through task sets, which serve to bias the representations formed so that a correct response is most likely: The stimulus representation is formed via a *stimulus task set*, which biases the system toward representing the task-relevant dimension of the stimulus (e.g., emphasizing "up" in a vertical task when presented with a stimulus in the top left quadrant); the two response representations are formed via two *response task sets*, one representing the response executed on the previous trial (*previous response set*) and the alternative response from the previous trial (*alternative response set*). These response sets thus represent the task-relevant dimension from the previous trial, which "spills over" and influences processing on the current trial (e.g., task set inertia [TSI]; Allport, Styles, & Hsieh, 1994). Stimulus sets also maintain their values into the next trial and therefore must be reconfigured on task switch trials.

Processing in the model follows four stages. Initially, the task sets need to be reconfigured so that the currently relevant task dimension is emphasized. While it is assumed that stimulus sets can be reconfigured—a process Meiran calls stimulus-set biasing—during preparation stages ahead of stimulus onset (i.e., during the cuing interval), response sets are not reconfigured ahead of stimulus onset but rather occur after response selection, which establishes the response sets and representations that are carried forward to the next trial (TSI): On task-repetition trials, response sets will therefore already be biased in favor of the relevant task but are biased toward the incorrect task on switch trials. Once task sets have been configured, they need to be applied so that the mental representations can be formed. For the stimulus set, this results in stimulus identification, whereby the relevant dimension of the target display is emphasized. Then, the representation of the stimulus is compared with the representation of each response in a *similarity-matching procedure*, which determines which of the two responses is most similar to the stimulus. Based on this process, each of the two responses gains *potency*, with higher potency for stronger similarity between the stimulus representation and the representation of the response. Finally, the potencies are translated into *response strength* (the difference in potencies between the two responses), which determines which response is selected and how fast the resulting response is, with RT inversely proportional to the response strength. The concept of response strength captures competition/interference in response selection: If there is similar potency between the two responses, the response strength will be reduced, resulting in a slower, less accurate, response.

Control by Action Representation and Input Selection of Meiran et al. (2008)

Meiran and colleagues (2008) developed the Control by Action Representation and Input Selection (CARIS) modeling framework to investigate whether task switching performance could be better explained as arising from proactive control—that is, activating task-relevant rules before executing a task (Meiran, 1996; Meiran et al., 2000; Rogers & Monsell, 1995; Rubenstein et al., 2001; Sohn &

Anderson, 2001)—or reactive control—where task-relevant stimuli bias internal processing during task performance itself (Allport et al., 1994).

CARIS has two levels of representation, which share some similarity to those assumed by Meiran (2000): A preselective representation, which contains information relevant to all tasks without any prioritization (e.g., a representation of a "top left" stimulus, without emphasizing a "top" or a "left" response) and a representation that enters response selection, which is a transferred version of the preselective representation with greater weight given to information relevant to the current task. There is a shared representation space for perceived stimuli and actions, with direct interaction possible between perception-related (i.e., stimuli) and action-related (i.e., response) representations. The formation of the input and action codes follows from two transformations. The first transformation forms a graded task representation (e.g., going from a "upper left" target to a target representation that emphasizes "upper") and is referred to as the *input set* (this was the stimulus set in Meiran, 2000); the second transformation forms a graded response representation (e.g., going from the response key that represents "up left" to a key representation that emphasizes "up") and is referred to as the action set (this was the response set in Meiran, 2000).

Unlike Meiran (2000), control is achieved in CARIS via two processes: An explicit *task decision process*, whereby cue encoding activates an abstract representation of which task the model is focusing on, and *rule implementation*, which uses the result of the task decision process to determine a biasing process that eventually determines what information will enter into response selection processes (with preference for task-relevant information). This biasing process can be set by the current goal (determined by the cue, representing proactive control) or by the immediate experience of the model (i.e., a perseverative setting, reflecting reactive control) and acts by filtering the representation of the stimulus and the possible responses. Response selection follows similar processes described by Meiran (2000).

Meiran et al. (2008) examined three models, each of which represented a unique strategy, depending on whether selection of task-relevant information is driven by a controlled, proactive process—triggered by the task cue—or whether selection is based on perseverative activation of the previous trial's representation; a third strategy combines these two. When selection is controlled, the task decision is set by the task cue; when selection is perseverative, it is set based on the task executed on the previous trial.

These strategies were realized by implementing three models. Model 1 assumed that input selection is controlled, determined by the current task's cue, and that action selection perseverates from the previous trial. Successful performance in this model arises as the input set is able to bias information processing so as to emphasize task relevant information. Model 2 had the opposite assumptions, that input selection is perseverative (determined by the task performed on the previous trial) and that action selection is the controlled process, which biases information so as to emphasise the relevant information from the current trial. The final model assumed that both input selection and action selection are controlled by the current task, with no perseverative effect from the previous task.

Meiran et al. (2008) concluded that a combination of Model 1 and Model 2 fit the data best (called Model 1–2), depending on the current condition's preparation interval: Model 1 fit the data better at short intervals, and Model 2 fit best at long intervals. This is inconsistent with a view of proactive control, and rather supports a reactive, transient, control process. The inconsistency with a proactive explanation arises as Model 1–2 suggests that a controlled implementation of the input set at short preparation intervals—as predicted by Model 1—becomes a perseverative implementation of the input set at long preparation intervals—as predicted by Model 2. Proactive accounts rather suggest that controlled parameters retain their value until proactive control changes them. The observation that input sets at long preparation intervals are determined by the previous trial's representation is not consistent with this idea. Instead, the data and modeling suggests that performance on trial *n*-1 biases the system towards performing that task on the current trial, and control processes intervene to bias the system toward the correct task; this, Meiran et al. argue, is the essence of a reactive control process.

The switch from Model 1 to Model 2 at extended preparation intervals also suggests that when presented with a task cue—that is, cues that merely signal the task (e.g., "vertical") rather than specify the response sets (e.g., "up-down")—attention is initially attracted to input-related aspects of the cue (which triggers biasing of the input set), with attention to action-related aspects (i.e., Model 2) only arising later with long cue exposures. When the action set has not been configured at short preparation intervals, there exists perseverative influence of the previous trial's action representation; this is overcome at longer preparation intervals because the action set can be configured before stimulus onset.

It is important to note, however, that this proposal differs markedly from that of Meiran (2000), which was a proactive control model. CARIS, on the other hand, is described as a reactive control model, where internal processing is biased during task performance. It suggests that task performance creates perseverative tendencies of both the input and the action set and that reactive control must ensure these effects are controlled so as not to induce errors on the current trial. In addition, CARIS has an explicit task decision stage, which Meiran's original model did not have. As we shall see, this stage contributes to the model's account of the switch cost.

Logan and Schneider's Models

Logan and Bundesen (2003) present a model together with new empirical data (see also Mayr & Kliegl, 2003, and Meiran, this volume) that directly challenged the pervading idea that the switch cost in the explicitly cued task switching paradigm reflected the time-course of a task set reconfiguration process. It is important to note that Logan and colleagues do not suggest that task switching does not require cognitive control; rather, they question that the switch cost *measures* cognitive control processes (Logan, 2003). Researchers of task switching have been rather allured by the switch cost due to the belief that it captures cognitive control in operation; as a consequence, the field has arguably passed over other effects that may better capture such processes (see Altmann, 2003a, 2003b; Altmann & Gray, 2008). Thus, the models of Logan and colleagues are an important challenge to the primacy of the switch cost as an index of cognitive control.

The premise of all of Logan and colleagues' models—models of varying explanatory scope all based on the *compound-cue* model (Logan & Bundesen, 2003; Schneider & Logan, 2005)—is that task switching performance in the explicitly cued paradigm can be explained by cue-driven memory retrieval of the correct response from long-term memory (LTM): On each trial, participants encode a representation of the presented cue in short-term memory (STM), then a representation of the stimulus; these can together be used to probe LTM for the correct response. For example, the cue "OddEven" and the stimulus "7" uniquely retrieve an "odd" response from memory. On every trial, the presented cue is compared with representations in STM and LTM, with cue encoding being complete when a match to a representation is found (Logan & Bundesen, 2003). The comparison to representations in STM and LTM occurs in parallel (Bundesen, 1990), with faster cue-encoding times occurring when the presented cue is similar to a representation in STM. This occurs on task-repetition trials when the cue-encoding process is primed due to persisting activation from the previous trial's cue representation in STM; thus, it takes less time to form the cue representation on task-repetition trials, which leads to faster RTs. On switch trials, the current cue does not match the representation in STM and must rely on comparison to LTM (which is a slower process), producing prolonged cue-encoding times. Thus, the switch cost in this model is viewed as a repetition *benefit* rather than a switch cost. In addition, the compound-cue model suggests that the cuing procedure does not actually require task switching: On every trial, cues and stimuli are encoded to retrieve a response from LTM. All that changes from trial-to-trial is the compound-cue used to probe memory.

Logan and Bundesen (2003) formalized this compound-cue model and compared it with two other formal models: The reconfiguration model assumed task switching requires an endogenous act of control that occurs after cue encoding is complete only on task switch trials (Rogers & Mosnell, 1995; see also Logan & Schneider, 2010, for a further comparison between models that do and do not assume task set reconfiguration); this reconfiguration process retrieves the correct task set from LTM. Additionally, the model assumes that cue-encoding time is identical for repetition and switch trials (i.e., there is no benefit for repeated cues). The final model combined the assumptions of the compound-cue and reconfiguration model, assuming that cue-repetition priming *and* reconfiguration occur. Across several experiments, Logan and Bundesen (2003) demonstrated that the compound-cue model provided a superior account of the data than the other two models (see also Arrington & Logan, 2004; Logan & Bundesen, 2004).

In addition, as the compound-cue model states that the switch cost is merely a cost of switching cues (rather than having to switch task sets), the model made the novel prediction that merely a switch in cue (without a switch in task) would produce equivalent "switch costs" as when both the cue and the task switch. This prediction was tested using two cues per task (see also Mayr & Kliegl, 2003; Meiran, this volume), which produces three types of sequence: Cue repetitions (where the cue and the task repeats, e.g., OddEven—OddEven); task switches (where the cue and the task switches, e.g., LowHigh—OddEven); the new task sequence made possible with this 2:1 cue–task mapping is *cue switches*, where the cue switches but the task itself repeats (Parity—OddEven). The model predicts equivalently slower RTs for cue switches and task switches compared with task repetitions, because in both scenarios the cue presented on the current trial does not match the contents of STM, and thus must rely on comparison to LTM for successful encoding. Although Logan and Bundesen (2003) found no difference between RTs for cue-switch and task switch trials, several studies—some with methodological differences from that of Logan and Bundesen—have found significant differences, suggesting not all of the task switch cost can be explained by cue switching in all switching studies (Arrington et al., 2007; Brass & von Cramon, 2004; Grange & Houghton, 2010a; Jost et al., 2007; Logan & Bundesen, 2004; Mayr & Kliegl, 2003; Monsell & Mizon, 2006; Schneider & Logan, 2006). Although these studies report switch costs over and above cue-switch effects, not all authors agree on their interpretation.

The compound-cue retrieval process itself was elaborated by Schneider and Logan (2005; see also Schneider & Logan, 2009) who modeled the process as the biased accumulation of evidence toward the correct response over incorrect responses (i.e., a random walk process). The bias in the model does not arise from a cognitive control process (cf. Logan & Gordon, 2001) but rather from the presentation of the cues and stimuli on each experimental trial; each item presented to the participant is assumed to provide evidence for different response categories: The cue "Magnitude," for example, would provide evidence for the response categories "Low" and "High," and a target "6" would provide evidence for "Even" and "High" (i.e., higher than 5). In combination, the evidence for the correct response category "High" would reach retrieval threshold faster than the other response categories racing in the evidence accumulation process and would thus be selected as the appropriate response. Schneider and Logan (2005; see also Schneider & Logan, 2009) presented several experiments that confirmed the assumptions of this compound-cue retrieval process. Despite its success, we later review some evidence—both behavioral and from neuroimaging work—that challenges some of the assumptions of this model.

Computational Models

One advantage of computational models over mathematical models is that they aim to reproduce behavior observed by experimental participants; this differentiates them from mathematical models discussed in the previous section, which serve to describe behavior (Fum et al., 2007). A computational model—typically implemented as a computer program—"is given input and then must perform internal operations to create a behavior. By observing the behavior, the researcher can assess how well it matches behavior produced by a real mind" (Gazzinaga, Ivry, & Mangun, 2002, p. 102). Computational models have the advantage over mathematical models in that they are capable of tracking complex interactions between different processes because the nature of the modeling environment—that is, computational simulation—is intrinsically dynamic. Such simulations are well suited to investigating the nature of cognitive control during task switching.

The two computational models of task switching discussed here were constructed in the cognitive modeling architecture ACT-R (Anderson, 2007; Anderson et al., 2004) but differ notably in their construction and assumptions. Cognitive architectures are *unified theories of cognition* (Newel, 1990), in that they attempt to go beyond modeling a single task under investigation by working toward models that can perform a wide range of cognitive tasks. ACT-R comprises modules specialized for certain roles (perception, declarative memory, motor output, etc.) that are coordinated by production rules (*if-then* conditional statements stored in procedural memory), which monitor the buffers of the modules and select appropriate actions accordingly. For example, in a task switching study, if the model is presented with a task cue with the goal to retrieve the cue's meaning from memory, a production rule might fire that initiates this action. ACT-R assumes that knowledge can be divided into declarative memory (memories that are consciously accessible, such as facts, etc.) and procedural memory (memories that are not consciously accessible, such as actions and skills; see Anderson, 2007, for elaboration).

ACT-R models perform experiments in the same way participants do, as all aspects of performance are modeled, from stimulus perception through to motor output. The symbolic components of ACT-R (e.g., discrete memories, production rules etc.) are associated with subsymbolic quantities (governed by mathematical equations that determine the activation levels of memories and the utility of production rules). In a task switching context, for a particular experimental trial an ACT-R model would require the firing of several production rules, with each rule requesting retrieval of certain "chunks" of information from memory. Such chunks might inform the model that, for example, a square cue is associated with an "odd/even" task; another chunk might be retrieved that informs the model that a digit "7" is odd; and yet another chunk might be retrieved that informs the model as to the correct stimulus–response rule (e.g., "if odd, press left"). As declarative memory in a typical model might consist of several chunks—and a real human mind will certainly contain *many* times that—it is important that the system ensures the correct chunk is the most retrievable (otherwise errors occur). In ACT-R, the probability and speed of retrieving a certain chunk from declarative memory is directly proportional to its activation value; highly practiced and recently performed chunks are active and are retrieved with greater probability and with greater speed. Importantly for later discussion, activation levels of chunks in ACT-R decay passively as function of time. Below we discuss two

ACT-R models—Sohn and Anderson (2001), and Altmann and Gray (2008)—which propose different theories for how the cognitive system handles task switching scenarios.

Sohn and Anderson (2001)

The model of Sohn and Anderson (2001) attempted to delineate the different contribution of executive and automatic control in task switching contexts. Executive control—or proactive control (Braver, 2012)—is endogenous, goal-directed, and volitional, and serves to activate and sustain goal-relevant processes; automatic control—or reactive control—is driven by external stimuli that have associative links to a particular goal and/or action, and exert their influence regardless of the current goal. In a task switching context, executive control can be encouraged by increasing the opportunity for advanced preparation (e.g., Meiran, 1996) whereas automatic control is influenced by repetition or carryover effects (e.g., Allport et al., 1994). The experiment that was modeled by Sohn and Anderson varied whether participants had foreknowledge of the presence or absence of an upcoming switch in task. On each trial, participants were presented with pairs of tasks to be performed on bivalent stimuli (e.g., a letter and a number presented concurrently). The color of the stimuli determined the task to be performed (e.g., green cued the letter task determining whether it was a vowel or a consonant; red cued the number task determining whether it was odd or even). The first and second task of each trial could either be the same (in which case task 2 was a task repetition), or different (a task switch); the time between the response to task 1 and the onset of the task 2 stimuli—the response-stimulus interval, or RSI—was manipulated.

As the color of the stimulus signaled the relevant task, performance could be conducted in a purely reactive manner; that is wait for the stimulus to appear, and respond accordingly. However, to encourage executive control, some blocks of trials introduced *foreknowledge* to participants regarding whether there would be a switch of task from task 1 to task 2 or not. Thus, in this condition, participants could use the RSI between task 1 and task 2 to proactively prepare for the second task (including any proactive preparations for a task switch). In the no-foreknowledge condition, no such proactive preparation could be conducted. Thus, this experimental paradigm is well suited to separate the contributions of proactive and reactive control on performance.

The model consisted of seven chunks in declarative memory that are crucial to task switching performance: Two chunks hold information of the cue-to-task mapping (e.g., green cue is associated with a letter task); four chunks hold information of the stimulus response mappings (e.g., "consonant is associated with a "z" response"); importantly for the assumptions of the cognitive control processes in this model, two chunks encoded how to switch between two tasks, depending on the currently relevant task (e.g., "if current task is a digit task, a switch would require performing the letter task"). As we shall see, these chunks together with a switch-specific production rule formalize the notion of reconfiguration (Rogers & Monsell, 1995). Automatic control is influenced by the degree of activation of these chunks in declarative memory. On task-repetition trials, the relevant chunks will still be active in declarative memory (as they have not decayed so much), which can lead to positive priming (i.e., faster, more accurate performance). On the contrary, on switch trials the system will be attempting to access chunks that were performed longer ago, and thus have decayed (offering less priming). These dynamics become important when discussing how the model explains a portion of the switch cost.

Two of the model's production rules in the model are especially relevant to explaining task switch effects. The "encode-task" production fires when the color of a stimulus has been encoded but the system does not know what the current task is (i.e., on task 1, or on task 2 in the no-foreknowledge condition); its purpose is to trigger retrieval from declarative memory of the mapping between stimulus color and relevant task. Importantly, this production is not required for task 2 in the foreknowledge condition, as the participant will know the identity of task 2 by combining information from task 1 with the foreknowledge given (i.e., repeat task 1 or switch from task 1); thus, in this condition the model can skip to a production further down the processing chain. As retrieving information from declarative memory takes time, skipping this production is non-trivial to final performance.

The second production rule of interest is a "prepare-switch" production, which can only fire in the foreknowledge condition. This production can fire when the system has completed task 1 and is aware that task 2 requires a switch from the current task. In such scenarios, the RSI can be used to retrieve the relevant switching information from declarative memory; the likelihood of this retrieval being complete by stimulus onset increases with the RSI. Thus, in the foreknowledge condition, the model assumes that proactive control can be deployed to execute switch-specific operations, making it a formal instantiation of a reconfiguration-like process (Rogers & Monsell, 1995). Another production that competes for selection during the RSI is a "think" production, which represents intrusions of task-irrelevant cognitions. This competition between productions introduced during the RSI relates to De Jong's (2000) Failure to Engage hypothesis, which states that it is possible, but difficult, to fully prepare for a task switch. The probability that the task-relevant production "prepare switch" will be selected increases with increased RSI, as production selection occurs every 200ms, and it need only be selected once for full preparation to occur.

Altmann and Gray (2008)

Although constructed in the same architecture as the Sohn and Anderson (2001) model, Altmann and Gray's (2008) "cognitive control model" (CCM) explains task performance in a strikingly different manner. Of special note is the absence of any reconfiguration-like processes (there is no analogue to the "prepare switch" production of the Sohn & Anderson model).

The CCM proposes that when presented with a cue in a task switching context, a new representation of this cue is encoded in episodic memory; Altmann and Gray (2008) call this representation a "task code". The problem arises as to how the system can maintain this task code in the face of interference from competing, older, task codes in episodic memory. In the model—and in ACT-R more generally—memory returns the most active item when a retrieval request is made; thus, the system must ensure that the relevant code is the most active among all competitors. The problem is compounded because the activation levels of task codes are assumed to decay passively as a function of time; thus, the system must ensure not only that the currently relevant code is more active than competing codes, but also that it is maintained at a sufficient level of activation to guide behavior until a new cue is signaled. When a new cue *is* presented, the new code created must then become the most active, and so on. Although decay might seem problematic for the system, Altmann and Gray (2008) argue that it serves a vital function of reducing the likelihood of a catastrophic build-up of highly active old (and hence, likely irrelevant) task codes in memory. They contrast this with the notion of a controlled process such as inhibition of representations of recently performed tasks (Mayr & Keele, 2000; see Gade et al., this volume); decay is an obligatory process.

The declarative memory structure of the model is separated into semantic and episodic memory representations. Cues and stimuli presented to the model prime perceptual codes in declarative memory, which serve to identify the percepts presented. There are chunks which represent task meanings (e.g., "parity"), stimulus categories (e.g., "Even" and "Odd"), and responses (e.g., "left response," "right response"). Activation spreads through this network, boosting activations of chunks that are associatively linked. For example, a cue of "Even/Odd" would spread activation to the task meaning chunk "Parity," which would in turn spread activation to the stimulus categories "Odd" and "Even" and then on to the associated responses "Left" and "Right". The stimulus that is presented would additionally spread activation to the stimulus categories (for example, a "7" stimulus would spread activation to stimulus categories "Odd" and "Higher than 5") and response categories. Episodic memory consists of representations of the current task code, but importantly also older task codes, which also send activation through the network (for example, if a code representing the parity task was recently performed, it would still send some spreading activation to the chunk representing the parity task in semantic memory, which would prime that chunk on the current trial). Unlike the elements in semantic memory that have stable activations over the lifetime of the model, the activation of elements in episodic memory are dynamic; we will come to see in later sections that the dynamics of episodic memory representations lead to a plethora of task switching effects.

Behavior in the model is also governed by production rules. When presented with a task cue, a production fires that retrieves the cue's meaning from semantic memory, and also creates a new task code in episodic memory; as the activation of this new code is at zero, a new production then fires, which "pumps" the activation of the newly created code (the number of "pumps" required is a parameter in the model). Stimulus onset triggers trial processing, which consists of three stages: (a) **task focusing**, whereby a production retrieves a task code—the most active in the set, but not necessarily always the *correct* code—from episodic memory; (b) this code is then used to **identify the stimulus category** along its relevant dimension (e.g., "odd"); and (c) use this category to make a **response**. Note that using the combination of an encoded cue and an encoded stimulus to retrieve a response from memory prompts comparison to the compound-cue proposed by Logan and colleagues (Logan & Bundesen, 2003; Schneider & Logan, 2005); note, however, that the compound-cue model does not have a task focusing stage that is the source of several task switching effects in the Altmann and Gray model.

Artificial Neural Networks

Neural networks—or, connectionist models—model cognitive processes within a framework based on the form of computation believed to be realized by the brain (Houghton, 2005; Plaut, 2000). They consist of a set of interconnected processing "units" or "nodes", each associated with a numerical activation value, representing the degree to which whatever the unit represents is "mentally present". Such an activateable unit is analogous to a group of similarly tuned neurons, whose average firing level signals the presence of a particular cognitive entity or variable. Each unit signals its activation value to others to which it is connected via modifiable, weighted links (analogous to modifiable synapses), which may be excitatory or inhibitory. Activation spreads through a network via these connections. At each time step in a simulated network, each unit forms the sum of its inputs, which then determines its degree of activation. Excitatory inputs to a unit will tend to increase activation, while inhibitory inputs will reduce it. An important feature of such models is that they incorporate associative learning mechanisms, which can change the weighting of the connections between units, thereby changing the network's behavior (for instance its response to a given stimulus).

In the context of modelling task switching and cognitive control, neural network models typically operate by having a group of units which are responsive to stimulus properties, and another group whose activations represent the strength of particular responses. These groups will be linked (perhaps through associative learning) so that particular configurations of stimulus properties activate associated responses. Depending on the construction (or learning history) of the network, a given stimulus configuration may lead to the activation of multiple incompatible responses (see the discussion of Stroop stimuli, below). There are standard neural network architectures (such as lateral inhibition amongst local representations) that can cope with this situation, by allowing the initially most active response to become dominant through a competitive process. Such a "winner take all" mechanisms will lead to the production of just the most active response, generally with a response time whose latency reflects the degree of competition generated by the other incompatible responses (Norman & Shallice, 1986).

In such a context, the need for an additional cognitive control process arises when there is a high probability that the reponse generated by this basic architecture is not the correct, or desired, one in a given situation. Current models typically propose the existence of at least one additional set of processing units, sitting outside of the associative stimulus–response pathway sketched above, whose activation represents a particular task set (in an experimental context, these task units may represent a relatively arbitrary stimulus response relationship, e.g., if the letter is a vowel, make a left key press). The explanations the models provide of task set and task switching effects involve the interaction of the task set units with the lower-level stimulus–response processes. At a cognitive level, the activation of task set units is typically associated with effortful working memory processes; at an anatomical level, it is believed to correspond to the involvement of the prefrontal cortex (particularly dorso-lateral prefrontal cortex) in modulating the interaction between sensory and motor systems.

Gilbert and Shallice (2002)

The Gilbert and Shallice (2002) model is a connectionist model of switching between naming words and naming the color they are printed in, that is, two tasks usually defined on "Stroop" stimuli. As such the model takes as its starting point the earlier model of the Stroop task due to Cohen, Dunbar, and McClelland (1990). It shares with this model its analysis of the central control problem in performing the Stroop task, which is how to override the prepotent tendency to name the word when the target task is to name the ink color (in short, how to respond to incongruent Stroop color words).

The model was one of the first models of task switching to be given a precise computational form, and suggested a specific mechanism (associative learning between stimulus representation and task units) that could lead to item specific switch costs. The model may be seen as a task specific implementation of the classical Norman and Shallice (1986) model of cognitive control, in which response competition is resolved by a "Contention Scheduling" (CS) mechanism. This simply selects the most active response from any set of incompatible alternatives (as discussed above). Left to itself it hence favors automatic and habitual responses. When such responding must be modulated or overridden, the Supervisory Attentional System (SAS) is postulated to maintain a representation of the individual's current task goals that can modulate the competition in the CS system to favor non-habitual responses. Anatomically, the SAS is held to represent a function of the prefrontal cortex, perhaps in the modulation of corticobasal ganglionic loops involved in response selection and suppression.

The structure of the model is shown in Figure 8.1. It maps from a representation of an input word in a particular color through to two sets of response units, one set for reading the word, and another for naming the color. Top-down "task-set" input is provided by two task-units, one for word reading and the other for color naming. The two feed-forward processing pathways (word vs. color naming) are segregated, with the bias towards word-reading implemented as stronger (by a factor of almost 2) stimulus–response connections in that pathway. However, there are co-operative/competitive interactions among the two groups of output units such that units coding for the same response (e.g., "red") have reciprocal excitatory connections, while non-compatible response units have reciprocal

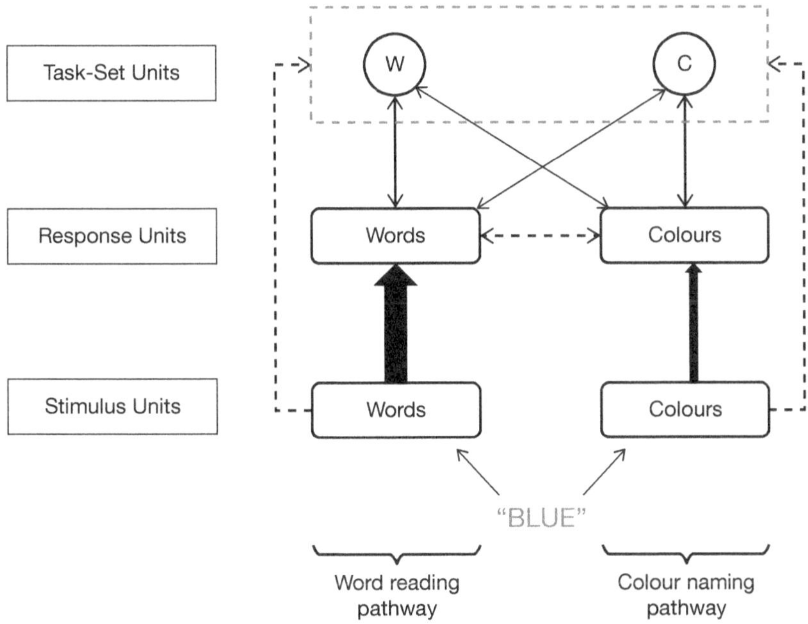

Figure 8.1 Architecture of the Gilbert and Shallice (2002) model of the Stroop task. The input stimulus ("BLUE") activates both lexical and color stimulus representations that feed forward to associated response codes. The word reading pathway is stronger (*thicker solid arrow*). Task-set units (W [word reading], C [color reading]) can bias the cooperative/competitive interactions (*thick dashed arrow*) between the pools of response units to favor one task or the other. Single-trial learning takes place between stimulus features and task units (thin dashed arrows), generating a switch cost.

negative connections (lateral inhibition). This induces response competition between the (three) pairs of compatible response codes (corresponding to the CS mechanism), which can be modulated by the top-down input from the task units (corresponding to the influence of the SAS over the CS, in the Norman & Shallice, 1986, framework). For instance, if the color naming task-unit is active it provides excitatory support to the color response units while inhibiting the word reading units. The parameters governing these interactions must be set by hand to ensure that the model is capable of producing the less-favored response (color naming) when presented with an incongruent Stroop stimulus.

The model accounts for basic findings in pure Stroop task blocks in a straightforward way. First, word naming is faster than color naming because the (built-in) stronger weights in the word pathway lead to more rapid accumulation of activation in the word response units. Second, for incompatible Stroop stimuli, word reading interferes with color naming more than vice versa because the more rapid activation of the incompatible word response more strongly inhibits color-naming than vice versa, even when the color naming task-unit is sufficiently active to eventually overcome this interference.

Brown et al. (2007)

The Brown et al. (2007) model relates to the continuing debate regarding the relative contribution of top-down and bottom-up processes to the switch cost. Top-down processes involve voluntary acts of task-set reconfiguration whereby the task set is effortfully installed into working memory (Rogers & Monsell, 1995). Bottom-up processes may refer in general to the learning of or adaptation to any aspect of a previous trial. If these adaptation mechanisms facilitate repetition of the task set applied to that trial, but cause interference when a new task is required, then they will tend to generate a switch cost (Wylie & Allport 2000; Waszak, Hommel, & Allport, 2003). The model is especially concerned with the role of the detection of various types of conflict in producing adaptive reactions that affect the way subsequent stimuli are processed. This is the kind of role often attributed anatomically to the anterior cingulate cortex (ACC; Botvinick, Braver, Barch, Carter, & Cohen, 2001).

As the model is particularly concerned with the adjustments made by the cognitive system to detection of various types of conflict in particular trials, it aims at modeling empirical effects in which the switch cost is modulated by various sequential relationships between trials. Prominent among these effects are:

1. Carryover congruency effects: Following a trial with an incongruent stimulus (which affords more than one response in the experimental context), RTs on a following switch trial are relatively slowed, while following a non-switch trial RT is facilitated. This suggests that the detection of incongruency reinforces the activation of the relevant task set. This impairs switching to a new task set on a following trial, but has a beneficial effect when the task repeats (Goschke, 2000).
2. Response repetition effects: Response repetition across trials has been found to have a facilitatory effect on reaction times when the task repeats, but to have the opposite effect when the task switches (Rogers & Monsell, 1995).

The basic architecture of the model is shown in Figure 8.2. A feed-forward stimulus–response pathway associates stimuli with responses via a set of mapping, or "plan" units. The activity of the plan units can be modulated by top-down input from a separate group of "task" units. The current state of the task units is determined bottom-up by a task cue that is supplied by the trial structure of the experiment. The connections between the task and response plan units are adaptable, allowing associative learning to take place between currently planned responses and the active task set (similar to the stimulus to task-set learning that takes place in the Gilbert & Shallice, 2002, model). In addition the plan to response unit connections were modifiable, allowing the model to implement a version of response facilitation.

This basic structure—which is very similar to other models discussed in this chapter (e.g., the Gilbert & Shallice, 2002, model)—is supplemented by two

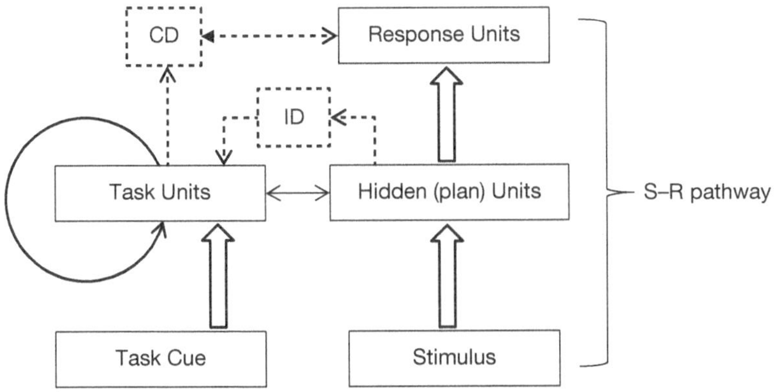

Figure 8.2 Architecture of the Brown et al. (2007) model. Stimulus codes are associated with responses via a layer of hidden units representing stimulus–response (S–R) relationships, referred to as plan units. A separate layer of task units modulates the state of the plan units to reflect the requirements (S–R mapping) of the current task. An exogenous task cue activates an appropriate task unit on each trial. The basic architecture is supplemented by two control modules and associated pathways, shown by bold dashed lines, the Incongruency Detector (ID), and the Change Detector (CD). See text for details.

control modules whose function is to detect two forms of conflict (Figure 8.2, bold dashed lines). The first is termed the Incongruency Detector (ID) whose job is to respond to conflict between incompatible response activations in the plan layer. When the ID is activated it boosts the activation of the currently active task unit, which in turn modulates the activity of the plan layer to favor the task compatible response. This effect occurs across trials; that is, the detection of conflict on one trial increases task set activation on the following trial, reducing conflict on that trial.

The other control module is termed the Change Detector (CD). This receives inputs from the task set units and also the output response units (Figure 8.2). Its job is to detect changes taking place in either of these structures. So it is activated when the task set switches (across trials), but also if the response changes from one trial to the next. According to Brown et al. (2007), the CD "detects brief periods of conflict as co-activation when the new task set representation becomes active and the previous one has not yet been deactivated by lateral inhibition" (p. 54), and likewise for the activation of output response units. This assumes that both task unit and response unit activation persists across trials. The effect of activation of the CD is to remove a "tonic arousal signal" to the response units, slowing all responses. The effect persists beyond the current trial leading the slowing of the next response, even when no change is detected. These dedicated mechanisms add a certain complexity to the model, and it contains a total of 21 free parameters, all set by hand (Brown et al., Table 6).

In brief, the ID monitors for conflict within a trial caused by the activation of more than one response "plan," while the CD monitors for conflict between trials caused by persisting activation of elements of the previous task and response when new tasks and responses are activated. Activation of the ID reduces conflict on the next trial by increasing the top-down signal from task units. The effect of the CD on the other hand cannot be so readily interpreted as resolving conflict, its effect being, effectively, to "inhibit" all response activation.

OVERVIEW OF EXPLANATORY SCOPE OF EACH MODEL

Task Sets

As mentioned in various components of Grange and Houghton, Schneider and Logan, and Meiran (all in this volume), task sets in task switching are often underspecified; Schneider and Logan (this volume) discuss this issue in depth and argue that the solution to the ambiguity as to the definition of a task set is to formalize the representations and processes needed for task performance in a computational/mathematical model. As a consequence, the nature of the task set has to be explicitly defined so that the model is capable of performing the task. On a broad level, they propose that a task set can be defined as the set of representations and processes that enable execution of the task at hand; in computational terms, Logan and Schneider (2010) define a task set as "a set of parameters in a computational model that is sufficient to program the model to perform particular task-relevant computations" (p. 416; see also Logan & Gordon, 2001). Thus, examination of how the models described above perform tasks will illuminate what constitutes a task set in the different theoretical approaches.

Meiran (2000)

The Meiran (2000) model proposes that task sets comprise of three components: The stimulus-set, which is determined by the cue for the current trial, and two response-sets, one representing the relevant response-set from the previous trial and the other representing the alternative response-set from the previous trial; the response-sets are determined by the response that was executed on the previous trial, and thus reflect carryover effects. Without these task sets, participants would be unable to respond to bivalent stimuli on incongruent trials. The stimulus-set is essential for accurate performance, as without it responding would become completely perseverative, as the response potencies would be solely influenced by the response-sets from the previous trial and the stimulus display. Without the stimulus-set, then, task switching would not be able to occur. These task sets influence the internal mental representations that are formed in the model, acting as a filter. In order to ensure the system can change its focus of attention during a task switch, the stimulus-set must be biased toward the currently relevant task; this process of stimulus-set biasing formalizes the concept of reconfiguration, and is a time-consuming process that can occur during active preparation for a task.

Meiran et al. (2008)—CARIS

Task sets in CARIS comprise the control parameters and representations that allow successful task performance. These can either be parameters that affect the representation of the input selection or the action representation, and which one is preferred seems to be influenced by the preparation time (action set preferred at longer cuing intervals) and the type of cue used: response cues attract attention towards the action set, whereas task cues attract attention to the input set. Meiran et al. (2008) state that these task sets are ad-hoc configurations, and there are many other parameters that might constitute the task set that they did not model.

Logan's Models

The task set in the compound-cue model of Logan and colleagues is a representation of the cue and a representation of the target, which are both used together to probe LTM for the correct response. Although the model does not assume task set reconfiguration for successful performance, there are some parameters in the model that a cognitive control process could operate on (Logan & Schneider, 2010). One is a parameter that acts as a gain control, enhancing the top-down bias towards categorizing an object as a member of a particular response category. This bias allows alternative responding to identical stimulus input. For example, the digit "2" in a common task switching context might provide evidence for "Even" and "Lower than 5" response categories; by biasing the system towards a magnitude task would mean the response category "Lower than 5" would be selected; if the task were to switch but present the same stimulus "2," a cognitive control process might alter the bias parameter to now favor the parity task, and thus "Even" would be selected (Logan & Gordon, 2001; Logan & Schneider, 2010). This bias parameter is not manipulated by a control process in Schneider and Logan's model as they suggest that the cue presented can bias the system towards the correct response category without the need for an endogenous act of control altering the bias parameter. The other parameter that might constitute a component of the task set is the criterion for response threshold of the evidence accumulation process. In such random walk and diffusion-type models, a higher response threshold produces slower but more accurate performance: More evidence is required before a response is executed (which takes time) but the probability increases that the correct response threshold is reached first (increasing accuracy). Although in Schneider and Logan's model the bias and criterion parameters were always fixed (i.e., no task set reconfiguration occurred), these are essential aspects of the task set that determine behavior of the model.

Sohn and Anderson

In the ACT-R models of Sohn and Anderson (2001) and Altmann and Gray (2008), performance is achieved by coordinated retrieval of task-relevant chunks from declarative memory via production rules. The declarative memory representations that allow for successful performance in the Sohn and Anderson model are chunks that perform cue-to-task translations, chunks that map stimuli to particular responses, and chunks that hold knowledge about switching transitions. Cue-to-task translations are required because the cues are non-transparent (Grange & Houghton, 2010a, 2010b; Logan & Schneider, 2006) in that they need to be interpreted. For example, a green stimulus in their experiment means the subject must perform a "consonant/vowel" discrimination. Thus, a chunk in memory pairs the color green with the letter task. Participants must also maintain the novel stimulus–response mappings that were learned in the experimental context. For example, presented with a consonant in the letter task, participants must recall that the correct response is "z". One production rule that is central to performance in this model is the "Prepare-Switch" production, which fires when a switch in task is required (in the foreknowledge condition), and changes the goal of the model to perform the opposite task to the one just executed. Although the model can perform successfully without this production—that is, the model can (and does, in the no-foreknowledge condition) perform in a reactive manner by waiting for stimulus onset and ascertaining from the color of the stimulus what the required task is—this production can fire during the preparatory period in the foreknowledge condition. Technically, then, according to Schneider and Logan's (this volume) definition, this production does not form part of the model's task set. Rather, this production *alters* the task set by changing the task that the model is focusing on, and is thus akin to a reconfiguration-like stage.

Altmann and Gray (2008)

The Altmann and Gray (2008) model also relies on declarative memory representations and production rules as the task set, but crucially has no reconfiguration-like production. The model's behavior is driven by semantic representations of the current task and stimulus category (determined by the percept of cue and stimulus, respectively, presented on the current trial) and of the stimulus–response mapping. Performance is achieved by retrieval of a task code from episodic memory, which is then added to the model's focus of attention; this guides the model's behavior until a new task cue is presented. Successful performance occurs when an episodic representation of the current task code is retrieved, but this retrieval process can be influenced by previous trials' task codes, which can positively prime performance in the case of task repetitions; due to noise in the activation values of episodic task codes, incorrect task codes can sometimes be retrieved, leading to errors.

The episodic task code created upon cue presentation is a central aspect of the task set, which is activated to a sufficient level to guide behavior. Thus, the "pumping" of activation of the new task code is essential to stable and correct behavior in the model (and is thus a "necessary" process in the model; Schneider & Logan, this volume).

Gilbert and Shallice (2002)

Broadly, a task set in a neural network model of task switching may be defined as the internal state of the network at a given time which biases it to respond to a multivalent stimulus configuration in a particular way. For instance, in the Gilbert and Shallice model the connection-strengths from stimulus to response are stronger in the word-reading pathway (reflecting greater practice on this task). As such this pathway will tend to dominate and determine behavior unless the task control mechanism intervenes and biases the network in favor of the other pathway when it is relevant. To achieve this, the task demand units—with separate units for each task—send activation to their associated pathways and inhibition to the alternative pathway. In addition, response units send activation to the task demand units; these connections are recurrent, such that activation is fed back from the response units to the task demand units. However, the key bias parameter for task selection comes from an additional top-down control input, which informs the model which task is relevant. Importantly, the parameter for top-down control input for performing the color task is greater than the top-down control input for performing the word task; although this allows the model to overcome the tendency to perform the word task, the mechanism by which this top-down control input is set is not specified.

Brown et al. (2007)

In the Brown et al. (2007) model, task sets are activated as a consequence of the task cue presented on the current trial. The model has a unique layer representing the task set that maintains a "persistent representation" of the currently relevant task set. In combination with input from the stimulus, this task set representation aids the formation of a unique pattern of activation in the hidden or "plan" layer, which determines the response to be executed. Task sets are also modulated by the incongruency detector, which enhances activity of the currently relevant task set when conflict between incongruent response processes is registered, "thus amplifying the processing of task-relevant stimulus–response processes" (p. 52).

Switch Costs

As the switch cost has been of primary interest to researchers in task switching—driven primarily by the belief that it reflects a time-consuming cognitive control process—examination of how different models explain the switch cost provides evidence as to the plausibility that the switch cost is indeed reflective of higher-order processing. Where relevant, different models' explanations of cue-switch costs are also discussed.

Meiran (2000)

According to Meiran (2000) the switch cost reflects the insertion of a time-consuming task set reconfiguration process (Meiran, 1996; Rogers & Monsell, 1995) on task switch trials, whereby the stimulus-set is biased toward the cued task. This allows a mental representation of the stimulus to be formed whereby the task-relevant dimension is emphasized over the task-irrelevant dimension. Thus, this model does propose that the switch cost reflects the time-course of cognitive control processes. This stimulus-set biasing stage occurs after cue onset and must occur before stimulus identification if accurate performance is to be achieved; no such reconfiguration is required on task-repetition trials because the stimulus-set is already biased toward the correct task. The stimulus-set biasing process can occur before stimulus onset if the preparation interval is sufficient; thus, at long preparation intervals, the model predicts no influence of stimulus-set biasing processes on RT.

The model explains residual switch costs as reflecting the negative effect of irrelevant response dimensions being emphasized on switch trials (due to the carryover of the response-sets from the previous trial). This reduces the similarity matching score between the mental representation of the stimulus and the representation of the correct response; this, in turn, reduces the potency of the correct response, which reduces the response strength during response selection, leading to a slower RT. This process is not affected by preparation interval because the model assumes that response-sets cannot be updated during preparatory intervals, and are rather updated after response selection.

Meiran et al. (2008)—CARIS

Switch costs in CARIS arise from two main processes. First, there is a pervasive influence of the previous trial's representation, which is in agreement with the task set inertia hypothesis (Allport et al., 1994): This aids performance on task-repetition trials, but hinders performance on task switch trials as components of the incorrect task are emphasized. As such, values of control parameters need to be changed, which takes time. The second component of the switch cost is the insertion of the explicit task decision stage. Interestingly, Meiran et al. (2000) conclude that this parameter reflects cue-encoding processes that are inflated for a change in cue that signals a task switch (cf. Logan & Bundesen, 2003; Mayr & Kliegl, 2003). Thus, although CARIS did not model data with two cues per task, conceptually CARIS should be able to predict cue-switch costs.

Switch costs in CARIS are reduced at extended preparation intervals partly due to more time for processing the switch in cue. Secondly, with longer cuing intervals, action-set control is implemented (Model 2), which is likely a more efficient strategy than input-set control. This is discussed by Meiran et al. in relation to the observation of smaller switch costs with response-category cues (e.g., "Odd-Even") than task cues (e.g., "Parity"; Mayr & Kliegl, 2003).

Logan and Colleagues

In the compound-cue model of Logan and colleagues, the switch cost is viewed as a repeated-cue-encoding benefit on task-repetition trials: Encoding a representation of the current trial's cue is primed by residual activation of the previous trial's cue in STM. Cue encoding on task switch trials, in contrast, does not benefit from priming in STM, and must therefore be achieved by comparison to traces in LTM, which is a slower process. This difference in cue-encoding times manifests as a switch cost; thus, from this account, the switch cost does not reflect the time-course of a cognitive control process. This account is supported by the observation that cue-switch trials—where the cue switches but the task repeats—produce robust costs to performance compared with cue-repetition trials—where the cue and the task repeats.

Although the original compound-cue model predicts identical performance for cue- and task switch trials—as in both cases the cue from the previous trial has switched, and has to be encoded via comparison to LTM traces (see Logan & Bundesen, 2003)—subsequent incarnations of the model accounted for the sometimes-reported observation that task switch RTs were slower than cue-switch RTs. These reported differences were a challenge to the original model. Some authors suggest this difference is the "true" switch cost, reflecting a time-consuming reconfiguration process that is not confounded by cue switching (Mayr & Kliegl, 2003; Monsell & Mizon, 2003); indeed, if cue-switch effects are now controlled empirically, any difference in performance must be due to processes unique to task switching (recall that the compound-cue model suggests task switching is not required in the explicit cuing paradigm).

Schneider and Logan (2005) highlighted that with two cues per task, the cues for each task are necessarily related either semantically (e.g., the cue "OddEven" is semantically related to the cue "Parity") or by learned episodic association (e.g., a square and a circle cue both signal a Magnitude judgment). Thus, by this notion, cue-switch trials should produce faster RTs than task switch trials, because although the cue does not match the cue active in STM, it is primed via semantic relatedness to the cue from the previous trial (Logan & Schneider, 2006); as a result, cues on cue-switch trials are encoded faster than cues on task switch trials (which benefit little, if at all, from semantic or associative priming from the cue presented on the previous trial). In the modeling framework, this can be formalized by assuming different cue-encoding times for cue-repetition, cue-switch, and task switch trials (Schneider & Logan, 2005; Logan & Schneider, 2006); the process of compound-cue retrieval of response categories from LTM is assumed to progress in an identical way once cue encoding is complete, and is thus unaffected by task transition. Therefore, even the observation of task switch costs over and above the costs of switching cues does not necessarily reflect the time-course of a cognitive control process.

However, there is increasing evidence that challenges the compound cue model. Arrington et al. (2007) found "true" task switch costs independent of cue-encoding effects by having participants make an overt response during cue presentation as to which task was being cued. By asking participants to make a response during the cue presentation period as to which task is being signaled ensures that all cue-encoding processes occur during this stage (the cue needs to be fully encoded before the task can be known); the target only appears once the response to the cue has been made. Thus, RT to the target is not contaminated by cue-encoding processes (which are already complete), whereas RT to the cue should be influenced by cue encoding processes. The finding of task switch effects—i.e., slower RT to task switch trials than to either cue-repetition or cue-switch trials—in target RT provides strong evidence against the compound-cue model, leading the authors to conclude that "The present results have falsified the conclusion [drawn] in several articles that cue-encoding effects are responsible for all cue- and task-transition effects in explicit task-cuing experiments" (Arrington et al., 2007, p. 497).

There is also growing evidence from the neuroimaging literature that cue-switch and task switch trials are processed in a qualitatively different manner (which is predicted by a "reconfiguration" hypothesis, but not by the compound-cue model). For example, Jost et al. (2008) analyzed event-related potentials (ERPs) in a cued task switching experiment with two cues per task. ERPs allow tracking of the brain's response to external stimuli even when an overt response is not made, which is ideal for tracking the neural response to cues in task switching (see Karayanidis & Jamadar, this volume, for more about ERPs). Jost et al. found both qualitatively and quantitatively different responses to cues that signaled a task switch than mere cue-switch sequences. The compound-cue model would not predict such a difference, as in both cases there is a switch in cue from that of the previous trial. Using similar logic, De Beane and Brass (2011)—using functional magnetic resonance imaging (see Richter & Yeung, this volume)—showed differential neural response to areas thought to underlie preparatory control (e.g., frontoparietal regions) during task switch trials compared with cue-switch trials. Together, the neuroimaging work suggests—in contrast to the compound-cue model—that cue-switch effects and task switch effects arise from different psychological processes.

Sohn and Anderson

Sohn and Anderson (2001) proposed a two-component hypothesis of the switch cost, stating a portion of it was due to repetition priming of task-relevant chunks in declarative memory (i.e., a task-repetition benefit; cf. Allport et al., 1994) and another portion of it was caused by active, top-down task preparation processes, which are executive processes that alter the course of information processing to allow task switching to take place; such preparation processes only manifest in RT when they are not completed by stimulus onset, so the contribution of preparatory processes to the switch cost decreases with increasing chances for preparation (cf. Meiran, 1996; Rogers & Monsell, 1995).

Recall that in their experiments, participants were exposed to foreknowledge and no-foreknowledge conditions, with task-specific preparation only being possible in the former condition. In this condition, Sohn and Anderson suggest the switch costs consists of both repetition priming and preparatory processes. When the RSI between task 1 and task 2 is of sufficient length in this condition, full preparation can occur—although, it does not necessarily occur all of the time (De Jong, 2000)—explaining the reduction of switch cost at extended RSIs. Preparation in the model consists of the firing of certain production rules which control when information retrieval from declarative memory occurs. During a task-repetition trial in the foreknowledge condition, the model—after performing task 1—will know that the task will repeat, and as such will not need to wait for task 2's stimulus to appear in order to know the identity of the color of the stimulus (which cues the relevant task); importantly, then, the "encode-task" production is not required. This production rule retrieves from memory the color-to-task pairing (e.g., that green stimuli cue the letter task), a process that takes time in ACT-R. Instead, the model can fire the "task-prepared" production immediately after task 1 has been performed and task 2's stimuli have onset; this production encodes the stimulus, which triggers further productions that produce a response. During switch trials, however, the model must change the task that it is focusing on. During the RSI between task 1 and task 2, the "prepare-switch" production has the potential to fire, which requests retrieval from declarative memory of the inverse of the task performed at task 1. Again, memory retrieval takes time, so a prolonged RSI affords more time for this process to occur ahead of stimulus onset, not affecting RT. However, this production rule competes during the RSI on task switch trials with a "think" production, which—if selected—reflects the occurrence of task-irrelevant cognitions (and hence reflects a formalization of De Jong's, 2001, failure to engage hypothesis). In ACT-R, productions that match the current condition and have the potential to fire compete against each other, and the production with the highest utility is selected and acted upon (a process called production resolution). Although in the implemented model the "prepare-switch" has the highest utility (set by the modelers), utilities are associated with transient noise, meaning that sometimes productions with lower set utilities can be selected. Extending the RSI increases the likelihood that the model will successfully prepare for a switch as production resolution occurs every 200 ms. Only one resolution must be won by the prepare-switch production for a switch in task to be implemented.

Thus, the model assumes that in the foreknowledge condition, the switch cost reflects the time-course of important cognitive control operations (akin to reconfiguration). This is not the case for the switch cost in the no-foreknowledge condition: As participants cannot be aware of an impending switch in this condition, the switch cost here can only be due to repetition priming, as preparation processes for a task repetition cannot differ from those for a task switch. The activation levels of all of the task-relevant chunks that were retrieved for performance of task 1 will persist—albeit in a decaying fashion—and prime performance of task 2. In the model, the repetition benefit comes from two sources: Repeating the same color-to-task translation, and repeating the same stimulus–response rule. Although the former will occur on all task-repetition trials, the latter requires a repetition of stimulus category, which does not always occur. Increasing the RSI in this condition will reduce the switch cost according to the model because the repetition benefit will decrease due to the decaying activation of task-relevant chunks in declarative memory.

The model of Sohn and Anderson (2001) thus suggests that a portion of the switch cost does indeed reflect cognitive control processes. The experimental work, however, suggests that some thought needs to be employed if one wishes to separate this component of the switch cost from the repetition benefit, which does not reflect cognitive control.

Altmann and Gray

Unlike Sohn and Anderson (2001), Altmann and Gray argue strongly that no portion of the switch cost is to be attributed to a reconfiguration-like process whose sole purpose is to switch the task the model is focusing upon. In addition, unlike all models presented in this chapter, the Altmann and Gray model explain task switching effects from a variety of different experimental paradigms using the same basic processes and mechanisms. In this model—whether the paradigm is an alternating runs paradigm, explicit cuing paradigm, or extended runs design—the switch cost is explained as being a product of repetition priming during cue-identification. The "identify-cue" production is the first stage of encoding a new task code that governs behavior until such time as a new cue is presented. The production requires that a new cue has been presented; when it fires, it retrieves the meaning of the cue from memory and brings it to the focus of the model's attention and creates a new task code in episodic memory. On task-repetition trials, this process is primed because the episodic task code from the previous task is still in the focus of attention which spreads activation to the relevant meaning in semantic memory. This primed activation speeds the retrieval of this meaning from memory. Such priming does not provide any benefit on switch trials.

The effect of advanced preparation on performance was examined by modeling the explicit-cuing paradigm with the CCM. In this model, it is assumed that identical preparation processes run on task switch trials as on task-repetition trials. This puts it in stark opposition to "reconfiguration" hypotheses, which suggest that preparation for switch trials is unique, including a specialized process for performing the switching operation. Generally, the preparation effect in the CCM can be explained by the task-encoding processes having a greater likelihood of finishing before stimulus onset at longer preparation intervals. These processes not only include the identify-cue production, but also the repeated pumping of the new task code's activation to ensure it is more active than its competitors in episodic memory. These task-encoding processes are essential on task switch *and* task repetition trials.

Although the switch cost did not reduce at longer preparation intervals in the data modeled by Altmann and Gray (2008; see also Altmann, 2004; Koch, 2001), such a reduction is often found in task switching studies (Kiesel et al., 2010; Vandierendonck et al., 2010). Altmann demonstrated that this reduction seems to rely on the preparation interval being manipulated within-subjects. In the CCM, this interaction between sequence and preparation can occur due to dynamic shifts in encoding efficiency (see Altmann & Gray for more information). Importantly, though, the reduction of switch cost at longer preparation intervals is not caused by a reconfiguration process occurring before stimulus onset (Rogers & Monsell, 1995).

Gilbert and Shallice (2002)

For this model it is worth noting that—just given the architecture shown in Figure 8.1 and its processing principles—one could imagine a number of ways in which a switch cost might come about. For instance, on switch trials (e.g., from word reading to color naming), the relevant task-demand unit must become the most active. Simply assuming that this process is still taking place on switch trials—but is complete on non-switch trials—would be expected to generate a switch cost. Alternatively (or in addition) rapid potentiation of the "just-used" processing pathway would provide benefits on repeat trials and costs on switch trials, resulting in an overall switch cost. These two possibilities would correspond respectively to reconfiguration (Rogers & Monsell, 1995) and carryover (Allport & Wylie, 2000) accounts of the switch cost. There is nothing in the architecture per se that would lead one to prefer one account over the other.

However Gilbert and Shallice (2002) promote a version of the carryover account, in which the model learns associations between features of the current trial (i.e., properties of the stimulus) and the task units. This requires the inclusion of a pathway connecting the stimulus to the task units, shown as two thin dashed arrows in Figure 8.1. This learning is rapid (single trial) and also vanishes equally quickly, with the learned weights being reset to zero after the following trial (when learning of that trial then takes place). This means that on a switch trial, any feature of the input that is repeated from the previous trial will reactivate the previous task set, with which it has become associated. This causes heightened competition among the task-units, impeding the dominance of the now relevant task. However by the first repeat trial, this learning of the previous task has disappeared (by fiat) to be replaced by learning that occurred on the switch trial. This is compatible with the requirements of the task repeat trial, leading to facilitation, and consequently, a switch cost. The model is used to simulate a number of effects where the switch cost is modulated by stimulus repetition (e.g., Allport & Wylie, 2000). The built-in asymmetry between the word-reading and color-naming pathways also allows the model to capture certain interactions between stimulus repetition and task.

The authors conclude that their simulations provide support for a carryover account of switch costs. However, there are a number of caveats. First, at a theoretical level, the model includes a learning pathway between the stimulus and task units whose sole function is to produce the required carry over effects. This is the only part of the model that learns, with no learning taking place between the stimulus and response representations, even though these are supposed to reflect the relative frequency of previous association (leading to stronger connections in the word-reading pathway). So for instance, the model shows no effects of response repetition on task switch (Hübner & Druey, 2006; Rogers & Monsell, 1995), or repeat trials (Mari-Beffa, Cooper, & Houghton, 2012). Furthermore, the learning that does take place is made to rapidly disappear, only affecting the subsequent trial. This produces a strong advantage for the first repeat trial, but no further advantage for successive repeat trials. While this fits with data that show little or no processing advantage after the first non-switch trial of extended runs (Rogers & Monsell, 1995), it seems that this is simply built in to the model.

A second problem is that the "top-down" activation of the relevant task set unit appears as *deus ex machina* whose source is not explained. When a particular task is required to be performed the associated task unit receives top-down input, with greater input to the color than to the word task unit. Furthermore, before the start of each trial the activation of the task units is reset to precisely 80% of whatever activation they had at the end of the previous trial, a form of inhibition. Again no mechanism for achieving this is specified. In short, the model contains unspecified mechanisms that carry out, to all intents and purpose, task-set reconfiguration. It would appear that these could produce a switch cost on their own, but the authors do not explore this possibility.

Brown et al. (2007)

The model provides two mechanisms that combine to produce the overall switch cost. First it implements a version of the task-set interference account of the switch cost via the modifiable connections of the plan units to the task units. Reactivation of a state of the plan units associated with a previous task will tend to reactivate that task set, interfering with reconfiguration on switch trials. This is a mechanism very similar to that in the Gilbert & Shallice (2002) model described earlier, and is not discussed further here. In addition to this, the change detection mechanism becomes activated when it detects a change in the state of the task units. This activation reduces tonic facilitation of the response units (in effect, an inhibitory influence) that slows responding on the upcoming trial. This latter mechanism is a rather direct implementation of a "switch cost producer"; however, its effects are made to last beyond the following trial, so that it contributes to more than just the switch cost. The slowing of responses also leads to increased accuracy (other things being equal). It would be reasonable to interpret this change detection mechanism as playing a role in task set reconfiguration (Rogers & Monsell, 1995). After all, it is activated when a change of task set is detected, and its effect is to retard responding. This gives all components of the model more time to settle into the fully "reconfigured" state before a response is made, increasing accuracy at the cost of speed. In this sense, the model endorses both task set interference and reconfiguration accounts of the switch cost.

As the model deals with sequential effects pertaining to conflict-related phenomena and their influence on switch costs, we discuss these in this section. The model implements carryover effects of incongruent stimuli in a fairly direct way. The sole function of the ID module is to detect conflict among the response plan units (not the response units themselves), which only occurs when processing incongruent bivalent stimuli. On the basis of this, the activation of the current task unit is increased, which leads to "amplified processing of the task-relevant pathway [which] overrides conflict from the inappropriate response process" (Brown et al., 2007, p. 52). If the following trial is a switch trial, then this increased activation of the current task set impedes reconfiguration, and slows responses over and above the slowing caused by the mechanisms already described. If the following trial is a non-switch trial, then responding is facilitated due to potentiation of the relevant task pathway.

Interactions between response repetition/alternation and task switch/nonswitch arise due to learning between the plan and response units. Making a particular response in the context of a specific plan state (the latter controlled by top-down input from the task set units) leads to a strengthening of the association between the two. At the same time, other plan unit connections to the same response are weakened. Clearly, if the response is repeated in the context of the same plan state (i.e., same task set), then responding is facilitated. However, if the same response is required but with a different task set, the weakened plan-to-response connections slows responses. This a mechanisms similar to that proposed by Meiran (2000).

In summary, the model provides a very fine grained account of trial-by-trial adjustments of control settings, which allows the simulation of the experimental results the model was based on. In doing so, it incorporates a variety of mechanisms also found in other models. In Brown et al. (2007) the model is mostly evaluated with respect to averaged data, both across subjects and across trials of the same condition. However, given its highly detailed specification (and large number of parameters), the model should be capable of simulating human performance on a trial-by-trial basis, by fitting to runs produced by individual subjects. This would offer a more stringent test of the mechanisms it proposes.

"Run" Effects

Runs—in a task switching context—generally refer to when participants are presented with a task cue that indicates which task is to be performed on a succession of targets (see Altmann, this volume). Thus, a cue is followed by a run of targets, upon which the cued task must be performed (e.g., C_XXXX where C_x is the cue for task x, and X are the targets). Cues can either indicate a repetition of the previously relevant task (e.g., C_AAAAA—C_AAAAA) or a switch from the previous task (e.g., C_AAAAA—C_BBBBB). On this run, the cue is only presented with the first target; after this, targets are presented in isolation, and the relevant task must be maintained in memory; this is in contrast to the standard explicit cuing paradigm where a cue is provided on every trial. These extended-runs designs produce novel task switching effects, which help constrain plausible theories of cognitive control. The Altmann and Gray (2008) model is the only model that extensively deals with extended runs designs, so much of the discussion below centers on this model.

Within-Run Slowing

Within-run slowing refers to the finding that—in the extended runs design—responses become progressively slower throughout the run. This is true for switch and repeat runs. The Altmann and Gray (2008) model—to our knowledge—is the only model to address this effect theoretically. Recall that successful performance in their model is achieved by retrieval of a task code from episodic memory, which allows the system to identify the imperative stimulus along its relevant dimension. Recall also that task codes decay in episodic memory as a function of time. The observed within-run slowing effect is thus thought to reflect the system accessing a decaying representation. The consequence of the decay is that it increases the probability that a retrieval failure will occur when an attempt is made to access this task code; retrieval failures waste the current retrieval cycle, meaning the system has to wait for a new retrieval cycle before another retrieval attempt can be made (prolonging eventual retrieval time). Note that this also manifests in error rates (so called within-run error increase); this effect arises in the model as decay of the relevant task code increases the similarity in activation in itself and the most active old task code in episodic memory, thus increasing the probability that the incorrect task code is retrieved and acted upon (which Altmann & Gray, 2008, refer to as task focusing errors). Note that both of these effects—and indeed the model architecture itself—rests on the assumption that memoranda decay passively as a function of time, a topic we return to in the penultimate section.

Full-Run Error Switch Cost

This effect pertains to the observation that error rates for switch runs are higher than for repetition runs for incongruent stimuli (where the stimulus affords different response, depending on the task). This is true across the whole run of trials, rather than being isolated to position one. This effect is explained by the model as the increased occurrence of task focusing errors on task switch runs than on task-repetition runs. This is caused by the fact that—on task switch trials—the most active old task code in episodic memory will more likely be from the incorrect task (which was used on the previous run); on task-repetition runs, the most active old task code in memory will most likely be for the currently relevant task, such that "incorrect" retrieval of this code will not lead to a performance error.

FUTURE DIRECTIONS OF MODELING

In this chapter, we have provided a broad overview of several key models of cognitive control in task switching. Despite the impressive advances made, there remain—to our mind—two key directions that would benefit from future modeling/empirical efforts. Of course, these suggested directions reflect our own research interests, but we believe they constitute important areas for fully developing our understanding of cognitive control in task switching.

We do not discuss more general directions, such as the importance of developing models of more recent task switching paradigms, such as the task-span procedure, the transition-cuing procedure, and the voluntary task switching procedure. Although such avenues are of immense importance, such paradigms are in their relevant infancy, and as such a body of empirical data has yet to accrue. Despite this, Schneider and Logan (2007) have already shown how the transition-cuing procedure might be implemented within their compound-cue model. As Arrington, Reiman, and Weaver (this volume) attest, there exists ample empirical evidence to start constructing models of voluntary task switching. Indeed, one such model has been presented by Vandierendonck, Demanet, Liefooghe, and Verbruggen (2012); this "chain-retrieval model" suggests that task selection is achieved by retrieval of sequences (chains) of tasks from LTM, which are then used to control task performance. This model, however, was primarily derived to address task *choice* behavior, and as such does not address task performance in detail. It would be interesting to explore how general this model might be beyond voluntary task switching procedures. In addition, a useful extension of this model would be to formalize task performance processes, and to address how task choice processes might impact this.

Below we address two important avenues for future exploration. The first addresses the concept of decay, and the second addresses the need to develop formal models of inhibitory control in task switching.

Addressing Decay

The first direction is largely empirical in nature, dealing with the concept of decay processes. There has been much debate recently as to whether memory traces decay passively as a function of time, or whether memory traces are forgotten/lost due to proactive interference from competing items (Altmann, 2009; Altmann & Schunn, 2012; Barrouillet & Camos, 2009; Lewandowsky, Oberauer, & Brown, 2009a, 2009b, 2009c; Neath & Brown, 2012; Oberauer & Lewandowsky, 2012). Aside from the data presented by Altmann and Gray (2008; see also Altmann, 2002; Altmann & Gray, 2002) regarding within-run slowing—which in itself provides strong evidence for decay (but see Lewandowsky, Oberauer, & Brown, 2009c, for an interference model that is able to reproduce within-run slowing without recourse to decay)—there is other empirical evidence in task switching that supports the existence of a decay process that affects the activation of task sets. One prominent example is from manipulating the response–cue interval (RCI); extending the RCI is thought to allow the previous task's activation levels to decay. Indeed, it has been shown that extending the RCI prolongs task-repetition RTs (e.g., Meiran et al., 2000; but see Altmann, 2004; Koch, 2001), which is perfectly in-line with a decay account: At extended RCIs, the previous task's activation will be decayed, and will prime behavior less than at short RCIs, where the activation will not have had time to decay. The net effect is a reduction of switch cost at extended RCIs.

However, the decay theory of task sets was challenged by Horoufchin et al. (2011a, 2011b), who manipulated RCI randomly on a trial-to-trial basis and found that the decrease of task switch cost was not related to the *absolute* time of RCI, but was dependent upon the sequential variation of the RCI from one trial to the next: Specifically, switch costs were only reduced at long RCIs when the RCI for the previous trial was short. Horoufchin et al. (2011a, b) suggested manipulating the RCI sequentially in this manner affects the temporal distinctiveness (TD) of a previous task's episodic trace—that is, how "isolated" the representation of the task is in memory. This in turn affects the probability of retrieving this episodic trace on the current trial (see Brown, Neath, & Chater, 2007, for a formalization of this mechanism addressing the memory literature; see Grange & Cross, 2013, for a formalization of this account in a task switching context). Thus, from this perspective, the effect is caused by variation of task set interference, and not due to a decay process (although, see Grange and Cross, 2013, who demonstrate that a decay-based model can explain at least a subset of the temporal distinctiveness effect).

We mention this because any empirical falsification of a decay-like process in task switching would also potentially lead to a falsification of any model that has decay at its core. This is not only the case for the Altmann and Gray (2008) model, but also for many other models discussed in this chapter (e.g., Logan & Bundesen, 2003; Schneider & Logan, 2005; Sohn & Anderson, 2001). For example, the compound-cue model (Logan & Bundesen, 2003; Schneider & Logan, 2005) assumes STM traces of cue representations decay passively as a function of time. This decay process is thought to explain the differential cue-encoding times for cue-repetition and cue-switch trials (Schneider & Logan, 2005).

Thus, a targeted research program examining the effects in task switching attributable to decay would be an excellent avenue with which to explore in more detail the validity and explanatory scope of most extant models. Of course, such a research program would benefit considerably by fitting and comparing models—ones that assume decay, and ones that do not.

Modeling Inhibition in Task Switching

Little of human or animal behavior consists of repeating the same action over and over again without interruption. Even within a sustained high-level task—for example to type the first sentence of a paper—the lower level task of which word to type next is constantly changing. And within each word, the target letter mostly switches from one letter to the next. Many current models of such serial processes include an inhibitory component which suppresses the currently dominant response, be it at the level of words (Brown, Preece & Hulme, 2000; Burgess & Hitch, 1999), letters (Glasspool & Houghton, 2005), or some other behaviour (Bullock & Rhodes, 2003; Cooper & Shallice, 2000). In this broader context of the sequencing of changing behaviours, it is somewhat suprising to note the relative absence of an appeal to any inhibitory mechanism playing a role in task switching models. Although the neural network models have inhibitory connections in their architecture, there is yet to be a model produced that comprehensively addresses the best evidence for inhibition in task switching: The so-called *n*-2 repetition cost (Mayr & Keele, 2000; see also Koch, Gade, Schuch, & Philipp, 2010, and Gade et al., this volume). When switching between three tasks (A, B, and C), it has been consistently shown that RTs are slower when returning to a recently executed task (e.g., an ABA sequence) compared with returning to a task not recently performed (CBA sequence). These costs are thought to reflect the persisting inhibition of task "A" when it was disengaged at *n*-1. Inhibition in task switching has been shown to be a flexible process, targeting those aspects of the trial structure (i.e., cue–target–response) that generate the greatest inter-trial conflict (Houghton, Pritchard, & Grange, 2009): There exists evidence that inhibition can target cue-related processes (Grange & Houghton, 2009, 2010b, 2011; Houghton et al., 2009), stimulus processing (Sdoia & Ferlazzo, 2008), and response-related processes (Koch, Gade, & Phillip, 2004; Philipp, Jolicoeur, Falkenstein, & Koch, 2007; Schneider & Verbruggen, 2008; Schuch & Koch, 2003).

It is important to note that the *n*-2 repetition cost in itself already provides a great challenge for many models of task switching that assume task performance is achieved by *activating* relevant representations (e.g., Altmann & Gray, 2008; Schneider & Logan, 2005; Sohn & Anderson, 2001); such models would predict an *n*-2 repetition *benefit*, as the activation from task A at *n*-2 would persist and prime behavior on the current trial in an ABA sequence, in direct contrast to what is found (see Grange, Juvina, & Houghton, 2013).

To date, only one model of *n*-2 repetition costs exists in the literature (Grange et al., 2013; see also Grange & Juvina, 2014). Using ACT-R (Anderson, 2007), Grange et al. were able to model *n*-2 repetition costs by applying a short-term inhibitory component to a subsymbolic equation that governs the activation levels of discrete memories (chunks) in declarative memory, which are central to task performance. For example, the model's memory contained chunks that translated a cue percept into a representation of its meaning, and then used this meaning to retrieve the correct target from memory. By applying a short-term inhibitory mechanism to these chunks, *n*-2 repetition costs were found at the mean RT level.

Although not intended to be a complete model of inhibition in task switching, the Grange et al. (2013) model does provide a framework from which to build such a comprehensive model. One potential shortcoming of the model is that it uses a self-inhibition mechanism, in that a task's representation is inhibited as soon as it is executed; this might be problematic, as there exists evidence that—rather than being deployed in an automatic fashion such as this—inhibition is dependent on the presence of intertrial conflict at *n*-1. That is, inhibition of a task only seems to occur when the system detects conflict between competing alternatives. For example, Schuch and Koch (2003) showed no *n*-2 repetition cost when the trial at *n*-1 did not require an overt response (i.e., it was a "no-go" trial). Schuch and Koch took this absence as evidence that, as there was no response required at *n*-1, no conflict was generated at the level of response processes between this task and the previous task, and as such no inhibition was deployed.

Although we are currently exploring in ongoing modeling work to what extent a self-inhibition mechanism can explain such "conflict-driven" effects, an essential direction for future modeling would be to establish how conflict-driven inhibition occurs during task switching more widely, by addressing the conflict-driven inhibition evidence.

This research direction has several challenges. First, as already noted, there exists evidence that conflict-driven inhibition is not particular to one aspect of the trial structure (cue–target–response), but can arise from modulation of interference among any one of these components (Houghton et al., 2009). Thus, a successful model would need to be general enough so that it could explain such diverse loci of conflict-driven inhibition. Such a model would likely need to generalize beyond one particular experimental paradigm, as the evidence in favor of conflict-driven inhibition arises from markedly different experimental paradigms.

An additional—and key—challenge is to first establish the mechanism by which conflict is detected, and second to establish how this conflict is transferred into an inhibitory signal; such formal specification is essential to avoid *deus ex machina*.

One candidate is the conflict-monitoring mechanism proposed by Botvinick et al. (2001) in their influential theory of the anterior cingulate cortex (ACC). In this model, the ACC continuously monitors the degree of response conflict in the system; the system responds to high degrees of conflict by increasing the top-down input of task-relevant parameters into the model: Thus, high conflict leads to high levels of top-down control, and low conflict leads to low levels of top-down control. Thus, it will be interesting to explore how conflict-detection might operate in the task switching paradigm (see also Brown et al., 2007) and to explore how this conflict detection is translated into a directed inhibitory signal. (It should be noted that the top-down input of the Botvinick et al. model was increased activation to task-relevant parameters, with no inhibitory input arising as a consequence of the conflict detection.) Not only should the inhibition be proportional to the degree of conflict detected (to avoid overkill), the inhibition must "know" somehow which element of the task set structure to target. How this is achieved is currently not known.

Such developments of understanding how an inhibitory mechanism "knows" how much and where to deploy inhibition will provide a great step forward in our understanding of how task switching is achieved, and how the system resolves the stability–flexibility dilemma (Goschke, 2000; see Grange & Houghton, this volume).

NOTE

1. There are many other advantages to cognitive modeling, which have been highlighted in several influential articles (Farrell & Lewandowsky, 2011; Fum et al., 2007; Lewandowsky & Farrell, 2010; Lewandowsky, 1993; Sun, 2002); throughout this article, we refer mostly to the arguments put forward by Fum et al. (2007).

REFERENCES

Allport, A., & Wylie, G. R. (2000). Task switching, stimulus–response bindings, and negative priming. In S. Monsell & J. Driver (Eds.), *Control of cognitive processes: Attention and performance. XVIII* (pp. 35–70). Cambridge, MA: MIT Press.

Allport, A., Styles, E. A., & Hsieh, S. (1994). Shifting intentional set: Exploring the dynamic control of tasks. In C. Umilta & M. Moscovitch (Eds.), *Attention and performance. XV: Conscious and nonconscious information processing* (pp. 421–452). Cambridge, MA: MIT Press.

Altmann, E. M. (2002). Functional decay of memory for tasks. *Psychological Research, 66*, 287–297.

Altmann, E. M. (2003a). Task switching and the pied homunculus: Where are we being led? *Trends in Cognitive Sciences, 7*, 340–341.

Altmann, E. M. (2003b). Think globally, ask functionally. *Behavioral & Brain Sciences, 26*, 609–620.

Altmann, E. M. (2004). Advance preparation in task switching: What work is being done? *Psychological Science, 15*, 616–622.

Altmann, E. M. (2009). Evidence for temporal decay in short-term episodic memory. *Trends in Cognitive Sciences, 13*, 279–279.

Altmann, E. M., & Gray, W. D. (2008). An integrated model of cognitive control in task switching. *Psychological Review, 115*, 602–639.

Altmann, E. M., & Schunn, C. D. (2012). Decay versus interference: A new look at an old interaction. *Psychological Science, 23*, 1435–1437.

Anderson, J. R. (2007). *How can the human mind occur in the physical universe?* New York, NY: Oxford University Press.

Anderson, J. R., Bothell, D., Byrne, M. D., Douglass, S., Lebiere, C., & Qin, Y. (2004). An integrated theory of the mind. *Psychological Review, 111*, 1036–1060.

Arrington, C. M., & Logan, G. D. (2004). Episodic and semantic components of the compound stimulus strategy in the explicit task cuing procedure.*Memory & Cognition, 32*, 965–976.

Arrington, C. M., Logan, G. D., & Schneider, D. W. (2007). Separating cue encoding from target processing in the explicit task-cuing procedure: Are there "true" task switch effects? *Journal of Experimental Psychology: Learning, Memory, and Cognition, 33*, 484–502.

Baddeley, A. D. (1986). *Working memory*. Oxford, UK: Clarendon Press.

Barrouillet, P., & Camos, V. (2009). Interference: Unique source of forgetting in working memory? *Trends in Cognitive Sciences, 13*, 145–146.

Botvinick, M. M., Braver, T. S., Barch, D. M., Carter, C. S., & Cohen, J. D. (2001). Conflict monitoring and cognitive control. *Psychological Review, 108*, 624–652.

Brass, M., & von Cramon, D. Y. (2004). Decomposing components of task preparation with functional MRI. *Jounral of Cognitive Neuroscience, 16*, 609–620.

Braver, T. S. (2012). The variable nature of cognitive control: A dual mechanisms framework. *Trends in Cognitive Sciences, 16*, 106–113.

Brown, G. D. A., Neath, I., & Chater, N. (2007). A temporal ratio model of memory. *Psychological Review, 114*, 539–576.

Brown, G. D. A., Preece, T., & Hulme, C. (2000). Oscillator-based memory for serial order. *Psychological Review, 107*, 127–183.

Brown, J. W., Reynolds, J. R., & Braver, T. S. (2007). A computational model of fractionated conflict-control mechanisms in task-switching. *Cognitive Psychology, 55*, 37–85.

Bullock, D., & Rhodes, B. (2003). Competitive queuing for serial planning and performance. In M. Arbib (Ed.), *Handbook of brain theory and neural networks*, 2nd edition (pp. 241–244). Cambridge, MA: MIT Press.

Bundesen, C. (1990). A theory of visual attention. *Psychological Review, 97*, 523–547.

Burgess, N., & Hitch, G. (1999). Memory for serial order: A network model of the phonological loop and its timing. *Psychological Review, 106*, 551–581.

Cohen, J. D., Dunbar, K., & McClelland, J. L. (1990). On the control of automatic processes: A parallel distributed processing account of the Stroop effect. *Psychological Review, 97*, 332–361.

Cooper, R., & Shallice, T. (2000). Contention scheduling and the control of routine activities. *Cognitive Neuropsychology, 17*, 297–338.

Dawson, M. R. (2004). *Minds and machines*. Malden, MA: Blackwell Publishing.

De Baene, W., & Brass (2011). Cue-switch effects do not rely on the same neural systems as task-switch effects. *Cognitive, Affective and Behavioral Neuroscience, 11*, 600–607.

De Jong, R. (2000). An intention-activation account of residual switch costs. In S. Monsell & J. Driver (Eds.), *Attention and performance. XVIII: Control of cognitive processes* (pp. 357–376). Cambridge, MA: MIT Press.

Farrell, S., & Lewandowsky, S. (2010). Computational models as aids to better reasoning in psychology. *Current Directions in Psychological Science, 19*, 329–335.

Fum, D., Missier, F. D., & Stocco, A. (2007). The cognitive modeling of human behavior: Why a model is (sometimes) better than 10,000 words. *Cognitive Systems Research, 8*, 135–142.

Gazzaniga, M. S., Ivry, R. B., & Mangun, G. R. (2002). *Cognitive neuroscience: The biology of the mind.* New York: Norton & Co.

Gilbert, S. J., & Shallice, T. (2002). Task switching: A PDP model. *Cognitive Psychology, 44*, 297–337.

Glasspool, D. W., & Houghton, G. (2005). Serial order and consonant-vowel structure in a graphemic output buffer model. *Brain & Language, 94*, 304–330.

Goschke, T. (2000). Intentional reconfiguration and involuntary persistence in task set switching. In S. Monsell & J. Driver (Eds.), *Control of cognitive processes: Attention and performance* (Vol. *18*, pp. 331–355). Cambridge, MA: MIT Press.

Grange, J. A., & Cross, E. (2013). Can time-based decay explain temporal distinctiveness effects in task switching? Manuscript submitted for publication Available from Social Science Research Network, http://dx.doi.org/10.2139/ssrn.2372657.

Grange, J. A., & Houghton, G. (2009). Temporal cue–target overlap is not essential for backward inhibition in task switching. *Quarterly Journal of Experimental Psychology, 62*, 2069–2080.

Grange, J. A., & Houghton, G. (2010a). Cue-switch costs in task-switching: Cue priming or control processes? *Psychological Research, 74*, 481–490.

Grange, J. A., & Houghton, G. (2010b). Heightened conflict in cue–target translation increases backward inhibition in set switching. *Journal of Experimental Psychology: Learning, Memory,& Cognition, 36*, 1003–1009.

Grange, J. A., & Houghton, G. (2011). Task preparation and task inhibition: A comment on Koch, Gade, Schuch, & Philipp (2010). *Psychonomic Bulletin & Review, 18*, 211–216.

Grange, J. A., & Juvina, I. (2014). The effect of practice on n–2 repetition costs in set switching. Manuscript submitted for publication. Available at Social Science Research Network, http://dx.doi.org/10.2139/ssrn.2378373

Grange, J. A., Juvina, I., & Houghton, G. (2013). On costs and benefits of *n*-2 repetitions in task switching: Towards a behavioural marker of cognitive inhibition. *Psychological Research, 77*, 211–222.

Horoufchin, H., Philipp, A. M., & Koch, I. (2011a). Temporal distinctiveness and repetition benefits in task switching: Disentangling stimulus-related and response-related contributions. *Quarterly Journal of Experimental Psychology, 64*, 434–446.

Horoufchin, H., Philipp, A.M., & Koch, I. (2011b). The dissipating task-repetition benefit in cued task switching: Task-set decay or temporal distinctiveness? *Journal of Experimental Psychology: Human Perception and Performance, 37*, 455–472.

Houghton, G. (Ed.) (2005). *Connectionist models in cognitive psychology.* Taylor & Francis, US.

Houghton, G., Pritchard, R., & Grange, J. A. (2009). The role of cue–target translation in backward inhibition of attentional set. *Journal of Experimental Psychology: Learning, Memory and Cognition, 35*, 466–476.

Hübner, R., & Druey, M. D. (2006). Response execution, selection, or activation: What is sufficient for response-related repetition effects under task shifting? *Psychological Research, 70*, 245–261.

Jost, K., Mayr, U., & Rosler, F. (2008). Is task switching nothing but cue priming? Evidence from ERPs. *Cognitive, Affective, and Behavioral Neuroscience, 8*, 74–84.

Kiesel, A., Steinhauser, M., Wendt, M., Falkstein, M., Jost, K., Philipp, A., & Koch, I. (2010). Control and interference in task switching—A review. *Psychological Bulletin, 136*, 849–874.

Koch, I. (2001). Automatic and intentional activation of task sets. *Journal of Experimental Psychology: Learning, Memory, and Cognition, 27*, 1474–1486.

Koch, I., Gade, M., & Philipp, A. M. (2004). Inhibition of response mode in task switching. *Experimental Psychology, 51*, 52–58.

Koch, I., Gade, M., Schuch, S., & Philipp, A. M. (2010). The role of inhibition in task switching—A review. *Psychonomic Bulletin & Review, 17*, 1–14.

Lewandowsky, S. (1993). The rewards and hazards of computer simulations. *Psychological Science, 4*, 236–243.

Lewandowsky, S., & Farrell, S. (2010). *Computational modeling in cognition: Principles and practice.* Thousand Oaks, CA: Sage.

Lewandowsky, S., Oberauer, K., & Brown, G. D. A. (2009a). No temporal decay in verbal short-term memory. *Trends in Cognitive Sciences, 13*, 120–126.

Lewandowsky, S., Oberauer, K., & Brown, G. D. A. (2009b). Response to Barrouillet and Camos: Interference or decay in working memory? *Trends in Cognitive Sciences, 13*, 146–147.

Lewandowsky, S., Oberauer, K., & Brown, G. D. A. (2009c). Response to Altmann: Adaptive forgetting by decay or removal of STM contents? *Trends in Cognitive Sciences, 13*, 280–281.

Logan, G. D. (2003). Executive control of thought and action: In search of the wild homunculus. *Current Directions in Psychological Science, 12*, 45–48.

Logan, G. D., & Bundesen, C. (2003). Clever homunculus: Is there an endogenous act of control in the explicit task-cuing procedure? *Journal of Experimental Psychology: Human Perception and Performance, 29*, 575–599.

Logan, G. D., & Bundesen, C. (2004). Very clever homunculus: Compound stimulus strategies for the explicit task-cuing procedure. *Psychonomic Bulletin & Review, 11*, 832–840.

Logan, G. D., & Gordon, R. D. (2001). Executive control of visual attention in dual task situations. *Psychological Review, 108*, 393–434.

Logan, G. D., & Schneider, D. W. (2006a). Interpreting instructional cues in task switching procedures: The role of mediator retrieval. *Journal of Experimental Psychology: Learning, Memory, and Cognition, 32*, 347–363.

Logan, G. D., & Schneider, D. W. (2006b). Priming or executive control? Associative priming of cue encoding increases "switch costs" in the explicit task-cuing procedure. *Memory & Cognition, 34*, 1250–1259.

Logan, G. D., & Schneider, D. W. (2010). Distinguishing reconfiguration and compound-cue retrieval in task switching. *Psychologica Belgica, 50*, 413–433.

Marí-Beffa, P., Cooper, S., & Houghton, G. (2012). Unmixing the mixing cost: Contributions from dimensional relevance and stimulus–response suppression. *Journal of Experimental Psychology: Human Perception and Performance*, *38*, 478–488.

Mayr, U., & Keele, S. W. (2000). Changing internal constraints on action: The role of backward inhibition. *Journal of Experimental Psychology: General*, *129*, 4–26.

Mayr, U., & Kliegl, R. (2003). Differential effects of cue changes and task changes on task-set selection costs. *Journal of Experimental Psychology: Learning, Memory, and Cognition*, *29*, 362–372.

Meiran, N. (1996). Reconfiguration of processing mode prior to task performance. *Journal of Experimental Psychology. Learning,Memory, and Cognition*, *22*, 1423–1442.

Meiran,N. (2000). Modeling cognitive control in task-switching. *Psychological Research*, *63*, 234–249

Meiran, N. (2010). Task switching: Mechanisms underlying rigid vs. flexible self control. In R. Hassin, K. Ochsner, & Y. Trope. (Eds.), *Self control in society, mind and brain*. (pp. 202–220). New York, NY: Oxford University Press.

Meiran, N., Chorev, Z., & Sapir, A. (2000). Component processes in task switching. *Cognitive Psychology*, *41*, 211–253.

Meiran, N., Kessler, Y., & Adi-Japha, E. (2008). Control by Action Representation and Input Selection (CARIS): A theoretical framework for task switching. *Psychological Research*, *72*, 473–500.

Monsell, S., & Mizon, G. (2006). Can the task-cuing paradigm measure an measure an endogenous task-set reconfiguration process? *Journal of Experimental Psychology: Human Perception and Performance*, *32*, 493–516.

Neath, I., & Brown, G. D. A. (2012). Arguments against memory trace decay: A SIMPLE account of Baddeley & Scott. *Frontiers in Cognition*, *3*, 35. doi:10.3389/fpsyg.2012.00035

Newell, A. (1990). *Unified theories of cognition*. Cambridge, MA: Harvard University Press.

Norman, D. A., & Shallice, T. (1986). Attention to action: Willed and automatic control of behaviour. In R. J. Davidson, G. E. Schwartz, & D. Shapiro (Eds.), *Consciousness and self-regulation: Advances in research and theory, Vol. 4*. New York, NY: Plenum.

Oberauer, K., & Lewandowsky, S. (2013). Evidence against decay in verbal working memory. *Journal of Experimental Psychology: General*, *142*, 380–411.

Oberauer, K., Lewandowsky, S., Farrell, S., Jarrold, S., & Greaves, M. (2012). Modeling working memory: An interference model of complex span. *Psychonomic Bulletin & Review*, *19*, 779–819.

Philipp, A. M., Jolicoeur, P., Falkenstein, M., & Koch, I. (2007). Response selection and response execution in task switching: Evidence from a go-signal paradigm. *Journal of Experimental Psychology: Learning, Memory, and Cognition*, *33*, 1062–1075.

Plaut, D. C. (2000). Connectionist modeling. In A. E. Kazdin (Ed.), *Encyclopedia of psychology*. Washington, DC: American Psychological Association.

Roberts, S., & Pashler, H. (2000). How persuasive is a good fit? A comment on theory testing. *Psychological Review*, *107*, 358–367.

Rogers, R. D., & Monsell, S. (1995). Costs of a predictible switch between simple cognitive tasks. *Journal of Experimental Psychology: General*, *124*, 207–231.

Rubinstein, J. S., Meyer, D. E., & Evans, J. E. (2001). Executive control of cognitive processes in task switching. *Journal of Experimental Psychology: Human Perception and Performance*, *27*, 763–797.

Schneider, D. W., & Logan, G. D. (2005). Modeling task switching without switching tasks: A short-term priming account of explicitly cued performance. *Journal of Experimental Psychology: General, 134*, 343–367.

Schneider, D. W., & Logan, G. D. (2006). Priming cue encoding by manipulating transition frequency in explicitly cued task switching. *Psychonomic Bulletin & Review, 13*, 145–151.

Schneider, D. W., & Logan, G. D. (2009). Selecting a response in task switching: Testing a model of compound cue retrieval. *Journal of Experimental Psychology: Learning, Memory, and Cognition, 35*, 122–136.

Schneider, D. W., & Verbruggen, F. (2008). Inhibition of irrelevant category-response mappings. *Quarterly Journal of Experimental Psychology, 61*,1629–1640.

Schuch, S., & Koch, I. (2003). The role of response selection for inhibition of task sets in task shifting. *Journal of Experimental Psychology: Human Perception & Performance, 29*, 92–105.

Sdoia, S., & Ferlazzo, F. (2008). Stimulus-related inhibition of task set during task switching. *Experimental Psychology, 55*, 322–327.

Sohn, M.-H., & Anderson, J. R. (2001). Task preparation and task repetition: Two-component model of task switching. *Journal of Experimental Psychology: General, 130*, 764–778.

Sun, R. (2002). *Duality of the mind*. Mahwah, NJ: Lawrence Erlbaum Associates.

Vandierendonk, A., Demanet, J., Liefooghe, B., & Verbruggen, F. (2012). A chain-retrieval model for voluntary task switching. *Cognitive Psychology, 65*, 241–283.

Vandierendonck, A., Liefooghe, B., & Verbruggen, F. (2010). Task switching: Interplay of reconfiguration and interference control. *Psychological Bulletin, 136*, 601–626.

Waszak, F., Hommel, B., & Allport, A. (2003). Task-switching and long-term priming: Role of episodic stimulus–task bindings in task-shift costs. *Cognitive Psychology, 46*, 361–413.

Wylie, G., & Allport, A. (2000). Task switching and measurement of "switch costs". *Psychological Research, 63*, 212–233.

9

Event-Related Potentials Reveal Multiple Components of Proactive and Reactive Control in Task Switching

FRINI KARAYANIDIS AND SHARNA D. JAMADAR

INTRODUCTION

A large body of behavioral studies has used variations of the task switching paradigm to study cognitive control processes associated with rapidly, flexibly and efficiently shifting between different contextual demands (see Kiesel et al., 2010; Vandierendonck et al., 2010, for recent reviews of behavioral studies). These studies have firmly established a role for both proactive and reactive control processes in task switching performance (Braver, Gray, & Burgess, 2007). Proactive control includes processes that are associated with bringing the system to a state of readiness to repeat or change task and that can be manipulated by varying the opportunity for preparation prior to target onset (e.g., cue informativeness, preparation interval). Reactive control includes processes that optimize target processing by minimizing the impact of carryover interference (e.g., backward interference, positive or negative priming) and posttarget interference (e.g., irrelevant character priming). Indeed, it is the ability to simultaneously manipulate both proactive and reactive control processes that has made the task switching paradigm particularly attractive as a platform to study cognitive control. However, as conventional behavioral measures represent the cumulative endpoint of these processes, they do not offer direct insight into the multiple sensory, cognitive and motor processes that contribute to the overt response. This limitation is particularly relevant to task switching paradigms, where the emphasis is on understanding not only the unique contributions of preparation in anticipation of the target (i.e., proactive control) and target-driven interference (i.e., reactive control) but also how these processes interact to bring about efficient and flexible performance under changing task contexts. Critical to addressing these questions is the ability to temporally distinguish proactive and reactive control processes that contribute to overt behavior.

In task switching paradigms, the effect of preparation on behavioral performance is evaluated by comparing the degree to which *switch cost* (*switch-repeat*) is reduced on trials with long compared with short preparation intervals. In cued-trials paradigms, this is typically manipulated by varying the cue–target interval (CTI). This *reduction in switch cost* is taken as evidence that this preparation interval was used to differentially prepare for switch versus repeat trials. The leftover from this double subtraction [*Long CTI (switch-repeat)—Short CTI (switch-repeat)*] is considered to represent the additional time taken to overcome differential interference on target processing for switch versus repeat trials (i.e., the *residual switch cost*). Many interpretations of the concepts of switch cost, reduction in switch cost, and residual switch cost are based strongly on an additive-factors logic (Sternberg, 1969). Three assumptions underlie this logic: (a) switch trials are identical to repeat trials with the exception of an extra process involved in shifting task set, (b) task switching under prepared conditions is identical to task switching in unprepared conditions with the exception that this extra shifting process occurs before target onset, and (c) completing this shifting process before target onset does not necessarily alter the nature or strength of target-driven interference (e.g., Rogers & Monsell, 1995; Rubinstein et al., 2001). However, straightforward application of this additive factors logic to the task switching paradigm is indirectly challenged by a range of behavioral findings. For example, early work by Allport et al. (1994) showed that carryover of task activation between trials may contribute to switch cost—leading to the concept of task-set inertia. De Jong (2000) provided evidence that residual switch cost may arise not only from target-driven interference but also from failure to use the preparation interval to shift task set on some proportion of switch trials. Koch and colleagues showed that trial sequence effects eliminate switch cost by differentially increasing response time (RT) on repeat trials (Koch & Philip, 2005; Schuch & Koch, 2003; see also Jamadar, Michie, & Karayanidis, 2010b), indicating that repeat and switch trials may involve both common and distinct underlying processes. This logic is more directly challenged by event-related potential (ERP) studies showing evidence for multiple preparation processes, some of which are common to both switch and repeat trials and others more specific to switch trials (e.g., Jamadar et al., 2010b; Karayanidis et al., 2011a).

ERPs are extracted from the electroencephalogram (EEG) and are variations in brain electrical activity time-locked to different types of events (Rugg & Coles, 1995). With a temporal resolution in the order of milliseconds, ERPs provide a unique measure of the timeline of sensory, cognitive, and motor processes that is unmatched by other neuroimaging methods. In the context of task switching paradigms, ERPs can differentiate activity time-locked to the cue from that locked to the target, thereby offering direct measures of processes associated with switch and repeat trials in cue-locked and posttarget intervals, respectively. This can help define the nature of these processes and test the underlying assumptions of theoretical models proposed to account for them. Cue-locked ERP waveforms can directly measure proactive control processes by providing a detailed time-course of differential preparation for switch and repeat cues during the CTI. Target-locked ERP waveforms measure switch versus repeat differences after target onset and can test assumptions arising from the use of the additive factors logic (i.e., that control processes necessary to overcome target-driven interference are independent of preparation during the CTI).

Differences between switch and repeat trials have been consistently reported in ERPs time-locked to both cue onset and target onset. Two ERP effects of task switching have been established most robustly and have been linked to temporally distinct processes in task switching (for a recent review, see Karayanidis et al., 2010). These include a relative increase in positivity for switch versus repeat trials during the CTI and a relative reduction in positivity for switch versus repeat trials after target onset. In this essay, we will examine what these ERP effects have told us about the nature of proactive and reactive control processes that contribute to task switching performance. We focus primarily on the cued-trials paradigm because, by providing control over the onset and duration of the preparation interval, it can temporally dissociate the contributions of proactive and reactive control processes on task switching performance.

ERP EVIDENCE OF PROACTIVE CONTROL IN TASK SWITCHING

Early work in this area has focused on establishing whether cue-locked ERPs show evidence for some kind of anticipatory preparation. That is, does advance knowledge that the upcoming target requires a change or repeat of task produce systematic ERP differences in the interval leading up to that target. Different paradigms have produced a variety of cue-locked ERP differences between switch and repeat trials. The most consistent effect is a relative positive shift for switch compared with repeat trials (see Figure 9.1A) that is maximal over central and parietal scalp and peaks around 400–600 ms post-cue (e.g., Karayanidis et al., 2003; Kieffaber & Hetrick, 2005; Nicholson et al., 2005; Swainson et al., 2006). We refer to this as the *switch-positivity* [see (a) in Figure 9.1A] to differentiate it from other preparation-related effects occurring within the CTI.

Although the switch-positivity is the most robust cue-locked component, other ERP effects are also evident during the CTI. Lavric and colleagues (Elchlepp et al., 2012; Lavric et al., 2006) reported a PCA component corresponding to an anterior negativity/posterior positivity complex, which is likely to correspond to what we call here the switch-positivity. Swainson and colleagues (Astle et al., 2006, 2008a; Mueller et al., 2007, 2009) found a slow frontal negativity that is sensitive to response-set mapping and may be associated with preparatory remapping of effectors to response category (see Karayanidis et al., 2010, for a review). This component appears to be more readily evident when using a different reference configuration to that more commonly used in task switching studies (i.e.,

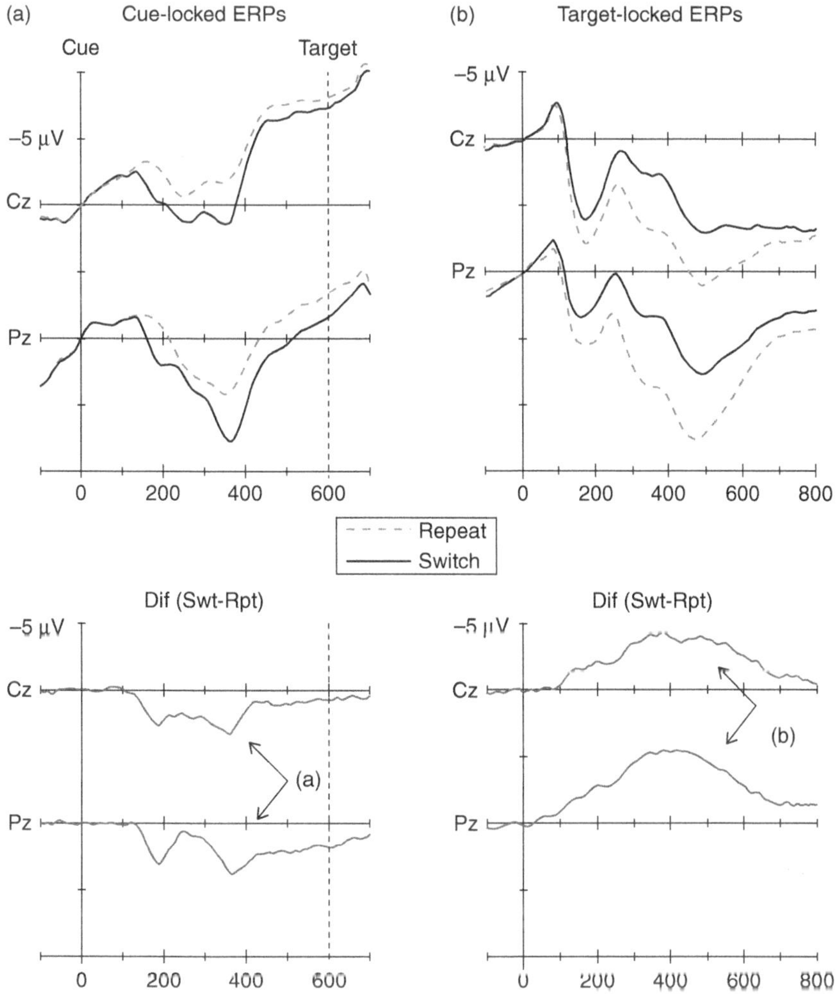

Figure 9.1 Grand average ERP waveforms time-locked to the onset of the cue (A) and the target (B). Waveforms are shown at central (Cz) and parietal (Pz) midline electrodes that tend to show largest trial type differences. The bottom panel shows (switch–repeat) difference waveforms with arrows pointing to (a) switch-positivity in cue-locked ERPs and (b) switch-negativity in target-locked ERPs. The *y*-axis depicts amplitude in microvolts. The *x*-axis depicts time in milliseconds.
Data adapted from Nicholson et al. (2005) using condition with 150-ms response–cue interval and 600-ms cue–target interval.

common average versus linked-mastoid reference). How this component corresponds to response-set related effects on the switch-positivity obtained with a mastoid reference is not yet established.

In the following sections, we first discuss the nature of differential preparation to switch task, as measured by the switch-positivity. We then discuss preparation processes common to both switch and repeat trials, focusing on other cue-locked ERP effects.

Evidence for Preparation to Switch: Switch-Positivity

The switch-positivity has been consistently reported with a range of alternating runs (DeSanctis et al., 2009; Karayanidis et al., 2003, 2006) and cued-trials task switching paradigms (Kieffaber & Hetrick, 2005; Lavric et al., 2008; Nicholson et al., 2005, 2006a, 2006b; Swainson et al., 2006), as well as with variations of the Wisconsin Card Sorting Task (WCST; Adrover-Roig et al., 2010; Barceló et al., 2000, 2006). A similar switch-positivity has been reported in voluntary switching paradigms (e.g., Karayanidis & Mansfield, 2010; Orr, Gehring, & Weissman, 2010), where it varies as a function of the number of task choices (Forstmann, Ridderinkhof, Kaiser, & Bledowski, 2007). The switch-positivity is robust to sequence effects induced by the inclusion of no-go trials (Astle et al., 2006; Gajewski & Falkenstein, 2011; Jamadar et al., 2010b), which have been shown to eliminate RT switch cost (Schuch & Koch, 2003), indicating that sequence effects do not disrupt differential preparation for switch versus repeat trials. Although most ERP task switching studies typically record from young university students, the switch-positivity has also been recorded across a range of other participant groups, including healthy elderly (Adrover-Roig et al., 2010; DeSanctis et al., 2009; Goffaux et al., 2008; Karayanidis et al., 2011b), children and adolescents (Karayanidis et al., forthcoming; Manzi et al., 2011), people with mild cognitive impairment (Sinai et al., 2010), and people with schizophrenia (Finke et al., 2011; Jamadar et al., 2010c; Karayanidis et al., 2006; Kieffaber et al., 2007).

In cued-trials paradigms, this robust switch-positivity has been elicited by a broad range of cues. It is found with both visual and auditory task cues (i.e., cues mapped to the upcoming task, e.g., Astle et al., 2006; Goffaux et al., 2006; Kieffaber & Hetrick, 2005; Lavric et al., 2008; Nicholson et al., 2005; Poulsen et al., 2005; Swainson et al., 2006; Wylie et al., 2009), regardless of whether the cues are explicit (e.g., the words *letter* and *number* cueing the letter and number tasks, respectively) or implicit (e.g., one location, shape or color mapped to the letter task and another to the number task). It is also elicited by both regular and intermittent transition cues (i.e., cues explicitly indicating a switch or repeat trial rather than the task to be performed, e.g., Astle et al., 2008a, 2008b; Cunillera et al., 2012; Hsieh & Chen, 2006; Hseih & Wu, 2011; Rushworth et al., 2002, 2005). The switch-positivity is also elicited by response feedback that indirectly signals a change in task, by indicating that a response using the previously relevant task rules is no longer correct (e.g., Barceló et al., 2006, 2008). ERP studies comparing 1:1 and 2:1 cue-task mapping have shown a robust switch-positivity to task-change cues, over and above any effect of cue-change/task-repeat cues (Jost et al., 2008; Nicholson et al., 2006a), indicating that differential activity for switch versus repeat trials within the preparation interval is not simply an artifact of cue identity change on task switch compared with task repeat trials (e.g., Logan & Bundesen, 2003).

The fact that this differential cue-locked positivity for switch versus repeat trials is larger over parietal sites and peaks around 400–600 ms has led some researchers to conclude that it represents a larger P3b component being elicited for switch compared with repeat trials (e.g., Kieffaber & Hetrick, 2005; West et al., 2011). In classic oddball ERP paradigms, the P3b is elicited by unpredictable, infrequent, task-relevant stimuli (e.g., Squires, Squires, & Hillyard, 1975). A long-standing theory of P3b is that it represents some type of "context updating" or updating of one's mental representation of the current environment (Donchin, 1981, see also Polich, 2007; but see Verleger, Jaskowskis, & Wascher, 2005). This interpretation appears to be intuitively compatible with a task-set shifting process that is necessary for switch but not repeat trials. However, many characteristics of the switch-positivity are not readily compatible with conditions known to affect the P3b. First, although the relative enhancement of positivity for switch versus repeat trials is often superimposed on a centroparietal P3-like positivity that is evident for both trial types in cued trials paradigms (e.g., Lavric et al., 2008; Nicholson et al., 2005, 2006a, 2006b; Swainson et al., 2006), in alternating runs paradigms it occurs over a broad negative waveform (Karayanidis et al., 2003, 2006). Second, although the switch-positivity tends to be larger centroparietally, it is typically evident broadly across the scalp. Third, the switch-positivity can emerge either before or after target onset, depending on the length of the preparation interval (Karayanidis et al., 2003; Nicholson et al., 2005). Further, although switch trials show a larger positivity than repeat trials in cue-locked waveforms, they have *reduced* positivity in target-locked waveforms (see later). The fact that switch trials are inherently more difficult than repeat trials and that the P3b component typically reduces in amplitude as function of task difficulty (e.g., Israel et al., 1980; Wickens et al., 1983) suggests that the target-locked, rather than the cue-locked, switch–repeat difference may be more compatible with P3b modulation (see later). Finally, as reviewed in detail later, there is evidence for multiple preparation-related positivities emerging in the CTI. Further experimental evidence is necessary to show whether one or more preparation positivity is modulated by the same experimental parameters known to modulate P3b. In the meantime, we have argued that the use of more generic and descriptive labels, such as *switch-positivity*, provides theoretically neutral placeholders that describe the phenomenon without implying premature allegiance to any particular theoretical position.

The replicability of this cue-locked switch-positivity across a range of paradigms provides categorical evidence for a role of proactive cognitive control processes in preparing for an upcoming switch in task. Given that this differential preparation is likely to involve shifting from a readiness to perform one task to readiness to perform another task, it is tempting to label the switching-positivity as an index of anticipatory task-set reconfiguration (cf. Rogers & Monsell, 1995). Indeed, such an interpretation is supported by evidence that a larger switch-positivity in the preparation interval is associated with a smaller RT switch cost (Karayanidis et al.,

2009, 2011a, 2011b; Lavric et al., 2008). However, defining the functional significance of the switch-positivity using a label that is itself ill defined is unhelpful. Rather, together with other ERP activity in the CTI, this switch-positivity offers a tool that can be used to define the nature of proactive control processes in task switching. This can be achieved by examining changes in ERP measures during the preparation interval as a function of experimental manipulations, individual variability and group differences (for further discussion, see Karayanidis et al., 2010). This information is crucial to fractionating the concept encompassed by the descriptive term "task-set reconfiguration" into constituent processes. Many ERP studies have developed variations of the task switching paradigm to address theoretical questions about the nature of switch-related preparation processes. For example, is switch preparation a single process or a set of processes that are differentially activated, depending on task parameters? Can a task set be fully prepared before target onset? If not, what can be prepared before target onset and what can only be prepared after the identity of the target has been revealed? Next, we review ERP studies that have addressed these and other questions by examining variation in the cue-locked switch-positivity as a function of the task properties that are used to define the switch trial.

Defining the Nature of Preparation to Switch

Most task switching paradigms require a switch in *both* stimulus set (i.e., shift from one classification rule to another) and response set (i.e., shift from one response rule to another).[1] For example, commonly used tasks are the letter and digit tasks (e.g., Rogers & Monsell, 1995). The shift from classifying a letter as vowel/consonant to classifying a digit as odd/even requires changing both stimulus set (*attend to letters versus attend to numbers*) and response set (*map left index finger to vowel versus odd and right index finger to consonant versus even*). Most ERP studies of task switching require switching both stimulus sets and response sets and hence cannot differentiate between preparation to shift attention to the new stimulus set and preparation to remap effectors to new response sets.

However, these same tasks could be designed to involve shifting only stimulus sets if the question was changed so as to require identical response mapping for both tasks (e.g., "Is the letter a vowel?" and "Is the number even?" since both map onto a Yes/No response). In addition, degree of interference at the stimulus-set level can be manipulated by using univalent versus bivalent sets. For example, the target can be univalent or bivalent by including exemplars from only one stimulus set (*A#*) or both stimulus sets (*A4*), respectively. Similarly, it is possible to design tasks that require only a shift in response set without a shift in stimulus set. For instance, a single stimulus set (e.g., letters) could involve a reversal of stimulus–response (S–R) mappings (*left = odd, right = even* versus *left = even, right = odd*) or a change in effectors (*index/middle fingers of left hand mapped to letter task options and of right hand mapped to number task options*). The former example illustrates a bivalent response set (i.e., overlapping S–R mapping) and the latter illustrates a univalent response set (i.e., distinct S–R mapping for each task). These manipulations are useful in identifying whether proactive and reactive control operate on stimulus-related or response-related processes. Next, we review several ERP studies that have shown that the cue-locked switch-positivity is elicited by preparation to switch either stimulus set or response set.

It is conceivable that the nature or amount of anticipatory preparation differs depending on whether the paradigm uses univalent or bivalent targets. That is, given that univalent targets unambiguously signal the currently relevant task and elicit less between-task interference than bivalent targets, there would be no requirement for advance preparation. A robust switch-positivity has been consistently found when shifting attention to the relevant stimulus set even when response set is univalent (e.g., Kieffaber & Hetrick, 2005). It is also elicited when the tasks are based on different dimensions of the same stimulus set (e.g., parity and numerosity of a single digit; Nicholson et al., 2006a), so that task switching is defined in terms of shifting attention between stimulus attributes (*parity* versus *numerosity*) rather than between stimulus features (*letters* versus *numbers*). However, although the switch-positivity is elicited in anticipation of both univalent and bivalent targets, its amplitude tends to be larger for the latter (Elchlepp et al., 2012; Karayanidis et al., 2003; Kieffaber & Hetrick, 2005; Poulsen et al., 2005). This is consistent with a larger switch-positivity being associated with greater need for preparation and inconsistent with a P3b component, which tends to reduce in amplitude with task difficulty.

The scalp distribution of the switch positivity does not differ when switching between visual tasks that are processed in neurally distinct areas (e.g., verbal versus spatial tasks; Miniussi et al., 2005). Switching between visual and auditory tasks mapped to the same response set produced three components in a spatio-temporal principal components analysis (PCA; Kieffaber & Hetrick, 2005). Two of these switch-related components were sensitive to stimulus properties whereas the third was linked to switching independently of stimulus properties. Elchlepp et al. (2012) also showed that multiple PCA components can be extracted in the CTI and that these are differentially affected by switching for univalent and bivalent stimulus sets. These findings support multiple underlying components contributing to the switch-positivity, with at least one component reflecting a more central or generic preparation process related to switching stimulus set.

Response-set shifting also elicits a switch-positivity. The centroparietal switch-positivity has been shown even with simple reversal of S–R mapping, that is, when alternating response sets for the same stimulus set (Astle et al., 2011; Rushworth et al., 2002). West et al. (2009) compared switching of stimulus set or response set alone or both together. The early component of the parietal switch-positivity (circa 400–600 ms) did not differ as a function of the type of switching, whereas the later component (post 600 ms) was larger when having to shift either stimulus set alone or both stimulus and response sets. Astle et al. (2008a) reported a switch-positivity with both univalent (index and middle fingers of both hands) and bivalent (index and middle fingers of dominant hand) S–R mappings for identical bivalent stimulus sets (e.g., vowel/consonant versus uppercase/lowercase tasks). The effect was prolonged for bivalent mappings, indicating that the duration of the switch-positivity is affected by the need to remap stimulus set to response set. The switch-positivity was evident regardless of whether the task defined an overt (e.g., button press) or a covert (e.g., mental counting) response.

In sum, the switch-positivity is consistent with a task-independent and response modality-independent proactive control process that prepares the system to shift task set regardless of whether this is defined on the basis of stimulus or response properties. The general consistency of this finding is compatible with de Jong's (2000) notion of an intention-activation process; a unitary process that shifts the system from a state of readiness to perform one task to a state of readiness to perform another (see also Brown, Lehmann, & Poboka, 2006). However, despite the almost ubiquitous nature of the switch-positivity, the above studies also paint a more complex picture. There is some variability in the size, duration and/or distribution of the switch-positivity as a function of stimulus- and response-related task parameters. Moreover, PCA analyses show more than one underlying components, some of which were task specific, whereas others were elicited independently of task properties. Therefore, it appears that this switch-preparation is unlikely to involve either a unitary process or an all-or-none process. More recent studies have developed paradigm manipulations or analysis approaches that help address this issue.

Evidence for Multiple Switch-Related Preparation Processes

Cue-locked ERPs depict moment-by-moment variation in electrical activity for switch versus repeat trials over the preparation interval. However, switch and repeat trial waveforms for each participant are derived by averaging individual trial EEG activity. So, like mean RT, this ERP waveform represents the *average* difference between switch and repeat trials for that participant, smoothing out trial-by-trial variability. In addition, the voltage of the ERP waveform at any point in time reflects the summated activity of two or more underlying ERP components that may be generated in spatially distinct areas and partially overlap in time (e.g., Luck, 2005). Therefore, variability in the size and duration of the differential switch-positivity across different task conditions may reflect differential modulation of the amplitude of the same ERP component or differential activation of some but not other partially overlapping ERP components. Recent studies have capitalized on the above properties of the ERP waveform to address the nature of preparation processes using analyses that examine intraindividual variability in preparation and paradigms that manipulate what can be prepared.

The size of the RT switch cost varies across the range of the RT distribution for switch and repeat trials, with fast responses being associated with smaller switch cost than slow responses (Figure 9.2; Brown et al., 2006; de Jong, 2000; Karayanidis et al., 2011a). This has been taken as evidence in favor of an all-or-none preparation process with residual RT switch cost resulting from a mixture of fully prepared and fully unprepared switch trials (de Jong, 2000). If variability in RT switch cost is due to differential preparation at fast (prepared) versus slow (unprepared) ranges of the RT distribution, we would expect that the amplitude of the switch-positivity would vary as a function of RT. Several ERP studies have shown, in fact, that the switch-positivity is larger for fast compared with

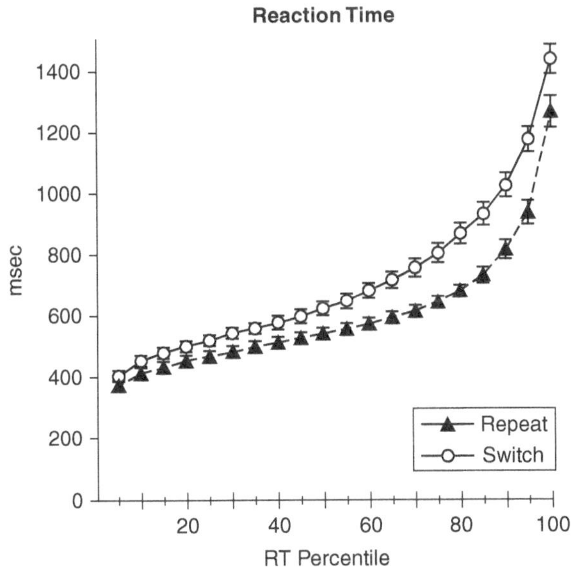

Figure 9.2 Mean RT for switch and repeat trials at each of 20 percentile ranks from the same data set as shown in Figure 9.1.
Adapted from Karayanidis et al. (2011).

slow RT responses using median, tercile, or quintile splits of the RT distribution (Elchlepp et al., 2012; Jost et al., 2008; Lavric et al., 2008). This relationship between switch-positivity amplitude and RT switch cost supports the notion that the switch-positivity provides a measure of preparation to switch. However, as the RT distribution for switch trials is shifted to the right of that for repeat trials, even quintile averages are likely to involve RT differences between switch and repeat trials. Therefore, any ERP differences may represent more generic differences in arousal or attention leading to slower versus faster responses.

Karayanidis et al. (2011a) used orthogonal polynomial trend analysis (OPTA; Woestenburg et al., 1983) to model the cue-locked ERP waveform for switch and repeat trials at each RT percentile (Figure 9.3). Consistent with a larger switch-positivity being associated with greater switch preparation, the amplitude of the differential switch-positivity progressively reduced with increasing RT switch cost across the RT distribution (Figure 9.3A). Analysis of RT-related variation in cue-locked ERPs for switch and repeat trials separately provided further evidence regarding the nature of preparation processes. Both repeat and switch waveforms showed a positive deflection within the latency range of the peak of the switch-positivity (Figure 9.3B). However, while the positivity for switch trials was largest for fast trials and reduced with increasing RT, the positivity for repeat trials did *not* vary with RT. In fact, the smallest positivity for switch trials (associated with the slowest switch trial RT) was significantly larger than the positivity for repeat trials. In addition, the positivity remained significantly larger for switch than for repeat trials, even when selecting switch and repeat trials from different

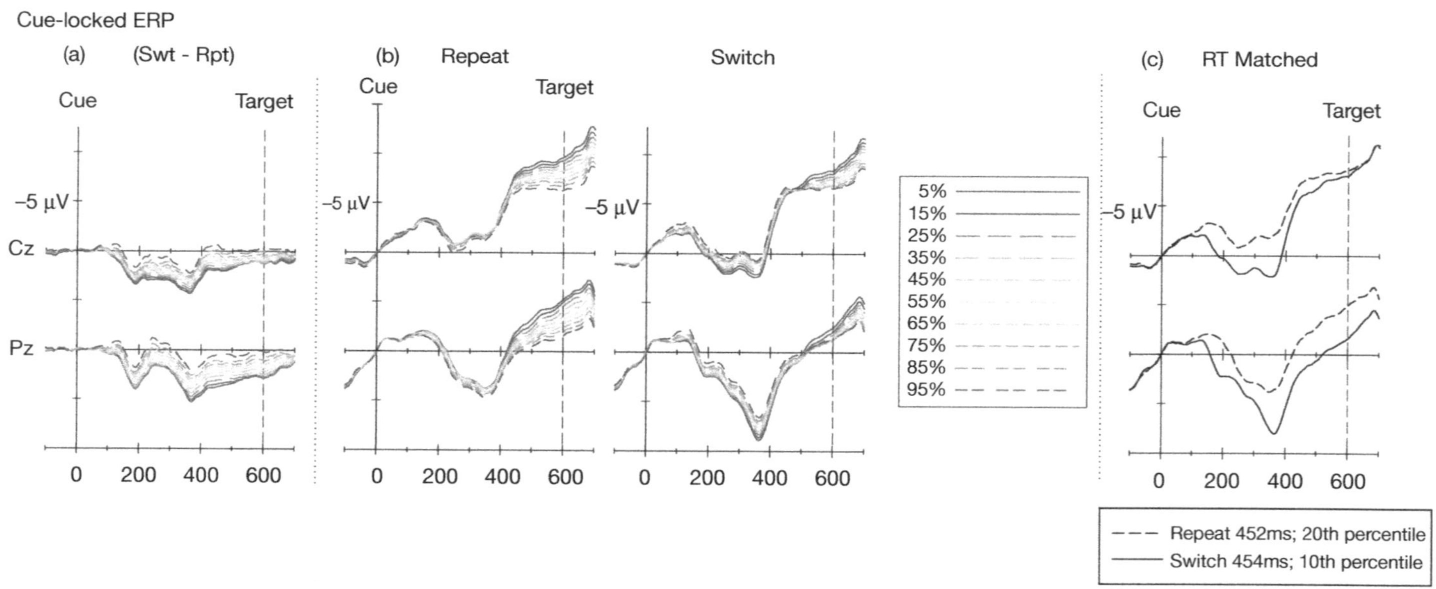

Figure 9.3 Cue-locked ERP waveforms in 10% increments starting at the fifth RT percentile. (A) Switch–repeat difference waveforms derived at each RT percentile interval. (B) ERP waveforms for repeat and switch trials. (C) Switch and repeat trials at the earliest percentile where RT is matched.

Adapted from Karayanidis et al. (2011a) using data from Nicholson et al. (2005) shown in Figure 9.1.

percentiles so as to be equated for RT. Together, these findings provide strong evidence for a switch-specific ERP component that is superimposed on a more generic positivity occurring for both switch and repeat trials. The generic positivity does not vary as a function of RT, whereas the amplitude of the switch-specific positivity varies inversely with switch trial RT. This switch-specific positivity is consistent with a graded rather than an all-or-none switch-specific preparation process.

Other evidence suggests that switch preparation is also not a unitary process. Using a novel three-task design that varied the type of information provided by the cue, Nicholson et al. (2006b) found distinct early and late switch-positivities associated with different levels of switch preparation. This paradigm differentiates between two types of switch cues (*switch-to* and *switch-away* cues). Both switch cues validly inform of an upcoming switch in task. However, *switch-to* cues also identify the task to be performed on the upcoming target (i.e., are equivalent to typical switch cues), whereas *switch-away* cues do not. For these *switch-away* cues, the participant knows that they will not repeat the same task but have to wait for the target itself to determine which of the other two tasks they need to perform. Both *switch-to* and *switch-away* cues elicited an early switch-positivity over 250–400ms relative to repeat cues (see (a) in Figure 9.4A). This early switch-positivity was not elicited by *noninformative* cues that were equally likely to result in a switch or repeat trial and therefore did not promote preparation to switch (Karayanidis et al., 2009).

For both *switch-to* and *switch-away* cues, the amplitude of the early switch-positivity was inversely related with RT, nondecision time, and response threshold. Non-decision time is a latent variable derived from an evidence accumulation model, which is affected by duration of encoding and response processes (Ratcliff & Rouder, 1998). In task switching paradigms, nondecision time has been shown to be inversely related to the amplitude of the switch-positivity (Karayanidis et al., 2009), suggesting that greater preparation may optimize encoding and response processes, and/or reduce the amount of switch-related processes that need to be completed after target onset (see also Schmitz & Voss, 2012). Response threshold indicates the amount of information required to arrive at a decision. Overall, switch trials are associated with higher response threshold than repeat trials, consistent with more evidence required on the more difficult switch trials. In addition, for switch trials, a larger switch-positivity was associated with lower response threshold. This is also consistent with the switch positivity reflecting switch preparation, such that greater preparation reduces the amount of information needed to arrive at a decision. So, the early switch-positivity was only elicited by cues that validly cued a switch trial and was related to degree of preparation. *Switch-to* cues also elicited a second switch-positivity within the CTI (see (b) in Figure 9.4A). However, for *switch-away* cues, this second switch-positivity emerged only *after* the onset of the target that indicated the identity of the task.

These findings are consistent with two distinct switch-related preparation processes. The *early switch positivity* is elicited only when the cue indicates with certainty that the preceding task will *not* be repeated—consistent with suppression or

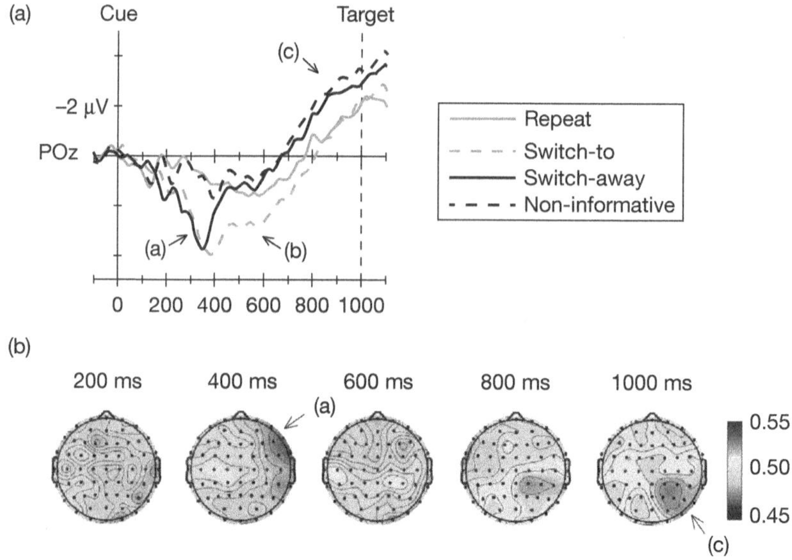

Figure 9.4 (A) Cue-locked ERP waveforms for each trial type at POz. (a) Early switch-positivity associated with switch preparation, (b) late switch-positivity, (c) pretarget negativity associated with task preparation. (B) Topographical plots showing misclassification of *repeat* and *switch-away* activity as *switch-to* activity within the alpha band based on Karayanidis et al. (2009) data shown in (A). (a) Right frontal cluster in timeframe of early switch-positivity indicates region related to switch preparation. (b) Right parietal cluster in timeframe of pretarget negativity indicates region related to task preparation. Red = *repeat* misclassified as *switch-to*, blue = *switch-away* misclassified as *switch-to*.
A, Adapted from Karayanidis et al. (2009). B, Adapted from Mansfield et al. (2012).

disengagement of the now irrelevant task set or activation of the intention to shift task (see Meiran, Hsieh, & Chang, 2011 for other evidence of suppression of irrelevant task rules). This is consistent with the finding that the early switch-positivity is associated with alpha frequency band activity over the right inferior frontal cortex (IFC; Mansfield et al., 2012; see (a) in Figure 9.4B), a region that has been strongly linked to inhibitory control (Aron et al., 2004; Jamadar et al., 2010a). The *later switch positivity* emerges only when the identity of the task is revealed (i.e., before target onset for *switch-to* cues and after for *switch-away* cues)—consistent with updating or reloading the now relevant task set. This process is likely to be mediated by frontoparietal pathways involved in task implementation (see Ruge, Jamadar, Zimmermann, & Karayanidis, 2013). These findings provide strong evidence that the concept of "task-set reconfiguration" or the shift from a readiness to complete one task to readiness to complete another involves multiple processes.

Together the above studies provide firm evidence that the differential switch-positivity elicited during the CTI is related to preparation to switch task and contribute to our understanding of the nature of switch preparation in task switching. There is consistent evidence that switch preparation is not a unitary process. Some processes are elicited irrespective of task parameters whereas others are linked to the specific nature of the tasks being switched. Emerging evidence suggests that an early process may be linked to setting the intention to switch. Later task-specific preparation processes appear to be differentially modulated by task parameters, including the nature of the tasks, whether task sets are univalent or bivalent and whether switching is defined on stimulus sets and/or response sets. At least some switch preparation processes are graded, with greater activation being associated with proportionately smaller RT for switch trials. These latter processes appear to be involved in setting action plans, consistent with evidence for switch-related activation in posterior parietal cortex (for a review, see Ruge et al., 2013). In addition, there is increasing evidence that preparation to switch does not simply represent greater activation of one or more processes commonly activated for both switch and repeat trials, although as discussed in the next section, there is evidence for common preparation processes as well. While the above studies have gone a long way towards identifying and defining switch-specific preparation processes, the link between different switch-positivities and precise cognitive processes remains weak. Later, we discuss promising directions from more recent work that examines the association between ERP measures of proactive and reactive control processes and latent model parameters from evidence accumulation models that are associated with specific decision-related processes.

Evidence for Common Preparation Processes for Switch and Repeat Trials

While we made the case for switch-specific preparation processes, cue-locked ERPs also show evidence for preparation processes common to both switch and repeat trials. In this section, we briefly discuss three cue-locked ERP components that are elicited for both switch and repeat trials.

Pretarget Negativity

Within the CTI, the centroparietal positivity that is larger for switch trials is frequently succeeded by a centrally maximal pretarget negativity that peaks at target onset and is often larger for repeat trials (e.g., Goffaux et al., 2006; Jamadar et al., 2010b; Kieffaber & Hetrick, 2005; Nicholson et al., 2005; Swainson et al., 2006). Given the relatively short intervals that produce optimal preparation (circa 600–1200 ms), it is often difficult to temporally differentiate between the earlier switch-positivity and the later pretarget negativity. This is especially the case in switch-repeat difference waveforms that result in a large and broad positivity emerging around 300 ms and resolving around target onset at central and parietal sites (Figure 9.1A).

Karayanidis et al. (2011a) provided strong evidence that the switch-positivity and the pretarget negativity are functionally dissociable components. While, as noted above, the amplitude of the parietal positivity varied inversely with RT only for switch trials, the pretarget negativity varied with RT for *both* trial types (Figure 9.3B). A larger pretarget negativity was associated with faster responding to the upcoming target, consistent with a late CNV or stimulus-preceding negativity (e.g., Brunia, 1999) related to task preparedness and/or anticipatory attention. In addition, unlike the preceding parietal positivity, when controlling for RT, the pretarget negativity did not differ in amplitude between switch and repeat trials (Figure 9.3C). This indicates that, given the opportunity to prepare for an upcoming switch trial (as indexed by the switch-positivity), a similar state of general task preparedness (as indexed by the pretarget negativity) reduces residual switch cost. The fact that these prepared switch trials show continue to show a significant residual RT switch cost suggests that, even on highly prepared switch trials, target-driven interference can be reduced but not eliminated (see later).

Other findings also support the notion that this pretarget negativity is associated with anticipatory attention and/or task preparedness. The pretarget negativity differentiated between cues that provide valid information about the identity of the upcoming task (i.e., repeat and switch-to cues) and cues that do not (i.e., cues indicating that a change in task is definite (switch-away) or likely (noninformative); see (c) in Figure 4A in Karayanidis et al., 2009). The former cues provide certainty about the relevant stimulus–response mapping whereas, for the latter cues, this mapping is not specified until target onset. Multivariate pattern classification analysis differentiated between these two cue types (task predictive versus task nonpredictive) in alpha frequency band activity over the right parietal cortex (see (c) in Figure 9.4b; Mansfield et al., 2012). This is consistent with the link between superior parietal lobule (SPL) activation and task readiness (Forstmann et al., 2006; Ruge et al., 2009; see Ruge et al., 2013), a process conceptualized as either reinforcing (in the case of *repeat* cues) or re-loading (in the case of *switch-to* cues) the relevant task set.

Informative-Positivity and Mixing-Positivity

Most ERP studies have only reported ERPs from conditions with an optimal preparation interval (i.e., circa 600–1000 ms). This is mostly because short preparation intervals result in an overlap of cue-locked and target-locked ERP components, making it more difficult to disentangle cue-related from target-related processes (see Jost et al., 2008; Karayanidis et al., 2003; Nicholson et al., 2005, for comparison of ERPs at short and longer preparation intervals). Additionally, varying preparation interval does not only alter the time available to process the cue and differentially prepare for the upcoming switch or repeat trial. It can also result in interference of cue processing on target processing[2] and differential readiness for the onset of the second event in the cue–target sequence. To control for these effects on target-locked ERPs and also examine cue-locked preparation processes common to both switch and repeat trials, some cued-trials switching paradigms compare conditions with a fixed long CTI where the cue is either informative (i.e., signals the timing of the target *and* the identity of the task) or noninformative (i.e., signals the timing of the target, *but not* the identity of the task).

In cued-trials paradigms, ERPs to noninformative cues diverge from both switch and repeat informative cues around 300ms post-cue (Jamadar et al., 2010a, 2010b). We have referred to this relative parietal positivity for informative relative to noninformative cues as the *informative-positivity*, to differentiate it from the later *switch-positivity* that emerges for informative switch relative to informative repeat cues (Figure 9.5A). This informative-positivity is larger when informative and noninformative trials are presented in separate blocks than when they are intermixed (Jamadar et al., 2010b) and appears to be compatible with a general preparation process common to both repeat and switch trials. While the scalp distribution of informative-positivity is similar to that of the switch-positivity, these waveforms are associated with fMRI activation in different cortical networks. Switch-positivity amplitude is associated with differential (*switch-repeat*) activation in posterior parietal cortex (Figure 9.5C), whereas informative-positivity amplitude correlates with differential (*informative–noninformative*) activation in right dorsolateral prefrontal cortex (Figure 9.5B; Jamadar et al., 2010a). Moreover, seeded source localization analyses confirmed that posterior parietal cortex (superior parietal lobule) and dorsolateral prefrontal cortex (superior frontal gyrus) are likely sources of the switch-positivity and informative-positivity, respectively (Jamadar et al., 2010a). These data support the contention that the informative-positivity and the switch-positivity are distinct cognitive processes generated in different neural pathways.

Repeat trials in mixed-task blocks (*mixed-repeat*[3]) show slower and less accurate performance than repeat trials in single-task blocks (*all-repeat*), an effect referred to as the *mixing cost*. In cue-locked ERPs, both mixed-repeat and switch trials show a larger positivity compared with all-repeat trials, which we have previously referred to as the *mixing-positivity* (Goffaux et al., 2008; Jost et al., 2008; Karayanidis et al., 2011b; Kray et al., 2005; see also Hsieh & Chen, 2006). Both the behavioral mixing cost and the mixing-positivity occur despite the fact that all-repeat and mixed-repeat cues are physically identical. They differ in that, in single-task blocks, the cue provides redundant information. This mixing-positivity is elicited even when the physical identity of the cue varies across trials in both single-task and mixed-task blocks (Jost et al., 2008; Karayanidis et al., 2011b). Therefore, this differential positivity cannot reflect differences related to physical properties of the cue, and is consistent with greater need for trial-by-trial cue processing and preparation on mixed-task blocks.

In conclusion, the informative-positivity is consistent with a goal activation process elicited for both switch and repeat cues and generated in dorsolateral prefrontal cortex and the switch-positivity is compatible with a later task activation process elicited only for switch cues and generated in posterior parietal cortex (Jamadar et al., 2010a; see also Jamadar et al., 2010c). Goal activation may be conceptualized as translating the cue information to formulate the intention to switch or repeat task, whereas task activation may be conceptualized as reloading the new task set in anticipation of the target.

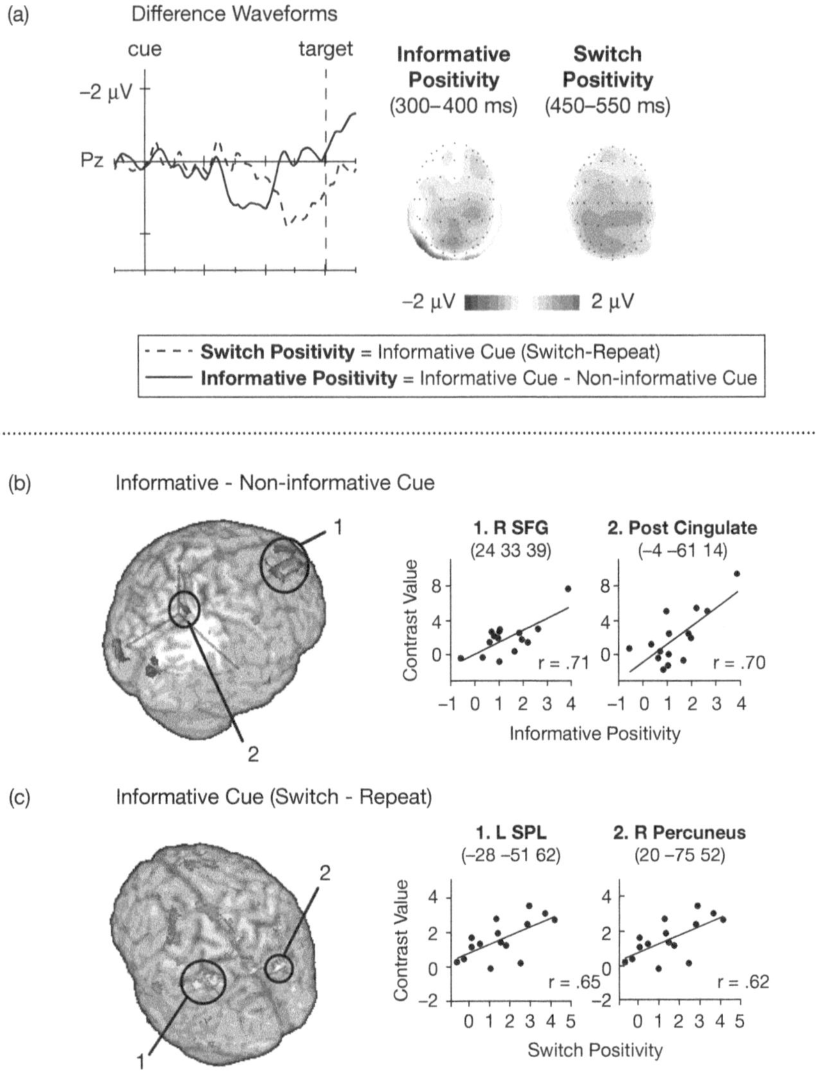

Figure 9.5 (A) Difference waveforms showing early cue-locked differential positivity for (informative–noninformative) cue conditions (informative-positivity) and late cue-locked differential positivity for informatively cued (switch–repeat) conditions (switch positivity). Scalp topographies of the informative-positivity and the switch-positivity (right). (B) Multiple regression analyses of fMRI Informative > noninformative cue contrast with cue-locked informative positivity amplitude over 300–400 ms. (C) Multiple regression analyses of fMRI switch > repeat contrast with switch-positivity amplitude over 450–550 ms. For both B and C, scatterplots show the relationship between BOLD contrast value and ERP measures within each region of interest (ROI). ROIs were defined by the clusters in the multiple regression analysis. L, left; R, right; SFG, superior frontal gyrus; SPL, superior parietal lobule; Post Cingulate, posterior cingulate.
Adapted from Jamadar et al. (2010a).

ERP EVIDENCE OF REACTIVE CONTROL IN TASK SWITCHING

Although ERP studies of task switching have focused primarily on preparation-related processes occurring during the CTI, ERPs also show robust effects of task switching in the posttarget interval. Target-locked ERPs are characterized by a large frontocentral N2 component followed by a later centroparietal positivity. Switch trials typically show a larger N2 and smaller P3 relative to repeat trials (Figure 9.1B). Consequently, across a range of paradigms, (*switch–repeat*) difference waveforms show a broad centroparietally maximal negative waveform (see (b) in Figure 9.1B; Barceló, 2003; Hsieh & Chen, 2006; Karayanidis et al., 2003; Kieffaber & Hetrick, 2005; Lavric et al., 2008; Miniussi et al., 2005; Nicholson et al., 2005; Poulsen et al., 2005; Wylie et al., 2003). When the target is preceded by a long and informative preparation interval, this relative negative shift for switch trials emerges as early as 150 ms and peaks around 600 ms posttarget (Karayanidis et al., 2003; Mueller et al., 2009; Nicholson et al., 2005). When there is little opportunity for anticipatory preparation, its onset is delayed by more than 300ms and it is often preceded by a differential switch-positivity (Karayanidis et al., 2003; Nicholson et al., 2005, 2006a). This relative negative shift for switch trials has been shown in children (Karayanidis et al., forthcoming; Manzi et al., 2011), older people (e.g., Karayanidis et al., 2011b; West & Travers, 2008), and people with schizophrenia (Jamadar et al., 2010c; Karayanidis et al., 2006).

For reasons similar to those discussed earlier with regard to the cue-related switch-positivity, we have previously referred to this effect as a *switch-negativity* to denote that it does not appear to be temporally or spatially linked to any single ERP component (e.g., Karayanidis et al., 2003; Nicholson et al., 2005). However, there is amassing evidence that differential modulation of switch and repeat trials in target-locked ERPs may indeed represent, at least partly, modulation of the P3b component (e.g., Barceló et al., 2008; Goffaux et al., 2006; Hsieh & Liu, 2005, Kieffaber & Hetrick, 2005; for a review, see Karayanidis et al., 2010). Morphologically, in both cued-trials and alternating runs paradigms, this differential switch effect is superimposed on a parietally maximal positivity that has a similar peak amplitude, latency, duration, and topography to the P3b. Like the P3b, the amplitude of this target-locked positivity is smaller (a) for the more difficult switch trials, (b) under bivalent than univalent task conditions for both switch and repeat trials (e.g., Karayanidis et al., 2003), and (c) in individuals with schizophrenia who consistently show reduced P3b across various task switching paradigms (Finke et al., 2011; Jamadar et al., 2010c; Kieffaber et al., 2007; see Jeon & Polich, 2003, for a review of P3 in schizophrenia). Finally, PCA consistently shows that the differential switch effect is obtained on the latent P3b component (Elchlepp et al., 2012; Kieffaber & Hetrick, 2005; Lavric et al., 2008).

Importantly, regardless of the label applied to this posttarget switch effect, it has been assumed that the relative negativity for switch versus repeat trials results from modulation of a single ERP component which represents an additive process that must be completed for switch trials in order to make them equivalent to repeat trials (e.g., a posttarget reconfiguration process, Rogers & Monsell, 1995; see Introduction). This is not surprising, given the broad continuous morphology of this target-locked (*switch–repeat*) difference (see (b) in Figure 9.1B). However, target-locked ERPs consist of numerous partially overlapping components that are associated with sensory, cognitive and motor processes leading from stimulus processing to response activation. In long preparation conditions, switch trials show a larger frontocentral N2 and a smaller centroparietal P3b than repeat trials. Across a range of paradigms, manipulations that increase N2 amplitude for switch trials also tend to reduce P3b amplitude (Gajewski & Falkenstein, 2011). In fact, N2 and P3 are so tightly coupled that they are often conceptualized as an N2/P3 complex. Thus, the question remains whether the switch-negativity represents a single additional component for switch trials superimposed on both N2 and P3b or multiple ERP components differentially affected on switch and repeat trial types.

There is strong evidence that both P3 and N2 consist of functionally distinct subcomponents. In the current context, the relevant subcomponents are the P3b and the anterior (frontocentral) N2 (Folstein & van Petten, 2008; Johnson et al., 1993), respectively. P3b amplitude decreases with increasing attentional and working memory load (Donchin et al., 1986; Kok, 1997) and with decreasing stimulus discriminability (Linden, 2005). The anterior N2 component is elicited in paradigms that require control processes such as interference, inhibition, and error monitoring (see Folstein & van Petten, 2008, for a review). For example, the N2 is larger for stimuli associated with high interference in paradigms such as the Eriksen Flanker task (e.g., Gehring et al., 1992; Hsieh et al., 2012) and the Simon task (e.g., Spapé et al., 2011). Although typically the N2 peaks around 200 ms posttarget, in some paradigms it can peak later or show a broader peak, often resulting in what appears as two partially overlapping components. For instance, incongruent trials during color-naming in the Stroop tasks (e.g., West & Alain, 2000) elicit a later negativity (N450) within the latency range of the N400 component, which is elicited typically by semantic incongruity. Folstein and van Petten (2008) make a case for distinct anterior N2 components related to deviance detection and control of interference.

In the following section, we review studies showing differential switch-related modulation of interference and decision processes. We conclude that the differential negativity for switch versus repeat trials over central and parietal sites is consistent with modulation of both anterior N2 and P3b.

Posttarget Interference and Reactive Control

Under fully prepared conditions, the task switching paradigm can be conceptualized as an interference paradigm. In task switching, interference may be present for both switch and repeat trials as a result of either carryover of positive and/or negative priming from the immediately preceding trials or the presence of incongruent bivalent stimuli (e.g., Wylie & Allport, 2000). Persistent residual mixing-cost even for highly prepared and practiced conditions (e.g., Whitson et al., 2012) and strong sequence effects on repeat trial RT (e.g., Jamadar et al., 2010b; Schuch & Koch, 2003) indicate that target-driven interference is present for repeat trials presented in mixed-task blocks. Persistent residual switch cost with bivalent stimuli even under highly prepared and practiced conditions (e.g., Whitson et al., 2012) and for the fastest (fully prepared) switch trials (Karayanidis et al., 2011a) indicates that this target-driven interference is greater on switch trials and cannot be completely overcome with preparation.

Few studies have systematically examined target-driven interference in task switching. In target-locked ERPs, anterior N2 has been shown to be smallest for all-repeat trials and to progressively increase for (mixed-) repeat and switch trials in a mixed-task block (Goffaux et al., 2006; Jost et al., 2008; Karayanidis et al., 2011b). This increase in N2 amplitude with increasing level of interference is accompanied by a progressive reduction in parietal P3b, consistent with greater difficulty of decision processes. Larger N2 and smaller P3 for switch versus repeat trials have been reported in other studies (Hsieh & Liu, 2008; Karayanidis et al., 2003; Poulsen et al., 2005). These studies manipulated stimulus valence and showed that N2 was larger and P3b smaller for bivalent compared with univalent stimuli. The valence effect on N2 did not differ for switch and repeat trials. However, in both Hsieh and Liu (2008) and Karayanidis et al. (2003), the valence effect on P3 was larger for switch trials, with smaller amplitude and earlier resolution of the switch–repeat differential for univalent trials. This pattern is consistent with independent switch-related modulation of N2 and P3.

Between-task interference in task switching has also been examined by looking at sequence effects (i.e., the carryover of task-set information into subsequent trials). These studies also show a pattern compatible with differential modulation of N2 and P3b. Jamadar et al. (2010b) examined sequence effects introduced by intermixing no-go trials with typical switch and repeat trials (experiment 1). On no-go trials, the task is prepared but not implemented, so one would expect reduced carryover of task-set activation after a no-go trial. Hence, trials following a no-go trial (i.e., *no-go*/go) should show less interference than *go*/go trials. Consistent with this, Jamadar et al. (2010b) found that *no-go*/go trials elicited smaller N2 and larger P3b than *go*/go trials.[4] In contrast, Gajewski and colleagues showed enhanced N2 and reduced P3b for *no-go*/go sequences relative to *go*/go sequences (see Gajewski et al., 2010 for N2 and Gajewski & Falkenstein, 2011 for P3 analyses of the same data set). The key to this discrepancy is a difference in the way these studies defined no-go stimuli. In Jamadar et al (2010b), the target on no-go trials was selected from a set of nonalphanumeric characters that did not belong to either stimulus set. As there was no association between the no-go target stimulus and a response, the no-go target could not activate any response. In Gajewski et al.'s study, the target on no-go trials belonged to the relevant stimulus set but was accompanied by a visual no-go cue (i.e., change in background color). Hence, the target could activate an S–R link and an associated response, but this response would have to be inhibited. So, compared with *go*/go sequences, *no-go*/go trials would have more carryover of interference in Gajewksi et al.'s study

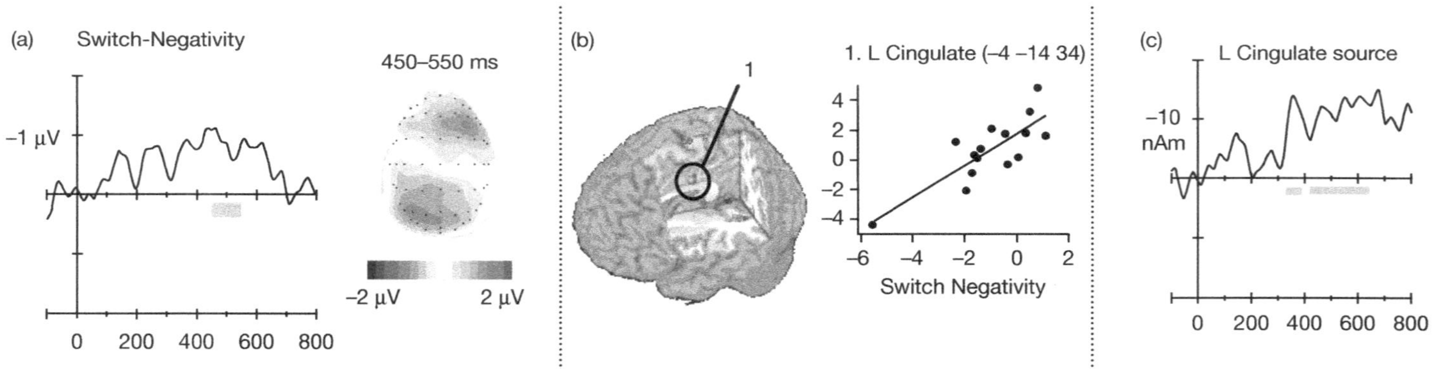

Figure 9.6 (A) Difference waveform showing target-locked differential negativity for informatively cued (switch–repeat) condition (switch-negativity) and its scalp topography. (B) Multiple regression analysis of fMRI switch > repeat contrast with switch-negativity amplitude over 450–500 ms. Scatterplot shows the relationship between the BOLD contrast in the left cingulate ROI and switch-negativity amplitude. The correlation remained significant after removal of the outlier. ROI was defined by the clusters in the multiple regression analysis. (C) Source waveform for target-locked switch-negativity with dipole seeded in left cingulate. Bars represent areas of significant deviation from baseline. Adapted from Jamadar et al. (2010a).

than in Jamadar et al.'s. This fits nicely with the larger N2/smaller P3 in Gajewski et al.'s study and the smaller N2/larger P3 in Jamadar et al.'s study.

Repeat trial sequences also show effects consistent with carryover of interference as reflected in N2 and P3b. Wylie et al. (2003) used an alternating runs paradigm with three task repetitions (AAABBB). Here, switch trials (i.e., AB) would be expected to show greater interference than repeat trials (i.e., BB), but also short repeat sequences (i.e., ABB) should show greater interference than long repeat sequences (i.e., BBB). As predicted, switch trials showed a smaller P3 than short repeat sequences, which in turn had a smaller P3b than long repeat sequences (Wylie et al., 2003). N2 shows a similar pattern in their Figure 9.4.

So, posttarget ERPs in task switching show a pattern of N2 and P3b modulation similar that seen in interference paradigms and consistent with differential activation of reactive control processes for the more difficult switch trials. In a combined ERP-fMRI study, Jamadar et al. (2010a) showed that the amplitude of the switch-negativity correlated with fMRI activity in the anterior cingulate cortex (ACC; Figure 9.6B), a region known to be involved in interference detection and suppression (Botvinick et al., 2004). This relationship was confirmed by seeded source analysis which showed that the ACC is a likely generator of the switch-negativity (Figure 9.6C; Jamadar et al., 2010a). Jamadar et al. (2010c) found that the earlier "N2" part of the differential switch-negativity and the later "P3b" part of the switch-negativity were associated with different patterns of fMRI activation. In healthy controls, the early switch-negativity overlapping N2 was correlated with greater switch > repeat activation in frontopolar cortex (medial frontal gyrus), whereas the late switch-negativity overlapping P3b was also correlated with activity in bilateral ACC and right PPC (inferior parietal lobule). This frontopolar cortex source was confirmed in an EEG study using three-dimensional tomographic source analysis (Jamadar et al., 2010d). Jamadar et al. (2010c) showed that, in participants with schizophrenia, the relationship between ACC activation and the switch-negativity was stronger than in controls and emerged on the earlier component overlapping N2, consistent with greater target-driven interference. Together these results suggest that, even under prepared conditions, targets on switch trials are associated with greater carryover or target-driven interference than repeat trials, as indicated by effects on N2 and activation of ACC. This results in a greater need to recruit reactive control processes in order to reduce the impact of interference on decision and response selection, as indicated by activity in the frontopolar cortex, a region highly implicated in contextual control (Koechlin & Summerfield, 2007).

Effect of Preparation on Target-Driven Interference

Although it is now widely agreed that opportunity for proactive control improves task switching performance, it remains unclear how advance preparation affects posttarget processing of switch and repeat trials. Preparation reduces but typically does not eliminate RT switch cost and error switch cost. Most studies showing

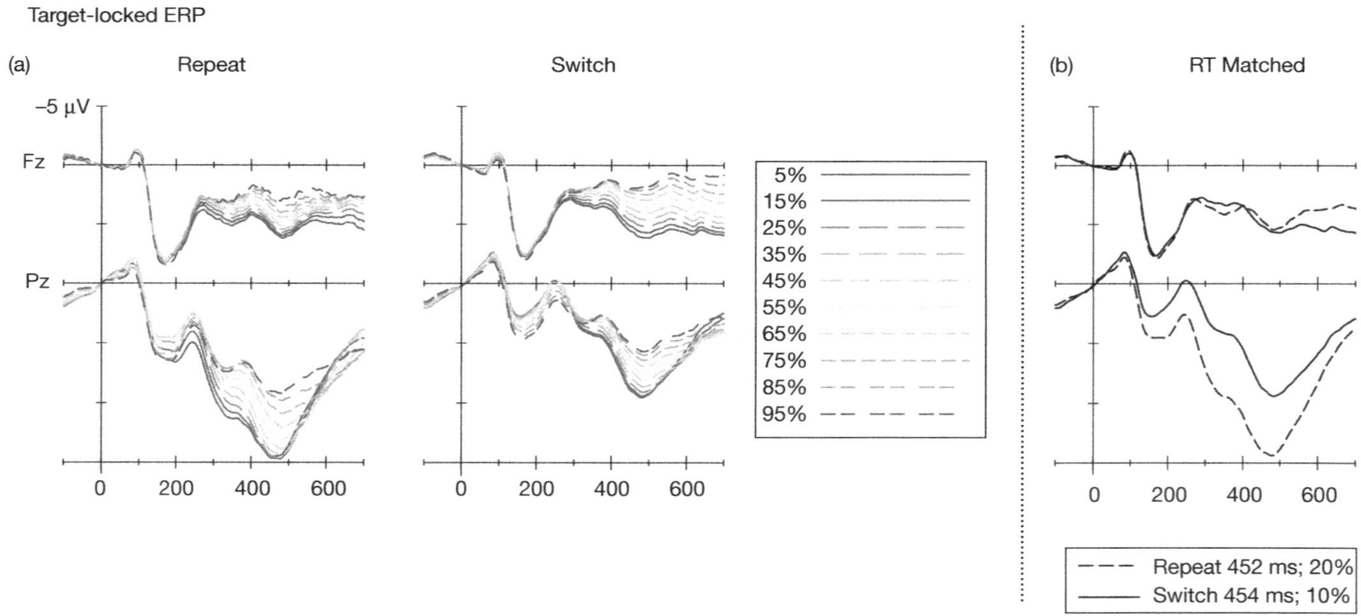

Figure 9.7 Target-locked ERP waveforms in 10% increments starting at the fifth RT percentile. (A) ERP waveforms for repeat and switch trials. (B) Switch and repeat trials at the earliest percentile where RT is matched.
Provost et al. (forthcoming) using target-locked data from Nicholson et al. (2005) shown in Figure 9.1. These represent the target-locked ERPs that correspond to the same condition as the cue-locked ERPs shown in Figure 9.3.

large posttarget N2 and P3b differences between switch and repeat trials have used a long preparation interval (see section B.1), indicating persistent differences at target processing level. The fact that the size of this (switch-repeat) difference is larger or more prolonged when the preparation interval is short (e.g., Jost et al., 2008; Karayanidis et al., 2003; Nicholson et al., 2005), suggests that preparation reduces the impact of target-driven interference on switch trials.

More direct evidence that preparation can reduce target-driven interference is shown by intrasubject variability in target-locked ERPs across the RT distribution (Provost et al., forthcoming). Both repeat and switch trials showed a smaller anterior N2 and a larger parietal P3b for fast "prepared" compared with slow "unprepared" trials (Figure 9.7A). In addition, when matched for RT, switch trials did not differ from repeat trials in anterior N2 and but continued to show a large reduction in parietal P3b (Figure 9.7B). So, preparation reduces target-driven interference for both switch and repeat trials. However, even when comparing fast prepared responses for switch and repeat trials that are matched for RT (second quintile for switch and fourth for repeat), target-locked ERPs show no evidence of interference, but still differences in decision processes. These findings are consistent with the notion that proactive control reduces but does not eliminate posttarget interference for switch trials. They also indicate trial-by-trial variability in the relative activation of proactive and reactive control processes for both switch and repeat trials. Further work is needed to define the conditions that increase probability of implementation of proactive control in order to reduce target-driven interference and the resulting need for reactive control.

Is Reconfiguration an Obligatory Process?

Early models of task switching proposed that reconfiguration is a discrete, obligatory process that shifts the system to a state of readiness to activate the new task set (e.g., Meiran, 2000; Rogers & Monsell, 1995; Rubinstein et al., 2001). With long preparation intervals, it is assumed that reconfiguration can be fully or partly completed before target onset, whereas with short preparation intervals, it must be initiated or completed after target onset. In the latter case, it is assumed that target-related processing cannot be initiated until these earlier processes are completed. We have already discussed ERP evidence that switch-related preparation is neither an all-or-none nor a unitary process (see earlier). We also showed that proactive control in task switching involves preparation exclusive to switch trials as well as preparation common to both switch and repeat trials. Hence, the concept of a discrete reconfiguration process seems to be replaced by a suite of proactive control processes that are differentially activated depending on task parameters and individual differences, but also vary in degree of activation across trials. However, a crucial question remains. Does task switching under unprepared conditions involve the same processes as switching under prepared conditions? That is, are these preparation processes necessary for task switching to be effective and, if so, when there is no opportunity for advance preparation, do these preparation processes simply shift temporally?

Some ERP data support the existence of an obligatory reconfiguration process. Under short preparation interval conditions, the switch-positivity emerges ~150–200 ms after target onset, and is followed by the typical posttarget differences between switch and repeat trials (Karayanidis et al., 2003; Nicholson et al., 2005). Similarly, partially informative cues that validly indicate an upcoming switch trial but not the identity of the task to be performed (*switch-away* trials) produce two temporally distinct switch-positivities. One that is time-locked to cue onset and another that emerges after target onset (Karayanidis et al., 2009; Mansfield et al., 2011; Nicholson et al., 2006d). The latter is consistent with task-specific reconfiguration being completed when task information becomes available.

However, other data do not support an obligatory preparation process. Non-informative cues allow anticipation of the timing of the target, but do not provide information about whether it will require a task repeat or switch. Therefore, the switch-positivity should be elicited after target onset and be followed by typical posttarget switch versus repeat differences. However, target-locked ERPs for noninformatively cued trials did not differ between switch and repeat trials (Jamadar et al., 2010b; Swainson et al., 2006) despite producing a large RT switch cost. In fact, compared with informatively cued trials, which showed the typical cue-locked and target-locked ERP effects, noninformative trials showed a suppressed N2 and very large early P3b for both switch and repeat trial types (see Figure 8 in Jamadar et al., 2010b). Differences between switch and repeat trials only emerged for these noninformatively cued trials in response-locked ERPs that are associated with activation of response preparation. These data indicate unequivocally that, at least under some unprepared task conditions, there is no evidence for a distinct reconfiguration process that is completed after target onset for switch trials.

These morphological differences between target-locked ERP waveforms for informative and noninformative trials suggest a qualitative difference in the way that prepared and unprepared trials are processed. We speculate here that, with substantial task practice, cue–task and stimulus–response mappings are strengthened, and hence the two tasks may blend into a single task set. So, under highly practiced conditions but with no opportunity for advance preparation, the simultaneous presentation of cue-related and target-related information may result in build-up of activation across the four possible S–R mappings (e.g., letter cue + vowel = left, number cue + odd = left etc.). In this instance, target-driven interference may not differ between switch and repeat trials and there may be less need for reactive control at the level of target processing. However, there may still be response-level interference because the same effector was previously used to respond to a different option. We conceptualize this interpretation within the compound-cue framework proposed by Schneider and Logan (2005).

In sum, existing evidence suggests that reconfiguration is not an obligatory process. However, more work is needed to understand the conditions under which reconfiguration becomes unnecessary or unhelpful.

Motor Preparation and Activation Processes

Above we discussed processes associated with general task preparedness, as represented by the pretarget negativity in cue-locked ERPs, and response preparedness, as indexed in switch versus repeat differences in response-locked ERPs. A more specialized measure of motor preparation is the lateralized readiness potential (LRP) which is typically measured by examining lateralized activation over the contralateral motor cortex of the responding hand, when responses are mapped to different hands. The LRP measures lateralized activity over the motor cortex contralateral to the responding hand (e.g., Coles, 1989). For the stimulus-locked LRP (sLRP), the interval between stimulus onset and sLRP onset is used as an index of the duration of premotoric processes leading up to response selection (Masaki, Wild-Wall, Sangals & Sommer, 2004). The response-locked LRP (rLRP) is time-locked to the onset of the response to that stimulus. The interval between rLRP onset and the response is said to represent the duration of subsequent motoric processes, including response programming and execution (Leuthold & Jentzsch, 2002; Osman, Moore, & Ulrich, 1995).

There is substantial evidence that response selection mechanisms as measured by sLRP onset are sensitive to task switching. Typically, LRP has been measured by using both simple S–R reversal tasks (Hsieh & Yu, 2003, 2005) and more complex tasks with bivalent response sets (Hsieh, 2006; Hsieh & Chen, 2007), Hsieh and colleagues have consistently shown that switch trials show a significant delay in sLRP onset compared with repeat trials. The size of this delay has been shown to not differ between prepared (informative) and unprepared (noninformative) task conditions, suggesting that preparation does not affect response selection. Using a long preparation interval, Ruge, Stoet, and Naumann (2006) found a mixing cost effect on sLRP onset, indicating that response selection is also delayed for repeat trials that are intermixed with switch trials. Hence, despite advance preparation for a validly cued mixed-repeat or switch trial, participants still show mixing-related and switch-related interference at response selection.

Unfortunately, these studies do not present preparation-related ERP waveforms which could have confirmed whether participants actually used the cues to prepare for mixed-repeat and switch trials. However, cue-locked data presented in Hsieh and Chen (2006, which correspond to the data set in Hsieh & Chen, 2007) showed a large switch-positivity in anticipation of the informative switch target, consistent with switch preparation. Despite differences in stimulus sets and task conditions, all of these studies used bivalent S–R mappings and/or bivalent response sets. It is therefore possible that these conditions produce sustained response interference that is triggered by S–R mapping and is not amenable to preparation. This interference may contribute to the persistent residual mixing cost and switch cost found even under prepared task conditions. This idea is consistent with a large congruency effect on sLRP onset latency for prepared switch and repeat trials (Kieffaber, O'Donnell, Shekhar, & Hetrick, 2007).[5] The fact that Karayanidis et al. (2006) found no sLRP onset difference between switch and repeat trials across a range of preparation intervals when using univalent stimulus sets with bivalent response sets suggests that this interference is triggered by S–R mapping rather than response-hand mapping.

Differences in response activation as reflected in rLRP are not strong. Most studies report no difference in rLRP onset latency between switch and repeat trials, under either informative or noninformative conditions (Hsieh, 2006; Hsieh & Chen, 2007; Hsieh & Yu, 2003; Jamadar et al., 2010b; Karayanidis et al., 2006). However, Hsieh and Liu (2005) reported earlier rLRP onset for mixed-repeat than switch trials and Ruge et al. (2006) showed earlier rLRP onset for mixed-repeat trials than all-repeat trials. These findings provide weak evidence for progressive prolongation of response planning on mixed-repeat and switch trials.

LRPs have also been used to show evidence for differential response preparation in anticipation of target onset. Using tasks univalently mapped to hand, Gladwin, Lindsen, and de Jong (2006) showed that fast RT switch trials were associated with earlier emergence of a large LRP for a change in response hand. This LRP was sensitive to the probability that advance preparation of the response hand would be a useful task strategy (de Jong, 2006). Steinhauser, Hubner, and Druey (2009) found greater LRP activation during the CTI in favor of the response not executed on the preceding trial, consistent with a response-switch bias effect. In other words, during the preparation interval, participants build up a bias toward suppressing the tendency to repeat the same response and in favor of preparing a response with the other hand.[6] This response-switch bias was greater when there was a risk that the target would elicit the incorrect response (i.e., incongruity). It remains to be determined how these processes are linked to the pretarget negativity effects seen in cue-locked ERPs.

CONCLUSIONS

ERPs have proved to be a powerful tool in characterizing the cognitive architecture of task switching performance and testing predictions arising from existing theoretical models. Given their superior temporal resolution, ERPs provide a sensitive method for disentangling the influence of multiple proactive and reactive control processes. In addition, this methodology offers considerable inferential power as a result of the large body of research into the functional significance of ERP components during the past 60 years.

We highlighted a number of conclusions about the nature of proactive and reactive control processes in task switching performance that can be drawn on the basis of ERP findings. We show that proactive control processes in task switching involve both switch-specific and general preparation. Moreover, switch-specific preparation, as indexed by the cue-locked switch-positivity, consists of multiple underlying processes, which can be measured independently. Repeat trials that are intermixed among switch trials also engage proactive control, indexed by the informative-positivity. Both switch and repeat trials show trial-by-trial variation in task readiness, as indexed by the pretarget negativity, consistent with a more general task preparation process.

We present evidence that reactive control processes in task switching primarily involve resolution of carryover or target-driven interference and associated difficulty of decision processes. Advance switch preparation was shown to reduce this interference, as indexed by smaller N2 and P3b effects on prepared switch trials. We reviewed evidence that both response selection and response activation processes are also modulated by the requirement to change task, but note that the relationship between proactive control, reactive control and response-level interference effects has not been examined systematically.

Finally, we showed evidence that prepared and unprepared task switching may, under certain conditions, involve qualitatively distinct mechanisms, rather than simply a temporal shift in a discrete "reconfiguration" process. We speculate that this may suggest two modes of task switching: a more controlled mode that relies heavily on preparation and suffers high interference when this control is not efficiently applied, and a more cue/target-driven mode that does not require cognitive control but is based heavily on cue–target associations. We conceptualize this within the framework of shifting from a more controlled to a more automatic mode of responding, especially after considerable task practice or when there is no opportunity to prepare to change task set. The properties of these two modes of task switching and the degree to which they are mutually exclusive under different conditions remain to be determined. Indeed it is important to note a significant caveat of all above conclusions. Few ERP (or indeed behavioral) studies in task switching have been specifically designed to test the predictions arising from theoretical or computational models, and hence most conclusions are based on post-hoc interpretations of outcomes. Clearly, this is an area in need of attention.

FUTURE DIRECTIONS IN TASK SWITCHING RESEARCH: MULTIMODAL APPROACHES

Recent task switching research has started addressing the need for more theoretically driven approaches (e.g., Barceló et al., 2008). One approach has been to address theoretically driven hypotheses using multiple techniques to deal with gaps or weaknesses of each technique alone. For example, integrating across ERP and fMRI methodologies offers an opportunity to capitalize on the excellent temporal and spatial information provided by each technique, respectively. Some success has begun to emerge by integrating ERP and fMRI methods (Brass et al., 2005; Jamadar et al., 2010a; Swainson et al., 2003) to examine the spatiotemporal dynamics of control and interference. We briefly touched on some of this work in earlier sections (see also Karayanidis et al., 2010).

More recently, we have shown that combining latent variables from formal models of cognition, ERPs and both structural and functional brain imaging measures (Karayanidis et al., 2009, 2011b; Mansfield et al., 2011) provides a powerful approach that can help define task switching processes and the brain networks that mediate them. Evidence accumulation models estimate latent variables that characterize speed and accuracy of decision-making (e.g., Grasman et al., 2009;

Ratcliff, 1978). Response criterion (i.e., the amount of information required before arriving at a decision) and drift rate (i.e., the rate of accumulating information from the stimulus) determine decision time (i.e., the time to arrive at a decision on that trial). In typical two-choice RT paradigms, the remaining portion of RT (i.e., nondecision time) represents sensory and response processes. However, in the context of task switching, it also includes the degree to which preparation was efficiently completed before target onset (Karayanidis et al., 2009; Schmitz & Voss, 2012).

Response criterion varies on a trial-by-trial basis, being higher on the more difficult switch than the easier repeat trials (Karayanidis et al., 2009, 2011b; Schmitz & Voss, 2012). The amplitude of the cue-locked switch-positivity is inversely related with response criterion, indicating that individuals who show greater preparation tend to set a lower criterion setting (Karayanidis et al., 2009, 2011b). Mansfield et al. (2011) showed that lower criterion setting is associated with greater BOLD activation in the striatum for repeat trials and lower activation in the right STN for switch trials. These findings are consistent with neural models of response criterion adjustment (Forstmann et al., 2008, 2010) and suggest that criterion setting is involved in proactive control in task switching. Furthermore, the relationship between criterion on mixed-repeat trials and cue-locked mixing-positivity is mediated by age (Karayanidis et al., 2011b), indicating that more conservative preparation for the easier repeat trials may explain the robust finding of an age-related increase in mixing-cost. Relationships are also emerging between level of preparation and nondecision time (Karayanidis et al., 2009) as well as between target-driven interference and drift rate (Karayanidis et al., 2011b).

This approach shows promise for defining and testing new computational models of task switching that are theoretically and neurally grounded. It may also help define the factors that contribute to variability in cognitive control at both the group and the individual level. ERPs have already been useful in characterizing differences in task switching ability between clinical groups and healthy controls. At the group level, individuals with schizophrenia show intact preparatory but impaired posttarget ERPs in exogenously cued task switching (Finke et al., 2011; Jamadar et al., 2010c; Kieffaber et al., 2007). However, under endogenous cueing (i.e., alternating runs), they show impairments in both preparatory and posttarget processing, even in the absence of any overt behavioral difference (Karayanidis et al., 2006). Healthy aging is associated with ERP changes suggestive of greater need for proactive control, even for the easier mixed-repeat trials and greater application of reactive control in the resolution of interference (DeSanctis et al., 2009; Karayanidis et al., 2011b; Kray et al., 2005; West & Travers, 2008) as well as response selection (Adrover-Roig et al., 2010). Children show delayed preparatory processing (Karayanidis et al., forthcoming; Manzi et al., 2011) and impaired motor preparation (Bender et al., 2005).

Results are even more exciting and promising at the individual level. Emerging work in imaging genetics has shown links between task switching ERPs and *DAT1* (Garcia-Garcia et al., 2010), *ANKK1*, and *COMT* (Garcia-Garcia et al., 2011). Specifically, cue-locked ERPs were found to be modulated by individual differences in the availability of prefrontal dopamine. In a study integrating across decision model parameters, ERP and DTI methodologies, Mansfield et al. (forthcoming) shows that individual variability in response criterion is associated with differences in white matter organization in distinct frontostriatal pathways (see also Madden et al., 2008). Moreover, the relationship between switch-positivity and response criterion is mediated by white matter organization of the striatum. These multidisciplinary and integrative approaches offer promising future directions for developing robust models of cognitive control.

NOTES

1. This distinction has also been referred to as attentional set versus intentional set (e.g., Rushworth et al., 2005)
2. Nicholson et al. (2005) compared CTI 0 ms (cue + target together) and CTI 150 ms conditions. The CTI 150 ms condition showed a small reduction in switch cost indicating that some preparation may occur even with a very small CTI. ERP waveforms did not differ substantially between the two conditions. This argues against cue interference on target processing.
3. The terms *mixed-repeat* and *all-repeat* were introduced by Whitson et al. (2012) to differentiate between repeat trials in mixed-task or task switching blocks and repeat trials in single-task or repeat-only blocks.
4. The N2 was not explicitly measured but can be seen to vary in Figure 9.3.
5. It is worth noting that most studies tend to show large trial type differences in sLRP peak amplitude and peak latency consistent with differential preparation for switch trials, but these measures are not reported.
6. This pattern is actually the opposite in voluntary task switching paradigms, where prestimulus LRPs suggest there is a bias toward repetition that is overruled later in the processing stream (van Damme et al., 2010).

REFERENCES

Adrover-Roig, D., & F. Barceló (2010). Individual differences in aging and cognitive control modulate the neural indexes of context updating and maintenance during task switching. *Cortex*, *46*, 434–450.

Allport, A., Styles, E. A., & Hsieh, S. (1994). Shifting intentional set: Exploring the dynamic control of tasks. In C. Umilta & M. Moscovitch (Eds.), *Attention and performance. XV* (pp. 421–452). Cambridge, MA: MIT Press.

Aron, A. R., Robbins, T. W., & Poldrack, R. A. (2004). Inhibition and the right inferior frontal cortex. *Trends in Cognitive Sciences*, *8*, 170–177.

Astle, D. E., Jackson, G. M., & Swainson, R. (2006). Dissociating neural indices of dynamic cognitive control in advance task-set preparation: An ERP study of task switching. *Brain Research*, *1125*, 94–103.

Astle, D. E., Jackson, G. M., & Swainson, R. (2008a). Fractionating the cognitive control required to bring about a change in task: A dense-sensor event-related potential study. *Journal of Cognitive Neuroscience*, *20*, 255–267.

Astle, D. E., Jackson, G. M., & Swainson, R. (2008b). The role of spatial information in advance task-set control: An event-related potential study. *The European Journal of Neuroscience, 28,* 1404–1418.

Astle, D. E., Nixon, E., Jackson, S. R., & Jackson, G. M. (2011). Neural correlates of changing intention in the human FEF and IPS. *Journal of Neurophysiology, 107,* 859–867.

Barceló, F. (2003). The Madrid card sorting test (MCST): A task switching paradigm to study executive attention with event-related potentials. *Brain Research Protocols, 11,* 27–37.

Barceló, F., Escera, C., Corral, M. J., & Periánez, J. A. (2006). Task switching and novelty processing activate a common neural network for cognitive control. *Journal of Cognitive Neuroscience, 18,* 1734–1748.

Barceló, F., Munoz-Cespedes, J. M., Pozo, M. A., & Rubia, F. J. (2000). Attentional set shifting modulates the target P3b response in the Wisconsin card sorting test. *Neuropsychologica, 38,* 1342–1355.

Barceló, F., Periáñez, J. A., & Nyhus, E. (2008). An information theoretical approach to task-switching: evidence from cognitive brain potentials in humans. *Frontiers in Human Neuroscience, 1,* 13. doi:10.3389/neuro.09.013.2007

Bender, S., Weisbrod, M., Bornfleth, H., Resch, F., & Oelkers-Ax, R (2005). How do children prepare to react? Imaging maturation of motor preparation and stimulus anticipation by late contingent negative variation. *Neuroimage, 27,* 737–752.

Botvinick, M. M., Cohen, J. D., & Carter, C. S. (2004). Conflict monitoring and anterior cingulate cortex: an update. *Trends in Cognitive Sciences, 8,* 539–546.

Brass, M., Ullsperger, M., Knoesche, T. R., von Cramon, D. Y., & Phillips, N. A. (2005). Who comes first? The role of the prefrontal and parietal cortex in cognitive control. *Journal of Cognitive Neuroscience, 17,* 1367–1375.

Braver, T. S., Gray, J. R., & Burgess, G. C. (2007). Explaining the many varieties of working memory variation: Dual mechanisms of cognitive control. In A. R. A. Conway, C. Jarrold, M. J. Kane, A. Miyake, & J. N. Towse (Eds.), *Variation in working memory* (pp. 76–106). Oxford, UK: Oxford University Press.

Brown, S., Lehmann, C., & Poboka, D. (2006). A critical test of the failure-to-engage theory of task switching. *Psychonomic Bulletin & Review, 13,* 152–159.

Brunia, C. H. M. (1999) Neural aspects of anticipatory behavior. *Acta Psychologica, 101,* 213–242.

Coles, M. G. H. (1989). Modern mind-brain reading: Psychophysiology, physiology, and cognition. *Psychophysiology, 26,* 251–269.

Cunillera, T., Fuentemilla, L., Perianez, J., Marco-Pallares, J., Kramer, U. M., Camara, E., . . . & Rodriguez-Fornells, A. (2012). Brain oscillatory activity associated with task switching and feedback processing. *Cognitive, Affective & Behavioral Neuroscience, 12,* 16–33.

De Jong, R. (2000). An intention - activation account of residual switch costs. In S. Monsell & J. Driver (Eds.), *Attention and Performance. XVIII* (pp. 357–376). Cambridge, MA: MIT Press.

De Sanctis, P., Gomez-Ramirez, M., Sehatpour, P., Wylie, G. R., & Foxe, J. J (2009). Preserved executive function in high-performing elderly is driven by large-scale recruitment of prefrontal cortical mechanisms. *Human Brain Mapping, 30,* 4198–4214.

Donchin, E. (1981). Surprise!... Surprise? *Psychophysiology, 18,* 493–513.

Donchin, E., Karis, D., Bashore, T., Coles, M. G. H., & Gratton, G. (1986). Cognitive psychophysiology and human information processing. In M. G. H. Coles, E. Donchin, & S. W. Porges (Eds.), *Psychophysiology: Systems, processes and applications*. New York, NY: Guilford Press.

Elchlepp, H., Lavric, A., Mizon, G. A., & Monsell, S. (2012). A brain-potential study of preparation for and execution of a task-switch with stimuli that afford only the relevant task. *Human Brain Mapping, 33*, 1137–1154.

Finke, M., Barceló, F., Garolera, M., Cortinas, M., Garrido, G., Pajares, M., & Escera, C. (2011). Impaired preparatory re-mapping of stimulus–response associations and rule-implementation in schizophrenic patients—the role for differences in early processing. *Biological Psychology, 87*, 358–365.

Folstein, J. R., & van Petten, C. (2008). Influence of cognitive control and mismatch on the N2 component of the ERP: A review. *Psychophysiology, 45*, 152–170.

Forstmann, B. U., Anwander, A., Schäfer, A., Neumann, J., Brown, S., Wagenmakers, E.-J., . . . & Turner, R. (2010). Cortico-striatal connections predict control over speed and accuracy in perceptual decision making. *Proceedings of the National Academy of Sciences U S A, 107*, 15916–15920.

Forstmann, B. U., Dutilh, G., Brown, S., Neumann, J., von Cramon, D. Y., Ridderinkhof, K. R., & Wagenmakers, E.-J. (2008). Striatum and pre-SMA facilitate decision-making under time pressure. *Proceedings of the National Academy of Sciences U S A, 105*,17538–17542.

Forstmann, B. U., Brass, M., Koch, I., & von Cramon, D. Y. (2006). Voluntary selection of task sets revealed by functional magnetic resonance imaging. *Journal of Cognitive Neuroscience, 18*, 388–398.

Forstmann, B. U., Ridderinkhof, K. R., Kaiser, J., & Bledowski, C. (2007). At your own peril: An ERP study of voluntary task set selection processes in the medial frontal cortex. *Cognitive, Affective, & Behavioral Neuroscience, 7*, 286–296.

Gajewski, P. D., & Falkenstein, M. (2011). Diversity of the P3 in the task-switching paradigm. *Brain Research, 1411*, 87–97.

Gajewski, P. D., Kleinsorge, T., & Falkenstein, M. (2010). Electrophysiological correlates of residual switch costs. *Cortex, 46*, 1138–1148.

Garcia-Garcia, M., Barceló, F., Clemente, I. C., & Escera, C. (2010). The role of DAT1 gene on the rapid detection of task novelty. *Neuropsychologia, 48*, 4136–4141.

Garcia-Garcia, M., Barceló, F., Clemente, I. C., & Escera, C. (2011). COMT and ANKK1 gene-gene interaction modulates contextual updating of mental representations. *Neuroimage, 56*, 1641–1647.

Gladwin, T. E., Lindsen, J. P., & de Jong, R. (2006). Pre-stimulus EEG effects related to response speed, task switching and upcoming response hand. *Biological Psychology, 72*, 15–34.

Goffaux, P., Phillips, N. A., Sinai, M., & Pushkar, D. (2006). Behavioural and electrophysiological measures of task switching during single and mixed-task conditions. *Biological Psychology, 72*, 278–290.

Goffaux, P., Phillips, N. A., Sinai, M., & Pushkar, D. (2008). Neurophysiological measures of task-set switching: Effects of working memory and aging. *Journals of Gerontology Series B Psychological Sciences and Social Sciences, 63*, 57–66.

Hsieh, S. (2006). The lateralized readiness potential and P300 of stimulus-set switching. *International Journal of Psychophysiology, 60*, 284–291.

Hsieh, S., & Chen, P. (2006). Task reconfiguration and carryover in task switching: An event-related potential study. *Brain Research, 1084*, 132–145.

Hsieh, S., & Chen, P. (2007). The effect of task preparation in task switching as reflected on lateralized readiness potential. *International Journal of Psychophysiology, 63*, 98–104.

Hsieh, S., & Liu, H. (2008). Electrophysiological correlates of task conflicts in task-switching. *Brain Research, 1203*, 116–125.

Hsieh, S., & Liu, L. C. (2005). The nature of switch cost: Task set reconfiguration or carryover effect? *Cognitive Brain Research, 22*, 165–175.

Hsieh, S., & Wu, M. (2011). Electrophysiological correlates of preparation and implementation for different types of task shifts. *Brain Research, 1423*, 41–52.

Hsieh, S., & Yu, Y. T. (2003). Switching between simple response-sets: Inferences from the lateralized readiness potential. *Cognitive Brain Research, 17*, 228–237.

Isreal, J., Chesney, G., Wickens, C., & Donchin, E. (1980). P300 and tracking difficulty: Evidence for multiple resources in dual-task performance. *Psychophysiology, 17*, 259–273.

Jamadar, S., Hughes, M., Fulham, W. R., Michie, P. T., & Karayanidis, F. (2010a). The spatial and temporal dynamics of anticipatory preparation and response inhibition in task-switching. *Neuroimage, 51*, 432–449.

Jamadar, S., Michie, P. T., & Karayanidis, F. (2010b). Sequence effects in cued task switching modulate response preparedness and repetition priming processes. *Psychophysiology, 47*, 365–386.

Jamadar, S., Michie, P., & Karayanidis, F. (2010c). Compensatory mechanisms underlie intact task-switching performance in schizophrenia. *Neuropsychologia, 48*, 1305–1323.

Jamadar, S., Provost, A., Fulham, W. R., Michie, P. T., & Karayanidis, F. (2010d). Multiple sources underlie ERP indices of task-switching. In W. Christensen, E. Schier, & J. Sutton (Eds.), *ASCS09: Proceedings of the 9th Conference of the Australasian Society for Cognitive Science* (pp. 154–161). Sydney: Macquarie Centre for Cognitive Science. doi:10.5096/ASCS200924 http://www.maccs.mq.edu.au/news/conferences/2009/ASCS2009/html/jamadar.html

Jeon, Y. W., & Polich, J. (2003). Meta-analysis of P300 schizophrenia studies: Patients, paradigms and practical implications. *Psychophysiology, 40*, 684–701.

Johnson, R., Jr. (1993). On the neural generators of the P300 component of the event-related potential. *Psychophysiology, 30*, 90–97.

Jost, K., Mayr, U., & Rosler, F. (2008). Is task switching nothing but cue priming? Evidence from ERPs. *Cognitive, Affective & Behavioral Neuroscience, 8*, 74–84.

Karayanidis, F., Coltheart, M., Michie, P. T., & Murphy, K. (2003). Electrophysiological correlates of anticipatory and post-stimulus components of task-switching. *Psychophysiology, 40*, 329–348.

Karayanidis, F., Jamadar, S., Ruge, H., Phillips, N., Heathcote, A., & Forstmann, B. U. (2010). Advance preparation in task-switching: converging evidence from behavioral, brain activation, and model-based approaches. *Frontiers in Psychology, 1*, 25.

Karayanidis, F., Jamadar, S., & Sanday, D. (2013). Stimulus-level interference disrupts repetition benefit during task switching in middle childhood. *Front. Hum. Neurosci., 7*, 841. doi:10.3389/fnhum.2013.00841

Karayanidis, F., & Mansfield, E. L. (2010). Increasing the requirement for top-down control in task-switching: ERP evidence from a voluntary task-switching paradigm. Paper presented at 37th Australasian Experimental Psychology Conference, Melbourne, Australia.

Karayanidis, F., Mansfield, E. L., Galloway, K. L., Smith, J. L., Provost, A., & Heathcote, A. (2009). Anticipatory reconfiguration elicited by fully and partially informative cues that validly predict a switch in task. *Cognitive, Affective & Behavioral Neuroscience*, *9*(2), 202–215.

Karayanidis, F., Nicholson, R., Schall, U., Meem, L., Fulham, R., & Michie, P. T. (2006). Switching between univalent task-sets in schizophrenia: ERP evidence of an anticipatory task-set reconfiguration deficit. *Clinical Neurophysiology*, *117*(10), 2172–2190.

Karayanidis, F., Provost, A., Brown, S., Paton, B., & Heathcote, A. (2011a). Switch-specific and general preparation map onto different ERP components in a task-switching paradigm. *Psychophysiology*, *48*, 559–568.

Karayanidis, F., Whitson, L. R., Heathcote, A., & Michie, P. T. (2011b). Variability in proactive and reactive cognitive control processes across the adult lifespan. *Frontiers in Psychology*, *2*, 318.

Kieffaber, P. D., & Hetrick, W. P. (2005). Event-related potential correlates of task switching and switch costs. *Psychophysiology*, *42*, 56–71.

Kieffaber, P. D., O'Donnel, B. F., Shekhar, A., & Hetrick, W. P. (2007). Event related brain potential evidence for preserved attentional set switching in schizophrenia. *Schizophrenia Research*, *93*, 355–365.

Kiesel, A., Steinhauser, M., Wendt, M., Falkenstein, M., Jost, K., Philipp, A., & Koch, I. (2010). Control and interference in task-switching—a review. *Psychological Bulletin*, *136*, 849–874.

Koch, I., & Philipp, A. M. (2005). Effects of response selection on the task repetition benefit in task switching. *Memory & Cognition*, *33*, 624–634.

Koechlin, E., & Summerfield, C. (2007). An information theoretical approach to prefrontal executive function. *Trends in Cognitive Sciences*, *11*, 229–235.

Kray, J., Eppinger, B., & Mecklinger, A. (2005). Age differences in attentional control: An event-related potential approach. *Psychophysiology*, *42*(4), 407–416.

Lavric, A., Mizon, G., & Monsell, S. (2008). Neurophysiological signature of effective anticipatory task-set control: A task-switching investigation. *European Journal of Neuroscience*, *28*, 1016–1029.

Leuthold, H., & Jentzsch, I. (2002). Distinguishing neural sources of movement preparation and execution: An electrophysiological analysis. *Biological Psychology*, *60*, 173–198.

Linden, D. E. J. (2005). The P300: Where in the brain is it produced and what does it tell us? *The Neuroscientist*, *11*, 563–576.

Logan, G. D., & Bundesen, C. (2003). Clever homunculus: Is there an endogenous act of control in the explicit task-cuing procedure? *Journal of Experimental Psychology: Human Perception and Performance*, *29*, 575–599.

Luck, S. (2005). *An introduction to the event-related potential technique*. Cambridge, MA: MIT Press.

Madden, D. J., Spaniol, J., Costello, M. C., Bucur, B., White, L. E., Cabeza, R.,…& Huettel, S. A. (2009). Cerebral white matter integrity mediates adult age differences in cognitive performance. *Journal of Cognitive Neuroscience*, *21*, 289–302.

Mansfield, E. L., Karayanidis, F., Jamadar, S., Heathcote, A., & Forstmann,B.U. (2011). Preparatory adjustments of response threshold during task switching: A model based fMRI study. *Journal of Neuroscience*, *31*, 14688–14692.

Mansfield, E., Karayanidis, F., & Cohen, M. X. (2012) Switch-related and general preparation processes in task-switching: Evidence from multivariate pattern classification of EEG data. *Journal of Neuroscience, 32*, 18253–18258.

Mansfield, E. L., Karayanidis, F., Heathcote, A., & Forstmann, B. U. (forthcoming). Strategic adjustments of response caution: Combined evidence from diffusion MRI and electrophysiology.

Manzi, A., Nessler, D., Czernochowski, D., & Friedman, D. (2011). The development of anticipatory cognitive control processes in task-switching: an ERP study in children, adolescents, and young adults. *Psychophysiology, 48*, 1258–1275.

Masaki, H., Wild-Wall, N., Sangals, J., & Sommer, W. (2004). The functional locus of the lateralized readiness potential. *Psychophysiology, 41*, 220–230.

Meiran, N. (2000). Reconfiguration of stimulus task-sets and response task-sets during task-switching. In S. Monsell & J. Driver (Eds.), *Control of cognitive processes: Attention and Performance. XVIII* (pp. 377–400). Cambridge, MA: MIT Press.

Meiran, N., Hsieh, S., & Chang, C. C. (2011). "Smart inhibition": Electrophysiological evidence for the suppression of conflict-generating task rules during task switching. *Cognitive, Affective & Behavioral Neuroscience, 11*, 292–308.

Miniussi, C., Marzi, C. A., & Nobre, A. C. (2005). Modulation of brain activity by selective task sets observed using event-related potentials. *Neuropsychologia, 43*, 1514–1528.

Mueller, S. C., Swainson, R., & Jackson, G. M. (2007). Behavioural and neurophysiological correlates of bivalent and univalent responses during task switching. *Brain Research, 1157*, 56–65.

Mueller, S. C., Swainson, R., & Jackson, G. M. (2009). ERP indices of persisting and current inhibitory control: A study of saccadic task switching. *Neuroimage, 45*, 191–197.

Nicholson, R., Karayanidis, F., Bumak, E., Poboka, D., & Michie, P. T. (2006a). ERPs dissociate the effects of switching task sets and task cues. *Brain Research, 1095*, 107–123.

Nicholson, R., Karayanidis, F., Davies, A., & Michie, P. T. (2006b). Components of task-set reconfiguration: Differential effects of "switch-to" and "switch-away" cues. *Brain Research, 1121*, 160–176.

Nicholson, R., Karayanidis, F., Poboka, D., Heathcote, A., & Michie, P. (2005). Electrophysiological correlates of anticipatory task-switching processes. *Psychophysiology, 42*, 540–554.

Orr, J. M, Gehring, W. J, & Weissman, D. H. (2010). ERP predictors of voluntary task switching. Poster presentation at the Society of Neuroscience 2010 Annual Meeting, San Diego, CA.

Osman, A., Moore, C. M., & Ulrich, R. (1995). Bisecting RT with lateralized readiness potentials: precue effects after LRP onset. *Acta Psychologica, 90*, 111–127.

Polich, J. (2007). Updating P300: An integrative theory of P3a and P3b. *Clinical Neurophysiology, 118*, 2128–2148.

Poulsen, C., Luu, P., Davey, C., & Tucker, D. M. (2005). Dynamics of task sets: Evidence from dense-array event-related potentials. *Cognitive Brain Research, 24*, 133–154.

Provost, A., Jamadar, S., & Karayanidis, F. (forthcoming). Effect of preparation on target-driven interference processes.

Ratcliff, R., & Rouder, J. N. (1998). Modeling response times for two-choice decisions. *Psychological Science, 9*, 347–356.

Rogers, R. D., & Monsell, S. (1995). Costs of a predictable switch between simple cognitive tasks. *Journal of Experimental Psychology, 124*, 207–231.

Rubinstein, J. S., Meyer, D. E., & Evans, E. (2001). Executive control of cognitive processes in task switching. *Journal of Experimental Psychology: Human Perception and Performance, 27*, 763–797.

Ruge, H., Braver, T., & Meiran, N. (2009). Attention, intention and strategy in preparatory control. *Neuropsychologia, 47*, 1670–1685.

Ruge, H., Jamadar, S., Zimmerman, L., & Karayanidis, F. (2013). The many faces of preparatory control in task switching: Reviewing a decade of fMRI research. *Human Brain Mapping, 34*, 12–35.

Ruge, H., Stoet, G., & Naumann, E. (2006). Attentional set mixing: Effects on target selection and selective response activation. *Psychophysiology, 43*, 413–421.

Rugg, M. D., & Coles, M. G. H. (1995). *Electrophysiology of mind: Event-related brain potentials and cognition*. New York, NY: Oxford University Press.

Rushworth, M. F. S., Passingham, R. E., & Nobre, A. C. (2002). Components of switching intentional set. *Journal of Cognitive Neuroscience, 14*, 1139–1150.

Rushworth, M. F. S., Passingham, R. E., & Nobre, A. C. (2005). Components of attentional set-switching. *Experimental Psychology, 52*, 83–98.

Schmitz, F., & Voss, A. (2012). Decomposing task-switching costs with the diffusion model. *Journal of Experimental Psychology: Human Perception and Performance, 38*, 222–250.

Schneider, D. W., & Logan, G. D. (2005). Modeling task switching without switching tasks: A short-term priming account of explicitly cued performance. *Journal of Experimental Psychology: General, 134*, 343–367.

Schuch, S., & Koch, I. (2003). The role of response selection for inhibition of task sets in task shifting. *Journal of Experimental Psychology: Human Perception and Performance, 29*, 92–105.

Sinai, M., Phillips, N. A., Chertkow, H., & Kabani, N. J. (2010). Task switching performance reveals heterogeneity amongst patients with mild cognitive impairment. *Neuropsychology, 24*, 757–774.

Spapé, M. M., Band, G. P. H., & Hommel, B. (2011). Compatibility-sequence effects in the Simon task reflect episodic retrieval but not conflict adaptation: Evidence from LRP and N2. *Biological Psychology, 88*, 116–123.

Squires, N. K., Squires, K. C., & Hillyard, S. A. (1975). Two varieties of long-latency positive waves evoked by unpredictable auditory stimuli in man. *Electroencephalography & Clinical Neurophysiology, 38*(4), 387–401.

Steinhauser, M., Hubner, R., & Druey, M. (2009). Adaptive control of response preparedness in task switching. *Neuropsychologia, 47*, 1826–1835.

Sternberg, S. (1969). The discovery of processing stages: Extensions of Donders' method. In W. G. Koster (Ed.), *Attention and Performance. II* (pp. 276–315). North Holland, Amsterdam.

Swainson, R., Cunnington, R., Jackson, G. M., Rorden, C., Peters, A. M., Morris, P. G., & Jackson, S. R. (2003). Cognitive control mechanisms revealed by ERP and fMRI: Evidence from repeated task-switching. *Journal of Cognitive Neuroscience, 15*, 785–799.

Swainson, R., Jackson, S. R., & Jackson, G. M. (2006). Using advance information in dynamic cognitive control: An ERP study of task-switching. *Brain Research, 1105*, 61–72.

Van Damme, K., Szmalec, A., Liefooghe, B., & Vandierendonck, A. (2010). Are voluntary switches corrected repetitions? *Psychophysiology, 47*, 1176–1181.

Vandierendonck, A., Liefooghe, B., & Verbruggen, F. (2010). Task-switching: Interplay of reconfiguration and interference control. *Psychological Bulletin, 136*, 601–626.

Verleger, R., Jaskowski, P., & Wascher, E. (2005). Evidence for an integrative role of P3b in linking reaction to perception. *Journal of Psychophysiology, 19*, 165–181.

West, R., & Alain, C. (2000). Effects of task context and fluctuations of attention on neural activity supporting performance of the Stroop task. *Brain Research, 873*, 102–111.

West, R., Bailey, K., & Langley, M. M. (2009). An investigation of the neural correlates of attention and effector switching using ERPs. *Cognitive, Affective & Behavioral Neuroscience, 9*, 190–201.

West, R., Langley, M. M., & Bailey, K. (2011). Signaling a switch: Neural correlates of task switching guided by task cues and transition cues. *Psychophysiology, 48*, 612–23.

West, R., & Travers, S. (2008). Differential effects of aging on processes underlying task switching. *Brain and Cognition, 68*, 67–80.

Whitson, L. R., Karayanidis, F., & Michie, P. T. (2012). Task practice differentially modulates task-switching performance across the adult lifespan. *Acta Psychologica, 139*, 124–136.

Wickens, C. D., Kramer, A., Vanasse, L., & Donchin, E. (1983) Performance of concurrent tasks: A psychophysiological analysis of reciprocity of information processing resources. *Science, 221*, 1080–1082.

Woestenburg, J. C., Verbaten, M. N., Van Hees, H. H., & Slangen, J. L. (1983). Single trial ERP estimation in the frequency domain using orthogonal polynomial trend analysis (OPTA): Estimation of individual habituation. *Biological Psychology, 17*, 173–191.

Wylie, G., & Allport, A. (2000). Task switching and the measurement of "switch costs". *Psychological Research, 63*, 212–233.

Wylie, G. R., Javitt, D. C., & Foxe, J. J. (2003). Cognitive control processes during an anticipated switch of task. *European Journal of Neuroscience, 17*, 667–672.

Wylie, G. R., Murray, M. M., Javitt, D. C., & Foxe, J. J. (2009). Distinct neurophysiological mechanisms mediate mixing costs and switch costs. *Journal of Cognitive Neuroscience, 21*, 105–118.

10

Neuroimaging Studies of Task Switching

FRANZISKA R. RICHTER AND NICK YEUNG

INTRODUCTION

Discussions of the contributions of neuroimaging research to psychology have emphasized two distinct but related aims: to identify the neural basis of cognitive processes and, conversely, to use emerging neuroimaging data to inform cognitive theories (Coltheart, 2004; Henson, 2005; Poldrack, 2006). Here we review progress toward these aims in functional magnetic resonance imaging (fMRI) studies of task switching. In common with most cognitive neuroscience research, we take localization of function in the brain to be a necessary foundational step, but our real focus is the use of neuroimaging data to shed new light on the cognitive mechanisms of task switching. We therefore begin with a brief overview of brain regions that are consistently activated during task switching—presenting a new meta-analysis of 34 published fMRI studies—but devote the bulk of the chapter to an exploration of the implications of these neuroimaging findings for current theories of cognitive control in task switching.

Our discussion addresses four questions. The first is whether neuroimaging evidence supports theories emerging from behavioral studies of task switching. We focus in particular on the developing consensus that the switch cost—the drop in performance seen when people switch tasks as compared with repeatedly perform the same task—reflects a complex interplay between top-down cognitive control and competitive interactions between tasks (Kiesel et al., 2010; Monsell, 2003; Vandierendonck, Liefooghe, & Verbruggen, 2010). The second question is whether neuroimaging evidence provides support for the often-implicit assumption that "task switching" represents a coherent area of study—that is, that common mechanisms or common organizational principles govern task switching regardless of the particular tasks involved. The third question, in contrast, is whether consistent dissociations are observed among different forms of task switching, for example switching between perceptual attributes versus switching between different sets of potential responses. The fourth, more exploratory, question is whether switching of "retrieval set" in long-term memory—for example, when switching from remembering the name of a recent acquaintance to trying to remember where you first met them—shares principles and mechanisms with task switching as more traditionally studied. The goal of this section is to draw parallels between two research fields—on memory and cognitive control—that are typically treated separately but that promise to be mutually very informative.

A Note on Methodology

Before embarking on our main discussion, we first note that there are important challenges in translating theories and methods developed from reaction time (RT) studies into workable hypotheses and experiments for neuroimaging research. Our concerns are practical rather than existential: We disagree with those who claim that neuroimaging is of limited relevance to cognitive psychology (Coltheart, 2006; Page, 2006) and are broadly optimistic about the value of fMRI in providing an additional dependent measure to experimental psychologists (Henson, 2005), in particular one that can directly index behaviorally silent processes of task preparation that are the hallmark of top-down intentional control (cf. Ruge, Jamadar, Zimmermann, & Karayanidis, 2011).

Nonetheless, fMRI is not naturally suited to measuring rapid and flexible behavioral switching, given its poor temporal resolution: fMRI experiments almost exclusively measure the blood oxygenation level dependent (BOLD) response, which can pinpoint the location of activity to within a few millimeters but which unfolds sluggishly over several seconds as blood flow increases to active neural tissue. As such, these experiments typically use interevent intervals of several seconds—to allow separation of successive BOLD responses—rather than a few hundred milliseconds as is common in RT studies. This difference complicates any attempt to relate behavioral and neuroimaging findings: Effects observed in fMRI data may be peculiar to the design of the studies, for example reflecting increased working memory demands when subjects must remember for a few seconds on each trial which task they were instructed to perform. More troubling still, the very nature of a "task set"—the configuration of mental resources needed to process information and respond according to current task goals—may be significantly altered in slow-paced designs: Subjects might have little incentive to create a stable task set if they will only perform one trial of that task in the next several seconds. They might instead treat each trial as a distinct event, so that all trials effectively become switch trials (or, more accurately, *restart trials*; Allport & Wylie, 2000; see also Altmann, this volume), thus diminishing the contrast between task switch and repeat trials that is the essence of most task switching experiments.

Neuroimaging studies of task switching must therefore compromise between slow pacing to allow separation of BOLD responses and fast pacing to capture the rapid switching processes of theoretical interest. With this tension in mind, we now turn to a meta-analysis of methods and results of studies that have attempted to solve this conundrum.

META-ANALYSIS OF METHODS AND RESULTS

Figure 10.1 presents the results of an activation likelihood estimation (ALE) meta-analysis of 34 fMRI task switching studies (see References for details). The analysis made use of the GingerALE algorithm, which identifies overlap between foci reported across studies by modeling each as a three-dimensional Gaussian probability distribution (Eickhoff et al., 2009). In all of the studies included in the meta-analysis, healthy young-adult subjects were presented with a series of stimuli and were asked to switch back and forth between two or more predefined tasks across trials. This design creates a within-block contrast between switch trials (in which the task differs from the one performed on the previous trial) and repeat trials (in which the same task is performed on successive trials). Thus, with one or two exceptions noted later, these studies focused exclusively on event-related fMRI correlates of "local" task switching rather than the blockwise "mixing cost" contrast that compares neural activity during task switching against activity observed in contexts in which only one task is ever required (see Mari-Beffa & Kirkham, this volume).

Almost all studies in our meta-analysis used designs in which each trial began with an instructional cue indicating the task to be performed, followed by the imperative stimulus (see Meiran, this volume). Mostly these cues indicated which task should be performed, but in some studies they directly indicated whether a task switch or repetition was required (Forstmann, Brass, Koch, & von Cramon, 2005; Rushworth, Hadland, Paus, & Sipila, 2002). Commonly, subjects performed just one trial of the cued task, but some studies used longer runs of trials (see also Altmann, this volume) at least in part to encourage subjects to establish stable task sets even with long interevent intervals (Yeung, Nystrom, Aronson, & Cohen, 2006). Less common methodological variants included designs in which task order was predictable (Dreher, Koechlin, Ali, & Grafman, 2002; Kimberg, Aguirre, & D'Esposito, 2000) or depended on subjects' voluntary choices (Forstmann, Brass, Koch, & von Cramon, 2006; Walton, Devlin, & Rushworth, 2004; see also Arrington et al., this volume). Among the included studies, various methods were used to decorrelate BOLD responses to successive experimental events: using very long interevent intervals (e.g., 11 seconds between cue and stimulus in MacDonald, Cohen, Stenger, & Carter, 2000), introducing temporal jitter—across-trial timing variation—between events (Bunge, Kahn, Wallis, Miller, & Wagner, 2003; Crone, Wendelken, Donohue, & Bunge, 2006; De Baene & Brass, 2011; Luks, Simpson, Feiwell, & Miller, 2002), or presenting occasional trials with a cue but no imperative stimulus (Brass & von Cramon, 2002). The studies also varied substantially in the particular tasks used: Some required subjects to switch between classifications of distinct stimulus types (Wylie, Javitt, & Foxe, 2006; Yeung et al., 2006), others between different categorizations of the same stimulus type (Forstmann et al., 2005; Kimberg et al., 2000; Liston, Matalon, Hare, Davidson, & Casey, 2006; Luks et al., 2002), others between different responses used to signal the same overall categorization (Crone et al., 2006; Dove, Pollman, Schubert, Wiggins, & von Cramon, 2000; Pollmann, Dove, von Cramon, & Wiggins, 2000). For now, we gloss over these and other methodological differences, and similarly ignore the distinction between cue- and stimulus-related activity (discussed in more detail later): The meta-analytic results in Figure 10.1 simply present the broad contrast between switch and repeat trials across all of these studies.

The results reveal that task switching is associated primarily with activity in parietal and frontal regions, with a degree of left-lateralization (cf. Kim, Cilles, Johnson, & Gold, 2011; Wager, Jonides, & Reading, 2004). Parietal and frontal regions have a long-established association with attention and executive function (Miller & Cohen, 2001; Petersen & Posner, 2012) and this large-scale frontoparietal network very commonly activates in situations of high cognitive demand, leading to its labeling as an "executive" or "multiple demand" network (e.g., Duncan, 2010). The large activation cluster in left parietal cortex stretches from the junction with the temporal lobe (BA39) on the lateral surface, through the inferior and superior temporal lobules (BA40 and 7), to the precuneus (BA7) on the medial surface. This left-lateralized activity is mirrored in part by right hemisphere clusters in the precuneus (extending inferior and posterior into BA31 and BA19) and superior parietal lobule. In frontal cortex, an activation focus extends from the left middle frontal gyrus (BA46) through the precentral gyrus (BA6) to the medial surface including dorsal anterior cingulate cortex (BA32). Corresponding but somewhat weaker foci are observed in each of these regions in the right hemisphere. Smaller frontal activation foci are observed bilaterally in the insula (BA13/47), a region often coactivated with anterior cingulate cortex and other regions in dorsomedial PFC. Outside of frontoparietal cortex, activation clusters are evident bilaterally in occipitotemporal cortex (BA18/19), likely reflecting the use of visual stimuli in all but one of the studies included in the meta-analysis, and in the right cerebellum.

Collectively these results are consistent with previous meta-analyses that have focused on positron emission tomography (PET) as well as fMRI studies (Wager et al., 2004) and that have included a broader range of designs than "pure" task switching (e.g., Wisconsin Card Sorting Task studies in Kim et al., 2011, or working memory tasks in Wager et al., 2004). Having set the scene with this descriptive summary of typical neuroimaging findings, we now turn to interpretation and finer dissection of these results.

NEURAL CORRELATES OF SWITCH COSTS

The main behavioral index of task switching is the switch cost: increased RTs and error rates accompanying a change of task. In two influential reports, Rogers and Monsell (1995) and Allport et al. (1994) put forward distinct explanations of this cost. According to Rogers and Monsell (1995), the switch cost reflects "reconfiguration" of cognitive resources into a new task set. As formalized by Rubinstein et al. (2001), for example, task processing on switch trials is postponed while control processes of shifting the task goal and activating new stimulus–response associations are completed. On this account, the RT switch cost directly reflects the time

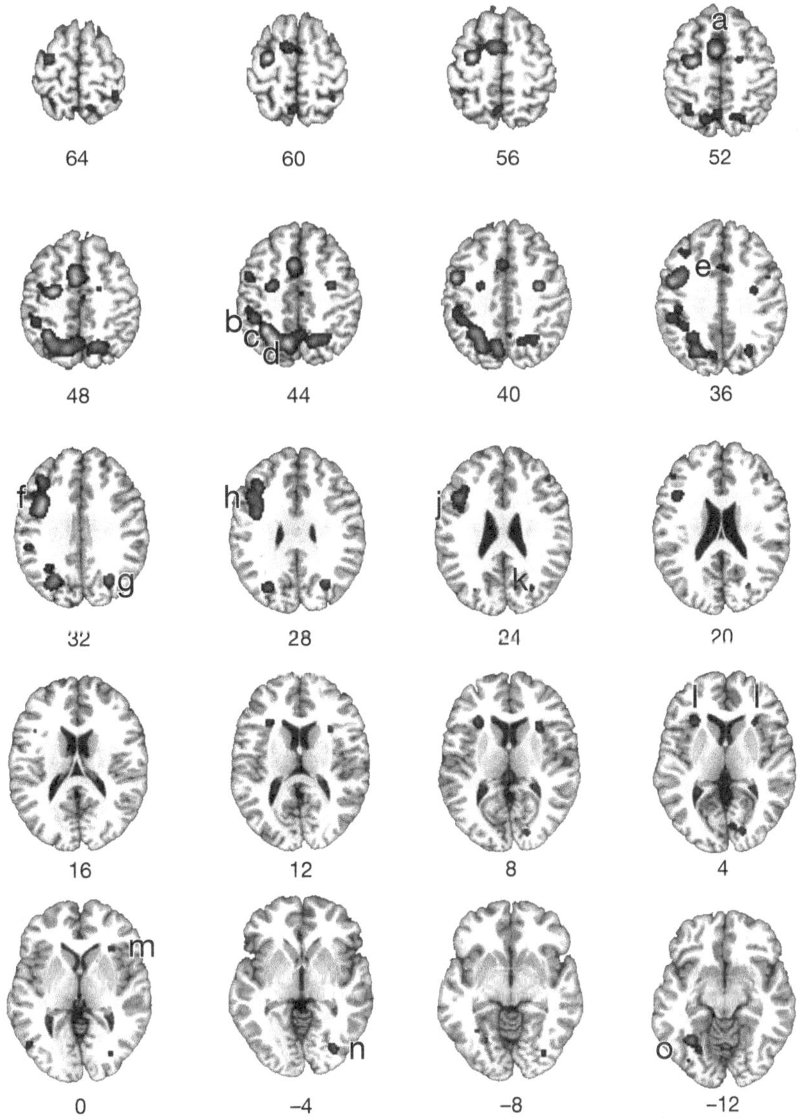

Figure 10.1 Results of the ALE meta-analysis of 34 fMRI task switching studies. Numbers below the images refer to z-coordinate at which each axial slice was taken. The likelihood maps were threshold at p <.05 applying false discovery rate to correct for multiple comparisons. For visualisation the maps were displayed onto the "colinbrain" Talairach template (Kochunov et al., 2002) using the Mango software (http://ric.uthscsa.edu/mango/). Letters a-p mark the areas closest to activation peaks described in the main text: (a) BA6, Medial Frontal Gyrus; (b) BA40, IPL; (c) BA40/7, SPL; (d) BA7, Precuneus; (e) BA32, Cingulate Cortex; (f) BA9/6, Middle Frontal Gyrus; (g) BA19, Precuneus; (h) BA9, Middle Frontal Gyrus; (i) BA7/31, Precuneus; (j) BA46, Middle Frontal Gyrus; (k) BA31, Precuneus; (l) BA13, Insula; (m) BA13/47, Insula; (n) BA18, Middle Occipital Gyrus; (o) BA19, Inferior Occipital Gyrus/Fusiform Gyrus.

taken to complete these reconfiguration processes. Allport et al. (1994) claimed otherwise, arguing that task performance is prolonged rather than postponed by task switching. Specifically, they claimed that task processes are performed less efficiently on switch trials because of competitive interactions between the new task and tasks just performed: "Inertia" of the previous task set interferes with the formation of a new one. On this view, the switch cost indexes a failure to form an effective task set, rather than indexing the successful completion of that process. Many theorists now propose that task switching reflects both reconfiguration and between-task competition (Kiesel et al., 2010; Vandierendonck et al., 2010). Of interest here is whether neuroimaging evidence supports this conclusion.

Switch versus Repeat Contrasts

A minimal neuroimaging prediction of all current theories is that neural activity should differ between switch and repeat trials, reflecting the need for reconfiguration and/or increased between-task competition when switching tasks. The meta-analysis results presented above certainly support this first-order prediction, but closer inspection reveals that pooling data in this way tends to mask inconsistency across individual studies. Thus, despite the robustness of the behavioral switch cost, and the fact that EEG studies consistently find switch-related effects (see Karayanidis & Jamadar, this volume), a notable minority of fMRI studies have failed to find differences between activity on switch and repeat trials (Brass & von Cramon, 2002, 2004; Bunge et al., 2003; Luks et al., 2002; Ruge et al., 2005). Indeed, according to a recent review, only half of fMRI studies looking at cue-related neural activity—when subjects are presumed to engage in active task-set reconfiguration—find greater activity in switch compared with repeat trials (Ruge et al., 2011).

Various factors might contribute to these surprising null results. FMRI as a measure might simply lack sensitivity to the effects of interest. More likely, the slow-pacing of fMRI designs may reduce the psychological distinction between switch and repeat trials. First, as noted above, the presence of long interevent intervals might discourage subjects from forming stable task sets. Second, compounding this effect, many studies have included a high frequency of switch trials that, paradoxically, may reduce the ability to find switch-related activity: Under these conditions, subjects come to expect and differentially prepare for task switches, reducing the difference between switch and repeat trials (Monsell & Mizon, 2006). Consistent with this analysis, many of the studies failing to find switch-related activity have included switches on 50% or more of trials (e.g., Brass & von Cramon, 2004; Crone et al., 2006), while studies reporting robust differences had few switches (e.g., 20 switch and 125 repeat trials in a study by Dove et al., 2000). Finally, the use of long cue–stimulus intervals (CSIs) may allow subjects to prepare so well for task switches that these trials become indistinguishable from repeat trials (Ruge et al., 2011). However, although it is true that some studies find switch-repeat differences when CSI is short but not when it is long

(Brass & von Cramon, 2004; Ruge et al., 2005), switch-repeat contrasts have produced null results even in studies using very short or zero CSIs, and even when a lenient statistical criterion is used (Gruber, Karch, Schlueter, Falkai, & Goschke, 2006). Therefore, while the general rule is that task switching is associated with activation in frontal and parietal cortex, there are many exceptions to the rule—and perhaps predictably so given the design constraints of fMRI task switching research.

Task-set Reconfiguration

Reconfiguration theories explain switch costs as the time needed to complete switch-specific control processes (Rubinstein et al., 2001). A basic prediction of these theories is that switching should activate regions associated with attention and executive functions, such as frontal and parietal cortex. Although straightforward, this prediction is not trivial given the suggestion that cued switching designs allow for a compound-stimulus strategy that obviates the need for task sets and task switching (Logan & Bundesen, 2003; see also Meiran, this volume). It is therefore reassuring that this basic prediction receives clear support from our meta-analysis results.

However, these observations do not provide unambiguous support for the reconfiguration theory. First, the prediction of switch-related activity differences is not unique to the reconfiguration view; for example, this activity might reflect the increased need to prepare for, or react to, increased between-task competition on switch trials. Second, switch-repeat differences in fMRI data might reflect neural adaptation effects in repeat trials rather than additional processes in switch trials (De Baene, Kuhn, & Brass, 2011). Adaptation, or *repetition suppression*, is commonly observed when neural representations are repeatedly activated—a physiological-level effect that need not bear any simple relationship to concurrent behavioral changes (Grill-Spector, Henson, & Martin, 2006). Thus, perhaps counterintuitively, switch-repeat differences could arise because of similarities, rather than contrasts, in the patterns of neural activity associated with switching and repeating tasks. Consistent with this interpretation, activity in frontal and parietal cortex has been shown to reduce gradually with consecutive task repetitions, as if reflecting the gradual accretion of adaptation, rather than showing the step-function decrease one would expect if successful reconfiguration at a task switch established an effective task set for all subsequent task repetitions (De Baene et al., 2011).

Current neuroimaging data provide even less support for the strongest and most distinctive prediction of reconfiguration theories: that if qualitatively different processes take place during switch trials, there should be corresponding switch-specific brain activations (i.e., brain regions that are activated on switch trials but, crucially, not on repeat trials). This prediction has rarely been borne out empirically: Areas activated during task switching are almost always active on task-repeat trials as well, just less so. This repeat-trial activation is apparent both during task preparation (e.g., Brass & von Cramon, 2004) and task performance (e.g., Braver, Reynolds, & Donaldson, 2003; Dove et al., 2000), throughout the entire network of frontal and parietal regions activated during switching (Dove et al., 2000), and even when the probability of task switching is very low (Slagter et al., 2006). It has therefore been suggested that similar processes take place in switch and repeat trials, with only quantitative differences in the amount or strength of processing required (Kiesel et al., 2010; Ruge et al., 2011; Shi, Zhou, Muller, & Schubert, 2010). There are some reports of exceptions to this general rule, with parietal lobe regions in particular showing some evidence of activation that might be limited to switch trials (Barber & Carter, 2005; Chiu & Yantis, 2009; Kimberg et al., 2000), but systematic replication and exploration of these scattered findings is currently lacking.

Between-task Competition

There is much stronger neuroimaging support for the view that switch costs reflect task-set inertia, the tendency to continue to activate tasks performed on previous trials (Allport et al., 1994). This hypothesis has been tested by asking subject to switch between tasks associated with dissociable brain regions, such as classifications of motion versus color (Wylie et al., 2006) or of faces versus words (Yeung et al., 2006). Activity in task-selective regions can then be used to measure subjects' attention to each of the tasks as they switch between them. Consistent with the task-set inertia hypothesis, switch trials are associated with persistent activity in regions selective for previously required but now irrelevant tasks, and the strength of this persistent activity predicts the size of the behavioral switch cost (Wylie et al., 2006; Yeung et al., 2006). This increase in between-task competition on switch trials is accompanied by activity in the usual network of frontal and parietal regions (Yeung et al., 2006), suggesting that successful switching depends crucially on effective monitoring and regulation of between-task competition (Desimone & Duncan, 1995; Miller & Cohen, 2001).

One mechanism for regulating between-task competition is the inhibition of irrelevant task sets (Koch, Gade, Schuch, & Philipp, 2010; see also Gade et al., this volume). Persuasive evidence of inhibition comes from *n*-2 repetition effects observed in paradigms in which subjects switch between three different tasks (*A*, *B*, and *C*). When comparing *ABA* with *CBA* trial sequences, subjects perform worse in the final *A* trial in *ABA* sequences, even though both sequences include equivalent *B*-to-*A* task switches (Mayr & Keele, 2000). This finding has been interpreted as evidence of "backward inhibition" during switching, such that in the *ABA* sequence, task *A* is inhibited as part of the initial switch to task *B*, making it more difficult to reactivate task *A* subsequently. In fMRI, activity in right ventrolateral prefrontal cortex is increased on the critical *ABA* trials (Dreher & Berman, 2002). This area is of particular interest given its association elsewhere with situations assumed to involve inhibition, such as go/no-go and stop signal tasks in which a prepotent response must be withheld (Aron, Robbins, & Poldrack, 2004). The region lies close to, but does not overlap with, the right insula activation focus identified in our meta-analysis, such that the contribution of inhibitory processes to task switching more generally remains unclear. Moreover, the fMRI findings leave open whether the activity identified reflects the application of inhibition or the need to deal with inhibition previously applied. Perhaps consistent with the latter interpretation, a recent study found that individual differences in the behavioral backward inhibition effect correlated with greater switching-related activity in dorsal premotor cortex (BA6) and the basal ganglia, but not in ventrolateral frontal cortex (Whitmer & Banich, 2012).

Conclusions

FMRI correlates of behavioral switch costs are not apparent in all studies, reflecting the challenge of studying dynamic switching with the sluggish BOLD signal. Where switch-repeat differences are apparent, they are widespread across frontal and parietal regions, stretching from the mid-lateral to medial cortical surfaces. These differences are typically quantitative rather than qualitative in nature—regional activity is increased, but not selectively observed, on switch trials—providing little evidence for switch-specific reconfiguration processes. Instead, task-set control processes appear to operate on both switch and repeat trials, regulating between-task competition that increases during switching because of persisting activation and inhibition of recently performed tasks.

SHARED ACTIVATION PATTERNS

The preceding section considered whether fMRI evidence complements theories and findings emerging from behavioral studies of task switching. The remainder focuses on questions for which neuroimaging offers a more distinct perspective. The first of these is whether any brain regions are active during task switching regardless of the specific tasks involved, a question that bears on the broader issue of whether task switching represents a coherent domain of study in which common mechanisms and principles operate across domains.

Types of Switching

Current evidence suggests a positive answer to this question. Although no single region exhibits switch-related activity in every published task switching study—an unreasonably strict criterion given the limitations of fMRI discussed above, together with inevitable measurement noise and variability in experimental design and analysis across studies—two key regions are consistently activated across studies with very differing designs: the inferior frontal junction (*IFJ*, Brass, Derrfuss, Forstmann, & von Cramon, 2005; Brass & von Cramon, 2004) and the superior parietal lobe (*SPL*, Serences, Schwartzbach, Courtney, Golay, & Yantis,

2004; Yantis et al., 2002). These regions fall within the large frontal and parietal clusters identified in our meta-analysis: The IFJ lies at the intersection of the inferior frontal sulcus and inferior precentral sulcus (BA6/8/44); within the SPL, switch-related activity is commonly observed in dorsal-lying regions, stretching towards the precuneus along the medial surface (BA7).

In recent work, Kim and colleagues (Kim et al., 2011a; Kim, Johnson, Cilles, & Gold, 2011b) have identified three distinct classes of task switching:

- *Perceptual switching*: when tasks differ in the relevant stimulus or stimulus attribute—e.g., if subjects are required to switch between classifying the color versus motion direction of a stimulus (Liston et al., 2006).
- *Response switching*: when tasks differ in their response set or mapping from stimuli to responses—e.g., if stimulus location is always the relevant attribute, but subjects switch between compatible and crossed stimulus–response mappings (Barber & Carter, 2005).
- *Set switching*: when tasks differ in their task rules—e.g., if subjects switch between different classification rules applied to different stimulus attributes (Monchi, Petrides, Petre, Worsley, & Dagher, 2001).

In an ALE meta-analysis of fMRI studies grouped according to these broad classifications, IFJ and SPL were the only regions identified as showing significant switch-related activity across all three types of switching (Kim et al., 2011a). A subsequent fMRI study provided converging support (Kim et al., 2011b): In a single design that allowed direct comparison between perceptual switching (between left versus right stimulus locations), response switching (between selecting the smaller versus larger of two-digit values), and set switching (between different digit comparisons), the IFJ and SPL were identified as exhibiting activity regardless of switch type (together with the precuneus). In what follows, we consider the possible functional roles of these two key regions.

Inferior Frontal Junction

Anatomically, the IFJ lies between the prefrontal (PFC) and premotor cortices (Figure 10.2, left panel). As such, it is uniquely well positioned to mediate between anterior PFC regions implicated in working memory and high-level cognitive control (Miller & Cohen, 2001) and more posterior premotor regions involved in conditional action selection (Passingham, 1993) (cf. Brass & von Cramon, 2002). In fact, functional connectivity studies—which use interregion activity correlations activity as an index of neural interactions—suggest that IFJ displays differential connectivity according to the particular task required (Stelzel, Basten, & Fiebach, 2011): IFJ-anterior PFC connectivity increases when subjects switch between abstract rules (e.g., between odd/even and magnitude number judgments), whereas IFJ-motor cortex connectivity increases when subjects switch between response hands. The IFJ also lies close to language-related areas

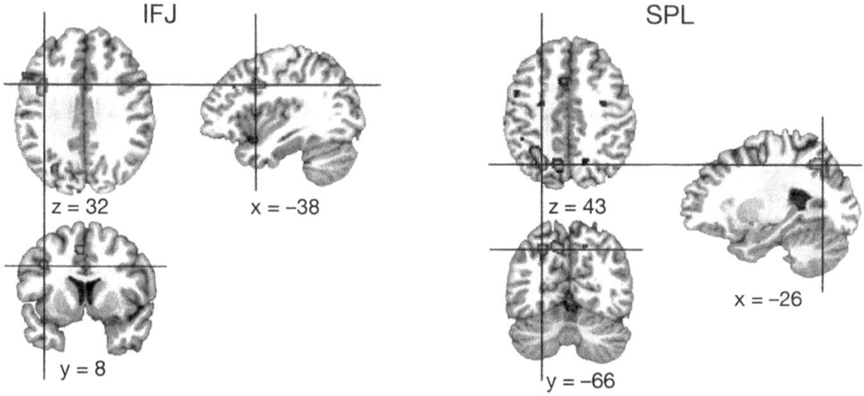

Figure 10.2 The inferior frontal junction (IFJ) and superior parietal lobe (SPL). These ALE maps were threshold at p <.0001 (corrected for multiple comparisons) to separate the IFJ and SPL activation foci from neighbouring ones apparent in the overall meta-analysis.

in inferior frontal cortex (cf. Amunts & von Cramon, 2006); indeed, activation is commonly observed in and around IFJ itself during phonological or semantic encoding of word stimuli (Bookheimer, 2002; Fiebach, Friederici, Smith, & Swinney, 2007). Anatomical proximity and functional overlap between regions involved in language and task switching is intriguing given evidence of the role of verbal self-instruction in switching (Miyake, Emerson, Padilla, & Ahn, 2004) and given the importance of hierarchical sequential structure in both language processing and movement control (Schubotz & Fiebach, 2006).

Task switching studies focusing on IFJ suggest a role in activating task rules (Brass & von Cramon, 2004). Thus, IFJ activity is observed when instructional task cues precede the imperative stimulus, allowing subjects to prepare the relevant task in advance (Brass & von Cramon, 2002, 2004). This preparatory activity increases with the specificity of the cue, for example being greater when cues indicate the required stimulus–response mapping than when cues solely indicate the relevant stimulus attribute to attend (Shi et al., 2010). Similarly, IFJ is more active when stimulus identity is revealed in advance of the task cue than vice versa, presumably because the former ordering permits more specific preparation (Ruge, Braver, & Meiran, 2009).

An inverse relationship is observed between IFJ activity during preparation and task performance: When advance cues are used, and preparatory IFJ activity is high, little activity is observed during task performance; when advance cues are absent, and preparation is correspondingly limited, robust IFJ activity is observed after stimulus onset (Brass & von Cramon, 2004; Ruge et al., 2005; Shi et al., 2010). Collectively these findings suggest that IFJ supports obligatory processes in task switching that either occur during preparation, if cues are provided, or during task performance, if not. Switch-related IFJ activity is also increased when stimuli are bivalent, affording responses in both possible tasks, compared with when stimuli are univalent, being uniquely associated with the required task (Crone et al., 2006).

Again this result is consistent with a role in activating task rules: When stimuli are univalent, multiple task sets can be maintained simultaneously without interference, reducing the need to re-activate task rules at each switch; with bivalent stimuli, task sets must be sequentially activated to prevent cross-talk (Rogers & Monsell, 1995).

Superior Parietal Lobe

The SPL (Figure 10.2, right panel) forms part of the dorsal visual stream that runs from occipital cortex through the parietal lobe and onwards to premotor cortex, supporting the visual control of action (Milner & Goodale, 2008). A reciprocal set of connections is widely held to carry attentional signals from frontal cortex to bias visual processing in favor of currently relevant objects (Desimone & Duncan, 1995). An influential hypothesis (Corbetta & Shulman, 2002) holds that the inferior and superior parietal lobes play complementary roles in this attentional biasing, with inferior regions involved in bottom-up attentional capture by salient stimuli (e.g., when flashed stimuli in the periphery draw attention exogenously to their location, Corbetta, Kincade, & Shulman, 2002) and the SPL involved in top-down attentional modulation according to current goals (e.g., when an arrow at fixation guides attention to the likely location of a target stimulus, Corbetta, Kincade, Ollinger, McAvoy, & Shulman, 2000).

Given this association between the SPL and top-down attentional control, it is unsurprising that the region is commonly activated during task switching (e.g., Wager et al., 2004). Activity in the SPL is found, for example, when switching between different spatial categorization tasks (Ruge et al., 2005) and when switching between counting arrows pointing to the right versus the left (Sylvester et al., 2003). SPL activity is not limited to location-based selection and switching, but is also observed when switching attention between stimulus attributes (e.g., color and motion; Liston et al., 2006; Liu, Slotnick, Serences, & Yantis, 2003) and between objects (Serences et al., 2004), when switching between categorization rules with no change in the relevant stimuli (Braver et al., 2003; Crone et al., 2006), when switching between more abstract sets like verbal categories (Gurd et al., 2002), and when shifting attention within working memory (Esterman, Chiu, Tamber-Rosenau, & Yantis, 2009), amongst many others (e.g., Wager et al., 2004; Wylie, Javitt, & Foxe, 2004; Yantis et al., 2002). Direct comparison indicates that common regions within SPL are activated by different types of switching—e.g., shifting attention across spatial locations and switching between abstract task rules—with cross-adaptation effects suggesting that representational overlap extends to the level of individual neurons (Chiu & Yantis, 2009). Collectively these findings suggest that the SPL plays a broader role in task switching than stimulus-oriented attentional control.

Indeed, the SPL coactivates very reliably with the IFJ in task switching studies, suggesting a high degree of overlap or interaction in function. One suggested division of labor between parietal and frontal regions is that the former are involved in implementing switches and maintaining task rules after they are retrieved, while the latter are additionally and more directly involved in preparatory processes such as rule retrieval (Bunge, 2004; Bunge et al., 2003). However, SPL activity is reliably seen during task preparation following instructional cues (e.g., Chiu & Yantis, 2009), and in these cases typically tracks the activation profile of IFJ across experimental conditions (e.g., Brass & von Cramon, 2004; Ruge et al., 2009; Shi et al., 2010), questioning any clear functional division between the two. Thus, while future comparisons between the SPL and IFJ may reveal dissociations in their respective functions in task switching, convincing direct contrasts are currently lacking. Moreover, given the strong anatomical connectivity between topographically mapped regions in the parietal lobe and premotor areas of frontal cortex (Rizzolatti & Luppino, 2001), one might expect any dissociations discovered to be subtle and quantitative rather than qualitative in nature.

Conclusions

Task switching research often proceeds on the assumption that common principles and mechanisms operate across different domains of switching. Neuroimaging evidence provides valuable reassurance on this point: Common regions in frontal and parietal cortex—particularly the IFJ and SPL—are active during switching with very different demands, from low-level spatial attention shifts to switching between abstract task rules. Substantive challenges nonetheless remain for future research, both in clarifying the respective roles of the IFJ and SPL, and in specifying these roles in more precise computational terms. Without this specification, accounts of IFJ-SPL activity couched in terms of activating and updating current task rules risk becoming circular re-descriptions of the process of task switching.

DISSOCIABLE ACTIVATION PATTERNS

We now turn to the question of whether neuroimaging findings suggest consistent dissociations among different switching domains. Several approaches have been proposed as to how to group different kinds of switching (e.g., Ravizza & Carter, 2008; Wager et al., 2004). However, one intuitive and very commonly made distinction, already been mentioned above, is between perceptual and response switching (Meiran, 2000; Rushworth, Paus, & Sipila, 2001). We first consider the evidence on this point. We then turn to evidence that separable regions are active specifically during switching between high-level, more abstract tasks (set switching), and finally consider whether dissociations are observed between regions active during task preparation and task performance.

Perceptual versus Response Switching

Perceptual switching covers a range of situations: shifting attention between locations (e.g., Chiu & Yantis, 2009; Yantis et al., 2002), between objects in a shared location (e.g., Cools, Clark, & Robbins, 2004; Ravizza & Carter, 2008; Yeung et al., 2006), and between different attributes of a single target (e.g., Liston et al., 2006; Wylie et al., 2006). In many studies, shifts of attention are accompanied by a change in the relevant classification (e.g., color blue or red versus movement leftward or rightward), but pure perceptual shifting is possible (e.g., applying the same classification rule to objects in different locations; Yantis et al., 2002). Response switching is a similarly broad category that includes switching from one effector to another with the same classification rule (Philipp, Weidner, Koch, & Fink, 2012), keeping the response set constant but reversing the mapping of stimuli to those responses (e.g., Barber & Carter, 2005; Crone et al., 2006; Dove et al., 2000; Pollmann et al., 2000; Shi et al., 2010), and switching between different categorization rules applied to a constant stimulus set (e.g., Brass & von Cramon, 2004; Luks et al., 2002).

In addition to their shared activation of the IFJ and SPL discussed above, perceptual and response switching have been found to activate dissociable regions within both frontal and parietal cortex. In frontal cortex, dorsolateral PFC (DLPFC, BA9/46) is consistently found to be more active during response switching than perceptual switching (Kim et al., 2011a, 2011b; Ravizza & Carter, 2008; Rogers, Andrews, Grasby, Brooks, & Robbins, 2000). The relative selectivity of DLPFC to response switching is only partly consistent with theories that place this region at the centre of the cortical network responsible for flexible behavioral control and switching (Miller & Cohen, 2001): Task switching research suggests a more specific role, for example in selecting stimulus–response sets (Hyafil, Summerfield, & Koechlin, 2009), preparing to implement specific rules (Ruge et al., 2011), or signaling to other regions to implement switches (Jamadar, Michie, & Karayanidis, 2010). Meanwhile, somewhat less consistently observed, but nevertheless evident in formal meta-analysis (Kim, Cilles et al., 2011), is a dissociation between lateral and medial premotor areas: Whereas dorsal premotor cortex (BA6) on the lateral surface exhibits greater activity during perceptual switching, the presupplementary motor area and dorsal anterior cingulate cortex (pre-SMA/ACC, BA6/32) on the medial surface show the opposite pattern (Kim et al., 2011b; Liston et al., 2006; Rushworth et al., 2002). The relative selectivity of dorsal premotor cortex to perceptual switching is perhaps surprising, but might reflect reconfiguration (or adaptation, De Baene et al., 2011) of stimulus–response associations represented in this region. Pre-SMA/ACC activity during response switching is less surprising given the presumed involvement of these regions in initiating, sequencing, and monitoring of actions (cf. Holroyd & Yeung, 2012). Activation in this region during task preparation, before any specific responses can be selected, suggests that pre-SMA/ACC performs these sequencing and monitoring functions at the level of whole tasks, not just individual actions (Brass & von Cramon, 2004; Weissman, Gopalakrishnan, Hazlett, & Woldorff, 2005; but see MacDonald et al., 2000).

Contrasts between perceptual and response switching have also been consistently observed in parietal cortex (Kim et al., 2011b; Liston et al., 2006; Ravizza & Carter, 2008; Rushworth et al., 2001). However, though dissociation is consistent, precise localization is not: For example, whereas formal meta-analysis suggests that perceptual switching results in greater activation in medial SPL and response switching more laterally (Kim et al., 2011a), the opposite effect is sometimes reported (Rushworth et al., 2001). This inconsistency presumably relates to design idiosyncrasies of individual studies, but in any case mitigates against strong conclusions about the nature of specialization within the parietal lobe. One intriguing possibility is that parietal regions exhibit finer functional specialization than is captured by a crude distinction between perceptual and response switching (Silver & Kastner, 2009), in contrast to frontal regions that are characterized by a higher degree of functional homogeneity (Duncan, 2010).

Two final caveats should be noted. First, specialization tends to be relative rather than absolute: Where studies present regional activation time-courses (not only statistical maps of between-condition differences) it is immediately clear that effects observed reflect quantitative preference rather than qualitative selectivity. For example, though DLPFC exhibits greater activity during response switching, the region is also activated to a significant degree during perceptual switching (Kim et al., 2011b; Ravizza & Carter, 2008). The second caveat is that activity in a region does not prove functional significance: Rushworth et al. (2002) found significant pre-SMA activity in both perceptual and response switching, but only the latter was disrupted by the application of transcranial magnetic stimulation to the region.

Set Switching

Set switching is once again a broad category: It has been applied to cases in which subjects switch between tasks that differ in both stimulus and response attributes (e.g., orthogonal classifications of color and of shape), cases in which a contrast is drawn between single task performance and task switching blocks (Braver et al., 2003; see also Mari-Beffa & Kirkham, this volume), and cases in which a partially completed task must be held in abeyance over a long period while another task is attempted (Koechlin, Basso, Pietrini, Panzer, & Grafman, 1999). The family resemblance across these situations is that switching cannot be achieved by modulating low-level perceptual or response processes, or by swapping sets of stimulus–response mappings; rather, the switch entails a more global change in behavior.

This high-level control of task set is associated with anterior parts in frontal cortex (BA10, e.g., Kim et al., 2011b), which are characterized by sustained rather than transient activity. Thus, whereas more posterior frontal regions such as DLPFC show cue- and stimulus-related activity that is enhanced during task switching, activity in anterior PFC is enhanced for the entire block (compared with single-task blocks) but shows little or no event-related activity (Braver et al., 2003). Similarly, in a study requiring subjects to switch between semantic and phonological classifications of word stimuli, anterior PFC activity was sustained throughout a long cue–stimulus interval, irrespective of the task to be performed, whereas activity in more posterior frontal regions was phasic and task selective (Sakai & Passingham, 2006). This preparatory activity in anterior PFC predicted subsequent behavioral performance and correlated with activity in different task-selective posterior PFC regions according to the required task, suggestive of a role for this region in maintaining high-level task goals through task-specific interactions with areas related to task performance. Perhaps consistent with this conclusion, anterior PFC regions show greater activity when abstract "transition cues" inform subjects whether the task is to be switched or repeated than when standard instructional cues indicate the particular task required (Forstmann et al., 2005).

An influential hypothesis holds that anterior PFC forms part of an integrated hierarchy of cognitive control. This hypothesis incorporates the long-held view that behavior can be characterized at different levels of abstraction (Lashley, 1951), from simple actions (e.g., a twitch of the finger) that are associated with particular motor goals (pressing a button), to conditional associations (indicating that a stimulus is green) that relate to higher-level tasks (classifying stimulus color), to abstract behaviors (completing a psychology experiment) with correspondingly abstract goals (collecting course credits). According to several recent theories, this hierarchy maps explicitly onto the rostrocaudal axis of frontal cortex, with successively more anterior regions containing increasingly abstract representations of actions (Badre & D'Esposito, 2007; Koechlin & Summerfield, 2007; Yoshida, Funakoshi, & Ishii, 2010). In support of this view, switching at different levels of hierarchical structure has been shown to activate regions selectively along this axis (Badre & D'Esposito, 2007; Koechlin, Ody, & Kouneiher, 2003). However, higher levels of abstraction tend to be associated with increased demands on working memory (cf. Wager et al., 2004), and recent evidence suggests that functional dissociations between anterior and posterior PFC regions may disappear if switching conditions are carefully matched for their demands on working memory maintenance and updating (Reynolds, O'Reilly, Cohen, & Braver, 2012). Thus, although an association between anterior PFC and set switching is consistently observed, the correct functional interpretation is yet to be conclusively determined.

Preparation versus Task Performance

As noted above, it is technically challenging to separate neural activity associated with preparation versus task performance using fMRI because of the slow time-course of the BOLD response: If experimental events are presented close in time, BOLD activity related to preparation and performance will temporally overlap; if events are spaced across several seconds to reduce temporal overlap, the very nature of preparation and task performance will likely change (e.g., via increased working memory demand). Nevertheless, several studies have attempted to compare brain activity during task preparation and task performance, reflecting the importance of this contrast for theories of task switching. In particular, many influential theories predict that similar activity patterns should be observed during preparation and performance, for example because the same obligatory processes must be carried out in either advance of an imperative stimulus—if the task to be performed is predictable or cued in advance—or after stimulus onset—if no preparation time is allowed, or preparation not attempted (Rogers & Monsell, 1995; Rubinstein et al., 2001). In contrast, a recent theory proposes a distinction between proactive and reactive modes of control—with the former characterized by advance preparation, and the latter by compensatory reactions when difficult conditions are experienced—which are thought to depend on at least partly distinct neural mechanisms (Braver, 2012).

One way to contrast preparation and task performance is to dissociate cue- and stimulus-related activity, either in time using long or jittered CSIs (MacDonald et al., 2000; Sakai & Passingham, 2003; Sohn, Ursu, Anderson, Stenger, & Carter, 2000) or across trials by independently manipulating the presence or absence of task cues and imperative stimuli (Brass & von Cramon, 2002, 2004). For example, Brass and von Cramon (2002, 2004) used "cue-only" trials, with no imperative stimulus, so that preparation could be studied in relative isolation from task performance, and opposite "no cue" trials so that task performance could be studied without preceding task preparation. A second approach has been to compare activity at short versus long CSIs, without necessarily attempting to dissociate BOLD responses to cue and stimulus events (e.g., Gruber et al., 2006; Ruge et al., 2005; Wylie et al., 2006): Regions exhibiting greater activity when the CSI is long are presumed to be involved in preparation (although any differences observed might also reflect the consequences of effective preparation on later task performance).

Together these studies have failed to find any consistent dissociations between preparatory and performance-related activation patterns. Many studies observe common areas of activity during preparation and task performance, in the frontal and parietal network described extensively above (e.g., Brass & von Cramon, 2002, 2004; Gruber et al., 2006; Ruge et al., 2009) as well as in task-selective parts of visual cortex (Wylie et al., 2006), 2006). Meanwhile, although some differences have been reported in individual studies, the results are inconsistent when taken collectively. For example, whereas Ruge et al. (2005) found no switch-specific preparatory activity but widespread frontal and parietal activity during task performance, Jamadar et al. (2010) observed the opposite pattern. Similarly, whereas Sohn et al. (2000) observed a dissociation between ventral PFC, more active during task preparation, and dorsal PFC, more active during task performance in the absence of preparation, the opposite pattern has also been observed (e.g., Badre & Wagner, 2006; Wylie et al., 2006). Many researchers have therefore concluded that task preparation involves strategic pre-activation of the same network of regions—instantiating the same task set—that is required during task performance (Gruber et al., 2006; Ruge et al., 2005; Wylie et al., 2006; but see Karayanidis et al., 2010, for a contrasting interpretation). Thus, to the extent that there are distinct proactive and reactive modes of control in task switching (Braver, 2012), these two modes would appear to rely on the flexible operation of a single network rather than qualitatively distinct neural mechanisms. However, this conclusion must be drawn with appropriate caution given the difficulty of teasing apart dynamically evolving processes of preparation and task performance using the temporally blunt fMRI BOLD response.

Conclusions

Neuroimaging methods are well suited to identifying dissociations between cognitive processes (Henson, 2005), and carving task switching at its joints in this way has been a major focus of research to date. This work has established that a coherent distinction exists between perceptual and response switching, that higher-level set switching has a consistent neural basis in anterior PFC, and that largely overlapping networks of regions seem to be activated during task preparation and task performance. The differences observed are almost exclusively quantitative rather than qualitative in nature—reflecting numerical differences in activity rather than full selectivity—a point not always explicitly acknowledged. This blurring might reflect the diversity of strategies adopted by experimental subjects, but perhaps also indicates that functional distinctions drawn to date (e.g., between perceptual and response switching) are only approximate characterizations of the underlying functional specialization of the brain regions in question.

TASK SWITCHING IN MEMORY RETRIEVAL

Cognitive control and long-term memory have separately received substantial scrutiny, but their interactions have only recently become a major focus of research (Chun & Johnson, 2011; Richter & Yeung, 2012). Interest in these interactions has arisen at least in part because of overlap in activity seen in neuroimaging studies of attention and memory, in both frontal (Buckner, 2003) and parietal regions (Cabeza, Ciaramelli, Olson, & Moscovitch, 2008). Particularly relevant to the present focus, concepts similar to that of task set have been defined in research on retrieval of episodic memories of specific personal events: those of *retrieval mode* (Tulving, 1983) and *retrieval orientation* (Rugg & Wilding, 2000). Retrieval mode refers to the state or set that a person enters in order to retrieve episodic events (e.g., last year's visit to Paris) as opposed to general semantic knowledge (e.g., that Paris is the capital of France). Retrieval orientation refers to the specific focus of an episodic retrieval attempt, for example, attempting to recall who you met on that trip to Paris versus recalling the food you ate. In this section, we argue that the concepts of retrieval mode and retrieval orientation (which we refer to together as *retrieval set*) share substantive overlap with the concept of task set as studied in task switching research.

As an example of retrieval set, suppose that subjects first learned a list of pictures and auditorily presented words (Figure 10.3), and are then presented with a series of retrieval cues (written words), some of which refer back to items experienced in the earlier list and some of which are new. Subjects are asked to perform one of two retrieval tasks: In one they indicate whether or not they have previously seen the item as a picture (versus the word being new or previously heard auditorily); in the other they indicate whether or not they have previously heard the item as an auditory word (versus the word being new or previously seen as a picture). Performing these two tasks entails distinct retrieval orientations—emphasizing

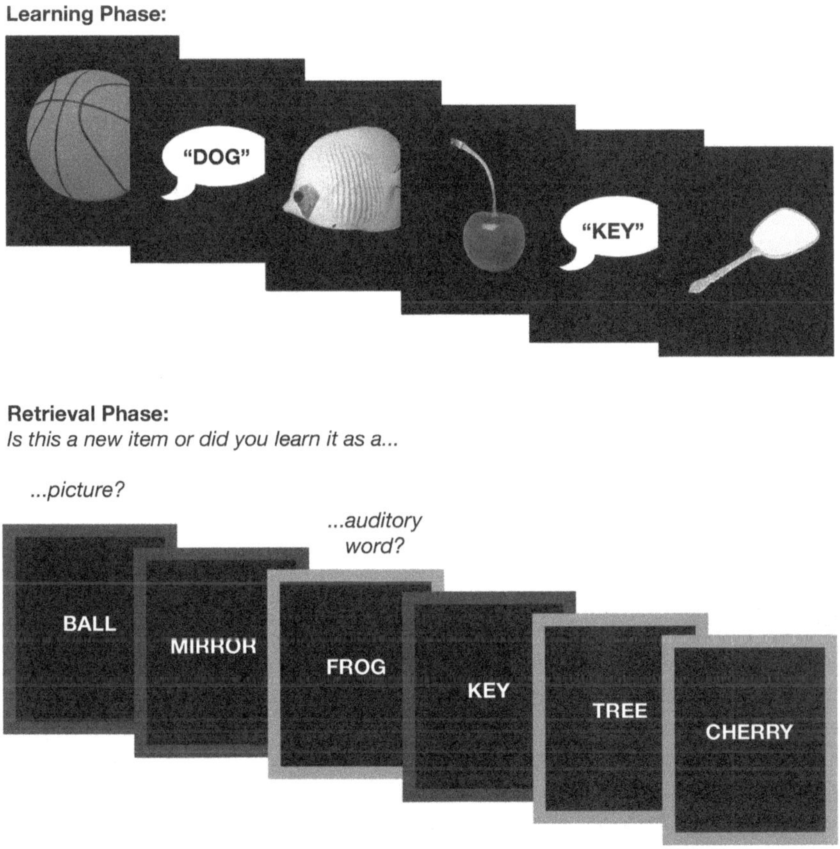

Figure 10.3 Schematic illustration of the retrieval orientation methodology. In an initial learning phase, subjects are presented with pictures and auditory words. In a later retrieval phase, they are presented with visual words referring to old pictures, old auditory words, or new items. A cue (here a coloured frame) indicates which of two retrieval tasks they have to perform. A dark frame instructs them to judge whether or not they have seen the item presented before as a picture. A light frame instructs them to indicate whether or not they have been presented with this item as an auditory word.

visual and auditory aspects of episodic memory, respectively—that, by hypothesis, rely on distinct mind sets. Crucially, these mind sets share clear parallels with the concept of task sets in task switching: Just as a retrieval set must be established when engaging in episodic retrieval, a task set must be established to perform a specific task (cf., Sakai, 2008).

More formally, in task switching research, task sets are typically defined operationally as allowing people to make distinct responses to the same stimulus according to their goals or intentions. For example, subjects can respond differently to the same colored shape depending on whether they are classifying it according to its color or its shape. Their ability to do so, and the observation that switching between classifications is associated with a behavioral cost, is taken as foundational evidence for the existence of task sets. Crucially, the structure of retrieval set studies is formally identical: Subjects are presented with a consistent stimulus type on each trial (the retrieval cue; e.g., a written word), and are required to make distinct responses according to their instructed goal (the retrieval set; e.g., judging whether the item was previously encountered as a picture). Indeed, many studies of retrieval set have required subjects to switch between different retrieval tasks, therefore resembling task switching studies in their experimental design. Thus, studies of task switching and retrieval set are structurally equivalent, with both requiring subjects to establish mental sets that can guide their responses to otherwise ambiguous external stimuli.

Neuroimaging of Retrieval Set

A number of studies have required subjects to switch between retrieval sets: for example, between episodic versus semantic memory tasks (Kompus, Olsson, Larsson, & Nyberg, 2009; Phillips, Velanova, Wolk, & Wheeler, 2009), between judging whether an item was seen recently versus was seen in the context of a particular task (Dobbins, Rice, Wagner, & Schacter, 2003; Dobbins & Wagner, 2005), between making old/new judgments versus detecting perceptual changes in the stimuli presented (Ranganath, Johnson, & D'Esposito, 2000), and between judging whether an item was seen in the context of a particular task versus judging whether an item is old or new (Dobbins & Han, 2006). However, disappointingly few of these studies report analyses of switch-related activity, instead focusing primarily on dissociations among the different retrieval tasks. The study by Phillips et al. (2009, Supplementary materials) is an important exception. In this study, switching between an episodic old/new judgment and a living/nonliving semantic task was associated with slowed RTs, increased activity in the SPL and medial frontal cortex, and modulation of memory-related activity in the region of the IFJ. Thus, switch-related activity in this study overlapped with core regions implicated in task switching as described above, lending preliminary support to the hypothesis that these processes rely on similar neural mechanisms.

Converging evidence comes from studies that have not studied switching specifically, but which have assessed memory tasks that require a specific retrieval orientation—such as recalling whether test items were seen previously in the context of a particular task—against a baseline of memory tasks without this requirement—such as performing nonspecific old/new judgments (Hayes, Buchler, Stokes, Kragel, & Cabeza, 2011; Dobbins & Han, 2006; Dobbins & Wagner, 2005). A familiar network of regions exhibits greater activity in the former case: areas of lateral frontal cortex stretching from ventrolateral regions, through IFJ, to DLPFC; foci in anterior PFC; and inferior lateral and superior medial regions of parietal cortex. Two further retrieval set effects are similarly reminiscent of task switching findings: First, many frontal and parietal regions show corresponding activity during retrieval set preparation and actual retrieval attempts (Dobbins & Han, 2006; Phillips et al., 2009), just as they do during preparation and performance in task switching (e.g., Gruber et al., 2006; Ruge et al., 2005). Second, anterior

PFC exhibits sustained activity across extended blocks of retrieval orientation (Woodruff, Uncapher, & Rugg, 2006), mirroring block-wise differences observed during task switching (Braver et al., 2003).

In addition to analysis of regions that are generically activated as retrieval sets are established and maintained, a substantial focus of memory research has been analysis of regions that exhibit selectivity for particular retrieval modes or orientations. In this context, a key feature of most fMRI designs is that common retrieval cues are used throughout (e.g., visually presented words), with only the to-be-retrieved information (e.g., episodic versus semantic information, or pictures versus auditory words) varying across trials. Set-specific activity has indeed been identified in this way (Dobbins et al., 2003; Dobbins & Wagner, 2005; Woodruff et al., 2006). Selectivity is observed in regions of sensory cortex associated with the material originally presented. For example, in a contrast between retrieval orientation to pictures versus auditory words (Hornberger, Rugg, & Henson, 2006), picture-orientation was associated with activity in visual cortex and inferior temporal lobe regions of the ventral visual stream, whereas orientation to auditory words produced activity in auditory cortex in the superior temporal lobe. Set-selectivity is also observed in frontal cortex (cf., Sakai & Passingham, 2006), with left-lateralized activity during recall of items previously categorized semantically and right-lateralized activity during recall of items categorized perceptually (Dobbins & Wagner, 2005).

Taken together, the above findings parallel those from neuroimaging studies of task switching in key respects: Frontal and parietal networks are activated during retrieval set formation and switching; anterior PFC regions exhibit sustained activity throughout periods of retrieval orientation; and preparation of retrieval sets is associated with activation in task-selective cortical regions as well as frontal-parietal control networks.

Meta-analysis of Task Switching and Retrieval Set

To place this comparison between task switching and retrieval set on a more formal footing, Figure 10.4 presents an ALE meta-analysis of regions that are commonly activated in fMRI studies of retrieval orientation and retrieval mode (see bibliography for details of the studies included). In the figure, the leftmost column ("RO") indicates areas of significant co-activation across published studies of retrieval set, with the second column ("RO=TS") signifying overlap with those activated during task switching. Activation foci are consistently smaller in the retrieval set meta-analysis than in our earlier task switching meta-analysis (contrast Figures 1 and 4, first column), likely reflecting the smaller sample of studies included. More crucially, the two ALE maps exhibit notable points of overlap in frontal and parietal cortex: Conjunction foci are evident in the core IFJ (BA6/9) and SPL (BA7) regions discussed extensively above, but also in DLPFC (BA9/46), insula (BA13), pre-SMA (BA6) and, perhaps reflecting the common use of visual stimuli in the studies of interest, in the inferior temporal lobe (BA37). These

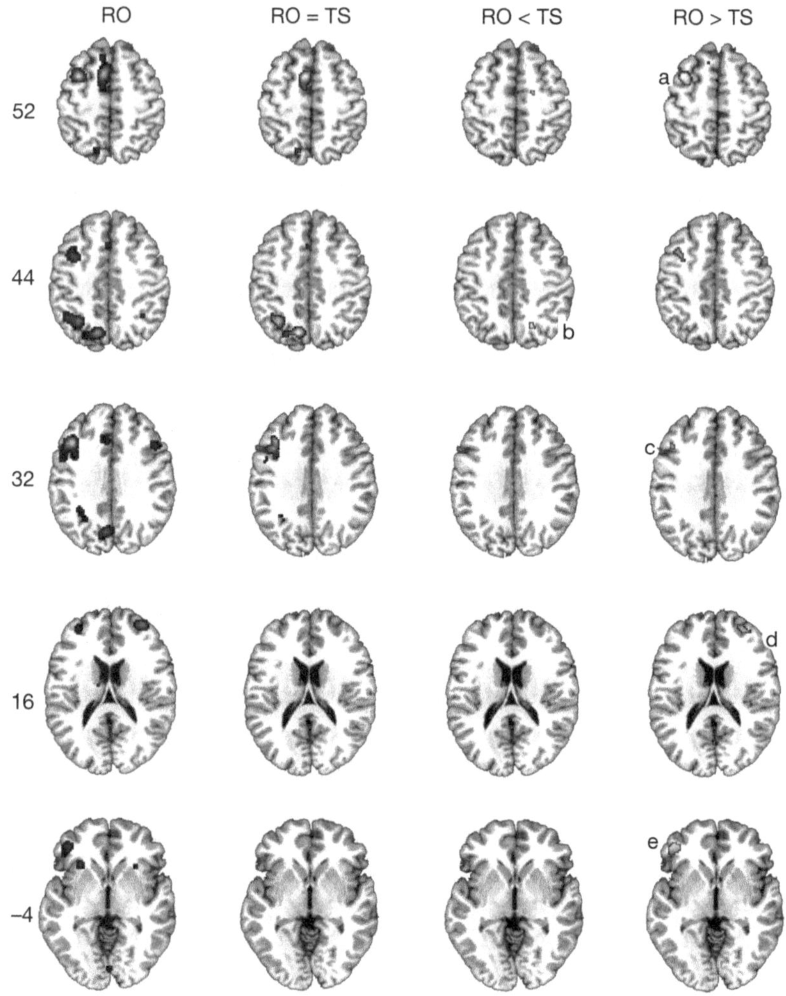

Figure 10.4 Results of ALE meta-analysis of 15 studies of retrieval set, and conjunction with activation foci in task switching. The first column (RO) indicates areas consistently activated in published studies of retrieval set; the second column (RO=TS) indicates overlap between these regions and those activated during task switching. Regions in the third column (RO<TS) indicate more consistent activity in task switching than retrieval orientation studies. Regions in the rightmost column (RO>TS) indicate more consistent activity in the retrieval studies than in task switching. Letters describe the closest areas to the peaks of activation in the following regions: (a) BA6 (retrieval orientation > task switching); (b) BA7 (task switching > retrieval orientation); (c) BA9 (retrieval orientation > task switching); (d) BA10 (retrieval orientation > task switching); (e) BA10 (retrieval orientation > task switching).

findings provide preliminary evidence of quantitative similarity between regions activated during task switching and retrieval set formation.

The meta-analytic contrast also identifies a few regions exhibiting significantly different activity in task switching and memory retrieval. Only one of these regions, a small area in the right precuneus (BA7), was reliably more active during task switching than retrieval orientation (area "b" in the column "RO<TS" in Figure 10.4). Several regions exhibited more consistent activity in memory than in task switching: a region in the middle frontal gyrus (BA6), as well as a region in more inferior middle frontal gyrus (BA11) extending into inferior frontal gyrus (BA47) and anterior PFC (BA10), with the activation in anterior PFC mirrored in the right hemisphere (areas "a", "c", "d", and "e" in the column "RO>TS" in Figure 10.4). In studies of episodic memory, the former region (BA6) has been found to be more active for old (remembered) than new items (Takahashi, Ohki, & Kim, 2008), for correct than incorrect judgments of familiarity (Iidaka, Matsumoto, Nogawa, Yamamoto, & Sadato, 2006), and for recognition of the context in which an item was seen than for simple recognition that the item is familiar (Dobbins, Foley, Schacter, & Wagner, 2002). These findings have implicated the region in monitoring and evaluating retrieved information (Dobbins et al., 2002) a function that is presumably less important when selecting among well-practiced stimulus–response mappings in task switching. Meanwhile, the anterior part of the inferior frontal gyrus (BA10/11/47) has been implicated in memory selection and control (Badre & Wagner, 2007; Young & Shapiro, 2011), for example, because it is more active when subjects attempt to retrieve memories that are only weakly associated with retrieval cues presented (Badre, Poldrack, Pare-Blagoev, Insler, & Wagner, 2005). This effect is particularly apparent in tasks involving semantic judgments (Badre & Wagner, 2007) and recency judgments (Duarte, Ranganath, & Knight, 2005), a feature that is relevant here given that such judgments are common in studies of retrieval set, but much rarer in task switching experiments.

Conclusions

There is substantial overlap in the neural mechanisms involved in the control of task sets and of retrieval sets in long-term memory. Taken with the conceptual and methodological similarities that are also apparent, there would appear to be much to gain from further integration of research in the two fields. Some of these gains will come from replication of key findings across domains: For example, switching-related activity in the IFJ and SPL is commonly interpreted as evidence that these regions are involved in selecting and maintaining task rules. Activity in these regions during long-term memory retrieval suggests that this conception of "task rule" cannot be restricted to the sorts of well-practiced response mappings typically used in task switching research, but must extend to rules relating to retrieval mode and orientation in long-term memory. Further gains from integrating research on task switching and long-term memory will come from exploring contrasts between the two fields. For example, one striking contrast is that task switching research has mostly ignored task-specific activations, focusing instead on generic mechanisms of cognitive control that are common across tasks, while the opposite is true in studies of retrieval set in long-term memory. It is somewhat odd that so much is now known about the mechanisms of task control, but so little about the nature of task sets thereby created, and there is clear scope for future research to investigate this issue.

THEMES AND FUTURE DIRECTIONS

Neuroimaging findings bear on several key issues in task switching research: the nature of task-set reconfiguration and between-task competition in task switching, the degree to which different domains of switching engage common or dissociable mechanisms, and the extent to which principles discovered in task switching research generalize beyond simple stimulus–response tasks to other domains such as long-term memory retrieval. In relation to the four questions we posed at the outset, our take-home summaries are as follows:

1. *Does neuroimaging evidence support theories emerging from behavioral studies of task switching?* FMRI studies have provided very little evidence of switch-specific reconfiguration processes: Task switching is associated with activity in a widespread network of frontal and parietal regions that are implicated in attention and cognitive control, but this network also exhibits robust activity on task repetition trials. These findings are more consistent with theories proposing that behavioral performance in task switching reflects the outcome of competitive interactions between task sets that are modulated, but not discretely controlled, by top-down biases.
2. *Does neuroimaging evidence support the notion that "task switching" represents a coherent area of study?* Task switching studies with very diverse demands very consistently report activity in common regions—the IFJ and SPL in particular—suggesting that core processes are shared across distinct switching domains. However, the precise functions of these core regions, and the division of labor between them, remain unclear in the absence of direct and focused contrasts.
3. *Are dissociations observed among different forms of task switching?* Consistent dissociations are indeed observed, for example between perceptual and response switching. However, these dissociations are almost exclusively relative rather than absolute: There is little or no convincing evidence of strict specialization of function in any region, at least in relation to current theories of the relevant functional divisions to test.
4. *Do common principles govern switching of task sets and switching of retrieval sets in long-term memory?* There is substantive overlap in theoretical ideas, methodological approaches, and neuroimaging findings in these two research fields. There are also important points of

contrast: Studies of retrieval set have rarely investigated the dynamic process of set formation and switching, but have more thoroughly investigated how neural activity varies with the specific retrieval sets required.

Overall, there has been clear progress in the past decade or so of neuroimaging research on task switching. Nevertheless, there are similarly clear opportunities for future development in this research field. A central aim of this chapter was to introduce one such development: the extension of principles and methods of task switching research to related topics of research. Such extensions are likely to be of mutual benefit: Task switching theories will benefit from the additional constraints imposed by having to explain, for example, why frontal and parietal regions associated with task switching are also active as subjects attempt to retrieve specific types of information from long-term memory. Theories of long-term memory will similarly benefit from applying current models of task-set control to the concept of retrieval set.

A second important opportunity for future research is the use of formal computational theories to generate fine-grained quantitative predictions for use in fMRI analysis (see also Karayanidis & Jamadar, this volume). In model-based fMRI, computational models are used to decompose observed behavior into multiple component processes (or *latent variables*), each of which can then be correlated with observed brain activity. Such approaches have been applied successfully in related fields of research in which, just as in task switching, the trial-to-trial dynamics of cognitive processes are of critical interest (Forstmann, Wagenmakers, Eichele, Brown, & Serences, 2011). This work has occasionally extended into the task switching domain, for example in modeling the impact of switching on evidence accumulation in perceptual categorization tasks (Madden et al., 2009; Mansfield, Karayanidis, Jamadar, Heathcote, & Forstmann, 2011). However, although several formal models of task switching have now been proposed (e.g., Altmann & Gray, 2008; Brown, Reynolds, & Braver, 2007; Gilbert & Shallice, 2002; Yeung & Monsell, 2003), these models have yet to receive systematic attention in neuroimaging research. Model-based fMRI may prove invaluable in individuating components of the frontal-parietal network discussed so frequently in this chapter. As we have seen, broad contrasts between switch and repeat trials, and between preparation and task performance, have typically revealed functional homogeneity rather than clear specialization. Quantitative, computationally specified hypotheses may be necessary in the next phase of neuroimaging research on task switching, to allow the field to move from broad generalizations about the role of frontoparietal regions in task switching to detailed accounts of the functioning of each component of that network.

A final key question for the future is how the different emphases of the two research fields of task switching (with its focus on mechanisms of task set control) and retrieval set (with its focus on task-specific processes) can be integrated. Control processes appear to be essential for the stable development of a memory task set, while task-specific processes provide valuable information about the nature of cognitive control. What has not yet been clearly established is how control processes and task-specific processes interact. One way in which neuroimaging can help clarify the relationship between control- and task-specific processes is by characterizing the interaction between activity in executive control regions and activity in task-relevant regions. An interesting method in this context is the analysis of functional connectivity between brain areas. Such connectivity has been studied in the context of connections between control related frontal areas (Sakai & Passingham, 2006; Stelzel et al., 2011). Investigating functional connectivity between control- and task-related areas across posterior as well as frontal regions could provide an important step in tying together the results of research on the control of task sets in traditional task switching studies and task-specific processes in retrieval orientation studies.

REFERENCES

Note: *Asterisked citations are those included in the task switching meta-analysis; hash-tagged citations were those included in the retrieval set meta-analysis. Specified in curly brackets after each reference are the relevant fMRI contrast used in the meta-analysis, the number of subjects (N), and the number of activation foci.*

Allport, D. A., Styles, E. A., & Hsieh, S. L. (1994). Shifting intentional set—Exploring the dynamic control of tasks. In C. Umilta & M. Moscovitch (Eds.), *Attention and performance. XV: Conscious and nonconscious information processing* (Vol. 15, pp. 421–452). Cambridge, MA: MIT Press.

Allport, D. A., & Wylie, G. (2000). "Task-switching," stimulus-response bindings, and negative priming. In S. Monsell & J. S. Driver (Eds.), *Control of cognitive processes: Attention and performance XVIII*. Cambridge, MA: MIT Press.

Altmann, E. M., & Gray, W. D. (2008). An integrated model of cognitive control in task switching. *Psychological Review, 115*(3), 602–639.

Amunts, K., & von Cramon, D. Y. (2006). The anatomical segregation of the frontal cortex: What does it mean for function? *Cortex, 42*(4), 525–528.

Aron, A. R., Robbins, T. W., & Poldrack, R. A. (2004). Inhibition and the right inferior frontal cortex. *Trends in Cognitive Sciences, 8*(4), 170–177.

Badre, D., & D'Esposito, M. (2007). Functional magnetic resonance imaging evidence for a hierarchical organization of the prefrontal cortex. *Journal of Cognitive Neuroscience, 19*(12), 2082–2099.

Badre, D., Poldrack, R. A., Pare-Blagoev, E. J., Insler, R. Z., & Wagner, A. D. (2005). Dissociable controlled retrieval and generalized selection mechanisms in ventrolateral prefrontal cortex. *Neuron, 47*(6), 907–918.

Badre, D., & Wagner, A. D. (2006). Computational and neurobiological mechanisms underlying cognitive flexibility. *Proceedings of the National Academy of Sciences of the United States of America, 103*(18), 7186–7191.

Badre, D., & Wagner, A. D. (2007). Left ventrolateral prefrontal cortex and the cognitive control of memory. *Neuropsychologia, 45*(13), 2883–2901.

Barber, A. D., & Carter, C. S. (2005). Cognitive control involved in overcoming prepotent response tendencies and switching between tasks. *Cerebral Cortex, 15*(7), 899–912.

Bookheimer, S. (2002). Functional MRI of language: New approaches to understanding the cortical organization of semantic processing. *Annual Review of Neuroscience, 25*, 151–188.

Brass, M., Derrfuss, J., Forstmann, B., & von Cramon, D. Y. (2005). The role of the inferior frontal junction area in cognitive control. *Trends in Cognitive Sciences, 9*(7), 314–316.

Brass, M., & von Cramon, D. Y. (2002). The role of the frontal cortex in task preparation. *Cerebral Cortex, 12*, 908–914.

* Brass, M., & von Cramon, D. Y. (2004). Decomposing components of task preparation with functional magnetic resonance imaging. *Journal of Cognitive Neuroscience, 16*(4), 1–12. {meaning switch versus cue switch, N = 14, Foci = 3; cue switch versus cue repeat, N = 14, Foci = 4; switch versus repeat (single cue), N = 14, Foci = 3}

Braver, T. S. (2012). The variable nature of cognitive control: A dual mechanisms framework. *Trends in Cognitive Sciences, 16*(2), 106–113.

* Braver, T. S., Reynolds, J. R., & Donaldson, D. I. (2003). Neural mechanisms of transient and sustained cognitive control during task switching. *Neuron, 39*, 713–726. {switch versus repeat, N = 13, Foci = 5}

Brown, J. W., Reynolds, J. R., & Braver, T. S. (2007). A computational model of fractionated conflict-control mechanisms in task-switching. *Cognitive Psychology, 55*(1), 37–85.

Buckner, R. L. (2003). Functional-anatomic correlates of control processes in memory. *Journal of Neuroscience, 23*(10), 3999–4004.

Bunge, S. A. (2004). How we use rules to select actions: A review of evidence from cognitive neuroscience. *Cognitive Affective & Behavioral Neuroscience, 4*(4), 564–579.

Bunge, S. A., Kahn, I., Wallis, J. D., Miller, E. K., & Wagner, A. D. (2003). Neural circuits subserving the retrieval and maintenance of abstract rules. *Journal of Neurophysiology, 90*(5), 3419–3428.

Cabeza, R., Ciaramelli, E., Olson, I. R., & Moscovitch, M. (2008). The parietal cortex and episodic memory: An attentional account. *Nature Reviews: Neuroscience, 9*(8), 613–625.

Chiu, Y. C., & Yantis, S. (2009). A domain-independent source of cognitive control for task sets: Shifting spatial attention and switching categorization rules. *Journal of Neuroscience, 29*(12), 3930–3938.

Chun, M. M., & Johnson, M. K. (2011). Memory: Enduring traces of perceptual and reflective attention. *Neuron, 72*(4), 520–535.

Coltheart, M. (2004). Brain imaging, connectionism, and cognitive neuropsychology. *Cognitive Neuropsychology, 21*(1), 21–25.

Coltheart, M. (2006). What has functional neuroimaging told us about the mind (so far)? *Cortex, 42*(3), 323–331.

* Cools, R., Clark, L., & Robbins, T. W. (2004). Differential responses in human striatum and prefrontal cortex to changes in object and rule relevance. *Journal of Neuroscience, 24*(5), 1129–1135. {switch versus repeat (object rule), N = 16, Foci = 11}

Corbetta, M., Kincade, J. M., Ollinger, J. M., McAvoy, M. P., & Shulman, G. L. (2000). Voluntary orienting is dissociated from target detection in human posterior parietal cortex. *Nature Neuroscience, 3*(3), 292–297.

Corbetta, M., Kincade, J. M., & Shulman, G. L. (2002). Neural systems for visual orienting and their relationships to spatial working memory. *Journal of Cognitive Neuroscience, 14*, 508–523.

Corbetta, M., & Shulman, G. L. (2002). Control of goal-directed and stimulus-driven attention in the brain. *Nature Reviews Neuroscience, 3*, 201–215.

* Crone, E. A., Wendelken, C., Donohue, S. E., & Bunge, S. A. (2006). Neural evidence for dissociable components of task-switching. *Cerebral Cortex, 16*(4), 475–486. {switch versus repeat (univalent trials), N = 21, Foci = 25}

* De Baene, W., & Brass, M. (2011). Cue-switch effects do not rely on the same neural systems as task-switch effects. *Cognitive, Affective, & Behavioral Neuroscience, 11*(4), 600–607. {task Switch versus cue repeat, N = 19, Foci = 5}

* De Baene, W., Kuhn, S., & Brass, M. (2012). Challenging a decade of brain research on task switching: Brain activation in the task-switching paradigm reflects adaptation rather than reconfiguration of task sets. *Human Brain Mapping, 33*(3), 639–651. {adaptation repeat vs switch, N = 21, Foci = 5}

* Derrfuss, J., Brass, M., & von Cramon, D. Y. (2004). Cognitive control in the posterior frontolateral cortex: Evidence from common activations in task coordination, interference control, and working memory. *Neuroimage, 23*(2), 604–612. {switch versus repeat, N = 20, Foci = 8}

Desimone, R., & Duncan, J. (1995). Neural mechanisms of selective visual attention. *Annual Review of Neuroscience, 18*, 193–222.

* DiGirolamo, G. J., Kramer, A. F., Barad, V., Cepeda, N. J., Weissman, D. H., Milham, M. P.,…McAuley, E. (2001). General and task-specific frontal lobe recruitment in older adults during executive processes: A fMRI investigation of task-switching. *NeuroReport, 12*(9), 2065–2071. {switch versus repeat (young subjects), N = 8, Foci = 68}

Dobbins, I. G., Foley, H., Schacter, D. L., & Wagner, A. D. (2002). Executive control during episodic retrieval: multiple prefrontal processes subserve source memory. *Neuron, 35*(5), 989–996.

Dobbins, I. G., & Han, S. (2006). Cue- versus probe-dependent prefrontal cortex activity during contextual remembering. *Journal of Cognitive Neuroscience, 18*(9), 1439–1452. {source/context versus old/new (probe), n = 15, foci = 10, source/context versus old/new (cues), N = 15, Foci = 22}

Dobbins, I. G., Rice, H. J., Wagner, A. D., & Schacter, D. L. (2003). Memory orientation and success: Separable neurocognitive components underlying episodic recognition. *Neuropsychologia, 41*(3), 318–333. {source versus recency task, N = 11, Foci = 25, recency versus source task, N = 11, Foci = 18}

Dobbins, I. G., & Wagner, A. D. (2005). Domain-general and domain-sensitive prefrontal mechanisms for recollecting events and detecting novelty. *Cerebral Cortex, 15*(11), 1768–1778. {(conceptual source versus novelty detection) + (perceptual source versus novelty detection), N = 14, Foci = 31, perceptual source retrieval versus conceptual source retrieval, N = 14, Foci = 23}

* Dove, A., Pollman, S., Schubert, T., Wiggins, C. J., & von Cramon, D. Y. (2000). Prefrontal cortex activation in task switching: An event-related fMRI study. *Cognitive Brain Research, 9*, 103–109. {switch versus repeat, N = 16, Foci = 13}

Dreher, J. C., & Berman, K. F. (2002). Fractionating the neural substrate of cognitive control processes. *Proceedings of the National Academy of Sciences of the United States of America, 99*(22), 14595–14600.

Dreher, J. C., Koechlin, E., Ali, S. O., & Grafman, J. (2002). The roles of timing and task order during task switching. *NeuroImage, 17*, 95–109.

Duarte, A., Ranganath, C., & Knight, R. T. (2005). Effects of unilateral prefrontal lesions on familiarity, recollection, and source memory. *Journal of Neuroscience, 25*(36), 8333–8337.

Duncan, J. (2010). The multiple-demand (MD) system of the primate brain: Mental programs for intelligent behaviour. *Trends in Cognitive Sciences, 14*(4), 172–179.

Eickhoff, S. B., Laird, A. R., Grefkes, C., Wang, L. E., Zilles, K., & Fox, P. T. (2009). Coordinate-based activation likelihood estimation meta-analysis of neuroimaging data: A random-effects approach based on empirical estimates of spatial uncertainty. *Human Brain Mapping, 30*(9), 2907–2926.

Esterman, M., Chiu, Y. C., Tamber-Rosenau, B. J., & Yantis, S. (2009). Decoding cognitive control in human parietal cortex. *Proceedings of the National Academy of Sciences of the United States of America, 106*(42), 17974–17979.

Fiebach, C. J., Friederici, A. D., Smith, E. E., & Swinney, D. (2007). Lateral inferotemporal cortex maintains conceptual-semantic representations in verbal working memory. *Journal of Cognitive Neuroscience, 19*(12), 2035–2049.

Forstmann, B. U., Brass, M., Koch, I., & von Cramon, D. Y. (2005). Internally generated and directly cued task sets: An investigation with fMRI. *Neuropsychologia, 43*(6), 943–952.

Forstmann, B. U., Brass, M., Koch, I., & von Cramon, D. Y. (2006). Voluntary selection of task sets revealed by functional magnetic resonance imaging. *Journal of Cognitive Neuroscience, 18*(3), 388–398.

Forstmann, B. U., Wagenmakers, E. J., Eichele, T., Brown, S., & Serences, J. T. (2011). Reciprocal relations between cognitive neuroscience and formal cognitive models: Opposites attract? *Trends in Cognitive Sciences, 15*(6), 272–279.

Gilbert, S. J., & Shallice, T. (2002). Task switching: A PDP model. *Cognitive Psychology, 44*, 297–337.

Grill-Spector, K., Henson, R., & Martin, A. (2006). Repetition and the brain: Neural models of stimulus-specific effects. *Trends in Cognitive Sciences, 10*(1), 14–23.

Gruber, O., Karch, S., Schlueter, E. K., Falkai, P., & Goschke, T. (2006). Neural mechanisms of advance preparation in task switching. *NeuroImage, 31*(2), 887–895.

* Gurd, J. M., Amunts, K., Weiss, P. H., Zafiris, O., Zilles, K., Marshall, J. C., et al. (2002). Posterior parietal cortex is implicated in continuous switching between verbal fluency tasks: An fMRI study with clinical implications. *Brain, 125*(5), 1024–1038. {switch versus repeat, N = 11, Foci = 2}

Hayes, S. M., Buchler, N., Stokes, J., Kragel, J., & Cabeza, R. (2011). Neural correlates of confidence during item recognition and source memory retrieval: Evidence for both dual-process and strength memory theories. *Journal of Cognitive Neuroscience, 23*(12), 3959–3971. {source versus item memory, N = 16, Foci = 15}

Henson, R. (2005). What can functional neuroimaging tell the experimental psychologist? *Quarterly Journal of Experimental Psychology. A, Human Experimental Psychology, 58*(2), 193–233.

Holroyd, C. B., & Yeung, N. (2012). Motivation of extended behaviors by anterior cingulate cortex. *Trends in Cognitive Sciences, 16*(2), 122–128.

Hornberger, M., Rugg, M. D., & Henson, R. N. A. (2006). fMRI correlates of retrieval orientation. *Neuropsychologia, 44*(8), 1425–1436. {retieval orientation auditory versus retieval orientation picture, N = 18, Foci = 7, retieval orientation picture versus retieval orientation auditory, N = 18, Foci = 4}

Hyafil, A., Summerfield, C., & Koechlin, E. (2009). Two mechanisms for task switching in the prefrontal cortex. *Journal of Neuroscience, 29*(16), 5135–5142.

Iidaka, T., Matsumoto, A., Nogawa, J., Yamamoto, Y., & Sadato, N. (2006). Frontoparietal network involved in successful retrieval from episodic memory. Spatial and temporal analyses using fMRI and ERP. *Cerebral Cortex, 16*(9), 1349–1360.

* Jamadar, S., Hughes, M., Fulham, W. R., Michie, P. T., & Karayanidis, F. (2010). The spatial and temporal dynamics of anticipatory preparation and response inhibition in task-switching. *NeuroImage, 51*(1), 432–449. {switch versus repeat (informatively cued), N = 18, Foci = 18}

Jamadar, S., Michie, P., & Karayanidis, F. (2010). Compensatory mechanisms underlie intact task-switching performance in schizophrenia. *Neuropsychologia, 48*(5), 1305–1323.

Karayanidis, F., Jamadar, S., Ruge, H., Phillips, N., Heathcote, A., & Forstmann, B. U. (2010). Advance preparation in task-switching: converging evidence from behavioral, brain activation, and model-based approaches. *Frontiers in Psychology, 1*, 25.

Kiesel, A., Wendt, M., Jost, K., Steinhauser, M., Falkenstein, M., Philipp, A. M., et al. (2010). Control and interference in task switching: A review. *Psychological Bulletin, 136*(5), 849–874.

Kim, C., Cilles, S. E., Johnson, N. F., & Gold, B. T. (2012). Domain general and domain preferential brain regions associated with different types of task switching: A meta-analysis. *Human Brain Mapping, 33*(1), 130–142.

* Kim, C., Johnson, N. F., Cilles, S. E., & Gold, B. T. (2011). Common and distinct mechanisms of cognitive flexibility in prefrontal cortex. *Journal of Neuroscience, 31*(13), 4771–4779. {switch versus repeat (stimulus switching), n = 16, Foci = 11, switch versus repeat (response switching), N = 16, Foci = 12, switch versus repeat (cognitive set switching), N = 16, Foci = 15}

* Kimberg, D. Y., Aguirre, G. K., & D'Esposito, M. (2000). Modulation of task-related neural activity in task switching: An fMRI study. *Cognitive Brain Research, 10*, 189–196. {switch versus repeat, N = 9, Foci = 9}

Koch, I., Gade, M., Schuch, S., & Philipp, A. M. (2010). The role of inhibition in task switching: A review. *Psychonomic Bulletin & Review, 17*(1), 1–14.

Kochunov, P., Lancaster, J., Thompson, P., Toga, A. W., Brewer, P., Hardies, J., et al. (2002). An optimized individual target brain in the Talairach coordinate system. *NeuroImage, 17*(2), 922–927.

Koechlin, E., Basso, G., Pietrini, P., Panzer, S., & Grafman, J. (1999). The role of the anterior prefrontal cortex in human cognition. *Nature, 399*, 148–151.

Koechlin, E., Ody, C., & Kouneiher, F. (2003). The architecture of cognitive control in the human prefrontal cortex. *Science, 302*, 1181–1185.

Koechlin, E., & Summerfield, C. (2007). An information theoretical approach to prefrontal executive function. *Trends in Cognitive Sciences, 11*(6), 229–235.

Kompus, K., Olsson, C. J., Larsson, A., & Nyberg, L. (2009). Dynamic switching between semantic and episodic memory systems. *Neuropsychologia, 47*(11), 2252–2260. {epsiodic versus semantiv retrieval, N = 16, Foci = 6}

Lashley, K. S. (1951). The problem of serial order in behaviour. In L. A. Jeffres (Ed.), *Cerebral Mechanisms in Behaviour* (pp. 112–136).

* Li, Z. H., Sun, X. W., Wang, Z. X., Zhang, X. C., Zhang, D. R., He, S., & Hu, X. P. (2004). Behavioral and functional MRI study of attention shift in human verbal working memory. *Neuroimage, 21*(1), 181–191. {switch versus repeat (attention shifting), N = 12, Foci = 10}

* Liston, C., Matalon, S., Hare, T. A., Davidson, M. C., & Casey, B. J. (2006). Anterior cingulate and posterior parietal cortices are sensitive to dissociable forms of conflict in a task-switching paradigm. *Neuron, 50*(4), 643–653. {switch versus repeat (both colour and motion), N = 19, Foci = 8, switch versus repeat (colour only), N = 19, Foci = 4}

Liu, T. S., Slotnick, S. D., Serences, J. T., & Yantis, S. (2003). Cortical mechanisms of feature-based attentional control. *Cerebral Cortex, 13*(12), 1334–1343.

Logan, G. D., & Bundesen, C. (2003). Clever homunculus: Is there an endogenous act of control in the explicit task-cuing procedure? *Journal of Experimental Psychology Human Perception and Performance, 29*(3), 575–599.

* Luks, T. L., Simpson, G. V., Feiwell, R. J., & Miller, W. J. (2002). Evidence for anterior cingulate cortex involvement in monitoring preparatory attentional set. *NeuroImage, 17*(2), 792–802. {switch versus repeat (informative cue), N = 11, Foci = 2, switch versus repeat (neutrally cued), N = 11, Foci = 2}

MacDonald, A. W., Cohen, J. D., Stenger, V. A., & Carter, C. S. (2000). Dissociating the role of dorsolateral prefrontal and anterior cingulate cortex in cognitive control. *Science, 288*, 1835–1838.

Madden, D. J., Spaniol, J., Costello, M. C., Bucur, B., White, L. E., Cabeza, R.,...Huettel, S. A. (2009). Cerebral white matter integrity mediates adult age differences in cognitive performance. *Journal of Cognitive Neuroscience, 21*(2), 289–302.

Mansfield, E. L., Karayanidis, F., Jamadar, F., Heathcote, A., & Forstmann, B. U. (2011). Adjustments of response threshold during task switching: A model-based functional magnetic resonance imaging study. *Journal of Neuroscience, 31*(41), 14688–14692.

Mayr, U., & Keele, S. W. (2000). Changing internal constraints on action: The role of backward inhibition. *Journal of Experimental Psychology: General, 129*(1), 4–26.

Meiran, N. (2000). Modeling cognitive control in task-switching. *Psychological Research, 63*, 234–249.

Miller, E. K., & Cohen, J. D. (2001). An integrative theory of prefrontal cortex function. *Annual Review of Neuroscience, 24*, 167–202.

Milner, A. D., & Goodale, M. A. (2008). Two visual systems re-viewed. *Neuropsychologia, 46*(3), 774–785.

Miyake, A., Emerson, M. J., Padilla, F., & Ahn, J. C. (2004). Inner speech as a retrieval aid for task goals: The effects of cue type and articulatory suppression in the random task cuing paradigm. *Acta Psychologica, 115*(2–3), 123–142.

Monchi, O., Petrides, M., Petre, V., Worsley, K., & Dagher, A. (2001). Wisconsin card sorting revisited: Distinct neural circuits participating in different stages of the task identified by event-related functional magnetic resonance imaging. *Journal of Neuroscience, 21*, 7733–7741.

Monsell, S. (2003). Task switching. *Trends in Cognitive Sciences, 7*(3), 134–140.

Monsell, S., & Mizon, G. A. (2006). Can the task-cuing paradigm measure an endogenous task-set reconfiguration process? *Journal of Experimental Psychology Human Perception and Performance, 32*(3), 493–516.

Page, M. P. A. (2006). What can't functional neuroimaging tell the cognitive psychologist? *Cortex, 42*(3), 428–443.

* Parris, B. A., Thai, N. J., Benattayallah, A., Summers, I. R., & Hodgson, T. L. (2007). The role of the lateral prefrontal cortex and anterior cingulate in stimulus-response association reversals. *Journal of Cognitive Neuroscience, 19*(1), 13–24. {flip versus hold, N = 22, Foci = 20}

Passingham, R. E. (1993). *The frontal lobes and voluntary action*. Oxford, UK: Oxford University Press.

Petersen, S. E., & Posner, M. I. (2012). The attention system of the human brain: 20 years after. *Annual Review of Neuroscience, 35*, 73–89.

* Pessoa, L., Rossi, A., Japee, S., Desimone, R., & Ungerleider, L. G. (2009). Attentional control during the transient updating of cue information. *Brain Research, 1247*, 149–158. {switch versus repeat, N = 20, Foci = 8, switch versus repeat; pop out task, N = 20, Foci = 2, switch versus repeat; visual detection task, N = 20, Foci = 10}

Philipp, A. M., Weidner, R., Koch, I., & Fink, G. R. (2012). Differential roles of inferior frontal and inferior parietal cortex in task switching: Evidence from stimulus-categorization switching and response-modality switching. *Human Brain Mapping*.

Phillips, J. S., Velanova, K., Wolk, D. A., & Wheeler, M. E. (2009). Left posterior parietal cortex participates in both task preparation and episodic retrieval. *NeuroImage, 46*(4), 1209–1221. {switch versus repeat, N = 12, Foci = 2, episodic versus semantic, N = 12, Foci = 12, switch* old/new interaction, N = 12, Foci = 2, switch* episodic/semantic*old/new interaction, N = 12, Foci = 1}

Poldrack, R. A. (2006). Can cognitive processes be inferred from neuroimaging data? *Trends in Cognitive Sciences, 10*(2), 59–63.

* Pollmann, S., Dove, A., von Cramon, D. Y., & Wiggins, C. J. (2000). Event-related fMRI: Comparison of conditions with varying BOLD overlap. *Human Brain Mapping, 9*(1), 26–37. {switch versus repeat, N = 11, Foci = 7}

Pollmann, S., Weidner, R., Muller, H. J., Maertens, M., & von Cramon, D. Y. (2006). Selective and interactive neural correlates of visual dimension changes and response changes. *Neuroimage, 30*(1), 254–265. {Switch versus Repeat (dimension (colour, shape etc)-features/attentional shift), N = 21, Foci = 4, Switch versus Repeat (response shift, ie pressing left or right?), N = 21, Foci = 16}

Ranganath, C., Johnson, M. K., & D'Esposito, M. (2000). Event-related fMRI of prefrontal cortex during general versus specific tests of episodic memory. *Journal of Cognitive Neuroscience*, 133–133. {specific versus general memorty judgement, N = 8, Foci = 1}

* Ravizza, S. M., & Carter, C. S. (2008). Shifting set about task switching: Behavioral and neural evidence for distinct forms of cognitive flexibility. *Neuropsychologia, 46*(12), 2924–2935. {switch versus repeat (perceptual switching), N = 20, Foci = 3, switch versus repeat (perceptual switching) (marginal), N = 20, Foci = 4, switch versus repeat (rule switching), N = 20, Foci = 3}

Reynolds, J. R., O'Reilly, R. C., Cohen, J. D., & Braver, T. S. (2012). The function and organization of lateral prefrontal cortex: A test of competing hypotheses. *PLoS ONE, 7*(2), e30284.

Richter, F. R., & Yeung, N. (2012). Memory and cognitive control in task switching. *Psychological Science, 23*(10), 1256–1263.

Rizzolatti, G., & Luppino, G. (2001). The cortical motor system. *Neuron, 31*(6), 889–901.

Rogers, R. D., Andrews, T. C., Grasby, P. M., Brooks, D. J., & Robbins, T. W. (2000). Contrasting cortical and subcortical activations produced by attentional-set shifting and reversal learning in humans. *Journal of Cognitive Neuroscience, 12*(1), 142–162.

Rogers, R. D., & Monsell, S. (1995). Costs of a predictable switch between simple cognitive tasks. *Journal of Experimental Psychology: General, 124*, 207–231.

Rubinstein, J., Meyer, D. E., & Evans, J. E. (2001). Executive control of cognitive processes in task switching. *Journal of Experimental Psychology: Human Perception and Performance, 27*(4), 763–797.

* Ruge, H., Brass, M., Koch, I., Rubin, O., Meiran, N., & von Cramon, D. Y. (2005). Advance preparation and stimulus-induced interference in cued task switching: further insights from BOLD fMRI. *Neuropsychologia, 43*(3), 340–355. {switch versus repeat (in response to cue and target), N = 18, Foci = 2}

Ruge, H., Braver, T., & Meiran, N. (2009). Attention, intention, and strategy in preparatory control. *Neuropsychologia, 47*(7), 1670–1685.

Ruge, H., Jamadar, S., Zimmermann, U., & Karayanidis, F. (2013). The many faces of preparatory control in task switching: Reviewing a decade of fMRI research. *Human Brain Mapping, 34*(1), 12–35.

* Ruge, H., Muller, S. C., & Braver, T. S. (2010). Brief Reports: Anticipating the consequences of action: An fMRI study of intention-based task preparation. *Psychophysiology, 47*(6), 1019–1027. {switch versus repeat, N = 18, Foci = 15}

Rugg, M. D., & Wilding, E. L. (2000). Retrieval processing and episodic memory. *Trends in Cognitive Sciences, 4*(3), 108–115.

* Rushworth, M. F. S., Hadland, K. A., Paus, T., & Sipila, P. K. (2002). The role of the human medial frontal cortex in task switching: A combined fMRI and TMS study. *Journal of Neurophysiology, 87*(5), 2577–2592. {switch versus repeat (response switch), N = 10, Foci = 4, switch versus repeat (visual switch), N = 10, Foci = 2}

* Rushworth, M. F. S., Paus, T., & Sipila, P. K. (2001). Attention systems and the organization of the human parietal cortex. *Journal of Neuroscience, 21*(14), 5262–5271. {response switch right versus left, N = 20, Foci = 16, visual switch color versus shape, N = 20, Foci = 10}

Sakai, K. (2008). Task set and prefrontal cortex. *Annual Review of Neuroscience, 31*, 219–245.

Sakai, K., & Passingham, R. E. (2003). Prefrontal interactions reflect future task operations. *Nature Neuroscience, 6*(1), 75–81.

Sakai, K., & Passingham, R. E. (2006). Prefrontal set activity predicts rule-specific neural processing during subsequent cognitive performance. *Journal of Neuroscience, 26*(4), 1211–1218.

Schubotz, R. I., & Fiebach, C. J. (2006). Integrative models of Broca's area and the ventral premotor cortex. *Cortex, 42*(4), 461–463.

* Serences, J. T., Schwartzbach, J., Courtney, S. M., Golay, X., & Yantis, S. (2004). Control of object-based attention in human cortex. *Cerebral Cortex, 14*, 1346–1357. {Exp1: shifting versus holding attention, N = 15, Foci = 5, Exp2: shifting versus holding attention, N = 8, Foci = 2}

Shi, Y. Q., Zhou, X. L., Muller, H. J., & Schubert, T. (2010). The neural implementation of task rule activation in the task cuing paradigm: An event-related fMRI study. *NeuroImage, 51*(3), 1253–1264.

Silver, M. A., & Kastner, S. (2009). Topographic maps in human frontal and parietal cortex. *Trends in Cognitive Sciences, 13*(11), 488–495.

Simons, J. S., Davis, S. W., Gilbert, S. J., Frith, C. D., & Burgess, P. W. (2006). Discriminating imagined from perceived information engages brain areas implicated in schizophrenia. *NeuroImage, 32*(2), 696–703. {perceived/imagined versus baseline, N = 16, Foci = 9, left/right versus baseline, N = 16, Foci = 10}

Simons, J. S., Gilbert, S. J., Owen, A. M., Fletcher, P. C., & Burgess, P. W. (2005). Distinct roles for lateral and medial anterior prefrontal cortex in contextual recollection. *Journal of Neurophysiology, 94*(1), 813–820. {context memory for task or list versus baseline condition, N = 16, Foci = 7}

Simons, J. S., Henson, R. N. A., Gilbert, S. J., & Fletcher, P. C. (2008). Separable forms of reality monitoring supported by anterior prefrontal cortex. *Journal of Cognitive Neuroscience, 20*(3), 447–457. {self/ experimenter status versus baseline, N = 16, Foci =17}

Simons, J. S., Owen, A. M., Fletcher, P. C., & Burgess, P. W. (2005). Anterior prefrontal cortex and the recollection of contextual information. *Neuropsychologia, 43*(12), 1774–1783. {context type (memory for task or position) versus baseline, N = 16, Foci = 13}

* Slagter, H. A., Weissman, D. H., Giesbrecht, B., Kenemans, J. L., Mangun, G. R., Kok, A., et al. (2006). Brain regions activated by endogenous preparatory set shifting as revealed by fMR1. *Cognitive Affective & Behavioral Neuroscience, 6*(3), 175–189. {switch versus repeat (preparation mixed dimension task block), N = 14, Foci = 10}

* Smith, A. B., Taylor, E., Brammer, M., & Rubia, K. (2004). Neural correlates of switching set as measured in fast, event-related functional magnetic resonance imaging. *Human Brain Mapping, 21*(4), 247–256. {switch versus repeat, N = 20, Foci = 10, switch versus repeat (preparation single dimension task block), N = 14, Foci = 11}

* Sohn, M.-H., Ursu, S., Anderson, J. R., Stenger, V. A., & Carter, C. S. (2000). The role of prefrontal cortex and posterior parietal cortex in task switching. *Proceedings of the National Academy of Sciences of the USA, 97*(24), 13448–13453. {switch versus repeat (transition effects), N = 12, Foci = 6}

* Stelzel, C., Basten, U., & Fiebach, C. J. (2011). Functional connectivity separates switching operations in the posterior lateral frontal cortex. *Journal of Cognitive Neuroscience, 23*(11), 3529–3539. {switch versus repeat (response hand switching), N = 48, Foci = 13, switch versus repeat (abstract task rules switching), N = 48, Foci = 2}

* Swainson, R., Cunningham, R., Jackson, G. M., Rorden, C., Peters, A. M., Morris, P. G., & Jackson, S. R. (2003). Cognitive control mechanisms revealed by ERP and fMRI: evidence from repeated task-switching. *Journal of Cognitive Neuroscience, 15*(6), 785–799. {switch versus repeat (go trials), N = 12, Foci = 2}

* Sylvester, C. Y. C., Wager, T. D., Lacey, S. C., Hernandez, L., Nichols, T. E., Smith, E. E., et al. (2003). Switching attention and resolving interference: fMRI measures of executive functions. *Neuropsychologia, 41*(3), 357–370. {event-related switches, N = 14, Foci = 14, blocked counter-switches, N = 14, Foci = 9}

Takahashi, E., Ohki, K., & Kim, D. S. (2008). Dissociated pathways for successful memory retrieval from the human parietal cortex: Anatomical and functional connectivity analyses. *Cerebral Cortex, 18*(8), 1771–1778.

Tulving, E. (1983). *Elements of episodic memory.* Oxford, UK: Clarendon Press.

Vandierendonck, A., Liefooghe, B., & Verbruggen, F. (2010). Task switching: interplay of reconfiguration and interference control. *Psychological Bulletin, 136*(4), 601–626.

Vinogradov, S., Luks, T. L., Schulman, B. J., & Simpson, G. V. (2008). Deficit in a neural correlate of reality monitoring in schizophrenia patients. *Cerebral Cortex, 18*(11), 2532–2539. {source memory task versus item recognition task, N = 8, Foci = 5}

Vinogradov, S., Luks, T. L., Simpson, G. V., Schulman, B. J., Glenn, S., & Wong, A. E. (2006). Brain activation patterns during memory of cognitive agency. *NeuroImage, 31*(2), 896–905. {correct external versus word reasing, N = 8, Foci = 3}

Wager, T. D., Jonides, J., & Reading, S. (2004). Neuroimaging studies of shifting attention: A meta-analysis. *NeuroImage*, *22*(4), 1679–1693.

Walton, M. E., Devlin, J. T., & Rushworth, M. F. (2004). Interactions between decision making and performance monitoring within prefrontal cortex. *Nature Neuroscience*, *7*(11), 1259–1265.

Weissman, D. H., Gopalakrishnan, A., Hazlett, C. J., & Woldorff, M. G. (2005). Dorsal anterior cingulate cortex resolves conflict from distracting stimuli by boosting attention toward relevant events. *Cerebral Cortex*, *15*(2), 229–237.

Whitmer, A. J., & Banich, M. T. (2012). Brain activity related to the ability to inhibit previous task sets: An fMRI study. *Cognitive, Affective and Behavioral Neuroscience*, *12*, 661–670.

Woodruff, C. C., Uncapher, M. R., & Rugg, M. D. (2006). Neural correlates of differential retrieval orientation: Sustained and item-related components. *Neuropsychologia*, *44*(14), 3000–3010. {retieval orientation picture versus retieval orientation word, N = 16, Foci = 4, retieval orientation word versus retieval orientation picture, N = 16, Foci = 4, retieval orientation word versus retieval orientation picture (delayed HRF), N = 16, Foci = 2, sustained activity relative to baseline, picture versus word retrieval orientation, N = 16, Foci = 12}

Wylie, G. R., Javitt, D. C., & Foxe, J. J. (2004). Don't think of a white bear: An fMRI investigation of the effects of sequential instructional sets on cortical activity in a task-switching paradigm. *Human Brain Mapping*, *21*(4), 279–297.

* Wylie, G. R., Javitt, D. C., & Foxe, J. J. (2006). Jumping the gun: Is effective preparation contingent upon anticipatory activation in task-relevant neural circuitry? *Cerebral Cortex*, *16*, 394–404. {switch versus repeat (color cues), N = 14, Foci = 11, switch versus repeat (color targets), N = 14, Foci = 19, Switch versus Repeat (speed targets), N = 14, Foci = 4}

Yantis, S., Schwartzbach, J., Serences, J. T., Carlson, R. L., Steinmetz, M. A., Pekar, J. J., et al. (2002). Transient neural activity in human parietal cortex during spatial attention shifts. *Nature Neuroscience*, *5*(10), 995–1002.

Yeung, N., & Monsell, S. (2003). The effects of recent practice on task switching. *Journal of Experimental Psychology: Human Perception and Performance*, *29*, 919–936.

* Yeung, N., Nystrom, L. E., Aronson, J. A., & Cohen, J. D. (2006). Between-task competition and cognitive control in task switching. *Journal of Neuroscience*, *26*(5), 1429–1438. {switch versus repeat, N = 15, Foci = 12}

Yoshida, W., Funakoshi, H., & Ishii, S. (2010). Hierarchical rule switching in prefrontal cortex. *NeuroImage*, *50*(1), 314–322.

Young, J. J., & Shapiro, M. L. (2011). The orbitofrontal cortex and response selection. *Annals of the New York Academy of Sciences*, *1239*, 25–32.

11

Task Switching and Executive Dysfunction

ABHIJIT DAS AND GLENN R. WYLIE ■

INTRODUCTION

To function effectively in a continuously changing environment, it is important to dynamically adjust one's behavior in response to shifting environmental cues and contingencies. This flexibility of human cognition depends on specialized cognitive mechanisms, broadly defined as executive functions, which at once facilitate goal-directed behavior while suppressing inappropriate behavior. The instantiation of a new behavioral set (a "goal" or a "task") is considered to be one of the core functions of executive processes, and has been scientifically investigated using the task switching paradigm. In this paradigm, subjects are required to switch between two (or more) tasks on some trials and repeatedly perform each task on others; by comparing task switch trials to task-repeat trials, researchers have gained insight into the operation of (one aspect of) executive processes.

From a clinical viewpoint, the task switching paradigm is one of the tools routinely used by neuropsychologists for measuring executive functioning. One advantage of this paradigm is that (after practice) rule learning and concept formation are held constant, which is not the case with other tests such as the Wisconsin Card Sorting Test (WCST) and the EDS/IDS shifting in the CANTAB battery, sometimes used to study task switching. Consequently, this essay will not focus on the WCST and the CANTAB battery. Moreover, because executive functions are frequently impaired in clinical samples, the task switching paradigm provides an important tool for the study of executive dysfunction in these samples. The authors review the current scientific literature on task switching and executive dysfunction in stroke, Parkinson's disease (PD), Huntington's disease (HD), traumatic brain injury (TBI), and schizophrenia.

TASK SWITCHING: ONE COMPONENT OF EXECUTIVE FUNCTIONS

Task switching paradigms require participants to perform two or more intermingled tasks that are defined on the basis of distinct or partially overlapping stimulus–response (S–R) contingencies or task sets (Jersild, 1927; Wylie & Allport, 2000). For example, in the alternating runs paradigm (Rogers & Monsell, 1995), participants switch between two tasks in a completely predictable sequence (i.e., AABBAA). When the tasks alternate, the first trial of the newly relevant task (the switch trial) is typically associated with increased response time (RT) and decreased accuracy compared with trials on which the task is repeated (the repeat, or stay, trials). The RT difference on switch and stay trials is commonly referred to as the "switch cost." Switch costs are reduced as subjects are given more time to prepare for a forthcoming switch. For example, in the alternating runs paradigm, as the interval between a response to stimulus n and onset of stimulus $n + 1$ (the response–stimulus interval [RSI]) is increased from 150 to 600 ms, the switch cost decreases, though not to zero (Rogers & Monsell, 1995). However, as the RSI is increased beyond ~600 ms, there is little further reduction in the switch cost. This "residual" switch cost is attributed to a stimulus-elicited component of task set reconfiguration or alternatively, to S–R interference elicited after stimulus onset (Meiran, Levine, & Henik, 2000; Rogers & Monsell). Also there is a large literature on the difference in performance between single-task ("pure") blocks, and blocks in which the tasks are intermingled, or mixed (Los, 1996; Meiran & Gotler, 2001; Pashler, 2000; Wylie & Allport, 2000). Subjects' performance is worse in mixed blocks than in pure blocks: the "mixing cost" (which is different from the switching cost).

Switch costs have been thought of as an index of the operation of control processes (Meiran, 1996; Nicholson, Karayanidis, Poboka, Heathcote, & Michie, 2005; Rogers & Monsell, 1995; Rubinstein, Meyer, & Evans, 2001), though the precise interpretation of which neural operations are being performed remains debated. Some propose that the switch costs follow from a necessity to reconfigure brain networks: that is, to activate relevant processing pathways and deactivate irrelevant ones (Rogers & Monsell; Rubinstein et al., 2001). Some part of this reconfiguration is thought to occur during the preparation interval, when subjects are afforded a preparation interval (Wylie, Murray, Javitt, & Foxe, 2009). Others interpret switch costs as due in part to the coding of the cue stimulus itself (Logan & Bundesen, 2003), though more recent studies would suggest that encoding a new cue does not account for the full switch cost (Brass & von Cramon, 2004). In addition to these propositions, a substantial body of work (Mayr, Diedrichsen, Ivry, & Keele, 2006; Mayr & Keele, 2000; Wylie & Allport, 2000; Wylie, Javitt, & Foxe, 2003a, 2004b) suggests that a large portion of the switch cost arises from interference (competition) between task-related activity related to the current trial and persisting activity that is "left over" from the previous trial. That is, there appears to be persisting activity in neural circuits associated with the task that was relevant on the previous trial, and this activity interferes with the processing of the task on the current trial (Koch, Gade, Schuch, & Philipp, 2010; Mayr et al., 2006; Mayr & Keele, 2000; Waszak, Hommel, & Allport, 2003; Wylie & Allport, 2000; Wylie, et al., 2003a, 2004b; Wylie, Javitt, & Foxe, 2003b, 2004a, 2006). One way to help adjudicate between these models is to use neuroimaging methods or electrophysiological recordings, and while these approaches have proven worth, the debate persists. Another approach is to study the performance of specific clinical populations while they perform a task switching paradigm. By relating their performance to what is known about the underlying neuropathology, it may be possible to arrive at a better understanding of the mechanisms underlying executive control. This is because specific components of task switching are affected by specific diseases (see later). Moreover, these results have wide-reaching implications for theories of executive function and in the broader framework of psychological function and dysfunction.

We will review the literature from several clinical populations. For expository purposes, we will first introduce a working model of the brain systems involved in task switching as a framework. In the remainder of the review, we will relate the findings from specific populations to this framework, refining it as we proceed.

A FRAMEWORK FOR THE BRAIN SYSTEMS INVOLVED IN TASK SWITCHING

The neuroimaging literature on task switching has implicated numerous of brain areas. However, looking at the literature as a whole (and speaking of brain areas in broad terms), three brain "systems" appear to be involved: a left frontal system, a frontoparietal system, and a basal ganglia (BG) system.

Left frontal cortex appears to be involved in the representation of goals and in top-down modulation. In the context of task switching, this means maintaining representations of the two tasks and providing top-down, biasing modulation such that the currently relevant task is more active than the currently irrelevant task. Neuroimaging studies suggest that maintenance and establishment of the task set are functions attributable to the left dorsolateral prefrontal cortex (PFC), especially the middle frontal gyrus (MFG) (Garavan, Ross, Murphy, Roche, & Stein, 2002; MacDonald, Cohen, Stenger, & Carter, 2000).

A system involving frontal and parietal areas is also heavily implicated in task switching studies. Indeed, frontal and parietal regions are often active when attentional control is required; however, there appears to be a network involving right inferior frontal gyrus (IFG) and parietal cortex that may subserve the inhibitory processes that are critically important for successful task switching performance. The right IFG has been shown to be critical in many neuroimaging studies of response inhibition (Konishi et al., 1999; Konishi, Nakajima, Uchida, Sekihara, & Miyashita, 1998; Rubia, Smith, Brammer, & Taylor, 2003). Moreover, the right IFG has been shown to be active in a number of neuroimaging studies of switching task, strategy or dimensions, including reversal-learning (Nagahama et al., 2001), the WCST (Monchi, Petrides, Petre, Worsley, & Dagher, 2001; Nagahama, et al., 2001), and task-set switching (Brass et al., 2003). The importance of the right IFG in task switching was shown in a study in which switching (the WCST) and response inhibition were directly compared, and common activation was found in the right IFG (Konishi et al., 1999). This has also been shown in work using both EEG and functional MRI: Swainson et al. (2003) performed a study investigating a go-versus-wait factor and a switch-versus-non-switch factor and found that the right IFG locus was related neither to pure switching nor to pure response inhibition but was instead responsible for "switching into a suppression mode" (Swainson et al., 2003). Chiu and Yantis (2009) used rapid event-related MRI to scan subjects while they were cued to perform both shifts of spatial attention and switches between categorization rules. A conjunction analysis revealed a common transient signal evoked by switch cues in bilateral medial superior parietal lobule for both domains of control, which was interpreted as a single domain-independent control mechanism.

The BG appear to play an important role in task switching and are likely involved in mediating interference (stimulus and/or response interference). Because task switching experiments require the participant to maintain two task sets in an active state, one component of the control exerted at a task switch consists in one task set being facilitated while the other is inhibited. In some paradigms, the cue for this switch is explicit (e.g., the presentation of the word "switch"), while in others it is implicit (e.g., switching every other trial). As we shall see, the BG appear to be sensitive to whether a switch is cued externally (exogenously) or internally (endogenously), with specific deficits occurring in BG disorders like PD or HD. In addition, the BG play a unique role in inhibiting competing action plans and filtering irrelevant information (Filoteo et al., 2005). Both filtering (Meiran et al., 2000) and inhibition (Mayr et al., 2006) have been shown to play a major role in task switching in normal participants.

The three brain systems in this framework are widely distributed in the brain (indeed, they could hardly be more widely distributed), and this has two important sorts of consequences. First, focal damage to one part of this network (e.g., the BG) may produce deficits in task switching that are quite different from damage to another part of the network (e.g., left frontal cortex). Second, because the network is widely distributed, it is heavily reliant on the white matter that connects its disparate "nodes." Thus, white matter damage would be expected to impair task switching performance. Given this framework, let us now see how damage caused to these areas in specific disease conditions affects task switching performance.

STROKE

Given the distributed network of cortical and subcortical regions implicated in successful task switching and the vast connectivity of these cortical areas with other brain structures, one might expect that damage in a wide range of brain regions—caused by stroke—could result in difficulties in task switching. However, with very few exceptions (Aron, Monsell, Sahakian, & Robbins, 2004; McDowd, Filion, Pohl, Richards, & Stiers, 2003; Pohl et al., 2007; Yehene, Meiran, & Soroker, 2008), task switching performance has not been evaluated in stroke survivors.

McDowd et al. (2003) evaluated 55 adult chronic (>6 months) stroke survivors (31 with left hemispheric stroke and 24 with right hemispheric stroke) using both alternating runs and cued task switching paradigms. The performance of these stroke survivors were compared with 39 age-matched healthy controls. Only 39 of the stroke survivors, and 35 healthy controls, could complete the attention switching tasks with acceptable levels of accuracy (accuracy criterion of 75% correct). There was a group difference in accuracy in cued task switching but not in the alternating runs version, and reaction time (RT) was significantly slower for the stroke group in both conditions. The authors noted that task switching was a very difficult task for stroke survivors, and the stroke survivors, more than healthy controls, were unable to complete all of the tasks, suggesting that their data may underestimate actual stroke-related deficits (McDowd et al., 2003). Moreover, because the details of the locations of these stroke lesions were not mentioned, it is difficult to make specific conclusions about the relationship between lesion location and task switching performance.

Aron et al. (2004) evaluated 17 patients with a single focal lesion confined to the left PFC (LF) and 19 to the right PFC (RF) using a task switching paradigm. Both RF and LF patients showed significantly larger switch costs than controls. For RF patients, a part of the switch cost was attributable to impaired inhibition of inappropriate responses or task sets triggered by stimuli. This was shown by a reliable correlation between residual switch cost (subtracting the switch cost at long RSI from the switch cost at short RSI) and the extent of lesion to the IFG, specifically the POp. As residual switch cost is thought to represent persisting task-set inhibition (e.g., Allport et al., 1994; Allport & Wylie, 1999), this not only accords well with neuroimaging studies that show activation in right IFG during task switching but also strongly implicates this region in inhibitory processing during task switching. For LF patients, a part of the switch deficit appeared to be attributable to impaired top-down control of task set. This was shown by a reliable correlation between the degree of top-down control (the difference in RT between nonswitch trials of congruent and neutral stimuli) and the extent of lesion to the left MFG (Aron et al., 2004). This result also supports and extends neuroimaging findings: left MFG is not only involved in task switching, but this involvement appears to be related to top-down modulatory processes.

Mayr et al. (2006) recruited seven patients with focal lesions in the left and four patients with focal lesions in the right PFC to assess performance on trials that required rule switches versus rule repetitions (local switch costs) and between blocks of bivalent stimuli and blocks with univalent stimuli (global switch costs). They found that patients with left prefrontal lesions, but not patients with right prefrontal lesions, exhibited increased costs on trials in which the relevant dimension switched (local switch costs), but also on no-switch trials with bivalent stimuli (global costs). Therefore, their result supported the previous study by Aron et al. (2004). Ravizza et al. reported similar findings in their study where task switching abilities were impaired for stroke patients with prefrontal damage regardless of working memory demands (Ravizza & Ciranni, 2002).

Pohl et al. (2007) recruited 46 adults with subacute stroke (<1 month) and 38 adults without a history of stroke in order to evaluate the effects of unilateral subacute stroke on task switching. Specifically, their purpose was to compare the switching ability for a task under endogenous control (using an alternating runs paradigm) with that for a task under exogenous control (using a cued task switching paradigm). Given the additional demands of a task under endogenous control (because of the requirement to keep track of the sequence), they hypothesized that the performance of adults who had had a stroke would be particularly impaired in the endogenous condition (alternating runs). They found that error rates on switch trials were higher for participants with stroke than for control participants. Both groups had higher switch costs (in errors) when the switches were endogenously cued than when they were exogenously cued. Moreover, there was a reliable interaction between group and condition that was attributable to high switch costs (in errors) for participants with stroke in the endogenous condition. However, there was no group difference for RT, though both groups had significantly longer RT for the endogenous task. Thus, this study supports the idea that endogenous cuing is more difficult than exogenous cuing and that this is exacerbated in stroke survivors. However, there was no effect of lesion side on the switch cost (possibly due to small sample size). Moreover, without brain images, this study was unable to address questions regarding the relationship of lesion location or lesion extent to task switching abilities (Pohl et al., 2007).

Yehene et al. (2008) studied the performance of patients with lesions involving the BG to examine the specific role of the BG within the frontal–subcortical circuits in task switching. They recruited seven patients with focal lesions in the BG, and their performance was compared with that of four patients with focal lesions in the thalamus, six patients with focal lesions including the PFC, and seven age-matched controls. With one exception, all patients had focal lesions due to stroke. They found that all the BG patients and none of the other participants showed a marked reduction in accuracy on incongruent trials (where there was maximal interference from the competing S–R rule). These marked differences in accuracy were coupled with an increase in switch cost in the BG patients, who had the highest switch cost among all the groups. None of the patients' groups showed a significant preparation-related gain in RT in blocks involving task switching. Additionally, they identified two subgroups of BG patients. One group showed accuracy around 0.50 for both tasks. The other group of BG patients showed near-zero accuracy for one task and near total accuracy for the other task. The authors previously used a mathematical modeling approach to show that the best-fitting model was one that explains the increased error rate in incongruent (relative to congruent) trials as mostly due to the correct execution of the wrong task ("task errors") (Meiran & Daichman, 2005). Therefore, they concluded that

BG has a special role in action selection and/or in the inhibition of irrelevant information during task switching (based on their previous work and also on differences in switching cost and mixing cost across these groups).

Despite the fact that the literature on task switching in stroke survivors is quite small, it provides some very important findings. Right frontal areas appear to be important for inhibitory processes, while left frontal areas are important for top-down modulatory (biasing) processes. The BG are important for action selection and/or inhibition of currently irrelevant information. Put another way, the BG appear to be important for the resolution of interference from currently irrelevant task-sets or S–R mappings.

PARKINSON'S DISEASE

PD is characterized by the degeneration and depletion of dopaminergic neurons in the substantia nigra pars compacta providing input to the striatum (Betchen & Kaplitt, 2003). This results in altered neuronal firing patterns in the two principal pathways of the BG—the direct and indirect—which leads to a net increase in inhibitory output from the BG on thalamocortical circuits (Dagher & Nagano-Saito, 2007). These factors contribute to the hallmark motor symptoms of bradykinesia (slowed movement execution) and akinesia (impaired movement initiation) and other profound nonmotor symptoms. Dopaminergic depletion is also considered a factor underlying executive dysfunction often observed in PD, which resembles symptoms that follow frontal lobe damage. Therefore, the disease has been considered as a clinical model for impaired prefrontal function in the absence of morphological lesions (Owen et al., 1992; Werheid, Koch, Reichert, & Brass, 2007). Although the task switching paradigm appears to be ideal to study the postulated cognitive control deficits in PD, the empirical findings are mixed.

Patients with PD seem to exhibit increased switch costs only under specific conditions. For example, a study by Rogers et al. investigated 12 early stage, medicated PD patients with a task switching paradigm requiring letter or number categorization (Rogers et al., 1998). PD patients showed a small increase in RT switch costs but showed progressive increases in the error switch costs as a function of the number of trials performed in each block, while age- and IQ-matched control subjects showed only progressive reductions in the error switch cost. However, the increases in the error switch costs (in PD patients) were present only in those conditions in which there was interference or crosstalk between the tasks. Moreover, the error switch costs were not reduced in those conditions in which the task cues were words as opposed to the color of the stimulus window. Thus, in contrast to several previous results involving PD patients (e.g., Brown and Marsden, 1988), there was no indication that this particular change in task performance could be reversed with stronger task cues that somehow ameliorated a deficit in the internal control of attention or action (this is discussed further below). The authors also attributed a part of this progressive increase in error cost to fatigue.

Other researchers (e.g., Hayes et al., 1998) have found increased RT switch costs in PD patients. These researchers investigated switching using a color/shape classification task in optimally medicated PD patients. Not only were RT switch costs present in PD patients (experiment 1), these costs were additionally increased during the "off" phases of PD symptom expression in patients with symptom fluctuations (experiment 2) (Hayes, Davidson, Keele, & Rafal, 1998). However, baseline RT on nonswitch trials were exceptionally high for both control subjects and patients with PD compared with the study by Rogers et al. (1998) and thus it is difficult to be sure that the increased switch costs in the study by Hayes et al. (1998) were not due to a general slowing of cognitive processes in PD.

To address the inconsistencies between these two studies, Cools et al. (2001) incorporated several design features in their study of set shifting in PD. They modified the paradigm developed Rogers et al. (1998) and used a shorter version of the task, avoiding fatigue and thus increasing task sensitivity. Second, this shorter version allowed them to test a larger population of patients with PD, increasing their statistical power. Learning and working memory load were reduced by having subjects switch between easy and well-practiced tasks that were explicitly cued on each trial. They found increased switch costs only in "crosstalk" conditions, when the target stimulus was presented together with another stimulus signaling the alternative, competing task in other trials. In contrast, no significant increase in switch costs was found in the condition without crosstalk, in which the target was paired with a neutral symbol. In the crosstalk condition, switching from one rule to another interferes with response selection because the subjects have to select the task-relevant symbol while ignoring the other symbol, which was relevant before but now is the distracting stimulus. If the distracting stimulus was replaced by a neutral character (e.g., "§" or "?") instead of a number or a letter (the "no-cross-talk" condition), the deficits in task switching behavior in PD patients vanished. These results provided strong evidence for a specific cognitive set shifting deficit in patients with mild PD in a nonlearning context, which also cannot be explained by general slowing of cognitive processes. In a series of further studies, Cools et al. varied the level of dopaminergic stimulation and showed abnormally increased switch costs in the "crosstalk" condition exclusively in PD patients after a dopamine withdrawal (Cools, Barker, Sahakian, & Robbins, 2003; Cools, Stefanova, Barker, Robbins, & Owen, 2002). Taken together, these findings support the view that the BG and the availability of dopamine in frontostriatal neuronal circuits is related to overcoming interference from competing S–R associations that must be maintained but are currently not relevant.

Another line of task switching research has been aimed at testing the view that the "core" deficit in PD consists of maintaining internal representations about the upcoming task (Pollux, 2004; Pollux & Robertson, 2002). These findings are compatible with Brown and Marsden's (1988) hypothesis of a PD-associated deficit in "internal" action control, in the presence of preserved "external" control. Brown and Marsden used a Stroop-like switching task, in which the upcoming task was either announced by a descriptive cue immediately preceding the target ("external control" condition) or announced before each block to be kept "in mind" by the participants ("internal control" condition). In comparison to healthy controls, PD patients showed increased switch costs only in the "internal control" condition. However, Brown and Marsden's experimental paradigm had methodological limitations. Most notably, their measure of task switching was based primarily on the response immediately following an infrequent switch (every 10 trials). Woodward, Bub, and Hunter (2002) reexamined this paradigm using a more recently developed Stroop task switching paradigm. A PD group (N = 30) was compared with an age-matched control group (N = 34) on vocal RT for color naming and word reading in response to neutral and incongruent Stroop stimuli. Participants carried out four blocks of task-repetition trials and eight blocks of task switching trials. People with PD were found to be impaired on incongruent color naming when switching tasks but were unimpaired on incongruent color naming when repeating tasks, unimpaired on incongruent word reading when switching tasks, and unimpaired on incongruent word reading when repeating tasks. This set of results was not compatible with the assertion that impaired use of internal control is the basis of a deficit in PD, because impairment was absent for incongruent-switching word reading, and incongruent-repeated color naming, conditions that demand the use of internal control. It was, however, compatible with the view that the BG plays an important role in mediating interference from competing S–R associations, as was shown by Cools and colleagues.

This interpretation was further supported by a study in 2004 by Pollux in which 18 patients with PD and 18 healthy control subjects were presented with a switching task where stimuli elicited either one (no-conflict condition) or two (conflict condition) task-relevant S–R mappings. Furthermore, the RSI between trials was varied to allow investigation of the extent to which participants engaged in advanced preparation of task set. In line with previous findings, set-switching deficits of PD patients were only observed in the conflict condition. Prolonging the RSI led to a reduction of switch costs for control subjects in both the conflict and the no-conflict task, whereas this effect was attenuated for PD patients in the conflict condition. The author explained this preparation deficit in terms of a reduced ability to maintain cue-action representations active in working memory in high interference conditions (Pollux, 2004). The issue of preparation has also been investigated by Witt et al. (2006). These authors investigated the effects of foreknowledge in task switching performance by assessing the performance of predictable and unpredictable switches and repetitions in patients suffering from PD. In accordance with the results of Pollux (2004), the performance of PD patients did not differ from that of controls on predictable trials. Thus, PD patients do not show a deficit in the preparation of predictable cognitive switches, just as they showed no deficit when the RSI was long. However, PD patients were specifically impaired in unpredictable trials compared with controls (just as they were when the RSI was short). These results can be incorporated into the view that the BG play an important role in mediating interference: inasmuch as a short RSI (or no foreknowledge) serves to maximize interference on a switch of task, this sort of manipulation would serve to amplify any deficits associated with interference resolution.

If PD affects the ability to mediate interference from competing S–R associations, one might expect a task switching deficit in another aspect of performance—backward inhibition (Fales, Vanek, & Knowlton, 2006). In neurologically intact subjects, switching from one task to another involves inhibiting some aspects of the previous task set (Mayr & Keele, 2000). This backward inhibition (BI) is revealed as poorer performance when participants must switch back to this task set. BI is thus measured as the cost associated with an alternating switch. If participants are performing three tasks (A B C) in an intermixed fashion, alternating-switch costs are measured as an increase in RT, or a decrease in accuracy, for the third trial in the alternating sequence ABA compared with the third trial in a nonalternating sequence (CBA). This cost is caused by persisting inhibition that makes task A harder to reactivate in the first case. BI is thought to be an important mechanism for preventing perseveration by aiding in the disengagement from task sets that are no longer relevant. Therefore, BI may be an automatic process that is applied to facilitate switching between tasks. As patients with PD exhibit abnormal alternating-switch costs, abnormal BI in this group may contribute to task switching deficits. Altered BI would contribute to task switching problems in PD in two ways. Exaggerated BI in patients with PD would result in greater costs for intermixed trials as compared with blocked trials because of difficulty in reactivating previously inhibited task sets. On the other hand, decreased BI could contribute to task switching deficits by hindering the disengagement of the previous task set. To investigate these issues, Fales et al. evaluated 21 patients with mild/moderate PD and age-matched controls who performed three tasks (A B C) in an intermixed fashion. PD subjects and controls showed equivalent RTs. However, the patients made significantly more errors during an alternating switch (i.e., ABA) than did control participants. In contrast, there was no group difference in accuracy in the comparable condition of two consecutive switches between different tasks (i.e., CBA). In addition, accuracy for the two groups was similar for trials in which the task was repeated. These data suggest that PD is associated with increased backward inhibition. As we can consider BI as a form of interference, the subjects show a reduced ability to overcome this interference when reactivating a recently abandoned task set. Therefore, these results further highlight the role of the BG in overcoming interference in task switching.

While there appears to be good evidence that at least part of the deficit associated with PD has to do with an impairment in overcoming interference, others have investigated the role of "internal" (i.e., self-initiated) task preparation in PD. This research is based not only on the idea that "internal" action control is affected in PD while "external" action control is spared (e.g., Brown & Marsden, 1998), but also on research in the last decade that has increasingly indicated that self-initiated and externally triggered task preparation are dissociable cognitive processes. For example, some imaging studies suggest that these processes are related to brain activity in different prefrontal regions. Self initiated task preparation has been more strongly associated with medial prefrontal brain areas, whereas externally triggered task preparation has been rather associated with dorsolateral prefrontal areas (Forstmann, Brass, Koch, & von Cramon, 2006). Behavioral research in patients has provided further evidence supporting the view that the distinction of self-initiated and externally triggered task preparation may be useful for characterizing the cognitive deficits in PD. Several behavioral studies investigating learning of S–R mappings or visuomotor sequences in PD have revealed impaired self-initiation of previously learned responses or response sequences, but intact or even facilitated responses elicited by an external trigger such as a spatially corresponding visual cue (Praamstra & Plat, 2001; Werheid, Ziessler, Nattkemper, & Yves von Cramon, 2003; Werheid, Zysset, Muller, Reuter, & von Cramon, 2003). In light of these findings, a question arises: is a PD-associated deficit in self-initiated task preparation restricted to simple S–R mappings, or does it extend to more complex cognitive operations, as required in task switching paradigms? To answer this question, Werheid et al. (2007) aimed to investigate the impact of self-initiated task preparation on performance in a sequential switching task. They investigated PD patients and age-matched controls (n = 16) with a sequential switching task in which the upcoming task was predicted by two different types of cues. First, every task was predicted by an external visual cue of varying utility (long versus short precuing interval). Additionally, the tasks were predictable on the basis of a fixed task sequence (AABB), which placed relatively higher demands on self-initiated task preparation (particularly when the precuing interval was short). After considerable practice, the sequence was changed from predictable to random. Increased RTs following the removal of predictability in the sequence indicated prior use of predictability in both groups. However, in contrast to healthy age-matched controls, PD patients did not learn to use the predictable task sequence to a greater extent when the utility of the visual task cue was low due to a short precuing interval. This finding was interpreted as evidence for a specific impairment in self-initiated as opposed to externally triggered task preparation.

Cameron et al. investigated the internal versus external controversy in task switching in PD with a different paradigm (Cameron, Watanabe, Pari, & Munoz, 2010). They used a paradigm in which participants were prompted to plan one response (prosaccade or antisaccade) but then switch it, unexpectedly, to the alternative on a subset of trials (Cameron, Watanabe, & Munoz, 2007). Importantly, the switching difficulty was asymmetric, meaning that subjects could be switching to a response that was either more automatic (prosaccade), or less automatic (antisaccade). Moreover, the time within a given trial at which the switch occurred varied with respect to peripheral stimulus onset, such that if the switch in instruction occurred in advance of stimulus onset, it would constitute a change of task set alone. The authors previously showed with fMRI that activation in the caudate nucleus (the BG input nucleus in the oculomotor system) correlated to switching difficulty (Cameron, Coe, Watanabe, Stroman, & Munoz, 2009). They hypothesized that if PD patients had an underlying deficit in task switching, they would have shown increased switch costs in both saccade RT and the occurrence of direction errors, with particular impairment in switching from a prosaccade to an antisaccade. Their results not only supported this hypothesis but also showed that PD patients performed better than controls in switching from an anti to a prosaccade. This suggests that task switching deficits in PD are particularly pronounced when more automatic behavior needs to be overridden with alternative behavior. That is, when the interference from the competing task is particularly strong, PD patients have particular trouble switching.

In summary, the data from PD suggest that the BG play an important role in the resolution of interference from competing tasks or S–R associations. There is also some evidence that the BG is important for initiating internally generated actions.

HUNTINGTON'S DISEASE

HD is an inherited neurodegenerative disease of the BG with motor, cognitive, and psychiatric symptoms and is characterized neuropathologically by the loss of GABA-containing medium-size spiny neurons in the neostriatum (Lawrence et al., 1996). Patients with HD have a wide range of cognitive impairments encompassing both visuospatial memory and executive functions, a pattern distinct from those seen in other BG disorders; often called a "dysexecutive" syndrome.

An early study of task switching in HD was undertaken by Sprengelmeyer, Lange, and Homberg (1995). In this experiment, they used three conditions of 50 trials each. On each trial, a letter and a number were presented at the same time, equidistant from the center on the left and right halves of the screen. In the first condition, subjects identified the location of the letter (pressing the compatible key corresponding to the left and right halves of the screen); in the second condition, subjects identified the location of the number; and in the third condition they alternated between locating the letters and numbers. HD patients manifested a switching deficit relative to controls; however, the fact that switch and non-switch trials were confined to separate blocks makes it possible that HD subjects' performance on switch relative to non-switch trials was impaired by factors other than a switching deficit per se (e.g., arousal or strategy; see Rogers & Monsell, 1995).

Aron et al. (2003) undertook another study to address these issues in early HD patients and matched control groups. As the early HD patients show few choreic movements (thereby permitting performance of speeded RT tasks) and because their pathology is usually restricted to the striatum, their choice was justified for the study. Aron et al. performed two task switching experiments. The first of these experiments (using the same task and method as Cools et al., 2001; Rogers et al., 1998 in PD) was directed toward (a) assessing whether there was an overall switching deficit in HD patients, (b) assessing whether such a deficit interacted with the presence of cross-talk trials ("bivalent trials," in which the stimulus has elements of both potential task sets) to explore the possibility that HD patients had difficulty inhibiting a response to an irrelevant stimulus element, and (c) whether there was evidence in trials following a bivalent stimulus of the putative need to suppress the irrelevant task on the previous trial. The second experiment employed neutral (univalent), congruent (bivalent), and incongruent (bivalent) stimuli in crosstalk blocks only and manipulated preparation interval between blocks. This experiment was directed toward (a) assessing how a putative switching deficit in HD patients interacts with preparation time, (b) exploring further the influence of stimulus congruency on the switch trial in terms of overcoming interference from the irrelevant task, and (c) assessing whether a disruption in "response inhibition" in HD could account for elevated switch costs. They found that in the first experiment, HD patients had a switching deficit even in a "pure" condition where they had to switch, predictably, and with substantial preparation time (1000 ms), between stimuli having only one possible response, indicating a switching deficit different from that for patients with PD (Cools et al., 2001) or frontal lobe trauma (Rogers et al., 1998), and possibly relating to inadequate activation of S–R links or "response set." In the more elaborate second experiment, they could not account for the switching deficit of the patients in terms of inadequate preparation in advance of a switch, deficient suppression of task-set processing from the preswitch trial, or impaired suppression of interference due to the presence of a competing task set. Instead, they found that part of the switching deficit was due to elevated RT and errors on switch trials for a repeated response (same button press as on the preswitch trial) relative to an alternated response (different button press from the preswitch trial). The authors argued that this elevated "repetition effect" for the HD patients is due to excessive inhibition of the just performed response in advance of a switch. Alterations in the "response-setting" process alone (Experiment 1) and both the response-setting and "response inhibition" process (Experiment 2) probably arise from striatal pathology in HD, thus accounting for the task switching deficits.

Although the studies in HD shed some light on the role of the striatum (and GABA) in task switching, more work clearly needs to be done. One possibility is that the response generated on trial n is "automatically" inhibited after completion by nonstriatal mechanisms and that when striatal inhibitory processes are impaired (due to loss of GABA), it is difficult to overcome this inhibition on trial n + 1—that is, it is difficult to undo the inhibition. This may explain the elevated "repetition effect" for the HD patients. This explanation is analogous to the explanations of movement disorders typical of HD, where BG damage causes the release or reinstatement of inhibition to be erratic and uncontrolled. This results in an awkward start to movements, or for movements to be unintentionally initiated, or for movements to be halted before, or beyond, their intended completion (Crossman, 2000).

TRAUMATIC BRAIN INJURY

In TBI, focal lesions generally occur directly beneath the site of impact (coup injury), and sometimes opposite the site of impact as well (contrecoup injury). The frontal and temporal lobes and their subcortical connections tend to be the brain areas most likely to be injured following TBI. The impact also causes movement of the brain relative to the skull, resulting in widespread tearing and shearing of white matter connections (diffuse axonal injury) between the frontal cortex and related circuitry, such as the BG, thalamus, and cerebellum (McDonald, Flashman, & Saykin, 2002). This frequently results in long-term physical, motor, cognitive, and emotional impairments (Colantonio et al., 2004). It is common for a TBI patient to present with deficits in executive function (Greenwald, Burnett, & Miller, 2003). Many patients with TBI are faced with persistent cognitive deficits, including decreased mental flexibility, trouble with shifting sets, impaired attention, poor planning and organization, impaired judgment, deficits in verbal fluency, reduced working memory, and increased impulsivity (Godefroy, 2003; Levin & Kraus, 1994; McDonald, et al., 2002), affecting independent living and psychosocial functioning (Garth, Anderson, & Wrennall, 1997). The deficits in executive functioning are particularly evident in situations where response conflict is high, and inappropriate, prepotent response tendencies have to be overcome. Inasmuch as the task switching paradigm involves precisely these processes, there is a growing literature investigating task switching in TBI.

Mecklinger et al. investigated task switching in TBI patients, (Mecklinger, von Cramon, Springer, & Matthes-von Cramon, 1999) by using an alternating runs paradigm (Rogers & Monsell, 1998), in which 18 TBI patients had to switch between an object discrimination task and a spatial discrimination task. Patients with left brain damage (LBD) showed higher switch costs than patients with right brain damage (RBD) whereas patients with RBD showed higher interference from irrelevant (but in same visual domain) task sets. Unlike patients with RBD, the LBD patients also exhibited language or speech disorders. According to the authors these results suggested that the efficiency of suppressing internal interference from a recently activated task set depended on the availability of verbal representations of the upcoming task. This idea was further supported by the finding that the disproportionally high RT switch costs exhibited by patients with LBD and language and speech disorders were unaffected by practice. Conversely, the group with RBD showed a higher vulnerability to external interfering information. For these patients it seemed harder to suppress inappropriate task sets when another task was required. Therefore this study replicated the findings by Rogers et al. (1998). While the distinction between LBD and RBD is admittedly rather coarse, this pattern of results nevertheless suggests that that the executive processes in task switching rely on hemispherically distinct mechanisms with exacerbation of proactive interference effects following LBD and interference generated by the stimulus itself exacerbated by RBD.

Perlstein et al. (2006) used event-related potentials (ERPs) to study two compo nents of cognitive control, "evaluative" and "regulative" components, underlying task switching in the TBI population (N = 11). The evaluative component supports monitoring for the presence of response conflict and signals the need to implement control when adjustments are necessary. The regulative component, on the other hand, is involved in the actual implementation of top-down support for task-relevant processes, such as the allocation of attention to task relevant demands, negotiating response conflict, and preparation to override potential prepotent but contextually inappropriate response tendencies. They used a cued, task switching version of the classic Stroop task where participants were presented on a trial-by-trial basis with a task instructional cue (i.e., the words "color" or "word"), followed after one of two delays (1 or 5 seconds) by the Stroop stimulus. They used ERPs to temporally dissociate the regulative and evaluative components. Behaviorally, TBI patients showed clear evidence of impaired cognitive control, characterized by increased error rates on the incongruent color-naming task, and performed more poorly than controls on the long-, but not short-delay conflict condition, consistent with a context processing deficit. TBI patients were also impaired on a measure of working memory capacity, a measure that correlated with the ability to implement regulative control and overcome conflict. These findings suggest that patients with TBI are impaired on both regulative and evaluative components of cognitive control rather than a more generalized inability to inhibit prepotent response tendencies, or to a more generalized deficit like generalized slowing, poor attention, concentration, or motivation.

Functional neuroimaging has played a key role in investigating task switching in TBI. Easdon et al. used a "go-stop" task and showed that, compared with controls, TBI patients showed decreased blood-oxygen level dependent (BOLD) activation in the bilateral dorsolateral PFCs (Brodmann's area 9/46) when a stop-signal was presented and decreased activity in the bilateral PFC and cingulate region when a go-signal was presented (Easdon, Levine, O'Connor, Tisserand, & Hevenor, 2004). Soeda et al. used a Stroop task and found reduced activity in anterior cingulate cortex in TBI subjects compared with controls when naming the color of incongruent Stroop stimuli (Soeda et al., 2005). However, these studies had small samples (n = 5) and used fixed-effects analyses, thus limiting extrapolation of the results.

Scheibel et al. studied 14 subjects with TBI using a random-effect fMRI analysis while they performed a spatial S–R compatibility task (Scheibel et al., 2007). Contrary to previous studies they found increased activation within the left precentral gyrus and bilateral cingulate, medial frontal, middle frontal, and superior frontal gyri. The authors ascribed this increased activation, which did not correlate with performance accuracy, to increased and inefficient utilization of neural resources to compensate for cognitive processes involved in task switching following TBI.

This finding was supported by Sozda et al., who used an event-related functional magnetic resonance imaging paradigm to examine brain activity associated with task switching: a cued-Stroop task in severe TBI (sTBI) subjects (Sozda, Larson, Kaufman, Schmalfuss, & Perlstein, 2011). Compared with healthy controls sTBI patients showed greater activation in the anterior cingulate cortex (ACC) and an increase in the spatial extent of activation across cortical and subcortical regions.

However, there are several methodological limitations and alternative explanations of findings of fMRI studies in TBI that merit discussion. For example, TBI participants in imaging studies are notoriously heterogeneous. The heterogeneity of this population results from individual differences in injury mechanism, injury localization, time since injury, posttraumatic amnesia, and loss of consciousness (Sozda et al., 2011). Given that the usual sample size in TBI studies tends to be small, it is hardly possible to control for all these variables. Second, it is well established that the BOLD signal measured in fMRI studies is a complex function reflecting changing levels of cerebral blood flow, blood volume, and oxygen metabolism that occur as a result of neural activity. Therefore, any injury-related differences in BOLD activation may result from factors related to the physiology of TBI (e.g., atrophy, change of brain anatomy, surgery) rather than from cognitive differences.

Because the network of cortical and subcortical regions subserving task switching is widely distributed, the integrity of the white matter tracts between these areas is essential. One of the most important white matter tracts is the corpus callosum, connecting both homotopic and heterotopic cortical regions across the two cerebral hemispheres. The corpus callosum is composed of densely packed, myelinated axons and is commonly partitioned into ordered subareas based on anatomical and functional connectivity between cortical regions. On the hypothesis that white matter damage in the corpus callosum may explain some of the impairment in task switching in TBI, Caeyenberghs et al. (2011) studied the role of corpus callosum integrity using diffusion tensor imaging. They measured task switching with bimanual coordination in 21 TBI subjects using a circle-drawing task, either clockwise or counterclockwise, with each hand. A multiple regression analysis showed that deficits in switching task were related to disrupted interhemispheric communication between prefrontal, sensory, and parietal regions. This paper further highlights the distributed network of brain regions subserving task switching.

Using the same task design, Leunissen et al. combined fMRI and DTI to investigate the role of the interaction between the neocortex and the BG in TBI (Leunissen et al., 2013). Relative to controls, TBI subjects had significantly increased activation in the presupplementary motor area (pre-SMA) and left IFC, and showed underactivation of the subthalamic nucleus (STN) region. This altered functional engagement was related to the white matter microstructural properties of the tracts connecting pre-SMA, IFC, and STN: lower fractional anisotropy (a measure of white matter integrity) in the tract from left IFC to left pre-SMA was associated with higher activity in pre-SMA and lower STN activity. Moreover, subjects with higher pre-SMA activity during motor switching also showed lower FA in the tracts from left pre-SMA to left STN and right IFC to right pre-SMA. Therefore, worse behavioral performance in the TBI group was correlated with (a) higher functional activity in pre-SMA and IFC, (b) lower activity in STN, and (c) poorer integrity of the connections between these regions. Based on the results, the authors concluded that TBI patients with the most severe damage to white matter tracts connecting pre-SMA, IFC, and STN, fail to modulate the STN via pre-SMA and/or IFC, resulting in less proficient switching behavior.

Another study from this group used graph theory to examine changes in task switching networks by measuring functional connectivity and network metrics in task-specific functional MRI data recorded from healthy volunteers and patients with TBI (Caeyenberghs et al., 2012). Graph theory offers a broad array of measures to examine and quantify relationships between activations in different brain regions. The study found that switching performance was significantly worse in patients with TBI compared with control subjects. Furthermore, altered functional connectivity was demonstrated in patients with TBI. In particular, compared with controls, patients with TBI showed increased connectivity degree and strength, and higher values of local efficiency, possibly suggesting adaptive mechanisms in this group. However, the degree of increased connectivity was significantly correlated with poorer switching task performance and more severe brain injury.

These studies of the effect of TBI on task switching provide some valuable insight into task switching and executive dysfunction. First, these studies strongly establish the predominant role of left dorsolateral PFC in maintaining the task-set functions and providing top-down, biasing modulation such that the currently relevant task is more active than the currently irrelevant task (Mecklinger et al., 1999; Rogers et al., 1998). Second, the source of this task switching deficit is attributed to both regulative and evaluative components of cognitive control rather than a more generalized inability to inhibit prepotent response tendencies (Perlstein et al., 2006). Third, these studies found that people with TBI show increased activation in brain areas known to be involved in task switching, suggesting inefficient processing in these areas. More important, these neuroimaging studies highlight the importance of the integrity of the widespread task switching network as a whole: these studies found lack of white matter integrity in corpus callosum (Caeyenberghs et al., 2011) and specific white matter tracts connecting cortical and subcortical structures (Leunissen et al., 2013) correlate with poor task performance and "inefficient" cortical activity. Using graph theory Caeyenberghs et al. (2012) provided a possible explanation for what this "inefficient processing" may be: more local connectivity and less long-range connectivity. This interpretation makes sense given the fact that TBI is known to result in diffuse axonal injury and that white matter integrity in the corpus callosum has been linked to task switching performance. Last but not the least, these results help us redefine the role of pre-SMA in response conflict in task switching (Leunissen et al., 2013). Pre-SMA is involved in situations where subjects have to stop an impending movement or when two procedures compete with each other (Aron & Poldrack, 2006; Coxon et al., 2010). The pre-SMA exerts a strong influence on BG nuclei, with projections not only to the striatum but also to STN. These projections to STN, from pre-SMA (and also from IFC), may function to exert a "brake" on the BG motor loop (Aron & Poldrack, 2006; Hikosaka & Isoda, 2010). When several competing responses are activated, the STN receives excitatory input from the cortex and sends a strong global "no go" signal allowing alternative responses to be considered before selecting the appropriate action. This might be important for slowing response execution until response conflict is resolved (Aron, 2007).

SCHIZOPHRENIA

Disorders of "executive function" or controlled attention are integral to even the earliest characterizations of schizophrenia (Bleuler, 1911). Recent research has firmly established that executive dysfunctions are core features of schizophrenia and are strongly associated with functional impairments among individuals with this illness (Heinrichs & Zakzanis, 1998; Mesholam-Gately, Giuliano, Goff, Faraone, & Seidman, 2009). Executive control processes are those mechanisms that allow individuals to flexibly and dynamically adjust their performance in response to changing environmental demands and changing internal goal states. Numerous empirical studies have shown that individuals with schizophrenia show deficits on tasks designed to measure such executive control processes (Reichenberg & Harvey, 2007; Wylie, Clark, Butler, & Javitt, 2010). Deficits on these executive control tasks are associated with both negative and disorganized symptoms in schizophrenia (and those at risk for schizophrenia), and deficits in executive control are associated with poor functional outcome (Delawalla et al., 2006). Clinical observations of perseveration have suggested that schizophrenics may have deficits in switching between tasks and therefore task switching deficits have been well investigated in patients with schizophrenia.

Cools et al. studied task switching in 20 individuals with chronic schizophrenia compared with 11 healthy control subjects (2000). Schizophrenic subjects made more errors overall, on both switch and nonswitch trials, but they did not make more errors on switch trials than nonswitch trials compared with control subjects. Furthermore, schizophrenic subjects responded as fast as controls on both types of trials. Therefore, they found no evidence of a task switching deficit. However, they did find that individuals with schizophrenia were more influenced by the presence of the irrelevant task set (incongruent stimuli) than were the controls. The patients thus made more errors due to responding to the irrelevant dimension, independent of trial type.

Manoach et al. (2002) measured task switching and inhibition during saccadic eye movement tasks to determine whether individuals with schizophrenia show selective impairments in task switching. Schizophrenic and healthy control subjects performed trials requiring either prosaccades or antisaccades. During prosaccade trials, subjects were instructed to look toward a suddenly appearing target. During antisaccade trials, subjects they were instructed to look in the direction opposite the target. Whereas prosaccades are a prepotent, relatively automatic response, antisaccades require inhibition of the prosaccade and the generation of a novel response (looking away from a target). The authors presented prosaccade and antisaccade trials in a randomly mixed sequence. They found task switching to be unimpaired in schizophrenic subjects (n = 21) despite having impaired WCST performance (as a group, their mean standard score was in the mildly impaired range for total errors ($\mu = 82 \pm 16$) and for perseverative errors ($\mu = 83 \pm 18$). The authors argued that their result suggested inhibition and task switching were mediated by distinct neural networks and that only the network underlying inhibition was dysfunctional in schizophrenia.

Similar results were obtained by Burton et al. (2002) when they examined task switching and inhibition in the antisaccade paradigm, in 21 individuals with schizophrenia and 16 age-matched controls. Schizophrenic subjects had a threefold increase in error rate for antisaccades compared with controls, but the effect of task switching on their accuracy did not differ from that in normal subjects.

Moreover, the accuracy rate of trials combining antisaccades and task switching was equivalent to a multiplication of the accuracy rates from trials in which each was done alone. The latencies for the individuals with schizophrenia were disproportionately increased for antisaccades, but again they were no different from controls in task switching costs. The authors concluded, similar to Manoach et al., that the executive dysfunction in schizophrenia is not generalized but selective, sparing task switching from exogenous cues, in which the switch is limited to an S–R remapping.

In contrast to this, Meiran et al. did find increased switch costs in individuals with schizophrenia (2000). They studied task switching in 13 schizophrenic subjects and 14 age-matched healthy controls with a paradigm that required subjects to switch between two spatial judgment tasks. Individuals with schizophrenia responded more slowly than controls on all trials but also showed increased switch costs. However, they were as efficient as controls in engaging in an upcoming task set and were faster than controls in disengaging from the previous task set. Moreover, the increased switch cost was found unambiguously only when patients were given very little time (132 ms) to prepare for a forthcoming switching of task. Therefore, while is some evidence for a task switching deficit in schizophrenia under certain circumstances (a very short preparation interval), deficits in task switching do not appear to be general in schizophrenia.

Kieffaber et al. (2006) aimed to distinguish perceptual processes (sensory and perceptual encoding abnormalities) from decisional/intentional processes in task maintenance and switching in schizophrenia. They argued that task switching deficits in schizophrenia can be articulated as an impaired ability to modify sensory/perceptual biases in favor of task-relevant stimuli and/or stimulus features, whereas the task maintenance deficits can be articulated as an impaired ability to sustain optimal sensory/perceptual encoding processes, resulting in increased processing of irrelevant information. They recruited 30 participants with schizophrenia and 27 healthy controls to complete a cued attentional set switching task. In addition to analyses of mean RTs, the contributions of attentional and intentional processes to task performance were estimated using an ex-Gaussian distributional analysis. There was no evidence for an attentional set switching deficit in schizophrenia (i.e., switch costs were equivalent in schizophrenia and healthy comparison groups), but schizophrenia was associated with a set maintenance deficit indicated by increased RT and error rates when responding to incongruent stimuli. The ex-Gaussian distributional analysis attributed this deficit to an attentional, rather than intentional, dysfunction.

Karayanidis et al. used behavioral and event-related potential (ERP) indices of task switching to examine whether individuals with schizophrenia have a specific deficit in anticipatory task-set reconfiguration using a alternating runs paradigm with a predictable AABB task sequence (2006). In this study, the authors found that schizophrenia patients had overall increased RT, but no increase in corrected RT switch cost, similar to previous studies. In the schizophrenia group, anticipatory ERPs were reduced (compared with the control group), as were ERPs associated with stimulus processing. This electrophysiological group difference, despite no behavioral differences in task switching performance, suggested group differences in processing on switch and repeat trials. The authors concluded that these results were compatible with impaired implementation of endogenously driven processes in schizophrenia and greater reliance on external task cues, especially at long preparation intervals.

Kieffaber, O'Donnell, Shekhar, and Hetrick (2007) electrophysiologically evaluated the idea that set switching may be intact in schizophrenia when the task switch requires only a change in the relevance of perceptual dimensions (e.g., attentional set switches: regarding the selection of stimuli and/or stimulus dimensions; shape, color, etc.), but decision-to-response mappings (intentional set: selection of motor responses) are maintained across trials. This hypothesis makes the counterintuitive prediction that individuals with schizophrenia would show an intact, switch-sensitive P3b brain response to cued switches of attentional set. This prediction was tested in a group of 20 individuals with schizophrenia and 20 healthy comparison participants using event-related brain potential methodology and a cued task switching task. Attentional set switching costs were equivalent between the two groups despite a set maintenance deficit in schizophrenia. Moreover, a posteroparietal P3b component of the ERP was found to be equally sensitive to attentional set switching in schizophrenia and comparison groups, indicating a "healthy" brain response to switches of attentional set in schizophrenia. These results further support the notion that the dynamic control of task switching may be preserved in schizophrenia and that previously reported executive deficits may be specific to the control of intentional set and to deficits of task set maintenance.

Wylie et al. (2010) provided another dimension to the previous research. They identified the task switching defect found in schizophrenia, characterized not by increased switch costs but by increased mixing costs (i.e., the difference between repeat trials in single-task blocks and repeat trials in mixed-task, switching blocks, similar to the pattern seen in monkeys treated with the *N*-methyl-D-aspartate (NMDA) antagonist Pphencyclidine (PCP) (Stoet & Snyder, 2006)). They suggested that the pattern of set-shifting deficit observed in schizophrenia, like other aspects of neurocognitive dysfunction in schizophrenia, may be attributable to underlying NMDA receptor dysfunction (Javitt & Zukin, 1991). They compared subjects with schizophrenia (n = 16) and healthy controls (n = 17) in a task switching paradigm where the subjects viewed colored letters and had to respond alternately based on letter (X versus O) or color (red versus blue). Individuals with schizophrenia showed similar switch costs to controls, consistent with prior literature. However, individuals with schizophrenia showed increased congruence and mixing costs. In addition, relative to controls, schizophrenia subjects showed worse performance across conditions in the letter versus color tasks, suggesting deficits in form versus color processing. Overall, while confirming executive dysfunction in schizophrenia, this study indicated that not all aspects of executive control are impaired and that the task switching paradigm may be useful for evaluating neurochemical versus neuroanatomical hypotheses of schizophrenia.

Perhaps no other disease condition showcases the unique place of task switching under the broad rubric of "executive function" as well as does schizophrenia. Although executive dysfunction is an integral part of the symptoms associated with schizophrenia, task switching per se is usually unaffected. This shows that the executive dysfunction in schizophrenia is not generalized but selective, largely sparing task switching. Moreover, the ERP studies show that while there may be no differences in task switching performance as measured by behavior, there are changes in neural functioning that are evident during task switching. These changes may be due to NMDA receptor dysfunction, which also likely results in increased mixing costs.

CONCLUSION

Task switching is a unique cognitive function within the broad domain of "executive function" that helps us navigate through continuously shifting environmental cues and contingencies. It is subserved by a widespread network of cortical and subcortical brain structures that is overlapping but distinct from networks subserving other executive functions. Therefore, different disease conditions, with their varying pathophysiological mechanisms, differently affect task switching. The preceding review of task switching literature in clinical populations with executive dysfunction make this point plain. The research from individuals with schizophrenia shows that despite being integral to this clinical constellation of symptoms, executive dysfunction in schizophrenia is not generalized but selective, largely sparing task switching. Furthermore, the studies in task switching also suggest a possible biological explanation behind this phenomenon (NMDA receptor dysfunction). Another remarkable example comes through the research with HD subjects. In addition to having significant executive dysfunction, the HD subjects manifest a unique task switching deficit—the "repetition effect"—wherein there is elevated RT and errors on switch trials for a repeated response (same button press as on the preswitch trial) rather than to an alternated response (which is usual in healthy or other disease population like stroke, TBI or PD). This is explained through the unique pathophysiology underlying HD—the loss of GABA-containing medium-size spiny neurons in the neostriatum—which leads to alterations in inhibitory outputs arising from BG. Moreover, all the studies from Sstroke, PD, TBI, and HD show the importance of specific brain areas to successful task switching performance. Stroke shows the importance of left DLPFC and right IFJ; PD and HD show the importance of the BG. The studies from TBI, because TBI often results in widespread neural network damage in the brain, show how TBI patients with damage to white matter tracts connecting cortical and subcortical areas, fail to modulate the network subserving task switching and as a result produce less proficient switching behavior. Additionally, these studies also provide important clues to what these areas do. The left DLPFC appears to provide top-down biasing signals that support the currently relevant task; the right IFJ appears to be important for inhibition; the BG appears to be important for resolving interference. Finally, TBI shows that these regions work as a network, and when the white matter connections between them are damaged, then task switching performance suffers.

In this regard, these studies on task switching in clinical populations with established brain pathology and executive dysfunction provide a very important piece of information which is not possible to achieve through other means. Neuroimaging studies do not settle whether putatively "task switching-related" activations are necessary for successful task switching and behavioral studies in healthy individuals do not address the neural basis of task switching. That is, it is difficult to establish which brain areas are necessary for the generation of normal task switching performance from studies of healthy populations alone. Therefore, studies with clinical populations form a critical bridge between brain areas, task switching and executive dysfunction.

REFERENCES

Allport, D. A., Styles, E. A., Hsieh, S. (1994). Shifting intentional set: Exploring the dynamic control of tasks. In: Umilta C, Moscovitch, eds. *Attention and Performance XI* (pp. 107–132). Cambridge, MA: MIT Press.

Aron, A. R. (2007). The neural basis of inhibition in cognitive control. *The Neuroscientist, 13*(3), 214–228.

Aron, A. R., Monsell, S., Sahakian, B. J., & Robbins, T. W. (2004). A componential analysis of task-switching deficits associated with lesions of left and right frontal cortex. *Brain, 127*(Pt 7), 1561–1573.

Aron, A. R., & Poldrack, R. A. (2006). Cortical and subcortical contributions to Stop signal response inhibition: Role of the subthalamic nucleus. *The Journal of Neuroscience, 26*(9), 2424–2433.

Aron, A. R., Watkins, L., Sahakian, B. J., Monsell, S., Barker, R. A., & Robbins, T. W. (2003). Task set switching deficits in early stage Huntington's disease: Implications for basal ganglia function. *Journal of Cognitive Neuroscience, 15*(5), 629–642.

Barton, J. J., Cherkasova, M. V., Lindgren, K., Goff, D. C., Intriligator, J. M., & Manoach, D. S. (2002). Antisaccades and task switching: Studies of control processes in saccadic function in normal subjects and schizophrenic patients. *Annals of the New York Academy of Sciences, 956*, 250–263.

Betchen, S. A., & Kaplitt, M. (2003). Future and current surgical therapies in Parkinson's disease. *Current Opinion in Neurology, 16*(4), 487–493.

Bleuler, E. (1911). Dementia praecox or the group of schizophrenias. In J. t. Kinkin (Ed.), *Dementia praecox or the group of schizophrenias.* New York, NY: International Universities Press.

Brass, M., Ruge, H., Meiran, N., Rubin, O., Koch, I., Zysset, S., . . . von Cramon, D. Y. (2003). When the same response has different meanings: Recoding the response meaning in the lateral prefrontal cortex. *NeuroImage, 20*(2), 1026–1031.

Brass, M., & von Cramon, D. Y. (2004). Decomposing components of task preparation with functional magnetic resonance imaging. *Journal of Cognitive Neuroscience, 16*(4), 609–620.

Brown, R. G., & Marsden, C. D. (1988). Internal versus external cues and the control of attention in Parkinson's disease. *Brain, 111*(Pt 2), 323–345.

Caeyenberghs, K., Leemans, A., Coxon, J., Leunissen, I., Drijkoningen, D., Geurts, M.,... Swinnen, S. P. (2011). Bimanual coordination and corpus callosum microstructure in young adults with traumatic brain injury: A diffusion tensor imaging study. *Journal of Neurotrauma, 28*(6), 897–913.

Caeyenberghs, K., Leemans, A., Heitger, M. H., Leunissen, I., Dhollander, T., Sunaert, S.,... Swinnen, S. P. (2012). Graph analysis of functional brain networks for cognitive control of action in traumatic brain injury. *Brain, 135*(Pt 4), 1293–1307.

Cameron, I. G., Coe, B. C., Watanabe, M., Stroman, P. W., & Munoz, D. P. (2009). Role of the basal ganglia in switching: A planned response. *The European Journal of Neuroscience, 29*(12), 2413–2425.

Cameron, I. G., Watanabe, M., & Munoz, D. P. (2007). Contrasting instruction change with response change in task switching. *Experimental Brain Research, 182*(2), 233–248.

Cameron, I. G., Watanabe, M., Pari, G., & Munoz, D. P. (2010). Executive impairment in Parkinson's disease: Response automaticity and task switching. *Neuropsychologia, 48*(7), 1948–1957.

Chiu, Y. C., & Yantis, S. (2009). A domain-independent source of cognitive control for task sets: shifting spatial attention and switching categorization rules. *The Journal of Neuroscience, 29*(12), 3930–3938.

Colantonio, A., Ratcliff, G., Chase, S., Kelsey, S., Escobar, M., & Vernich, L. (2004). Long-term outcomes after moderate to severe traumatic brain injury. *Disability and rehabilitation, 26*(5), 253–261.

Cools, R., Barker, R. A., Sahakian, B. J., & Robbins, T. W. (2001). Mechanisms of cognitive set flexibility in Parkinson's disease. *Brain, 124*(Pt 12), 2503–2512.

Cools, R., Barker, R. A., Sahakian, B. J., & Robbins, T. W. (2003). L-Dopa medication remediates cognitive inflexibility, but increases impulsivity in patients with Parkinson's disease. *Neuropsychologia, 41*(11), 1431–1441.

Cools, R., Brouwer, W. H., de Jong, R., & Slooff, C. (2000). Flexibility, inhibition, and planning: Frontal dysfunctioning in schizophrenia. *Brain and Cognition, 43*(1–3),108–112.

Cools, R., Stefanova, E., Barker, R. A., Robbins, T. W., & Owen, A. M. (2002). Dopaminergic modulation of high-level cognition in Parkinson's disease: The role of the prefrontal cortex revealed by PET. *Brain, 125*(Pt 3), 584–594.

Coxon, J. P., Goble, D. J., Van Impe, A., De Vos, J., Wenderoth, N., & Swinnen, S. P. (2010). Reduced basal ganglia function when elderly switch between coordinated movement patterns. *Cerebral Cortex, 20*(10), 2368–2379.

Crossman, A. R. (2000). Functional anatomy of movement disorders. *Journal of Anatomy, 196*(Pt 4), 519–525.

Dagher, A., & Nagano-Saito, A. (2007). Functional and anatomical magnetic resonance imaging in Parkinson's disease. *Molecular Imaging and Biology, 9*(4), 234–242.

Delawalla, Z., Barch, D. M., Fisher Eastep, J. L., Thomason, E. S., Hanewinkel, M. J., Thompson, P. A., & Csernansky, J. G. (2006). Factors mediating cognitive deficits and psychopathology among siblings of individuals with schizophrenia. *Schizophrenia bBulletin, 32*(3), 525–537.

Easdon, C., Levine, B., O'Connor, C., Tisserand, D., & Hevenor, S. (2004). Neural activity associated with response inhibition following traumatic brain injury: An event-related fMRI investigation. *Brain and Cognition, 54*(2), 136–138.

Fales, C. L., Vanek, Z. F., & Knowlton, B. J. (2006). Backward inhibition in Parkinson's disease. *Neuropsychologia*, *44*(7), 1041–1049.

Filoteo, J. V., Maddox, W. T., Simmons, A. N., Ing, A. D., Cagigas, X. E., Matthews, S., & Paulus, M. P. (2005). Cortical and subcortical brain regions involved in rule-based category learning. *Neuroreport*, *16*(2), 111–115.

Forstmann, B. U., Brass, M., Koch, I., & von Cramon, D. Y. (2006). Voluntary selection of task sets revealed by functional magnetic resonance imaging. *Journal of Cognitive Neuroscience*, *18*(3), 388–398.

Garavan, H., Ross, T. J., Murphy, K., Roche, R. A., & Stein, E. A. (2002). Dissociable executive functions in the dynamic control of behavior: Inhibition, error detection, and correction. *NeuroImage*, *17*(4), 1820–1829.

Garth, J., Anderson, V., & Wrennall, J. (1997). Executive functions following moderate to severe frontal lobe injury: Impact of injury and age at injury. *Pediatric Rehabilitation*, *1*(2), 99–108.

Godefroy, O. (2003). Frontal syndrome and disorders of executive functions. *Journal of Neurology*, *250*(1), 1–6.

Greenwald, B. D., Burnett, D. M., & Miller, M. A. (2003). Congenital and acquired brain injury. 1. Brain injury: Rpidemiology and pathophysiology. *Archives of Physical Medicine and Rehabilitation*, *84*(3 Suppl 1), S3–S7.

Hayes, A. E., Davidson, M. C., Keele, S. W., & Rafal, R. D. (1998). Toward a functional analysis of the basal ganglia. *Journal of Cognitive Neuroscience*, *10*(2), 178–198.

Heinrichs, R. W., & Zakzanis, K. K. (1998). Neurocognitive deficit in schizophrenia: A quantitative review of the evidence. *Neuropsychology*, *12*(3), 426–445.

Hikosaka, O., & Isoda, M. (2010). Switching from automatic to controlled behavior: Cortico-basal ganglia mechanisms. *Trends in Cognitive Sciences*, *14*(4), 154–161.

Javitt, D. C., & Zukin, S. R. (1991). Recent advances in the phencyclidine model of schizophrenia. *The American Journal of Psychiatry*, *148*(10), 1301–1308.

Jersild, A. T. (1927). Mental set and shift. *Archives of Psychology*, *89*.

Karayanidis, F., Nicholson, R., Schall, U., Meem, L., Fulham, R., & Michie, P. T. (2006). Switching between univalent task-sets in schizophrenia: ERP evidence of an anticipatory task-set reconfiguration deficit. *Clinical Neurophysiology*, *117*(10), 2172–2190.

Kieffaber, P. D., Kappenman, E. S., Bodkins, M., Shekhar, A., O'Donnell, B. F., & Hetrick, W. P. (2006). Switch and maintenance of task set in schizophrenia. *Schizophrenia Research*, *84*(2–3), 345–358.

Kieffaber, P. D., O'Donnell, B. F., Shekhar, A., & Hetrick, W. P. (2007). Event related brain potential evidence for preserved attentional set switching in schizophrenia. *Schizophrenia Research*, *93*(1–3), 355–365.

Koch, I., Gade, M., Schuch, S., & Philipp, A. M. (2010). The role of inhibition in task switching: A review. *Psychonomic Bulletin & Review*, *17*(1), 1–14.

Konishi, S., Nakajima, K., Uchida, I., Kikyo, H., Kameyama, M., & Miyashita, Y. (1999). Common inhibitory mechanism in human inferior prefrontal cortex revealed by event-related functional MRI. *Brain*, *122*(Pt 5), 981–991.

Konishi, S., Nakajima, K., Uchida, I., Sekihara, K., & Miyashita, Y. (1998). No-go dominant brain activity in human inferior prefrontal cortex revealed by functional magnetic resonance imaging. *The European Journal of Neuroscience*, *10*(3), 1209–1213.

Lawrence, A. D., Sahakian, B. J., Hodges, J. R., Rosser, A. E., Lange, K. W., & Robbins, T. W. (1996). Executive and mnemonic functions in early Huntington's disease. *Brain, 119*(Pt 5), 1633–1645.

Leunissen, I., Coxon, J. P., Geurts, M., Caeyenberghs, K., Michiels, K., Sunaert, S., & Swinnen, S. P. (2013). Disturbed cortico-subcortical interactions during motor task switching in traumatic brain injury. *Human Brain Mapping, 34*(6), 1254–1271.

Levin, H., & Kraus, M. F. (1994). The frontal lobes and traumatic brain injury. *The Journal of Neuropsychiatry and Clinical Neurosciences, 6*(4), 443–454.

Logan, G. D., & Bundesen, C. (2003). Clever homunculus: is there an endogenous act of control in the explicit task-cuing procedure? *Journal of Experimental Psychology. Human Perception and Performance, 29*(3), 575–599.

Los, S. A. (1996). On the origin of mixing costs: Exploring information processing in pure and mixed blocks of trials. *Acta Psychol (Amst.), 94*, 145–188.

MacDonald, A. W., 3rd, Cohen, J. D., Stenger, V. A., & Carter, C. S. (2000). Dissociating the role of the dorsolateral prefrontal and anterior cingulate cortex in cognitive control. *Science, 288*(5472), 1835–1838.

Manoach, D. S., Lindgren, K. A., Cherkasova, M. V., Goff, D. C., Halpern, E. F., Intriligator, J., & Barton, J. J. (2002). Schizophrenic subjects show deficient inhibition but intact task switching on saccadic tasks. *Biological Psychiatry, 51*(10), 816–826.

Mayr, U., Diedrichsen, J., Ivry, R., & Keele, S. W. (2006). Dissociating task-set selection from task-set inhibition in the prefrontal cortex. *Journal of Cognitive Neuroscience, 18*(1), 14–21.

Mayr, U., & Keele, S. W. (2000). Changing internal constraints on action: The role of backward inhibition. *Journal of Experimental Psychology. General, 129*(1), 4–26.

McDonald, B. C., Flashman, L. A., & Saykin, A. J. (2002). Executive dysfunction following traumatic brain injury: Neural substrates and treatment strategies. *NeuroRehabilitation, 17*(4), 333–344.

McDowd, J. M., Filion, D. L., Pohl, P. S., Richards, L. G., & Stiers, W. (2003). Attentional abilities and functional outcomes following stroke. *The Journals of Gerontology. Series B, Psychological Sciences and Social Sciences, 58*(1), P45–P53.

Mecklinger, A. D., von Cramon, D. Y., Springer, A., & Matthes-von Cramon, G. (1999). Executive control functions in task switching: Evidence from brain injured patients. *Journal of Clinical and Experimental Neuropsychology, 21*(5), 606–619.

Meiran, N. (1996). Reconfiguration of processing mode prior to task performance. *Journal of Experimental Psychology Learning Memory & Cognition, 22*, 1423–1442.

Meiran, N., & Daichman, A. (2005). Advance task preparation reduces task error rate in the cuing task-switching paradigm. *Memory & cognition, 33*(7), 1272–1288.

Meiran, N., & Gotler, A. (2001). Modelling cognitive control in task switching and ageing. *Eur. Journal of Cognitive Psychology, 13*, 165–186.

Meiran, N., Levine, J., & Henik, A. (2000). Task set switching in schizophrenia. *Neuropsychology, 14*(3), 471–482.

Mesholam-Gately, R. I., Giuliano, A. J., Goff, K. P., Faraone, S. V., & Seidman, L. J. (2009). Neurocognition in first-episode schizophrenia: A meta-analytic review. *Neuropsychology, 23*(3), 315–336.

Monchi, O., Petrides, M., Petre, V., Worsley, K., & Dagher, A. (2001). Wisconsin Card Sorting revisited: Distinct neural circuits participating in different stages of the task identified by event-related functional magnetic resonance imaging. *The Journal of Neuroscience*, *21*(19), 7733–7741.

Nagahama, Y., Okada, T., Katsumi, Y., Hayashi, T., Yamauchi, H., Oyanagi, C., . . . Shibasaki, H. (2001). Dissociable mechanisms of attentional control within the human prefrontal cortex. *Cerebral Cortex*, *11*(1), 85–92.

Nicholson, R., Karayanidis, F., Poboka, D., Heathcote, A., & Michie, P. T. (2005). Electrophysiological correlates of anticipatory task-switching processes. *Psychophysiology*, *42*(5), 540–554.

Owen, A. M., James, M., Leigh, P. N., Summers, B. A., Marsden, C. D., Quinn, N. P., . . . Robbins, T. W. (1992). Fronto-striatal cognitive deficits at different stages of Parkinson's disease. *Brain*, *115*(Pt 6), 1727–1751.

Pashler, H. (2000). Task switching and multitask performance. In S. Monsell & J. Driver (Eds.), *In control of cognitive processes* (pp. 277–308). Cambridge, MA: MIT Press.

Perlstein, W. M., Larson, M. J., Dotson, V. M., & Kelly, K. G. (2006). Temporal dissociation of components of cognitive control dysfunction in severe TBI: ERPs and the cued-Stroop task. *Neuropsychologia*, *44*(2), 260–274.

Pohl, P. S., McDowd, J. M., Filion, D., Richards, L. G., Stiers, W., & Kluding, P. (2007). Task switching after stroke. *Physical Therapy*, *87*(1), 66–73.

Pollux, P. M. (2004). Advance preparation of set-switches in Parkinson's disease. *Neuropsychologia*, *42*(7), 912–919.

Pollux, P. M., & Robertson, C. (2002). Reduced task-set inertia in Parkinson's disease. *Journal of Clinical and Experimental Neuropsychology*, *24*(8), 1046–1056.

Praamstra, P., & Plat, F. M. (2001). Failed suppression of direct visuomotor activation in Parkinson's disease. *Journal of Cognitive Neuroscience*, *13*(1).

Ravizza, S. M., & Ciranni, M. A. (2002). Contributions of the prefrontal cortex and basal ganglia to set shifting. *J ournal of Cognitive Neuroscience*, *14*(3), 472–483.

Reichenberg, A., & Harvey, P. D. (2007). Neuropsychological impairments in schizophrenia: Integration of performance-based and brain imaging findings. *Psychological Bulletin*, *133*(5), 833–858.

Rogers, R. D., & Monsell, S. (1995). The costs of a predictable switch between simple cognitive tasks. *Journal of Experimental Psychology General*, *124*, 207–231.

Rogers, R. D., Sahakian, B. J., Hodges, J. R., Polkey, C. E., Kennard, C., & Robbins, T. W. (1998). Dissociating executive mechanisms of task control following frontal lobe damage and Parkinson's disease. *Brain*, *121*(Pt 5), 815–842.

Rubia, K., Smith, A. B., Brammer, M. J., & Taylor, E. (2003). Right inferior prefrontal cortex mediates response inhibition while mesial prefrontal cortex is responsible for error detection. *NeuroImage*, *20*(1), 351–358.

Rubinstein, J. S., Meyer, D. E., & Evans, J. E. (2001). Executive control of cognitive processes in task switching. *Journal of Experimental Psychology. Human Perception and Performance*, *27*(4), 763–797.

Scheibel, R. S., Newsome, M. R., Steinberg, J. L., Pearson, D. A., Rauch, R. A., Mao, H., . . . Levin, H. S. (2007). Altered brain activation during cognitive control in patients with moderate to severe traumatic brain injury. *Neurorehabilitation and Neural Repair*, *21*(1), 36–45.

Soeda, A., Nakashima, T., Okumura, A., Kuwata, K., Shinoda, J., & Iwama, T. (2005). Cognitive impairment after traumatic brain injury: A functional magnetic resonance imaging study using the Stroop task. *Neuroradiology*, *47*(7), 501–506.

Sozda, C. N., Larson, M. J., Kaufman, D. A., Schmalfuss, I. M., & Perlstein, W. M. (2011). Error-related processing following severe traumatic brain injury: An event-related functional magnetic resonance imaging (fMRI) study. *International Journal of Psychophysiology, 82*(1), 97–106.

Sprengelmeyer, R., Lange, H., & Homberg, V. (1995). The pattern of attentional deficits in Huntington's disease. *Brain, 118*(Pt 1), 145–152.

Stoet, G., & Snyder, L. H. (2006). Effects of the NMDA antagonist ketamine on task-switching performance: Eevidence for specific impairments of executive control. *Neuropsychopharmacology, 31*(8), 1675–1681.

Swainson, R., Cunnington, R., Jackson, G. M., Rorden, C., Peters, A. M., Morris, P. G., & Jackson, S. R. (2003). Cognitive control mechanisms revealed by ERP and fMRI: Evidence from repeated task-switching. *Journal of Cognitive Neuroscience, 15*(6), 785–799.

Waszak, F., Hommel, B., & Allport, A. (2003). Task-switching and long-term priming: Role of episodic stimulus-task bindings in task-shift costs. *Cognitive Psychology, 46*(4), 361–413.

Werheid, K., Koch, I., Reichert, K., & Brass, M. (2007). Impaired self-initiated task preparation during task switching in Parkinson's disease. *Neuropsychologia, 45*(2), 273–281.

Werheid, K., Ziessler, M., Nattkemper, D., & Yves von Cramon, D. (2003). Sequence learning in Parkinson's disease: The effect of spatial stimulus-response compatibility. *Brain and Cognition, 52*(2), 239–249.

Werheid, K., Zysset, S., Muller, A., Reuter, M., & von Cramon, D. Y. (2003). Rule learning in a serial reaction time task: An fMRI study on patients with early Parkinson's disease. *Brain Research. Cognitive Brain Research, 16*(2), 273–284.

Witt, K., Daniels, C., Schmitt-Eliassen, J., Kernbichler, J., Rehm, S., Volkmann, J., Deuschl, G. (2006). The impact of normal aging and Parkinson's disease on response preparation in task-switching behavior. *Brain Research, 1114*(1), 173–182.

Woodward, T. S., Bub, D. N., & Hunter, M. A. (2002). Task switching deficits associated with Parkinson's disease reflect depleted attentional resources. *Neuropsychologia, 40*(12), 1948–1955.

Wylie, G., & Allport, A. (2000). Task switching and the measurement of "switch costs." *Psychological Research, 63*(3–4), 212–233.

Wylie, G. R., Clark, E. A., Butler, P. D., & Javitt, D. C. (2010). Schizophrenia patients show task switching deficits consistent with N-methyl-d-aspartate system dysfunction but not global executive deficits: Implications for pathophysiology of executive dysfunction in schizophrenia. *Schizophrenia Bulletin, 36*(3), 585–594.

Wylie, G. R., Javitt, D. C., & Foxe, J. J. (2003a). Cognitive control processes during an anticipated switch of task. *The European Journal of Neuroscience, 17*(3), 667–672.

Wylie, G. R., Javitt, D. C., & Foxe, J. J. (2003b). Task switching: A high-density electrical mapping study. *NeuroImage, 20*(4), 2322–2342.

Wylie, G. R., Javitt, D. C., & Foxe, J. J. (2004a). Don't think of a white bear: An fMRI investigation of the effects of sequential instructional sets on cortical activity in a task-switching paradigm. *Human Brain Mapping, 21*(4), 279–297.

Wylie, G. R., Javitt, D. C., & Foxe, J. J. (2004b). The role of response requirements in task switching: Dissolving the residue. *Neuroreport, 15*(6), 1079–1087.

Wylie, G. R., Javitt, D. C., & Foxe, J. J. (2006). Jumping the gun: Is effective preparation contingent upon anticipatory activation in task-relevant neural circuitry? *Cerebral Cortex, 16*(3), 394–404.

Wylie, G. R., Murray, M. M., Javitt, D. C., & Foxe, J. J. (2009). Distinct neurophysiological mechanisms mediate mixing costs and switch costs. *Journal of Cognitive Neuroscience, 21*(1), 105–118.

Yehene, E., Meiran, N., & Soroker, N. (2008). Basal ganglia play a unique role in task switching within the frontal-subcortical circuits: Evidence from patients with focal lesions. *Journal of Cognitive Neuroscience, 20*(6), 1079–1093.

12

Task Switching in Psychiatric Disorders

SUSAN M. RAVIZZA AND RUTH E. SALO

INTRODUCTION

Task switching is the ability to change one's current mode of processing to respond to the demands of a new situation. This ability has been of interest to those studying cognitive function in psychiatric populations because many of these disorders are characterized by inflexible behaviors. The motivation for these studies is to determine whether such inflexible behaviors may be due to a deficit in task switching or in cognitive control more generally. For example, schizophrenia, autism, and unipolar depression can be framed as perseverative disorders in which patients appear unable to switch away from inappropriate thoughts or behaviors. One goal is to review studies that have investigated task switching abilities in clinical populations, to assess whether core deficits in task switching could underlie the inflexible behaviors observed in these disorders. A second goal is to use this research as a basis for expanding, confirming, or revising ideas about the nature of task switching.

It is perhaps not surprising that task switching has been investigated as a potential source of inflexible behaviors given the range of cognitive abilities that are required to perform a task switch. Some of these processes include selecting and retrieving task-relevant information from memory (Horoufchin, Phillip, & Koch, 2011; Mayr & Kliegl, 2000; Rubenstein, Meyer, & Evans, 2001), focusing attention on relevant features or locations in the environment (Chiu & Yantis, 2009; Meiran & Marciano, 2002; Wager et al., 2005), ignoring task-irrelevant stimuli (Meiran, Chorev, & Sapir, 2000; Rogers & Monsell, 1995), inhibiting previous task sets (Lien, Ruthruff, & Kuhns, 2006; Mayr & Keele, 2000) overcoming automatic prepotent response tendencies (Barber & Carter, 2004), response selection (Hubner et al., 2004) monitoring the external or internal conditions to determine if or when a task switch is necessary (Arrington & Yates, 2009; Brown & Marsden, 1988), and evaluating instructive and motivational feedback to modify performance (Ravizza et al., 2012). Disruption of any of these processes might affect task switching with the type of deficit dependent on the process or processes that are compromised. In some ways, attempting to find the existence of a task switching impairment in a clinical population is less instructive than determining the conditions under which a potential task switching impairment is observed. For example, neuropsychological research with Parkinson's disease patients has shown switching impairments only when response selection demands are high (Cools et al., 2001; Ravizza & Ciranni, 2002; Ravizza et al., 2012). Such a finding provides converging evidence for several ideas: (a) Parkinson's disease is related to a core impairment of action selection, which may affect other executive functions in addition to task switching; (b) response selection is a component that determines the length of time needed to switch between tasks; and (c) task switching is determined, in part, by computations provided by the dorsal striatum, the region compromised in Parkinson's disease. Thus, research determining the conditions in which those with Parkinson's disease demonstrate a task switching impairment has more impact on our understanding of the mechanism of task switching than merely detecting whether a task switching impairment is present or absent.

This focus on the mechanisms underlying task switching has become prevalent in neuropsychological research with patients with focal lesions (Aron et al., 2004; Owen et al., 1993; Ravizza & Ciranni, 2002; Ravizza & Ivry, 2001; Rogers et al., 1998; Yehene, Meiran, & Soroker, 2008), but investigations of task switching in clinical population have only recently attempted to provide a more mechanistic account of task switching impairments. This may be due to the greater focus on emotional and social impairments related to many psychiatric disorders rather than associated cognitive deficits. In schizophrenia, for example, medication effectiveness has typically been evaluated by assessing the level of improvement in psychotic symptoms such as hallucinations rather than its effectiveness at restoring potential deficits in cognition (Meltzer & McGurk, 1999). Cognitive dysfunction in psychiatric disorders has been argued to affect daily functions and studies have begun to examine these processes in more detail (Green, Kern, & Heaton, 2004a, Green et al., 2004b).

Initial investigations of task switching relied on standardized tasks known to target executive function and frontal pathology. The Wisconsin Card Sorting Task (WCST) is a measure that is frequently used to assess task switching impairments in various psychiatric disorders. In this task, participants must sort cards according to three possible categories—color, shape, or number. Categorical rules are not provided to participants who must generate a potential rule, monitor whether the sorting rule is appropriate based on instructive feedback ("Correct," "Incorrect"), and either maintain or shift the rule. When participants have successfully sorted ten consecutive cards using the appropriate categorical rule, the relevant rule changes without notice. Several psychiatric disorders are associated with poor performance on the WCST (Table 12.1). Given that one component of this task involves the ability to switch between categorical rules, it has some diagnostic utility; that is, if patients perform well on the test, task switching abilities, at least the ability to switch between rules, may be presumed to be intact. Its utility is decreased, however, in determining the presence of a task switching deficit if

Table 12.1. SUMMARY OF TASK SWITCHING STUDIES IN FOUR CLINICAL POPULATIONS

Disorder	WCST	EDS of CANTAB	Spatial Switching Task	Specific Impairment	Neural Findings
Schizophrenia	Impaired	Impaired	Normal	Rule switching	Switch cost not related to activity of frontal cortex; Hyperactivity of parietal cortex
Autism	Impaired	Mixed	Normal	Switching quickly between auditory and visual streams	Hyperactivity of parietal cortex
ADHD	Normal	Normal	Normal	Switching with response interference	Hypoactivity of fronto-parietal network
Depression	Impaired	Impaired	Normal	Less inhibition of previous task set; Using motivational feedback to lower shift cost	Hypoactivity of frontoparietal network

WCST = Wisconsin Card Sorting Task; EDS = extradimensional shift; CANTAB = Cambridge Neuropsychological Test and Assessment Battery.

participants perform poorly on the test. For example, performance would be poor if participants were impaired on the ability to generate a rule even if switching between rules were intact. This makes it difficult to determine how task switching impairments may differ between psychiatric disorders. In fact, performance on the WCST was equivalent in two groups of patients with different clinical diagnoses (i.e., unipolar depression or schizophrenia) and little symptom overlap; that is, both groups completed fewer categories and made more perseverative errors than healthy control subjects (Moritz et al., 2002). Thus, the WCST may not isolate cognitive processes to the degree necessary to dissociate between the types of impairment observed in separate psychiatric populations.

The Cambridge Neuropsychological Test Automated Battery (CANTAB) was developed to remediate some of the problems with the WCST. In particular, the CANTAB sought to isolate task switching abilities using incremental tests that build on more basic abilities and then progresses to more advanced processes. For example, simple visual discrimination and feedback processing assessments are presented earlier in the sequence than the test of task switching. Most relevant to task switching is the final levels of the test (i.e., extradimensional shifting [EDS]). Participants are presented with two compound stimuli composed of shapes with superimposed line figures, which are presented on the left and right sides of the computer screen. First, participants learn to select one of the shapes but then have to switch between dimensions and determine which of the line drawings should be selected. While the step-wise procedure allows for a better isolation of component processes, participants who fail the early levels are never tested on the EDS; that is, it is assumed that these participants will fail the EDS level. Thus, this series of tests cannot directly assess the mechanism producing a task switching failure as no data are collected on task switching. Similar to the WCST, different patient populations have not shown dissociable patterns of performance if they reach the EDS level (McKirdy et al., 2009).

As interest in cognitive deficits associated with psychiatric disorders has evolved, researchers have turned to nonstandardized experimental designs developed by cognitive psychologists. One paradigm, in particular, has been used to test task switching deficits in multiple groups of patients with psychiatric disorders (Meiran, 1996). In this task, participants switch between classifying stimuli, presented in one cell of a 2 × 2 grid, in two dimensions, horizontally or vertically. Arrow cues are presented before the onset of the stimulus and instruct the participant to make either a left/right or up/down decision on the current trial. This task can be modified to assess the contribution of various processes to the shift cost. For example, response keys can be univalent or bivalent; in the bivalent condition, two keys are used to respond, one for "left" and "up" and another for "right" and "down," whereas each judgment is mapped to a different key in the univalent condition. By modifying aspects of the design, different contributions to the shift cost can be assessed and it may be possible to observe different patterns of deficits across clinical populations.

Studies using nonstandardized tests to isolate task switching components are becoming more frequent, but are relatively rare compared with studies using the WCST or CANTAB. In particular, preparation effects have been examined by manipulating the time between the onset of the cue and the presentation of the task set in order to determine whether patients with clinical disorders can take advantage of advance planning to reduce the shift cost (Jamadar, Michie, & Karayanidis, 2010; Karayanidis et al., 2006; King et al., 2007; Meiran et al., 2010). Some work has examined whether switching is primarily impaired when switches must be endogenously driven rather than triggered by explicit cues (Poljac et al., 2010; Van Eylen et al., 2011). Studies have also investigated the role of response inhibition and its role in task switching given that many disorders have shown a diminished ability to inhibit abnormal behaviors (Cepeda, Cepeda, & Kramer, 2000; King et al., 2007; Stoet & Lopez, 2011). Other research questions have focused on whether task switching deficits are selective to switches between rules compared with switches of visuospatial attention (Ravizza et al., 2010) and whether clinical populations might have particular problems in inhibiting the previous task set (Whitmer & Banich, 2007). These studies have provided some insights into why those with a psychiatric disorder may have difficulty switching between tasks.

In the following sections, we will review studies targeting task switching performance in psychiatric disorders. While the term "task" can be somewhat unclear (Rogers & Monsell, 1995), we define a task as being an abstract construct composed of a group of rules or procedures that are applied to accomplish a particular goal. A change in task can be as simple as switching from identifying the color of an object to identifying its shape. A task switch can be distinguished from a stimulus switch or reversal both behaviorally and neurally (Dias, Robbins, & Roberts, 1996; Meiran, 1996). For example, responding that an object is red and then responding that the next object is blue would not be considered a switch in the task. The task, color identification, stays the same, but the stimulus to be identified within the task set has changed. This is usually called a stimulus switch, stimulus reversal, or an intradimensional switch and we do not review the literature on the ability of clinical populations to respond to this type of change.

We will review task switching performance in four types of psychiatric disorders—schizophrenia, autism, attention deficit/hyperactivity disorder, and unipolar depression. We have focused on these groups because of hypotheses that the abnormal behavior associated with these disorders may be due to a problem of cognitive control. Moreover, most of the work on task switching in psychiatric disorders has focused on the performance of these patients. In the first section, we will discuss recent neurobiological theories of the link between cognitive control deficits and psychiatric disorders. Next, we will focus on task switching performance in each of the psychiatric disorders that we are discussing. In each of these sections, we will discuss both behavioral and neural mechanisms that may be impaired for each group. At the end of the paper, we will discuss conclusions based on the work to date and the impact of this research for understanding cognitive control deficits in psychiatric disorders as well as the insights it provides into the nature of task switching.

COGNITIVE CONTROL IN PSYCHIATRIC DISORDERS

There are two recent neurobiological models that would account for the presence of executive function impairments and, by implication, task switching impairments in multiple psychiatric disorders (Marin, 2012; Menon, 2011). At the neuronal level, Marin (2012) argues that dysfunction of interneurons, the cells that establish inhibitory circuits in the brain, may be prevalent across many psychiatric disorders such as schizophrenia and autism. Interneurons are thought to be especially important for gating relevant signals into processing pathways given their role in modulating excitatory and inhibitory inputs to neurons. Information gating might be especially important for executive functions like task switching, which rely on an ability to update and maintain task relevant information for flexible responding. Primary support for this idea comes from research with mouse models of schizophrenia and post mortem studies of the brains of patients with schizophrenia. In particular, interneurons located in the dorsolateral prefrontal cortex show a decrease in the expression of enzymes (e.g., GAD67) that affect the ability of these neurons to inhibit excitatory pyramidal cells. As will be seen in the following review, all the disorders discussed here seem to be linked to problems of inhibition ranging from difficulty in selecting among competing response rules to being unable to inhibit depressive thoughts. While connections between dysfunction at the neural level and behavior have yet to be made, this theory suggests that task switching impairments may be linked to a larger deficit in behavioral inhibition.

At the level of brain networks, Menon (2011) argues that psychiatric disorders can be understood through assessing the interactions among three large-scale neural networks—the central executive, default mode, and salience networks. In particular, disruption of the central executive network, a frontoparietal system important for goal-directed behavior, is present in virtually every psychiatric disorder (Menon). However, it is the aberrant pattern of dynamic interplay of the three networks that determines how problems in cognitive control may be expressed in psychiatric disorders. For example, activity of the default mode network (neural regions that are reliably deactivated during task performance and associated with autobiographical cognition) is excessively coupled to activity of the salience network (neural regions that determines the relevance of incoming sensory or internal information) in depression. This might result in the prevalence of ruminating depressive thoughts that then affect processing of the central executive network. In contrast, schizophrenia may be associated with dysfunction of all three networks. The fact that functioning of each of these networks affects the others may account for the prevalence of cognitive control deficits in a wide range of psychiatric disorders.

Both theories suggest some commonalities in cognitive control deficits in psychiatric disorders. The potential similarities in the source of cognitive control deficits, however, have different forms of expression. As will be reviewed below, the patterns of impairment in task switching are different between groups (see Table 12.1).

Schizophrenia

Much of the research on task switching in clinical populations has focused on potential switching deficits in schizophrenia. The reason for this emphasis is that schizophrenia is associated with structural and functional abnormalities in neural regions that are presumed to be important for task switching performance; namely, the dorsolateral prefrontal cortex (DLPFC) and anterior cingulate cortex (ACC) (Andreasen et al., 1986, 1992; Barch et al., 2001, 2003a; Kerns et al., 2005; MacDonald et al., 2005; Niznikiewicz, Kubicki, & Shenton, 2003; Shepherd et al., 2012). These regions are engaged in fMRI studies of task switching (Brass & von Cramon, 2004; Hyafil, Summerfield, & Koechlin, 2009; Kim et al., 2011; Ravizza

& Carter, 2008; Wylie, Javitt, & Foxe, 2004; Yeung et al., 2006) and patients with damage to the DLPFC have shown deficits in task switching performance (Aron et al., 2004; Ravizza & Ciranni, 2002, Rogers et al., 1998). The onset of schizophrenia is typically observed in early adulthood, which is consistent with its association with frontal abnormalities as these regions continue to develop into the late teens. Also consistent with a frontal impairment, schizophrenia is associated with poor cognitive control on tasks in which responding is not habitual such as the Stroop task (Cohen et al., 1999, Westerhausen, Kompus, & Hugdahl, 2011). Interestingly, major behavioral deficits in task switching have not been found in this disorder despite cognitive impairments in other domains.

Schizophrenia is a complex disorder characterized by behavioral symptoms in three areas: (a) delusions and hallucinations, (b) affective symptoms such as blunted affect and anhedonia, and (c) disorganized thoughts and/or speech (DSM-IV-TR, American Psychiatric Association, 2000). It is the latter set of symptoms that are thought to be directly associated with reduced cognitive control, although certainly a loss of motivation associated with negative symptoms could indirectly affect cognition. In general, however, performance in several cognitive tasks has been correlated with the severity of disorganization symptoms (Barch et al., 2003a; Cohen et al., 1999; Kerns & Berenbaum, 2003). For example, disorganization was related to performance on the Stroop task, the AX Continuous Performance task, and a lexical ambiguation task (Cohen et al., 1999) as well as performance on the WCST (Dibben et al., 2009; Nieuwenstein et al., 2001). In the domain of task switching, task switching performance has not been found to be reliably related to the severity of disorganization symptoms. Two studies conducted by the same research group showed mixed results. One study reported that the severity of disorganized symptoms was related to extradimensional shifting (Pantelis et al., 1999) while the other found no relationship with extradimensional shifting (Pantelis et al., 2004). In a separate study, disorganization was not related to switching between sets of stimulus–response rules (Ravizza et al., 2010). Unfortunately, many studies of task switching have not reported correlations between symptoms and cognitive performance. It will be important for future research to determine if task switching, like other forms of cognitive control, is related to the level of disorganization observed in the behavior of schizophrenia patients.

The mixed results concerning the relationship of disorganization symptoms and task switching is also reflected in the fact that task switching deficits are not reliably observed across paradigms. Support for a task switching deficit in schizophrenia is primarily observed in studies of discrimination-learning using the CANTAB (Pantelis et al., 1999) or in the WCST (Laws, 1999). Patients with schizophrenia perform poorly in the CANTAB (Hutton et al., 1998; Pantelis et al., 2004) and they take longer than controls to learn which stimulus is the target even before shifting is required (Pantelis et al., 1999). Patients with schizophrenia also show a perseverative deficit on the WCST (Everett et al., 2001, although see Laws, 1999). Given our previous discussion of the WCST and CANTAB tests, however, it is difficult to be certain whether a deficit in task switching is the cause of poor performance in these participants or is due to impairment of some other process needed to perform well in this paradigm. In fact, one study that compared task switching performance between patients with schizophrenia and patients with unipolar depression did not report group differences on the CANTAB (McKirdy et al., 2009); that is, both groups showed impaired extradimensional shifting suggesting that motivational deficits might also be impairing performance in addition to the ability to switch tasks per se.

In paradigms that place lower demands on non–switch-related processes (e.g., processing feedback), task switching was found to be intact among patients with schizophrenia once response speed was corrected for general response slowing (Finke et al., 2011; Franke et al., 2007; Jamadar, Michie, & Karayanidis, 2010; Karayanidis et al., 2006; Kieffaber, 2007; Manoach et al., 2002; Meiran, 2000; Wylie et al., 2008). Moreover, the effect of advance preparation for reducing the shift cost was the same for patients and controls (Jamadar et al., 2010; Karayanidis et al., 2006).

Neuroimaging studies of task switching in schizophrenia provide some insight into these puzzling behavioral findings. Despite their normal performance, patients with schizophrenia show abnormal brain responses while task switching. ERP studies have reported that several components of the electrical signature are abnormal when comparing patients to controls. These studies demonstrated that the N1 component linked to early sensory processing activity and the P2 component associated with attentional control is abnormal for schizophrenia patients at the time when the task set is presented (Finke et al., 2011; Jamadar, Michie, & Karayanidis, 2010, Karayanidis et al., 2006); however, preparatory activity did not differ between groups in two of the studies (Finke et al., 2011; Jamadar et al., 2010). Abnormal brain response in the presence of intact behavior suggests that patients can compensate for potential neural dysfunction. Jamadar et al. (2010) provided evidence for compensation in a joint ERP and fMRI study. While performance was equivalent between controls and patients, shift cost was correlated with frontal and parietal regions in control participants whereas it was correlated only with the parietal regions for those with schizophrenia. Moreover, patients showed hyperactivity of the parietal cortex compared with controls whereas the difference in activity in the DLPFC was not significant. ERP activity for schizophrenia patients during task switch preparation was also correlated with parietal activity, but not frontal activity, in the fMRI experiment. This suggests that patients are able to use the parietal cortex to compensate for potential dysfunction of the frontal cortex in order to produce equivalent performance (Jamadar et al., 2010).

Compensation may not be possible in all cases, however, but will depend on differences in the computations need to switch between tasks. For example, task switching paradigms may vary in the demands placed on visuospatial attention as when participants must switch between selecting the color of an item or its shape. Other paradigms might emphasize the retrieval of information from memory, for example, when having to implement a different set of stimulus–response rules when the task switches. There is some evidence that schizophrenia is primarily associated with a task switching impairment when rules change from one trial to the next. In contrast, patients with schizophrenia do not seem to have a problem switching the focus of selective attention to a different visual feature. For example, one study asked participants to judge whether two objects were the same size or the same shape and the rules for responding were constant for each type of judgment (Kieffaber et al., 2007). Similar switch costs were observed when switching between size and shape judgments for patients and controls. More importantly, ERP activity did not differ between groups. In contrast to other studies that demonstrated intact behavior and abnormal neural activity in schizophrenia patients, this study found no group differences in either behavioral or neural function when the paradigm required a switch in the placement of visuospatial attention.

Another study directly contrasted performance in patients when either a rules or the relevant perceptual feature switched (Ravizza et al., 2010). In both conditions, participants switched between identifying letter or shape targets (Figure 12.1). In the rule-switching condition, stimuli were univalent, but participants had to retrieve a set of four S–R rules in order respond appropriately. In the visuospatial attention condition, the stimuli were bivalent, which placed high demands on attentional selection to orient toward the appropriate feature. However, rules were constant in the attention condition; that is, participants always respond to the spatial location of the target regardless of whether it was a shape or letter. Patients with schizophrenia displayed a higher shift cost in the rule switching condition even when shift cost was corrected for overall behavioral slowing. Consistent with the Kieffaber et al. (2007) study, patients with schizophrenia performed just as well as control participants when switching visuospatial attention to the relevant perceptual feature. These results are also consistent with the fMRI study of schizophrenia in which patients had hyperactivity of the parietal cortex; that is, a separate fMRI study using the same rule and attention switching design demonstrated that rule switching engaged the dorsolateral prefrontal cortex whereas visuospatial attention switching relied on the posterior parietal cortex, (Ravizza & Carter, 2008). This suggests that schizophrenia patients can compensate by engaging the parietal cortex to the degree that performance relies on selective attention to visual features of the stimulus (or the mapping between visual features and action) to guide behavior.

One problem with imputing a rule switching problem in schizophrenia is that several of the studies reviewed here implemented a switch in rules as part of the task and yet patients showed intact performance (Franke et al., 2007; Jamadar et al., 2010; Karayanidis et al., 2006; Manoach et al., 2002; Wylie et al., 2008). One way to reconcile the studies finding intact rule switching with the results of the Ravizza et al. (2010) study in which rule switching was impaired is to assess the amount or complexity of the rules that must be maintained. Most of the studies of rule switching had two S–R rules per task set (Franke et al., 2007; Jamadar et al., 2010; Karayanidis et al., 2006; Manoach et al., 2002; Wylie et al., 2008), whereas four S–R rules were used in each set in the Ravizza et al. (2010) study. One possibility is that larger rule sets may tax the working memory system to a greater degree than smaller rules sets. Frontally mediated working memory processes may be required to maintain and update larger or more complex rule

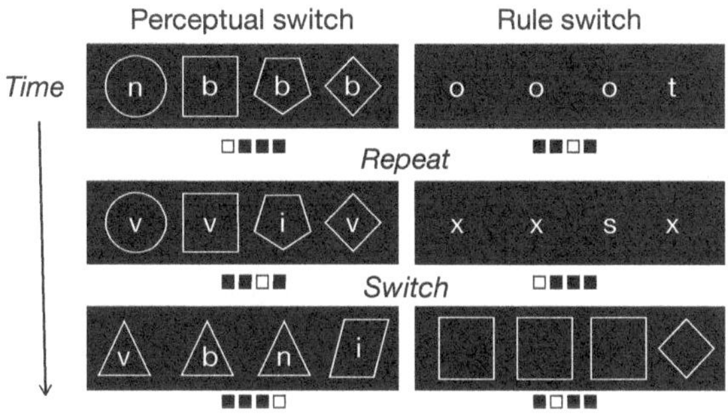

Figure 12.1 Examples of the two switch conditions used in Ravizza et al. (2010). In each condition, participants were asked to identify the odd-man-out (OMO). The four boxes under each display of letters and shapes indicate the appropriate key press for that trial. In the Perceptual condition (left side), participants responded by pressing a button that is spatially congruent to the odd-man-out. For example, the OMO in the top row is the letter "n" and participants would press the left-most key in a row of four response buttons to identify the spatial location of the OMO. Stimuli are bivalent, which requires participants to reorient visuospatial attention when the task switches; however, the rule of responding stays constant from one trial to the next. In the rule condition (right side), participants had to memorize and implement the correct response rules. Each letter was associated with one of the four response keys (s = "index", x = "middle", t = "ring", o = "little" finger). For example, the OMO in the top row, right-hand side is a "t" so pressing the key under the ring finger would be the correct response. Perceptual demands are lower in the condition; however, participants are required to retrieve the alternate set of response rules when the task switches. In these examples, the second trial in each condition is a repeat trial (letter to letter) and the third trial is a shift trial (letter to shape). Note that this sequence is used for illustrative purposes and that shift and repeat trials were randomized within each block of trials.

sets whereas the working memory processes subserved by the parietal lobe may be sufficient to bias simpler rule sets (Jamadar et al., 2010). Consistent with this idea, aspects of working memory have been found to be impaired in schizophrenia (cf. Barch et al., 2003b). A second possibility is that larger or more complex rule sets are more difficult to maintain because they are more vulnerable to interference from competing task sets. For example, Kieffaber et al. (2006) suggest that those with schizophrenia are less able to maintain a task set because of their difficulty in inhibiting irrelevant information (Kieffaber et al., 2006). Switching between larger sets of rules may also increase the intrusion of irrelevant task rules. Systematic investigations varying the amount or complexity of rules required for task switching would be helpful in assessing whether problems in rule processing underlie task switching deficits in schizophrenia.

The idea that schizophrenia is associated with an impairment in using rules to bias behavior is generally consistent with the hypothesis of frontal lobe function ing (Miller & Cohen, 2001). However, others have suggested that task switching is impaired because of a deficit in early sensory processing (Finke et al., 2011; Wylie et al., 2008). According to this view, an impairment in sensory processing may result in a weak representation of the task set, which results in less repetition priming benefits for those with schizophrenia. In support of this idea are ERP findings that schizophrenia patients showed an abnormal N1 sensory-linked response in both cue- and stimulus-locked signals and for both repeat and switch trials (Finke et al., 2011). It is unclear, however, how the sensory hypothesis would explain intact visuospatial attention switching in schizophrenia given that both rule- and perceptually based switching require sensory processing for performance. Moreover, the N1 component was not abnormal for visuospatial attention switching (Kieffaber et al., 2007). Rather than a pure sensory deficit, it may be that a deficit in biasing task rules affects the amplitude of the sensory response resulting in a weak representation of task rules in memory.

Research on task switching deficits in schizophrenia has resulted in several insights into the nature of task switching. First, this research has supported the idea that task switching is not a unitary process, but contains several component mechanisms such as rule biasing and visuospatial attention (Meiran, Kessler, & Adi-Japha, 2008; Rushworth et al., 2002). Second, this research suggests that parietally based compensation can remediate task switching deficits in some cases (Jamadar et al., 2010), although further work is necessary to fully understand the computational processes subserved by the parietal cortex in task switching. Third, this research suggests an interesting interaction between sensory processing impairments (Finke et al., 2011; Wylie et al., 2008) and how they affect or are affected by higher cognition.

Autism

Task switching has been of interest to those studying autism because this disorder is marked by a number of obsessive behaviors including inflexible routines, overly focused attention on specific objects, and repetitive movements (DSM-IV-TR, 2000). Investigators have attempted to link such inflexible behaviors to deficits in cognitive flexibility (see Geurts, Corbett, & Solomon, 2009, for a review). From this perspective, restricted behaviors that indicate an undue fascination with objects, interests or rituals may be a function of the diminished ability of those with autism spectrum disorder (ASD) to shift attentional focus to a new task. Much of this research has targeted task switching impairments in children with ASD as the social and communication impairments associated with this disorder are typically observed at a young age.

Courchesne and colleagues have suggested that the behavioral rigidity observed in ASD may be due to a difficulty in switching the focus of attention rapidly (Courchesne & Allen, 1997). They have demonstrated that rapidly switching attention between two streams of information (e.g., visual and auditory) is especially problematic for children with autism (Akshoomoff & Courchesne, 1992; Courchesne et al., 1994) (Figure 12.2b). If the task requires participants to switch between responding to a red square and a low-pitched tone, children with ASD are impaired when the time between targets is less than 2.5 seconds, but do not display deficits at longer time intervals. This line of research is supportive of the idea that behavioral inflexibility may be related to switching deficits particularly under time pressure.

Other forms of switching, however, are not as reliably impaired. Aside from the WCST in which those with ASD perform consistently worse than control participants, evidence is mixed as to whether task switching is generally impaired in this disorder. A recent review reported mixed findings across studies of cognitive flexibility deficits in ASD; in particular, impairments of extradimensional shifting and switching in the *modified* WCST were unreliable (Geurts, Corbett, & Solomon, 2009). One study found that those with ASD were actually *faster* to switch than controls when response interference was present presumably due to their greater focus on target features than on irrelevant features (Stoet & Lopez, 2011). Moreover, children's performance on a modified WCST was unrelated to the severity of repetitive and restricted behaviors thought to be a measure of behavior inflexibility in ASD (Dichter et al., 2010; although see, Yerys et al., 2009).

One idea that may explain the reliable task switching impairment observed in the studies of Courchesne and colleagues with the mixed findings on tasks like the modified WCST is the degree of explicit task instructions provided to the participant (Van Eylen et al., 2011). Very little explicit instruction is provided in the WCST given that a switch in the sorting rule is not signaled nor are any sorting rules provided to the participant at the outset. This is also the case in the visual/auditory switching task used by Courchesne and colleagues (Akshoomoff & Courchesne, 1992; Courchesne et al., 1994); that is, when participants detect a visual or auditory target, they have to remember that this signals a switch in monitoring the sensory stream and then initiate the switch. In task switching paradigms where the switch is explicitly cued, impairments are less likely to be observed in ASD. For example, Schmitz et al., 2006 asked adult participants to switch between making spatial judgments (i.e., left/right or up/down; Meiran, 1996) and arrow cues were used to indicate before every trial which task the participants should perform. No differences in the shift cost between ASD participants and controls were found. Moreover, no differences were observed between children with ASD and controls using modified versions of the WCST in which cues (Poljac et al., 2010) or stimulus–response rules were explicitly presented (Stoet & Lopez, 2011). Thus, ASD may be associated with the internal regulation of task switching using the implicit rules of the task (Van Eylen et al., 2011).

While this idea is intriguing, strong tests of this hypothesis remain to be done. First, it is critical to assess the effects of explicit cuing in conditions, which are matched for general difficulty (Knight & Silverstein, 2001). Requiring participants to generate, monitor, and implement switches when little explicit information is provided is a much more demanding situation than switching in response to an externally provided cue. Impairments in ASD might be due to a selective problem with internally generated switches or, alternatively, those conditions might be more sensitive to task switching deficits in general (MacDonald & Carter, 2002). Second, a direct comparison between implicit and explicit cuing conditions has not been performed within the same ASD group. Strong evidence for the explicit cuing hypothesis would be obtained by comparing how those with ASD perform when varying the degree of explicit cuing in conditions that are matched for difficulty.

While behavioral studies indicate task switching with explicit cues is intact in ASD, an fMRI study of task switching using explicit cues indicated that neural activity was abnormal. In the study of spatial switching described above with explicit cues, adults with ASD showed greater activation in the parietal cortex than control participants suggesting compensatory strategies (Schmitz et al., 2006). Note that this pattern of neural activity is strikingly similar to the fMRI study of task switching in schizophrenia in which the parietal cortex was hyperactive (Jamadar, Michie, & Karayanidis, 2010). Future work is necessary in order to determine the means by which the parietal cortex is compensating for performance. For example, perhaps the parietal lobe is engaged in processing explicit cues that allow those with ASD to switch tasks successfully. Other neural systems may be required when internal cues must prompt a switch and these neural systems are more compromised in ASD. In fact, activity in frontal regions is greater when task switching requires more endogenous control as is the situation when participants are not explicitly cued (Forstmann et al., 2005). This suggests that frontal lobe pathology may produce difficulty when task switching is more endogenously driven. As was suggested above, this hypothesis could be directly tested in ASD with the prediction that those with ASD would show less activation for endogenous task switching in regions of the prefrontal cortex.

Another fMRI study showed no difference in neural activity associated with task switching, however, it is unclear in this study whether task switching was necessary for performance (Shafritz et al., 2008). Participants were asked to identify targets while monitoring continuously presented stimuli. A shift was characterized as a change in the pre-specified target that participants were asked to identify within the run. Shifting impairments were assessed using behavioral and neural performance within the entire run of the task; this is quite different from typical experiments, which use the first trial after a switch occurs to assess switch performance (cf. Meiran et al., 1996; Rogers & Monsell, 1995). Indeed, control participants showed no shift cost in either accuracy or reaction time (RT) (Shafritz et al., 2008).

Task switching deficits have also been linked to the cerebellum in ASD. These studies compared the performance of an ASD group with the performance of those with damage to the cerebellum. In particular, Courchesne and colleagues argue that the impairments observed in switching between auditory and visual streams are a consequence of pathology of the cerebellum, which is known to be a marker of autism (Amaral, Schumann, & Nordahl, 2008). In the same way that the cerebellum coordinates rapid movements, this region is thought to facilitate rapid shifts of mental activity (Courchesne & Allen, 1997; Ozonoff et al., 2004). Thus, in the task described above, the cerebellum would help to shift attention between alternate sensory channels. In fact, further studies have shown that children with acquired cerebellar lesions perform equivalently to those with autism; that is, they are impaired when having to alternate attention between two information streams at rapid inter-target intervals (Akshoomoff & Courchesne, 1994; Courchesne et al., 1994). Moreover, event-related potentials recorded at the time indicate that cerebellar patients miss targets rather than simply fail to respond (Akshoomoff & Courchesne, 1994). Note, however, that these findings were not replicated in a larger sample of children with acquired cerebellar lesions in which no deficit in attention switching abilities was observed (Schoch et al., 2004).

The cerebellum is known to facilitate the coordination of movement and these studies used a control task requiring participants to focus their attention on one stream of information while making an equivalent number of movements (Akshoomoff & Courchesne, 1992; Akshoomoff & Courchesne, 1994; Courchesne et al., 1994) (Figure 12.2a). However, there was a difference in the general difficulty between the attention switching and focused attention conditions. The difference in difficulty introduces a potential confound to the interpretation of their results; indeed, it is not surprising that those with a clinical or neuropsychological disorder would be more impaired at the more difficult task. It may be that difficulty with responding rapidly will have an observable effect only when mental resources are taxed sufficiently as when participants must move quickly while switching attention. Moreover, damage to the cerebellum has long been known to affect basic motor function such as limb movement, speech, and eye gaze. Instead of trying to equate movements between conditions of unequal difficulty, Ravizza and Ivry (2001) implemented a control condition where participants had to switch attention between visual and auditory streams, but had to manually respond to only one type of information (Figure 12.2c). For example, participants were told to respond to red squares only if they had been preceded by a low-pitch tone. A significant improvement was observed in performance in adult cerebellar patients when movements were halved compared with the switching task that required a response to every target. Moreover, this was only true for those with damage to the cerebellum; a group of patients with motor difficulty due to dysfunction of frontostriatal pathways (i.e., Parkinson's disease) did not improve when motor demands were reduced (Ravizza & Ivry, 2001). These results were verified in an fMRI study demonstrating that the cerebellum was not engaged in the alternating attention task when motor demands were reduced; activity in this region was only observed when rapid responding was coupled with shifts of attention (Bischoff-Grethe et al., 2002).

Thus, there are two potential explanations for the performance of autistic individuals in this attention switching task. The first is that attention switching is not impaired, but that the greater motor effort required when individuals with autism have to respond quickly does not leave enough mental resources to shift attention appropriately. Alternatively, ASD may truly be related to switching deficits, but that this impairment is the result of pathology to the striatum or frontal lobes (also associated with autism) rather than the cerebellum.

ASD research has posed interesting questions about task switching. For example, how can a disorder that is linked to such rigid and inflexible behaviors be so weakly associated with task switching deficits? It may be that a more systematic

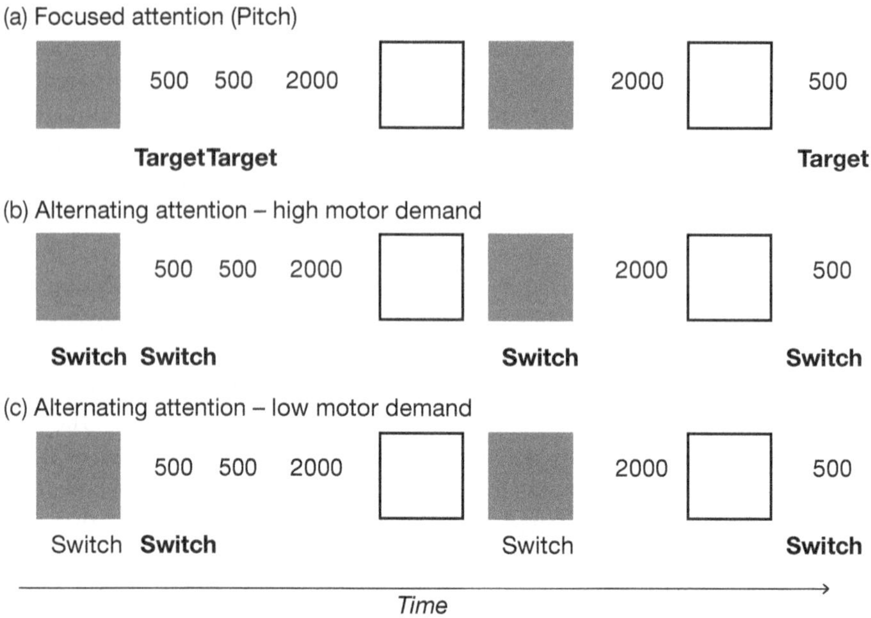

Figure 12.2 Examples of the conditions used in studies of switching between auditory and visual modalities in those with autism and cerebellar lesions. The Focused conditions (a; Color condition not pictured) served as a motor control in that participants made an equal number of responses but they did not have to switch between auditory and visual modalities. Words in bold-face indicate that a motor response was required for that stimulus. Participants only responded to low tones or red squares. The Alternating attention condition (b) required participants to switch between detecting red squares and low pitch tones while responding manually to each target. The Single-response conditions (c; Color condition not pictured) assessed the interaction of switching and motor performance. Participants were asked to alternate between auditory and visual modalities but motor demands were reduced given that participants only had to make a response to one of the targets. This is represented by the word "Switch" with bold-face indicating whether or not a motor response was required.

investigation of task switching impairments in ASD will reveal a reliably compromised cognitive process that affects both task switching performance and behavioral rigidity.

Attention Deficit/Hyperactivity Disorder (ADHD)

In some ways, ADHD symptoms are the opposite of those associated with autism. Instead of a rigid focus of attention on an object or detail, as is the case with ASD, those with ADHD demonstrate increased distractibility and impulsive behaviors (DSM-IV-TR, 2000). Given their symptom profile, those with ADHD might be expected to be quite good at switching between tasks as they might be able to disengage from task processing quickly. In line with this prediction, a meta-analysis of executive functioning in ADHD reported that performance on the WCST was only weakly associated with this disorder (Willcutt et al., 2005). This finding is in contrast to the strong link between WCST performance in both schizophrenia and autism described in the preceding sections.

There is also very little evidence in other paradigms that ADHD in children or adults is associated with a task switching deficit. Much of this work has been undertaken by Rubia and colleagues using the spatial switching paradigm (Meiran, 1996). This group has shown comparable switch costs and error rates between ADHD and control participants in three studies of spatial switching (Cubillo et al., 2010; Rubia et al., 2010; Smith et al., 2006). Switching performance in ADHD, however, was not BETTER than controls as might be predicted for those who could disengage from tasks quickly. Further work has demonstrated a subtle deficit when switching between color and shape judgments suggesting that those with ADHD might not prepare as well for a shift than controls. While switch cost was comparable between ADHD and control groups, a long preparation interval abolished the error cost in the control group but did not abolish the switch cost in the ADHD group (King et al., 2007).

Only one study has reported greater shift costs in children with ADHD compared with control participants, however, this was only the case when response interference from the irrelevant stimulus was high (Cepeda et al., 2000). Specifically, participants were asked to switch between making identity or quantity judgments for the numbers 1 and 3. Participants were presented with a set of 1 or a set of 3 numbers and those numbers were either the number "1" or the number "3" (i.e., "111," "333," "1," or "3"). They had to report the identity of the numbers or the quantity of the numbers. If the same response was correct for both the identity and quantity judgments, then responses to those stimuli were compatible rather than incompatible. For example, "111" is associated with incompatible responses; that is, the answer to the identity judgment is "1" and the answer to the quantity judgment is "3." In this experiment, the ADHD group had a greater shift cost, due to a higher RT in switch trials, than the control group, but only in the incompatible condition. Note, however, that the ADHD group was also slower overall and this overall slowing was not taken into account when calculating the shift cost. More instructive are the results of the ADHD group when medication (i.e., methylphenidate) status was manipulated. In this case, there was no main effect of RT (Experiment 2), but unmedicated children still had a higher shift cost in the incompatible condition compared with when they were in the medicated state (Cepeda et al., 2000).

These results are consistent with a meta-analysis of executive function disorders in ADHD (Willcutt et al., 2005). The relationship of ADHD to executive function was strongest when comparing tasks that required response inhibition such as the Stop signal Reaction time task (Willcutt et al.). Response interference was quite low in the spatial-switching task in which ADHD children performed well as each response was mapped to a different key (i.e., up, down, left, right) (Cubillo et al., 2010; Rubia et al., 2010; Smith et al., 2006). To date, however, switching under levels of high response interference has not been compared with an equally difficult control condition. Response incompatibility conditions are generally more difficult than the compatible conditions, making it difficult to interpret this effect as due to a selective problem with response interference rather than the increased sensitivity to shifting impairments in the more difficult condition. Interestingly, a recent study found response inhibition deficits in ADHD in blocks of single task performance, but response compatibility effects went away during task switching blocks (King et al., 2007). In this case, response inhibition deficits were found in the easier single task condition suggesting that response inhibition is a core deficit in ADHD. The mechanism by which response interference effects disappeared in the switching blocks requires further study.

Similar to schizophrenia and autism (Jamadar, Michie, & Karayanidis, 2010; Schmitz et al., 2006), children and adults with ADHD showed differences in neural activity compared with control participants even if switching performance was comparable (Cubillo et al., 2010; Rubia et al., 2010; Smith et al., 2006). In contrast to the findings of the two other clinical populations, the ADHD group showed *less* activity in neural regions rather than greater activity. Regions of hypoactivity were widespread and include the frontal, parietal, and temporal cortices as well as the striatum and cerebellum (Cubillo et al., 2010; Rubia et al., 2010; Smith et al., 2006), and symptoms of restlessness/inattention were negatively correlated with neural activity in these regions in one study (Cubillo et al., 2010).

This pattern of behavioral and neural responses is puzzling. In the case of schizophrenia, hyperactivity of the parietal lobe was argued to compensate for the intact behavioral performance observed in this group (Jamadar, Michie, & Karayanidis, 2010). In contrast, hypoactivity of brain regions when behavioral performance is intact suggests that those with ADHD were able to perform the task with less neural effort. While shifting was no better in ADHD than controls, the fMRI data suggest that ADHD might have some benefit to switching in that less neural activity is required to achieve the same level of performance.

fMRI studies of switching under conditions of high response interference in ADHD have not been undertaken. However, the pattern of performance in ADHD is similar to the type of task switching impairments observed in patients with Parkinson's disease; that is, task switching is primarily impaired in Parkinson's disease when there is high response interference (Cools et al., 2001; Ravizza & Ciranni, 2002). Both ADHD and Parkinson's disease are associated with abnormalities of striatal functioning; dopamine depletion in the dorsal striatum is the cause of Parkinson's disease and low striatal volumes has been found in ADHD (Castellanos et al., 1994). Behavioral impairments as well abnormal activity in the striatum might be observed in ADHD using a task switching paradigm in which response interference is high.

For ADHD, behavioral and cognitive flexibility seem to be consistent. In everyday functioning, those with ADHD are distractible and have a difficult time staying on task. This is mirrored by their relatively mild task switching impairments, the weak relationship with ADHD and performance on the WCST, and the fMRI findings of reduced neural engagement in the presence of intact switching behavior. Some evidence suggests that ADHD is associated with a core deficit in resolving response interference that may affect the ability to task switch. Further work in ADHD may provide insight into the role of response interference in task switching as well as possible cognitive mechanisms that might be beneficial for task switching performance.

Depression

Major or unipolar depression is a mood disorder characterized by feelings of chronic sadness and hopelessness, anhedonia, and difficulty concentrating (DSM-IV-TR, 2000). Of particular interest to task switching research is the relationship of depressive rumination to cognitive control. Rumination, a common feature of depression, is the repetitive focusing on the causes and symptoms of the negative affect experienced in depression (Nolen-Hoeksema & Morrow, 1991). People who ruminate more frequently often are more vulnerable to experiencing major depression and depression symptoms last longer in this group (Nolen-Hoeksema, 1991). Similar to those with ASD who fixate on details of an object, fixating on negative emotions and problems may be reflected in an inability to switch attentional focus to other topics. Most of the work on task switching has focused on the relationship of rumination to task switching performance (Davis & Nolen-Hoeksema, 2000; Meiran, 2010; Whitmer & Banich 2007), however, a recent study has examined the potential of disrupted motivational processing as a source of task switching impairments (Ravizza et al., 2012).

Depression is associated with poor performance on both the WCST and the extradimensional shifting component of the CANTAB (see Austin, Mitchell, & Goodwin, 2001, for a review; Heinzel et al., 2010). There is some evidence that rumination rather than overall level of depression is the key factor for performance on the WCST (Davis & Nolen-Hoeksema, 2000); that is, rumination was correlated with performance on the WCST even when self-reported depressive symptoms were factored out of the analysis. A study by Whitmer and Banich (2007) examined whether task switching in people with high and low levels of rumination was impaired because of a failure to inhibit previous task sets or difficulty in engaging the current task set. Participants had to switch between detecting targets in three dimensions—size, shape or orientation (Mayr & Keele, 2000). Shift cost was assessed as well as the effect of having to switch to a recently inhibited task set; for example, switching was compared when the task set was recently inhibited (e.g., size→ shape→ size) or not (e.g., size→ shape→ orientation). This effect is termed lag-2 inhibition (see Gade et al. of this volume). In this nonclinical sample, the level of depressive rumination was more predictive of inhibition effects than self-reported depressive symptoms. Neither depressive rumination nor depressive symptoms were predictors of the shift cost. The weak link between depressive rumination and switching performance was confirmed in another study of spatial switching (Meiran et al., 2010). Rumination was not linked to the shift cost, although high ruminators showed less of an effect of task preparation in reducing the shift cost. Taken together, these studies suggest that depressive rumination is not linked to problems in reconfiguring task set per se; that is, switch cost was not linked to depression in either study. Instead, depressive symptoms may be linked to a failure of inhibiting previously relevant information. Moreover, preparation effects may be due to either an inability to use this interval to inhibit previous task sets or because of lower motivation to prepare as we discuss in the following section.

Rather than a problem with task switching per se, it may be that depression is linked to problems in processing rewards or motivational feedback that indirectly affects task switching performance. For example, studies of the relationship of feedback processing with major depression or depressive symptoms have reported abnormal reactions to feedback, including enhanced reactivity to negative feedback (Santesso et al., 2008) and a lack of posterror slowing (Steele, Kumar, & Ebmeier,2007). A recent study showed that RT on switch trials improved in young adults when given nonmonetary, motivational feedback compared with no feedback (Ravizza et al., 2012). In this study, feedback consisted of the word "Correct!" and did not provide any information on speed of performance. Moreover, error rate was very low and, thus, participants rarely received any error feedback. Thus, simply presenting participants with feedback indicating that they were correct was enough to make them switch tasks more quickly. A further experiment demonstrated that the effect of feedback on the switch cost was related to the severity of self-reported depressive symptoms in older adults and those with Parkinson's disease (Ravizza et al., 2012). Thus, depression may be associated with deficits in using motivational feedback to improve task switching performance.

Depression in medication-naïve adolescents was also linked to hypoactivity in several regions important for cognitive control including the frontal and parietal cortex, anterior cingulate, and putamen in an fMRI study of task switching (Halari et al., 2009). However, behavioral performance between patients and controls did not differ. Reduced activation might mean that depressed individuals used less neural resources to obtain the same level of performance or the task was easy enough that even diminished activity in these regions was sufficient to perform the task. More fMRI studies are needed to get a more complete understanding of the neural effects of depression on task switching.

To date, research suggests that task switching may be affected in depression in situations when it is critical to inhibit previously relevant information and when feedback can motivate performance. Converging evidence could be used to validate these hypotheses; for example, activity of the striatum, associated with feedback processing, should be reduced for individual with depression if motivation is impaired. This research demonstrates that rumination may reflect a deficit in inhibiting previously relevant information that may indirectly affect task switching performance. Moreover, motivation, in the form of nonmonetary rewards affects task switching and emphasizes the importance of understanding the interaction of emotion and cognitive control.

CONCLUSION

The idea that task switching impairments underlie inflexible behaviors that are observed in clinical disorders is an intriguing hypothesis. What has emerged from research investigating task switching impairments in clinical population is that groups show difficulty in task switching only under some conditions. For example, those with ADHD seem minimally impaired in many different task switching paradigms and performance only declines when subjects have to overcome response interference while task switching (Cepeda et al., 2000). Based on this evidence, it seems unlikely that a core deficit in "task switching" is the cause of inflexible behaviors across these disorders. Instead, these inflexible behaviors may be associated with more general cognitive control processes that affect both the ability to task switch and the expression of behavioral flexibility. In the clinical disorders reviewed here, the cognitive control processes that are compromised appear to differ depending on the diagnosis.

Before summarizing the research findings and their interpretation, it is important to note that there are just a handful of studies investigating task switching performance in a mechanistic way in each group. The larger set of studies using standardized tests are not very informative about the specific processes that are impaired in each disorder although they can indicate the potential presence and, perhaps severity, of a task switching impairment. For example, it is noteworthy that those with ADHD do not show impairments in standardized tests of executive function. While we provide interpretation of research findings as they relate to specific cognitive mechanisms, we are cognizant of the fact that we are basing our discussion on a limited set of experiments. As such, these ideas should be taken as potential ways of interpreting the findings that need to be directly tested in future research.

Task switching is not uniformly impaired in schizophrenia. Instead, impairments are observed primarily when rules switch rather than when a switch occurs between relevant features of an object. Task paradigms that produce an observable deficit in task switching require participants to shift from one rule to another as in the WCST (Everett et al., 2001). In an experiment in which rule and visuospatial attention switches were directly compared, those with schizophrenia were selectively impaired on the rule switch condition (Ravizza et al., 2010). We suggested that reduced working memory abilities might explain why rule switching is selectively impaired in this disorder. Switching between features or locations rather than rules might not place high demands on working memory given that it is not necessary to update or retrieve task rules when the task switches. Consistent with this hypothesis are the reliable reports of working memory deficits associated with schizophrenia (cf. Barch et al., 2003b).

Those with an ASD, in contrast, perform well on rule switching paradigms such as the WCST (Guerts, Corbett, & Solomon, 2009) if rule switches are explicitly cued (Van Eylen et al., 2011). This is not the case for those with schizophrenia; that is, providing explicit cues to schizophrenia patients in the modified WCST improved performance, but did not eliminate deficits on this task (Hartman et al.,

2003). These findings have prompted some to claim that ASD is associated with problem in generating internally driven task switches (Van Eylen et al., 2011). There is some evidence supporting this in that task switching performance in this group is primarily disadvantaged when having to monitor when a task switch is necessary (Poljac et al., 2010; Stoet & Lopez, 2011; Van Eylen et al., 2011). While a promising idea, direct tests of this hypothesis have not been conducted in which external and internal switches are equated for difficulty. Moreover, it is still unclear what produces an impairment of internally driven task switching in ASD. There are several possibilities. It may be that they are unable to disengage from the current task without external prompting, they may lose track of how they last responded and so do not realize they are supposed to switch, or they may not be aware of more subtle environmental cues (e.g., error feedback) to switch tasks. These three possibilities might reflect deficits in either inhibition, working memory, or motivation.

In comparison to both ASD and schizophrenia, ADHD studies point to minimal deficits in task switching. Normal performance on the WCST (Willcutt et al., 2005) suggests that rule switching and switching with little explicit information is intact in this group. Instead, switching seems to be impaired when response interference is high (Cepeda et al., 2000). This is in contrast to both the ASD and schizophrenia groups. Those with ASD were actually faster to switch when response interference was high (Stoet & Lopez, 2011). Schizophrenia patients were impaired at rule switching even when response interference was low (Ravizza et al., 2010). ADHD is associated with impulsivity and distraction and it may be difficult for these individuals to ignore irrelevant stimulus or response information. In fact, it may be that a double dissociation could be obtained by comparing schizophrenia and ADHD groups in rule and visuospatial switching. Those with ADHD may perform well in the rule switching task in which there is little response or stimulus interference. In the visuospatial attention switching condition, the ADHD group may have difficulty selectively attending to the relevant feature when irrelevant stimuli are present.

Depression is associated with two potential deficits. The first is primarily linked to the severity of rumination in depression and the ability to inhibit previously relevant task sets (Whitmer & Banich, 2007). It is unclear whether this deficit is similar to the problem of inhibiting response interference associated with ADHD. It may be that inhibition fails at a higher level of abstraction in depression than ADHD; that is, inhibitory control may be reduced at the level of the task set in depression and the response or stimulus level for ADHD. For example, shifting performance was intact for depressed participants even when response interference was present (Whitmer & Banich, 2007). Note, however, that response compatibility was not assessed in this study. It is also unclear whether those with ADHD would show problems with failing to inhibit a previously relevant task set (i.e., lag-2 inhibition).

Another mechanism by which task switching may be affected in depression is through abnormal responses to motivational feedback (Ravizza et al., 2012). Depression is associated with anhedonia and studies have shown abnormal effects of rewards and punishments in this group (Santesso et al., 2008; see Eshel & Roiser, 2010 for a review). In general, the study of motivational feedback on task switching performance is understudied; however, rewards and punishments have been shown to modulate performance in working memory and cognitive control tasks such as the AX-CPT (Gilbert & Fiez, 2004; Locke & Braver, 2008; Taylor et al., 2004; see Pessoa, 2009, for a review). Thus, a second reason task switching may suffer is by reduced motivation to perform well.

In sum, it is heartening to observe that impairments in task switching are not identical across disorders. The implication is that the dysfunction of cognitive processes that produce an impairment of task switching may also be related to the different symptoms of behavioral inflexibility associated with each clinical disorder. However, we will argue that this link needs to more firmly established in the next section.

Challenges for Research of Task Switching in Clinical Disorders

We think that investigating task switching performance in clinical disorders is a promising way of understanding whether inflexible responding is due to a problem of cognitive control. There are some challenges, however, that need to be overcome in order to establish the link between clinical symptoms of inflexibility and cognitive control. In this section, we will suggest ways in which to meet these challenges including (a) relying more on cognitive control paradigms that isolate the phenomenon of interest, (b) equating conditions for their level of difficulty, (c) relating symptom severity to performance, and (d) making a priori predictions of the way brain activity relates to task switching performance.

There has been increasing use of paradigms that isolate particular cognitive processes of interest. Lag-2 inhibition (Whitmer & Banich, 2007), task set preparation (Jamadar, Michie, & Karayanidis, 2010; Karayanidis et al., 2006; King et al., 2007; Meiran et al., 2010), and response compatibility (Cepeda et al., 2000; King et al., 2007; Stoet & Lopez, 2011) have been systematically manipulated in behavioral studies with clinical populations. To make significant progress, it will be necessary to compare performance between groups on these tasks. For example, it is currently unknown whether there are similarities or differences in overcoming response or task interference in ADHD and depression. Moreover, using such tasks in the scanner is vital in order to make sense of the pattern of activity observed in fMRI studies. The goal is to associate cognitive functioning to brain abnormalities in clinical populations by varying the demand upon a cognitive process in isolation and observing whether brain activity tracks with increased demand upon that cognitive process in both typical and clinical populations.

When investigating whether a particular component of task switching is impaired, it is important to match this condition with another that is equated in difficulty. Task switching when response interference is present, for example, will be more difficult than when response interference is absent. The inclusion of a control condition that is difficult, but in a different manner, is critical in order to conclude that a clinical disorder is associated with a selective cognitive impairment (Knight & Silverstein, 2001). For example, response interference could be compared with a task with high stimulus interference (see Ravizza et al., 2012). Demonstrating that patients are impaired in response interference and not in an equally difficult control condition argues against the idea that the response interference condition is more sensitive to differences in control and patient groups (MacDonald & Carter, 2002).

A more specific understanding of the compromised processes is helpful in determining the cognitive sequelae of these disorders. However, it may also help in determining whether behavioral symptoms of the disorder are related to deficits in cognitive control. Some studies examined whether symptom severity was related to task switching performance, but not the majority. We argue that even if no relationship was found between symptom severity and performance, it is still important to report the null finding because it is possible that inflexible behaviors are not related to cognitive control, but are the result of some other cognitive/neural system. Moreover, clinical groups are variable in the severity and patterns of symptoms. For example, some schizophrenia patients report more symptoms of anhedonia whereas others are more disorganized. Linking symptoms with cognitive performance is important especially if no differences in performance are observed between patient and control groups. These differences in the patterns of symptoms may indicate different subgroups of patients that have more or less difficulty with cognitive control.

Data from behavioral and fMRI studies should provide converging evidence of task switching impairments. This has not been the case for fMRI studies of task switching in clinical disorders. Schizophrenia and ASD patients both show hyperactivity of the parietal cortex (see Table 12.1) while performance is intact. This has been argued to reflect compensatory strategies (Jamadar, Michie, & Karayanidis, 2010), but it is not clear whether this is true for both groups and, if so, whether both groups are compensating in the same way. ADHD and depression were associated with intact performance and hypoactivity of the parietal and frontal cortices. We suggested that this might reflect superior task switching abilities in ADHD since these individuals show little impairment in other forms of task switching. It is harder to make this case for depression since this group shows more widespread problems in task switching.

One reason for these ambiguous results is that these studies have, for the most part, used paradigms in which groups are not showing behavioral differences. A nice feature of equivalent performance between patient and control groups is that one cannot claim that neural differences in activity are due to differences in the experienced difficulty of the task. However, it becomes harder to decipher if neural activity was related to performance and, if so, how it was related. To overcome such problems, using a control condition in the scanner that is matched for difficulty could allow for the subtraction of neural regions that are just tracking general effort. Moreover, correlating activity with performance (Jamadar, Michie, & Karayanidis, 2010) or symptoms may be helpful in interpreting how brain abnormalities relate to cognitive functioning.

Insights on Task Switching From Clinical Research

Neuropsychological research has a rich tradition of informing theories of cognition. For example, studies of hippocampal amnesics lead to the idea of multiple types of memory and that memory could be thought of as a process rather than just a repository (Corkin, 2002). In the same way, we can evaluate how research with clinical populations informs our ideas of task switching.

From this review of the research, it is very apparent that task switching is a multicomponent construct. Each clinical group that we discussed has demonstrated a task switching impairment in some conditions but not others. Schizophrenia was associated with deficits in switching between rules but not when switching the focus of visuospatial attention. Those with ASD had no difficulty switching between tasks if explicit cues were provided, but had difficulty when there was less external guidance. Task switching impairments were observed only when response interference was present in the ADHD group. Depressed individuals may not be efficient task switchers under circumstances of high motivation or when strong inhibition of irrelevant task information is necessary. In all these groups, there was not a uniform deficit in task switching that was consistent across many different circumstances in which a task switch was required.

In fact, many of the problems observed with task switching might be attributed to deficits in other forms of cognitive control. For example, a core deficit in implementing response inhibition would affect task switching, multitasking, or reasoning. The pattern of results seen across these patient groups may have implications for theories of task switching, in particular, the idea that task switching is the process of reconfiguring mental states (see Monsell, 2003a for a review). This idea has been hotly debated in the literature with some arguing that switching requires the implementation of active reconfiguration (Monsell, 2003b), while others suggest that this process does not exist (Allport, Styles, & Hsieh, 1994; Altmann, 2003). According to the latter idea, task switching is not thought to invoke switch-specific processing; for example, one model suggests that semantic retrieval of task information occurs on every trial, but takes longer when the task changes because of a loss of priming from the previous task set rather than reconfiguration (Altmann & Gray, 2008).

The reconfiguration hypothesis would be supported if a group of patients were observed to have difficulty whenever a switch in the task was necessary regardless of other conditions like response interference or motivation. In the clinical realm, we do not find such a group, although perhaps those with ASD approach this criterion most closely. Those with ASD have difficulty switching between tasks without explicit cues, which might reflect a problem with task set reconfiguration that is remediated when given explicit guidance. As noted earlier, however, this type of task switching impairment in ASD has not been rigorously tested. It may be that we will not find a clinical or neuropsychological group that has a consistent and reliable task switching impairment because there is no "task switcher." Instead, other control processes such as working memory or inhibition may be responsible for producing impairments when a task switch is required. Thus, the results of research with clinical populations may be helpful in adjudicating between these two views of task switching.

In sum, the investigation of task switching abilities in clinical populations has been informative on a number of fronts. First, the knowledge of the conditions under which task switching deficits are observed provides insights into potential cognitive processes that are disturbed in each disorder. This is important in understanding the cognitive sequelae associated with clinical diagnoses. Second, each disorder is associated with behaviors and thoughts that are inflexible and are not adaptive for global functioning. If a link between these behaviors and cognitive control deficits is substantiated, this may have clinical relevance in terms of medication or remediation targets. Third, task switching impairments in clinical populations provide insight into our concept of "task switching." While we have listed some challenges that need to be met in order to make progress for this type of research, we think these investigations are informative to both cognitive and clinical psychologists.

REFERENCES

Akshoomoff, N. A., & Courchesne, E. (1992). A new role for the cerebellum in cognitive operations. *Behavioral Neuroscience, 106*(5), 731–738.

Akshoomoff, N. A., & Courchesne, E. (1994). ERP evidence for a shifting attention deficit in patients with damage to the cerebellum. *Journal of Cognitive Neuroscience, 6*(4), 388–399.

Allport, A., Styles, E. A., & Hsieh, S. (1994). Shifting intentional set: Exploring the dynamic control of tasks. In C. Umilta & M. Moscovitch (Eds.), *Attention and performance. XV: Conscious and Nonconscious information processing* (pp. 421–452). Cambridge, MA: MIT Press.

Altmann, E. M. (2003). Task switching and the pied homunculus: Where are we being led? *Trends in Cognitive Sciences, 7*(8), 340–341.

Altmann, E. M., & Gray, W. D. (2008). An integrated model of cognitive control in task switching. *Psychol Rev, 115*(3), 602–639.

Amaral, D. G., Schumann, C. M., & Nordahl, C. W. (2008). Neuroanatomy of autism. *Trends Neurosci, 31*(3), 137–145.

Andreasen, N., Nasrallah, H. A., Dunn, V., Olson, S. C., Grove, W. M., Ehrhardt, J. C., et al. (1986). Structural abnormalities in the frontal system in schizophrenia. A magnetic resonance imaging study. *Arch Gen Psychiatry, 43*(2), 136–144.

Andreasen, N. C., Rezai, K., Alliger, R., Swayze, V. W., 2nd, Flaum, M., Kirchner, P., et al. (1992). Hypofrontality in neuroleptic-naive patients and in patients with chronic schizophrenia. Assessment with xenon 133 single-photon emission computed tomography and the Tower of London. *Arch Gen Psychiatry, 49*(12), 943–958.

Aron, A. R., Monsell, S., Sahakian, B. J., & Robbins, T. W. (2004). A componential analysis of task-switching deficits associated with lesions of left and right frontal cortex. *Brain, 127*(Pt 7), 1561–1573.

Arrington, C. M., & Yates, M. M. (2009). The role of attentional networks in voluntary task switching. *Psychon Bull Rev*, *16*(4), 660–665.

American Psychiatric Association. (2000). *Diagnostic and statistical manual of mental disorders, fourth edition, text revised edition.* Washington, DC: Author.

Austin, M. P., Mitchell, P., & Goodwin, G. M. (2001). Cognitive deficits in depression: Possible implications for functional neuropathology. *British Journal of Psychiatry*, *178*, 200–206.

Barber, A. D., & Carter, C. S. (2004). Cognitive control involved in overcoming prepotent response tendencies and switching between tasks. *Cereb Cortex*, *15*(7), 899–912.

Barch, D. M., Carter, C. S., Braver, T. S., Sabb, F. W., MacDonald, A., 3rd, Noll, D. C., et al. (2001). Selective deficits in prefrontal cortex function in medication-naive patients with schizophrenia. *Arch Gen Psychiatry*, *58*(3), 280–288.

Barch, D. M., Carter, C. S., MacDonald, A. W., 3rd, Braver, T. S., & Cohen, J. D. (2003a). Context-processing deficits in schizophrenia: Diagnostic specificity, 4-week course, and relationships to clinical symptoms. *J Abnorm Psychol*, *112*(1), 132–143.

Barch, D. M., Sheline, Y. I., Csernansky, J. G., & Snyder, A. Z. (2003b). Working memory and prefrontal cortex dysfunction: Specificity to schizophrenia compared with major depression. *Biol Psychiatry*, *53*(5), 376–384.

Bischoff-Grethe, A., Ivry, R. B., & Grafton, S. T. (2002). Cerebellar involvement in response reassignment rather than attention. *Journal of Neuroscience*, *22*(2), 546–553.

Brass, M., & von Cramon, D. Y. (2004). Decomposing components of task preparation with functional magnetic resonance imaging. *J Cogn Neurosci*, *16*(4), 609–620.

Brown, R. G., & Marsden, C. D. (1988). Internal versus external cues in the control of attention in Parkinson's disease. *Brain*, *111*, 323–345.

Castellanos, F. X., Giedd, J. N., Eckburg, P., Marsh, W. L., Vaituzis, A. C., Kaysen, D., et al. (1994). Quantitative morphology of the caudate nucleus in attention deficit hyperactivity disorder. *Am J Psychiatry*, *151*(12), 1791–1796.

Cepeda, N. J., Cepeda, M. L., & Kramer, A. F. (2000). Task switching and attention deficit hyperactivity disorder. *J Abnorm Child Psychol*, *28*(3), 213–226.

Chiu, Y. C., & Yantis, S. (2009). A domain-independent source of cognitive control for task sets: Shifting spatial attention and switching categorization rules. *J Neurosci*, *29*(12), 3930–3938.

Cohen, J. D., Barch, D. M., Carter, C., & Servan-Schreiber, D. (1999). Context-processing deficits in schizophrenia: cConverging evidence from three theoretically motivated cognitive tasks. *J Abnorm Psychol*, *108*(1), 120–133.

Cools, R., Barker, R. A., Sahakian, B. J., & Robbins, T. W. (2001). Enhanced or impaired cognitive function in Parkinson's disease as a function of dopaminergic medication and task demands. *Cerebral Cortex*, *11*, 1136–1143.

Corkin, S. (2002). What's new with the amnesic patient H.M.? *Nat Rev Neurosci*, *3*(2), 153–160.

Courchesne, E., & Allen, G. (1997). Prediction and preparation, fundamental functions of the cerebellum. *Learning & Memory*, *4*, 1–35.

Courchesne, E., Townsend, J., Akshoomoff, N. A., Saitoh, O., Yeung-Courchesne, R., Lincoln, A. J., et al. (1994). Impairment in shifting attention in autistic and cerebellar patients. *Behav Neurosci*, *108*(5), 848–865.

Cubillo, A., Halari, R., Ecker, C., Giampietro, V., Taylor, E., & Rubia, K. (2010). Reduced activation and inter-regional functional connectivity of fronto-striatal networks in adults with childhood attention-deficit hyperactivity disorder (ADHD) and persisting symptoms during tasks of motor inhibition and cognitive switching. *J Psychiatr Res*, *44*(10), 629–639.

Davis, R. N., & Nolen-Hoeksema, S. (2000). Cognitive inflexibility among ruminators and non-ruminators. *Cognitive Therapy and Research*, *24*(6), 699–711.

Dias, R., Robbins, T. W., & Roberts, A. C. (1996). Dissociation in prefrontal cortex of affective and attentional shifts. *Nature*, *380*, 69–72.

Dibben, C. R., Rice, C., Laws, K., & McKenna, P. J. (2009). Is executive impairment associated with schizophrenic syndromes? A meta-analysis. *Psychol Med*, *39*(3), 381–392.

Dichter, G. S., Radonovich, K. J., Turner-Brown, L. M., Lam, K. S., Holtzclaw, T. N., & Bodfish, J. W. (2010). Performance of children with autism spectrum disorders on the dimension-change card sort task. *J Autism Dev Disord*, *40*(4), 448–456.

Eshel, N., & Roiser, J. P. (2010). Reward and punishment processing in depression. *Biol Psychiatry*, *68*(2), 118–124.

Everett, J., Lavoie, K., Gagnon, J. F., & Gosselin, N. (2001). Performance of patients with schizophrenia on the Wisconsin Card Sorting Test (WCST). *J Psychiatry Neurosci*, *26*(2), 123–130.

Finke, M., Barcelo, F., Garolera, M., Cortinas, M., Garrido, G., Pajares, M., et al. (2011). Impaired preparatory re-mapping of stimulus-response associations and rule-implementation in schizophrenic patients—the role for differences in early processing. *Biol Psychol*, *87*(3), 358–365.

Forstmann, B. U., Brass, M., Koch, I., & von Cramon, D. Y. (2005). Internally generated and directly cued task sets: An investigation with fMRI. *Neuropsychologia*, *43*(6), 943–952.

Franke, C., Reuter, B., Schulz, L., & Kathmann, N. (2007). Schizophrenia patients show impaired response switching in saccade tasks. *Biol Psychol*, *76*(1–2), 91–99.

Geurts, H. M., Corbett, B., & Solomon, M. (2009). The paradox of cognitive flexibility in autism. *Trends Cogn Sci*, *13*(2), 74–82.

Gilbert, A. M., & Fiez, J. A. (2004). Integrating rewards and cognition in the frontal cortex. *Cogn Affect Behav Neurosci*, *4*(4), 540–552.

Green, M. F., Kern, R. S., & Heaton, R. K. (2004a). Longitudinal studies of cognition and functional outcome in schizophrenia: Implications for MATRICS. *Schizophr Res*, *72*(1), 41–51.

Green, M. F., Nuechterlein, K. H., Gold, J. M., Barch, D. M., Cohen, J., Essock, S., et al. (2004b). Approaching a consensus cognitive battery for clinical trials in schizophrenia: the NIMH-MATRICS conference to select cognitive domains and test criteria. *Biol Psychiatry*, *56*(5), 301–307.

Halari, R., Simic, M., Pariante, C. M., Papadopoulos, A., Cleare, A., Brammer, M., et al. (2009). Reduced activation in lateral prefrontal cortex and anterior cingulate during attention and cognitive control functions in medication-naive adolescents with depression compared with controls. *J Child Psychol Psychiatry*, *50*(3), 307–316.

Hartman, M., Steketee, M. C., Silva, S., Lanning, K., & Andersson, C. (2003). Wisconsin Card Sorting Test performance in schizophrenia: The role of working memory. *Schizophr Res*, *63*(3), 201–217.

Heinzel, A., Northoff, G., Boeker, H., Boesiger, P., & Grimm, S. (2010). Emotional processing and executive functions in major depressive disorder: Dorsal prefrontal activity correlates with performance in the intra-extra dimensional set shift. *Acta Neuropsychiatrica*, *22*, 269–279.

Horoufchin, H., Philipp, A. M., & Koch, I. (2011). The dissipating task-repetition benefit in cued task switching: Task-set decay or temporal distinctiveness? *J Exp Psychol Hum Percept Perform*, *37*(2), 455–472.

Hubner, M., Kluwe, R. H., Luna-Rodriguez, A., & Peters, A. (2004). Response selection difficulty and asymmetrical costs of switching between tasks and stimuli: No evidence for an exogenous component of task-set reconfiguration. *J Exp Psychol Hum Percept Perform*, *30*(6), 1043–1063.

Hutton, S. B., Puri, B. K., Duncan, L. J., Robbins, T. W., Barnes, T. R., & Joyce, E. M. (1998). Executive function in first-episode schizophrenia. *Psychol Med*, *28*(2), 463–473.

Hyafil, A., Summerfield, C., & Koechlin, E. (2009). Two mechanisms for task switching in the prefrontal cortex. *J Neurosci*, *29*(16), 5135–5142.

Jamadar, S., Michie, P., & Karayanidis, F. (2010). Compensatory mechanisms underlie intact task-switching performance in schizophrenia. *Neuropsychologia*, *48*(5), 1305–1323.

Karayanidis, F., Nicholson, R., Schall, U., Meem, L., Fulham, R., & Michie, P. T. (2006). Switching between univalent task-sets in schizophrenia: ERP evidence of an anticipatory task-set reconfiguration deficit. *Clin Neurophysiol*, *117*(10), 2172–2190.

Kerns, J. G., & Berenbaum, H. (2003). The relationship between formal thought disorder and executive functioning component processes. *J Abnorm Psychol*, *112*(3), 339–352.

Kerns, J. G., Cohen, J. D., MacDonald, A. W., 3rd, Johnson, M. K., Stenger, V. A., Aizenstein, H., et al. (2005). Decreased conflict- and error-related activity in the anterior cingulate cortex in subjects with schizophrenia. *Am J Psychiatry*, *162*(10), 1833–1839.

Kieffaber, P. D., O'Donnell, B. F., Shekhar, A., & Hetrick, W. P. (2007). Event related brain potential evidence for preserved attentional set switching in schizophrenia. *Schizophr Res*, *93*(1–3), 355–365.

Kim, C., Johnson, N. F., Cilles, S. E., & Gold, B. T. (2011). Common and distinct mechanisms of cognitive flexibility in prefrontal cortex. *J Neurosci*, *31*(13), 4771–4779.

King, J. A., Colla, M., Brass, M., Heuser, I., & von Cramon, D. (2007). Inefficient cognitive control in adult ADHD: Evidence from trial-by-trial Stroop test and cued task switching performance. *Behav Brain Funct*, *3*, 42.

Knight, R. A., & Silverstein, S. M. (2001). A process-oriented approach for averting confounds resulting from general performance deficiencies in schizophrenia. *J Abnorm Psychol*, *110*(1), 15–30.

Laws, K. R. (1999). A meta-analytic review of Wisconsin Card Sort studies in schizophrenia: General intellectual deficit in disguise? *Cogn Neuropsychiatry*, *4*(1), 1–30; discussion 31–35.

Lien, M. C., Ruthruff, E., & Kuhns, D. (2006). On the difficulty of task switching: Assessing the role of task-set inhibition. *Psychon Bull Rev*, *13*(3), 530–535.

Locke, H. S., & Braver, T. S. (2008). Motivational influences on cognitive control: Behavior, brain activation, and individual differences. *Cogn Affect Behav Neurosci*, *8*(1), 99–112.

MacDonald, A. W., 3rd, & Carter, C. S. (2002). Cognitive experimental approaches to investigating impaired cognition in schizophrenia: A paradigm shift. *J Clin Exp Neuropsychol*, *24*(7), 873–882.

MacDonald, A. W., 3rd, Carter, C. S., Kerns, J. G., Ursu, S., Barch, D. M., Holmes, A. J., et al. (2005). Specificity of prefrontal dysfunction and context processing deficits to schizophrenia in never-medicated patients with first-episode psychosis. *Am J Psychiatry, 162*(3), 475–484.

Manoach, D. S., Lindgren, K. A., Cherkasova, M. V., Goff, D. C., Halpern, E. F., Intriligator, J., et al. (2002). Schizophrenic subjects show deficient inhibition but intact task switching on saccadic tasks. *Biol Psychiatry, 51*(10), 816–826.

Marin, O. (2012). Interneuron dysfunction in psychiatric disorders. *Nat Rev Neurosci, 13*(2), 107–120.

Mayr, U., & Keele, S. W. (2000). Backward inhibition during intentional shifts between task sets. *Journal of Experimental Psychology: General, 129*, 4–26.

Mayr, U., & Kliegl, R. (2000). Task-set switching and long-term memory retrieval. *Journal of Experimental Psychology: Learning, Memory, and Cognition, 26*(5), 1124–1140.

McKirdy, J., Sussmann, J. E., Hall, J., Lawrie, S. M., Johnstone, E. C., & McIntosh, A. M. (2009). Set shifting and reversal learning in patients with bipolar disorder or schizophrenia. *Psychol Med, 39*(8), 1289–1293.

Meiran, N. (1996). Reconfiguration of processing mode prior to task performance. *Journal of Experimental Psychology: Learning, Memory, and Cognition, 22*(6), 1423–1442.

Meiran, N., Chorev, Z., & Sapir, A. (2000). Component processes in task switching. *Cognitive Psychology, 41*, 211–253.

Meiran, N., Diamond, G. M., Toder, D., & Nemets, B. (2010). Cognitive rigidity in unipolar depression and obsessive compulsive disorder: Examination of task switching, Stroop, working memory updating and post-conflict adaptation. *Psychiatry Res, 185*(1–2), 149–156.

Meiran, N., Kessler, Y., & Adi-Japha, E. (2008). Control by Action Representation and Input Selection (CARIS): A theoretical framework for task switching. *Psychol Res, 72*(5), 473–500.

Meiran, N., Levine, J., Meiran, N., & Henik, A. (2000). Task set switching in schizophrenia. *Neuropsychology, 14*(3), 471–482.

Meiran, N., & Marciano, H. (2002). Limitations in advance task preparation: Switching the relevant stimulus dimension in speeded same-different comparisons. *Mem Cognit, 30*(4), 540–550.

Meltzer, H. Y., & McGurk, S. R. (1999). The effects of clozapine, risperidone, and olanzapine on cognitive function in schizophrenia. *Schizophr Bull, 25*(2), 233–255.

Menon, V. (2011). Large-scale brain networks and psychopathology: A unifying triple network model. *Trends Cogn Sci, 15*(10), 483–506.

Miller, E. K., & Cohen, J. D. (2001). An integrative theory of prefrontal cortex function. *Annu Rev Neurosci, 24*, 167–202.

Monsell, S. (2003a). Task switching. *Trends in Cognitive Sciences, 7*(3), 134–140.

Monsell, S. (2003b). Task-set reconfiguration processes do not imply a control homunculus: Reply to Altmann. *Trends in Cognitive Sciences, 7*(8), 341–342.

Moritz, S., Birkner, C., Kloss, M., Jahn, H., Hand, I., Haasen, C., et al. (2002). Executive functioning in obsessive-compulsive disorder, unipolar depression, and schizophrenia. *Arch Clin Neuropsychol, 17*(5), 477–483.

Nieuwenstein, M. R., Aleman, A., & de Haan, E. H. (2001). Relationship between symptom dimensions and neurocognitive functioning in schizophrenia: A meta-analysis of

WCST and CPT studies. Wisconsin Card Sorting Test. Continuous Performance Test. *J Psychiatr Res*, *35*(2), 119–125.

Niznikiewicz, M. A., Kubicki, M., & Shenton, M. E. (2003). Recent structural and functional imaging findings in schizophrenia. *Current Opinion in Psychiatry*, *16*, 123–147.

Nolen-Hoeksema, S. (1991). Responses to depression and their effects on the duration of depressive episodes. *J Abnorm Psychol*, *100*(4), 569–582.

Nolen-Hoeksema, S., & Morrow, J. (1991). A prospective study of depression and posttraumatic stress symptoms after a natural disaster: The 1989 Loma Prieta Earthquake. *J Pers Soc Psychol*, *61*(1), 115–121.

Owen, A. M., Roberts, A. C., Hodges, J. R., Summers, B. A., Polkey, C. E., & Robbins, T. W. (1993). Contrasting mechanisms of impaired attentional set-shifting in patients with frontal lobe damage or Parkinson's disease. *Brain*, *116*, 1159–1175.

Ozonoff, S., Cook, I., Coon, H., Dawson, G., Joseph, R. M., Klin, A., et al. (2004). Performance on Cambridge Neuropsychological Test Automated Battery subtests sensitive to frontal lobe function in people with autistic disorder: Evidence from the Collaborative Programs of Excellence in Autism network. *J Autism Dev Disord*, *34*(2), 139–150.

Pantelis, C., Barber, F. Z., Barnes, T. R., Nelson, H. E., Owen, A. M., & Robbins, T. W. (1999). Comparison of set-shifting ability in patients with chronic schizophrenia and frontal lobe damage. *Schizophr Res*, *37*(3), 251–270.

Pantelis, C., Harvey, C. A., Plant, G., Fossey, E., Maruff, P., Stuart, G. W., et al. (2004). Relationship of behavioural and symptomatic syndromes in schizophrenia to spatial working memory and attentional set-shifting ability. *Psychol Med*, *34*(4), 693–703

Pessoa, L. (2009). How do emotion and motivation direct executive control? *Trends Cogn Sci*, *13*(4), 160–166.

Poljac, E., Simon, S., Ringlever, L., Kalcik, D., Groen, W. B., Buitelaar, J. K., et al. (2010). Impaired task switching performance in children with dyslexia but not in children with autism. *Q J Exp Psychol (Hove)*, *63*(2), 401–416.

Ravizza, S. M., & Carter, C. S. (2008). Shifting set about task switching: Behavioral and neural evidence for distinct forms of cognitive flexibility. *Neuropsychologia*, *46*(12), 2924–2935.

Ravizza, S. M., & Ciranni, M. A. (2002). Contributions of the prefrontal cortex and basal ganglia to set shifting. *Journal of Cognitive Neuroscience*, *14*(3), 472–483.

Ravizza, S. M., Goudreau, J., Delgado, M. R., & Ruiz, S. (2012). Executive function in Parkinson's disease: Contributions of the dorsal frontostriatal pathways to action and motivation. *Cogn Affect Behav Neurosci*, *12*(1), 193–206.

Ravizza, S. M., & Ivry, R. B. (2001). Comparison of the basal ganglia and cerebellum in shifting attention. *Journal of Cognitive Neuroscience*, *13*(3), 285–297.

Ravizza, S. M., Moua, K. C., Long, D., & Carter, C. S. (2010). The impact of context processing deficits on task-switching performance in schizophrenia. *Schizophr Res*, *116*(2--3), 274–279.

Rogers, R. D., & Monsell, S. (1995). Costs of a predictable switch between simple cognitive tasks. *Journal of Experimental Psychology: General*, *124*(2), 207–231.

Rogers, R. D., Sahakian, B. J., Hodges, J. R., Polkey, C. E., Kennard, C., & Robbins, T. W. (1998). Dissociating executive mechanisms of task control following frontal lobe damage and Parkinson's disease. *Brain*, *121*, 815–842.

Rubia, K., Cubillo, A., Smith, A. B., Woolley, J., Heyman, I., & Brammer, M. J. (2010). Disorder-specific dysfunction in right inferior prefrontal cortex during two inhibition tasks in boys with attention-deficit hyperactivity disorder compared with boys with obsessive-compulsive disorder. *Hum Brain Mapp*, *31*(2), 287–299.

Rubinstein, J., Meyer, D. E., & Evans, J. E. (2001). Executive control of cognitive processes in task switching. *Journal of Experimental Psychology: Human Perception and Performance*, *27*(4), 763–797.

Rushworth, M. F. S., Hadland, K. A., Paus, T., & Sipla, P. K. (2002). Role of the human medial frontal cortex in task switching: A combined fMRI and TMS study. *Journal of Neurophysiology*, *87*, 2577–2592.

Santesso, D. L., Steele, K. T., Bogdan, R., Holmes, A. J., Deveney, C. M., Meites, T. M., et al. (2008). Enhanced negative feedback responses in remitted depression. *Neuroreport*, *19*(10), 1045–1048.

Schmitz, N., Rubia, K., Daly, E., Smith, A., Williams, S., & Murphy, D. G. (2006). Neural correlates of executive function in autistic spectrum disorders. *Biol Psychiatry*, *59*(1), 7 –16.

Schoch, B., Gorissen, B., Richter, S., Ozimek, A., Kaiser, O., Dimitrova, A., et al. (2004). Do children with focal cerebellar lesions show deficits in shifting attention? *J Neurophysiol*, *92*(3), 1856–1866.

Shafritz, K. M., Dichter, G. S., Baranek, G. T., & Belger, A. (2008). The neural circuitry mediating shifts in behavioral response and cognitive set in autism. *Biol Psychiatry*, *63*(10), 974–980.

Smith, A. B., Taylor, E., Brammer, M., Toone, B., & Rubia, K. (2006). Task-specific hypoactivation in prefrontal and temporoparietal brain regions during motor inhibition and task switching in medication-naive children and adolescents with attention deficit hyperactivity disorder. *Am J Psychiatry*, *163*(6), 1044–1051.

Shepherd, A. M., Laurens, K. R., Matheson, S. L., Carr, V. J., & Green, M. J. (2012). Systematic meta-review and quality assessment of the structural brain alterations in schizophrenia. *Neurosci Biobehav Rev*, *36*(4), 1342–1356.

Steele, J. D., Kumar, P., & Ebmeier, K. P. (2007). Blunted response to feedback information in depressive illness. *Brain*, *130*(Pt 9), 2367 –2374.

Stoet, G., & Lopez, B. (2011). Task-switching abilities in children with autism spectrum disorder. *European Journal of Developmental Psychology*, *8*(2), 244–260.

Taylor, S. F., Welsh, R. C., Wager, T. D., Phan, K. L., Fitzgerald, K. D., & Gehring, W. J. (2004). A functional neuroimaging study of motivation and executive function. *Neuroimage*, *21*(3), 1045–1054.

Van Eylen, L., Boets, B., Steyaert, J., Evers, K., Wagemans, J., & Noens, I. (2011). Cognitive flexibility in autism spectrum disorder: Explaining the inconsistencies? *Research in Autism Spectrum Disorders*, *5*, 1390–1401.

Wager, T. D., Jonides, J., Smith, E. E., & Nichols, T. E. (2005). Toward a taxonomy of attention shifting: Individual differences in fMRI during multiple shift types. *Cogn Affect Behav Neurosci*, *5*(2), 127–143.

Westerhausen, R., Kompus, K., & Hugdahl, K. (2011). Impaired cognitive inhibition in schizophrenia: A meta-analysis of the Stroop interference effect. *Schizophr Res*, *133*(1-3), 172–181.

Whitmer, A. J., & Banich, M. T. (2007). Inhibition versus switching deficits in different forms of rumination. *Psychol Sci*, *18*(6), 546–553.

Willcutt, E. G., Doyle, A. E., Nigg, J. T., Faraone, S. V., & Pennington, B. F. (2005). Validity of the executive function theory of attention-deficit/hyperactivity disorder: A meta-analytic review. *Biol Psychiatry, 57*(11), 1336–1346.

Wylie, G. R., Clark, E. A., Butler, P. D., & Javitt, D. C. (2008). Schizophrenia patients show task switching deficits consistent with N-methyl-d-aspartate system dysfunction but not global executive deficits: Implications for pathophysiology of executive dysfunction in schizophrenia. *Schizophr Bull, 36*(3), 585–594.

Wylie, G. R., Javitt, D. C., & Foxe, J. J. (2004). Don't think of a white bear: An fMRI investigation of the effects of sequential instructional sets on cortical activity in a task-switching paradigm. *Hum Brain Mapp, 21*(4), 279–297.

Yehene, E., Meiran, N., & Soroker, N. (2008). Basal ganglia play a unique role in task switching within the frontal-subcortical circuits: Evidence from patients with focal lesions. *J Cogn Neurosci, 20*(6), 1079–1093.

Yerys, B. E., Wallace, G. L., Harrison, B., Celano, M. J., Giedd, J. N., & Kenworthy, L. E. (2009). Set-shifting in children with autism spectrum disorders: reversal shifting deficits on the Intradimensional/Extradimensional Shift Test correlate with repetitive behaviors. *Autism, 13*(5), 523–538.

Yeung, N., Nystrom, L. E., Aronson, J. A., & Cohen, J. D. (2006). Between-task competition and cognitive control in task switching. *J Neurosci, 26*(5), 1429–1438.

13

Cognitive Flexibility in Childhood and Adolescence

SABINE PETERS AND EVELINE A. CRONE

EXECUTIVE FUNCTIONS

An important characteristic of human cognition is that people are constantly looking for ways to improve themselves. Rather than sticking to the status quo, people use flexibility and creativity to successfully adapt to an ever changing environment. For instance, children in school have to get used to switching between different subjects for each class. Instead of continuing to speak French during Spanish class, children tend to switch quite easily between classes. In situations like these, most people will recognize when they need to change their approach to adapt to a new environment.

For successful adaptation to a changing environment, executive functions are of paramount importance. Executive functions refer to the ability to behave in goal-directed actions in new and challenging situations, and to overcome automatic thoughts and behaviors (Garon, Bryson, & Smith, 2008). Executive functions are thought to consist of at least the subprocesses: (a) working memory, (b) inhibition, and (c) cognitive flexibility (Huizinga, Dolan, & van der Molen, 2006; Miyake et al., 2000), although the exact number of subprocesses and their structure remains a matter of debate.

COGNITIVE FLEXIBILITY

Cognitive flexibility is defined as the ability to adapt behavior to changing environmental demands. It is therefore essential for adaptive cognition, creative problem solving, and "out-of-the-box" thinking. Without cognitive flexibility, we would be stuck in rigid behavioral patterns and we would be having difficulty adapting to new situations. Cognitive flexibility is, because of its inherently adaptive nature, arguably the most important component of executive functioning, as well as the component that shows the most profound changes across child and adolescent development. However, cognitive flexibility cannot be seen as an entirely distinct executive function, because it relies heavily on two other executive functions: working memory and inhibition (Huizinga et al., 2006). Working memory is important for flexibility because it is necessary to remember your goals and keep relevant information online. Inhibition is important because for flexible behavior, automatic responses need to be inhibited to choose a response that is better suited to current demands.

Development of Cognitive Flexibility

Cognitive flexibility undergoes profound changes across child and adolescent development (Cragg & Chevalier, 2012). The development of cognitive flexibility is of considerable importance for successful school performance. For instance, cognitive flexibility scores are related to math scores and phonemic awareness in preschoolers (Blair & Razza, 2007), and task switching performance was found to be related to reading and math scores in a longitudinal study in preschool and primary school (Bull, Espy, & Wiebe, 2008). Furthermore, interventions aiming to improve executive functioning skills (including flexibility) improve school readiness in young children (Bierman, Nix, Greenberg, Blair, & Domitrovich, 2008). Additionally, impairments in cognitive flexibility are associated with a number of psychiatric disorders, such as autism spectrum disorder (Corbett, Constantine, Hendren, Rocke, & Ozonoff, 2009), obsessive-compulsive disorder (Chamberlain, Blackwell, Fineberg, Robbins, & Sahakian, 2005), and anorexia and bulimia nervosa (Tchanturia et al., 2012). Together, these studies highlight that cognitive flexibility is a cornerstone of cognitive development.

Measuring Cognitive Flexibility: Adaptive and Instructed Flexibility

Cognitive flexibility has been studied with many different experimental paradigms (Ionescu, 2012). Many researchers have argued for a better conceptual understanding of a complex and multifaceted construct such as cognitive flexibility (Cragg & Chevalier, 2012; Morton, 2010). Conceptually, a distinction can be made between instructed flexibility and adaptive flexibility. For instructed flexibility, individuals need to adapt behavior based on changing task rules, such as in task switching paradigms. Adaptive flexibility, on the other hand, requires an individual to infer rules based on feedback about prior behavior, such as in performance-monitoring paradigms.

We describe the development of these two different types of cognitive flexibility—instructed flexibility and adaptive flexibility—by focusing on task switching and performance-monitoring paradigms. Our focus will be on the development of school-aged children (6–17 years), a developmental group that can be directly compared with adults using the same paradigms (Cragg & Chevalier, 2012). Even though most of the research to date on the development of cognitive flexibility has focused on preschool years (Blair, Zelazo, & Greenberg, 2005), school-aged development is marked by continuing improvement of many types of cognitive flexibility. A better understanding of these developmental improvements will hopefully have consequences for improving education and interventions.

In the search for a more mechanistic understanding of subprocesses involved in cognitive flexibility, researchers have adopted a new approach to complement behavioral research. That is to say, the processes involved in cognitive flexibility and their developmental trajectory have been investigated from a neurocognitive perspective. This approach has proved highly valuable in situations where there are no overt behavioral indices (such as in the case of feedback processing; Crone, Zanolie, Van Leijenhorst, Westenberg, & Rombouts, 2008) or when different subprocesses may result in the same behavioral outcome (Morton, 2010). Therefore, we will focus on the development of both behavioral and neural processes involved in instructed and adaptive cognitive flexibility. We will first provide a brief overview of the neural mechanisms of cognitive flexibility in adults. Next, we describe several studies that investigated the neurocognitive development of cognitive flexibility. These studies are subdivided into instructed flexibility (measured with task switching paradigms) and adaptive flexibility (measured with performance monitoring paradigms).

Neural Mechanisms of Cognitive Flexibility in Adults

Using functional magnetic resonance imaging (fMRI), researchers have been able to identify the neural areas that are important for cognitive flexibility. Most studies in this area have focused on instructed flexibility, by using task switching paradigms. fMRI studies of task switching in adults have generally compared neural activity during switch trials with activation during nonswitch trials. The underlying rationale is that this subtraction paradigm allows the researcher to isolate the activity that is specific for switch trials. With this approach, it was found that task switching activates an extensive brain network including activity mostly in the lateral and medial prefrontal cortex (PFC) but also in the parietal lobes, cerebellum, and other subcortical areas (Monsell, 2003).

A recent meta-analysis analyzed data from different types of cognitive flexibility paradigms to investigate in more detail the specific contributions of these brain areas (Kim, Cilles, Johnson, & Gold, 2012). The main aim was to distinguish brain areas that are domain-general (activate across different types of flexibility) and which areas are specialized for different types of flexibility. Three different types of paradigms were distinguished by the authors: two types of instructed flexibility (perceptual attention switching and response switching) and adaptive flexibility (referred to as "context-based switching" by the authors). In response switching paradigms, participants are trained to make certain stimulus–response mappings (e.g., press left for circles, right for squares). After a switch, the correct stimulus–response mapping is changed (e.g., press left for squares, right for circles). In attention switching paradigms, participants respond with a key press to different dimensions of the same stimuli. For instance, prior to the switch participants could be asked to respond based on the color of the stimuli. After a switch, participants still see the same stimuli, but now they have to attend to a new dimension (e.g., shape) and ignore the previously correct dimension. In adaptive flexibility paradigms, participants are required to switch between task rules or cognitive "sets." The need to switch is inferred from performance feedback.

Kim et al. (2012) found a widespread network for all three switching types that consisted of medial and lateral PFC, but also parietal, temporal and occipital areas, the caudate nucleus, and the thalamus were found. This was consistent with previous meta-analyses that did not distinguish between different switching types (Buchsbaum, Greer, Chang, & Berman, 2005; Derrfuss, Brass, Neumann, & von Cramon, 2005; Wager, Jonides, & Reading, 2004). To investigate areas that are domain-general in nature, the researchers investigated which areas were activated for all three types of switching. Regions in the inferior frontal junction and posterior parietal cortex were found. The researchers therefore argue that that these areas are probably involved in representing and updating task sets, because these processes are essential in all three types of switching (Miyake et al., 2000).

Subsequently, they examined which areas were specifically activated for the three switching paradigms. The results revealed that in addition to domain-general regions associated with switching, there were also differences in brain activity for the three switching paradigms. For attention switching, compared with the other types of switching, preferential activity was found in several caudal PFC regions, posterior parietal cortex, and inferior temporal areas. For response switching, preferential activity was found in dorsolateral prefrontal cortex (DLPFC), several frontal gyri, and posterior parietal cortex. Adaptive flexibility tasks resulted in preferential activation in rostral PFC regions, middle frontal gyrus, cuneus, inferior temporal cortex, occipital areas, and subcortical structures. In summary, the findings of this meta-analysis indicated that there are several overlapping regions that are important for different types of task switching, but there are also separate neural networks underlying different types of instructive and adaptive flexibility. This illustrates that task switching is not a unitary process and highlights the importance of studying different types of switching.

In the next paragraphs, the behavioral and neural development of cognitive flexibility will be further described, based on the distinction between instructed and adaptive flexibility.

It is well known that at birth, the structure of the brain is not yet fully developed. Both gray matter (consisting of neurons) and white matter (structural connections between areas) are still maturing. This has been investigated with post-mortem studies and, more recently, with structural neuroimaging techniques. During child and adolescent development, linear increases have been observed in white matter connectivity (Barnea-Goraly et al., 2005; Giedd et al., 1999). For gray matter development, a nonlinear pattern has been found (Casey, Giedd, & Thomas, 2000). For the first two postnatal years of development, gray matter volume increases. After that period, gray matter decreases again with different brain areas differing in the rate at which they mature. The lateral PFC is one of the last areas to develop in adolescence (Casey et al., 2000) with estimates that gray matter in the lateral PFC reaches adult levels in the early 20s (Giedd, 2004). Similar results were found for the parietal cortex and the caudate (Giedd, 2004). It therefore seems that the areas that are important for task switching in adults undergo prolonged structural development during childhood and adolescence. This observation, combined with the results of behavioral studies in which increased switch costs for children were found, led a number of researchers to hypothesize that the development of cognitive flexibility may be related to brain maturation. Several studies have investigated the neural development of instructive flexibility, using two versions of task switching paradigms (response switching and attention switching) that were previously briefly described in the section on neuroimaging studies in adults.

Development of Instructed Flexibility

BEHAVIORAL DEVELOPMENT OF INSTRUCTED FLEXIBILITY

The task switching paradigm has proved to be a very valuable tool to investigate the development of instructed cognitive flexibility. Task switching paradigms have been developed in different varieties. For example, a distinction can be made between the alternating runs variant of the task switching paradigm, in which participants are instructed to switch after every *n*th trial, and the cue-based switching paradigm, in which a switch is indicated by a cue. In both paradigms, the demand to switch between tasks can result in "mixing costs" (increased reaction times when comparing a task block with switches to a task block without switches) and "switch costs" (increased reaction times when comparing switch trials within a switch block to nonswitch trials within a switch block) (Monsell, 2003).

Developmental comparisons have indicated higher switch costs for children compared with adults, in both alternating run paradigms (e.g., Huizinga et al., 2006) and cued switching paradigms (e.g., Crone, Bunge, van der Molen, & Ridderinkhof, 2006). Developmental improvements are most pronounced between ages 7 and 12, although improvements are still observed in adolescence (Huizinga et al., 2006). In a comprehensive review, Cragg and Chevalier (2012) summarized many different processes that may contribute to these developmental differences. First, they mention that developmental differences may result from an improvement in goal setting. For example, in the alternating run paradigm it is necessary to maintain the task set in mind (e.g., Task A, Task A, Task B, Task B, Task A, Task A), and in cued task switching it is necessary to "translate" the cue into the correct task representation. The finding of higher mixing costs (i.e., trials in a switch block compared with trials in a nonswitch block) in children relative to adults has been interpreted as developmental differences in goal setting (Chevalier & Blaye, 2009). Second, developmental differences may be related to overcoming the previously relevant rule. For example, Cepeda, Kramer, and Gonzalez de Sather (2001) showed that increasing the time between trials reduced switch costs in adults but not in children, suggesting that children experience larger interference from previous task set activation. Third, developmental differences may be related to interference from overlapping stimulus–response mappings. For example, Crone et al. (2006) showed that it is relatively more difficult for children to switch tasks when the switch trial is associated with the same response hand as on the previous trial compared with when the switch trial is associated with the opposite response hand, most likely because they experience more interference from the previous task-response mapping. Taken together, different underlying processes can account for developmental changes in switching, but exactly how and when these differences take place are not well understood. One way to entangle these developmental processes is by studying the neural mechanisms involved in task switching.

Neurocognitive Development of Instructed Flexibility

Developmental fMRI Studies of Response Switching

In response-switching paradigms, participants are instructed to switch between different stimulus–response mappings. Rubia et al. (2006) used a response-switching task in which adolescents (10–17 years, all males) and adults (20–43 year, all men) were presented with a grid divided into four squares, with either a horizontal or vertical bidirectional arrow in the middle. On each trial, a red dot appeared in one of the quadrants. When the arrow was horizontal, participants had to judge whether the dot was on the left or right side of the grid. When the arrow was vertical, participants had to judge if the dot was in the upper or lower half of the grid. Behavioral results revealed enhanced switch performance in adults compared with adolescents. When comparing switch trials to nonswitch trials, adults showed more activation than adolescents in right inferior PFC, left parietal cortex, anterior cingulate cortex, and putamen. The same areas were also found to be related to age in a region of interest and whole brain regression analysis, further confirming these findings. The most robust age correlations were found in the parietal cortex and basal ganglia, which the authors took to suggest that maturation of these areas is most important for the development of task switching capacity.

Researchers from the same laboratory performed a second study using a similar paradigm on a sample of 63 participants between 13–38 years old (38 males) (Christakou et al., 2009). The behavioral results showed that there were switch costs for both adults and adolescents, but no significant age differences were found. Despite the absence of behavioral differences, with increasing age there was more activity in the bilateral inferior frontal cortex, anterior cingulate cortex, caudate nucleus, putamen, thalamus, and inferior parietal lobe during switching. This was similar to the findings reported in a previous study using only male participants (Rubia et al., 2006).

A third response switching study was performed by Crone et al. (2006). Participants (17 children 8–12 years, 20 adolescents 13–17 years, 20 adults 18–24 years) were taught to associate three different cues with a prespecified stimulus–response mapping. Cues could be followed by bivalent stimuli (when depending on the rule, the same stimuli could be associated with a different response mapping) or univalent stimuli (stimuli that were always associated with the same response). Switching performance was better for adults and adolescents than for children. The pre-SMA was activated in all groups for rule switching compared with repetition. Interestingly, children also recruited this region more for bivalent repetition trials than for univalent repetition trials, indicating this region is not only active for rule switching but also rule representation. This suggests a less mature activity pattern in pre-SMA for children compared with adolescents and adults.

A potential confound in task switching studies is the performance difference that is often found between children and adults. Thomas et al. (2011) addressed this issue by using an algorithm that adjusts task difficulty to ensure a similar task performance for all age groups. Participants (21 adolescents 10–16 years and 21 adults 22–40 years) were accustomed to a certain stimulus–response mapping (press "1" for "X," press "2" for "O"). When cued with a background color change, they were required to inhibit the prepotent response and replace it with an alternate response (press "3"). Despite the fact that the task was designed to equalize accuracy, there were still significant differences in accuracy between adolescents and adults. The fMRI results indicated that when comparing switch to nonswitch trials, adults showed more activity in frontal and parietal areas (bilateral precentral gyri, precuneus, inferior and superior parietal lobule, paracentral lobule).

To summarize, the developmental fMRI studies investigating instructed flexibility with response switching paradigms generally find increased activation in frontal and parietal areas as well as the basal ganglia in adults compared with children or adolescents during switch trials.

Developmental fMRI Studies of Attention Switching

A different aspect of instructed flexibility is investigated with attention switching paradigms. In these tasks, participants are required to switch attention between different perceptual aspects of stimuli. Casey et al. (2004) were the first researchers to investigate attention switching in a developmental fMRI study. Adults (18–23 years, n = 7) and children (7–11 years, n = 7) performed a task in which they were instructed to judge which of three objects was unique. The unique attribute could be either color or shape and was alternated on each trial without cueing. Performance on these switch blocks was compared with control blocks, in which the relevant attribute was always color or always shape. Adults performed better on this task in terms of accuracy and reaction time than children. However, no switch costs were found, as indicated by similar behavioral performance on the switch blocks versus the control blocks. A possible explanation is that the task does not require deliberate top-down attention switching, but the unique stimulus "pops out," regardless of the dimension that was being attended to in the previous trial. Neural activity during switch trials compared with non-switch trials resulted in activation in the caudate nucleus in both adults and children. Adults showed more activation during switches than children in the superior frontal gyrus, superior parietal cortex, and middle temporal gyrus. However, the task seems to require a minimal amount of cognitive control because the "pop-out" effect of the unique stimulus is probably sufficient for participants to successfully perform the task.

Using a more traditional experimental paradigm for attention switching, Morton, Bosma, and Ansari (2009) instructed participants (14 children 11–13 years and 13 adults 19–25 years) to perform the Dimensional Change Card Sorting task. In this task, participants are instructed to sort cards according to changing stimulus dimensions (e.g., red and blue boats and flowers that must be sorted by either color or shape). Before each trial, participants are cued with the correct sorting rule. When comparing switch and nonswitch trials, adults showed more activation in the left posterior parietal cortex and the right thalamus compared with children. Children showed more activation than adults in the right superior frontal sulcus. Behavioral performance was similar for children and adults, suggesting that the age differences cannot be explained in terms of performance differences. The authors hypothesized that the parietal cortex is less efficient in children than in adults, leading to compensatory recruitment of the frontal sulcus area. The increased recruitment of superior parietal cortex with development concurs with the findings of Casey et al. (2004). An important difference is that Morton et al. (2009) found a frontoparietal network associated with switching, whereas this network was not found in the Casey et al. study. Possibly, this is due to the limited cognitive control demands in the experimental task of Casey et al. (2004).

The attention switching findings partly correspond to the results from response switching paradigms (Christakou et al., 2009; Crone et al., 2006; Rubia et al., 2006). That is to say, using both approaches, a frontoparietal/subcortical network associated with switching was found, that was generally more pronounced in adults than children. However, the exact loci of activation were slightly different, indicating that response switching and attention switching may rely on different underlying processes. In line with this hypothesis, similar findings were reported in the direct comparison of these two types of switching in the meta-analysis on adult studies by Kim et al. (2012). An unexpected result was that Morton et al. (2009) found increased activation in a frontal area in children relative to adults. Possibly, the dimensional task switching paradigm used in the Morton et al. study requires additional processes that are not present in response shifting. This may cause strategy differences between children and adults, which in turn can result in different patterns of neural activity. Children may, for instance, resort to more effortful strategies for updating working memory, which explains the increase in frontal activity. Together, these findings demonstrate that specific task demands can result in different patterns of neural activation across development. In the next paragraph, age differences in task specific demands will be further investigated in the development of adaptive flexibility.

Development of Adaptive Flexibility

BEHAVIORAL DEVELOPMENT OF ADAPTIVE FLEXIBILITY

A second type of cognitive flexibility is adaptive flexibility, which is switching based on performance feedback. Rather than switching based on an arbitrary cue, performance feedback indicates whether a switch is necessary in order to maintain optimal performance. This method of studying cognitive flexibility may more closely resemble real-life situations.

The task that has been the most widely used to study performance based switching is the Wisconsin Card Sorting Task (WCST; Milner, 1963). In the WCST, participants are instructed to sort cards with pictures following different sorting rules (based on number, color, and shape). After sorting, positive or negative performance feedback is provided, indicating whether the correct rule was applied. The rule can change without warning; therefore, the switch cue is the unexpected negative feedback after a certain number of correct sorts. When this happens, participants have to use positive and negative feedback to find the correct rule again.

Performance on the WCST improves dramatically in school-aged children, and reaches adult levels around the age of 12 years (Crone, Ridderinkhof, Worm, Somsen, & van der Molen, 2004). Interestingly, some authors have suggested that performance of children is similar to that of patients with damage to the lateral PFC (Chelune & Baer, 1986). Similar to prefrontal patients, children have difficulty switching to a new rule and perseverate in the old rule; even if feedback indicates it is no longer correct.

The WCST has been a promising starting point for the experimental research into the development of adaptive cognitive flexibility (performance-based switching). The WCST is a more complex task than the simple task switching paradigm, but it may therefore also more adequately reflect the complex nature of adaptive flexibility. Yet, several different subprocesses are necessary for successful performance-based switching. It is necessary to investigate these different processes in isolation to come to a full understanding of the development of performance-based switching.

One of the complications in the study of performance-based switching is that positive and negative feedback can have different meanings in different stages of an experimental task. For instance, Barcelo and Knight (2002) analyzed error types in the WCST and distinguished efficient errors (errors during the search for a new rule) and random errors (mistakes in a series of correct responses, due to distraction or memory errors). Along the same vein, positive feedback can also have different meanings. Zanolie, Van Leijenhorst, Rombouts, and Crone (2008) distinguished first positive feedback (the first positive feedback when the new correct rule is found) and correct responses (when participants are continuing to use the correct response). First positive feedback provides new information that is valuable for learning, whereas correct positive feedback merely confirms what the participant already knows. Because of these differences in informative value, it is important to distinguish different feedback types, since they may rely on different neural processes.

A second complication in the study of performance-based switching is that behavioral outcomes cannot be measured until the next trial occurs. FMRI provides an excellent tool to distinguish the processes underlying performance-based switching. An advantage of fMRI studies is that we can focus on the effects of learning signals (i.e., feedback) in the brain, instead of on the subsequent behavioral response. To date, several neuroimaging studies have investigated the neural underpinnings of feedback processing in adults.

The previously mentioned meta-analysis on different types of task switching in adults already indicated that there are both domain-general areas that are activated for all types of switching, as well as specific activations for adaptive flexibility (Kim et al., 2012). Most of the studies analyzed in this meta-analysis on adaptive flexibility used paradigms based on the WCST, but also included semantic classification tasks, letter matching tasks, visual detection tasks and intraextradimensional switching tasks. The focus in these studies was usually on the differences in activity for switch and nonswitch trials. Other studies have specifically investigated activations during the presentation of positive and negative performance feedback. This approach is also crucial for our understanding of adaptive flexibility because it allows researchers to investigate the neural reactions to an adaptive learning signal.

FMRI results in adults have indicated that for feedback processing, a network similar to the task switching network is activated, including DLPFC, medial PFC (particularly SMA/ACC), parietal areas, and the caudate (Holroyd et al., 2004; van Veen, Holroyd, Cohen, Stenger, & Carter, 2004; Zanolie et al., 2008). These areas have typically been found when comparing activity for negative feedback with activity for positive feedback. This contrast is similar to the comparison between switch and non-switch trials, because negative feedback by definition indicates a "switch" in behavior is necessary for optimal performance. However, not all studies have replicated this negative feedback network. For instance, Nieuwenhuis, Slagter, von Geusau, Heslenfeld, and Holroyd (2005) failed to find differential activity to negative feedback in the medial PFC using a time-estimation paradigm. Possibly, both positive and negative feedback signals are informative for adaptive learning, especially when both can be used to improve performance. Further research is necessary to unravel the exact contributions of the cognitive control network to feedback processing. In the next section, an overview of the developmental fMRI studies on adaptive flexibility will be provided.

Neurocognitive Development of Adaptive Flexibility

The first neuroimaging study to investigate adaptive flexibility in children used a WCST-like paradigm (Crone et al., 2008). The task was child-friendly and, instead of the extradimensional switches that are required in the WCST, there were three different rules based on only one dimension (location). Participants (17 children 8–11 years, 20 adolescents 14–15 years, and 20 adults 18–24 years) were instructed to "help a dog find its way home" (i.e., find the correct location of four possible options). Different positive and negative feedback types were distinguished. Adults showed more activation in ACC after negative feedback, which indicated a switch (and thus violated expectations) and in the DLPFC after error-related negative feedback. In contrast to adults, children did not differentiate between the different negative feedback types in the DLPFC and ACC. The results demonstrate that, with development, there is an age-related specialization in the ACC and DLPFC in their contribution to feedback monitoring. This led to the hypothesis that children have difficulty recognizing the informative value for learning in the different feedback types. Together these results indicate that over the course of development, ACC and DLPFC regions become more specialized for different types of feedback.

One of the difficulties with the Crone et al. (2008) study is that negative feedback was unexpected and therefore may have been more salient than positive feedback. Van Duijvenvoorde, Zanolie, Rombouts, Raijmakers, and Crone (2008) examined this question by focusing on learning from positive and negative feedback. Participants (18 children 8–9 years, 19 early adolescents 11–13 years, 18 adults 18–25 years) performed a task in which positive and negative feedback were used to find one of two correct sorting rules (sort by color or sort by shape). Two stimuli were always presented in pairs of trials: a guess trial and a repetition trial. On guess trials, the correct sorting rule (e.g., color or shape) was cued, and the participant had to infer the correct answer based on positive or negative feedback (with an expected value of 50% correct). On the subsequent trial, the participant was expected to apply the correct rule based on information retrieved from the guess trial. The behavioral results showed that adults were better at using performance feedback than adolescents, who in turn performed better than children. Additionally, children performed relatively more inaccurately after negative feedback than after positive feedback. This valence difference was reflected in neural activation patterns. For adults, DLPFC and superior parietal cortex were more active after negative feedback, whereas in children (8–9 years), these areas were activated more after positive feedback. The adolescents did not differentiate between positive and negative feedback, suggesting the turning point was around this age (11–13 years). For both adolescents and adults, but not for children, the SMA was more active after negative than positive feedback. Thus, SMA involvement during feedback learning seems to reach adults levels before the DLPFC.

Finally, in a third paradigm, feedback processing was studied using a probabilistic learning task. In such paradigms, feedback is correct on approximately 70–80% of the trials. These tasks are more complex than tasks that use determinative feedback (which is by definition 100% valid) because it requires attending to long-term goals. In a study by van den Bos, Guroglu, van den Bulk, Rombouts, and Crone (2009), participants (18 children 8–11 years, 27 adolescents 13–16 years, and 22 adults 18–22 years) were instructed to respond to one of two pictures. One picture resulted in positive feedback on 70–80% of the trials and the other picture resulted in positive feedback on 20–30% of the trials. Children, adolescents, and adults performed equally well on the task. Interestingly, when exploring alternative rules (the stimuli that do not result in the highest probability of positive feedback), children showed more activity in DLPFC and dACC after positive feedback, whereas adults showed more activation in these areas after negative feedback. Because these differences were only found when exploring alternative rules, this suggests that the developmental difference is not simply a valence effect (van Duijvenvoorde et al., 2008) but the informative value for learning that shows a different neural developmental trajectory.

Taken together, the studies that investigated the development of adaptive flexibility have demonstrated that, with increasing age, several brain areas in the cognitive control network become more specialized for different types of performance feedback. Activity in prefrontal areas (DLPFC, ACC) is more differentiated in adults for different types of positive and negative feedback, which suggests that with development, these areas become more sensitive to the informative value of feedback. The question for future research is how the development takes place in learning from positive to negative and learning from noninformative to informative feedback.

SUMMARY

The neural circuits underlying the development of instructed flexibility and adaptive flexibility were reviewed in this chapter. The development of instructed flexibility has been investigated with two types of task switching: response switching and attention switching. For both paradigms, better behavioral performance was generally found for adults compared with children (but see Christakou et al., 2009, and Morton et al., 2009, for exceptions). Concurrent with these behavioral differences, increased activity for adults compared with children for switching was found in frontal and parietal areas, the basal ganglia, and the thalamus. Morton et al. (2009) additionally found increased activity for children in the right superior frontal sulcus, suggesting possible strategy differences between adults and children. Second, for adaptive flexibility, a different developmental pattern was found. Performance-monitoring paradigms have found an age-related specialization of frontal and parietal areas for processing different types of feedback (noninformative versus informative, positive versus negative). These findings indicate that instructed flexibility and adaptive flexibility are separable processes that both contribute to cognitive flexibility. How and when these processes interact are important questions for future research.

Future Directions

As highlighted here, over the past decade several researchers have attempted to understand the neural development underlying the development of cognitive flexibility. Although the current body of literature has provided valuable insights into cognitive flexibility, several advancements can be made that will allow us to draw more firm conclusions about the development of cognitive flexibility. We recommend three directions for future research:

Longitudinal Studies

To date, only one study has investigated the neurocognitive development of cognitive flexibility with a longitudinal design (Koolschijn, Schel, de Rooij, Rombouts, & Crone, 2011). Included in this study on performance monitoring were the same participants who participated in the Crone et al. (2008) study (N at follow-up after 3.5 years: 10 adults, 12 adolescents, and 10 children). The results indicated that the neural networks involved during the WCST-like task changed over the 3.5-year interval: more activity was found in DLPFC, superior parietal cortex, and ACC. Intriguingly, these changes were strongly related to performance improvements, more so than to age per se. This suggests that in previous cross-sectional studies, which often found performance differences between age groups, performance differences can possibly partly explain neural differences between age groups.

The findings of this study highlight the importance of longitudinal designs in developmental psychology and developmental cognitive neuroscience. Longitudinal studies have important advantages over cross-sectional studies (where different age groups are compared as a proxy for development). With longitudinal designs, it is possible to truly investigate development within participants. In cross-sectional designs, within-subject development may be masked if between-subject variability in developmental trajectories is relatively large. Cohort effects (generational differences between age groups other than age) are not a confounding factor in longitudinal studies. Given the important behavioral improvements within individuals over time, longitudinal designs will be of critical importance for future research into the development of cognitive flexibility.

Network Analyses

Several studies in adults have indicated that, for cognitive flexibility tasks, it is not only important *which* areas are activated but also how these areas interact with each other (Madden et al., 2010; Stelzel, Basten, & Fiebach, 2011; van Schouwenburg, den Ouden, & Cools, 2010). Interaction between different brain areas can be described as *functional connectivity*. With functional connectivity analyses, it is possible to investigate temporal correlations between neural signals in different brain areas. It is assumed that a temporal correlation means that these regions work in concert. Research into the development of functional connectivity is an important future venture that undoubtedly will provide us with further insights into the neural development of cognitive flexibility (Morton, 2010; Stevens, 2009).

One developmental study that has investigated functional connectivity in adaptive flexibility was performed by Van den Bos, Cohen, Kahnt, and Crone (2012). They reanalyzed the data from a study on probabilistic feedback learning (van den Bos et al., 2009). For all trials, the "prediction error" was calculated using a simple reinforcement learning model. When feedback for a stimulus was better than expected, a positive prediction error was generated by the model for that stimulus, which in turn increases the decision weight for that stimulus (i.e., the chance that stimulus will be selected on the next trial is larger). When feedback was worse than expected, a negative prediction error was generated, resulting in a lower decision weight. The researchers found that the representation of the prediction error resulted in robust activation in the striatum, an effect that was similar across age groups. Interestingly, a functional connectivity analysis showed that with increasing age, the connectivity between activity in the striatum and medial

PFC increased. The strength of this connection was also related to the tendency to change expectations after negative feedback. These findings demonstrate that focusing on network analyses can provide additional information over focusing on activity in single brain areas.

Genetics

Finally, recent studies have indicated that there are profound genetic influences on executive functioning. This has been found with both quantitative and molecular genetics studies (Morton, 2010). In quantitative genetic studies, family members who share different percentages of their genes are compared in executive functioning skills. For instance, monozygotic twins share 100% of their genes, whereas dizygotic twins and siblings share 50% of their genes. A comparison of executive functioning in the different family members can provide an estimate of the amount of variation that is explained by genes or environmental influences. With this approach, it was found that executive functions have a surprisingly high heritability factor (Friedman et al., 2008). This means that monozygotic twins who grow up in completely different environments will still be very comparable in terms of their executive functioning.

Another approach to investigate genetic influences on executive functioning is to examine specific genetic variations in a particular gene. People who have one variation of the gene can be compared in executive functioning skills to people with another variation of the gene. With this approach, genetic differences that influence dopamine functioning have already been found in adults for learning from errors (Klein et al., 2007) and task switching (Colzato, Waszak, Nieuwenhuis, Posthuma, & Hommel, 2010; van Holstein et al., 2011) and in children for feedback processing (Althaus et al., 2009). Although little research has investigated genetic influences on the development of cognitive flexibility, the current body of literature provides strong indications that these influences are likely to be found in future studies.

Conclusion

Executive functions in general, and cognitive flexibility in particular, are important aspects of child development. Cognitive flexibility has been studied extensively in children, which has led to important insights on its developmental origins. Two main types of cognitive flexibility were described in this chapter: instructed and adaptive flexibility. Maturation of brain areas involved in cognitive flexibility tasks seems to play an important role in the development of both types of flexibility. Despite the great progress in this area of research, there are also still many open questions. Future studies should focus on combined approaches to using different types of cognitive flexibility in the same individuals, to investigate whether they rely on similar neural mechanisms. Additionally, developmental theories have been often inferred from studies on cross-sectional samples. For truly developmental models, longitudinal studies are essential.

To further advance our knowledge, functional connectivity within the cognitive flexibility network should be investigated, as well as possible influences of genetic variations on the development of cognitive flexibility. We expect that, together, these new insights will allow us to better track the developmental trajectory of cognitive flexibility from childhood, through adolescence into adulthood. This knowledge will eventually, we hope, help to create better learning environments across childhood development.

REFERENCES

Althaus, M., Groen, Y., Wijers, A. A., Mulder, L. J., Minderaa, R. B., Kema, I. P., et al. (2009). Differential effects of 5-httlpr and drd2/ankk1 polymorphisms on electrocortical measures of error and feedback processing in children. *Clinical Neurophysiology, 120*(1), 93–107.

Barcelo, F., & Knight, R. T. (2002). Both random and perseverative errors underlie wcst deficits in prefrontal patients. *Neuropsychologia, 40*(3), 349–356.

Barnea-Goraly, N., Menon, V., Eckert, M., Tamm, L., Bammer, R., Karchemskiy, A., et al. (2005). White matter development during childhood and adolescence: A cross-sectional diffusion tensor imaging study. *Cerebral Cortex, 15*(12), 1848–1854.

Bierman, K. L., Nix, R. L., Greenberg, M. T., Blair, C., & Domitrovich, C. E. (2008). Executive functions and school readiness intervention: Impact, moderation, and mediation in the head start redi program. *Development and Psychopathology, 20*(3), 821–843.

Blair, C., & Razza, R. P. (2007). Relating effortful control, executive function, and false belief understanding to emerging math and literacy ability in kindergarten. *Child Development, 78*(2), 647–663.

Blair, C., Zelazo, P. D., & Greenberg, M. T. (2005). The measurement of executive function in early childhood. *Developmental Nneuropsychology, 28*(2), 561–571.

Buchsbaum, B. R., Greer, S., Chang, W. L., & Berman, K. F. (2005). Meta-analysis of neuroimaging studies of the Wisconsin Card-Sorting Task and component processes. *Human Brain Mapping, 25*(1), 35–45.

Bull, R., Espy, K. A., & Wiebe, S. A. (2008). Short-term memory, working memory, and executive functioning in preschoolers: Longitudinal predictors of mathematical achievement at age 7 years. *Developmental Neuropsychology, 33*(3), 205–228.

Casey, B. J., Davidson, M. C., Hara, Y., Thomas, K. M., Martinez, A., Galvan, A., et al. (2004). Early development of subcortical regions involved in non-cued attention switching. *Developmental Science, 7*(5), 534–542.

Casey, B. J., Giedd, J. N., & Thomas, K. M. (2000). Structural and functional brain development and its relation to cognitive development. *Biological Psychology, 54*(1–3), 241–257.

Cepeda, N. J., Kramer, A. F., & Gonzalez de Sather, J. C. (2001). Changes in executive control across the life span: Examination of task-switching performance. *Developmental Psychology, 37*(5), 715–730.

Chamberlain, S. R., Blackwell, A. D., Fineberg, N. A., Robbins, T. W., & Sahakian, B. J. (2005). The neuropsychology of obsessive compulsive disorder: The importance of failures in cognitive and behavioural inhibition as candidate endophenotypic markers. *Neuroscience and Bbiobehavioral Reviews, 29*(3), 399–419.

Chelune, G. J., & Baer, R. A. (1986). Developmental norms for the Wisconsin Card Sorting Test. *Journal of Cclinical and Experimental Neuropsychology, 8*(3), 219–228.

Chevalier, N., & Blaye, A. (2009). Setting goals to switch between tasks: Effect of cue transparency on children's cognitive flexibility. *Developmental Psychology, 45*(3), 782–797.

Christakou, A., Halari, R., Smith, A. B., Ifkovits, E., Brammer, M., & Rubia, K. (2009). Sex-dependent age modulation of frontostriatal and temporo-parietal activation during cognitive control. *NeuroImage, 48*(1), 223–236.

Colzato, L. S., Waszak, F., Nieuwenhuis, S., Posthuma, D., & Hommel, B. (2010). The flexible mind is associated with the catechol-o-methyltransferase (COMT) Val158Met polymorphism: Evidence for a role of dopamine in the control of task-switching. *Neuropsychologia, 48*(9), 2764–2768.

Corbett, B. A., Constantine, L. J., Hendren, R., Rocke, D., & Ozonoff, S. (2009). Examining executive functioning in children with autism spectrum disorder, attention deficit hyperactivity disorder and typical development. *Psychiatry Research, 166*(2–3), 210–222.

Cragg, L., & Chevalier, N. (2012). The processes underlying flexibility in childhood. *Quarterly Journal of Experimental Psychology, 65*(2), 209–232.

Crone, E. A., Bunge, S. A., van der Molen, M. W., & Ridderinkhof, K. R. (2006). Switching between tasks and responses: A developmental study. *Developmental Science, 9*(3), 278–287.

Crone, E. A., Ridderinkhof, K. R., Worm, M., Somsen, R. J., & van der Molen, M. W. (2004). Switching between spatial stimulus–response mappings: A developmental study of cognitive flexibility. *Developmental Science, 7*(4), 443–455.

Crone, E. A., Zanolie, K., Van Leijenhorst, L., Westenberg, P. M., & Rombouts, S. A. (2008). Neural mechanisms supporting flexible performance adjustment during development. Cognitive, *Affective & Behavioral Neuroscience, 8*(2), 165–177.

Derrfuss, J., Brass, M., Neumann, J., & von Cramon, D. Y. (2005). Involvement of the inferior frontal junction in cognitive control: Meta-analyses of switching and stroop studies. *Human Brain Mapping, 25*(1), 22–34.

Friedman, N. P., Miyake, A., Young, S. E., Defries, J. C., Corley, R. P., & Hewitt, J. K. (2008). Individual differences in executive functions are almost entirely genetic in origin. *Journal of Experimental Psychology, 137*(2), 201–225.

Garon, N., Bryson, S. E., & Smith, I. M. (2008). Executive function in preschoolers: A review using an integrative framework. *Psychological Bulletin, 134*(1), 31–60.

Giedd, J. N. (2004). Structural magnetic resonance imaging of the adolescent brain. *Annals of the New York Academy of Sciences*, 1021, 77–85.

Giedd, J. N., Blumenthal, J., Jeffries, N. O., Castellanos, F. X., Liu, H., Zijdenbos, A., et al. (1999). Brain development during childhood and adolescence: A longitudinal MRI study. *Nature Neuroscience, 2*(10), 861–863.

Holroyd, C. B., Nieuwenhuis, S., Yeung, N., Nystrom, L., Mars, R. B., Coles, M. G., et al. (2004). Dorsal anterior cingulate cortex shows fMRI response to internal and external error signals. *Nature Neuroscience, 7*(5), 497–498.

Huizinga, M., Dolan, C. V., & van der Molen, M. W. (2006). Age-related change in executive function: Developmental trends and a latent variable analysis. *Neuropsychologia, 44*(11), 2017–2036.

Ionescu, T. (2012). Exploring the nature of cognitive flexibility. *New Ideas in Psychology, 30*(2), 190–200.

Kim, C., Cilles, S. E., Johnson, N. F., & Gold, B. T. (2012). Domain general and domain preferential brain regions associated with different types of task switching: A meta-analysis. *Human Brain Mapping, 33*(1), 130–142.

Klein, T. A., Neumann, J., Reuter, M., Hennig, J., von Cramon, D. Y., & Ullsperger, M. (2007). Genetically determined differences in learning from errors. *Science, 318*(5856), 1642–1645.

Koolschijn, P. C., Schel, M. A., de Rooij, M., Rombouts, S. A., & Crone, E. A. (2011). A three-year longitudinal functional magnetic resonance imaging study of performance monitoring and test-retest reliability from childhood to early adulthood. *Journal of Neuroscience 31*(11), 4204–4212.

Madden, D. J., Costello, M. C., Dennis, N. A., Davis, S. W., Shepler, A. M., Spaniol, J., et al. (2010). Adult age differences in functional connectivity during executive control. *NeuroImage, 52*(2), 643–657.

Milner, B. (1963). Effects of different brain lesions on card sorting: Role of frontal lobes. *Archives of Neurology, 9*(1), 90-&.

Miyake, A., Friedman, N. P., Emerson, M. J., Witzki, A. H., Howerter, A., & Wager, T. D. (2000). The unity and diversity of executive functions and their contributions to complex "frontal lobe" tasks: A latent variable analysis. *Cognitive Psychology, 41*(1), 49–100.

Monsell, S. (2003). Task switching. *Trends in Cognitive Sciences, 7*(3), 134–140.

Morton, J. B. (2010). Understanding genetic, neurophysiological, and experiential influences on the development of executive functioning: The need for developmental models. *Wiley Interdisciplinary Reviews-Cognitive Science, 1*(5), 709–723.

Morton, J. B., Bosma, R., & Ansari, D. (2009). Age-related changes in brain activation associated with dimensional shifts of attention: An fMRI study. *NeuroImage, 46*(1), 249–256.

Nieuwenhuis, S., Slagter, H. A., von Geusau, N. J., Heslenfeld, D. J., & Holroyd, C. B. (2005). Knowing good from bad: Differential activation of human cortical areas by positive and negative outcomes. *The European Journal of Neuroscience, 21*(11), 3161–3168.

Rubia, K., Smith, A. B., Woolley, J., Nosarti, C., Heyman, I., Taylor, E., et al. (2006). Progressive increase of frontostriatal brain activation from childhood to adulthood during event-related tasks of cognitive control. *Human Brain Mapping, 27*(12), 973–993.

Stelzel, C., Basten, U., & Fiebach, C. J. (2011). Functional connectivity separates switching operations in the posterior lateral frontal cortex. *Journal of Cognitive Neuroscience, 23*(11), 3529–3539.

Tchanturia, K., Davies, H., Roberts, M., Harrison, A., Nakazato, M., Schmidt, U., et al. (2012). Poor cognitive flexibility in eating disorders: Examining the evidence using the wisconsin card sorting task. *PloS one, 7*(1), e28331.

Thomas, L. A., Hall, J. M., Skup, M., Jenkins, S. E., Pine, D. S., & Leibenluft, E. (2011). A developmental neuroimaging investigation of the change paradigm. *Developmental Science, 14*(1), 148–161.

van den Bos, W., Cohen, M. X., Kahnt, T., & Crone, E. A. (2012). Striatum-medial prefrontal cortex connectivity predicts developmental changes in reinforcement learning. *Cerebral Cortex, 22*(6), 1247–1255.

van den Bos, W., Guroglu, B., van den Bulk, B. G., Rombouts, S. A., & Crone, E. A. (2009). Better than expected or as bad as you thought? The neurocognitive development of probabilistic feedback processing. *Frontiers in Human Neuroscience, 3*, 52.

van Duijvenvoorde, A. C., Zanolie, K., Rombouts, S. A., Raijmakers, M. E., & Crone, E. A. (2008). Evaluating the negative or valuing the positive? Neural mechanisms supporting feedback-based learning across development. *Journal of Neuroscience 28*(38), 9495–9503.

van Holstein, M., Aarts, E., van der Schaaf, M. E., Geurts, D. E., Verkes, R. J., Franke, B., et al. (2011). Human cognitive flexibility depends on dopamine D2 receptor signaling. *Psychopharmacology, 218*(3), 567–578.

van Schouwenburg, M. R., den Ouden, H. E., & Cools, R. (2010). The human basal ganglia modulate frontal-posterior connectivity during attention shifting. *Journal of Neuroscience, 30*(29), 9910–9918.

van Veen, V., Holroyd, C. B., Cohen, J. D., Stenger, V. A., & Carter, C. S. (2004). Errors without conflict: Implications for performance monitoring theories of anterior cingulate cortex. *Brain and Cognition, 56*(2), 267–276.

Wager, T. D., Jonides, J., & Reading, S. (2004). Neuroimaging studies of shifting attention: A meta-analysis. *NeuroImage, 22*(4), 1679–1693.

Zanolie, K., Van Leijenhorst, L., Rombouts, S. A., & Crone, E. A. (2008). Separable neural mechanisms contribute to feedback processing in a rule-learning task. *Neuropsychologia, 46*(1), 117–126.

14

Task Switching and Aging

JUTTA KRAY AND NICOLA K. FERDINAND ■

INTRODUCTION

The ability to control one's own processing allows the flexible adaption to changes in the environment and is assumed to be highly associated with intelligence (e.g., Duncan, 1995). Cognitive control has been generally defined as the ability to guide thoughts and actions in accord with external and internal task goals and is particularly required in situations that involve the switching and selection between multiple tasks, the maintenance of task-relevant and the inhibition of task-irrelevant information, as well as the monitoring of error and conflict information (e.g., Hofmann, Schmeichel, & Baddeley, 2012; Miller & Cohen, 2001; Smith & Jonides, 1999). As it is now well documented in cognitive aging research that a number of different intellectual abilities show an accelerated decline from early adulthood to old age, such as speed of processing, working memory, and reasoning (for reviews, see Bialystok & Craik, 2006; Craik & Salthouse, 2008), a better understanding of age differences in cognitive control seems useful in order to conduct appropriate cognitive interventions for elderly people. We will review findings on developmental changes in task switching in the adult lifespan. In the first section, we will provide a look at the general pattern of age differences in task switching components and discuss this in the light of prominent cognitive aging accounts. In the second section, we will report results on age differences in preparatory and response–selection processes during task switching, while the third section will focus on the question of whether and how we can improve cognitive control processes by strategy-based or process-based interventions, such as verbal mediation or task switching training, respectively. Finally, we will discuss the empirical findings in the context of theoretical explanations and aging models of cognitive control functioning.

AGE DIFFERENCES IN TASK SWITCHING COMPONENTS

Ageing research has taken a great interest in applying the task switching paradigm as it allows the study of a variety of control processes, such as task preparation, interference and switching processes within the same experimental paradigm (for a recent review, see Kiesel et al., 2010). Most of these aging studies used an experimental design with blocks of trials in which participants are instructed to switch between two tasks A and B (i.e., mixed-task blocks) as well as blocks of trials in which participants perform only task A or B (i.e., single-task blocks). Thereby, mixing costs can be examined by comparing performance between mixed-task and single-task blocks (also termed global or general switch costs; cf. Kray & Lindenberger, 2000; Mayr, 2001), and switching costs can be derived by comparing performance between switch and nonswitch trials within mixed-task blocks (also termed local or specific switch costs). Mixing costs are thought to reflect control processes that are required for maintaining multiple task sets and for selecting between them (i.e., being in a switching situation), while switching costs are thought to reflect the reconfiguration of task sets (i.e., performing a task switch). Note that there exist different variants of defining mixing costs as well as theoretical explanations of their origin (see Mari-Beffa & Kirkham, this volume). Evidence for the view that both types of costs, mixing and switching costs, are indeed separable and distinct components of task switching comes from structural equations approaches. For instance, Kray and Lindenberger (2000) used a confirmatory factor analysis and found that a two-component model with mixing and switching costs as separate but intercorrelated latent factors fitted the data better than a single-factor model.

Up to date, the majority of aging studies has found substantial age differences in mixing costs, suggesting age-related impairments in maintaining and selecting between task sets (Buchler, Hoyer, & Cerella, 2008; Cepeda, Kramer, & Gonzalez de Sather, 2001; Kray, 2006; Kray & Lindenberger, 2000; Kray, Eber, & Lindenberger, 2004; Kray, Eber, & Karbach, 2008; Lawo, Philipp, Schuch, & Koch, 2012; Mayr, 2001; Meiran, Gotler, & Perlman, 2001; Lien, Ruthruff, & Kuhns, 2008; Reimers & Maylor, 2005; van Asselen & Ridderinkhof, 2000; but see Kray, Li, & Lindenberger, 2002). Although some studies also reported evidence for age differences in switching costs (e.g., Meiran et al., 2001), a majority of studies showed that age differences in switching costs are much smaller than in mixing costs (e.g., Karayanidis, Whitson, Heathcote, & Michie, 2011; Kray & Lindenberger, 2000; Kray et al., 2004, 2008; Kray, Eppinger, & Mecklinger, 2005; Mayr, 2001; Mayr & Liebscher, 2001; Lien et al., 2008; Reimers & Maylor, 2005) and often fail to reach significance (e.g., Kray & Lindenberger, 2000; Hahn, Anderson, & Kramer, 2004; Salthouse et al., 1998). This indicates that older adults show no process specific limitations in task switching per se (i.e., in the implementation of a task switch at trial-to-trial transitions), but in being in a switch situation requiring the selection between tasks and their maintenance. This general pattern of differential age-related changes in task switching components has recently been confirmed by a meta-analysis that included 26 so far published aging studies on task switching (Wasylyshyn, Verhaeghen, & Sliwinski, 2011).

According to current theories of cognitive aging, one group of aging researchers favor theoretical explanations that propose a very limited number of determinants that can explain age-related changes in a large variety of cognitive tasks (e.g., Lindenberger, Mayr, & Kliegl, 1993; for a review, see Baltes, Staudinger, & Lindenberger, 1999). The most prominent among them is the speed-of-processing account suggested by Salthouse (1991, 1996). In fact, there is accumulated evidence for the view that age-related slowing in cognitive processing is the most powerful predictor for explaining age-related differences in fluid-like cognitive abilities (e.g., Salthouse et al., 1998). The other group of aging researchers emphasize process-specific limitations in cognitive tasks in the elderly, highlighting empirical evidence showing age-related differences in some aspects of cognitive control processes, such as in task coordination, but not in other aspects of cognitive control, such as selective attention (for reviews, see, e.g., Kramer & Kray, 2006; Verhaeghen & Cerella, 2002). Hence, the empirical results on age differences in the two task switching components as described above are in line with this latter view favoring process-specific limitations of cognitive processing in old age. In the following, we will review age differences in different types of the task switching paradigm that differ in their demands on task-preparation, task-maintenance and inhibition processes.

Age Differences in Task Preparation

Different variants of the task switching paradigm have been applied to investigate the nature of preparatory processes involved in the control of cognitive processes. Nearly all of those task switching studies have found that mixing and switching costs are substantially reduced when subjects have more time to prepare the next task, either when applying explicit cueing paradigms (for a review, see Meiran, this volume) or alternating-runs paradigms (cf. Rogers & Monsell, 1995).

Looking at age differences in advance task preparation, the findings so far indicate that young and older adults show a similar reduction in mixing and switching costs when explicit task cues are provided (Cepeda et al., 2001; Hartley, Kieley, & Slabach, 1990; Kray, 2006; Kramer, Hahn, & Gopher, 1999; Mayr & Liebscher, 2001; Meiran, Gotler, & Perlman, 2001; Hahn, Anderson, & Kramer, 2004), suggesting no specific deficit of older adults in processing and using task-cue information if they have enough time to prepare. In a so far unpublished study, Kray and Eber (2003) additionally examined whether the type of task cue has an impact on advance preparation during task switching. In this study, we investigated age differences in the reduction of mixing costs with a short (550 ms) and a long (1050 ms) preparation interval depending on a semantic or symbolic task cue. Semantic cues clearly indicated the task meaning (e.g., "Color" for a categorization task on the type of color, such as blue and yellow) and can be seen as transparent cues, while symbolic cues (e.g., "C" for the same task) are less meaningful and by this termed nontransparent cues (cf. Grange & Houghton, 2010). In particular, we assumed that symbolic cues need additional processing, that is, a translation of the cue into a phonological representation of the task goal, which is time consuming (e.g., Baddeley, Chincotta, & Adlam, 2001; Chevalier & Blaye, 2009; Emerson & Miyake, 2003; Miyake, Emerson, Padilla, & Ahn, 2004). Therefore, preparation

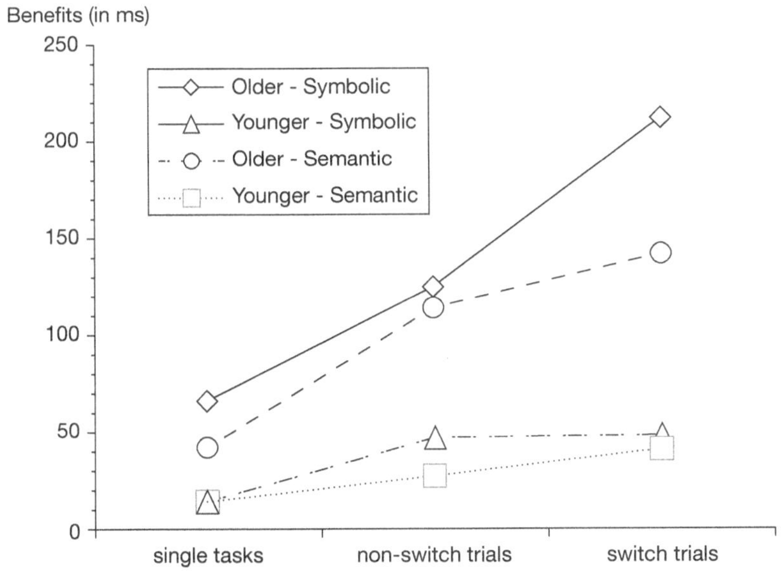

Figure 14.1 Preparation benefits defined as differences in mean RT for short preparation intervals (550 ms) versus mean RT for long preparation intervals (1050 ms) as a function of trial type (single, nonswitch, switch), cue type (semantic, symbolic), and age group (younger, older) (cf. Kray & Eber, 2003).

benefits should be larger for symbolic than for semantic task cues. Results of this study are fully in line with the predictions. Mixing costs were larger for symbolic than for semantic cues for younger and older adults and age was insensitive to the nature of task cues (see Figure 14.1). In this study, older adults showed even larger preparation benefits in nonswitch as well as in switch trials compared with younger adults.

In a similar vein, Hahn, Andersen, and Kramer (2004) showed further evidence for the age insensitivity to the processing of cue type. Results of their study showed that both younger and older adults can use task cues as well as response cues for reducing switching costs when they receive more time to prepare a switch. In contrast, Lawo et al. (2012) recently reported that older adults profit less from increased preparation time than younger adults do. However, in this study subjects had to switch between three tasks so that memory load to maintain task set representations was relatively high even if explicit cues were presented. Moreover, the preparation interval was prolonged to 1000 ms only, so it might still be the case that age differences disappear with even longer preparation intervals.

Also, under memory-based switching conditions in which the task sequence is predictable and no explicit cues are presented, younger as well as older adults are able to profit from increased preparation time (De Jong, 2001; Kramer et al., 1999; Kray, 2006; Kray & Lindenberger, 2000), and some studies report an even larger reduction in switching costs for older adults (cf. Cepeda et al., 2001). Interestingly, only one study so far showed that older adults were not able to use longer preparation times under memory-based switching conditions and in this case the memory load was relatively high because subjects had to keep track of four task repetitions before switching to the other task (cf. Kramer et al., 1999). Hence, age differences in preparatory processing may only occur under relatively high working memory load (cf. Kramer & Kray, 2006) or when working memory is impaired (Goffaux, Phillips, Sinai, & Pushkar, 2008).

Age Differences in the Voluntary Control of Behavior

Altogether, the above findings suggest that older adults profit from increased preparation time during task switching, independently of the absence or presence of task cues and the nature of cue information. Some researchers argue that age differences in task switching components are smaller when explicit task cues are present than when they are absent (e.g., Kray et al., 2002). However, it seems that age differences in mixing and switching costs are strongly influenced by participants' behavior in nonswitch conditions and this depends on a number of factors, such as the predictability of task switches. For example, Kray (2006) found that older adults showed smaller switching costs than younger adults when an explicit cueing paradigm was applied in which the sequence of tasks was random and by this unpredictable, and, in contrast to most other aging studies, task cues were only presented briefly for about 300 ms and then disappeared. In comparison to a memory-based switching condition and younger adults, older adults showed nearly no reaction time differences between nonswitch and switch trials. This finding was interpreted in the light of theoretical ideas suggested by Monsell and colleagues (2003), who propose that the voluntary control of behavior functions differently under cue-based than memory-based switching modes. In a random switching situation, cognitive control behavior is influenced by the expectation of subjects that a further task change is possible, and thereby, they adopt a less extreme bias between two task sets (i.e., they engage less in reconfiguring task settings). In contrast, in a predictable switching situation with the next switch being predictable with a 100% probability, subjects use a more extreme bias between both tasks, i.e., they nearly fully reconfigure the task settings from one task to the next, which produces greater switch costs on the first trial after a task switch. Hence, the unpredictability of events (task switches) may lead older adults to adopt a more conservative strategy than younger adults in the sense that they are less engaged in a new task. In a recent study, however, Lien et al. (2008) found no age differences in switching costs depending on the expectancy of a task switch, neither when applying an alternating runs paradigm nor an explicit cueing paradigm. Similarly, age differences in switching costs have been found to be insensitive to the frequency of task switches in explicit cueing paradigms (Kray et al., 2002).

Further evidence for the view that differences between younger and older adults in task switching situations are influenced by the strategic adaption of different control modes induced by task cues comes from a study by Spieler, Mayr, and LaGrone (2006). They suggest that older adults have problems with switching from a high control mode induced by a cued switching condition to a low control mode in which only one of the two tasks has to be performed in the following trials (see also Mayr & Liebscher, 2001). Using eye-movement techniques, they found that older, in contrast to young adults, had a strong tendency to inspect task cues even in single-task blocks in which the cue information is in principle redundant. When older subjects were forced to rely on an internal mode of control because no external task cues were provided, age differences in performance disappeared. Hence, if cues are present older adults prefer to "outsource" the maintaining of relevant task representations to the environment, probably to reduce memory load and to reduce demands on selecting between competing task-set representations even when it is not necessary (cf. Spieler et al., 2006).

Age Differences in Switching between Multiple Tasks and Stimuli

Most aging studies to date have focused on examining age differences in the efficiency of switching between two task sets, while rather few studies have also investigated age effects of switching between two in contrast to multiple tasks (e.g., Buchler et al., 2008; Kray et al., 2002). If memory load is critical for the explanation of age differences in task switching costs, then increasing the number of tasks should matter. One major problem with conducting experiments that compare switching performance between different numbers of tasks is that other factors, such as switch frequency, should be kept constant or be carefully controlled across this manipulation. For instance, in a study by Buchler et al. (2008), this was achieved by fixing the switching probability to 66% and determining task switching costs by continuously increasing the task-set size from one to four. In the Kray et al. (2002) study, the switching probability was manipulated and varied between 37.5%, 50%, and 75% for the task-set sizes two and four. Results indicated that (a) switch frequency had no impact on switching costs as well as on age differences therein; (b) mixing costs were insensitive to the increase of task-set size beyond two; and (c) switching costs increased with the number of tasks in the one (Kray et al., 2002) but not in the other study (Buchler et al., 2008). Interestingly, age differences in mixing costs were largely reduced and disappeared with intensive practice in the latter study although subjects had to switch between four simple computational tasks. Hence, it seems that the occurrence of age differences in mixing costs cannot be solely explained by an increase in memory load induced by the number of tasks. Mixing costs primarily occur when subjects need to switch from one task to the next (being in a switch situation) while the number of potentially relevant tasks does not matter. However, note that in both studies mentioned above, an explicit cueing paradigm was applied so that it remains an open question whether these findings also generalize to memory-based switching conditions in which subjects have to keep track of the task sequence.

Another factor that was thought to influence the switching between task sets is the number of different stimuli included in switching experiments. For instance,

Rogers and Monsell (1995) argued that the number of stimuli should be large in order to avoid that subjects will learn associations between attributes, task cues, and responses throughout the experiment. In other words, the use of small stimulus-set sizes in task switching experiments may result in a modification of association strengths between tasks, stimulus attributes, and responses with increasing practice so that reconfiguration at the level of higher-order "task sets" is no longer necessary. To our knowledge, there is only one aging study to date that examined whether the number of stimuli included in task switching experiments has an impact on age differences in switching costs. In that study, age differences in task switching costs were compared between conditions with a rather small stimulus set (n = 4) and a larger stimulus set (n = 96). Noteworthy, age differences in switching costs—that are sometimes found to be reliable and sometimes not—were only significant for the small stimulus-set size but absent for the large stimulus-set size condition. Further analysis of the age effects in the small stimulus-set size group revealed that younger and older adults differ in benefitting from practice as a function of response congruency. On congruent trials, in which the stimulus attributes of the two task sets were mapped onto the same response, younger and older adults show a similar reduction of switching costs with practice. In contrast, on incongruent trials, in which stimulus attributes of the two task sets were associated with different responses, a reduction of switching costs with practice was only obtained for younger adults but not for older adults. Hence, the results are in line with other findings suggesting that older adults have more problems in task switching than younger adults when there is interference induced at the level of stimulus and response sets by overlapping task-set representations (cf. Mayr, 2001; see also next section).

The Influence of Task Interference

A number of studies have investigated how interference between tasks or interference arising from a previously performed task influence task switching (see Gade et al., this volume). Task interference depends on the degree of overlap between the involved task representations and can be induced at different levels: at the level of stimuli and/or at the level of responses. Interference at the level of stimuli can be measured by comparing performance on congruent and incongruent stimuli, in which attributes of the two tasks are present, with performance on a "neutral" stimulus, in which only attributes of one task are present together with task-irrelevant attributes. For instance, in the Rogers and Monsell (1995) study, subjects saw digit-letter combinations (e.g., 5A). In the digit task, they had to decide whether the digit was odd or even by responding with a left or right response button, and in the letter task, they decided whether the letter is a consonant or vowel also by pressing the same left or right response button). As neutral trials, they used combinations of letters or digits with symbols (e.g., 5%, #A) that require no response. Interference at the response level occurs when attributes of the two tasks are mapped onto the same responses compared with when each attribute is mapped onto a separate response (in this example, two versus four response buttons, respectively).

Task interference (or task ambiguity) has been shown to influence task switching performance, for instance, switching costs are often found to be greater on incongruent than on congruent trials, suggesting that switching from one task to the next is hampered when attributes of the other task have to be suppressed (for reviews, see Kiesel et al., 2010, and Gade et al., this volume). Older adults seem to be insensitive to task interference when switching is required at trial-to-trial transitions (e.g., Eppinger, Kray, Mecklinger, & John, 2007; Kramer et al., 1999; Kray et al., 2005; see also Lawo et al., 2012).

Interestingly, task interference seems to influence age effects in mixing costs under specific conditions. For example, Mayr (2001) systematically investigated whether age differences in mixing costs are influenced by task interference occurring at the stimulus and response level. Results of his study indicated that age differences in mixing costs were reliable under conditions of high stimulus ambiguity and full response-set overlap, even though explicit task cues were provided. Age differences in mixing costs were reduced and disappeared when either stimulus attributes of the two tasks or response attributes of the two tasks were not overlapping (Mayr, 2001; see also Eppinger et al., 2007; but see Kray et al., 2005). Consequently, Mayr (2001) suggested that older adults have a specific deficit in differentiating between partially overlapping task-set representations and therefore show the tendency to update internal control settings all the time when being in a switch situation, that means in nonswitch and switch trials. Hence, younger and older adults differ in their task switching behavior primarily on nonswitch trials. As a consequence, age differences in mixing costs are much larger relative to age effects in costs occurring within mixing blocks.

COGNITIVE INTERVENTIONS: HOW CAN AGE DIFFERENCES IN TASK SWITCHING BE REDUCED?

The research findings on age differences in task switching reported so far demonstrate that not all kinds of cognitive control processes are equally sensitive to age. As a general phenomenon, age differences primarily occur when older adults are in a switch situation and when the environmental context induces uncertainty which task should be performed next (e.g., high task interference, absence of task cues). Some researchers, like Duncan (1995), suggest a close link between the efficiency of cognitive control, cognitive impairments of patients after frontal lobe damage and of older adults, and individual differences in fluid intelligence, and that all these phenomena are due to problems of abstract goal selection in the context of ambiguity.

In the following, we will summarize research from two research approaches on cognitive interventions: The first is a strategy-based intervention approach in which subjects are instructed to apply a verbal strategy during task switching, and the second is a process-based intervention approach in which cognitive control processes are practiced throughout different types of task switching training conditions. Given that the number of elderly people will substantially increase in the next decades, it seems mandatory to develop and to prove effective cognitive interventions that can improve cognitive control functioning in old age.

Strategy-Based Interventions: Effects of Verbal Labeling

One way to support task-preparatory processes and to enhance the retrieval of currently relevant tasks is promoting inner speech processes (cf. verbal mediation). Such internal control devices may be especially useful for elderly people because of their lifelong practice in using language for action control. The general idea, that verbal processes play a critical role in planning and regulating goal-directed behavior, has a long tradition in psychology and has been put forward, among others, by famous psychologists such as Vygotsky (1962) and Luria (1961).

In the last decade, the role of inner speech processes has also been examined in the context of task switching, primarily in young adulthood. A variety of these studies applied an articulatory suppression approach in order to disrupt the use of inner speech processes during task switching. For instance, subjects were instructed to repeat aloud an over-learned sequence of words during task preparation, such as naming the days of the week. Results are quite consistent across these studies in showing that mixing costs are substantially increased when inner speech was disrupted by articulatory suppression (e.g., Baddeley et al., 2001; Bryck & Mayr, 2005; Emerson & Miyake, 2003; Goschke, 2000; Miyake et al., 2004; Saeki & Saito, 2004). It is noteworthy that mixing costs were largest when explicit external cueing devices were absent or relatively abstract as compared with semantic task-cues or symbolic cues that directly activate the currently relevant task (e.g., Baddeley et al., 2001; Chevalier & Blaye, 2009; Emerson & Miyake, 2003; Miyake et al., 2004). Thus, if explicit task cues are missing, subjects spontaneously recruit inner speech in order to appropriately retrieve and maintain currently relevant task goals.

Along this line, we investigated in our studies whether verbal labeling such as verbalizing the next task (task labeling) or response (response labeling) is an appropriate strategy to enhance task preparation in older as well as in younger adults, and whether especially older adults would profit from such a verbal self-instruction strategy as they are known to rely less on the spontaneous use of strategies (Kray et al., 2004, 2008; Kray, Blaye, & Lucenet, 2010). In one of these studies (Kray et al., 2006), we used an alternating runs paradigm without explicit task cues, originally introduced by Rogers and Monsell (1995), so that participants had to keep track of the task sequence in mixing blocks as it has already been shown that the recruitment of inner speech is maximized when external cues are missing (e.g., Emerson & Miyake, 2003). Participants had to perform a simple color-categorization (gray or colored) or animal-categorization task (can swim or fly). In order to determine the impact of verbal processes, we compared performance between three types of conditions: In the control condition, no verbalization was required, while in the task labeling condition, subjects were to

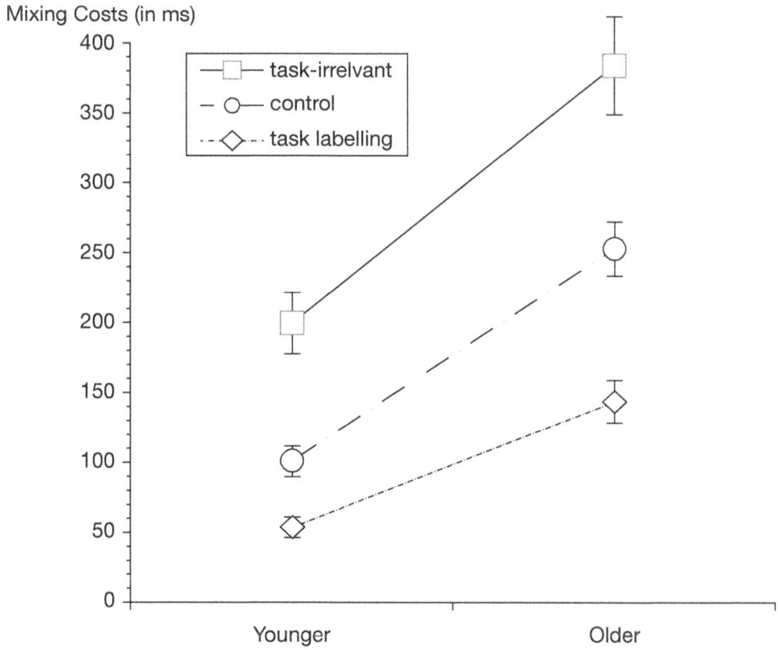

Figure 14.2 Mixing costs as a function of verbalization condition (task-irrelevant, control, task labeling) and age (younger, older) (cf. Kray et al., 2008). Error bars refer to the SEMs.

verbalize aloud the upcoming task, that is, they said "color" or "animal" during the preparation phase. In the third condition, participants had to verbalize one task-irrelevant word of an over-learned sequence during the preparation phase (i.e., "the, the, the" which corresponds to the three different German articles "der, die, das"). Importantly, in both labeling conditions participants were explicitly instructed to begin with labeling at the onset of the fixation cross. Results indicated that (a) mixing costs were greater when subjects verbalized task-irrelevant words as compared with the control condition, fully in line with previously reported findings showing articulatory suppression effects; (b) mixing costs were smaller in the task labeling than in the control condition, suggesting that although subjects perform a secondary task, younger as well as older adults show substantial benefits of using verbal self-instructions (see Figure 14.2). Furthermore, (c) older adults even showed larger reductions of mixing costs under the task labeling condition than younger adults did, supporting the view that older adults usually make less spontaneous use of verbal strategies. Finally, (d) these costs and benefits of task-irrelevant and task-relevant labeling remained reliable across three sessions of practice, suggesting that verbal processes still play an important regulatory function after the initial implementation of a task and its response rules.

Because of the high demands on keeping track of the task sequence in an alternating runs paradigm, Bryck and Mayr (2005) recently suggested a specific task-sequencing function of verbal processes. In line with this view, they reported that the articulatory suppression effect on mixing costs was strongly reduced if the task sequence was spatially cued by the position of a grid in which the stimuli were presented. Along this line, we recently investigated whether effects of task labeling on mixing costs also vary with the presence of environmental spatial cues and whether young as well as older adults have a preference for external control devices (Kray et al., 2010), consistent with the outsourcing idea proposed by Spieler and colleagues (2006). Therefore, we assessed task switching performance in a control condition without labeling and in a task labeling condition, similar to the one described before, under a high and a low task-sequencing condition. For the high task-sequencing load group all stimuli appeared in one grid. The low task-sequencing load group performed the switching task with spatial cues. Here, the stimuli appeared in one of two grids with the grid position indicating whether task A or task B should be performed. We expected that with lower task-sequencing demands, verbal labeling should be less beneficial.

Verbalization benefits depended on whether participants started the task switching experiment with the control or the task-labeling condition. For the group that started with the control condition, we found a substantial reduction of mixing costs under task labeling conditions and this reduction was even more pronounced for elderly subjects. In fact, age differences in mixing costs disappeared for the task-naming condition. However, we found no reliable interactions with task-sequencing load. For the group that started with the task-labeling condition, we found no verbalization benefits on mixing costs and no modulation of this effect with the task-sequencing load. Hence, verbalization benefits on mixing costs were only found when subjects already had some practice in task switching. This was further supported by a control study that we conducted with a subsample of older adults who completed a second session which was identical to the first. Indeed, task-labeling benefits in mixing costs occurred in the second session. Hence, it seems that verbal labeling becomes beneficial more quickly if subjects have at least some practice in task switching alone without performing an additional verbal task (cf. Kray et al., 2010).

Why is task labeling such a useful cognitive intervention especially for older adults? We believe that task labeling promotes optimal task preparation in two ways: First, it optimizes the timing of preparation. Note that in our studies subjects were also instructed on *when* to begin with the task-retrieval process, namely with the appearance of the fixation cross, and task retrieval should be most efficient if it starts early during the preparation interval. Second, it ensures the application of preparation. Given that investing in advance preparation is also exhausting, subjects sometimes tend to engage in advance preparation and sometimes not, suggesting that they are not always optimally prepared for the next task (cf. failure-to-engage account by De Jong, 2001; Nieuwenhuis & Monsell, 2002; see also reactive control mode described in the next section). Thus, task labeling may increase the likelihood to engage in advance preparation in nearly all of the trials and thereby strongly reduces mixing costs. As there is at least some evidence that older adults fail to spontaneously use verbal strategies in contrast to younger adults (Meichenbaum, 1974), they particularly profit from the induced task-labeling strategy. An alternative explanation would be that task labeling more strongly activates currently relevant task-set representations so that older adults may suffer less from stimulus interference (see earlier), which in turn strongly reduces age differences in task switching (cf. Kray et al., 2010).

Process-Based Interventions: Practice Effects and Transfer of Training

Another approach to improve task switching performance in the elderly is to simply practice the involved cognitive control processes. If mixing and switching costs are still present after intensive practice, this would further support the view that they reflect higher-order control processes that are still needed, even if the application of task-specific rules is well automatized (cf. Kray & Lindenberger, 2000). From a developmental perspective, practice- or training-induced cognitive interventions have been applied to determine the potential range as well as the limits of cognitive plasticity in younger and older adults. In particular, studies using a testing-the-limits approach (cf. Baltes & Kliegl, 1992; Kliegl & Baltes, 1987)—in which participants receive practice until they reach an asymptotic performance level—are useful in order to separate aging losses that are due to experience and practice from biological aging losses (e.g., Baltes et al., 1999).

Following this line of reasoning, a number of previous studies have indicated that mixing and switching costs are reduced but still reliable after practice (e.g., Minear & Shah, 2008) and that younger as well as older adults show substantial plasticity in task switching already after moderate and after extensive practice (Buchler et al., 2008; Cepeda et al., 2001; Karbach & Kray, 2009; Kramer et al., 1999; Kray et al., 2008; Kray & Eppinger, 2006; Kray & Lindenberger, 2000). Some of these studies even found evidence for reduced age differences in mixing costs after practice, with older adults showing larger improvements than younger adults (Cepeda et al., 2001; Kray & Lindenberger, 2000, Kray et al., 2008), and some reported that age differences in task switching disappeared after extended practice (Buchler et al., 2008; Kramer et al., 1999). Although these findings are promising in themselves because they imply considerable plasticity in cognitive control processes even in old age, it would have enormous practical implications if the cognitive improvements after practice in task switching are transferable to untrained, structurally similar as well as different, cognitive tasks, even more so because the transfer of cognitive training improvements has been found to be restricted in elderly people (for a review, see, e.g., Lövdén et al., 2010).

In one of our recent lifespan studies (Karbach & Kray, 2009), we specifically examined the transfer scope of practice-induced changes in task switching under different kinds of training conditions. For this purpose, we applied a pretest-training-posttest design in which participants received four sessions of practice either in task switching (treatment groups) or in both single tasks (active control group). To determine the transfer scope we used a comprehensive cognitive test battery including an untrained but structurally similar switching task as well as tests and tasks measuring visual and verbal working memory, inhibition, and reasoning. To examine the effects of different training conditions, we compared transfer effects between three treatment groups: The first group performed the same switching tasks across all four sessions, the second group was additionally instructed to use verbal self-instruction as this strategy has been found to reduce age differences in task switching in a previous study (Kray et al., 2008), and the third group practiced task switching with verbal self-instructions but received new switching tasks in each of the four sessions (variable training condition). The most important results of this study were that (a) younger as well as older adults showed substantial practice-induced improvements in task switching (i.e., a reduction in switching costs) throughout the training sessions; (b) transfer effects to an untrained switching task were found, that is, a larger reduction of mixing costs (cf. Minear & Shah, 2008) and switching costs from pre-test to post-test in the treatments relative to the control group (see Figure 14.3), (c) this transfer effect was greater for older than for younger adults; and finally (d) a relatively broad transfer scope was obtained in younger as well as in older adults, that is, better performance in visual and verbal working memory, inhibitory control as well as in reasoning tasks at posttest relative to pretest performance. Regarding the different treatment effects, we also found similar effects for younger and older adults. None of the age groups showed a reliably larger transfer of training when the groups additionally received the strategy-based intervention, namely a verbal-self instruction training (see also Karbach, Mang, & Kray, 2010), but they showed larger transfer when the training was variable and participants performed new switching tasks in each of the four training sessions (see Figure 14.3). Hence, results of this study have important practical implications as they suggest that practice of higher-order control processes (i.e., task switching training) leads to improvements in a number of cognitive tasks all related to fluid intelligence. This means that cognitive training interventions that aim at enhancing cognitive control processing appear to be quite successful in promoting general transfer, i.e., improved performance in a number of intellectual tasks (cf. Karbach & Kray, 2009).

However, the results also indicated that the strategy-based intervention, namely practice of verbal self-instruction, did not lead to even larger transfer effects. One possible explanation for the lack of verbal self-instruction transfer might be related to the degree of similarity between the training and the transfer situation. To examine this, a new training study including only older adults was conducted and transfer effects were compared between two further groups that applied the verbal strategy also at posttest. While the one group applied the verbal strategy also during training, the other group applied it only at posttest. In line with our assumption, transfer effects were now larger for the training group that applied the verbal strategy during training and posttest as compared with the group that performed the verbal strategy only during training. However, the control group which used the verbal strategy only at posttest showed an even larger transfer effect, indicating that a strategy-based intervention is not easily transferred to or interfered with a new situation, although applying a verbal strategy during task switching as such is useful (Karbach et al., 2010).

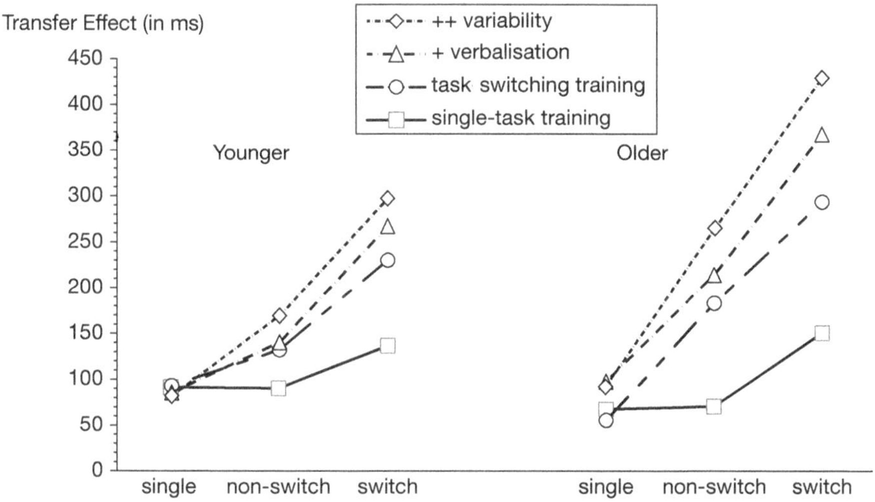

Figure 14.3 Transfer effects (pretest minus posttest performance) as a function of training conditions (single-task training, task switching training, task switching + verbalization training, task switching + verbalization + variability training), trial type (single, nonswitch, switch), and age (younger, older) (cf. Karbach & Kray, 2009).

Summary

To summarize, older adults particularly have problems when they are in a switch situation which requires task-set selection and maintenance, but less when they have to switch from one task to the next. This phenomenon cannot be simply explained by increasing demands of memory load as increasing the number of tasks did not enlarge mixing costs or age differences therein. Increasing the number of tasks from one to two seems critical to induce selection problems in the elderly that can be reduced with intensive practice or with prolonged preparation time and be increased with task interference and uncertainty. Although task-preparatory processes are relatively preserved in old age, cognitive intervention studies show that optimal task preparation can be promoted by practice and verbal labeling strategies so that age differences in task-set selection sometimes disappear. Task switching training can be seen as a useful cognitive intervention that improves cognitive control processing and transfers to a number of other intellectual abilities.

THEORETICAL EXPLANATIONS OF AGE DIFFERENCES IN TASK SWITCHING

Given the large body of evidence on differential age effects in task switching, indicating age-related differences in mixing costs and smaller ones in switching costs, theories promoting process-specific cognitive limitations in the elderly seem more plausible than theories arguing for general processing limitations in old age. Interestingly, a number of other aspects of executive control, such as the control of interference in Stroop or negative priming tasks, show no age-specific effects beyond the effects of general slowing. Using multilevel modeling for a meta-analytic approach, Verhaeghen and colleagues recently showed that mixing costs as well as dual-task costs require an additional processing stage, producing age effects beyond general slowing (Verhaeghen & Cerella, 2002; see also Wasylyshyn et al., 2011).

Along this line, some aging researchers propose that older adults have a specific problem in selecting between higher-order tasks (i.e., task sets) at least in the context of task ambiguity or uncertainty (Kray et al., 2002; Mayr, 2001). Task ambiguity induced by overlapping task representations or task uncertainty induced by unpredictability of task order or absence of cues increase demands on task selection so that older adults, in contrast to younger adults, retrieve currently relevant task settings even if it is not necessary (cf. Mayr, 2001).

It is also reasonable to assume that mixing costs arise because of changes in setting response criteria in mixed compared with single-task blocks (cf. Los, 1996) and that older adults use more conservative response criteria, that is, they "wait" much longer for response selection in mixed-task relative to single-task blocks compared with younger adults (cf. De Jong, 2001). If older adults use a more conservative response threshold in mixing blocks, then a response deadline procedure forcing subjects to respond faster should reduce age differences in mixing costs. Indeed, De Jong (2001) reported some evidence for this view. Interestingly, in one study in which we did not find age differences in mixing costs, we applied a response deadline procedure as well (see Kray et al., 2002). However, even if older adults have a tendency to prolong response execution, one still has to understand in which conditions this arises to come up with a theoretical interpretation of age-specific deficits in task switching.

Evidence From the Neurosciences of Ageing

To better understand the origin of age differences in task switching, some researchers have used neurophysiological measures like event-related potentials (ERPs). The advantage of an ERP approach is the online-measurement of information processing in different phases of task performance, thereby allowing the investigation of age differences in cue- and target-related as well as in response-related processing stages. By this, it is possible to identify the differential contribution of the processes involved in task and response preparation and execution (see also Karayanidis & Jamadar, this volume) and to determine the process-specific impairments of the elderly in a more fine-grained fashion.

For instance, task-preparatory processes were often examined with cued task switching paradigms. A typical cue-related activity in the ERP is reflected in a positive deflection that onsets at about 300 ms after cue presentation over parietal scalp regions. This component, the P300, is typically interpreted as a reflection of working memory updating (e.g., Donchin & Coles, 1988) and is substantially larger in mixed- than in single-task blocks. A number of aging studies have found that this component is only somewhat delayed in the elderly but not attenuated (Eppinger et al., 2007; Kray et al., 2005; West, 2004; West & Travers, 2008); it is attenuated only for low-performing elderly subjects (De Sanctis et al., 2009). These findings fit nicely with the previously reported behavioral results, showing no specific deficit of older adults in processing and retrieving task-cue information. Moreover, while the P300 differentiates switch from nonswitch trials within mixed task blocks in younger adults, this is not the case for older adults. This is also in line with the theoretical consideration that older adults tend to update task sets all the time when being in a switching situation (see Eppinger at al., 2007; Friedman et al., 2008; West & Moore, 2005).

In contrast to this, age effects were found in a different component, the contingent negative variation (CNV) that occurs before target presentation. For older adults, but not for younger adults, the CNV was larger in mixed- than single-task blocks (Kray et al., 2005). However, in a study by West (2004), slow potentials were larger for mixed than single blocks and were attenuated over occipital areas for older participants. These findings were taken to reflect a reduced ability to maintain task representations over time or to configure appropriate task-rule mappings during preparation.

Examining target-related ERP activity, West and Travers (2008) found that younger adults showed an enhanced parietal P300 in single compared with mixed blocks, while this difference was absent for older adults. They interpreted this finding as reflecting differences in attentional demands: While the two conditions posed clearly different attentional demands on younger adults, they seemed to be equally demanding for the elderly. Also, Adrover-Roig et al. (2010) showed that the P300 after target presentation was clearly parietally distributed for younger adults, but it was more evenly distributed over the scalp for older participants. This age-related anterior shift may reflect compensatory resource allocation that is specifically linked to target evaluation and response selection processes (for a similar finding, see De Sanctis et al., 2009).

This latter view is also supported by studies using functional and structural imaging methods. For instance, DiGirolamo and colleagues (2001) found that younger adults showed greater activation in dorsolateral prefrontal cortex and medial frontal cortex during switching than during single blocks, while older adults showed no such differentiation. Older adults also recruited significantly larger brain areas in both conditions than did younger adults. This may indicate that although older subjects recruit similar brain areas during switch and single blocks, they compensate for reduced cognitive abilities by using larger brain areas even in tasks that do not necessarily require this (see also Gold et al., 2010).

Moreover, Madden and colleagues (2010) were able to show that the magnitude of switching-related activation in a frontoparietal network was comparable for younger and older adults, which is consistent with the lack of age-related differences in behavioral switching costs. However, they also found that several regions of this network, especially prefrontal regions related to cue and target processing, were more strongly activated in older than younger adults, while other regions, especially the occipital cortex, exhibited greater activation for younger adults. This is in line with the age-related anterior shift found in ERP studies, showing that older adults activate multiple prefrontal regions rather than limiting activation to those regions specifically supporting the required processes.

To explain age differences in cognitive control, Braver and colleagues put forward the context processing model (Braver & Barch, 2002; Braver & West, 2007). In this framework, context is defined as a subset of representations within working memory, which influence the processing of other representations. These context representations are housed in the dorsolateral prefrontal cortex and actively maintained depending on the task demands. A fundamental function of lateral prefrontal cortex is seen in exerting a top-down bias on posterior and subcortical brain systems that are engaged in task-specific processing. In their model, they further propose that dopamine projections to the prefrontal cortex are regulating the access to context information via a gating mechanism. When there is phasic dopamine activity, incoming information can update context representations. As it is well known that aging is accompanied by pronounced changes in the prefrontal cortex (e.g., Cabeza, Nyberg, & Park, 2005; Raz, 2000), Braver and colleagues assume that in healthy aging, this context processing mechanism is impaired. As a consequence, age-related impairments can be observed in multiple cognitive domains. For example, when less dopamine is projected to the prefrontal cortex, context representation is less reliable and the activation and maintenance of task-relevant information is hindered, which matches the above reported ERP studies examining slow potentials just before target presentation (Kray et al, 2005; West, 2004).

In this context, in their dual mechanisms of control framework Baver and colleagues recently suggested two qualitatively distinct modes of control, which are differentially engaged by younger and older adults (e.g., Braver, 2012; Braver, Gray, & Burgess, 2007; Jimura & Braver, 2010): In proactive control, goal-relevant information is actively maintained before the occurrence of a demanding event, to optimally bias cognitive processes in a goal-driven manner. In contrast, reactive control is recruited as a late correction mechanism that is mobilized as needed and requires the reactivation of context information. This assumption is supported, for instance, by findings from Jimura and Braver (2010), showing that younger adults exhibited larger sustained activity in prefrontal areas in mixed than single blocks, while older adults showed transient activity in the same region, especially on switch trials. They concluded that sustained prefrontal activation reflects active maintenance of task sets, by this reflecting a proactive control strategy in young participants. The transient activation observed in older adults was interpreted as reflecting a compensatory mechanism of interference resolution and thus as evidence for a reactive control strategy (see also Karayanidis et al., 2011). Hence, it seems plausible to assume that the age differences in mixing costs, observed in a variety of task switching studies, can be a result of impairments in context updating, and that strategy-based interventions, such as verbal labeling, as well as process-based interventions, such as task switching training, are useful tools to promote proactive control in the elderly.

CONCLUSION

The findings reviewed in this chapter indicate process-specific limitations of older adults in task switching. While switching from one task to the next is relatively spared, task maintenance and selection is impaired in the elderly as compared with young adults. Evidence from behavioral as well as neuroscience approaches suggest that older adults have problems with the appropriate representation and biasing of task-relevant information in switching situations, due to age-related deterioration in prefrontal lobe regions. These problems can be enhanced by task uncertainty, such as overlapping task representations (i.e., task interference), the absence of cues, or unpredictability of upcoming tasks and preparation times, and can be reduced by intensive practice or verbal labeling. Given this knowledge, it will be a challenge for future research to further specify which types of cognitive training interventions are best suited for improving optimal task-set representations in elderly people that also lead to long-term maintenance and broad generalization of training improvements as well as which one can be easily applied in everyday life.

REFERENCES

Adrover-Roig, D., & Barceló, F. (2010). Individual differences in aging and cognitive control modulate the neural indexes of context updating and maintenance during task switching. *Cortex*, *46*, 434–450.

Baddeley, A., Chincotta, D., & Adlam, A. (2001). Working memory and the control of action: Evidence from task switching. *Journal of Experimental Psychology: General*, *130*(4), 641–657.

Baltes, P. B., & Kliegl, R. (1992). Further testing of limits of cognitive plasticity: Negative age differences in a mnemonic skill are robust. *Developmental Psychology*, *28*, 121–125.

Baltes, P. B., Staudinger, U. M., & Lindenberger, U. (1999). Lifespan psychology: Theory and application to intellectual functioning. *Annual Review of Psychology*, *50*, 471–507.

Bialystok, E., & Craik, F. I. M. (2006). *Lifespan cognition: Mechanisms of change*. New York, NY: Oxford University Press.

Braver, T. S. (2012).The variable nature of cognitive control: A dual mechanisms framework. *Trends in Cognitive Sciences*, *16*, 106–113.

Braver, T. S., & Barch, D. M. (2002). A theory of cognitive control, aging cognition, and neuromodulation. *Neuroscience and Biobehavioral Reviews*, *26*, 809–817.

Braver, T. S., & West, R. (2007). Working memory, executive control and aging. In F. I. M. Craik & T. A. Salthouse (Eds.), *The handbook of aging and cognition, third edition*. New York, NY: Psychology Press.

Braver, T. S., Gray, J. R., & Burgess, G. C. (2007). Explaining the many varieties of working memory variation: Dual mechanisms of cognitive control. In A. Conway, C.

Jarrold, M. Kane, A. Miyake, & J. Towse (Eds.), *Variation in working memory* (pp. 76–16). New York, NY: Oxford University Press.

Bryck, R. L., & Mayr, U. (2005). On the role of verbalization during task set selection: Switching or serial order control? *Memory & Cognition, 33*, 611–623.

Buchler, N. G., Hoyer, W. J., & Cerella, J. (2008). Rules and more rules: The effects of multiple tasks, extensive training, and aging on task switching performance. *Memory & Cognition, 36*, 735–748.

Cabeza, R., Nyberg, L., & Park, D. (2005). *Cognitive neuroscience of aging: Linking cognitive and cerebral aging*. New York, NY: Oxford University Press.

Cepeda, N. J., Kramer, A. F., & Gonzalez de Sather, J. C. M. (2001). Changes in executive control across the life span: Examination of task-switching performance. *Developmental Psychology, 37*, 715–730.

Chevalier, N., & Blaye, A. (2009). Setting goals to switch between tasks: Effect of cue transparency on children's cognitive flexibility. *Developmental Psychology, 45*, 782–797.

Craik, F. I. M., & Salthouse, T. A. (2008). *The handbook of aging and cognition (3rd ed.)*. New York, NY: Psychology Press.

De Jong, R. (2001). Adult age differences in goal activation and goal maintenance. *European Journal of Cognitive Psychology, 13*, 71–89.

De Sanctis, P., Gomez-Ramirez, M., Sehatpour, P., Wylie, G. R., & Foxe, J. J. (2009). Preserved executive function in high-performing elderly is driven by large-scale recruitment of prefrontal cortical mechanisms. *Human Brain Mapping, 30*, 4198–4214.

DiGirolamo, G. J., Kramer, A. F., Barad, V., Cepeda, N. J., Weissman, D. H., Milham, M. P., & McAuley, E. (2001). General and task-specific frontal lobe recruitment in older adults during executive processes: A fMRI investigation of task-switching. *NeuroReport, 12*, 2065–2071.

Donchin, E., & Coles, M. G. H. (1988). Is the P300 component a manifestation of context updating? *Behavioral and Brain Sciences, 11*, 357–374.

Duncan, J. (1995). Attention, intelligence, and the frontal lobes. In M. Gazzaniga (Ed.), *The cognitive neurosciences* (pp. 721–733). Cambridge, MA: MIT Press.

Emerson, M. J., & Miyake, A. (2003). The role of inner speech in task switching: A dual-task investigation. *Journal of Memory and Language, 48*, 148–168.

Eppinger, B., Kray, J., Mecklinger, A., & John, O. (2007). Age differences in response monitoring: Evidence from ERPs. *Biological Psychology, 75*, 52–67.

Friedman, D., Nessler, D., Johnson, R., Ritter, W., & Bersick, M. (2008). Age-related changes in executive function: An event-related potential (ERP) investigation of task-switching. *Aging, Neuropsychology, and Cognition, 15*, 1–34.

Grange, J. A., & Houghton, G. (2010). Cue-switch costs in task-switching: Cue priming or control processes? *Psychological Research, 74*, 481–490.

Goffaux, P., Phillips, N. A., Sinai, M., & Pushkar, D. (2008). Neurophysiological measures of task-set switching: Effects of working memory and aging. *Journals of Gerontology, Series B: Psychological Sciences and Social Sciences, 63*, P57–P66.

Gold, B. T., Powell, D. K., Xuan, L. Jicha, G. A., & Smith, C. D. (2010). Age-related slowing of task switching is associated with decreased integrity of frontoparietal white matter. *Neurobiology of Aging, 31*, 512–522.

Goschke, T. (2000). Involuntary persistence and intentional reconfiguration in task-set switching. In S. Monsell & J. Driver (Eds.), *Attention and performance. XVIII: Control of cognitive processes* (pp. 331–355). Cambridge, MA: MIT Press.

Hahn, S., Andersen, G. J., & Kramer, A. F. (2004). Age influences on multi-dimensional set switching. *Aging, Neuropsychology, and Cognition, 11*, 25–36.

Hartley, A. A., Kieley, J. M., & Slabach, E. H. (1990). Age differences and similarities in the effects of cues and prompts. *Journal of Experimental Psychology: Human Perception and Performance, 16(3)*, 523–537.

Hofmann, W., Schmeichel, B. J., & Baddeley, A. D. (2012). Executive functions and self-regulation. *Trends in Cognitive Sciences, 16*, 174–180.

Jimura, K., & Braver, T. S. (2010). Age-related shifts in brain activity dynamics during task switching. *Cerebral Cortex, 20*, 1420–1431.

Karayanidis, F., Whitson, L. R., Heathcote, A., & Michie, P. T. (2011). Variability in proactive and reactive cognitive control processes across the adult lifespan. *Frontiers in Psychology, 2*, 318.

Karbach, J., & Kray, J. (2009). How useful is executive control training? Age differences in near and far transfer of task-switching training. *Developmental Science, 12*, 978–990.

Karbach, J., Mang, S., & Kray, J. (2010). Transfer of verbal self-instruction training in older age. *Psychology and Aging, 25*, 677–683.

Kiesel, A., Steinhauser, M., Wendt, M., Falkenstein, M., Jost, K., Philipp, A.M., & Koch, I. (2010). Control and interference in task switching—A review. *Psychological Bulletin, 136*, 849–874.

Kliegl, R., & Baltes, P. B. (1987). Theory-guided analysis of mechanisms of development and aging through testing-the-limits and research on expertise. In C. Schooler & K. Schaie (Eds.), *Cognitive functioning and social structure over the life course* (pp. 95–119). Westport, CT: Ablex Publishing.

Kramer, A. F., & Kray, J. (2006). Aging and attention. In E. Bialystok & F. I. M. Craik (Eds.), *Lifespan cognition: Mechanisms of change* (pp. 57–69). New York, NY: Oxford University Press.

Kramer, A. F., Hahn, S., & Gopher, D. (1999). Task coordination and aging: Explorations of executive control processes in the task switching paradigm. *Acta Psychologica, 101*, 339–378.

Kray, J. (2006). Task-set switching under cue-based versus memory-based switching conditions in younger and older adults. *Brain Research, 1105*, 83–92.

Kray, J. & Eber, J. (2003). Können Kinder semantische und symbolische Hinweisreize gleichermaßen zur Steuerung von Handlungen nutzen wie junge und ältere Erwachsene? Poster präsentiert auf der *16. Tagung der Fachgruppe Entwicklungspsychologie*, Mainz. [Kray, J. & Eber, J. (2003). Are children as well as younger and older adults able to use semantic and symbolic cues for the regulation of behavior? *Paper presented at the 16. "Tagung der Fachgruppe Entwicklungspsychologie"*, Mainz, Germany.]

Kray, J., & Eppinger, B. (2006). Effects of associate learning on age differences in task-set switching. *Acta Psychologica, 123*, 187–203.

Kray, J., & Lindenberger, U. (2000). Adult age differences in task switching. *Psychology and Aging, 15*, 126–147.

Kray, J., Blaye, A., & Lucenet, J. (2010). Can older adults enhance task switching performance by using verbal self-instructions? The influence of working-memory load and early learning. *Frontiers in Aging Neuroscience, 2*, 147.

Kray, J., Eber, J., & Karbach, J. (2008). Verbal self-instructions in task switching. A compensatory tool for action-control deficits in childhood and old age? *Developmental Science, 11*, 223–236.

Kray, J., Eber, J., & Lindenberger, U. (2004). Age differences in executive functioning across the lifespan: The role of verbalization in task preparation. *Acta Psychologica, 115*, 143–165.

Kray, J., Eppinger, B., & Mecklinger, A. (2005). Age differences in attentional control. An event-related potential approach. *Psychophysiology, 42*, 407–416.

Kray, J., Li, K. Z. H., & Lindenberger, U. (2002). Age-related changes in task-switching components: The role of task uncertainty. *Brain and Cognition, 49*, 363–381.

Lawo, V., Philipp, A. M., Schuch, S., & Koch, I. (2012). The role of task preparation and task inhibition in age-related task-switching deficits. *Psychology and Aging, 27*(4), 1130–1137.

Lien, M., Ruthruff, E., & Kuhns, D. (2008). Age-related differences in switching between cognitive tasks: Does internal control ability decline with age? *Psychology and Aging, 23*, 330–341.

Lindenberger, U., Mayr, U., & Kliegl, R. (1993). Speed and intelligence in old age. *Psychology and Aging, 8*, 207–220.

Los, S. A. (1996). *On the origin of mixing costs: Exploring information processing in pure* and mixed blocks of trials. *Acta Psychologica, 94*, 145–188.

Lövdén, M., Bäckman, L., Lindenberger, U., Schaefer, S., & Schmiedek, F. (2010). A theoretical framework for the study of adult cognitive plasticity. *Psychological Bulletin, 136*, 659–676.

Luria, A. R. (1961). The development of the regulatory role of speech. In J. Tizard (Ed.), *The role of speech in the regulation of normal and abnormal behavior* (pp. 50–96). New York, NY: Liveright.

Madden, D. J., Costello, M. C., Dannis, N. A., Davis, S. W., Shelpler, A. M., Spaniol, J., Bucur, B., & Cabeza, R. (2010). Adult age differences in functional connectivity during executive control. *NeuroImage, 52*, 643–657.

Mayr, U. (2001). Age differences in the selection of mental sets: The role of inhibition, stimulus ambiguity, and response-set overlap. *Psychology and Aging, 16*, 96–109.

Mayr, U., & Liebscher, T. (2001). Is there an age deficit in the selection of mental sets? *European Journal of Cognitive Psychology, 13*, 47–69.

Meichenbaum, D. (1974). Self-instructional strategy training: A cognitive prothesis for the aged. *Human Development, 17*, 273–280.

Meiran, N., Gotler, A., & Perlman, A. (2001). Old age is associated with a pattern of relatively intact and relatively impaired task-set switching abilities. *Journals of Gerontology, Series B: Psychological Sciences and Social Sciences, 56*, P88–P102.

Miller, E. K., & Cohen, J. D. (2001). An integrative theory of prefrontal cortex function. *Annual Review of Neuroscience, 24*, 167–202.

Minear, M., & Shah, P. (2008). Training and transfer effects in task switching. *Memory & Cognition, 36*, 1470–1483.

Miyake, A., Friedman, N. P., Emerson, M. J., Witzki, A. H., Howerter, A., & Wager, T. (2000). The unity and diversity of executive functions and their contributions to complex "frontal lobe" tasks: A latent variable analysis. *Cognitive Psychology, 41*, 49–100.

Miyake, A., Emerson, M. J., Padilla, F., & Ahn, J.-C. (2004). Inner speech as a retrieval aid for task goals: The effects of cue type and articulatory suppression in the random task cuing paradigm. *Acta Psychologica, 115*, 123–142.

Monsell, S., Sumner, P., & Waters, H. (2003). Task-set reconfiguration with predictable and unpredictable task switches. *Memory and Cognition, 31*, 327–342.

Nieuwenhuis, S., & Monsell, S. (2002). Residual costs in task switching: Testing the failure-to-engage hypothesis. *Psychonomic Bulletin & Review, 9*, 86–92.

Raz, N. (2000). Aging of the brain and its impact on cognitive performance: Integration of structural and functional findings. In F. I. M. Craik & T. A. Salthouse (Eds.), *The handbook of aging and cognition, second edition*. Mahwah, NJ: Lawrence Erlbaum Associates.

Reimers, S., & Maylor, E. A. (2005). Task switching across the life span: Effects of age on general and specific switch costs. *Developmental Psychology, 41*, 661–671.

Rogers, R. D., & Monsell, S. (1995). Cost of a predictable switch between simple cognitive tasks. *Journal of Experimental Psychology: General, 124*, 207–231.

Saeki, E., & Saito, S. (2004). Effect of articulatory suppression on task-switching performance: Implications for models of working memory. *Memory, 12*, 257–271.

Salthouse, T. A. (1991). *Theoretical perspectives on cognitive aging*. Hillsdale, NJ: Erlbaum.

Salthouse, T. A. (1996). The processing-speed theory of adult age differences in cognition. *Psychological Review, 103*, 403–428.

Salthouse, T. A., Fristoe, N., McGuthry, K. E., & Hambrick, D. Z. (1998). Relation of task switching to speed, age, and fluid intelligence. *Psychology and Aging, 13*, 445–461.

Smith, E. E., & Jonides, J. (1999). Storage and executive processes in the frontal lobes. *Science, 283*, 1657–1661.

Spieler, D., Mayr, U., & LaGrone, S. (2006). Outsourcing cognitive control to the environment: Adult age differences in the use of task cues. *Psychonomic Bulletin & Review, 5*, 787–793.

van Asselen, M., & Ridderinkhof, K. R. (2000). Shift cost of predictable and unexpected set shifting in young and older adults. *Psychologica Belgica, 40*, 259–273.

Verhaeghen, P., & Cerella, J. (2002). Aging, executive control, and attention: A review of meta-analyses. *Neuroscience and Biobehavioral Reviews, 26*, 849–857.

Vygotsky, L. S. (1934/1962). *Thought and language*. Cambridge, MA: MIT Press.

Wasylyshyn, C., Verhaeghen, P., & Sliwinski, M. J. (2011). Aging and task switching: A meta-analysis. *Psychology and Aging, 26*, 15–20.

West, R. (2004). The effects of aging on controlled attention and conflict processing in the Stroop task. *Journal of Cognitive Neuroscience, 16*, 103–113.

West, R., & Moore, K. (2005). Adjustments of cognitive control in younger and older adults. *Cortex, 41*, 570–581.

West, R., & Travers, S. (2008). Differential effects of aging on processes underlying task switching. *Brain and Cognition, 68*, 67–80.

INDEX